HUMAN RIGHTS PROTECTION IN THE EUROPEAN LEGAL ORDER: THE INTERACTION BETWEEN THE EUROPEAN AND THE NATIONAL COURTS

HUMAN RIGHTS PROTECTION IN THE EUROPEAN LEGAL ORDER: THE INTERACTION BETWEEN THE EUROPEAN AND THE NATIONAL COURTS

Edited by
Patricia Popelier
Catherine Van de Heyning
Piet Van Nuffel

intersentia
Cambridge – Antwerp – Portland

Intersentia Ltd
Trinity House | Cambridge Business Park | Cowley Road
Cambridge | CB4 0WZ | United Kingdom
mail@intersentia.co.uk

Distribution for the UK:
Hart Publishing Ltd.
16C Worcester Place
Oxford OX1 2JW
UK
Tel.: +44 1865 51 75 30
Email: mail@hartpub.co.uk

Distribution for the USA and Canada:
International Specialized Book Services
920 NE 58th Ave. Suite 300
Portland, OR 97213
USA
Tel.: +1 800 944 6190 (toll free)
Email: info@isbs.com

Distribution for Austria:
Neuer Wissenschaftlicher Verlag
Argentinierstraße 42/6
1040 Wien
Austria
Tel.: +43 1 535 61 03 24
Email: office@nwv.at

Distribution for other countries:
Intersentia Publishers
Groenstraat 31
2640 Mortsel
Belgium
Tel.: +32 3 680 15 50
Email: mail@intersentia.be

Human rights protection in the European legal order: The interaction between the European and the national courts
Patricia Popelier, Catherine Van de Heyning and Piet Van Nuffel (eds.)

Doesburg, Theo van (1883-1931): Simultaneous Counter-Composition, 1929-30. New York, Museum of Modern Art (MoMA). Oil on canvas, 19 3/4 × 19 5/8' (50.1 × 49.8 cm). The Sidney and Harriet Janis Collection. Acc. n.: 588.1967. © 2011. Digital image, The Museum of Modern Art, New York/Scala, Florence

ISBN 978-1-78068-010-1
NUR 828

GPRC
Guaranteed
Peer Reviewed
Content

British Library Cataloguing in Publication Data. A catalogue record for this book is available from the British Library.

CONTENTS

The interaction between European and national courts as to human rights protection: The editors' introduction 1

1. Human rights protection by the European Court of Justice in the shadow of the European Convention on Human Rights 3
2. The attitude of the European Court of Human Rights *vis-à-vis* European Union law 6
3. Interaction between the European Court of Justice and the European Court of Human Rights 7
4. Impact of the co-existence of European protection mechanisms on the national constitutional courts 8
5. Impact of the ECHR on national constitutional courts 10
6. Impact of EU fundamental rights on national constitutional courts 11
7. Preserving human rights or preserving protection mechanisms? 12

I. THE INTERACTION BETWEEN THE EUROPEAN COURT OF JUSTICE AND THE EUROPEAN COURT OF HUMAN RIGHTS 15

Chapter 1. The use of the ECHR and Convention case law by the European Court of Justice
Bruno De Witte 17

1. Introduction 17
2. The Convention: A source of special guidelines or of binding norms? 19
3. Systematic or eclectic use of the Convention? 24
4. Consequences of the Lisbon Treaty 33

Chapter 2. The EU as a party to the European Convention of Human Rights: EU law and the European Court of Justice case law as inspiration and challenge to the European Court of Human Rights jurisprudence
Catherine Van de Heyning and Rick Lawson 35

1. Introduction 35
2. Inspiration and challenge 39
   2.1. The Luxembourg case law as inspiration for the European Court of Human Rights jurisprudence – and more 39

2.1.1. The jurisprudence of the EU courts as inspiration for the Strasbourg jurisdiction . . . 39
2.1.2. Taking into account EU law as 'law of the land' . . . 42
2.1.3. The ECtHR as a means to enforce compliance with EU law . . . 45
2.1.4. Regard of the Luxembourg case law, not reliance? . . . 46
2.2. European Union law as challenge for the European Court of Human Rights' jurisprudence . . . 49
2.2.1. The *Bosphorus* doctrine and its application . . . 49
2.2.2. The doctrine after accession to the ECHR . . . 56
3. Future prospects of the relationship between the Strasbourg and Luxembourg courts . . . 61
4. Concluding remarks . . . 64

Chapter 3. No place like home: Discretionary space for the domestic protection of fundamental rights
Catherine Van de Heyning . . . 65

1. Legitimate reasons for constitutional discretionary space: Diversity and subsidiarity . . . 67
2. Maximisation clauses: Application and critique . . . 71
2.1. Article 53 ECHR in the Strasbourg case law . . . 71
2.2. The rebirth of the maximisation clause? . . . 73
2.2.1. The maximisation clause in the EU Charter . . . 73
2.2.2. A new direction for the maximisation clause in the Strasbourg case law . . . 74
2.3. Limits of a maximisation clause . . . 78
3. Alternative approaches providing discretionary space . . . 82
3.1. Margin of appreciation and the domestic legal order . . . 83
3.1.1. Margin of appreciation doctrine . . . 83
3.1.2. A limited discretionary space . . . 86
3.2. A doctrine not without flaws . . . 87
3.3. Restraint towards domestic judgments . . . 91
4. No place like home: Promising new direction? . . . 94

Chapter 4. European human rights, supranational judicial review and democracy. Thinking outside the judicial box
Samantha Besson . . . 97

1. Introduction . . . 97
2. The notion of supranational judicial review . . . 102
3. Supranational judicial review in Europe . . . 104
3.1. Supranational judicial review by the ECtHR . . . 105
3.1.1. The status of ECHR rights in domestic law . . . 105

3.1.2. The jurisdiction of the ECtHR . . . 106
3.1.3. The effects of a ECtHR's judgement in domestic law . . . 108
3.2. Supranational judicial review by the ECJ . . . 112
3.2.1. The status of EU fundamental rights in domestic law . . . 112
3.2.2. The jurisdiction of the ECJ on fundamental rights. . . . 116
3.2.3. The effects of an ECJ's judgement in domestic law . . . 118
3.3. European supranational judicial review compared. . . . 120
4. The democratic legitimacy of supranational judicial review . . . 123
4.1. The democratic legitimacy of judicial review *tout court*. . . . 123
4.2. The democratic legitimacy of judicial review in the supranational context . . . 126
4.2.1. Reassessing the issue . . . 126
4.2.2. Different questions . . . 128
4.2.3. Different answers . . . 133
5. European legal pluralism and the relationship between European courts . . . 138
5.1. The role of European human rights review in circumstances of legal pluralism . . . 138
5.2. The consequences for the relationships between European courts. . . 140
6. Conclusion . . . 143

II. THE IMPACT OF THE COEXISTENCE OF THE EUROPEAN COURTS ON THE NATIONAL CONSTITUTIONAL COURTS . . . 147

Chapter 5. Belgium. The supremacy dilemma: The Belgian Constitutional Court caught between the European Court of Human Rights and the European Court of Justice
Patricia Popelier . . . 149

1. The protection of fundamental rights by the Belgian courts . . . 149
1.1. First track: Case law of the Court of Cassation (Supreme Court). . . . 149
1.2. Second track: The establishment of the Belgian Constitutional Court. . . . 150
2. The relationship between national law and international law according to Belgian law . . . 151
2.1. The primacy of international law: A (moderated) monist view. . . . 151
2.2. EU law. . . . 153
3. The influence of ECHR and EU law on the national protection of human rights . . . 154
3.1. The influence of the ECHR on the national protection of human rights. . . . 154
3.2. The influence of EU law on the national protection of human rights. . . . 156

4. The relation between the national and the European protection of human rights 158
4.1. The position of the Constitutional Court in human rights proceedings 158
4.1.1. An exhaustive remedy? 158
4.1.2. Reference to the Constitutional Court in the case of analogous human rights 159
4.2. Consequences of the *Simmenthal* case 161
4.3. Preliminary references to the European Court of Justice 164
4.4. The maximisation clause 166
5. The protection of human rights in converging legal orders: The *Money Laundering Case* 168
6. Conclusion 170

Chapter 6. East European Countries. On secret legislation, blanket data recording, arrest warrants and property rights: Questions on the rule of law and judicial review in the EU in the light of post-communist constitutions
Anneli Albi 173

1. The centrality of the rule of law in the post-communist constitutional reforms and the commitment to the ECHR 173
2. Past criticisms regarding judicial review and rights protection by the ECJ 177
3. Recent questions on the review of EU measures 181
3.1. On secret legislation: *Heinrich* case 181
3.2. On blanket electronic surveillance: The EU Electronic Data Retention Directive 2006/24 184
3.3. The European Arrest Warrant: An erosion of *nulla poena sine lege*? 185
3.4. On property rights and legal certainty: From the 'Banana saga' to a 'Sugar saga' 189
3.4.1. Retroactive fines on undertakings: Overview of direct actions and domestic cases 190
3.4.2. Impossibility of removing stocks held by private individuals and households 191
4. Supremacy of EU law: A case for rigorous rather than minimal judicial review? 195
5. Teleological interpretation and effectiveness of EU law: Questions regarding balancing, limits, fines and double standards 199
6. Revisiting the role of constitutions and constitutional courts in EU scholarly discourse: Beyond the lens of sovereignty and euro-friendliness 204

Chapter 7. France. The impact of European fundamental rights on the French Constitutional Court
Laurence BURGORGUE-LARSEN 211

1. Introduction. The 'Europeanization' of the French Constitution 211
2. The Constitutional Council and European Union Law. 214
   2.1. The Constitutional Council and Primacy. 214
   2.2. The Constitutional Council and the Reference for a Preliminary Ruling (Article 267 TFEU) 218
3. The Constitutional Council and the Power of the European Convention on Human Rights 225
   3.1. The Constitutional Council is controlled by the European Court of Human Rights. 226
      3.1.1. *Decision* control by the Constitutional Council 226
      3.1.2. *Procedure* control before the Constitutional Council. 229
   3.2. The Constitutional Council under the influence of the European Court of Human Rights' case law. 234

Chapter 8. Germany. The Federal Constitutional Court of Germany in the context of the European integration
Rainer ARNOLD 237

1. The dual function of the Constitutional Court. 237
   1.1. Constitutional Court and the EU: Some basic observations 237
   1.2. The Constitutional Court and traditional international law. 238
   1.3. The jurisdictional means of control. 239
   1.4. Approximation of the national and inter/supranational orders by interpretation. 241
2. The basic order of the European Communities and its acceptance by the Federal Constitutional Court 241
   2.1. The three elements of the supranational order. 241
   2.2. The EU not a State but a 'Staatenverbund' – The vagueness of this term. 242
3. Constitutional limits of the European integration. 244
   3.1. Formal and substantive limits – Article 23 §1 BL 244
   3.2. Three substantive integration limits developed by the jurisprudence. 245
      3.2.1. Constitutional parallelism 245
      3.2.2. The *ultra vires* concept. 245
      3.2.3. Constitutional identity 246
   3.3. Values and substitutive parallelism: A functional integration approach. 246

3.3.1. The dignity of man as a basis of fundamental rights 246
3.3.2. Supranational fundamental rights for the supranational order 246
3.3.3. From unwritten to written fundamental rights in the EU . . . 246
3.3.4. Joining the ECHR. 247
3.4. National or supranational fundamental rights? – The *Solange I* and *II* decisions 247
3.5. The functional-substitutive approach of the Constitutional Court . . 249
3.6. Rule of law 249
3.7. Limits of integration: *Ultra vires* and constitutional review 250
3.7.1. The principle of *compétences d'attribution* and *ultra vires* actions 250
3.7.2. The obligation to address the ECJ 250
3.7.3. The Maastricht decision and the *ultra vires* concept 251
3.7.4. The journey back to EU law conformity: The *Mangold* case . . 251
3.8. Limits of integration: Constitutional identity 252
3.8.1. Constitutional identity through Article 79 §3 BL? 252
3.8.2. National identity in the sense of Article 4 §2 of the new EU Treaty 252
3.8.3. The term of constitutional identity going back to the *Solange* jurisprudence 253
3.8.4. A functional approach to identity? 253
3.8.5. The involvement of the ECJ. 254
3.8.6. Harmonising the national and supranational perspectives on constitutional identity 254
4. The Constitutional Court as a protector of supranational law. 255
4.1. The Constitutional Court as a guardian of the ECJ 255
4.2. What is a violation of this guarantee? 255
4.3. The 'cooperation' between the Constitutional Court and the ECJ . . . 256
5. The Constitutional Court and the European Convention of Human Rights (ECHR) 257
5.1. The ECHR as an international treaty transformed into German law 257
5.2. Constitutionalising the ECHR 257
5.3. The monistic effect of rule of law 257
5.4. The *Görgülü* decision and its deficiencies 258

Chapter 9. Italy. The impact of the European courts on the Italian Constitutional Court
Giuseppe Martinico and Oreste Pollicino 261

1. The protection of fundamental rights by the Italian courts 261
2. The relation of national law and international law according to Italian law 262
   2.1. Italian dualism as a starting point of the national Constitutional Court 262
   2.2. EU Law 264
      2.2.1. The Italian Constitutional Court before EU law: The counter-limits doctrine 265
      2.2.2. Preliminary references to the European Court of Justice 266
      2.2.3. The impact of the EU Charter of Fundamental Rights on Italian case law 269
3. The European Convention on Human Rights 273
   3.1. The Simmenthal doctrine for the ECHR? The viewpoint of the national non-constitutional judges 275
   3.2. The landmark decisions of 2007 276
      3.2.1. The new parameter of Article 117, paragraph 1, of the Constitution 277
      3.2.2. A possible alternative judicial path for the Constitutional Court? 279
      3.2.3. A look at the follow up to such decisions 282
4. The key role of the ordinary judges: From the risk of a 'double standard' to the reaction of the ordinary judges 285

Chapter 10. The Netherlands. A Case of constitutional leapfrog. Fundamental rights protection under the Constitution, the ECHR and the EU Charter in the Netherlands
Monica Claes and Gert Jan Leenknegt 287

1. Introduction 287
2. Introducing the actors: A brief overview of the Dutch court system 289
3. Constitutional review: Not a judicial matter 290
4. Dutch law and international law 293
5. The Dutch Constitution and the European Union: Don't ask, don't tell .. 295
6. EU law in Dutch courts: Routine, or is it? 298
7. The ECtHR: A substitute constitutional court? 301
8. Competition from the other Europe? The ECJ and fundamental rights .. 302
9. Caught in the middle? Dutch courts and conflicts between ECtHR and ECJ case law 305
10. Talking to the neighbours: On judicial dialogues 306

Chapter 11. Spain. The impact of the European Convention of Human Rights and the Charter of Fundamental rights of the European Union on Spanish constitutional law: Make a virtue of necessity
Enrique Guillén López 309

1. Preliminary observations. Law and rights in the formation of a new Europe 309
2. The theoretical framework of the impact of the doctrine of the European Court of Human Rights and the European Court of Justice on the fundamental rights expressed in the Spanish constitutional system. The legal instruments for integration 313
3. The European Convention on Human Rights and the case law of the European Court of Human Rights, conflict and dialogue 319
   3.1. The theoretical framework behind the Constitutional Court. Article 10.2 as an interpretative mandate and not as a mechanism for creating new rights (Constitutional Court judgment 236/2007) . 320
   3.2. The Constitutional Court is as an instrument for the protection of fundamental rights enshrined in the Spanish Constitution – and not other rights 321
   3.3. Analysis of the internal constitutional case law cited for various rights under the European Convention on Human Rights. Analysis of the rights that may create a new framework 322
      3.3.1. Sexual equality (Article 14 of the European Convention on Human Rights) 323
      3.3.2. Right to a fair trial (Article 6 of the European Convention on Human Rights) 324
      3.3.3. Right to respect for private and family life (Article 8.1 European Convention on European Rights) 326
      3.3.4. Confidential correspondence (Article 8 of the European Convention on European Rights) 328
      3.3.5. Freedom of expression (Article 10 European Convention on Human Rights) 329
      3.3.6. Right to free elections (Article 3 of the Additional Protocol) . 330
      3.3.7. Protection of property (Article 1 of the Additional Protocol) 330
   3.4. Condemnatory judgments made against Spain by the European Court of Human Rights 332
4. Fundamental rights within the European Union and the Spanish constitutional system 333
5. Conclusions 340

Chapter 12. The United Kingdom. The influence of European law on the protection of fundamental human rights in United Kingdom law
Brice Dickson 343

1. Introduction 343
2. Fundamental human rights protection at the EU level 345
3. Pre- and post-2000 approaches to the ECHR 350
4. Influences on the UK Parliament 352
5. Influences on the relationship between UK judges and the UK Parliament. 353
6. Influences on the UK's common law per se. 355
   6.1. The right to privacy and refusal to develop the common law 356
   6.2. Developing the common law beyond the ECHR 359
   6.3. Hesitation and doubts 361
7. Conclusion 363

Chapter 13. Protection of European human rights by highest courts in Europe: The art of triangulation
Wim Voermans 365

1. At the heart of the matter: Observing European human rights requires constitutional balancing. 365
2. The European compound human rights system: Sharing rights and courts 367
3. Constitutional calibration of European human rights review. 370
   3.1. The search for coherence 370
   3.2. The dilemma of autonomy. 373
4. Coordination and conflict resolution strategies. 375
5. In conclusion: Adding to Europe's common human rights gene pool 378

About the authors and editors 379

THE INTERACTION BETWEEN EUROPEAN AND NATIONAL COURTS AS TO HUMAN RIGHTS PROTECTION

The editors' introduction

These are fascinating times for academics who study the mechanisms of human rights protection in Europe. After half a century of control exercised by the European Court of Human Rights (ECtHR) and the Court of Justice of the European Union (Chapter 1 "European Court of Justice" or ECJ) 'living apart together' – as De Witte puts it (see Chapter 1) –, negotiations have been launched that should lead to the European Union acceding to the European Convention on Human Rights (hereinafter the 'Convention' or ECHR). Furthermore, since the entry into force of the Lisbon Treaty, the European Union has availed itself with an own Charter of Fundamental Rights (the 'Charter'), which, while referring to the ECHR as leading source of inspiration, is set to be the new standard of fundamental rights to which the ECJ will hold both the (other) institutions of the European Union (EU) and the EU Member States when they implement EU law.

If one adds to this picture the fact that most European states have laid down in their national constitution guarantees for the respect of fundamental rights, ensuring the protection of human rights in Europe becomes a highly complex exercise. Where courts are faced with a human rights claim, they not only have to examine the validity of that claim, but also need to have a clear understanding of the human rights catalogue that is to be applied, that is to say human rights as guaranteed by the national constitution, human rights as protected under EU law, based or not on the Charter, and/or human rights as identified in the Convention.

In March 2009, we discussed in Antwerp this complex picture of human rights protection with a selected group of academics and members of the ECJ, the ECtHR and national supreme and constitutional courts. In this seminar, which the Faculty of Law and the Centre for Law and Cosmopolitan Values of Antwerp University organised together with the Institute for European Law of Leuven University, the idea was tabled to have our discussions further developed in a collection of articles that would zoom in on various aspects of the interaction between courts in the complex European system of human rights protection.

With this book, we are now glad to present the results of this international academic cooperation. In a first part, we present a selection of articles on the co-existence at European level of the dual system of human rights protection as ultimately safeguarded by the ECtHR and the ECJ, respectively. Interaction between these two European Courts has come into being, which goes beyond the attention paid to each other's case law towards actual common consensus-building on their respective roles. On the interaction between the European courts, we present contributions of Bruno De Witte (on the use by the ECJ of the ECHR and Strasbourg case law), Catherine Van de Heyning and Rick Lawson (on the use by the ECtHR of EU law and ECJ case law), Catherine Van de Heyning (on the maximisation clause in the ECHR and the Charter) and Samantha Besson (on supranational judicial review and its connection with democracy).

Secondly, we have invited a number of distinguished colleagues to study the impact of this dual mechanism of European human rights protection on the protection of human rights within specific EU Member States. This makes the picture even more complex, in particular where national constitutional courts seek to preserve the fundamental rights ensured in the national constitution and have this protection of 'constitutional' rights taking over from the search for compatibility with 'European' human rights. Nonetheless, the complexity of human rights mechanisms is not always perceived as problematic. Indeed, some authors emphasize the need to seek for the highest protection of human rights, if need be at the national level, rather than to apply some pre-existing understanding that human rights are best protected at the European level.

The contributions received on the complexity of human rights protection seen from the national perspective have been collected in the second part of our book, in which we are happy to present articles by Patricia Popelier (on the Belgian constitutional court), Anneli Albi (on Eastern European constitutional courts), Laurence Burgorgue-Larsen (on the French *Conseil constitutionnel*), Rainer Arnold (on the German constitutional court), Giuseppe Martinico and Oreste Pollicino (on the Italian constitutional court), Monica Claes and Gert Jan Leenknegt (on the judicial protection of human rights in the Netherlands), Enrique Guillén Lopez (on the Spanish constitutional court) and Brice Dickson (on human rights protection by United Kingdom courts).

In order to guide the reader through the articles collected in this book, we thought it useful to briefly recall the European context that constitutes the common starting point of all authors and to which each of them has contributed its specific expertise. Unexpectedly, the views presented in the contributions are not always convergent. Some authors express more trust in human rights protection at European level than others. In our view, however, bringing together these different views allows to unfold some common threads, which we set out below, only as a matter of introduction of the various contributions, who all speak better for themselves. For a general conclusion on our research subject, we refer to the final contribution of Wim Voermans, in which he discerns coordination and conflict strategies to solve the dilemma between respect for international obligations on the one hand and a mandate to protect constitutional rights on the other.

1. HUMAN RIGHTS PROTECTION BY THE EUROPEAN COURT OF JUSTICE IN THE SHADOW OF THE EUROPEAN CONVENTION ON HUMAN RIGHTS

The co-existence of two European courts protecting fundamental rights is a development that was hardly foreseeable when, just after the disaster of the Second World War, the political class in Western Europe agreed on the need to swiftly repair the European economy, on the one hand, and to fundamentally reconcile their peoples along while securing that gross human rights violations would never occur, on the other. Instead of having one supranational organ established to pursue these economic and political objectives, two organisations would eventually be charged with these tasks. The Council of Europe became the prime promoter of human rights and political reconcilement between the European states, surveying the observation of the rights entrenched in the ECHR under the control of the ECtHR. Another organisation was to look after economic cooperation and reconstruction of European industry – the European Community, nowadays the European Union. Nonetheless, the founding fathers of the European Community had as well a political concept in mind with the establishment of this economic organization. As Robert Schuman stated in his declaration of 9 May 1950, the united production of coal and steel would be 'the first concrete foundation of a European federation indispensable to the preservation of peace'.

With the establishment of the European Communities, the ECJ was given the task to have the law observed in the interpretation and application of the constituent Treaties. No need was felt for the inclusion within the Treaties of human rights guarantees. Most probably, the Member States considered that the competences given to the Communities would not interfere with human rights and that the protection of human rights was best left to the national states that had also signed the ECHR. However, the initial refusal of the ECJ in *Geitling* and *Stork* to have Community acts reviewed against the fundamental rights guaranteed in national law[1] met hard opposition from the highest national courts. That resistance was reinforced by the case law of the ECJ that declared the supremacy of Community law over all national law, as this rendered the national constitutional protection of rights and freedoms ineffective in consideration to Community law.[2]

It is well known that it was the clear opposition of the German and Italian constitutional courts that led the ECJ to react in *Internationale Handelsgesellschaft* by making it clear that the protection of fundamental rights would also be ensured in Community law.[3] In *Nold* the Court elaborated on the sources of these fundamental rights: on the one hand, they would be found in the constitutional traditions common to the Member States and, on the other, in international human rights treaties on which the Member States had collaborated or of which they are signatories.[4] Case by case, the ECJ recognised rights and freedoms entrenched in international treaties, especially the ECHR, and identified certain constitutional traditions of the Member States as general principles of Community law, now EU law. Yet, the continued critique against the European Communities for lacking a protection of human rights ensued in the entrenching of human rights as a Union's objective in the Maastricht Treaty and, eventually, in the elaboration of an own bill of rights with the proclamation of the Charter.

As far as the scope of its fundamental rights protection is concerned, the ECJ now has an elaborated case law according to which all EU acts should respect fundamental rights. In addition, the ECJ will scrutinize national norms on their compatibility with fundamental rights whenever they fall 'within the scope of European Union law'. That is the case, first, where national authorities through their implementation of EU law, act as 'agents' for the European Union.[5] Second, national norms will be scrutinized on their compatibility with fundamental rights when they derogate from the economic freedoms laid down in the Treaties.[6] Article 51(1) of the Charter builds on this case law where it provides that the rights, freedoms and principles of the Charter apply to Member States "only when they are implementing Union law".

1 Case 1/58 *Stork* v *High Authority* [1959] ECR 17; Case 40/59 *Geitling* v *High Authority* [1960] ECR 423.
2 Case 26–62, *Van Gend & Loos* [1964] ECR 1; Case 6/64 *Costa* v *ENEL* [1964] ECR 585.
3 Case 11/70, *Internationale Handelsgesellschaft* [1970] ECR 1125.
4 Case 4/73, *Nold* v *Commission* [1974] ECR 491.
5 Case 5/88, *Wachauf* [1989] ECR 2609.
6 Case 260/89 *ERT* [1991] ECR 2925.

As regards the source for EU fundamental rights, it is now clear – since the entry into force of the Lisbon Treaty – that the ECJ is not only to apply the Charter, but also, as "general principles of the Union's law", fundamental rights as guaranteed by the ECHR and as they result from the constitutional traditions common to the Member States (Article 6(1) and (3) TEU). With respect to the status of the ECHR in the EU legal order, De Witte forcefully argues in this book that Article 6(3) TEU leaves no more doubt that the ECHR is to be considered as a binding source of EU law (see Chapter 1). It is true that, before the entry into force of the Lisbon Treaty, the case law of the ECJ and the General Court (GC) were often ambiguous. Although the ECJ and the GC recognised the "special significance" of the ECHR for the protection of EU fundamental rights, they also stressed that the rights identified in the ECHR applied only as general principles of EU law. Occasionally, the GC went even so far as considering that the ECHR was not a part of Community law.[7] Yet, in practice, the ECHR had undisputable become the prime source of fundamental rights protection. Article 6(3) TEU has merely codified this result.

Nonetheless, critique has remained that the level of protection offered by the ECJ still falls foul of the standards set by the ECtHR. Given the ECJ's frequent reliance on the ECHR and its ample citations of ECtHR case law, the critique on the ECJ has softened, but the protection of human rights is still held by some as unsatisfactory. As De Witte argues in his contribution, the problem is not so much one of divergences between the Luxembourg and Strasbourg case law. Indeed, such divergences have been very rare and, where present, have long been corrected. In his view, the problem is rather that the ECJ would make an eclectic and unsystematic use of the ECHR and the Strasbourg case law. Part of the dissatisfaction seems to be rooted in the specific type of the courses of action for which the ECJ is competent, with both direct actions and preliminary reference cases having their own limits. For example, both De Witte (Chapter 1) and Besson (Chapter 4) criticise the fact that the ECJ does not raise fundamental rights claims of its own motion. However, although some domestic constitutional courts dealing with direct actions have competence to rule *ultra petita* in this sense, this would probably be a more sensitive matter in the case of a supranational court.

Since the entry into force of the Lisbon Treaty, the ECJ has made clear that it considers the Charter as it basic frame of reference in terms of fundamental rights. De Witte refers to the recent trend set by the ECJ to base its fundamental rights reasoning on the Charter rather than on the ECHR, even where ECHR rights are also relevant (Chapter 1). Article 52 of the Charter requires the rights in

7 Case T-347/94, *Mayr-Melnhof Kartongesellschaft* v *Commission* [1998] ECR II-1751, para. 311; Case T-112/98, *Mannesmannröhren-Werke* v *Commission* [2000] ECR II-729, paras 59–60.

the Charter that are drawn from the ECHR to have the same meaning and scope as the corresponding ECHR rights. In that connection, De Witte warns for the "potential trap" of the ECJ sticking too closely to the minimum standard developed in Strasbourg without asking themselves whether the EU legal order should give further protection. This concern is echoed in some of the contributions that deal with the interpretation of the Charter by domestic courts (Chapter 10).

2. THE ATTITUDE OF THE EUROPEAN COURT OF HUMAN RIGHTS *VIS-À-VIS* EUROPEAN UNION LAW

From the Strasbourg side, the focal question has been whether the ECtHR should act against possible Convention breaches by Member States where they act in compliance with obligations under EU law. Particularly problematic are those situations where EU norms do not leave any discretionary space to the Member States. In such situation, where Convention rights would be found to be infringed, it would appear most reasonable to hold the EU responsible. However, as long as the European Union has not acceded to the ECHR, the ECtHR has no competence over acts of the EU institutions.[8]

In this respect, the position of the ECtHR has travelled through roughly three stages. Initially, the ECtHR held that where an international organisation offered an 'equivalent protection' of human rights, it would not scrutinise national norms adopted in compliance with obligations ensuing from membership of that organisation as this would be 'incompatible with the provisions of the Convention ratione materiae'.[9] This interpretation was subject to criticism, however, as the existence of 'equivalent protection' was assessed solely on the basis of the general policies of the international organisation and not on the basis of the human rights protection offered in the specific case. In subsequent cases, the ECtHR applied a more direct scrutiny of national norms, emphasizing that Member States should not automatically evade ECHR responsibility when delegating powers to an international organisation. In *Cantoni*, the ECtHR thus held that the fact that a Member State literally copied a provision from a Community Directive did not remove its responsibility to comply with the Convention.[10]

---

8 See *Guérin Automobiles* v *the 15 EU Member States*, no. 51717/99, 4 July 2000 (unreported); *Segi and Gestoras Pro-Amnistía and Others* v *Germany, Austria, Belgium, Denmark, Spain, Finland, France, Greece, Ireland, Italy, Luxembourg, the Netherlands, Portugal, the United Kingdom and Sweden*, nos. 6422/02 and 9916/02, ECHR 2002-V; *Senator Lines* v *the 15 Member States of the European Union*, no. 56672/00, 2004-IV 331.

9 *Melchers & Co* v *Federal Republic of Germany*, no. 13258/87, [1990] 64 *DR* 138.

10 *Cantoni* v *France*, no. 17862/91, [1996] *Reports*, Series A, 1996-V.

The third, most recent stage corresponds to the well known *Bosphorus* judgment,[11] where ECtHR has considered that Member States' actions pursuant to legal obligations arising from membership of an international organization are justified out of the general interest of international cooperation whenever this organisation can be considered to protect human rights in an 'equivalent' manner to the ECHR at the relevant time. For the ECtHR, the European Union provides 'equivalent protection' both in substantive and procedural terms, so that there is a presumption of Convention compliance where the Member State implements legal obligations of the EU. This presumption may be rebutted if in the particular case the protection of the Convention right is found to be 'manifestly deficient'. However, the ECtHR emphasized that the Member States remain fully responsible for any measure or action falling outside their strict international legal obligations. Thus, in *M.S.S. v Belgium and Greece*, the ECtHR recently considered that the Dublin Regulation leaves a Member State some freedom to assess an asylum application instead of the Member State designated by the Regulation, which triggered the finding of the ECtHR that the first Member State violated the ECHR by returning an asylum seeker to another State where his Convention rights risked to be endangered.[12]

In her analysis of the respective roles of the two European courts, Besson comes up with an interesting analysis of the ECtHR and the ECJ's position in their respective political and "democratic" context. Her "thinking outside the judicial box" clarifies the circumstances in which the ECtHR has been given the task to scrutinise the European States' compliance with human rights and confronts it with the totally different background against which the ECJ came to develop its human rights case law. Besson comes up with an interesting explanation in democratic terms of the *Bosphorus* case law, as she argues that not only the "subsidiary" position of the ECtHR towards the ECJ but also the "subsidiary" position of the ECtHR towards national constitutional courts corresponds with the closer ties of the ECJ and the national courts to European and national democracies (Chapter 4).

3. INTERACTION BETWEEN THE EUROPEAN COURT OF JUSTICE AND THE EUROPEAN COURT OF HUMAN RIGHTS

In their contributions, both Besson and De Witte refer to the intensive interaction that exists between the ECJ and of the ECtHR. Through this cooperation, the two European courts have definitely reinforced each other's authority

11 *Bosphorus Hava Yollari Turizm Ve Ticaret* v *Ireland*, no. 45036/98, [2006] 42 EHRR 1.
12 *M.S.S.* v *Belgium and Greece*, no. 30696/09.

(Chapter 4). This cooperation is not limited to references in their judgments to each other's case law, but also includes formal and regular contacts between members of both courts. Remarkably, the purpose of such meetings is not only to exchange information on their respective case law and expertise as to the treatment of cases at supranational level. It follows from a joint communication issued by the Presidents of the two courts at the occasion of a meeting in January 2011 that they also seek to achieve consensus on important issues related to the applicable human rights standard and the mechanism of enforcement of human rights.[13] On the first issue, both Presidents consider it "*important to ensure that there is the greatest coherence between the Convention and the Charter insofar as the Charter contains rights which correspond to those guaranteed by the Convention*" and believe that "*a 'parallel interpretation' of the two instruments could prove useful*". As far as the review exercised by the ECtHR on Member States' acts implementing EU law, both courts believe that, after the accession of the EU to the Convention, it should be avoided that the ECtHR is to adjudicate on applications calling into question provisions of EU law where the ECJ did not have the opportunity to review the consistency of that law with the fundamental rights of the Charter (e.g. because national courts did not put a preliminary reference to the ECJ). In their view, "*a procedure should be put in place, in connection with the accession of the EU to the Convention, which is flexible and would ensure that the* [ECJ] *may carry out an internal review before the* [ECtHR] *carries out external review*".

4. IMPACT OF THE CO-EXISTENCE OF EUROPEAN PROTECTION MECHANISMS ON THE NATIONAL CONSTITUTIONAL COURTS

Whereas the interrelationship between the ECJ and ECtHR has developed into a classic theme of European and human rights scholarship, we believed that far less has been reflected upon – or at least published on – the impact of the co-existence of two European human rights mechanisms on national courts, in particular on the national constitutional courts, which are generally entrusted with controlling compliance with fundamental rights at national level.

In this respect, legal doctrine has traditionally paid attention to the problem that arises where the ECJ and the ECtHR do not ensure the same level of protection. In practice, however, such situations have been rare, even though doctrinal writings have some malicious tendency to always revisit the few divergences,

13 Joint communication from Presidents Costa and Skouris, annex to Press Release no. 75 of 27 January 2011 ("Joint Statement Issued by the Presidents of the Two European Courts").

which have moreover mostly disappeared (Chapter 1). The question how to deal with divergent European case law has frequently been answered by reference to Article 53 of both the Convention and the Charter, according to which that document does not prevent the application of any higher level of protection where that would follow from any other human rights document. Such "maximisation clause" is often presented as a tool to resolve potential conflicts while giving preference, at the same time, to a level of protection that would arguably benefit from greater democratic legitimacy or would allow to better take into account the specificities of a given community. In her contribution, Van de Heyning warns, however, not to put too high expectations on Article 53 of the Charter as its ECHR counterpart has never played any significant role in the ECtHR's case law. Moreover, a maximisation clause is unfit to give guidance in the event of a conflict between several fundamental rights (Chapter 3). She refers to alternative avenues explored by the ECtHR, such as leaving a margin of appreciation to the Member States and/or exercising restraint towards domestic rulings which demonstrate that a proper balancing has been undertaken that duly took into account the Convention rights. The question arises whether such alternative approaches would be equally acceptable from the ECJ as they are from the ECtHR. In his contribution, De Witte indeed criticises the ECJ where it chooses to leave Member States a margin of appreciation as to the ultimate balancing of human rights rather than to strike itself the right balance (Chapter 1).

Interestingly, the potential risk of divergences between the case law of the European courts does not seem to be the central concern in the contributions that look at the issue from a national perspective. These contributions deal with other themes, such as the (different) status of Convention rights and EU law in the respective national legal orders and the various tools by which Convention rights and EU fundamental rights are enforced, describing the whole spectrum from the "soft" rule to have national rules interpreted as much as possible in conformity with European human rights up to the "hard" solution of invalidating national law that conflicts with European human rights. Many of the contributions warn for the risk of looking at the issue in a uni-dimensional way. They argue that implementing a European human rights standard does not necessarily mean providing the appropriate level of protection. Interestingly, that viewpoint does not only come from Member States, such as Germany and Italy, where national constitutional courts have always been vigilant not to sacrifice the level of human rights protection guaranteed by the national constitution for the mere sake of the supremacy of European law. Let us run through some of the themes that are being discussed in the following articles.

First of all, the picture that our colleagues present from the national perspective makes clear that, even where national constitutional courts seek to implement human rights as laid down in the ECHR or EU law, ECHR fundamental rights are not always endowed with the same legal force as fundamental rights that are recognised within the EU legal order. In France, the constitutional court hardly refers to the ECHR or the ECtHR case law (Chapter 7). Both in Germany and Italy, where constitutional courts have for some time been hesitant to recognise the true supranational nature of EU law, such legal status has definitely not been given to the ECHR, which still has the same status as any other international treaty (Chapters 8 and 9). In the UK, the situation was quite similar until the adoption of the Human Rights Act (Chapter 12). A totally different picture emerges in Belgium, where the constitutional court has from the outset been open to review national legislation in the same way against EU law as against the ECHR (Chapter 5). The same openness towards EU law and the ECHR exists in the Netherlands, which is perhaps less surprising, given the absence of any Dutch constitutional court (Chapter 10). Interestingly, the leading role of EU fundamental rights would appear to match with the leading role that Besson would seem willing to grant to the ECJ as far as fundamental rights within the EU legal order are concerned.

5. IMPACT OF THE ECHR ON NATIONAL CONSTITUTIONAL COURTS

As regards the ECHR, most of the Member States analysed in this book have by now recognised the obligation for national courts to have provisions of national law interpreted as far as possible in conformity with Convention rights (Belgium, Germany, Italy, the Netherlands, United Kingdom). Dickson explains that, when adopting its Human Rights Act, the United Kingdom, rather than accepting the possibility of courts invalidating national legislation, opted for the possibility of courts to issue a declaration of incompatibility, to which the political institutions may respond with legislative changes (Chapter 12). With respect to Germany, Arnold describes that, despite the "dualist" approach taken towards the ECHR, national legislation has often been made subject to ECHR scrutiny (Chapter 8). Whereas the Italian constitutional court has accepted to direct scrutinise legislation against the ECHR, it has at the same time asserted the sole jurisdiction to exercise that control (Chapter 9). The Spanish constitutional court appears to refuse reviewing legislation against any other fundamental rights than those laid down by the constitution, even though its case law is reported to be clearly influenced by the Strasbourg case law (Chapter 11). Likewise, the French constitutional court appears to control compliance with the ECHR while avoiding any reference to Strasbourg case law (Chapter 7). Again, the Belgian constitutional court reveals a very 'open' attitude towards controlling compliance with ECHR rights. Popelier argues that the Belgian constitutional court systematically interprets the fundamental rights laid down by the national constitution in the light of Convention rights, even to the point that, where necessary to ensure coherence, the constitutional rights are being interpreted restrictively (Chapter 5).

6. IMPACT OF EU FUNDAMENTAL RIGHTS ON NATIONAL CONSTITUTIONAL COURTS

In order to ensure the effectiveness of EU law, national courts are to interpret provisions of national law in conformity with EU law and, where a provision of national law would conflict with EU law, including EU fundamental rights, to disapply such provision. In some Member States, however, the constitutional court does not see it as falling within its task of overseeing compliance with the national constitution to control the compatibility of national legislation in the light of EU law. That is the case for the German constitutional court, which, conversely, identified three situations where the compatibility of EU law itself with the German constitution would need to be assessed, that is where the EU would act *ultra vires*, where fundamental rights would not be protected at the same level as under the German constitution and, finally, since the ruling on the Lisbon Treaty, where the constitutional identity of the State would be at stake (Chapter 8). The Spanish constitutional court also formulated reservations with respect to the primacy of EU law over the national constitution, but eventually accepted it as not contrary to the Spanish constitution (Chapter 11). In contrast, the Belgian constitutional court has no difficulties in assessing the compatibility of national legislation with EU law, including EU fundamental rights (Chapter 5). The French *Conseil constitutionnel* initially refused to exercise such control. However, since the recent introduction of the priority constitutional review, it can no longer avoid that exercise (Chapter 7). Remarkably, national courts in both Italy and Spain are reported to have frequently applied the provisions of the Charter (Chapters 9 and 11).

Another interesting theme is the question whether or not the constitutional court of a Member State is ready to engage in dialogue with the ECJ through the preliminary rulings procedure (Article 267 TFEU). It is well known that the Belgian constitutional court has been the first constitutional court to refer to the ECJ, both for questions related to the interpretation of EU law as for doubts on the validity of EU acts (see Chapter 5). The Austrian constitutional court has followed that example, whereas, rather recently, only the Lithuanian and Italian constitutional courts have had recourse to the preliminary rulings procedure. Martinico and Pollicino explain in their contribution that the Italian constitutional court has limited its willingness to refer to the ECJ to proceedings where it is seized with a direct appeal and, in all other cases, still seems to avoid direct interaction with the ECJ, even though it sometimes prevents conflicts by awaiting a ruling of the ECJ before rendering judgment itself (Chapter 9). Nonetheless, it is telling that the German constitutional court, which has never referred to the ECJ, recently accepted that there may be exceptional situations where it would refer to the ECJ, in particular where doubts would arise in a given case as to whether the EU acted *ultra vires* (Chapter 8). As regards the French constitutional court, Burgorgue-Larsen points out that the constitutional court accepts that, where it is seized by judicial organs with a priority constitutional review, such organs themselves also refer to the ECJ, but does not yet seem to realise that following the *Melki* judgment of the ECJ[14] the constitutional court itself may be in a position where such reference becomes unavoidable (Chapter 7).

7. PRESERVING HUMAN RIGHTS OR PRESERVING PROTECTION MECHANISMS?

Finally, it becomes clear from the contributions in this book that, in many Member States, the complexity following from the co-existence of the ECtHR and the ECJ is supplemented with another layer of complexity where there is more than one national court asserting the role of highest guardian of human rights. Member States with a constitutional court may face situations where the highest court of the ordinary judiciary branch – the supreme court – disputes with the constitutional court on the exact delimitation of powers as to the final interpretation of 'European' and 'constitutional' human rights. In France, it appears that for a long period of time the constitutional court has managed to avoid scrutinising legislation on its conformity with human rights. However, as Burgorgue-Larsen points out, once a constitutional court starts taking its role as guardian of the national constitution seriously, it unavoidably needs to take a stance on the interpretation and application of human rights (Chapter 7). In both Belgium and Italy, the national constitutional court has asserted the role of primary guardian of fundamental rights, which has led – at least in Belgium – to tensions between the constitutional court and the supreme court as to the power to interpret and apply 'European' and 'constitutional' human rights. In Belgium and France, the legislator recently opted for a system of references to the constitutional court that requires ordinary judges faced with questions of interpretation of human rights that are protected both at European and national (constitutional) level to refer first to the constitutional court. As far as Belgium is concerned, Popelier argues that it follows from the conception of this system that its first purpose is not to offer the highest protection of human rights against

14 Cases C-188/10 and C-189/10 *Melki and Abdeli* (ECJ 22 June 2010).

the legislator but to avoid situations where other courts than the constitutional court would assess the validity of national legislation. Protection of national legislation would thus seem to obtain priority over human rights protection (Chapter 5).

This leads us to our final remark, which concerns the principal question touched upon, in a direct or indirect way, in most of the contributions collected in this book, namely whether human rights should be best protected at the European level, through the ECHR and/or the incorporation of human rights into EU law, or rather at national level, through the safeguards laid down in the national constitutions. In her contribution, Albi warns against any presumption that conferring the ultimate responsibility for human rights protection at the European level would necessarily lead to the highest protection of human rights. As already mentioned, it is interesting to see that such conclusion is not found on the well-known case law of the German and Italian constitutional court, but on recent case law of Eastern-European constitutional courts where human rights – so argues Albi – are being protected at a higher level than in comparable case law of the ECJ (Chapter 6).

It is certainly true that, in itself, neither the choice for the European protection mechanisms, nor the preference for safeguards at national level, necessarily leads to the highest level of protection of human rights. Moreover, given the direct connection of human rights with ideological, cultural or religious preferences, there is no 'objective' way to determine the most optimal protection of human rights in a given situation: in any such discussion, be it at European or at national level, lawyers will be seen to defend opposing views. Any obligation to give one mechanism of human rights protection priority over another mechanism may in itself be disputed, certainly if the mechanisms are known to lead to diverging assessments of the appropriate level of protection. The least one can say, however, is that the possibility of dialogue between judges at European and national level has the potential to deepen each other's understanding of the values and interests at stake and may thus lead to a better balanced outcome. Interestingly, there may be situations whether the requirement for judges to comply with a specific protection mechanism could be said to form itself part of human rights protection, namely where the right to effective judicial remedies is at stake. Thus, the German constitutional court has considered the obligation for German judges to respect the requirements following from Article 267 TFEU as being linked to the right of any party to be judged by the "legally appointed" judge (*gesetzliche Richter*, see Arnold, Chapter 8).

We hope that the reader finds in this collection valuable information and feed for further thinking. Last but not least, we express our gratitude to all the colleagues who have contributed to this book.

Piet VAN NUFFEL, Patricia POPELIER and Catherine VAN DE HEYNING

I. THE INTERACTION BETWEEN THE EUROPEAN COURT OF JUSTICE AND THE EUROPEAN COURT OF HUMAN RIGHTS

CHAPTER 1

THE USE OF THE ECHR AND CONVENTION CASE LAW BY THE EUROPEAN COURT OF JUSTICE

Bruno De Witte*

1. INTRODUCTION

The Court of Justice of the European Union (ECJ) and the European Court of Human Rights (ECtHR) have been living apart together since 1975, when the ECJ for the first time referred to the text of the European Convention as a source for the interpretation of Community law.[1] Since that time, the formal accession of the European Community to the ECHR became a matter of scholarly and political debate. Like the monster of Loch Ness, the accession question arose from time and time and then disappeared again from the European agenda. The Court of Justice helped to complicate matters by holding in 1996, in its Opinion 2/94, that the European Community did not have the competence to seek accession to the ECHR under the then current EC Treaty.[2] This Opinion has been criticized, and rightly in my view, for being needlessly restrictive and diffident towards the ECHR. As a result of the Opinion, it became necessary for a specific provision to be inserted in the founding Treaties of the European Union in order to authorize this accession. The Treaties of Amsterdam and Nice failed to enact such a specific provision, but the Constitutional Treaty and its avatar the Treaty of Lisbon finally contained the required authorization. Under the Treaty of Lisbon, the European Union is not only entitled but positively required to seek accession to the ECHR.[3] Whether this treaty duty becomes reality will depend

* Thanks to Vasiliki Kosta, PhD researcher at the European University Institute, for valuable research assistance.

1 Case C-36/75 *Rutili v Minister for the Interior*, [1975] ECR 1219, para. 32.

2 ECJ, Opinion 2/94 on Accession by the Community to the ECHR, [1996] ECR I-1759, para.35.

3 Article 6(2) TEU (as revised by the Treaty of Lisbon): "The Union shall accede to the European Convention for the Protection of Human Rights and Fundamental Freedoms. Such accession shall not affect the Union's competences as defined in the Treaties." For a discussion of the legal issues arising in this accession process, see, in particular: O De Schutter, "L'adhésion de

on the outcome of the on-going negotiations and, ultimately, on the cooperation of the non-EU parties to the European Convention, including Russia, and on the ratification by all the member states of the Council of Europe.

In its Opinion 2/94, the Court of Justice had expressed a clear preference for continuing to live 'apart' from the European Court of Human Rights, but it showed that it nevertheless wanted to operate 'together' with the Strasbourg court. It acted 'as if', trying to organise the relationship between EU law and Convention law in such a way that these legal orders did not grow apart and that the legal reality resembled to what it would be like if the EU were a party to the ECHR.[4] The wheels of cooperation are also being oiled extra-judicially by means of regular institutional meetings of members of the two Courts, as well as occasional meetings of individual judges during academic conferences or other European legal events. On such occasions, the members of both courts express satisfaction about the way in which they respect each other's role. In particular, in relation to the subject of this intervention, the members of the ECHR express their appreciation for the active application of ECHR standards by the Court of Justice of the European Union. The members of the ECJ are similarly upbeat. They see a clear crescendo in the attention given in Luxembourg to the ECHR and its court's case law. For example, Allan Rosas, a judge at the Court of Justice, notes the following stages in the case law of his court:

> 'fundamental rights outside the competence of the Court; fundamental rights as part of the general principles of Community law (since 1969); explicit reference to the ECHR (since 1974); characterization of the ECHR as having "special significance" (since 1989); and reference to individual judgments of the European Court of Human Rights (since the 1990s).'[5]

The mutual congratulations are strategically *appropriate*, since they help to bolster the legitimacy of both international courts as protectors of human rights

l'Union européenne à la Convention européenne des droits de l'homme: feuille de route de la négociation" [2010] *Revue trimestrielle des droits de l'homme,* pp. 535–571; and T Lock, "EU Accession to the ECHR: Implications for Judicial Review in Strasbourg" [2010] *European Law Review*, pp. 777–798.

4 "Tant que l'adhésion de l'Union européenne à la Convention n'est pas devenue une réalité juridique tangible, il est toujours aussi passionnant d'étudier la manière avec laquelle les deux Cours agissent "comme si", comme si cette fameuse adhésion était effective afin de ne pas générer la création et le développement d'une Europe des droits de l'homme à plusieurs vitesses." (L Burgorgue-Larsen, (2007) "Jurisprudence européenne comparée", (2008) *Revue du droit public* 1435–1461, p. 1435).

5 A Rosas, "The European Union and Fundamental Rights/Human Rights" in C Krause and M Scheinin (eds), *International Protection of Human Rights: A Textbook* (Institute for Human Rights, Åbo Akademy University 2009), p. 457.

in the face of possible criticism by national, judicial and political, actors.[6] The congratulations are also *justified* since both courts are genuinely concerned to respect each other's role in the European legal space. In the case of the ECJ, there is an additional reason to take the ECHR seriously: as long as the EU has not acceded to the Convention, the Court in Strasbourg has agreed not to scrutinize national measures implementing EU law if, and as long as, the EU legal order provides 'equivalent protection' to the Convention rights. This is the gist of the famous *Bosphorus* doctrine of the ECtHR, formulated in 2005 and more recently reaffirmed (by a majority of the Chamber judges) in the *Kokkelvisserij* decision of 20 January 2009.[7]

So, is everything going well in the best of all possible worlds? Not entirely, perhaps. I will discuss in the following pages two questions that still appear problematic when examining the Court of Justice's 'take' on the ECHR and on the case law from Strasbourg. The first question, which is primarily of theoretical importance, is that of the formal legal status of the ECHR in the EU legal order which is still somewhat unsettled, rather strangely so after many years of interaction between the legal orders (section 2). The second question, which is more important in practice, is that of the effective reliance by the ECJ on the ECHR and the relevant case law: it will be argued that the ECJ takes an eclectic and unsystematic approach to the Convention (section 3). In the final section 4, I will propose a few reflections on future developments of the ECJ's use of the Convention now that the Treaty of Lisbon has entered into force.

2. THE CONVENTION: A SOURCE OF SPECIAL GUIDELINES OR OF BINDING NORMS?

Neither the European Community nor the European Union have (so far) become parties to any of the core regional and universal human rights instruments: the European Convention on Human Rights, the European Social Charter, the two UN Covenants, the UN Conventions on Race Discrimination, on Discrimination against Women and on the Rights of Children, or the main conventions of the

---

6 See L Scheeck, "La diplomatie commune des cours européennes" in P Mbongo and A Vauchez (eds), *Dans la fabrique du droit européen* (Bruylant, Brussels 2009) 105–137.

7 *Cooperatieve Producentenorganisatie van de Nederlandse Kokkelvisserij v the Netherlands* (admissibility decision) App. no. 13645/05 (ECtHR, 20 January 2009). The case dealt with the compatibility of the role of the Advocate-General at the ECJ with the fair trial guarantee of the ECHR. It thus raised one of the few potential areas of open contrast between the ECHR and EU law. The prudent attitude of the ECtHR allowed it to bypass this potential conflict already at the admissibility stage. See the case comment by C Van de Heyning in (2009) *Common Market Law Review*, pp. 2117–2125.

International Labour Organisation.[8] In this respect, the European Union finds itself in a very different position from that of its Member States. To the extent that those Member States have transferred many powers to the EU in fields covered by those international instruments, they can no longer fully ensure compliance with their international obligations, and there arises a potential gap in the protection of human rights.

The gap has been plugged, to some extent, by the Court of Justice of the European Union through its well-established use of international human rights instruments as 'sources of inspiration' for the development of the unwritten general principles of Community law (now called, after the entry into force of the Treaty of Lisbon, general principles of Union law). These principles are part of primary EU law and a frequently used basis for the judicial review and interpretation of EU acts, and of Member State measures coming within the scope of EU law. The Court of Justice presents this rather complex legal situation in the following typical way:

> 'it should be recalled that, according to settled case-law, fundamental rights form an integral part of the general principles of law the observance of which the Court ensures, and that, for that purpose, the Court draws inspiration from the constitutional traditions common to the Member States and from the guidelines supplied by international treaties for the protection of human rights on which the Member States have collaborated or to which they are signatories. The ECHR has special significance in that respect.'[9]

According to this formula, the ECHR has 'special significance', but its formal status seems to be the same as that of other international instruments, namely that of offering 'guidelines' from which the Court 'draws inspiration' in fine-tuning its own general principles of EU law.

The General Court has spelled out the 'negative' side of this positively sounding formula by stating explicitly that the Convention is not applicable as such within the Community legal order. It did so, among other cases, in the *Treuhand* judgment[10]:

---

8 Only very recently did the European Community conclude its first true human rights treaty, namely the UN Convention on the Rights of Persons with Disabilities. See L Waddington, "Breaking New Ground: The Implications of Ratification of the UN Convention on the Rights of Persons with Disabilities for the European Community", in OM Arnardottir and G Quinn (eds), *The UN Convention on the Rights of Persons with Disabilities – European and Scandinavian Perspectives* (Martinus Nijhoff Publishers, Dordrecht 2009), pp. 111–140.

9 Case 479/04 *Laserdisken ApS v Kulturministeriet* [2006] ECR I-8089, para. 61; identical or almost identical paragraphs appear in most ECJ judgments dealing with fundamental rights, including in the famous *Kadi* judgment: ECJ, Joined Cases C-402/05 P and C-415/05 P *Kadi and Al Barakaat v Council* [2008] ECR I-6351, para. 283.

10 Case T-99/04 *AC-Treuhand v Commission* [2008] ECR II-1501, para. 45 (emphasis added).

'It should be pointed out, at the outset, that the *Court has no jurisdiction to assess the lawfulness of an investigation under competition law in the light of provisions of the ECHR, inasmuch as those provisions do not as such form part of Community law.* That said, the fact remains that the Community judicature is called upon to ensure the observance of the fundamental rights which form an integral part of the general principles of law and, for that purpose, it draws inspiration from the constitutional traditions common to the Member States and from the guidelines supplied by international instruments for the protection of human rights, on which the Member States have collaborated and to which they are signatories. In that regard, the ECHR has special significance, as confirmed by Article 6(2) EU.'

This position corresponds to the generally accepted view in the EU legal literature. Most authors praise the ECJ for making frequent reference not just to the text of the Convention but also to the Strasbourg court's case law, but add that the ECHR is still not formally binding on the EU institutions as long as the Union has not acceded to the Convention. For example, Allan Rosas, judge at the ECJ and a leading expert on international human rights law, recently wrote: 'as the EU is not a Contracting Party to the ECHR, the Convention is not a binding Community law instrument but plays a role rather as an authoritative guideline for determining the general principles of Community law which the Court applies.'[11] The current President of the European Court of Human Rights declared himself in agreement with this view. In a lecture held at King's College London in October 2008 he stated: 'It is of course true that formally speaking the Convention is not binding under European Union law.'[12]

Even though this is the received wisdom, it does not seem a very satisfactory account of the current state of the law, in the light of the wording of Article 6(3) TEU, which states:

'Fundamental rights, *as guaranteed by the European Convention* for the Protection of Human Rights and Fundamental Freedoms and as they result from the constitutional traditions common to the Member States, shall constitute general principles of the Union's law.'[13]

Although this sentence was slightly rephrased compared to its pre-Lisbon version (when it figured in Article 6(2) EU Treaty), the wording of its core normative

---

11 A Rosas, "The European Union and Fundamental Rights/Human Rights", n. 5 above, at 457–8; see, similarly, G Harpaz, "The European Court of Justice and its Relations with the European Court of Human Rights: The Quest for Enhanced Reliance, Coherence and Legitimacy", [2009] *Common Market Law Review* 105, p. 108–115.

12 J-P Costa, "The Relationship between the European Convention on Human Rights and European Union Law – A Jurisprudential Dialogue between the European Court of Human Rights and the European Court of Justice", Lecture at King's College London, 7 October 2008, p. 2 (available on the Court's website).

13 Emphasis added.

statement has remained unaltered ever since the Maastricht Treaty, when the sentence was first introduced in the EU Treaty. That statement indicates that the rights of the Convention *are* general principles of EU law and not just a *source of inspiration* for those principles. So, the language of the EU Treaty seems to very clearly express the will of the Member States to make the ECHR rights formally binding on the EU institutions, rather than just a source of inspiration which the Court *may decide* to use in shaping 'its' unwritten general principles. At the time of the Maastricht Treaty, the expression of that will of the Member States was rather half-hearted, since Article F(2) (as it then was) was not among the provisions of the EU Treaty which the Court was allowed to apply and enforce. This anomaly was corrected by the Treaty of Amsterdam which made Article 6(2) – as it was then renumbered – judicially enforceable. It is true that Article 6(2) TEU pre-Lisbon, and Article 6(3) TEU now, did not make the Convention applicable *as such* within the EU legal order, but only through the formal intermediary of the general principles of Union law. But the text makes it clear that the Convention rights *are actually* incorporated within the category of general principles without leaving any discretion in this regard to the ECJ; one could say that the Court's traditional power to 'fill' with content the category of the unwritten general principles had been partially taken away by the Member States when they adopted the Maastricht Treaty.

There is therefore no doubt, in my view, that Article 6(3) TEU gives formal binding status to the entire content of the ECHR within the EU legal order, and it is quite curious that the Court of Justice and most of the legal literature have failed to draw that conclusion. Perhaps this is due to a confusion between two separate legal questions: the question whether the European Union (and, until its recent demise, the European Community) is bound by the ECHR *under international law* (it is not, since it has not signed and ratified the Convention) and the question whether the ECHR is binding for the EU institutions *as a matter of European Union law* (this is so, in view of the unambiguous language of Article 6 TEU). A similar distinction can be made with regard to the Geneva Convention on Refugees. Neither the EC nor the EU have become parties to that Convention, so that the European Union, as an *international* subject, is not bound by it; but the Geneva Convention has been made binding *internally* for the EU institutions when developing their asylum policy, by means of Article 78(1) TFEU.[14]

14 Article 78(1) TFEU: "The Union shall develop a common policy on asylum, subsidiary protection and temporary protection with a view to offering appropriate status to any third-country national requiring international protection and ensuring compliance with the principle of *non-refoulement*. This policy must be in accordance with the Geneva Convention of 28 July 1951 and the Protocol of 31 January 1967 relating to the status of refugees, and other relevant treaties." Before the entry into force of the Lisbon Treaty, a quasi-identical provision was to be found in Article 63(1) EC Treaty.

On a closer look, one does find some judgments of the Court of Justice in which it drops the 'special significance' terminology and refers directly to the ECHR as if it considered the Convention to be formally binding. Among the examples of this approach which, I submit, expresses a more accurate reading of current EU law, one could mention the *Elgafaji* judgment of 2009, in which the Court stated *obiter* that 'the ECHR forms part of the general principles of Community law, observance of which is ensured by the Court'.[15] In *Orfanopoulos,* the Court mentioned 'the right to respect for family life as guaranteed by Article 8 of the ECHR, which is among the fundamental rights which, according to the Court's settled case law, are protected in Community law.'[16] In *Varec*, the ECJ applied both Articles 6 and 8 ECHR in a straightforward manner without mentioning the *détour* of 'general principles'.[17] In *Schneider Electric* (a competition law case), the General Court held simply that 'observance of all persons' right to a hearing before an independent and impartial tribunal is guaranteed by Article 6(1) of the Convention, to which reference is made by Article 6(2) of the Treaty on European Union, and which was reaffirmed by the second paragraph of Article 47 of the Charter of Fundamental rights of the European Union.'[18] Here, as in *Varec*, the passage through the general principles channel is completely elided.[19]

This tendency of the Court of Justice to anchor the ECHR more strongly into the EU legal order is pursued with some hesitation (in many other recent cases, the Court reverts to the 'special significance' formula which I quoted above), but it should be pursued more vigorously, since it corresponds to the wording of Article 6(3) TEU. It would also make the EU's future accession to the ECHR (now imposed by Article 6 TEU) an easier step to take from the 'domestic' EU perspective. Indeed, if the Court of Justice were to recognize that the ECHR is formally binding on the EU institutions already now, then the future accession would not cause any major change in the Court's use of the Convention. That would not render the accession meaningless, of course. Whereas the current reference to the ECHR, in Article 6 TEU, is quite generic, accession would require the European Union to nail its colours to the mast by deciding which Protocols of the Convention to ratify (for example, should it ratify Protocol No. 12 containing a general prohibition of discrimination which few of its Member States have so far ratified?) and whether or not to make reservations upon ratification. As regards the role of the Court of Justice, accession would make EU

---

15 Case C-465/07 *Meki Elgafaji, Noor Elgafaji v Staatssecretaris van Justitie* [2009] ECR I-0921, para. 28.

16 Joined Cases C-482/01 and C-493/01 *Georgios Orfanopoulos et al. v Land Baden-Württemberg* [2004] ECR I-5257, para. 98.

17 Case C-450/06 *Varec SA v Etat belge* [2008] ECR I-581, para. 44 ff.

18 Case T-351/03 *Schneider Electric v Commission* [2007] ECR II-2237, para. 181.

19 Another example still of a direct reference to the ECHR as a binding source of EU law is Case C-404/07 *György Katz v István Roland Sós*, [2008] ECR I-7607, para. 48–49.

acts directly reviewable by the ECtHR, and might thus 'concentrate the mind' of the Court of Justice to shadow the Strasbourg case law even more closely than today, so as to avoid being second-guessed or overruled by the Strasbourg court in human rights cases. Indeed, the current practice of the ECJ does not always – despite the friendly rhetoric – closely follow the case law of the Human Rights Court, as will be illustrated in the following section.

3. SYSTEMATIC OR ECLECTIC USE OF THE CONVENTION?

After discussing the formal legal status of the ECHR in the EU legal order, I will now look more closely at the *actual use* made by the Court of Justice, and the General Court, of the European Convention and its case law. The received view on this matter is formulated as follows by former Advocate-General Jacobs:

> 'The ECJ has treated (…) the European Convention on Human Rights as if it were binding upon the Community, and has followed scrupulously the case-law of the European Court of Human rights, even though the European Union itself is not a party to the Convention.'[20]

In fact, the Court of Justice has not always followed the case-law of its sister court, and even now it does not do so 'scrupulously'. Explicit references to judgments of the European Court of Human Rights have appeared in the ECJ's case law only at a relatively recent date, namely in 1996, that is, more than twenty years after the ECHR was first acknowledged as a source of inspiration. The first such reference occurred in the case of *P & S* in which the ECJ gave judgment on 30 April 1996,[21] that is, one month after it had closed off the possibility of EC accession to the ECHR in its Opinion 2/94.[22] So, this new willingness to refer not only to the Convention text but also to the interpretation by the Strasbourg court could be seen as a compensation for the fact that the Court of Justice had made it impossible – at least until a hypothetical treaty revision – for Community acts to become subject to review directly by the ECtHR. Since 1996, references to judgments of the ECtHR have become quite frequent in the ECJ's fundamental rights case law, including in some of the leading cases such as *Kadi* (2008).[23]

20 F Jacobs, *The Sovereignty of Law* (Cambridge University Press, Cambridge 2007), p. 54.

21 Case C-13/94 *P. v S. and Cornwall County Council* [1996] ECR I-1827.

22 ECJ, Opinion 2/94 [1996] ECR I-1759 (see n. 2 above) was delivered on 28 March 1996.

23 ECJ, *Kadi and Al Barakaat v Council* (n. 9 above), para. 360, 363 and 368 (reference to ECtHR judgments about the right to property) and para. 344 (reference to ECtHR judgments about the right to effective judicial protection). See also the follow-up judgment of the General Court, Case T-85/09, *Kadi v Commission*, judgment of 30 September 2010, para. 176 (with a lengthy reference to a ECtHR judgment about procedural fairness).

Indeed, as was noted,[24] the Luxembourg judges have not cited any other body of 'external' case law with such regularity.

For a long time, legal writing has focused on exploring *divergences* between the case law of both Courts, but those divergences were always very rare, and the few that existed (such as, on whether business firms were protected by the right to privacy, alongside individual people)[25] have long been corrected. The ECJ hardly ever departs from the Strasbourg case law and never openly contradicts it.[26] Does this mean, as Francis Jacobs claims in the extract cited above, that the ECJ has *followed scrupulously* the case law of the ECtHR? Not exactly, it seems to me. Rather, as I will argue in the following pages, the Court of Justice has made an *eclectic and unsystematic use* of the ECHR and the Strasbourg case law, which is not so dissimilar from the eclectic use which is now made by the Strasbourg court of the fundamental rights jurisprudence of the ECJ.[27] I will highlight, in the following pages, some forms and patterns of eclectic use that emerge from the recent practice of the Court of Justice.

The European Court of Human Rights does not impose an obligation on domestic courts to cite the ECHR, or its judgments, leaving it to those domestic courts to avoid breaches of the Convention from arising with whatever legal means they may, or wish, to use. Similarly, the fact that the Convention is binding on the EU (as argued in the previous section) does not put the Court of Justice under an obligation to cite the Convention case law. Yet, the ECJ also considers, more generally and more controversially, that it does not need to deal with arguments of Convention rights violation by the EU institutions if such

---

24 S Douglas-Scott, "A Tale of Two Courts: Luxembourg, Strasbourg and the Growing European Human Rights *Acquis*" [2006] *Common Market Law Review* 629, p. 650.

25 The Court of Justice accepted the ECtHR's extensive interpretation of the right to privacy, and overruled its own more restrictive reading that it had followed in earlier judgments, in Case C-94/00, *Roquette frères SA v DGCCRF* [2002] ECR I-9011, para. 29. See, for instance, S Marciali, "Les rapports entre les systèmes européens de protection des droits fondamentaux", in J Rideau (dir.), *Les droits fondamentaux dans l'Union européenne – Dans le sillage de la constitution européenne* (Bruylant, Brussels 2009) 345–377, pp. 349–350.

26 The one area in which the ECJ seemed definitely unwilling to follow the lead of the ECtHR (although there never was an open clash) was in respect of its own institutional functioning, namely on the question whether the fair trial right of Article 6 ECHR required that parties to an ECJ case should be able to respond to the Opinion of the Advocate-General. See, for a discussion of this mini-saga of national and European case law: M Lasser, *Judicial Transformations – The Rights Revolution in the Courts of Europe* (Oxford University Press, Oxford 2009), chapter 6.

27 Douglas-Scott (n. 24 above, p. 655) refers, in the same vein, to "inchoate borrowings" by both courts (ECJ and ECtHR) from each other's jurisprudence. On the "reverse" borrowing, by Strasbourg from Luxembourg, see R Lawson, "Ex Boreale Lux – On the Influence of the ECJ on the Interpretation of the ECHR", in M Bulterman, L Hancher, A McDonnell and H Sevenster (eds), *Views of European Law from the Mountain – Liber Amicorum for Piet Jan Slot* (Kluwer, The Hague 2009) 439–454.

arguments are not raised by the parties to the case. A good illustration of this position is the judgment of 2009 in *Ireland v Parliament and Council*. The Court of Justice was asked to decide whether Directive 2006/24, which imposes a duty on information service providers to retain electronic communication data for a certain period of time in order to make them available for possible criminal investigations, had been correctly based on Article 95 EC Treaty (the EC's internal market competence) or should rather have been based, as Ireland claimed, on the legal basis provided by Title VI of the EU Treaty (the EU's criminal law competence). The content of that directive had been contested, at the time of its adoption, by several NGOs as containing excessive restrictions of the fundamental right to privacy of the users of information services, which is protected by Article 8 ECHR. However, the fundamental rights issue was not raised by the parties before the ECJ, because the applicant state Ireland, in reality, would have preferred the EU measure on data retention to be *more* rather than less restrictive of privacy and, therefore, had no inclination to challenge it by invoking fundamental rights. The Court of Justice laconically commented that 'the action brought by Ireland relates solely to the choice of legal basis and not to any possible infringement of fundamental rights arising from interference with the exercise of the right to privacy contained in Directive 2006/24', and it did not deal with fundamental rights in the rest of the judgment since doing so would be *ultra petita*.[28] Thus, fundamental rights protection, as embodied in the ECHR, is treated by the ECJ, in this case, as an issue to be addressed only if the parties to the case raise it, rather than as a matter of constitutional order to be raised by the Court on its own motion where necessary. This stands uneasily next to a statement made by the Court of Justice a few months before, in the *Kadi and Al Barakaat* judgment, that 'the protection of fundamental rights, including the review by the Community judicature of the lawfulness of Community measures as regards their consistency with those fundamental rights' constitutes a principle 'that forms part of the very foundations of the Community legal order.'[29] If a directive is widely suspected of being in breach of the 'very foundations of the legal order', and even if none of the parties to a case raises that question, should the Court not raise it of its own motion? Also, one may wonder whether the Court of Justice will be able to stick to this orthodox conception of the *ultra petita* principle once the EU will have acceded to the Convention. Indeed, by not addressing a serious issue of Convention compatibility when none of the parties raise it, the Court would then expose the Union to an adverse ruling of the ECtHR in a future case.

In other cases, the Court goes one step further by not addressing the ECHR-based arguments *even* when they are put forward by the parties to the case,

28 Case C-301/06 *Ireland v Parliament and Council*, judgment [2009] ECR I-593, para. 57.
29 Judgment of 3 September 2008, n. 9 above, para. 304.

because it considers that the case can be decided on other grounds. A rather spectacular example of this approach was the *Passenger Names Records* case, in which the European Parliament had challenged a Commission and a Council act preparing the conclusion of an agreement with the United States on making available personal data of air travellers to the US authorities in the context of the fight against terrorism. The acts were challenged on two very different grounds, namely (1) that the Commission and the Council, when concluding the agreement, had used the wrong legal basis and (2) that they had breached the fundamental right to privacy, protected by Article 8 ECHR. The Court of Justice chose to annul the measures on the first ground without addressing the constitutionally more important ground of breach of fundamental rights.[30] Such an approach can, generally speaking, be defended on grounds of judicial economy ('one problem at a time'), but it is disputable whether this is also appropriate when fundamental rights stemming from the ECHR are at stake.[31] Here again, accession to the Convention would make this approach more 'risky' from a strictly legal point of view.

Similar examples can be found among the Court's preliminary rulings. Thus, in the case *Europa 7*, the referring Italian court had asked, as its first question, whether the Italian practice for the attribution of broadcasting licences was in violation of Article 10 ECHR, but the Court of Justice, after having found that the practice was in breach of (other) norms of EU law, namely those on the freedom to provide services, decided that an answer to the ECHR-related question was superfluous[32] – although one could well argue that the issue of a possible breach of freedom of expression was indeed very relevant to the further stages of the dispute before the Italian court.

In other cases, though, the Court of Justice *does* raise of its own accord fundamental rights issues even when the parties did not mention them – not, it is true, for reviewing the legality of an EU measure, but for *interpreting* EU law in a rights-friendly sense. An example of this is the *Promusicae* ruling of 2008. In this case, that originally arose before Spanish courts, the association of

---

30 ECJ, Joined Cases C-317/04 and C-318/04 *Parliament v Council and Commission* [2006] I-4721.

31 See similarly Case C-376/98 *Germany v Parliament and Council* (2000) ECR I-8419 (the "first" tobacco advertising case), in which the ECJ decided to annul the directive banning advertising for tobacco products on the ground that its legal basis did not cover all of its content, without addressing the issue of a possible violation of the freedom of expression of tobacco producers and advertisers, an issue which had also been raised by the German government in its application.

32 Case C-380/05 *Centro Europa 7 Srl v Ministero delle Comunicazioni et al.* [2008] ECR I-0349, para. 120–122. Compare with Advocate-General Poiares Maduro, who referred (in para. 39 of his Opinion in this case) to the ECHR and to a ECtHR ruling for the interpretation of the relevant norms of Community law.

Spanish music producers had invoked the terms of an EC copyright directive in order to compel a provider of information services to disclose traffic data that would identify infringers of copyright on the internet (the customers had used the KaZaA file exchange programme). To strengthen their argument, the music producers also invoked the articles of the EU Charter of Fundamental Rights protecting the right to property, including intellectual property, and the right to effective judicial protection. The defendant, Telefónica, invoked another piece of EC legislation, namely the Electronic Data Protection directive, in order to refuse the request. When asked to interpret the relevant norms of EC law, the Court of Justice decided to take a broader fundamental rights perspective than that proposed by the applicant. It agreed that the right to property should weigh on the interpretation of the case, but it added that the service providing firm could also have invoked a fundamental right (although it did not), namely the right to protection of the privacy and personal data of its customers, which is contained in Article 8 of the ECHR. The ECJ concluded:

> 'The present reference for a preliminary ruling thus raises the question of the need to reconcile the requirements of the protection of different fundamental rights, namely the right to respect for private life on the one hand and the right to protection of property and to an effective remedy on the other.'[33]

Thus, the ECJ neutralized the interpretative force of the Convention as invoked by one party by constructing, of its own motion, another Convention-based argument on the other side of the dispute. Disappointingly, though, whilst imposing on the Member States, and their courts, the obligation to strike a fair balance between the various fundamental rights, the Court of Justice did not give any useful indications on *where* to strike it in the given case.[34] In this case, the Court may be blamed for giving ringing but cheap endorsement to the importance of protecting fundamental rights (including ECHR rights) even when not expressly invoked by the parties, but taking no interest in how the actual balance between conflicting rights will turn out. It thus accepts that the balance will be struck rather differently from one country to another, and also, that some national courts may fall foul of the Convention. In cases such as this one, when national authorities and courts clearly act within the scope of EU law but receive no substantive guidance on the interpretation of fundamental rights from the view of the Court of Justice, the question arises whether the 'protective screen of EU law', recognized by the ECtHR in *Bosphorus*, still applies. Can one say that the ECJ offers 'equivalent protection', in the sense of the *Bosphorus*

33 Case C-275/06 *Productores de Musica de España (Promusicae) v Telefonica de España SAU* [2008] ECR I-271, para. 65.

34 For further discussion of this case from the angle of fundamental rights protection, see V Kosta, "Internal Market Legislation and the Private Law of the Member States – The Impact of Fundamental Rights"[2010] *European Review of Contract Law* 409, p. 424–9.

doctrine, when it merely refers to the provisions of the ECHR without pronouncing itself on their application to the facts of the case? In such cases, the national authorities effectively act 'on their own' so that there seems every reason to apply the normal standards of Strasbourg scrutiny to their performance, rather than the deferential standard for EU-based member action that was formulated in *Bosphorus*.

The situation exemplified by the *Promusicae* case, in which contrasting fundamental rights are pitted against each other, becomes rather more frequent in EU legal practice, and shows that the fundamental rights jurisprudence (and the EU legal order as a whole) is maturing to such an extent that it now replicates the fundamental rights constellations with which national constitutional courts are familiar. Still, the impression arises that it is mostly a matter of good or bad luck whether such a potential fundamental rights clash is identified by the ECJ or not. Take, for example, the *Dynamic Medien* case which raised the question whether the German authorities could impose additional national controls, for age classification purposes, on videos and DVDs imported from the UK where they had already received a minimum-age label. Advocate-General Mengozzi, in his Opinion on the case, had referred to the ECHR as providing a standard of freedom of expression with which EU Member States have to comply when restricting the freedom of goods, but the Court chose not to complicate the assessment and refrained from mentioning Convention law and its guarantee of freedom of expression, insisting instead on a fundamental rights argument pointing in the other direction, namely the fact that the German authorities had complied with a duty of states under the UN Convention on the Rights of the Child to restrict the marketing of goods that may harm children.[35]

As with the UN Child Convention in *Dynamic Medien*, references to the ECHR and case law of the ECtHR may also lead, occasionally, to an outcome which is restrictive of individual rights and protective of the policy discretion of state authorities. In *Kabel Deutschland*, the Court of Justice interpreted a piece of EU legislation, the Universal Service Directive (which was part of the legislative 'package' on electronic communications adopted in 2002), as allowing the Member States to restrict the freedom of cable TV operators to choose which channels to broadcast through the imposition of so-called 'must carry' rules.[36] In reaching that result, the Court relied on the existence of a *positive* obligation for States, under Article 10 ECHR, to guarantee the viewers' freedom to receive information by preserving a pluralist offer of broadcasting services – but the

[35] Case C-244/06 *Dynamic Medien Vertriebs GmbH v Avides Media AG* [2008] ECR I-0505, para. 39–41; Opinion of Advocate-General Mengozzi of 13 September 2007, para. 91.

[36] Case C-336/07 *Kabel Deutschland Vertrieb und Service GmbH v Niedersächsische Landesmedienanstalt für privaten Rundfunk* [2008] ECR I-9459, paras. 33–38.

Court did so without referring to the ECtHR judgments in which this interpretation of Article 10, which is not evident from the text, was formulated. Along the same lines, we may also cite the *Hans Werhof* judgment on the interpretation of the EC directive on safeguarding employees' rights in case of a transfer of undertakings. The Court of Justice decided to interpret the text of the directive in the light of the freedom of association – that is, the 'negative' freedom of an employer *not to join* an association, thereby using the Convention (which had not been mentioned at all by the referring national judge) in order to reach a rather paradoxical result, namely that of limiting the rights of employees under a social policy directive.[37]

It often happens that the ECHR is not mentioned by the Court of Justice at all, despite references to it by other actors involved in the case, whether the referring national court, or the parties to the case, or the Advocate-General. For example, in *Satamedia*, a data protection case stemming from Finland, Advocate-General Kokott had referred in great detail to the relevant Strasbourg case law on conflicts between data protection and freedom of expression, but the Court chose to deal with the conflict on the basis of EC legislation and the general principles of Community law, without reference to the Convention articles nor to the available judgments from Strasbourg.[38] Part of the explanation for this attitude may be the subject matter of the case. It seems that there are certain areas, such as data protection, where the ECJ feels now sufficiently confident to rely on its own precedents rather than on Convention law.

This is also, and even more clearly, the case in relation to the rights of defence and the right to be heard in EU administrative law. Although these rights are protected, to some extent at least, by Article 6 ECHR,[39] the Court of Justice prefers to treat them as self standing EU general principles with only an occasional nod to the ECHR.[40] To the extent that those rights have been given

37 Case C-499/04, *Hans Werhof* [2006] ECR I-2397.

38 Case C-73/07, *Tietosuojavaltuutettu v Satakunnan Markkinapörssi Oy, Satamedia Oy* [2008] ECR I-5887, para. 52–62; opinion of Advocate-General Kokott of 8 May 2008, para. 37–45. See the critical comment on this case by P Oliver, "The Protection of Privacy in the Economic Sphere before the European Court of Justice" [2009] *Common Market Law Review* 1483, at 1459 ff.

39 On the meaning of the notion of "civil rights and obligations", to which the fair trial guarantees of Article 6 ECHR apply, see e.g. A Mowbray, *Cases and Materials on the European Convention on Human Rights* (Oxford University Press, Oxford 2007) 341 ff.

40 See, for characteristic examples of this, Case C-349/07 *Sopropé v Fazenda Pública* [2008] ECR I-10369; and Case C-385/07 P *Der Grüne Punkt – Duales System Deutschland* [2009] ECR I-6155, para. 177 (Article 6 ECHR is mentioned, but not the case law of the ECtHR, and the question of whether there was a fair hearing within a reasonable time is pursued in the light of the ECJ's own precedents). A counter-example, in which the ECJ *did* refer to ECtHR case law in a fair hearing case, is Case C-276/01 *Joachim Steffensen* [2003] ECR I-3735, para. 75–77. For a general discussion of this question, see A Ward, "National and EC Remedies under the

protection in the EU legal order which extends beyond the minimum protection offered by the ECHR, this attitude is justified: there is no need to refer to the ECHR if the standard of fundamental rights protection offered by EU law is more generous. But there are two 'weak spots' of the EU legal order in this domain.

The first of those weak spots concerns the *right of access to a court,* which is protected by Article 6 and Article 13 ECHR, and which the EU legal order does not guarantee in certain respects and in certain areas. This is a deficiency which, to some extent has been inflicted on the EU legal order by the 'Masters of the Treaties', and which the Court of Justice cannot remedy,[41] but the Court's restrictive approach to the standing of private individuals to challenge EU measures under the former Article 230 EC (now Article 263 TFEU) is largely of its own making and is problematic in the light of Article 6 ECHR.[42] When the General Court, in the famous *Jego Quéré* judgment of 2002, sought to broaden the notion of individual concern that served as a condition for the standing of private litigants under Article 230 EC, it argued that a change was needed in order to comply with Articles 6 and 13 ECHR;[43] whereas the Court of Justice, when it rejected its junior court's novel approach some months later in *Union de Pequeños Agricultores* and confirmed the restrictive *Plaumann* test for individual access, also referred to Article 6 and 13 of the Convention, but did not discover in those Convention articles a requirement to modify its restrictive case law.[44] Neither the General Court nor the Court of the Justice referred, in those judgments, to the relevant case law of the ECtHR. It is probably fair to say that the question of the adequacy of the standing of private individuals to challenge EU acts was seen by both courts as primarily a matter of 'domestic EU law' rather than one of compliance with the Convention.[45] The second area of uncertainty concerning Article 6 ECHR is in relation to EU competition proceedings. The Court of Justice has accepted the Convention jurisprudence according to which severe administrative sanctions (such as competition law sanctions) are equivalent to criminal sanctions for the purpose of Article 6, but some of the

EU Treaty: Limits and the Role of the ECHR", in C Barnard and O Odudu (eds), *The Outer Limits of European Union Law* (Hart Publishing, Oxford 2009), pp. 329–361.

41 This was the case, in particular, for the intergovernmental pillars of the EU in the pre-Lisbon era; see A Hinarejos, *Judicial Control in the European Union – Reforming Jurisdiction in the Intergovernmental Pillars* (Oxford University Press, Oxford 2009).

42 See a detailed discussion of this issue by T Corthaut and F Vanneste, "Waves between Strasbourg and Luxembourg: The Right of Access to a Court to Contest the Validity of Legislative or Administrative Measures" [2006] *Yearbook of European Law* 475.

43 GC, Case T-177/01 *Jégo-Quéré v Commission* [2002] ECR II- 2365, para. 47.

44 ECJ, C-50/00 P *Union de Pequeños Agricultores v Council* [2002] ECR I- 6677, para. 39.

45 See, however, the ECJ judgment in Case C-229/05 P *Osman Öcalan et al.* [2007] ECR I-439, para. 76 ff., where the Court interprets the standing rules of (then) Article 230 EC in the light of Article 34 ECHR, which is the provision defining the conditions for individual applications to the European Human Rights Court.

detailed aspects of the Commission's antitrust investigations have been argued to fall foul of the evolving Article 6 case law of the ECtHR.[46]

In the field of immigration law, there is less reason for the CJ to steer its own course without referring to ECHR cases. Yet, in a recent case involving the conditions of detention of irregular migrants, in application of the so-called 'Return Directive' of 2008,[47] the Court of Justice interpreted the relevant article of the directive without referring to the rich case law of the Strasbourg Court on Article 5 ECHR in respect of the detention of irregular migrants – despite a brief reference to Article 5 by the Advocate-General.[48] This may be a missed opportunity since the question of the adequate protection of the fundamental rights of immigrants is one in which the Court of Justice is still struggling to find its marks and could therefore usefully draw on the rich Strasbourg jurisprudence.

A final example of the 'eclectic use' of the ECHR is where the Court of Justice uses Strasbourg case law for the interpretation of an act of EU law which does not fall within the scope of the ECHR. In the *Michael Weiss* case, the ECJ first held that Article 6(3)(a) ECHR, that protects the right to be informed in a language which one understands in *criminal* proceedings, was not directly relevant for a question relating to language use in *civil* proceedings.[49] Nevertheless, the Court went on to consider three judgments of the ECtHR relating to criminal cases in order to interpret the scope of the corresponding EC rule relating to civil law.[50]

---

46 There is a lively debate among competition lawyers on this question. See, among others, IS Forrester, "Due Process in EC Competition Cases: A Distinguished Institution with Flawed Procedures" [2009] *European Law Review* 817; HMH Speyart, "A Tale of Three Cities: Grondrechtelijke aandachtspunten bij de toepassing van het mededingingsrecht" [2010] *Nederlands tijdschrift voor Europees recht* 343; G Di Federico, *La riforma del procedimento comunitario antitrust e i diritti di difesa* (2009).

47 Directive 2008/115 of the European Parliament and of the Council of 16 December 2008 on common standards and procedures in Member States for returning illegally staying third-country nationals, OJ 2008 L 348/98.

48 Case C-357/09 PPU *Said Shamilovich Kadzoev (Huchbarov)* [2009] ECR I-11189; View of Advocate-General Mazak of 10 November 2009, para. 52. For criticism of the Court's failure to interpret the directive in the light of Article 5 ECHR, see J-F Amedro, "La Cour de Justice de l'Union européenne et la rétention des étrangers en situation irrégulière dans le cadre de la directive retour" [2010] *Revue trimestrielle des droits de l'homme* 893, p. 908 ff. For an analysis which seeks to infuse the implementation of the Return Directive with human rights standards derived from Article 5 ECHR, see the report of the EU Fundamental Rights Agency, *Detention of Third-Country Nationals in Return Procedures*, November 2010.

49 The question arose in the course of interpreting EC Regulation 1348/2000 on the service, between Member State judicial authorities, of judicial and extrajudicial documents in civil and commercial matters.

50 Case C-14/07 *Ingenieurbüro Michael Weiss und Partner GbR v Industrie- und Handelskammer Berlin* [2008] ECR I-3367, paras. 57 and 70–71.

4. CONSEQUENCES OF THE LISBON TREATY

The post-Lisbon Treaty regime is marked by the coexistence of potentially three sources of fundamental rights protection in the European Union: the general principles of Union law, whose existence is reaffirmed in very similar terms as before in Article 6(3) TEU; the EU Charter of Fundamental Rights which has become binding as primary EU law by means of the 'incorporation' clause of Article 6(1) TEU; and the ECHR, which is now still binding by way of its incorporation in the general principles, but which will become directly binding on the EU after the Union's accession. Moreover, Article 52 of the EU Charter of Rights provides that the Charter rights that are drawn from the Convention shall have the same meaning and scope as the corresponding Convention rights, and the Explanations of the Charter add that this also means that they should be interpreted in accordance with the case law of the European Court in Strasbourg.

What will happen with those different sources of EU fundamental rights in the practice of the Court of Justice? It is likely that the Court will, from now on, rely primarily on the EU Charter, and will use the general principles as referred to in Article 6(3) TEU mainly as a vehicle for recognizing other and more far-reaching rights than those contained in the Charter. In some of its post-Lisbon judgments, the Court of Justice indeed bases its fundamental rights reasoning on the Charter rather than on the Convention, even where Convention rights are also relevant for the case at hand.[51] If this trend were confirmed, references to the ECHR itself will become scarcer than today, since the main 'conduit' for those references – the general principles of EU law – will not be used as often as before. The Convention may, however, continue to play an important role with regard to the UK and Poland. To the extent that the Protocol on the application of the Charter in those countries has sought to limit its judicial enforcement, the Convention may well continue to be the main standard for reviewing the compliance of those two countries with EU fundamental rights.[52] The Convention will, obviously, also be considered by the Court of Justice if, as a result of the accession to the Convention, national courts will ask specifically whether EU acts comply with the ECHR and also if, as a result of the accession negotiations, some kind of special procedure were to be created allowing the Court of Justice to examine compliance with the Convention of EU acts prior to a judgment by the ECtHR.[53]

---

51 For example: Case C-403/09 PPU *Jasna Detiček v Maurizio Sgueglia*, judgment of 23 December 2009, para. 53 ff.; ECJ, Joined Cases C-92/09 and C-93/09 *Schecke and Eifert v Land Hessen*, judgment of 9 November 2010, para. 45 ff.

52 A Bultrini, "I rapporti tra Carta dei diritti fondamentali e Convenzione europea dei diritti dell'uomo dopo Lisbona: potenzialità straordinarie per lo sviluppo della tutela dei diritti umani in Europa", *Il Diritto dell'Unione Europea* (2009) 700–720, p. 707.

53 The creation of a special mechanism of this kind was suggested by the Court of Justice in a Discussion Document of 5 May 2010 (available on curia.europa.eu) and, more recently,

However, references to the *case law* of the Strasbourg court should, in principle, remain as abundant as before, because of the horizontal clause in the Charter mandating reliance on the ECHR (and its interpretation) when using Convention-based rights of the Charter. The Court of Justice has dutifully complied with this rule of interpretation already several times since the entry into force of the Lisbon Treaty.[54] There is a potential trap, though, in this cross-reference, within the Charter, to Strasbourg case law, namely that the EU courts (and the national courts applying EU law) may stick too closely to the minimum standard developed in Strasbourg, without asking themselves whether the EU legal order should give further reaching protection to the particular Convention-inspired right at stake. The temptation to use the ECHR as both a minimum and maximum standard of protection was already visible in some pre-Lisbon judgments of the Court of Justice. In the *Family Reunification* judgment, to name a famous case, the Court cited extensively from ECtHR cases dealing with the right to family life,[55] and reviewed the EC directive on family reunification against that standard, without stopping to consider that, perhaps, the EU legal order could be more generous in its protection of the right to family reunification than the Strasbourg court which is notoriously prudent in this area. Now, with the expansion of EU competences in fields such as immigration law and criminal law and procedure, there will be an increasing number of occasions for the Court of Justice to examine whether EU law may give more protection to certain fundamental rights than the minimum standard formulated by the ECtHR. In doing so, the Court will face the general question of whether, or to what extent, it should act as a 'second European human rights court', establishing a second, and higher, 'floor of rights' (above that resulting from the ECtHR's case law) which all EU Member States must respect whenever they act within the, notoriously broad, scope of EU law.

---

supported by a Joint communication of the presidents of the two Courts (*Joint communication from Presidents Costa and Skouris*, Press release of the European Court of Human Rights, 27 January 2011, no. 75).

54 See Case C-400/10 PPU, *J. McB v L.E.*, judgment of 5 October 2010, para. 53 ff.; and Case C-279/09 *DEB Deutsche Energiehandels- und Beratungsgesellschaft mbH v Bundesrepublik Deutschland*, judgment of 22 December 2010, para. 45 ff.

55 Case C-540/03 *European Parliament v Council* [2006] ECR I-5769.

CHAPTER 2

THE EU AS A PARTY TO THE EUROPEAN CONVENTION OF HUMAN RIGHTS

EU law and the European Court of Justice case law as inspiration and challenge to the European Court of Human Rights jurisprudence

Catherine Van de Heyning and Rick Lawson*

1. INTRODUCTION

The contribution of De Witte in this volume discusses the impact that the European Union's accession to the European Convention of Human Rights will have on the European Court of Justice. The EU courts already take considerable notice of the Strasbourg case law and apply its jurisprudence as if binding. In essence the EU accession to the Convention as envisaged in the Lisbon Treaty will consolidate the current position of the Convention in EU law and the EU courts' jurisprudence. Seen from the opposite perspective, i.e. the point of view of Strasbourg, the EU accession may appear at first sight as the equivalent of a regular state accession: it does not necessarily imply any particular effects on the ECHR judiciary control system. That is not the case, however. As the president of

---

* C Van de Heyning is FWO researcher on fundamental rights at the University of Antwerp. Prof. Rick Lawson is head of the European law department at Leiden University, the Netherlands. Part of this article builds on a previous publication: RA Lawson, 'Ex Boreale Lux – On the Influence of the ECJ on the Interpretation of the ECHR', in A McDonnell et al. (eds.), *Views from the Mountain* (Kluwer 2009), pp. 439–454. The critique and suggestions of professor Wouter Vandenhole (University of Antwerp) have been of great value for this paper.

the ECtHR, Jean-Paul Costa, noticed in 2009, the accession of the EU to the ECHR "may have far-reaching" consequences.[1]

Over the last decades, the jurisdiction of the ECtHR and the EU courts has become increasingly intertwined. The EU courts and the ECtHR share common jurisdiction *ratione loci*, namely the 27 Member States of both the European Union and the Council of Europe. Both consider similar fundamental rights issues. Both apply and interpret the fundamental rights laid down in the ECHR. In the absence of any formal relationship, a harmonious development of the case-law should not be taken for granted. Indeed, the late 1980s and early 1990s featured what one may call, with a bit of exaggeration, 'gunboat diplomacy' between the two European Courts. After the ECJ observed in *Hoechst* that the protective scope of Article 8 ECHR "is concerned with the development of man's personal freedom and may therefore not be extended to business premises",[2] the ECtHR responded in *Niemietz* that such an approach was too restrictive and that there was "no reason of principle" why activities of a business nature would be excluded from the protection of Article 8 ECHR.[3] After the ECJ observed in *Orkem* that neither Article 6 ECHR nor the Strasbourg case-law seemed to recognise the right not give evidence against oneself,[4] the ECtHR simply stated in *Funke* that Article 6 ECHR *does* contain the right to remain silent and not to contribute to incriminating himself.[5] When in the *Grogan* case Advocate General Van Gerven submitted that Article 10 ECHR allowed Ireland to prohibit the distribution of information about foreign abortion facilities,[6] the ECtHR arrived at the very opposite conclusion in *Open Door Counselling*.[7] And to mention a last example: after the ECJ decided in *Emesa Sugar* that parties appearing before it do not have a right to comment on the Opinion of the Advocate General,[8] the

---

[1] See the memorandum of 3 July 2009, submitted with a view to the High Level conference on the future of the European Court of Human Rights (Interlaken, 18–19 February 2010). The text of the memorandum can be found on the website of the Council of Europe (www.coe.int).

[2] ECJ, joined case 46/87 and 227/88, *Hoechst v. Commission,* [1989] ECR p. 2924. This is not to say that the ECJ deliberately took a position different from that of the Strasbourg Court; there simply was no Strasbourg case-law on the issue. But the point remains that the mere existence of *Hoechst* seemed trigger a specific reaction in Strasbourg.

[3] ECtHR, 16 December 1992, *Niemietz v. Germany* (Appl. No. 13710/88), par. 29. All ECtHR cases cited are judgments unless indicated otherwise. For the sake of convenience, only reference is made to the application numbers of cases, and not to their official publication in *Series A* (until 1996) or the *Reports* (thereafter). All cases cited are easily accessible at www.echr.coe.int.

[4] ECJ, case 374/87, *Orkem v. Commission,* [1989] ECR pp. 3350–3351. The same caveat as in footnote 3 applies.

[5] ECtHR, 25 February 1993, *Funke v. France* (Appl. No. 10828/84), par. 44.

[6] Opinion of AG Van Gerven in case 374/87, *SPUC v. Grogan,* [1991] ECR p. I-4727.

[7] ECtHR, 29 October 1992, *Open Door Counselling v. Ireland* (Appl. No. 14234/88), par. 72 *et seq.*

[8] ECJ, case C-17/98, *Emesa Sugar,* [2000] ECR p. I-665; most recently confirmed in ECJ, case C-484/06, *Koninklijke Ahold*, judgment of 10 July 2008, par. 20.

ECtHR affirmed in *Kress* that the right to adversarial proceedings requires that such a possibility is given.[9]

But things have changed. Nowadays the ECJ relies extensively on Strasbourg case-law where appropriate.[10] It even encourages the EU Member States to comply with their obligations under the Human Rights Convention when implementing EU law.[11] The ECtHR reciprocates by taking into account the applicable rules of EU law, as we will see later on. Crucially, in *Bosphorus* the ECtHR accepted that the EU legal order offers an 'equivalent protection' of fundamental rights, and introduced the presumption that Member States comply with their obligations under the Convention when they do no more than implement legal obligations resulting from EU law.[12]

No doubt the human dimension has played an important role in this *rapprochement* between Strasbourg and Luxembourg. Several judges currently serving in the ECJ were based in Strasbourg before; the former Registrar of the European Court of Human Rights, Paul Mahoney, became President of the Civil Service Tribunal; and conversely former ECJ president Gil Carlos Rodríguez Iglesias acted as chairman of the *Group of Wise Persons* that had to develop proposals to rescue the Strasbourg Court from its huge case-load. Recent case-law confirms that Jean Monnet was right: fee movement of workers fosters mutual understanding.

But whatever the explanation may be, the two European Courts are now in harmony. In a speech held in London in October 2008, President Costa noted that

> "coherence between the European Convention on Human Rights and European Union law has been gradually emerging. The case-law of both European Courts discussed previously shows that they are ready to cooperate in order to ensure consistency of fundamental rights protection in their respective domains. In fact, they do more than co-operate. The examples of cross-fertilisation in the jurisprudence of both Courts indicate that a convergence between the two legal orders begins to develop.
> There are no formal rules regarding the relationship between the Court of Justice and the European Court of Human Rights. If there were conflicts between them, there

9 ECtHR, 7 June 2001, *Kress v. France* (Appl. No. 39594/98), par. 76: "the parties may reply to the Government Commissioner's submissions by means of a memorandum for the deliberations, a practice which – and this is vital in the Court's view – helps to ensure compliance with the adversarial principle".

10 See for instance ECJ, case C-540/03, *Parliament v. Council (Family Reunification Directive)*, par. 55. On occasion the ECJ, referring to Strasbourg case-law, arguably went further than the Human Rights Court itself would have done in similar circumstances: ECJ, case C-60/00, *Carpenter*, 2002 [ECR] p. I-6279, par. 41–45.

11 See for instance ECJ, case C-105/03, *Pupino*, par. 60, for an admonition to the national courts not to lose sight of the requirements flowing from Article 6 ECHR.

12 ECtHR, 30 June 2005, *Bosphorus v. Ireland* (Appl. No. 45036/98), par. 165.

> would be no obvious way of resolving them. Therefore, the two European Courts have a particular responsibility in that regard. On a practical level – both Courts meet regularly and discuss issues of common interest… I remain optimistic. As my fellow judge, Lech Garlicki, has commented, "judges are, in general, reasonable creatures and their whole professional training prompts them to look for compromise solutions and not for confrontations".[13]

Looking at recent case-law, the picture that emerges from President Costa's speech seems accurate. It is true that both European Courts co-operate in a constructive way, and it is also true that – much as controversies allow for great case notes – a coherent body of interpretation of fundamental rights is in the interest of all.

In this context of a rather peaceful *modus vivendi,* establishing a formal link between both courts is, paradoxically, not without risks. It might disturb the current peaceful coexistence. As will be discussed in this contribution, the introduction of a formal procedure linking both courts might invoke questions regarding the hierarchy of both courts which might invoke a reaction of the ECJ to protect its autonomy. The following statement of the European Parliament bears witness of the fear that formalizing the relationship between both courts might result in a loss of autonomy of the ECJ:

> "it would be unwise to formalise relations between the Court of Justice of the European Union and the European Court of Human Rights by establishing a preliminary ruling procedure before the latter or by creating a body or panel which would take decisions when one of the two courts intended to adopt an interpretation of the ECHR which differed from that adopted by the other…
> [The EP]. Is clearly aware of the fact that the European Court of Human Rights may find a violation in a case that has already been decided by the Court of Justice of the European Union and stresses that this would in no way cast a doubt on the credibility of the Court of Justice of the European Union as an ultimate umpire in the EU judicial system".[14]

Yet, several judges of the ECtHR have supported this evolution. In a 2004 speech ECtHR president Wildhaber stated that EU accession to the ECHR "has now been commonly accepted as a necessity".[15] Several reasons have been put forward: to ensure coherence between the fundamental rights case law of both courts and avoid open conflicts, to remove the blank gaps of protection currently

13 JP Costa, *The Relationship between the European Convention on Human Rights and European Union Law – A Jurisprudential Dialogue between the European Court of Human Rights and the European Court of Justice,* lecture at the King's College, London, 7 October 2008.

14 European Parliament resolution of 19 May 2010 on the institutional aspects of the accession of the European Union to the European Convention for the Protection of Human Rights and Fundamental Freedoms (2009/2241(INI)), par. 15–16.

15 Speech Luzius Wildhaber, Conference on the position of constitutional courts following integration into the European Union (Bled, 30 September 2004).

existing with respect to EU norms and to increase the participation of the EU in ECtHR proceedings. A joint communication released in February 2011 by the presidents of the ECtHR and the ECJ gives evidence of the involvement of both courts in the process and indicates that both courts believe that the decisions during the accession negotiations will impact on their functioning.[16]

This contribution will consider both the current role of the ECJ case law in cases before the ECtHR and the future prospects after an accession. A first section will consider how EU law and the ECJ jurisprudence specifically inspire as well as the ECtHR adjudication. This section firstly reviews to what extent the Strasbourg court refers to the ECJ case law and whether or not the jurisprudence is considered guiding for the interpretation of the Convention rights and freedoms. Such reference might not be surprising as the ECtHR also refers to other international standards and decisions of international tribunals and committees. It is scrutinized whether the ECJ case law takes a special position as interpretive tool for the Convention rights and freedoms. A second section discusses how EU law challenges the adjudication of the ECtHR. The question whether or not the ECtHR can review violations resulting from EU norms implemented at the national level has become more pressing due to the ever growing impact of EU law on the domestic legislation of the High Contracting Parties. The ECtHR produced the *Bosphorus* doctrine in answer to this challenge. It will be discussed whether this doctrine will continue to apply once the EU has become a party to the Convention. The attention will then be shifted from the ECtHR case law to the institutional question regarding the accession. We will consider whether the direction taken with regards to the accession and the accession itself will ensure a more coherent protection of fundamental rights in the European legal space. A third section will regard the main challenges ahead for an enhanced cooperation between the ECtHR and the ECJ.

2. INSPIRATION AND CHALLENGE

2.1. THE LUXEMBOURG CASE LAW AS INSPIRATION FOR THE EUROPEAN COURT OF HUMAN RIGHTS JURISPRUDENCE – AND MORE

2.1.1. The jurisprudence of the EU courts as inspiration for the Strasbourg jurisdiction

The ECtHR has a long tradition of referring to other international treaties and the jurisprudence of international courts and tribunals as guiding sources for

16 Joint communication from Presidents Costa and Skouris. Available at: www.echr.coe.int.

the interpretation of the Convention rights and freedoms. Already in the famous case of *Golder* of 1975, the Court was prepared to be guided by the Vienna Convention on the Law of Treaties.[17] The account taken of international law by the Strasbourg Court does not stop at an occasional reference to international treaties. The ECtHR has postulated that the Convention should be interpreted in conformity with international law, especially with the international human rights treaties. It has consistently held that the Convention needs to be read "in the light of the rules set" by international law and cannot be interpreted "in a vacuum"; the "relevant rules of international law" must be "taken into account" when interpreting the Convention, notwithstanding the autonomy of the ECHR.[18] In short, the ECtHR considers that the Convention is not the sole framework for reference for the interpretation of the rights and freedoms entrenched in the ECHR.[19]

On many occasions did the ECtHR refer to international human rights treaties and decisions from United Nations bodies and committees as "relevant law". These documents provide a general image of the current interpretation of human rights or international law. The ECtHR might not explicitly mention these documents in its operative part or specify in which manner the international norms have affected the ECtHR's case law in the case at hand.

International law can also be relied upon to observe the existence of a new tendency or consensus in the international legal order justifying a dynamic interpretation of a specific Convention right or limiting the margin of appreciation granted to the States Parties. Remarkably, the Court considers that it is not necessary for the State concerned to have ratified the entire collection of human rights instruments which will be taken into consideration. It will be sufficient that the international instruments and national practice all point towards a similar evolution to establish the existence of a common ground which can be taken into consideration for the interpretation of the Convention.

For example, in the case of *Marckx* on inheritance law the ECtHR considered two international conventions not yet ratified by Belgium.[20] The ECtHR held that

---

17 App. No. 4451/70, *Golder v. United Kingdom*, February 21, 1975, at 29.

18 See e.g. App. No.35763/97, *Al-Adsani v. United Kingdom* (2002) 34 E.H.R.R. 273 at 55, App. No.37112/97, *Fogarty v. United Kingdom*, unreported, November 21, 2001 at 35, and App. No.34503/97, *Demir and Baykara*, unreported, 12 November 12, par. 67–68.

19 *Demir and Baykara* (see previous footnote), par. 67.

20 See App. No. 6833/74, *Marckx v. Belgium* (1979) 2 E.H.R.R. 330 at 20–41. Sometimes the ECtHR will apply more caution naming the ratification of a treaty by the MS when taking account of international treaties when interpreting the ECHR. For example, in T. v. United Kingdom whereby the ECtHR when naming the CRC adds that this Treaty is binding upon the United Kingdom as well as on the other States of the European Council because of their ratification of the Treaty. App. No. 24724/94, *T. v. United Kingdom* (2000) 30 E.H.R.R. 121.

these conventions were the expression of a clear evolution of domestic law of many Member States, even if the conventions had been ratified by only a small number of high contracting parties. The ECtHR indicated that international norms become relevant to the interpretation of the Convention whenever consensus emerges from specialized international human rights instruments and from the practice of contracting States.[21] In that context, the ECtHR referred to EU law and more recently to the EU Charter of Fundamental Rights as an indication of a growing consensus or evolution in international fundamental rights law.[22]

The case law of the EU courts, especially the ECJ, has also featured in the Strasbourg case law. In general, we can observe two types of references to the ECJ fundamental rights case law. First, in a number of cases the ECJ case law on a specific fundamental rights issue is referred to as "relevant law" in combination with other EU law sources or the jurisprudence of other international or regional courts (e.g. Inter-American Court). Thus, in the case of *Sergey Zolotukhin* the ECJ case law on the *non bis in idem* principle is mentioned along jurisprudence of the Inter-American Court of Human Rights and the US Supreme Court.[23] The ECJ case law can also be referred to as relevant to the interpretation of general concepts of law e.g. as to the meaning of serious negligence in environmental cases.[24]

Accordingly the ECJ jurisprudence with regards to discrimination on the basis of gender has repeatedly featured as "relevant law" in the ECtHR case law. A possible explanation may be found in the extensive ECJ jurisprudence and EU directives on gender discrimination. The EU Treaties early on provided for a prohibition of gender discrimination. Unlike EU law, the Convention does not entrench an autonomous gender discrimination clause. Article 14 ECHR which holds a prohibition to discriminate solely on the basis of gender will only be applied by the ECtHR in conjunction with another Convention provision. E.g. a refusal of national authorities to register the new gender of transsexuals will be remedied through a reliance on Article 14 ECHR in conjunction with Article 8 ECHR, namely respect for family and private life. Due to the autonomous provision on gender discrimination in the Treaties, the ECJ rather than the ECtHR which has been standard-setting in the Member States on this topic. In *I v. United Kingdom* and *Christine Goodwin v. United Kingdom* the ECJ case law

---

21 App. No.34503/97, *Demir and Baykara*, unreported, 12 November 2008 at 85–86.

22 ECtHR, *Schalk and Kopf v. Austria*, App. no. 30141/04, 24 June 2010, par. 52, ECtHR, *Sergey Zolotukhin v. Russia*, App. No. 14939/03 (unreported, 10 October 2009), par. 79 and ECtHR, *Goodwin v United Kingdom* (2002) 35 EHRR 18, par. 100.

23 ECtHR, *Sergey Zolotukhin v. Russia*, App. No. 14939/03 (unreported, 10 October 2009), par. 35–38.

24 ECtHR, *Mangouras v. Spain*, App. No. 12050/04 (), par. 39.

on gender discrimination featured prominently in the description of the relevant case law on the topic.[25] Against the background of the ECJ jurisprudence and other relevant international law, the ECtHR concluded that an evolution had taken place with regards to the treatment of transsexuals on gender issues. The Court found that the United Kingdom could no longer claim that a wide margin of appreciation should be granted on the grounds of a lack of consensus on gender issues with regards to transsexuals.[26]

A second type of references to the ECJ case law follows from reliance by the applicants or the defending government. They might refer to the ECJ case law in order to persuade the ECtHR to revise its existing case law. Thus, in *D.H.* the applicants referred to the ECJ case law on racial discrimination.[27] We observe similar references in dissenting or concurring opinions of judges who refer to the ECJ case law in order to propose a revision of the established case law. In his separate opinion in the case of *Demir and Baykara v. Turkey* judge Zagrebelsky addressed the legal consequences that flow from a decision of the Court to depart from existing case-law. He pointed to the approach of the European Court of Justice, according to which 'new' case-law does not apply (retrospectively and automatically) to the case pending before it or to similar situations.[28] He argued that the ECtHR should follow the same line. In her dissenting opinion in *Andrejeva v. Latvia* judge Ziemele relied on the ECJ case law in order to argue that the acts of the USSR in Latvia ought to be recognized as illegal and invalid by the ECtHR.[29]

2.1.2. Taking into account EU law as 'law of the land'

Sometimes EU law plays a different role in cases before the ECtHR: it is, as it were, part of the 'law of the land', the domestic law of the State Party concerned. A number of ECHR rights and freedoms, such as the right to respect for family life, allow for restrictions. Certain conditions apply, however: any restriction must be, inter alia, in accordance with the law. 'Law' means domestic law in this context, but since *Van Gend & Loos* and *Costa v. ENEL* we know that, as far as the EU Member States are concerned, it would be wrong to ignore EU law. The European Court of Human Rights has drawn the logical consequence in a couple of cases, for instance when ruling on situations where the domestic authorities failed to respect the rights that the applicant derived from Community law.

25 ECtHR, Goodwin v United Kingdom (2002) 35 EHRR 18, par. 43 and I v. United Kingdom App. No. 25680/94 (11 July 2002).
26 ECtHR, Goodwin v United Kingdom (2002) 35 EHRR 18, par. 43.
27 DH v Czech Republic (2008) 47 EHRR 3.
28 Separate Opinion Judge Zagrebelsky, *Demir and Baykara* App. No.34503/97, 12 November, 2008 par. 85–86.
29 Dissenting Opinion Judge Ziemele, *Andrejeva v. Lithuania* App. no. 55707/00, 18 February 2009.

The French case of *Aristimuño Mendizabal* provides a clear example.[30] The applicant, who described herself as "a Bask citizen of Spanish nationality", had been refused the residence permit to which she was entitled as an EU citizen. Instead she was given, over a period of fourteen years, a series of no less than 69 short-term permissions to stay on French territory. Apparently the French authorities were hesitant to allow her a full-fledged residence status in view of her ties with ETA. Be that as it may, the resulting uncertainty interfered with her right to respect for family life (Article 8 ECHR). The Court had little difficulties in finding a breach of that provision given that the authorities had not acted in conformity with the law, "que la "loi" en question soit française ou communautaire".[31] In its judgment the ECtHR referred extensively to secondary Community legislation and quoted the *Baumbast* and *Commission v. Belgium* judgments.

A similar approach was followed in *Dangeville* and two subsequent cases where companies suffered damage as a result of non-implementation of the Sixth VAT Directive.[32] The Strasbourg Court interpreted the right to property in the light of Community law and held that the applicant companies should have benefited from the rights enshrined in the Directive. Co-incidentally all cases mentioned involved France. Since it is unlikely that failures to comply with EU law occur only in that country, it would seem that lawyers in other countries are still to discover the Strasbourg route to enforce rights derived from EU law.

One such attempt was recently made by no-one less than George Soros. The American financial guru was convicted in France for insider trading on the stock market in 1988. Relying on Article 7 ECHR (no punishment without law), Mr Soros complained in Strasbourg that the law applicable at the relevant time had been too unclear for him to realise that he was doing anything wrong. He also complained of the failure to apply EC Directive 89/592 provisions to his case which were more favourable to him than the French law that was applied. In September 2010 the Court declared the case admissible.[33]

---

30 ECtHR, *Aristimuño Mendizabal v. France* App. No. 51431/99, 17 January 2006.

31 ECtHR, 17 January 2006, *Aristimuño Mendizabal v. France* (Appl. No. 51431/99), par. 69: "La Cour estime donc que l'article 8 doit être interprété en l'espèce à la lumière du droit communautaire et en particulier des obligations imposées aux Etats membres quant aux droits d'entrée et de séjour des ressortissants communautaires". Only a French version of the judgment is available.

32 ECtHR, 16 April 2002, *Dangeville v. France* (Appl. No. 36677/97), par. 46: "The Court notes that, by requiring payment of VAT on transactions negotiated by insurance brokers during the period from 1 January to 30 June 1978, the French legislation was incompatible with the provisions of Article 13-B-a of the Sixth Directive of the Council of the European Communities of 17 May 1977". See also ECtHR, 22 July 2003, *S.A. Cabinet Diot & S.A. Gras Savoye v. France* (Appl. No. 49217/99) and ECtHR, 25 January 2007, *Aon Conseil et Courtage S.A. a.o. v. France* (Appl. No. 70160/01).

33 ECtHR, 15 Sept. 2010, *Soros v. France* (Appl. No. 50425/06), adm. decision.

Two problems have to be addressed in this connection. One is that the ECtHR cannot avoid interpretations of EU law, something which obviously belongs to the realm of the ECJ. To what extent is an EU citizen actually entitled to reside in another Member State? Indeed in one of the VAT cases the ECtHR was divided on the interpretation of one of the *Roquette Frères* judgments of the ECJ.[34] The ECtHR may find itself in the awkward position that it has to descend into the labyrinth of EU law. Leaving *acte clair* situations aside, and cases where the national courts have already obtained a preliminary ruling from the ECJ before the case got to Strasbourg, the Court may be in need of authoritative clarification. Assuming that the introduction of a formal preliminary rulings procedure between Strasbourg and Luxembourg is neither realistic nor desirable, a possible remedy would be to invite the European Commission to intervene in each case where EU law plays a role.[35]

The other problem is to identify these cases. For instance in the case of *Üner*,[36] which dealt with the Dutch authorities' decision to deport a Turkish national to his country of origin, it might have been useful to look at relevant rules under the EC-Turkey Association Agreement. The Strasbourg Court, however, did not do so, without stating a reason for this omission. But only a few months later, in *Maslov*, it did take into account Article 28 §3(b) of Directive 2004/38/EC in a case that involved the expulsion by Austria of a Bulgarian youth with a criminal record.[37] And in *Saadi v. the UK*, which relates to the detention of an asylum seeker in 2001, the Court referred to Directive 2005/85, the transposition deadline of which was only by 1 December 2008.[38] Is there any system behind all this? Assuming that it is not feasible for the Strasbourg Court to apply EU law of its own motion in appropriate cases, there seems to be no alternative but to leave it up to the vigilant individual (and his lawyers) to point out relevant rules.

As a matter of fact the *Maslov* case features another example of 'Luxembourgish influences'. Mr Maslov was convicted to a prison sentence in 2000, and a ten-year exclusion order was imposed on him in 2001. That decision became final in 2002, but it was only in 2003 that he was actually expelled. In the intervening period – i.e. between 2000 and 2003 – he did not commit any further offences, and the

---

34 ECtHR, 25 January 2007, *Aon Conseil et Courtage S.A. a.o. v. France* (Appl. No. 70160/01), dissenting opinion of Judges Costa and Kovler (who noted in para 7 "il nous semble fâcheux qu'il y ait un semblant de divergence entre les deux Cours suprêmes européennes, qui évitent soigneusement de telles divergences ").

35 To some extent this is already practice: see the Commission's intervention in cases such as *Bosphorus (supra* note 13), *Senator Lines* (ECtHR, 10 March 2004, Appl. No. 56672/00) and *Emesa Sugar* (ECtHR, 13 January 2005, Appl. No. 62023/00).

36 ECtHR (GC), 18 October 2006, *Üner v. Netherlands* (Appl. No. 46410/99), par. 82.

37 ECtHR (GC), 23 June 2008, *Maslov v. Austria* (Appl. No. 1638/03), par. 82.

38 ECtHR (GC), 29 January 2008, *Saadi v. UK* (Appl. No. 13229/03), par.par. 40 and 56. The Chamber, which had dealt with *Saadi* initially, had not referred to the Directive.

question was whether this period of good conduct should be taken into account when reviewing the expulsion order under the ECHR. The Austrian government argued that developments which occurred after the final domestic decision should not be taken into account, but the Strasbourg Court did not agree:

> its task is to assess the compatibility with the Convention of the applicant's actual expulsion, not that of the final expulsion order. *Mutatis mutandis*, this would also appear to be the approach followed by the European Court of Justice which stated in its *Orfanopoulos and Oliveri* judgment that Article 3 of Directive 64/221 precludes a national practice whereby the national courts may not take into consideration, in reviewing the lawfulness of the expulsion of a national of another Member State, factual matters which occurred after the final decision of the competent authorities.[39]

This is a clear example of the Strasbourg Court seeking inspiration in the practice of the ECJ.

2.1.3. *The ECtHR as a means to enforce compliance with EU law*

There have also been several cases in which the Strasbourg Court extended a helping hand to its Luxembourg counterpart. In the case of *Hornsby*, a British couple – both graduate teachers of English – wanted to settle in Greece and teach English. However, the Greek authorities simply refused to grant them a working permit, and even ignored domestic court judgments ordering them to grant the required papers. Even infringements proceedings, leading up to a judgment by the ECJ,[40] did not help the Hornsbys. The Court found a violation of Article 6 ECHR:

> "the administrative authorities form one element of a State subject to the rule of law and their interests accordingly coincide with the need for the proper administration of justice. Where administrative authorities refuse or fail to comply, or even delay doing so, the guarantees under Article 6 enjoyed by a litigant during the judicial phase of the proceedings are rendered devoid of purpose".[41]

Needless to say that this case provides great support for the practical realisation of rights derived from Community law.

One year later, Strasbourg was even more generous in the case of *Pafitis*. The applicant complained about the length of proceedings in a case before the Greek courts. Part of the delay had been caused by a preliminary rulings procedure,

39 *Ibid.*, par. 93; see ECJ, cases C-482/01 and C-493/01. The Human Rights Court also referred to the ECJ's *Commission v. Spain* judgment of 31 January 2006 (Case C-503/03).

40 ECJ, Case C-147/86, *Commission v. Greece* [1988] ECR, p. 1637.

41 ECtHR, 19 March 1997, *Hornsby v. Greece* (Appl. No. 18357/91), par. 41.

which had taken more than two and a half years. The ECtHR, however, decided that it could not take this period into consideration in its assessment of the length of the proceedings:

> "even though it may at first sight appear relatively long, to take it into account would adversely affect the system instituted by Article 177 of the EEC Treaty and work against the aim pursued in substance in that Article".[42]

This is a rare example of the Court dealing with competing interests by simply favouring one of the other *because* otherwise the former would suffer.

Of great potential use is the '*Coëme* doctrine', after a Belgian case in which a trial court refused to refer questions for a preliminary ruling to a higher Belgian Court. The European Court of Human Rights held that the arbitrary refusal to start a preliminary rulings procedure may in itself amount to a violation of Article 6 ECHR.[43] Indeed, the Court is currently considering a Belgian case in which the domestic courts declined to refer questions for a preliminary ruling to the ECJ. The Strasbourg Court will have to address the interesting *and* delicate question whether this refusal must be qualified as "arbitrary".[44]

2.1.4. Regard of the Luxembourg case law, not reliance?

The ECJ jurisprudence has thus been mentioned by the ECtHR, but – until fairly recently – only in a limited number of cases. When looking back at the Strasbourg case-law until around 2007, it would seem that the ECtHR referred more often to EU norms and measures than to the case law of the EU courts. In addition, the ECJ case law did not feature prominently in the operative part of ECtHR's judgments but was instead mentioned as relevant law among other sources or considered by governments, applicants or dissenting judges in an attempt to convince the Court of a new direction. One may speculate why the ECtHR might have been hesitant to rely on the ECJ's case law explicitly in its assessment of the case.

One argument, though not very convincing, would be that the ECJ case law in general did not provide for much interesting case law with regards to the interpretation of fundamental rights. It may be true that, in the early years at least, the number of fundamental rights cases before the ECJ are still limited and the compact, civil law-style manner of reasoning might not lend itself for guidance with regards to fundamental rights issues. However, with regards to

42 ECtHR, 26 February 1998, *Pafitis v. Greece* (Appl. No. 20323/92), par. 95.
43 ECtHR, 22 June 2000, *Coëme v. Belgium* (Appl. No. 18357/91), par. 114.
44 See the case *Ullens de Schooten*, (Appl. Nos. 3987/07 en 38353/07), pending. Both cases were communicated to the Belgian government on 28 August 2008. Rumour has it that the Commission declined the ECtHR's invitation to intervene as a third party.

discrimination on the basis of gender or race the ECJ has been a frontrunner. The same applies to the protection of personal data under the right to privacy.[45]

A more compelling argument might be that the ECtHR felt bound to refrain from explicitly relying on the ECJ case law in the operative part because of the regional character of the EU in contrast to the ICJ or UN bodies.[46] Not all High Contracting Parties of the ECHR are Member States of the EU. By relying explicitly on ECJ case law the ECtHR might be accused from binding states to international norms on which they did not consent. Therefore, the ECtHR would be slow to read the Convention in the light of the ECJ case law.[47] A counter-argument would then be that the ECtHR had accepted that not all Member States should be bound by a specific international treaty for it to be considered as indicating a new trend or growing consensus with regards to human rights issues. Still, the regional character might matter as it is not considered to constitute the framework in which the ECtHR operates as e.g. international treaty law, but rather a coexistent regional legal order. Such position might be read into the dissenting opinion Judge Loucaides. He argued that the ECJ case law could not constitute an obstacle to a certain approach on the Convention rights and freedoms as the ECJ concerning discrimination "examined the question of discrimination in a different legal context, and in any case it is not binding on us".[48]

Be that as it may – especially in the last two years many references to EU law, and to ECJ case-law were made by the ECtHR. A few examples. In *Scoppola* the Grand Chamber adopted a new approach to Article 7 ECHR, relying heavily on the EU Charter and ECJ case-law.[49] Less than a month later, the Grand Chamber

---

45 The protection of personal data is now even entrenched in the EU Charter on Fundamental Rights as a separate right additional to the general respect of privacy. Article 8 EU Charter.

46 E.g., the ECtHR relied on the ICJ on several occasions in the operative part of a judgment: ICJ Advisory Opinion concerning Continued Presence of South Africa in Namibia in ECtHR, *Loizidou v Turkey* (1996) 23 EHRR 513, par. 45 or to the ICJ LaGrand case in ECtHR, *Stoll v Switzerland* (2007) 44 EHRR 53, par. 59.

47 It should be reminded that also if the ECJ case law would be considered as international law in the light of which the convention ought to be read, its impact would be limited. The ECtHR held that it would only read the ECHR in the light of international law "as far as possible". ECtHR, *McElhinney* App. No.31253/96 (21 November 2001, par. 36 or ECtHR, *Al-Adsani v. United Kingdom* (2002) 34 EHRR 273 par. 55. Where a clear incompatibility exists the Bosphorus doctrine (infra) applies. ECtHR.

48 Dissenting opinion Judge Loucaides, Stec and Others v. United Kingdom (2005) 41 EHRR SE 18. Professor Vandenhole correctly observed that this dissenting opinion does not stipulate whether this limitation of influence on the ECtHR case law is limited to EU discrimination law or also applies to EU fundamental rights law.

49 ECtHR (GC), 17 Sept. 2009, *Scoppola v. Italy* (Appl. No. 10249/03), par. 105: 'The Court considers that a long time has elapsed since the Commission gave the above-mentioned *X v. Germany* decision and that during that time there have been important developments internationally. In particular … mention should be made of the proclamation of the European Union's Charter of Fundamental Rights. The wording of Article 49 par. 1 of the Charter

changed its position again, this time concerning the applicability of Article 6 ECHR to summary injunction proceedings: in the case of *Micallef* the case-law of the ECJ was used as an argument.[50] Then the Court dealt with the phenomenon of international child abduction in *Neulinger & Schuruk*. In finding an international consensus that 'best interests of the child' should be the primary consideration, the Grand Chamber pointed 'in particular' to Article 24 §2 of the European Union's Charter of Fundamental Rights.[51] In *Mangouras* the Grand Chamber noted, basing itself on an extensive analysis of EU law, that criminal sanctions were used more frequently to ensure compliance with environmental law; 'these new realities have to be taken into account in interpreting the requirements of Article 5 §3'.[52]

This trend may only increase as a result of the accession of the EU to the ECtHR.[53] It is to be expected that the ECJ will be taken into account when interpreting the ECHR in a similar fashion as regard is given to the national courts' case law. The Strasbourg court might limit the margin of appreciation for domestic authorities or interpret a Convention right progressively on the grounds of a growing consensus visible in the case law of domestic courts and the ECJ. Whether or not the ECJ will become a source of inspiration will depend on its capacity to provide for a well-reasoned and progressive fundamental rights case law. The accession will result a more crucial change: the EU institutions will be able to present their point of view directly before the ECtHR as defending party. In these interventions the EU institutions can highlight the ECJ case law on the topic under scrutiny. As a party to the ECHR, the Court will have to answer the EU institutions' considerations in a similar manner as it responds to Member States' government argumentation. The ECtHR currently refers to domestic case law when responding to the national authorities' considerations. It might consider the ECJ in the same manner. Moreover, the EU can propose three judges of which the ECtHR will select one judge. This judge will be able to provide a better understanding of EU law and the ECJ case law. In conclusion, the ECJ case law might inspire the ECtHR interpretation of the Convention rights and freedoms, but only implicitly as a source of law among other relevant national and international legal opinions.

---

differs – and this can only be deliberate (…) – from that of Article 7 of the Convention in that it states: 'If, subsequent to the commission of a criminal offence, the law provides for a lighter penalty, that penalty shall be applicable' (…). In the case of *Berlusconi and Others*, the Court of Justice of the European Communities, whose ruling was endorsed by the French Court of Cassation (…), held that this principle formed part of the constitutional traditions common to the Member States'.

50 ECtHR (GC), 15 Oct. 2009, *Micallef v. Malta* (Appl. No. 17056/06), par. 32 en 78.

51 ECtHR (GC), 6 July 2010, *Neulinger & Shuruk v. Switzerland* (Appl. No. 41615/07), par. 135.

52 ECtHR (GC), 28 Sept. 2010, *Mangouras v. Spain* (Appl. No. 12050/04), par. 36–43 en 87.

53 R Lawson, "Human Rights: the best is yet to come" (2005) 1 *European Constitutional Law Review* 27, p. 28.

2.2. EUROPEAN UNION LAW AS CHALLENGE FOR THE EUROPEAN COURT OF HUMAN RIGHTS' JURISPRUDENCE

2.2.1. *The Bosphorus doctrine and its application*

While the ECJ case law might be of growing importance as inspiration for the ECtHR, it definitely challenges the Strasbourg system of Convention protection. All EU Member States are High Contracting states to the ECHR as accession to the Convention is a necessary condition for membership of the EU. This means that a vast part of the ECHR Member States are bound by EU law, including the ECJ case law. The ever growing competences of the EU and permeation of national law by the ECJ jurisprudence begs the question of the jurisdiction of the ECtHR. Does the transfer of competences to a supranational organization as the EU imply that all measures taken in compliance with the obligations resulting from EU membership are immune from ECtHR scrutiny? The ECtHR elaborated the *Bosphorus* doctrine in order to answer this question. The doctrine does not apply to the EU alone, but is relevant for all obligations resulting from international treaties or the membership of an international organisation.

A distinction needs to be made between direct actions and indirections actions.[54] The first concerns complaints directed against the EU for measures which violate the conventional rights and freedoms. Indirect actions target measures implemented by Member States in compliance with their obligations under EU law. The application is in such case directed against a Member State. The Court indicated that in case of direct actions it would not hold international organisations themselves accountable due to a lack of jurisdiction.[55] At the time of the Bosphorus ruling the EU was clearly not a party to the ECHR. Complaints addressed against the EC or the EU are therefore simply rejected since cases can only be brought against the High Contracting Parties. However, this situation has not prevented claims against the Union from being brought in Strasbourg indirectly: applicants tried to bring a complaint against the Member States instead (indirect actions). As long as EU accession to the ECHR has not been accomplished similar complaints will be lodged. In deciding these cases, the position of the Convention bodies has evolved and continues to evolve.

Two scenarios of indirect actions may be distinguished at the outset. The first one involves complaints addressed against all Member States, the argument

---

54 The terminology of direct and indirect actions was applied by the ECtHR and ECJ presidents in a joint communication considering the effects of the accession on the relationships between both courts. Joint communication from Presidents Costa and Skouris. Available at: www.echr.coe.int.

55 ECtHR, *Bosphorus Hava Yollari Turizm Ve Ticaret AS v. Ireland* (2006) 42 EHRR 1.

being that the Member States may be held collectively or individually responsible for violations of the Convention by Union institutions – for instance an alleged violation of privacy by the European Commission. The second scenario involves complaints addressed against a particular Member State, not so much for its own conduct but for acts of the Union in connection with that State – for instance an allegedly unreasonable amount of time taken by the ECJ to issue a preliminary ruling in a case pending before the domestic court of a particular Member State. Whereas the former group represents attempts to establish a 'pure' form of Member State responsibility, it will be noted that there is a rather thin line between the latter group and the *Cantoni* and *Bosphorus* type of cases that will be discussed below.

Interestingly, in one of its very first decisions – in 1958! – the European Commission of Human Rights observed that if a State party to the ECHR concludes another international agreement which disables it from performing its obligations under the Convention, it will be answerable for any resultant breach of its obligations thereunder.[56] Since there is no reason to assume that this principle does not apply to international agreements establishing an international organisation, the Commission's decision seemed to open the door to 'Member State responsibility' for the conduct of international organisations. Indeed, in the 1980s the Commission dealt with a series of cases in which it expressly left open the possibility that the Member States are answerable for violations of the ECHR by Community institutions. All cases were rejected, however, on other grounds.[57]

The case of *Senator Lines* seemed destined to become the leading case in this area; it was assigned to the Grand Chamber of the European Court of Human Rights. The applicant in the case was a German company that complained of a breach of the right to a fair trial (Article 6 ECHR) by the Court of First Instance and the European Court of Justice. Senator Lines' application was directed against the 15 Member States of the European Union, the argument being that the Member States may be held collectively or individually responsible for violations of the Convention by Community institutions. Unfortunately the case was declared inadmissible in March 2004 on factual grounds.[58]

Subsequently it was the case with the impressive name of *Cooperatieve Producentenorganisatie van de Nederlandse Kokkelvisserij U.A.* v. *the Netherlands*

---

56 ECommHR, decision of 10 June 1958, Appl. No. 235/56, *X & X.* v. *FRG*, 2 *Yearbook ECHR* (1958–1959) p. 300.

57 See, e.g., ECommHR, decision of 9 December 1987, Appl. No. 11123/84, *Tête* v. *France*, *DR* 54, p. 76; ECommHR, decision of 19 January 1989, Appl. No. 13539/88, *Dufay* v. *EC and its Member States* (not reported).

58 ECtHR, *Senator Lines GmbH* v. *Austria* App. No. 56672/00, 10 March 2004.

which squarely raised the question to what extent an individual Member State may be held responsible for ECJ decisions which are implemented by the domestic courts or by other authorities. An association of fishermen, the *Kokkelvissers*, was involved in litigation before a Dutch court. Pursuant to Article 234 TEC, the Dutch court referred questions to the European Court of Justice for a preliminary ruling. Whilst the case was pending before the ECJ, the *Kokkelvissers* sought leave to submit written observations in order to respond to the Advocate General's submissions. The Statute of the ECJ and its Rules of Procedure make no provision for this. However, the *Kokkelvissers* based their request on the right to a fair trial, as laid down in Article 6 ECHR. More in particular they relied on well-established case law of the ECtHR according to which the concept of a fair hearing implies the right to adversarial proceedings. This requires that the parties to criminal or civil proceedings must have the opportunity to have knowledge of and comment on all evidence adduced or observations filed, with a view to influencing the court's decision.[59] Interestingly, the ECtHR has determined in a series of cases, the first of which dates from 1991, that this principle also applies to the submissions of the Advocates General before the highest national jurisdictions.[60] The *Kokkelvissers* took the view that this case law also applies to the Opinion delivered before the ECJ by the Advocate General and accordingly sought leave to reply to it.

However, in line with the previous case of *Emesa*,[61] the ECJ refused leave to submit written observations in response to the AG's Opinion. Following the preliminary ruling of the ECJ, the Dutch court decided the case accordingly. The *Kokkelvissers* then brought a complaint in Strasbourg against the Netherlands in lieu of the Union proper. The main argument was that the Netherlands were responsible for the fact that the Dutch court, in applying the ECJ's preliminary ruling, relied on a judgment delivered in breach of Article 6. That argument was not successful:

> "The nexus between a preliminary ruling by the ECJ under Article 234 of the EC Treaty and the domestic proceedings which give rise to it is obvious. It is the domestic court which, finding itself faced with a question of Community law to which it requires an answer in order to decide a case pending before it, seeks the ECJ's assistance in terms of its own choosing; the interpretation which the ECJ then gives of Community law is authoritative and cannot be ignored by the domestic court.

---

59 See, e.g., ECtHR, judgment of 18 March 1997, Appl. No. 21497/93, *Mantovanelli* v. *France*, *Reports* 1997-II, p. 436, par. 33; ECtHR, judgment of 3 March 2000, Appl. No. 35376/97, *Krcmár* v. *Czech Republic*, par. 40.

60 See among many authorities ECtHR, judgment of 30 October 1991, Appl. No. 12005/86, *Borgers* v. *Belgium*, *Series A 214-B*, paras. 26–29; ECtHR, judgment of 20 February 1996, Appl. No. 19075/91, *Vermeulen* v. *Belgium*, *Reports* 1996-I, p. 224, paras. 29–30.

61 ECJ, Order of 4 February 2000, Case C-17/98, *Emesa Sugar (Free Zone) NV* v. *Aruba* [2000] *ECR* I-665.

> However, as already noted, there is a presumption that a Contracting Party has not departed from the requirements of the Convention where it has taken action in compliance with legal obligations flowing from its membership of an international organisation to which it has transferred part of its sovereignty as long as the relevant organisation is considered to protect fundamental rights, as regards both the substantive guarantees offered and the mechanisms controlling their observance, in a manner which can be considered at least equivalent to that for which the Convention provides. As a corollary, this presumption applies not only to actions taken by a Contracting Party but also to the procedures followed within such an international organisation itself and, in particular, to the procedures of the ECJ. In that respect, the Court also reiterates that such protection need not be identical to that provided by Article 6 of the Convention; the presumption can be rebutted only if, in the circumstances of a particular case, it is considered that the protection of Convention rights was manifestly deficient.
> Consequently, the Court must examine whether, in the present case, the procedure before the ECJ was accompanied by guarantees which ensured equivalent protection of the applicant's rights. In that respect, it gives weight to the possibility offered by Rule 61 of the ECJ's Rules of Procedure ... to order the reopening of the oral proceedings after the Advocate General has read out his or her opinion if it finds it necessary to do so and to the fact, as apparent from the ECJ's decision of 28 April 2004 in the present case, that a request for such reopening submitted by one of the parties to the proceedings is considered on its merits. In the present case, the ECJ found that the applicant association had submitted no precise information which made it appear either useful or necessary to reopen the proceedings.
> The Court further notes that the Administrative Jurisdiction Division of the Council of State could have submitted a further request for a preliminary ruling to the ECJ if it had found itself unable to decide the case based on the first such ruling. ...
> It follows that in so far as it is directed against the Kingdom of the Netherlands, the application must be rejected as manifestly ill-founded, pursuant to Article 35 §§3 and 4 of the Convention".[62]

Are there still any lessons that one might draw from this case-law? Quite apart from the outcome of specific cases, there is an element of unfairness in cases where EU Member States are being held responsible for situations that are to a considerable extent beyond their control. The Dutch government has very little to say about the way in which the ECJ regulates its procedure. If all Member States are involved in a case, as in *Senator Lines*, they may have a difficult time in agreeing on a common line of defence. Conversely, for the EU it is difficult to stand by as cases like *Senator Lines* and *Kokkelvissers* are pleaded in Strasbourg: they are in reality about the EU. Finally, for the applicant it may be somewhat intimidating to have to bring proceedings against a group of States.

---

62 ECtHR, decision of 20 January 2009, Appl. No. 13645/05, *Cooperatieve Producentenorganisatie van de Nederlandse Kokkelvisserij U.A. v. the Netherlands.* More on Kokkelvisserij see C Van de Heyning, "Case note under the ECJ judgment Kokkelvisserij" (2009) 46 *CMLRev.*6.

For all these reasons, EU accession to the European Convention has to be welcomed.

In a separate series of cases, the ECtHR has made it clear that it considers itself incompetent to deal with labour disputes between an EU employee and the EU institutions if there was no involvement of an ECHR High Contracting Party.[63] At the same time, the Court meant to deter Member States from transferring competences to international organisations in order to avoid their measures being scrutinized by the ECtHR.[64] This would thwart the promise of the ECHR as an effective and practical protection of human rights for all individuals who find themselves subject to the European legal space.[65] The threat of such immunity through transfer of competences became conceivable with the ever growing competences of the EU. Union law permeates a vast part of domestic law. The ECtHR sought to ensure the effectiveness of international organisations on the one hand without allowing the Convention protection to become hypothetical on the other hand.

In 2005 the ECtHR elaborated the *Bosphorus* doctrine which was to constitute a framework to deal with such cases. The case was first scrutinized by the ECJ.[66] The case concerned the question whether an EU measure implementing UN Security Council resolutions with regards to the civil war in the Federal Republic of Yugoslavia violated the right to peaceful enjoyment of property. The claimant stated that Ireland violated his property rights, as protected by Article 1 of the First Protocol to the Convention, by enforcing the EU Council Regulation 990/93. The ECJ held that property rights may be restricted substantially when pursuing an interest of equal substantial importance, e.g. the implementation of UN Security Council regulations.[67] The Court held that the Security Council regulations were to prevail because they pursued an objective fundamental to the international community, *in casu* to put an end to war and stop massive violations of human rights.[68] The applicant hence approached the ECtHR.

Before the Strasbourg Court the European Commission argued that the ECtHR should not intervene if the EU provided for an equivalent doctrine. The Commission argued that the EU law effectiveness would be undermined if the ECtHR required every state to scrutinise an EU act on compliance with the

63 ECtHR, *Connelly v. France* App. no. 73274/01 (9 December 2008).

64 ECtHR, *Bosphorus Hava Yollari Turizm Ve Ticaret AS v. Ireland* (2006) 42 EHRR 1, par.

65 ECtHR, *Airey v. Ireland* (1979–80) 2 EHRR 305, ECtHR, *Beer and Regan v Germany* 33 EHRR 54 (1999), para. 24, para. 57 and ECtHR, *Matthews v UK* (1999) 28 EHRR 361, para. 34.

66 ECJ, C-84/95 *Bosphorus Hava Yollari Turizm Ve Ticaret AS v. Minister of Transport* [1996] ECR I-03953.

67 *Ibid.*, par. 24.

68 *Ibid.*, par. 25–26.

Convention. Moreover, the EU Commission suggested that the ECtHR would declare itself final arbiter and thus, hierarchically higher than the ECJ if it would scrutinise EU acts for compatibility with the ECHR.[69] In its assessment the ECtHR balanced the effectiveness of human rights protection with the possibility for Member States to accede to international organizations for reasons of international cooperation.[70]

The doctrine in the first instance considers the question which violations are directly imputable to the Member State and which infringements follow directly from their obligations under international organisation (so-called indirect actions). The ECtHR emphasized that the Member States remain fully responsible for any measure or action falling outside its "strict international legal obligations".[71] The degree of discretion determines whether or not the Bosphorus doctrine applies. In the *Bosphorus* case the Court found that a national court was left no discretion but to apply judgments of the ECJ after a preliminary reference procedure.[72] Where, however, a regulation provides for exceptions to the general rule allowing Member States to examine individual cases the Member State has sufficient discretion to be held imputable to ECHR violations. This was e.g. the case in *MSS v. Belgium and Greece* which considered the obligations of Member States under the 'Dublin Regulation' on asylum.[73] Regulation 343/2003 provided that each Member State could examine an application for asylum lodged by a non-EU national even if such examination was not its responsibility under the criteria laid down in the Regulation (the so-called sovereignty clause). The ECtHR held that in such case the Member State remains responsible as it could refrain from transferring an applicant if it considered that the receiving country did not fulfill its obligations under the Convention.[74]

With consideration to those measures which are not directly imputable to the Member State, the ECtHR will take a more restraint approach on the condition that the international organisation under the auspices of which the decision was taken provides a fundamental rights protection equivalent to the ECHR. If the protection of the international organisation is found to be equivalent to the ECHR a presumption emerges that the measure under scrutiny does not violate the ECHR. The Court specified that the 'equivalent' as 'comparable' and not 'identical'.[75] In the case *Bosphorus* the Court noted that fundamental rights had

69 ECtHR, *Bosphorus Hava Yollari Turizm Ve Ticaret AS v. Ireland* (2006) 42 EHRR 1, par. 124.
70 *Ibid.*, par. 152 – 153.
71 *Ibid.*, par. 157.
72 *Ibid.*, par. 147.
73 ECtHR, *Mss v. Belgium* App. no. 30696/09 (21 January 2011), par. 339.
74 *Ibid.*, 339–340.
75 ECtHR, *Bosphorus Hava Yollari Turizm Ve Ticaret AS v. Ireland* (2006) 42 EHRR 1, par. 3, par. 155.

not been enshrined in the original texts of the Treaties of the European Union, but were now recognised as general principles of EU law and a condition for the legality of Community acts. The ECtHR highlighted that the ECtHR had been considered to be of "special significance" and that the ECJ refers extensively to the Convention. The Court highlighted the entrenchment of fundamental rights in the Treaties and the drafting of the EU Charter of fundamental rights. The ECtHR further scrutinized the controlling mechanisms, especially the procedures before the ECJ.[76] The Court concluded in *Bosphorus* that the EU provided an 'equivalent protection' both by substantive guarantees as by mechanisms controlling the observance. Therefore, a presumption of equivalence applies to EU measures and norms. In the case *MSS v. Belgium and Greece* the Court emphasized that for the finding of equivalence it attaches particular importance to the role of the ECJ as controlling mechanism for fundamental rights violations.[77]

In *Bosphorus* dissenting judges criticized the finding of equivalence of EU law by the ECtHR. They highlighted that in certain fields the ECJ lacked competence, namely in the field of EU Foreign and Security policy.[78] They argued that without the protection of the ECtHR due to the presumption of equivalence, victims of Convention violations by EU norms in this field would be left defencelessness.[79] However, the case *MSS v. Belgium and Greece* confirms that the presumption does not apply to the whole of EU law, but only to these fields of policy which were formerly categorized as first pillar issues.[80] The reason therefore lies in the special attachment of the ECtHR to the role played by the ECJ as protector of fundamental rights. The presumption only applies to EU law where the EU court system can intervene and effectively protect fundamental rights.

That must not necessarily imply that the ECJ must have considered the case for the finding of equivalence. E.g. in the case *Cooperative des Agriculteurs de Mayenne* the ECtHR found the presumption to apply even though no preliminary reference had been sent to the ECJ and thus, the Court had not considered the issue.[81] The French *Conseil d'Etat* did, however, consider the Community regulations. Lock argues that the EU court system is not limited to the ECJ or the General Court but also encompasses the domestic courts applying and

76 ECtHR, *Bosphorus Hava Yollari Turizm Ve Ticaret AS v. Ireland* (2006) 42 EHRR 1, par. 161–165.

77 ECtHR, *Mss v. Belgium* App. no. 30696/09 (21 January 2011), par. 338.

78 At the time of *Bosphorus* the ECJ also lacked competence to consider the so-called third pillar issues, namely internal and justice affairs. This has been remedied by the Lisbon Charter and the critique does no longer hold for this field of policy.

79 Dissenting judges, ECtHR, Bosphorus Hava Yollari Turizm Ve Ticaret AS v. Ireland (2006) 42 EHRR 1.

80 ECtHR, ECtHR, *Mss v. Belgium* App. no. 30696/09 (21 January 2011), par. 338.

81 ECtHR, *Cooperative des Agriculteurs de Mayenne* App. No. 16931/04 (10 October 2006).

interpreting EU law.[82] Therefore, the procedural protection of citizens must not be left ineffective if the ECJ does not consider the case as long as the national courts ensure the protection of fundamental rights.

This presumption can only be rebutted if the measure or act in question leaves the ECHR protection manifestly deficient. The Bosphorus doctrine was criticized for establishing a high threshold with the wording of "manifestly deficient" that it appeared illusory to think that the ECtHR would judge this level reached.[83] In the case *Kokkelvisserij*, which was mentioned above, the ECtHR gave an indication how it would apply the doctrine.[84] The fact that the EU provides an overall adequate protection of fundamental rights appears a settled fact as the Court does not examine whether such statement is indeed correct.[85] However, the effective scrutiny of the preliminary procedure highlights that the *Bosphorus* finding of equivalence of EU law does not provide automatic immunity from all scrutiny.[86] The ECtHR will consider whether the protection is not manifestly deficient with, however, some restraint. This is apparent in the flexible reading of the ECtHR former case law on adversarial proceedings and the restraint applied when establishing the effectiveness of the ECJ procedure enabling interventions. It exemplifies that while the Bosphorus doctrine requires the ECtHR to present in-depth arguments why the protection was not manifestly deficient, the threshold for finding a violation is considerably high.[87] It is to be awaited whether the accession to the ECHR will result in a stricter scrutiny or whether mechanisms will be introduced in order for the ECtHR to review EU law directly.

2.2.2. The doctrine after accession to the ECHR

With the EU accession to the ECHR one of the premises of the *Bosphorus* doctrine alters, namely the lack of competence with regards to EU law. The EU

---

82 T Lock, "Beyond Bosphorus: The European Court of Human Rights' Case Law on the Responsibility of Member States of International Organisations under the European Convention on Human Rights" (2010) 10 *Human Rights Law Review* 3.

83 S Douglas-Scott, "A Tale of Two Court: Luxembourg, Strasbourg and the Growing European Human Rights acquis" (2006) 43 *Common Market Law Review* 629, pp. 638–639.

84 ECtHR, *Kokkelvisserij v. The Netherlands, Application* (App. no. 13645/05) (ECtHR, 20 January 2009).

85 This is not self-evident as several judges claimed the EU fundamental rights protection not equivalent due to the limited individual access to the EU courts. ECtHR, dissenting opinion, ECtHR, *Bosphorus Hava Yollari Turizm Ve Ticaret AS v. Ireland* (2006) 42 EHRR 1, par. 162.

86 The ECtHR did not agree with the *Emesa Sugar* reasoning on all points. Instead, the ECtHR provided its own reasoning with, however, considering the Emesa judgment as relevant community practice.

87 Lock criticizes the ECtHR for not applying the Bosphorus doctrine consequently in all cases concerning international law obligations. T Lock, "Beyond Bosphorus: the European Court of Human Rights' Case law responsibility of Member States of International Organisations under the European Convention on Human Rights" (2010) 10 *Human Rights Law Review* 3.

accession to the Convention will not simply imply that the ECtHR can scrutinize all measures of EU law including ECJ judgments in the same manner as Member State actions and norms. The accession will be concluded through negotiations between the Council of Europe and the European Union in order to ensure that the necessary adjustments are put in place.[88]

In these negotiations account has to be taken of the limits the ECJ set to such accession in its 2/94 Order when the possibility of accession was first put before the Court. The EU Commission argued before the ECJ that the 'immunity' of Community norms of external scrutiny on the compatibility with the ECHR amounted to a "conspicuous gap in the European legal system".[89] The Commission advocated that an accession to the ECHR would not endanger EU autonomy since the Convention imposes only minimum standards and the control machinery of the ECHR would have no direct effect on the Community legal order. However, the French, Portuguese, Spanish, Irish and UK governments argued that the accession could endanger the autonomy of the Community Legal Order since it would submit the appreciation of EU norms to the scrutiny of another court than the ECJ.[90] The ECJ stipulated that submitting the EU to decisions of an international court was compatible with the Treaty as long as it did not endanger the autonomy of the EU legal order.[91]

Especially the position of the ECJ following an EU accession to the ECHR was examined. Several national governments advocated that an accession would seriously limit the autonomous interpretation of EU law by the ECJ and be incompatible with the monopoly of the ECJ to interpret and apply EU law.[92] The ECJ stressed the need to respect the EU courts independence in particular the monopoly of the ECJ in the interpretation of EU law.[93] This concern was taken on board. Protocol No. 8 to the Lisbon Treaty stipulates that an accession cannot affect Article 344 TFEU (former Article 292) which holds that the Member States will only settle their disputes concerning the interpretation of EU law by the

---

88 A draft agreement on the accession of the EU to the Convention was already proposed in March. Several options were still put on an equal footing. Still, certain elements such as the concept of the co-respondent mechanism appear agreed upon. See Council of Europe, 6th working agreement of the CDDH informal working group on the accession of the European Union to the European Convention on human rights with the European Commission (15-18 March, Strasbourg), CDDH-UE (2011)04 (hereafter: Draft agreement on the accession).

89 Commission Communication on the accession of the Community to the ECHR and the Community legal order, 19 October 1990, SEC(90)2087final, par. 1.

90 ECJ, Opinion 2/94 *Accession by the Community to the. European Convention for the Protection of Human. Rights and Fundamental Freedoms* [1996] ECR I–1780–1782.

91 ECJ, Opinion 1/91, Re the Draft Treaty on a European Economic Area [1991] *ECR* I-6079.

92 ECJ Opinion 2/94 *Accession by the Community to the. European Convention for the Protection of Human. Rights and Fundamental Freedoms* [1996] ECR I-1781.

93 ECJ, Opinion 1/91 *Re the Draft Treaty on a European Economic Area* [1991] ECR I-6079.

means provided by the Treaty.[94] It indicates that the drafters intended to preserve the ECJ as prime interpreter of EU Law as provided by the Treaty and that an accession would not alter that fact. In the discussion whether to start accession talks after the Lisbon Treaty ratification, the ECJ advocated that the invalidation of EU norms remained the sole task of the Court and this characteristic of the EU judicial protection system should be preserved.[95] The prerogative of the ECJ to invalidate EU norms is thus considered a crucial element in the accession talks.

In a joint communication the presidents of the ECJ and the ECtHR considered how this autonomy could be safeguarded while ensuring that the EU would live up to its obligations under the Convention.[96] They discussed the effects of an EU accession with regards to direct actions, namely procedures directed against EU norms, and to indirect actions, namely applications against domestic law implementing EU law. In the first case the ECtHR would have considered before the accession that it lacks jurisdiction to consider the case. After the accession the Strasbourg court gains this competence. In such cases Article 35(1) ECHR applies which demands applicants to first exhaust all domestic remedies, in this case EU remedies. This means that applicants will first have to demand the EU courts to consider the issue before submitting a complaint to the Strasbourg Court. It is to be expected that in such cases the established ECtHR case law with regards to the exhaustion of remedies applies. E.g. the Court has held that Article 35(1) ECHR demands applicants to exhaust those procedures which are effective and available. The requirement of "availability" suggests that applicants can directly bring a case before the Strasbourg court against EU norms against which no complaint can be lodged before the ECJ, e.g. measures which fall in the field of Foreign and Security policy.[97]

The indirect actions are considered to be governed by the *Bosphorus* doctrine before the accession. The exhaustion criterion plays here as well: the applicants will have to refer the matter first to the domestic courts which can refer the question to the ECJ by means of a preliminary reference. However, only the highest courts are obliged to refer the question and several of those courts,

94 Article 3 of the protocol 6 relating to Article 6(2) of the Treaty on European Union on the accession of the Union to the European Convention on the Protection of Human rights and Fundamental Rights, Off. Publ., 9th May 2005. See as well Article 6 *Draft agreement on the accession*.

95 ECJ, Discussion document of the Court of Justice of the European Union on certain aspects of the accession of the European Union to the European Convention for the Protection of Human Rights and Fundamental Rights (hereafter: *ECJ Discussion document)* (5 May 2010, Luxembourg), par. 9. Available at www.curia.int.eu.

96 Joint communication from Presidents Costa and Skouris. Available at: www.echr.coe.int.

97 Individuals need to exhaust those domestic remedies which are capable of providing redress and have a reasonable chance of success. ECtHR, *Akdivar and Others v Turkey* (1996) 23 EHRR 143, para. 68 and ECtHR, *Sejdovic v Italy* (2006) 42 EHRR 360, para. 46.

especially constitutional courts, refrain from sending such questions.[98] The presidents of the ECJ and ECtHR advocate that in such cases the ECtHR will have to adjudicate an application with consideration to EU law even though the ECJ will not be given the chance to review the case itself. As the applicant cannot force domestic courts to refer a preliminary question to the ECJ, this procedure will not be considered to fall under the obligation to exhaust all remedies as entrenched in Article 35(1) ECHR.

Does the proposed procedure undermine the subsidiarity of the Strasbourg mechanism and encroach upon the autonomy of the EU control mechanism? First, the presidents submit that these situations are exceptional and thus, the limited number of such applicants is not capable to undermine the autonomy of the EU courts as such.[99] Second, reference could be made to the ECtHR case law which actively support the authority of the ECJ. As mentioned, the Court held that article 6 ECHR which entrenches the right to a fair process might be infringed by the national authorities' refusal to execute a judgment of the EU Courts.[100] In order to fully safeguard the principle of subsidiarity the judges propose the introduction of a new procedure which would enable the ECJ to carry out an internal review of fundamental rights violations before the ECtHR. In the Draft Agreement on the accession, which was elaborated by the Informal working group on the accession of the European Union with the European Commission, the basic principles of the proposal of the ECJ and the ECtHR judges were upheld. The Draft introduces the co-respondent mechanism. It would allow the EU and member states to act in proceedings as co-respondents if there appears a "substantive link" between the ECHR violation and EU legal acts or measures.[101] Option B of the co-respondent mechanism in the Draft Agreement adopted a proposal similar to the one favoured by the ECtHR and ECJ judges in their Joint communication. This proposal considers that when the EU acts as co-respondent before the ECtHR, the ECJ will have the opportunity to rule on the validity or the conformity of the EU act with fundamental rights as set out in the notification of the application to the parties, if the ECJ has not done so yet.[102] The Draft Agreement does not mention the distinction between direct and indirect actions, but distinguishes on the basis of the existence of a substantive link. Only if such link exists, the EU can act as a co-respondent and

98 Most constitutional courts do not refer preliminary questions. The Belgian and Austrian Constitutional courts have made several references. Recently, the Lithuanian and Italian constitutional courts have also made a preliminary reference. Other courts have not engaged in a preliminary procedure. For more see G Martinico, "Judging in the multilevel legal order: exploring the techniques of "hidden dialogue" (2010) 21 *King's Law Journal* 24.

99 Joint communication from Presidents Costa and Skouris. Available at: www.echr.coe.int.

100 ECtHR, 19 March 1997, *Hornsby v. Greece* (Appl. No. 18357/91).

101 This proposal featured in both options A en B of the co-respondent mechanism versions in Article 4 *Draft Agreement on the Accession*.

102 This proposal only featured in option B, par. 3 in Article 4 *Draft Agreement on the Accession*.

the question can be referred to the ECJ first. The co-respondent proposal in the Draft Agreement adds that such ECJ ruling should proceed by the applicable rules of EU law, but should be delivered quickly so that the proceedings before the European Court of Human Rights are not unduly delayed. The latter addition clearly indicates the concern of the EU and the Council of Europe that the accession would lead to unreasonable lengthy proceedings. While this procedure before the ECJ was only adopted in one of the two options of the co-respondent mechanism, we expect it to be favoured by the negotiators because it enables the reconciliation of ECHR control with the autonomy of the EU mechanism and is supported by the presidents of the ECJ and the ECtHR.

As long as no formal procedures connecting both courts are established, the Bosphorus doctrine will continue to be applied in indirect actions. The accession only brings about the competence of the ECtHR with regards to EU norms *ratione materiae*. The Bosphorus reasoning with regards to indirect actions remains valid, namely to allow Member States to live up to their obligations under international law without, however, rendering the ECHR protection futile. However, if the ECtHR and ECJ presidents' proposal on indirect actions would be applied the scope of the *Bosphorus* doctrine will be limited to international law except for EU law.[103] Instead indirect actions will be governed by the mechanisms set up by the EU and Council of Europe during the accession talks. If the co-respondent mechanism is adopted, should the degree of discretion of the Member States still play any role? We would argue it does not. If a substantive link between the ECHR violation and EU law exists, the EU can intervene in the proceedings as co-respondent and the ECJ should be given the possibility to consider the case first. If the violation follows from Member State measures falling within their discretion, the violation is imputable to the Member State alone. In such case it appears that the former reasoning of the ECtHR should be followed by which the ECtHR can directly consider the violation after the exhaustion of all domestic remedies.

The question arises whether a formal linkage between the ECJ and the ECtHR implies that the Strasbourg Court should dedicate even more attention to the ECJ case law. We already observed that the accession might imply that the Luxembourg jurisprudence might play a more visible role as inspiration with regards to the interpretation of the Convention rights and freedoms. If a new procedure is introduced whereby the ECJ would first consider the case on fundamental rights issues, it could be questioned to what extent the ECtHR should be obliged to consider its arguments. In any case, the accession would mean that EU institutions could defend their point of view directly before the

103 T Lock, "The ECJ and the ECtHR: the future relationship between the two European Courts" (2009) 8 *The law and Practice of International Courts and Tribunals* 3, p. 396.

ECtHR in direct actions and the ECJ case law would be regarded in a similar manner as the relevant case law of domestic courts in cases against Member States. It would be wise to pay equivalent attention to the ECJ case law in the matter in indirect actions to safeguard the current peaceful relationship between both courts.

3. FUTURE PROSPECTS OF THE RELATIONSHIP BETWEEN THE STRASBOURG AND LUXEMBOURG COURTS

The accession negotiations had not been settled when this contribution was finalized. Yet, there are good reasons to believe that the communication of the presidents of the ECtHR and the ECJ will have a considerable impact on the official accession talks. Safeguarding the current cooperative relationship between the ECtHR and the ECJ and ensuring their respective autonomy had been of great concern. The protocol annexed to the Lisbon Treaty considering the accession to the ECHR explicitly mentions this point. Due to the intention to safeguard the peaceful interaction between the ECtHR and the ECJ it seems wise to follow the lead from these courts with regards to their future interactions after accession. The *Draft Agreement* agreed upon by the CDDH and the EU Commission adopts a mechanism to accommodate the interests of the ECJ and the ECtHR, namely the co-respondent mechanism. The proposal still upholds two options for this new mechanism with only the B option entrenching the ideas of the Joint Communication of the judges. We could expect this B version of the co-respondent mechanism to be favoured because of the support of the actors who will have to put the mechanism into practice, namely the ECJ and the ECtHR.

Such procedure of coordination would balance the protection by the ECtHR with the subsidiarity principle. However, the establishment of a procedure to allow the ECJ to consider the fundamental rights issues first even though all available and effective procedures were exhausted has been met with critique.[104] First, certain participants of the CDDH working group highlighted that such procedure would imply a difference in treatment between the EU and Member States. No such procedure is provided for Member States.[105] E.g. if a domestic courts refuses to send a preliminary question to the constitutional court with regards to a fundamental rights violation inherent to domestic legislation, the constitutional court is not given the chance to consider the issue before the ECtHR. The new procedure would violate the principle of equality between the

104 *Ibid.*, par. 6.
105 We are indebted to professor De Witte for his point of view on this issue.

high contracting parties. It could be argued that such argument can be refuted on the ground that a difference in treatment is justifiable because of the difference in institutional construction between an international organisation and a domestic state. While a Member State is sovereign except for those fields were it transferred its competences completely to an international organisation, the EU has only attributed competences. When approving the EU accession the high contracting countries must have been aware of the adjustments necessary to allow such international organisation. E.g., the original text of the ECHR was to be altered as it only considered the accession of Member States.

Second, the judges mentioned that such new procedure should not result in lengthy proceedings. The communication emphasizes that it should be clearly determined to which cases such procedure would apply. The judges argue that the ECJ should introduce an accelerated procedure for such cases in order to ensure that the proceedings before the ECHR are not postponed unreasonably. The latter remark touches upon a problematic feature of both courts, namely the length of procedures. E.g. in the case *Koua Poirrez* the total of procedures including an application before the ECJ and the ECtHR lasted over twelve years. The introduction of new procedures in order to coordinate fundamental rights protection by the ECtHR and the ECJ should give special attention to this issue.[106]

The main question is whether the accession will remedy the reasons why the EU and Council of Europe considered such accession necessary.[107] The accession intended to ensure a greater coherence between the EU fundamental rights and the ECHR jurisprudence and avoid open conflicts between the ECJ and ECtHR case law. The accession will remove the current blank spots of Convention protection, namely where a violation originates directly from EU law. However, it is not sure that the accession will remove the potential for open conflicts. The ECtHR will consider fundamental rights cases which have been scrutinized on the same merits by the ECJ. With the proposal of the judges such ECJ scrutiny might even take place while the application is pending before the ECtHR.

---

106 E.g. Tridimas argued against a system of preliminary reference procedures between the ECJ and the ECtHR out of fear for unreasonable lengthy proceedings. Such procedure would only be acceptable if accompanied with a time-limit. Takis Tridimas, *The General Principles of EU Law* (Oxford University Press, Oxford 2006), p. 356. See also Jospeh R Wetzel, "Improving Fundamental Rights Protection in the European Union: Resolving the conflict and confusion between the Luxembourg and Strasbourg Court" (2002–2003) 71 *Fordham Law Review* 2823, pp. 2851–2852 and Robin CA White, "The Treaty of Lisbon: some human rights issues" (2008) *The Jean Monet Seminar Series*, pp. 26–29. Available at: http://home.um.edu.mt.

107 There were several other reasons for the accession apart from ensuring coherence and avoiding open conflicts, e.g. to ensure that the EU would have to live up to the same standards it demands from states willing to accede to the EU. For more HC Krüger and J Polakiewicz, "Proposals for a coherent human rights protection system in Europe – The European Convention on Human Rights and the EU Charter of Fundamental Rights" (2001) 22 *Human Rights Law Journal* 1, pp. 1–13.

In principle the ECtHR is not bound by the findings of the ECJ in the same way as it is not bound by the considerations of domestic courts. If the ECtHR would completely dismiss the finding of the ECJ open conflicts will only be avoided if the latter court accepts the reasoning behind the judgment. It should be reminded that a judgment of the ECtHR is declaratory and does not invalidate or annul the impugned act from the European legal space.[108] The EU institutions will have to remove the act or the ECJ will have to find the norm invalid. It will beg the question whether or not the ECJ is bound by the ECtHR judgment and is required to remove the norm. The established case law of the ECtHR considers that national authorities remain free as to the means to remedy the violation.[109] However, they are requested not only to provide a remedy for the victim, but also to remove the causes of the violation.[110] The same would thus apply to the EU institutions and hence, the ECJ. In such case sentiments of lost autonomy might emerge resulting in tensions equivalent as those between the ECJ and the domestic constitutional or supreme courts.[111] Without a formal mechanism the ECJ was left more manoeuvring space to avoid open conflicts without having to settle whether or not the ECtHR jurisprudence is directly binding.

A problem arises for the Member States as well. In principle they cannot set aside EU norms under the ECJ *Foto-Frost* doctrine.[112] Fundamental rights concerns are not accepted as a legitimate exception. However, in case the ECtHR finds an EU norm to violate the ECHR and the domestic court cannot refer a preliminary question to the ECJ, the domestic court will be left with the difficult choice whether or not to apply the EU norm as long as it is not removed. If the Member State applies the norm, it will disregard a judgment of the ECtHR. If it refuses to apply the norm, it will neglect the supremacy of EU law over all national norms. The accession negotiations should explicitly consider this, albeit exceptional, situation in order to allow the domestic courts to act in good faith.

While open conflicts are still possible after the accession, the risk should not be overestimated. The fact that the ECJ and the ECtHR jointly propose coordination mechanisms displays the current cooperative attitude of both courts. It can be expected that both courts will endeavour to avoid such conflicts as they have

---

108 The protection hence relies on the actions of Member States. ECtHR, *Assanidze* (2004) 39 EHRR 653, para. 202 and ECtHR, *Ocalan v. Turkey* (2005) 41 EHRR 45, para. 210.

109 ECtHR, *Brumarescu v. Romania* (2001) 33 EHRR 35, para. 20 and ECtHR, *Iatridis v. Greece* (2000) 30 EHRR 97, para. 33.

110 J Polackiewicz, "The execution of judgments of the ECHR" in R Blackburn and J Polackiewicz (eds), *Fundamental Rights in Europe* (Oxford University Press, Oxford 2001), p. 62.

111 E.g. the recurrent interaction between the German Constitutional Court and the ECJ (so-called Solange cases).

112 C-314/419 *Foto-Frost v. Hauptzollamt Lübeck* [1985] ECR I-4199. In the case Cilfit the ECJ already indicated under which conditions last resort courts are not required to send preliminary references. For more see the Cilfit contributions in M Poiares Maduro and L Azoulai, *The Past and Future of EU Law* (Hart Publishing, Oxford 2010).

before the accession and not abuse the coordination mechanisms they developed themselves. The major challenge after the accession will remain to deliver justice in time. The problem is currently most pressing at the ECtHR itself due to an ever growing influx of – mostly inadmissible – applications without an equivalent expansion of its capacity. These EU cases will come on top of the heavy caseload resulting in an even more considerable backlog. Protocol 14 ECHR does provide for better filter mechanisms and a new admissibility criterion (significant disadvantage).[113] Yet, the accession might mean an additional number of applications. Remedying the duplication of work could, in contrast, decrease the total length of procedures. In conclusion, it should be advisable that during the negotiations not all efforts are dedicated to avoid open conflicts and safeguard the respective autonomy of the courts, but that the focus should be put on the question how to ensure the best protection between the ECJ and the ECtHR within a reasonable timeframe.

4. CONCLUDING REMARKS

Without attempting to be exhaustive we have seen that EU law, and the ECJ's case-law more in particular, has had quite an impact on the jurisprudence of the European Court of Human Rights. In some cases EU law is applied as 'law of the land' (*Aristimuño Mendizabal, Dangeville)*, in others as an authority or source of inspiration (*Marckx, Maslov)*. In some cases the Strasbourg Court lends a helping hand to Luxembourg (*Hornsby, Pafitis*). Especially in recent years the ECtHR has relied very frequently on EU law, and on the case-law of the ECJ.

Meanwhile, the Lisbon Treaty has paved the way for Union accession to the ECHR, and at the same time has given legal binding force to the Charter of Fundamental Rights. The first impression is that this arrangement settles the relationship between the European Court of Justice and the European Court of Human Rights. But there are some outstanding issues. The two European Courts will have to devise ways to minimise the risks of diverging interpretations that might be detrimental to both. In addition, it will be very interesting to see if the ECJ develops in the direction of a human rights court, not only with respect to the institutions but also *vis-à-vis* the Member States, and if so, how this will affect the balance between Strasbourg and Luxembourg. To be continued.

113 Several authors argue that the improvements will only provide little redress for the enormous caseload. M Scheinin, "Access to Justice before International Human Rights Bodies" in Fancesco Francioni (ed.) Access to Justice as a Human Right (Oxford: OUP, 2007), p. 150, P Mahoney, "Parting Thoughts of an Outgoing Registrar of the European Court of Human Rights" (2005) 26 *Human Rights Law Journal* 9 p. 346 and S Greer, "Protocol 14 and the Future of the European Court of Human Rights" (2005) *Public Law* 83, p. 104.

CHAPTER 3
NO PLACE LIKE HOME
Discretionary space for the domestic protection of fundamental rights

Catherine VAN DE HEYNING

Fundamental rights have played an important historic role in shaping the relationship between the domestic highest courts and the European Courts. The conflict between the European Court of Justice (ECJ) and the German Constitutional Court on this point is well-known (*Solange* cases): the latter refused to accept the supremacy of EU law over all German law as long as EU law did not provide for a protection of fundamental rights equivalent to the German domestic protection, notably the protection of constitutional rights and freedoms entrenched in the Basic Law. Ever since, the ECJ has elaborated a vast case law on fundamental rights protection drawing on international treaties, especially the ECHR, and the common constitutional traditions of the Member States. The EU protection of fundamental rights did not stop at providing a check on the compatibility of EU law with fundamental rights. The ECJ highlighted that it could review the compatibility of domestic norms with fundamental rights if they would fall within the scope of EU law.[1] The ECJ thus became an active protector of fundamental rights, albeit within the scope of EU law. The EU Charter of Fundamental Rights consolidates this evolution towards fundamental rights protection at the EU level. In the *Banana* judgment, several decades after the first *Solange* case, the German Constitutional Court confirmed that the EU level had reached an acceptable level of fundamental rights protection.[2]

This emergence and consolidation of a substantive fundamental rights protection at the EU level did, however, not demolish the domestic constitutional fences against the supremacy claims of EU law. The protection of fundamental rights by

1 C-260/89, ERT [1991] ECR I-2925.
2 German Constitutional Court 2 BvL 1/97, 7 June 2000.

the ECJ and even active scrutiny means that the constitutional and EU level could significantly disagree on what the protection of particular rights entails. This is especially the case where two conflicting rights need to be balanced in a particular case. The constitutional legal order might give more weight to one right over the other whereas the ECJ might decide otherwise. It is observed that several constitutional courts only conditionally accept the supremacy of EU law over all domestic law.[3] Both the German as French constitutional court indicated that they would only accept the supremacy of EU law as long as it would not touch upon the national constitutional identity.[4] Thereby, the constitutional courts indicate that they maintain the last word in those situations where they consider that EU law touches upon the most sensitive issues of domestic constitutional protection. Therefore, the *Solange* approach of the German constitutional court has not withered but transformed. The emphasis is now put on constitutional particularity rather than a general level of fundamental rights. A similar position towards the ECtHR could be witnessed in the *Gorgülü* judgment of the German Constitutional court which has been labelled by some as the Strasbourg *Solange* judgment.[5]

It has been argued that this continued friction on ultimate say and supremacy is unhelpful for the protection of fundamental rights. BESSELINK has argued in an article of 1998 for an alternative approach based on the maximisation of fundamental rights protection.[6] He claimed that the decision on which court ought to have the last say in conflict cases should not be decided on the grounds of supremacy rules, but on the basis whether EU law or domestic law provides the best fundamental rights protection of the citizen.[7] Such approach appears echoed in the new Article 53 of the Charter of Fundamental Rights which claims that the Charter will not restrict the already recognised protection, thus the domestic and international protection of fundamental rights. This clause mimics a similar ECHR provision. Does such "best protection" rule provide an effective

---

3 Damian Chalmers, "Constitutional modesty" (2005) 30 *European Law Review* 4, p. 459.

4 Apparent in cases French Constitutional Court, decision 2006–540 DC 29 July 2006, par. 19 and German Constitutional Court, 2 BvE 2/08, 2 BvE 5/08, 2 BvR 1010/08, 2 BvR 1022/08, 2 BvR 1259/08 and 2 BvR 182/09, 30 June 2009, par. 240.

5 In this judgment, the German constitutional court had limited the loyalty of the German courts to the Strasbourg jurisprudence insofar as it was compatible with the core element of the German Constitution. At the same time, however, the Court indicated that it would interpret the German constitution in conformity with the Convention. German Constitutional Court, 2 BvR 1481/04, 14 October 2004.

6 Leonard Besselink, "Entrapped by the maximum standard: on fundamental rights, pluralism and subsidiarity in the European Union" (1998) 35 *Common Market Law Review* 629.

7 He considers that the application of domestic standards if they provide a better protection than the EU standard result from the principle of subsidiarity and would result in a local maximum standard. Ibid., p. 677.

tool to avoid conflicts and ensure a better protection of fundamental rights?[8] The Strasbourg court had to deal early on and frequently with the potential differences between constitutional and conventional protection of fundamental rights and freedoms. Notwithstanding some isolated and exceptional events, the ECtHR approach has resulted in the absence of open conflicts without the protection of the Convention being immobilized out of fear for potential discords with the domestic constitutional level. Possibly, the ECtHR case law provides an answer or at least interesting conceptions on this issue.

This contribution starts by shortly outlining the main reasons behind the claim for a certain discretionary space for the constitutional legal order with regards to fundamental rights protection, mainly the value of diversity, democratic legitimacy and the principle of subsidiarity. The paper continues with a discussion on the existing maximisation clauses within the ECHR and the EU Charter. This section will scrutinize the viability of such clauses within the current practice of supranational adjudication of fundamental rights. A third section will discuss alternative approaches elaborated by the ECtHR to ensure discretionary space for the constitutional protection of fundamental rights. This contribution will conclude by assessing the potential of mechanisms to ensure a certain margin of discretion for the Member States and the role the domestic courts should play.

1. LEGITIMATE REASONS FOR CONSTITUTIONAL DISCRETIONARY SPACE: DIVERSITY AND SUBSIDIARITY

The European and the constitutional legal orders protect in general equivalent fundamental freedoms and rights. Moreover, the EU Charter and the Convention apply directly in the domestic legal order either through the ratification of the Lisbon Treaty and the incorporation of the Convention in domestic law or through the direct effect of international law in monist legal orders. These rights are autonomously interpreted by the supranational courts. That does not mean that the European courts do not take account of the domestic evolutions when setting their standard of fundamental rights protection. The ECtHR and the ECJ have to a certain extent linked their assessment of fundamental rights to the evolutions in the Member States. The ECtHR revises its established case law in

---

8 It should be noted that the scope of this contribution is restricted to the discussion of concrete jurisprudential tools for judges to ensure effective protection of fundamental rights within a supranational context. It does not discuss an alternative reasoned approach of the European legal space such as e.g. the concept of constitutional pluralism provides. On this issue, I would like to refer to the contribution of Samantha Besson.

favour of a more stringent interpretation of a conventional right or freedom on the grounds of a tendency within the Member States towards such interpretation (the living instrument doctrine). E.g. in *Goodwin,* the ECtHR overturned its previous case law on the protection of transsexuals under Article 8 ECHR on the grounds of a perceivable change in the recognition by the national authorities of transsexuals. The ECJ established that it would recognise rights stemming from the common constitutional traditions.[9] E.g. in *Omega*, the Court accepted the right to dignity as an autonomous fundamental right on the ground of the recognition of such right in several constitutional orders.[10] Thus, both systems endeavour to progress their protection of human rights along the evolutions within the domestic constitutional orders.[11]

Therefore, it could be questioned whether the protection of fundamental rights at the domestic level and the European level could actually diverge. Fundamental rights provisions are in general open-ended and vague. Courts are, therefore, demanded to interpret these provisions and apply them in concrete cases. They will be required in many cases to balance the protection of rights with legitimate public interests or other rights.[12] Such balancing does not take place in a vacuum, but against a given judicial, social, cultural and political background. As a consequence, certain rights might be given more weight in one legal culture in comparison to other legal orders. Balancing has become a crucial element of the Strasbourg's approach towards the proportionality of potential restrictions of conventional rights and freedoms. Confronted with diverse balancing by the national authorities or domestic courts, the Strasbourg Court can either scrutinize the reasoning put forward justifying the outcome of the national balance itself or allow for a certain margin of decision for the Member States.[13] The Court has indicated that it will apply judicial restraint towards the domestic legal orders under certain conditions and only scrutinize the margins of their

---

9 Besselink correctly highlights that this approach does not mean an incorporation of the fundamental rights standards of the member states into a European standard. The fundamental rights protection was until the Lisbon Treaty only incorporated as a general principle of EU law. Leonard Besselink, "Entrapped by the maximum standard: on fundamental rights, pluralism and subsidiarity in the European Union" (1998) 35 *Common Market Law Review* 629, p. 633.

10 ECJ, C-36/02 *Omega* [2004] ECR I-9609.

11 It should be mentioned, however, that both concepts have been criticized for being based on limited comparative research and analysis. Several authors demand for coherent and transparent criteria for the ECJ and the ECtHR to base their reasoning on. Gerald Neuman, "Human Rights and constitutional rights: harmony and dissonance" (2003) 55 *Stanford Law Review* 1863, p. 1885.

12 More on balancing in case of conflicts of rights, see Lorenzo Zucca, "Conflicts of fundamental rights as constitutional dilemmas" in Eva Brems (ed.), *Conflicts between fundamental rights* (Antwerp, Intersentia 2008), pp. 19–37.

13 Eva Brems, "Human rights: minimum and maximum perspectives" (2009) 9 *Human Rights Law Review* 3, p. 351.

appreciation of the proportionality of the measures taken restricting fundamental rights. There are several grounds on the basis of which the European courts applied judicial restraint towards the domestic assessment of fundamental rights protection: first, the idea that national authorities might be better placed to appreciate the situation, second and closely connected, the democratic legitimacy of the domestic legislator and finally, the observation of diverse practices and interpretations of fundamental rights protection.

First, the supranational position of the European Court might justify a certain level of restraint towards the protection of rights by the domestic courts, especially the constitutional courts. The ECtHR is in principle a subsidiary protection mechanism.[14] Therefore, the main responsibility for the protection of the conventional rights and freedoms remains with the national authorities. The domestic courts play a particular important role in the enforcement of these rights. Therefore, the ECtHR has argued that the domestic courts should be given in first instance the possibility to review the compatibility of the domestic practices and acts with the Convention.[15] The reasoning of the domestic courts on the compatibility of the domestic legislation enables the ECtHR to "benefit of the views of the national courts".[16] The Court considers these views important as the domestic courts are in direct and continuous contact with the vital forces of their countries and therefore, can provide important insights on the interpretation and appreciation of the domestic norms and interests.[17] The Court accepts that on this basis the domestic courts should be granted a certain margin of appreciation with regards to the balancing between the conventional rights and legitimate interests. Besselink has argued that the principle of subsidiarity entrenched in the TEU (and more recently in a separate recommendation)[18] could justify restraint towards domestic standards of fundamental rights offering a better protection than the EU norms.[19]

Second, the democratic legitimacy of the domestic legislator has been accepted as a potential reason for applying greater restraint when scrutinizing the appreciation of fundamental rights protection by national authorities. Bellamy notes that rights and liberties are "intimately tied up with the democratic

14 The admissibility criterion of exhaustion of domestic remedies bears witness to the subsidiarity of the Strasbourg mechanism.
15 ECtHR, Azinas v. Cyprus (2004) 40 EHRR 8, par. 38.
16 ECtHR, *Burden v United Kingdom* (2008) 47 EHRR 38, par. 42 and ECtHR, *Kennedy v. United Kingdom* (App. no. 26839/05) (unreported, 18 May 2010), par. 109.
17 ECtHR, *Handyside v United Kingdom* (1976) 1 EHRR 737, par. 48.
18 Article 5 par. 1 TEU and protocol 2 on the application of the principles of subsidiarity and proportionality. The article 1 of this protocol requires every institution, thus including the ECJ, to respect the principle of subsidiarity.
19 Leonard Besselink, "Entrapped by the maximum standard: on fundamental rights, pluralism and subsidiarity in the European Union" (1998) 35 *Common Market Law Review* 629, p. 676.

process, which gives them their force, form and content".[20] The ECtHR has accepted that under certain circumstances restraint should be applied towards national authorities because they have more democratic legitimacy to strike the difficult balance between rights and legitimate public interests, especially in economic and social policy.[21]

Third, the observation that the interpretation of rights takes place within a specific legal, political, cultural and social framework might also justify a certain level of freedom with regards to the protection of rights. The protection of rights is closely connected with the conception of the "good" in society. Notwithstanding the existence of a certain common consensus about the core of fundamental rights among the EU Member States, there is no similar in-depth common notion of what the "good" entails. Hence, divergences of the framing of fundamental rights can be expected. To a certain extent, the ECtHR accepts the protection of diversity as a valuable reason for allowing a margin to the Member States. The Court provides for a wide margin of appreciation with regards to the proportionality test where it cannot discern a common practice or consensus. E.g. in the case *Leyla Sahin*, the Court argued that the absence of a common approach towards religious signs in educational institutes within the European legal space justified a wide margin for the Member State to scrutinize a prohibition of veils in universities.[22] Such position could be criticized. If diversity of human rights protection is considered a protectable value, a common tendency or lack of it should not be of great importance.[23] Rather, it should be examined whether the reason for such diverse interpretation is legitimate and respects the limits of the provided margin. In fact, in the case *Leyla Sahin* the ECtHR drew much attention to the particular political and historical situation of Turkey and its concept of secularism to find that the margin had not been overstepped.[24]

The Lisbon Treaty entrenches a recognition of the constitutional diversity of the Member States. A new provision claims that the EU must respect the national identities inherent in their political and constitutional fundamental structures.[25]

20 Richard Bellamy, *Liberalism and Pluralism* (London, Routledge 1999), p. 175.

21 ECtHR, *Hatton v. United Kingdom* (2003) 37 EHRR 28, par. 97.

22 ECtHR, *Leyla Sahin v. Turkey* (2005) 41 EHRR 8, par. 109.

23 *Vice versa*, it could also be argued that the lack of a common tendency should not be accepted in all circumstances as a legitimate reason for judicial restraint. Sardurski demonstrates that the accession of several new member states with a limited protection of fundamental rights implied a necessary threat to a rather general consensus to the core of human rights protection of fundamental rights protection among the established member states. Wojciech Sadurski, "Partnering with Strasbourg: Constitutionalisation of the European Court of Human Rights, the accession of Central and East European states to the council of Europe, and the idea of pilot judgments" (2009) 9 *Human Rights Law Review* 3, pp. 400–401.

24 ECtHR, *Leyla Sahin v. Turkey* (2005) 41 EHRR 8, par. 114.

25 Article 4 par. 2 TEU. Luxemburg implicitly referred to this provision holding that a national clause should be respected by EU law because of its close connection with the constitutional

To a certain extent, the ECJ also recognises diversity as a legitimate interest for a margin of discretion with regards to its fundamental rights scrutiny of domestic norms falling within the scope of EU law. The Court accepts that the Member States should be accorded a certain margin of discretion in the appreciation whether a restriction to a right was proportionate because the conception of fundamental rights differs from Member State to Member State on the grounds of divergent moral and cultural views.[26]

If it is accepted that the supranational position of courts and the value of diversity are legitimate reasons for a certain restraint towards the constitutional protection of rights and freedoms, the European Courts will have to apply interpretational tools ensuring that judicial restraint does not endanger the common protection or, as Brems labels it, the borderline of fundamental rights protection.[27] Such restraint should not endanger the supervisory function of the ECtHR or its function to ensure a progressive protection of fundamental rights within the European legal space.[28] With regards to the ECJ, the danger is even greater. There is a clear potential that the effectiveness of EU law as such is affected if certain Member States could apply different norms on the grounds of a divergent domestic protection of fundamental rights. E.g. hidden market restrictions could be presented as constitutional rights issues. Still, in both the EU Charter as the ECHR a maximum clause was entrenched to safeguard a domestic "better protection" of fundamental rights. The practice of the ECtHR with regards to this clause suggests, however, little perspective for its EU Charter counterpart.

2. MAXIMISATION CLAUSES: APPLICATION AND CRITIQUE

2.1. ARTICLE 53 ECHR IN THE STRASBOURG CASE LAW

Article 53 ECHR holds that the ECHR cannot be relied upon to limit the protection of fundamental rights and freedoms provided for by the member states or international treaties. This article indicates the subsidiary nature of the

identity of Luxemburg. See ECJ, Opinion AG Cruz Villalon, C-R3/08 European Commission v. Grand Duchy of Luxembourg [2010] I-0000, par. 141.

26 C-244/06 *Dynamic Medien Vertriebs GmbH v. Avides Media AG* [2008] ECR I-0000, par. 44.

27 Eva Brems, "Human rights: minimum and maximum perspectives" (2009) 9 *Human Rights Law Review* 3, p. 350.

28 The Council of Europe's Whitepaper on Cultural diversity considers that respect for cultural diversity cannot result in cultural relativism. The ECHR must remain a "moral compass". Council of Europe, "White Paper on Intercultural Dialogue – Living together as equals in dignity", Strasbourg 2008, p. 9.

protection afforded by the ECHR.[29] This maximisation clause could be regarded as a conflict rule: where the ECtHR is confronted with a conflicting conventional and national interpretation of fundamental rights or freedom, the Strasbourg interpretation should only be given precedence if it offers a better protection of the right. This conflict rule does not decide the precedence on the basis of the hierarchical position of the norm nor of a specific court, but instead on the basis of substantive criteria.

The ECtHR has only in very exceptional cases referred to Article 53 ECHR.[30] In fact, the potential scope of the maximisation clause was early on limited by the ECtHR. In *Handyside* is one of these exceptional cases where the ECtHR relied on Article 53 ECHR (ex Article 60). The Court highlighted:

> "Article 60 (art. 60), never puts the various organs of the Contracting States under an obligation to limit the rights and freedoms it guarantees. In particular, in no case does Article 10 para. 2 (art. 10–2) compel them to impose "restrictions" or "penalties" in the field of freedom of expression; it in no way prevents them from not availing themselves of the expedients it provides for them (cf. the words "may be subject")".[31]

This case indicated the potential scope of Article 53 ECHR in connection to the interpretation of other conventional rights and freedoms. However, the ECtHR forcefully elaborated the doctrine of the margin of appreciation and extended its scope to Article 10 ECHR. The discretionary space provided for the Member States was thus granted on the grounds of the margin of appreciation doctrine and not on the basis of Article 53 ECHR. Thereby, Article 53 ECHR early on lost its potential, while the jurisprudentially created margin of appreciation doctrine became the leading mechanism in the ECtHR case law in order to accommodate diversity and the consequences of its position as supranational court. Some discussion has taken place whether Article 53 ECHR could serve as a basis for widening the scope of the review of the Court. The Court has indicated that applicants cannot rely on Article 53 ECHR to claim that their rights under national law or international law have been violated.[32] In such cases, the ECtHR will find itself incompatible to consider the case. The Court is only competent to

---

29 Santiago Ripol Carulla, *El sistema Europeo de protección de los derechos humanos y el Derecho español* (Barcelona, Tirant Lo Blanch 2007), p. 44.

30 Jonas B Liisberg, "Does the EU Charter of Fundamental Rights Threaten the Supremacy of Community Law?" (2001) *jean monet program* 4/01, p. 22 and Rick Lawson, "Beyond the Call of Duty? Domestic Courts and the standards of the European Court of Human Rights" in Stefan Vogenauer and Henk Sneijders (eds.) *Content and Meaning of National Law in the context of Transnational Law* (Munich, Sellier European law publishers, 2009), p. 28.

31 ECtHR, Handyside v United Kingdom (1976) 1 EHRR 737, par. 54.

32 See e.g. ECtHR, *Markoupolou et al. v. Greece* (App. Nos. 20665/92, 20666, 20668, 21732, 21991–92, 21991, 21999, and 22219/93) (unreported, 6 April 1992), par. 4 and ECtHR, *E.M. v. Greece* (App. No. 22225/93) (unreported, 1 December 1993), par. 4.

regard violations of the ECHR. Article 53 ECHR has, thus, not been relied upon to expand the scope of review of the Court. In later cases, the ECtHR confirmed this case law, albeit by relying on Article 19 rather than Article 53 ECHR.[33]

The maximisation clause has, moreover, not been applied as a conflict rule. It appears a deliberate choice since in the ECtHR did not even mention Article 53 ECHR in the case *Open Door* where the defendant country explicitly relied on Article. Ireland considered that the ECtHR could not consider a violation of the freedom of expression by the Irish prohibition of advertisement for abortion abroad, because the Irish legal system thereby safeguarded the right to life.[34] The ECtHR suggested that the maximisation clause did not apply, without explicitly referring to it, because the infringement did not consider the standard of protection of the right to life as claimed by Ireland but instead the application of the freedom of expression where the same reasoning could not be upheld.[35] Instead of following the reasoning of Ireland on the grounds of Article 53 ECHR, the Court applied a different conception to decide the potential conflict of standards of protection between the ECtHR and the Irish legal system, i.e. the margin of appreciation.[36]

2.2. THE REBIRTH OF THE MAXIMISATION CLAUSE?

2.2.1. The maximisation clause in the EU Charter

Notwithstanding the very limited role of the maximisation clause in the Strasbourg case law, a similar clause was entrenched in the EU Charter. The ratification of the Lisbon Treaty rendered the Charter legally binding. Article 53 of the EU Charter reads:

> "[n]othing in this Charter shall be interpreted as restricting or adversely affecting human rights and fundamental freedoms as recognised ... by Union law and international law and by international agreements to which the Union, the Community or all the Member States are party, including the European Convention for the Protection of Human Rights, and *by the Member States' constitution*".[37]

It should be noted that potential role of the Charter does not extend the current role of the ECJ with regards to the protection of fundamental rights within EU

33 See ECtHR, *Potereau v. France and Belgium* (App. No. 41546/98) (unreported, 2 March 1999), par. 5 and ECtHR, *Emin and others v. Greece* (App. No. 34144/05) (unreported, 27 March 2008), par. 17.

34 ECtHR, *Open Door Counselling v Ireland* (1993) 15 EHRR 244, par. 78.

35 *Ibid.*, par. 79.

36 *Ibid.*, par. 68.

37 Article 53 EU Charter of Fundamental Rights.

law. First, EU norms can be scrutinized on their compatibility with EU fundamental rights law in as far as the ECJ has jurisdiction to examine these norms. This implies that EU norms falling within the foreign and security policy of the EU fall outside the scope of the ECJ's scrutiny of the compatibility with the Charter. Second, the Charter will only apply to national authorities when they are implementing EU law. Therefore, within a completely domestic situation where the national authorities do not act as EU agents, the ECJ will have no jurisdiction to test the compatibility with the Charter. In such cases, only the fundamental rights review of the ECtHR applies. The maximisation clause is a specific expression of the principle of subsidiarity as mentioned in the Charter as a guiding principle of its application.[38] Due to the very limited role of the maximisation clause it was questioned whether the EU Charter clause would be actually applied in a significant manner by the ECJ.[39]

2.2.2. A new direction for the maximisation clause in the Strasbourg case law

Recently, a potentially new direction on Article 53 ECHR surfaced in the Strasbourg case law. In the case *E.B. v. France*, the ECtHR did refer to Article 53 ECHR to advocate that Member States can go beyond the common interpretation of Article 8 ECHR by providing single parents the possibility to adopt children, as long as they respected the other Convention articles, *in casu* the protection of discrimination.[40] This reasoning was repeated in a recent case where Austria provided for the possibility to extend accident and sickness insurance cover under a statutory insurance scheme to cohabiting partners.[41] In this case, the ECtHR held that Article 8 ECHR did not require to extend the same social security benefits of married couples to cohabiting couples, but if the Member States decided in favour of such extension it could not exempt homosexual couples from these benefits. The ECtHR noted on the relevance of Article 14 ECHR that:

> "[it] also applies to those additional rights, falling within the general scope of any Convention Article, for which the State has voluntarily decided to provide. This principle is well entrenched in the Court's case-law".[42]

In the earlier case *Karner v. Austria*, the ECtHR had already come to a similar conclusion with regards to the entitlement of tenancy by the serving partner in

38 Article 51 par. 1 EU Charter of Fundamental Rights.

39 Anne-Marieke Widmann, "Article 53: undermining the impact of the Charter of Fundamental Rights" (2002) 8 *Columbia Journal of European Law* 2, pp. 342–358 and Jonas Bering Liisberg, Does the EU Charter of Fundamental Rights Threaten the Supremacy of Community Law?" (2001) *Jean Monet working Paper*, nr. 4/01 available at www.jeanmonetprogram.org.

40 ECtHR, *E.B. v. France* (2008) 47 EHRR 21, par. 49.

41 ECtHR, *P.B. and J.S. v. Austria* (App. no. 18984/02) (22 July 2010), par. 34.

42 ECtHR, *P.B. and J.S. v. Austria* (App. no. 18984/02) (22 July 2010), par. 32.

cohabiting relationships.[43] However, in this case the ECtHR did not rely on Article 53 ECHR. Instead, the ECtHR considered that the Member States were given a margin with consideration to the measures taken to protect the traditional family, but that this margin was narrow in cases where the measures implied a difference of treatment on the basis of sexual orientation.[44] The Court found that Austria could not provide that the narrow interpretation of the Rent Act was necessary and thus, found the measure to violate Article 14 ECHR in conjunction with the Article 8 ECHR.[45] It could be contended that the difference between these Austrian cases might signal a new approach and a reintroduction (or maybe even introduction) of Article 53 ECHR in the Strasbourg jurisprudence. LAWSON considers that Article 53 ECHR might be read as a freedom for Member States to provide a more "generous" interpretation or protection of the conventional rights and freedoms as long as they do not infringe upon other conventional rights, e.g. the right to equal treatment.[46] However, when comparing the approach in the two Austrian cases, it could be questioned what Article 53 ECHR adds to the proportionality test applied in *Karner*. These cases are still too limited to label them as a new direction and it needs to be seen whether the ECtHR will rely more often on Article 53 ECHR to allow for more progressive interpretations of the conventional rights and freedoms by the Member States.

In the same period, Article 53 ECHR has played a curious role in the determination of the applicability of article 6 ECHR claims. The ECtHR had early on considered that the concept "civil rights and obligations" as mentioned in Article 6 ECHR were autonomous standards, independent from the categorization in domestic law. The question was raised whether Article 53 ECHR did not oblige to follow the domestic law's conception of civil rights and obligations where this would result in a wider protection of rights of individuals. In *Okyay v. Turkey*, the ECtHR relied on the maximisation clause to examine the applicability of Article 6 ECHR.[47] The Turkish government conceded that the claims presented by the applicants were considered to constitute interests only in to Turkish law and not civil rights.[48] On this ground, the government argued that the case did not fall within the ambit of Article 6 ECHR. The Court noted, however, that Turkish constitution did actually protect the claims of the

43 ECtHR, *Karner v. Austria* (2003) 38 EHRR 528.
44 *Ibid.*, par. 41.
45 *Ibid.*, par. 42.
46 Rick Lawson, "Beyond the Call of Duty? Domestic Courts and the standards of the European Court of Human Rights" in Stefan Vogenauer and Henk Sneijders (eds.) *Content and Meaning of National Law in the context of Transnational Law* (Munich, Sellier European law publishers, 2009), p. 25.
47 ECtHR, Okyay v. Turkey (App. No. 36220/97) (unreported, 12 July 2005).
48 *Ibid.*, par. 62.

applicants, namely the right to a healthy and balanced environment.[49] The Chamber judgment mentioned that the defendant state could not rely on the ECHR to restrict the understanding of a "civil right" in the domestic legal system, namely the right to a healthy environment in the Turkish constitution.[50]

This reasoning was supported by several judges in their dissenting opinion in the case *Vilho Eskelinen.*[51] In this case, the ECtHR overturned its former case law established in *Pellegrin* where the Court had held that disputes raised by servants of the State such as police officers over their conditions of service fell in general out of the ambit of Article 6 ECHR.[52] The Court considered in *Vilho Eskelinen* that the functional criterion set in *Pellegrin* could lead to anomalous results.[53] In consequence, the Court strictly limited the possibility for Member States to rely on the applicant's status as a civil servant in excluding the protection of Article 6 ECHR. Several judges argued that that the existence of access to a domestic court in such cases was not sufficient reason to overturn the former case law for the new interpretation risked generating more uncertainty.[54] The judges advocated that the court could rely on Article 53 ECHR to uphold its own criteria but enable domestic courts to provide a wider protection of Article 6 ECHR. The reliance of several, albeit dissenting, judges (including the ECtHR president) on Article 53 ECHR with regards to the scope of Article 6 ECHR suggested an evolution to a wider conception of this article by the Court in further cases.

In the case *Micallef v. Malta*, the *Okyay* reasoning was reiterated by the Chamber judgment.[55] In this case, the applicants argued that Article 6 should also apply to injunction proceedings because the domestic courts had provided such interpretation of the conventional right.[56] The applicants argued that on the basis of Article 53 ECHR the ECtHR could not limit the interpretation of Article 6 ECHR of the domestic courts. The national government, however, conceded that the case did not fall within the ambit of Article 6 ECHR as injunction proceedings did not concern the determination of the merits of the right or obligation. The Court reiterated its stance on the autonomous interpretation of the concept "civil rights" independent from the determination in domestic law. The Court added, however, that the subsidiarity of the Convention mechanism implies that the ECtHR jurisprudence reinforces the protection of human rights and, on the

49 *Ibid.*, par. 65.
50 *Ibid.*, par. 68.
51 ECtHR, *Vilho Eskelinen v Finland* (2007) 45 EHRR 43.
52 ECtHR, Pellegrin v France (2001) 31 EHRR 26.
53 *Ibid.*, par. 51.
54 Dissenting Opinion Costa, Wildhaber, Türmen, Borrego Borrego and Jociene, ECtHR, *Vilho Eskelinen v Finland* (2007) 45 EHRR 43, par. 6.
55 ECtHR, *Micaleff v. Malta* (App. No. 17056/06) (unreported, 15 January 2008).
56 *Ibid.*, par. 45.

grounds of Article 53 ECHR, does not limit it.[57] Judge Bonello supported this argument by advocating that it would lead to "judicial schizophrenia" if Article 6 ECHR protection "flourishes in the domestic jurisdiction, but falls effortlessly dead on the doorstep of the Strasbourg Court.[58] Therefore, the ECtHR concluded that on the basis of Article 53 ECHR the concept of "civil right" could not be interpreted as limiting an enforceable right in domestic law.[59] The domestic interpretation of Article 6 ECHR was thus interpreted without setting a new general standard.

However, this case law is difficult to reconcile with the autonomous standard doctrine of the ECtHR and the evolution of the ECtHR towards a fine-tuner.[60] If the *Okyay* doctrine would be accepted, the standard provided by national legislation would become the reference norm and not the autonomous standard. The access to the Strasbourg court for a review of fair trial rights and access to court would thus become dependent on the domestic conception of a civil right by the domestic law or jurisdiction. This unease was already present in the Chamber judgment in the case *Micaleff* where the Court considered that:

> "[t]he Court does not countenance the view that human rights protection in any particular area should be weaker in Strasbourg than it is in domestic tribunals".[61]

On appeal, however, the Grand Chamber did not mention Article 53 ECHR, notwithstanding the references by the defending authorities and the intervening Czech authorities.[62] Instead, the Court emphasized the autonomous interpretation of the concept "civil right".[63] The Court mentions that in general it has not accepted that interim procedures fall in the scope of Article 6 ECHR, albeit with certain exceptions.[64] The ECtHR notes that the protection of such rights under Article 6 ECHR is not limited to the Maltese legal order, but has

---

57 *Ibid.*, par. 44.

58 Concurring Opinion Judge Bonello, ECtHR, Micaleff v. Malta (App. No. 17056/06) (unreported, 15 January 2008), par. 15. Judge Bonnello referred to the case *Vilho Eskelinen* in which the ECtHR indicated that if controversy existed in the domestic jurisdiction whether or not a case fell within the scope of the article 6 ECHR, the case would only highly exceptionally be found inapplicable by the Court. ECtHR, Vilho Eskelinen v Finland (2007) 45 EHRR 43.

59 ECtHR, *Micaleff v. Malta* (App. No. 17056/06) (unreported, 15 January 2008), par. 45.

60 This terminology of fine tuner has been used by Sadurksi. He argues that the ECtHR has acquired certain features of constitutional adjudication. See Wojciech Sadurski, "Partnering with Strasbourg: Constitutionalisation of the European Court of Human Rights, the accession of Central and East European states to the council of Europe, and the idea of pilot judgments" (2009) 9 *Human Rights Law Review* 3, p. 7.

61 ECtHR, *Micaleff v. Malta* (App. No. 17056/06) (unreported, 15 January 2008), par. 44.

62 ECtHR, Micallef v. Malta [2010] 50 EHRR 37, par. 74–89.

63 *Ibid.*, par. 74.

64 *Ibid.*, par. 75.

been provided by several Member States and the ECJ.[65] In the light of this general tendency, the ECtHR decides in favour of an evolutive interpretation of Article 6 ECHR.[66] Article 6 ECHR will thus in general be applicable to interim procedures as well.[67] This case suggests that Article 53 ECHR will most likely continue to play a limited role in the ECtHR jurisprudence. The acceptance that the ECtHR interpretation of a right would be less extensive than the protection by the domestic courts is hardly compatible with the ECtHR's current position as supreme and authoritative interpreter of the Convention.[68] Therefore, the ECtHR prefers to let the standard of protection evolve along the rising protection in the Member States where possible or provide a margin of appreciation in cases of balancing rights and freedoms.

It is unclear how this Grand Chamber judgment in Mitcallef corresponds with the cases *E.B. v. France* and *P.B. and J.S. v. Austria.* Does the ECtHR make a difference between Article 6 ECHR and other conventional rights and freedoms e.g. Article 8 ECHR? Or, should the importance of *E.B. v. France* and *P.B. and J.S. v. Austria* not be overestimated since it was not confirmed by a Grand Chamber judgment yet? It is still too early to draw a conclusion on whether or not the ECtHR has taken a new direction. The concept of a maximisation clause has certain weaknesses which make it a provision unfit to deal with the most tangent issues of conflict between domestic and Strasbourg jurisprudence, e.g. the conflict between rights and interests and between universal rights and diversity.

2.3. LIMITS OF A MAXIMISATION CLAUSE

There are several reasons why a maximisation clause might not be the appropriate tool to deal with conflicts of rights. These defaults might be the reason why the ECtHR has only scarcely relied upon Article 53 ECHR and why we might expect an only very marginal role of its equivalent in the EU Charter. First, both maximisation clauses are at odds with the concept of autonomous standards as applied by the ECJ and ECtHR case law. Both courts argued that they set an autonomous standard of the protection of fundamental rights. The ECtHR advocated that the definition of the terms of the Convention is autonomous

65 *Ibid.*, par. 78.

66 *Ibid.*, par. 80–81.

67 *Ibid.*, par. 86.

68 Lawson contends that it might indicate the rejection by the ECtHR of Article 6 ECHR as having a minimum character. Rick Lawson, "Beyond the Call of Duty? Domestic Courts and the standards of the European Court of Human Rights" in Stefan Vogenauer and Henk Sneijders (eds.) *Content and Meaning of National Law in the context of Transnational Law* (Munich, Sellier European law publishers, 2009), p. 26.

from the domestic determination.[69] The Court considered that a wide discretion for Member States to frame themselves whether they would fall within the scope of the Convention would render the ECHR ineffective and be contrary to the purpose and object of the Convention.[70] The ECJ held in a similar fashion that the EU was an autonomous legal order. The Court advocated that an autonomous and uniform interpretation of concepts in EU law is necessary in order to ensure a uniform application of EU law.[71] By allowing another interpretation of rights and freedoms to prevail in case such interpretation is considered to offer a better protection, the autonomous standard upheld by the ECtHR loses its harmonizing effect.

With respect to the Charter it has been questioned whether this article is compatible with the supremacy claim of EU law over all national law, including constitutional norms and freedoms. In the case *Simmenthal*, the ECJ held that EU law prevails over the national constitutions.[72] A strict regard of supremacy implies that the level of fundamental rights protection is not the decisive factor with regards to the question which norm will be applied. The prevailing rule is determined on the grounds of its EU pedigree. Behind this jurisprudence lays the endeavour to ensure a coherent and uniform application of EU law within all national Member States to enhance the functioning of the single market without restrictions. In Hauer, the ECJ already held that:

> "[t]he introduction of special criteria for assessment stemming from the legislation or constitutional law of a particular Member State would, by damaging the *substantive unity and efficacy of community law*, lead inevitably to the destruction of the unity of the common market."[73]

The introduction of a maximisation clause demands a reconsideration of this concept of supremacy.[74] It would mean that EU law would prevail over all

---

69 ECtHR, *Neumeister v. Austria* (1968) 1 EHRR 83, par. 14 and ECtHR, *Engel v. Netherlands* (1976) 1 EHRR 647, par. 81.

70 By emphasizing that to come to this conclusion it did not rely on Articles 17 ECHR (abuse of rights) or 18 ECHR (limitation on use of restriction of rights), the ECtHR made it clear that its delineating power did not intend to prevent member states from deliberately circumventing the responsibilities under the Convention, but also to set itself limits even though the member states argued in good faith without any intent to abuse or avoid the ECHR protection. ECtHR, *Engel v. Netherlands* (1976) 1 EHRR 647, par. 81.

71 ECJ, C-66/08 *Koszłowski* [2008] ECR I-6041, par. 41–42.

72 ECJ, C-106/77 *Amministrazione delle Finanze dello Stato v Simmenthal* [1978] ECR I-629.

73 Case 44/79, Liselotte Hauer v. Land Rheinland Pfalz [1979] *ECR* 3727, par. 14.

74 Besselink argued before the construction of the Charter that the accession to the ECHR by the EU would pose a problem to the supremacy doctrine because of Article 53 ECHR. The same thus certainly applies to the equivalent of Article 53 ECHR in the EU Charter. Leonard Besselink, "Entrapped by the maximum standard: on fundamental rights, pluralism and subsidiarity in the European Union" (1998) 35 *Common Market Law Review* 629, p. 666.

national law with the exception where the domestic protection sets a higher standard than EU law. The European court might thus not be inclined to apply the maximisation clause as it holds a challenge to the supremacy principle which ensures the ECJ's position as supreme court within the EU.[75] WETZEL argues such incompatibility between Article 53 ECHR and the supremacy principle only applies when supremacy is understood as uniformity.[76] Instead, Article 53 ECHR should be understood as influencing the minimum standard of EU fundamental rights protection. Where the ECJ finds a domestic standard to provide for a stricter protection, the minimum standard should be increased.

Second, reliance on Article 53 ECHR might also appear unattractive as it diminishes the reach as well as the authority of the ECtHR case law. By relying explicitly on Article 53 ECHR, the Court would knowledge that a domestic legal system provides a better protection of fundamental rights than the ECHR and even that its own interpretation might be capable of limiting or prejudicing this protection.[77] This could suggest that the Convention plays no role of importance for this legal system, at least for what concerns this specific right. Thereby, the ECtHR also loses its position to review the compatibility of the domestic legal practice with the Convention and thus, risks disconnecting the protection of this right at the Strasbourg level with the domestic level as the protection fall out of the scope of its review.[78] This can be contrasted with the construction of the margin of appreciation whereby the ECtHR grants the Member States discretionary space but indicates that this margin is not unlimited. The specific issue does not disappear from the scope of the ECtHR review.

Moreover, a maximisation clause (even more in general the idea of maximum and minimum langue of human rights) does not appear an effective and operational conflict rule. In the case where it is maintained that the ECHR as interpreted by the Strasbourg court limits the national protection of fundamental rights, an examination has to take place which of both legal systems offers a better protection. Such scrutiny will in practice be very difficult in cases where fundamental freedoms and rights are balanced against other fundamental rights

---

75 Anne-Marieke Widmann, "Article 53: undermining the impact of the Charter of Fundamental Rights" (2002) 8 *Columbia Journal of European Law* 2, p. 351.

76 Joseph Wetzel, "Improving fundamental rights protection in the European Union: resolving the conflict and confusion between the Luxembourg and Strasbourg courts" (2003) 71 *Fordham Law Review* 2823, p. 2856.

77 It has been noted that Article 53 ECHR might be of more use for the reliance on international treaties. Emmanuel Decaux, "Article 60," in Louis-Edmond Pettiti (Ed.), *La Convention Européenne des Droits de l'Homme – Commentaire Article par Article*, (1995), p. 897. Indeed, the ECtHR considers that it will interpret the Convention in the light of international treaties, albeit as far as possible.

78 Gerald Neuman, "Human Rights and constitutional rights: harmony and dissonance" (2003) 55 *Stanford Law Review* 1863, p. 1887.

or legitimate interests.[79] The protection of fundamental rights and freedoms is not quantifiable so that such assessment can taken place on objective and clear criteria.[80] Obviously, it is possible to compare fundamental rights standards as to the level of protection for if it would not the ECtHR could not review whether a level of protection afforded by a Member State falls below the minimum standard protected by the Convention.[81] With regards to the margin of appreciation, for instance, the ECtHR declares that the Member State cannot overstep the margin, namely it cannot go as far as touching upon the core or the essence of the right. Thus, where the protection of a right falls clearly below the protection afforded by the ECtHR or the ECJ, fundamental rights standards can clearly be compared. What is actually meant by the statement that rights are not quantifiable, is that in cases where two rights are balanced and whereby the conflict can only be resolved by providing a lesser protection of one of both, one cannot simply calculate the limitation of one right in relation to the increase of protection of the other right in search for a the best equilibrium between both rights. The weight given to one right or another or specific legitimate interests depends on the societal appreciation. As mentioned, the interpretation and application of rights is coloured by the social, cultural and historical background of the legal order.[82]

A clear example is provided by the privacy cases concerning famous persons before the European Court of Human Rights and the German Constitutional Court. Both courts were confronted with the question whether restrictions to the freedom of press could be allowed in order to protect the right of privacy of celebrities. The German Constitutional Court clearly favoured the freedom of press claiming that certain restrictions to the right of privacy could be made regarding famous persons.[83] The ECtHR, in contrast, considered that these

---

79 Rick Lawson, "Beyond the Call of Duty? Domestic Courts and the standards of the European Court of Human Rights" in Stefan Vogenauer and Henk Sneijders (eds.) *Content and Meaning of National Law in the context of Transnational Law* (Munich, Sellier European law publishers, 2009), p. 28 and Leonard Besselink, "Entrapped by the maximum standard: on fundamental rights, pluralism and subsidiarity in the European Union" (1998) 35 *Common Market Law Review* 629, p. 639.

80 Dworkin argues that we cannot compare two limitations to freedom (e.g. restriction of political speech and restriction of speeding on the highway), understood as to do as one likes, on the basis of which act is most restricted by government. Such operalisation of liberty would not match our own feeling of what basic liberties are and what not. In contrast, the determination of fundamental liberties and legitimate restrictions to them can only be assessed on a principled basis. Ronald Dworkin, *Taking Rights seriously* (Cambridge, Harvard University Press 1977), p. 335.

81 Joseph Wetzel, "Improving fundamental rights protection in the European Union: resolving the conflict and confusion between the Luxembourg and Strasbourg courts" (2003) 71 *Fordham Law Review* 2823, p. 2857.

82 Anne-Marieke Widmann, "Article 53: undermining the impact of the Charter of Fundamental Rights" (2002) 8 *Columbia Journal of European Law* 2, p. 355.

83 German Constitutional Court, 1 BvR 653/96, 15 December 1999, par. 116–118.

restrictions were too extensive and implied an infringement of the right to privacy.[84] This example indicates the limited applicability of the Convention. It cannot be said that the ECtHR or the German Constitutional Court provided a better protection of the freedom of expression or the right to privacy as such. Rather, they decided to a different outcome after have balanced both rights providing more weight to either right. The ECtHR argued that the outcome of the German Constitutional Court touched upon the core protection of the right to privacy. In this case, the ECtHR did not rely on Article 53 ECHR to decide the case, but, instead, relied on the margin of appreciation to define the width of the scope for the domestic legal system to define the issue.

This case indicates that a maximisation clause might not be of considerable use to decide potential conflicts of between constitutional legal orders and the ECtHR on the application of fundamental rights and freedoms. Such cases are in general not a question of the highest protection, but rather of the extent of diversity the conventional system allows and who is to decide on such matters. Especially where rights and interests are balanced practices between Member States might importantly diverge due to a different constitutional, historical or social background. One constitutional order might attach more weight to a right in contrast to another court. The ECtHR established the doctrine of the margin of appreciation in order to allow for discretionary space for the national authorities to decide such matters while maintaining marginal control.

3. ALTERNATIVE APPROACHES PROVIDING DISCRETIONARY SPACE

A maximisation clause is no effective and workable conflict rule to ensure that the best protection of rights is established within the interaction between the European courts. We assessed already that the main point of conflict is not the demand for a certain objective level of protection of fundamental rights protection at the supranational level. Rather, it is the respect demanded for the constitutional differences or particularities with regards to fundamental freedoms and rights. The constitutional courts indicate to maintain the ultimate say in case supranational law would touch upon the core of their constitutional rights protection. It can therefore not be remedied by providing a particular protection at the supranational level, but only by interpretational tools to allow national authorities to diverge from the supranational rule in case conflicts arise with such fundamental values. Other approaches are possible. The ECtHR has elaborated alternative mechanisms to ensure such discretionary space. First, the

---

84 ECtHR, *Von Hannover v Germany* (2004) 40 EHRR 1, par. 79–80.

margin of appreciation doctrine was introduced providing the Member States a certain degree of discretionary freedom, albeit not without restrictions. Second, in certain cases the ECtHR has held that it would show restraint towards the findings of a constitutional or a supreme court with regards to the balancing of fundamental rights and interests.

3.1. MARGIN OF APPRECIATION AND THE DOMESTIC LEGAL ORDER

3.1.1. *Margin of appreciation doctrine*

The margin of appreciation is not mentioned in the text of the Convention and was not discussed in the preparatory works.[85] The European Court of Human Rights established the doctrine in order to determine the discretionary space left to the Member States in cases of public emergency as entrenched in Article 15 ECHR. The ECtHR provided a certain discretionary space for the Member States in scrutinizing whether the measures were proportionate or whether an emergency existed.[86] The recognition of discretionary space for Member States was extended in a first phase to the interpretation of the restriction clauses of Article 8–11 ECHR. The doctrine of the margin of appreciation was extensively elaborated in the case *Handyside*.[87] The Court considered that the subsidiary character of the Convention demanded the Court to grant the national authorities a discretionary margin to consider whether an interference with a right was necessary to ensure the protection of a legitimate interest. The Court elaborated this doctrine into one of the cornerstones of the application of the Convention. The Court mentioned that such margin would apply to the consideration of the proportionality of restrictions of the rights with an explicit limitation clause (Article 8–11), but also to other rights which can be restricted *inter alia* Article 6 ECHR,[88] Article 1 protocol 1[89] or Article 14 ECHR.[90] The margin of appreciation has thus become a corollary of the proportionality test.[91]

---

85 Howard Yourow, *The Margin of Appreciation doctrine in the Dynamics of the European Human Rights jurisprudence* (Dordrecht, Nijhoff Publishers 1996), p. 196.

86 The ECtHR scrutinized only whether the finding by Ireland that an emergency existed could reasonably be deduced. ECtHR, *Lawless v Ireland* (No 3) (1961) 1 EHRR 15, par. 28.

87 ECtHR, *Handyside v United Kingdom* (1976) 1 EHRR 737.

88 ECtHR, *Fogarty v United Kingdom* (2001) 34 EHRR 302, par. 33.

89 ECtHR, *Chassagnou v. France* (2000) 29 EHRR 615, par. 75 and ECtHR, *Sporrong and Lonroth v Sweden* (1983) 5 EHRR 35, par. 69.

90 ECtHR, *Larkos v Cyprus* (1999) 30 EHRR 597, par. 29 and ECtHR, ECtHR, *Chassagnou v. France* (2000) 29 EHRR 615, par. 91.

91 On the relation between the margin of appreciation and the proportionality test see Yutaka Arai-Takahasi, *The Margin of Appreciation Doctrine and the Principle of Proportionality in the ECHR* (Antwerp, Intersentia, 2002), pp. 14–15.

The ECtHR put forward different reasons to apply the margin of appreciation test. First, the margin has been considered a consequence of the subsidiary nature of the ECHR machinery. The margin enables balancing the effectiveness of the ECHR protection with the sovereignty of the Member States. The margin might be considered a "natural product" of the distribution of powers between the supranational and domestic level.[92] National authorities have more (democratic) legitimacy to strike the difficult balance between rights and legitimate public interests, especially in economic and social policy.[93] Second, the margin can be applied out of pragmatic considerations, namely that domestic authorities are better suited to assess certain elements of the proportionality test. It could be claimed that the domestic legal orders have a comparative advantage[94] as they are "direct and continuous contact with the vital forces of their countries".[95] E.g. with respect to moral issues, the ECtHR noted that they vary 'from time to time' and 'from place to place'.[96] National authorities are better suited than an international court to define what these moral requirements entail. Thereby, the ECtHR can combine a marginal supervision of a common norm with cultural diversity.[97] National authorities might also be better suited to decide in so-called "multi-polar" cases, namely where the issue before the court (also) involves the balancing of two private interests, e.g. with regards to the question whether the identity of the biological mother of an adoptive child can be revealed. A third reason for the margin of appreciation doctrine is the diversity within the European legal space of political and social contentions of the good society.[98] When restricting certain rights in favour of a legitimate public interest, Member States are left with a certain margin as to the choice of measures and the necessity of the restrictions. E.g. the ECtHR leaves the decision whether certain restrictions were necessary to prevent disorder.[99] The ECtHR will not provide a definition of what it understands under disorder, but leaves

92 Eva Brems, "The Margin of Appreciation Doctrine in the case-law of the European Court of Human Rights" (1996) 56 *Zeitschrift für ausländisches öffentliches Recht und Völkerrecht*, p. 304. In this perspective, the margin performs an institutional function, namely allocating responsibility to the domestic courts. Gerald Neuman, "Human Rights and constitutional rights: harmony and dissonance" (2003) 55 *Stanford Law Review* 1863, p. 1884.

93 ECtHR, *Hatton v. United Kingdom* (2003) 37 EHRR 28, par. 97.

94 Yuval Shany, "Toward a general margin of appreciation doctrine in international law" (2006) 16 *European Journal of International Law* 5, p. 913.

95 ECtHR, *Handyside v United Kingdom* (1976) 1 EHRR 737, par. 48.

96 ECtHR, *Sunday Times v United. Kingdom* (1979) 2 EHRR 245, par. 59.

97 Oren Gross and Fionnuala Ni Aolain, "From discretion to scrutiny: revisiting the application of the margin of appreciation doctrine in the context of Article 15 of the European Convention on Human Rights" (2001) 23 *Human rights Quarterly*, p. 627 and Paul Mahoney, "Marvelous richness of diversity or individious cultural relativism?" (1998) 19 *Human Rights Law Journal* 1.

98 This follows the suggestion of Koskenniemi that as long as there is no wide agreement on the good life as concept, statehood remains the best guarantee for citizens against authoritarian impulses. Martti Koskenniemi, "The Future Statehood" (1991) 32 *Harvard International Law Journal* 2, p. 397.

99 ECtHR, *De Wilde, Ooms and Versyp v Netherlands* (1979–80) 1 EHRR 373, par. 93.

such assessment as well as the necessity of the measures to the Member States. As LETSAS argues, this conception of the margin (substantive concept) follows from the acceptance that most conventional rights and freedoms are limitable.[100]

The Court noted that the margin of appreciation was not only afforded to the national legislator, but also to the domestic judiciary.[101] E.g. with consideration to the assessment of custody and access of parents under Article 8 ECHR, the national courts enjoy a wide margin.[102] The ECtHR also considered according the national courts a margin when interpreting the domestic rules regarding the prevention of undermining military discipline.[103] The ECtHR likewise granted a margin of appreciation to the national courts when balancing the housing needs against the applicant's right to respect for her home.[104] The ECtHR thus allows a margin for the national courts to balance the rights and freedoms when it considers those courts better placed to make judgments on the proportionality. This might follow, on a more principled basis, from the consideration that the ECtHR has been established as a subsidiary control mechanism but that the conventional rights should in the first place be protected by the domestic courts.[105] The balance between rights and legitimate interests struck by the domestic courts, might be given a certain discretion because they might be better suited to appreciate the necessity of the measures due to their constant and direct contact with the societal needs and because they might better fit the protection of rights in the societal, economic, cultural and historical context of the Member State.

The Court will review the decisions of the domestic courts but with consideration to the wide or narrow margin afforded. As the ECtHR mentioned:

---

100 George Letsas, "Two concepts of the margin of Appreciation" (2006) 26 *Oxford Journal of Legal Studies* 4, p. 711.

101 ECtHR, *Handyside v United Kingdom* (1976) 1 EHRR 737, par. 48 and ECtHR, *A. v. United Kingdom* (App. No. 3455/05) (unreported, 19th February 2009), par. 174.

102 ECtHR, *Elsholz v Germany* (2000) 34 EHRR 1412, par. 48–53, ECtHR, *Sahin v Germany* (2003) 36. EHRR 765, par. 77 and ECtHR, *Sommerfeld v Germany* (2003) 38 EHRR 756, par. 74.

103 ECtHR, *Engel and Others v The Netherlands* (1976) 1 EHRR 647, par. 100.

104 ECtHR, *Blecic v. Croatia* (2004) 41 EHRR 185, par. 60–61. It should be mentioned that this case was overturned by the Grand Chamber on the basis of the lack of competence ratione temporis. The Grand Chamber did not consider the merits.

105 Lady Justice DBE Arden, "Is the Convention Ours? Seminar to mark the official opening of the judicial Year of the European Court of Human Rights" (29 January 2010, Strasbourg), p. 7. Available at: www.judiciary.gov.uk and Oren Gross and Fionnuala Ni Aolain, "From discretion to scrutiny: revisiting the application of the margin of appreciation doctrine in the context of Article 15 of the European Convention on Human Rights" (2001) 23 *Human rights Quarterly*, p. 627.

> ""it is in no way [its] task to take the place of the competent national courts but rather to review under Article 10 (art. 10) the decisions they delivered in the exercise of their power of appreciation".[106]

From the case law, it appears that the fact that national courts have scrutinized the proportionality of domestic measures might be accepted as a reason to provide a margin of appreciation to the Member States. E.g. in the case *Hirst*, the ECtHR found that the national courts had not been able to consider the proportionality of the restriction of the ECHR and therefore, there was no reason to provide the Member State with a wide margin.[107] That does not mean that the ECtHR will follow the reasoning of the national court.[108]

3.1.2. A limited discretionary space

The margin is not unlimited. Where the national authorities overstep this margin touching upon the core of the protection, the ECtHR would scrutinize itself whether the balance was proportionate. Granting a margin does not equal providing for arbitrary power.[109] First, the Member States cannot discriminate when taking measures restricting ECHR rights, even when falling within the margin of appreciation.[110] Moreover, the legislator's judgment of the weight of the rights and interests involved, will be counterbalanced with procedural guarantees, namely the decision-making process.[111] The fact that a margin is accorded does not mean that citizens should not be given the possibility to contest the restrictions. Finally, no restriction can go as far as touching upon the very essence or core of the right. The ECtHR emphasizes that no restriction can be allowed which leaves the right wholly ineffective. Therefore, the margin of appreciation doctrine provides a discretionary space within limits which the Court will guard, albeit marginally. As the Court noted:

> "The domestic margin of appreciation thus goes hand in hand with a European supervision".[112]

The discretionary space for the Member States depends on the width of the accorded margin. In cases only a small margin is accorded, the national

---

106 ECtHR, *Handyside v United Kingdom* (1976) 1 EHRR 737, par. 50.

107 ECtHR, *Hirst v United Kingdom* (No 2) (2005) 42 EHRR 41, par. 78–80.

108 ECtHR, *Sunday Times v United. Kingdom* (1979) 2 EHRR 245, par. 59. See in this respect e.g. ECtHR, *Neumeister v. Austria* (1968) 1 EHRR 83, par. 4 and *König v Federal Republic of Germany* (1979–80) 2 EHRR 170, par. 88–96.

109 ECtHR, *Frette v France* (2002) 38 EHRR 438, par. 41.

110 ECtHR, *Belgian Linguistic case (No 2)* (1968) 1 EHRR 252, par. 9, ECtHR, *National Union of Belgian Police v Belgium* (1975) 1 EHRR 578, par. 44 and ECtHR, *Sahin v. Germany* (2003) 36 EHRR 43, par. 90.

111 ECtHR, *Hatton v. United Kingdom* (2003) 37 EHRR 28, par. 99.

112 ECtHR, Handyside v United Kingdom (1976) 1 EHRR 737, par. 49.

authorities will have to prove compelling state interest or weighty reasons for restriction the conventional rights and freedoms. Where the ECtHR decides on a wide margin, the national authorities will only have to establish that the decision was taken on a rational basis. The ECtHR has elaborated several criteria to define whether a wide or small margin will be accorded. First, the practices of other Member States will be taken into account when assessing the width of the margin, especially with consideration to moral issues. Where no consensus exists among the Member States, the margin for the Member States will be wide. When a common tendency exists or a common practice can be discerned, the national authorities will be left with a mall margin. Second, the Court mentioned that the width of the margin will vary along the nature of the issues and the importance of the interests at stake. E.g., where the policy measures interfere with a particularly intimate part of the applicant's life, the margin will be small.[113]

3.2. A DOCTRINE NOT WITHOUT FLAWS

The margin of appreciation was not introduced in order to allow for a different but equivalent protection of constitutional rights at the domestic level, but to provide more in general a discretionary space for Member States to assess whether a restriction of rights was proportionate. It is remarkable that the critique on the doctrine and the application of the doctrine has not ceased notwithstanding the observation that the margin of appreciation is well-established case law and has been applied in countless cases. These critiques address both the legitimacy of the doctrine itself (namely, a conflict with the universality of universal rights) as the application of the doctrine in specific cases (incoherent and not transparent).[114] Two critiques are systematically reiterated in the jurisprudence.

The first critique concerns the criteria on which the ECtHR will decide to accord a margin of appreciation. The assessment of proportionality is vital for the

113 ECtHR, *Dudgeon v. United Kingdom* (1982) 4 EHRR 149, par. 52.

114 See *inter alia* Paolo G Carrozza, "Subsidiarity as a structural principle of international human rights law" (2003) 97 The *American Journal of International law*, pp. 38–79, George Letsas, *A theory of interpretation of the European Convention on Human Rights* (Oxford University Press, Oxford 2007), pp. 80–98, Oren Gross and Fionnuala Ni Aolain, "From discretion to scrutiny: revisiting the application of the margin of appreciation doctrine in the context of Article 15 of the European Convention on Human Rights" (2001) 23 *Human rights Quarterly*, pp. 625–649, Eyal Benvenisti, "The Margin of Appreciation, consensus and universal standards" (1999) 31 *N.Y.U. Journal of International Law & Policy* 4, pp. 843–854, Pieter Van Dijk and Godefridus Van Hoof, *Theory and Practice of the European Court of Human Rights* (The Hague, Kluwer 1998), pp. 92–95 and Ronald S MacDonald, "The Margin of Appreciation" in Ronald S MacDonald, Franz Matscher and Herbert Petzold (eds.) *The European system for the Protection of Human Rights* (Martinus Nijhoff Publishers, Dordrecht 1993).

judgment whether a violation of the Convention has occurred. Therefore, the ECtHR case law on the application of the proportionality should be as clear, coherent and transparent as possible in order to ensure proper guidance for the domestic courts. Infringements of the Convention rights are justified where they are provided by law serve a legitimate interest and are proportionate. The ECtHR has clearly established the criteria with respect to what is to be understood as "law" and "legitimate interest". With regards to the proportionality test the ECtHR will rely on the margin of appreciation in case rights and legitimate interests need to be balanced. It is argued that in cases where the ECtHR applies the substantive concept of the margin doctrine, namely where the Court finds an interference with a freedom which it judges not to amount to a violation, the ECtHR does not offer a clear indication on where the boundary between the protection of the right and the restriction due to a legitimate interest should be drawn.[115] The margin it itself lacks a "normative force" guiding how the individual rights and public interests should be balanced.[116] The ECtHR does not argue clearly why the infringement is justified, but simply states that the case falls within the margin of appreciation and then, proceeds to scrutinize whether the margin afforded is wide or small. In fact, the decision that the case falls within the margin in such situation, is by itself a determination that the restriction is justifiable.[117] Such vague and case-by-case approach fails to provide clear guidelines for the domestic courts in their future case law to assess the proportionality of restrictions in similar cases.[118]

Thereby, the margin of appreciation becomes a mere tool of conflict avoidance, but fails to enhance closer cooperation by clearly indicating the line of proportionality and the task of the domestic courts in such balancing.[119] A clear contest of such practice was launched by Judge De Meyer who argued that the doctrine should be abandoned without delay:

---

115 Eyal Benvenisti, "The Margin of Appreciation, consensus and universal standards" (1999) 31 *N.Y.U. Journal of International Law & Policy* 4, p. 847 and Robert Blackburn, "Current developments, Assessment, and prospects" in Robert Blackburn and Jörg Polakiewicz (eds), *Fundamental Rights in Europe* (Oxford, Oxford University Press 2001), p. 82.

116 George Letsas, *A theory of interpretation of the European Convention on Human Rights* (Oxford University Press, Oxford 2007), p. 86.

117 Ronald S MacDonald, "The Margin of Appreciation" in Ronald S MacDonald, Franz Matscher and Herbert Petzold (eds.) *The European system for the Protection of Human Rights* (Martinus Nijhoff Publishers, Dordrecht 1993), p. 85.

118 Paolo G Carrozza, "Subsidiarity as a structural principle of international human rights law" (2003) 97 The *American Journal of International law*, p. 71.

119 Such limited justification for the introduction and application of interpretational tools is not limited to the margin of appreciation, but also applies to other doctrine as e.g. the living instrument doctrine. Mowbray argues that the Court in general eschews general theorizing and prefers and incremental evolution of its principles. Alastair Mowbray, "The Creativity of the European Court of Human Rights" (2005) 5 *Human Rights Law Review* 1, p. 61.

> "On that subject the boundary not to be overstepped must be as clear and precise as possible. It is for the Court, not each State individually, to decide that issue, and the Court's views must apply to everyone within the jurisdiction of each State".[120]

A second problematic feature is the reliance on the existence of a European consensus to assess the width of the margin. First, the case law as to when a common consensus will be found is incoherent and not transparent. In many cases, the ECtHR notices the absence of such consensus without, however, providing a profound account of the practices of the Member States. It is also unclear how "common" such practice must be. E.g. in the case *Hirst*, the United Kingdom argues that there is no common practice in affording voting rights to prisoners and moreover, that many Member States limit voting rights in such circumstance.[121] The ECtHR argued that, indeed, there might some disagreement among the Member States on this issue, but that less than 13 Member States provide a similar limitation. Moreover, in certain cases the ECtHR notes that the existence of a common consensus is not determinative for the justification of the restriction,[122] in other cases much weight seems to be put on such common consensus.[123] The lack of comparative research and clarity on the determining factors seriously undermine the legitimacy to rely on this element to delineate the discretionary freedom of Member States. Second, and more fundamentally, it could be questioned whether the existence of a common consensus is a sufficiently legitimate basis to provide for a stricter or wider review of the proportionality of restriction of ECHR rights and freedoms. A Member State might have completely legitimate reasons to restrict a specific right in order to safeguard the protection of another right or legitimate aim, without, however, the existence of a common tendency. Such doctrine completely fails to take into account the most vulnerable rights, namely the rights of minorities.[124]

Fundamental rights are not applied in the vacuum, but against a social, legal and cultural background. As the ECtHR correctly notices, the European legal space is characterized by economic, social and cultural diversity. Against this background, national courts might be better suited to assess how rights should be fitted within this framework. It appears unclear how a distinctive and rather unique position of a domestic constitutional order on the restriction of rights should be accorded less discretion than the position of another domestic order

120 Dissenting Opinion Judge De Meyer, ECtHR, Z. v. Finland (App. no. 22009/93)(unreported, 25 February 1997).

121 ECtHR, *Hirst v United Kingdom (No 2)* (2005) 42 EHRR 41, par. 81.

122 *Ibid.*, par. 81–82.

123 See E.g. complaints of Judge Rozakis in his Concurring Opinion, ECtHR, Odièvre v. France (Appl. no. 42326/98) (unreported, 13 February 2003).

124 Eyal Benvenisti, "The Margin of Appreciation, consensus and universal standards" (1999) 31 *N.Y.U. Journal of International Law & Policy* 4, p. 853.

which follows a common tendency among courts without, however, a similar elaborated reasoning. The common consensus element is relied upon by the ECtHR as a persuasive tool towards the Member States in order for an easier acceptance of its case law. Where the Court provides for a new interpretation of a right (living instrument doctrine) such consensus might play a legitimate role as interpretative tool considering the supranational status of the Court.[125] However, with regards to the restriction of rights, the common consensus doctrine does not appear legitimate. Rather, the Court would better provide a wider discretionary power where the restriction has been justified by a weighty balancing of the rights and interests by a domestic court than the superfluous and many times ill-researched observation of a common consensus. In such context, the ECtHR provides for some diversity in the protection of human rights with regards to the heterogeneous cultural, social and political traditions of the Member States while ensuring that domestic courts actively guarantee the protection of rights through balancing. It would result in an active coordination between the ECtHR and the domestic courts to provide the best guarantee of rights in the way Merills portrayed:

> "the margin of appreciation is a way of recognizing that the international protection of human rights and sovereign freedom of action are not contradictory but complementary. Where the one ends, the other begins".[126]

These critiques do not mean that the margin of appreciation could not be a valuable tool: it allows at its best a tool to both provide for a certain discretionary space for national authorities to apply conventional rights and freedoms within their specific legal, social and cultural order while maintaining a certain supranational supervision.[127] A margin might thus be a justified tool if the ECtHR ensures a more coherent case law and provides for sufficient guidance as to the criteria for its application and the borders of the margin. The focus should be put on the boundary conditions of the margin. The ECtHR already established that a margin cannot result in a discriminatory treatment of citizens. Other such limiting conditions could be elaborated to guarantee that providing a margin of appreciation for Member States does not generate lower standards of fundamental rights protection. WAITER highlights the fundamental conditions for such margin as elaborated in the COE White paper on cultural diversity: democracy

---

125 Even in such cases, the reliance on the consensus doctrine might be criticized as it suggests that the only way to demand member states to abide by the evolving duties, is by demanding their consent. The Court thereby "eschews" responsibility for its decisions. Eyal Benvenisti, "The Margin of Appreciation, consensus and universal standards" (1999) 31 *N.Y.U. Journal of International Law & Policy* 4, p. 852.

126 John G Merrills, *The Development of International Law by the European Court of Human Rights* (Manchester University Press, New York 1988) p. 157.

127 Krisch praises the flexibility of the doctrine. Nico Krisch, "The Open architecture of European Human Rights Law" (2008) 71 *Modern Law Review*, p. 207.

(legitimate decision making and exercise of power), rule of law (legal certainty and access to court) and equal dignity (non-discrimination).[128] GREER argued that the margin of appreciation could be accorded to domestic courts, but not to other national authorities.[129] The ECHR is a legal document and therefore, its interpretation should be settled by judicial authorities and not left to the discretion of the national authorities. From the supranational position of the ECtHR, it can be argued that such margin is justifiable with regards to the domestic courts' judgments when interpreting the Convention as they might be better suited to understand the context or scrutinize the necessity of the measures.

3.3. RESTRAINT TOWARDS DOMESTIC JUDGMENTS

The ECtHR has indicated that it is in principle not a fourth instance court.[130] It could be concluded that this auto-limitation of the ECtHR *vis-à-vis* errors of the national courts is an exercise in defining the division of tasks between the Strasbourg court and the national courts: the national courts interpret the national legislation and settle the facts, the ECtHR scrutinizes whether the outcome of these decisions violates the Convention. The Court has taken a step further implying that its own proper scrutiny with regards to the potential violation of the ECHR is to be undertaken with regards to the finding of the (highest) national courts. Such attitude transcends a position of auto-limitation and could be regarded as a cooperative attitude.

The Court held that the national courts should first be given the opportunity to consider the compatibility of domestic law with the Convention. This reasoning can easily be deduced from the admissibility requirement of exhaustion of all national remedies.[131] The ECtHR adds, however, that the Court should be informed of the views of these national courts "as being in direct and continuous contact".[132] Therefore, the national authorities should put the same arguments before the ECtHR as they have advocated before the domestic courts.[133] This

128 Patricia Wiater, "Intercultural Dialogue in the Framework of European Human Rights Protection" (COE, White Paper Series vol. 1, Strasbourg), pp. 27–49.

129 Steven Greer, *The European Convention on Human Rights* (Cambridge University Press, Cambridge 2006), p. 226.

130 This follows from the admissibility requirement that all domestic remedies need to be exhausted. The Court indicated that this only applies to effective domestic procedures and no excessive formalism will be applied. ECtHR, *Azinas v. Cyprus* (2004) 40 EHRR 8, par. 38.

131 ECtHR, *Burden v United Kingdom (*2008) 47 EHRR 857, par. 42 and ECtHR, *Akdivar and others v. Turkey* judgment (1996) 23 EHRR 143, par. 65.

132 ECtHR, *A. v. United Kingdom* (App. No. 3455/05) (unreported, 19th February 2009), par. 154.

133 ECtHR, *Pine Valley Developments Ltd v Ireland* (1991) 14 EHRR 319, par. 47 and ECtHR, *Kolompar v Belgium* (1992) 16 EHRR 197, par. 31–32.However, this requirement does not

implies at least that the ECtHR will take account of the reasoning of the national court when scrutinizing the compatibility with the ECHR.

In addition, the Court signalled that it would take a specific restraint approach in case it was presented with a substantively reasoned opinion of one of the domestic highest courts. The Court believes that in such circumstances the Court should take on board the reasoning of the highest courts. Such position first surfaced in Z *v. United Kingdom*.[134] The Court was called upon to judge whether the right to access to court had been infringed because the House of Lords had no entitlement under Article 6 ECHR to obtain a hearing concerning the facts of the case. The Strasbourg Court remarked that the House of Lord had undertaken a careful balancing of the policy reasons against the imposition of liability on the local authority in the applicants' circumstances.[135]Therefore, the ECtHR concluded that it was not for the Court to decide on the outcome of the striking-out proceedings since this would effectively involve "substituting its own views as to the proper interpretation and content of domestic law".[136] This position of regard for the domestic highest courts has been repeated in several cases concerning the identification of a claim as a "civil right" under Article 6 ECHR.[137] The Court considers that notwithstanding the autonomous interpretation of this term by the ECtHR, it would take the provisions of the relevant domestic law and their interpretation by the domestic courts as a starting-point for its assessment.[138] In its assessment, the Court would apply special restraint towards the findings of the domestic highest courts' judgments which thoroughly scrutinized the case. As the Court pointed out:

> "[W]here, moreover, the superior national courts have analysed in a comprehensive and convincing manner the precise nature of the impugned restriction, on the basis of the relevant Convention case-law and principles drawn therefrom, this Court would need strong reasons to differ from the conclusion reached by those courts by substituting its own views for those of the national courts on a question of interpretation of domestic law".[139]

---

imply that the national authorities cannot challenge the reasoning of its own highest court before the ECtHR as e.g. the United Kingdom with regards to the findings of the House of Lords. ECtHR, *A. v. United Kingdom* (App. No. 3455/05) (unreported, 19th February 2009), par. 157.

134 ECtHR, Z v United Kingdom (2001) 34 EHRR 97.

135 *Ibid.*, par. 100.

136 *Ibid.*, par. 101. The Court decided that the applicants' conventional rights had been infringed, but that the problem had not been the access to court under Article 6 ECHR, but rather the lack of an effective remedy under Article 13 ECHR. *Ibid.*, par. 102.

137 ECtHR, *Roche v United Kingdom* (2005) 42 EHRR 599, ECtHR, *K.T. v. Norway* (2009) 49 EHRR 4 and ECtHR, *Markovic v Italy* (2006) 44 EHRR 1045.

138 ECtHR, *Masson and van Zon v Netherlands* (1995) 22 EHRR 491, par. 49.

139 ECtHR, *Roche v United Kingdom* (2005) 42 EHRR 599, par. 120.

This jurisprudence has also been extended to other issues, e.g. the existence of emergency situations under Article 15 ECHR.[140] The account for the highest domestic courts' judgments is, however, not without limits. In the case *A v. United Kingdom*, the ECtHR considered that:

> "where the highest domestic court has examined the issues relating to the State's derogation and concluded that there was a public emergency threatening the life of the nation but that the measures taken in response were not strictly required by the exigencies of the situation, the Court considers that it would be *justified in reaching a contrary conclusion only if satisfied that the national court had misinterpreted or misapplied Article 15* or the Court's jurisprudence under that Article or reached a conclusion which was *manifestly unreasonable*".[141]

One cannot but find a striking similarity in this reasoning with regards to the balancing exercise of the highest national courts and the restraint shown towards the EU in *Bosphorus*: the terminology of "manifestly unreasonable" and "manifestly deficient" share a close resemblance.[142] How should this jurisprudence be read? First, it should be reminded that the ECtHR considered itself that such circumstances were unusual.[143] Only in the case where a domestic highest court considered the protection of the ECHR and in the case where it was to undertake a balancing exercise between interests and a Convention right would such margin apply. In most cases where a constitutional court or highest court would find a violation or find the balance struck by the national authorities unreasonable, this would result in the removal or disapplication of the concerned norm and the reparation of the negative effects for the applicant. In such situation, the case would not result in an application before the ECtHR as the victim would no longer hold any interest. In the case of the UK, however, the national judge – including the highest court – can only observe the violation of the Convention and issue a Declaration of Incompatibility. It is, thus, left to the national authorities to repair such damage and change then norms. Thus, a judgment claiming a violation of the ECHR does not result necessarily in the loss of interest before the ECtHR.[144]

Second, this jurisprudence is rather recent. It might be too soon to imply that the ECtHR has taken up a completely new attitude towards the domestic courts.[145] It

140 ECtHR, *A. v. United Kingdom* (App. No. 3455/05) (unreported, 19th February 2009).

141 ECtHR, *A. v. United Kingdom* (App. No. 3455/05) (unreported, 19th February 2009), par. 174.

142 ECtHR, *Bosphorus Hava Yollari v. Ireland* (2006) 42 EHRR 1.

143 ECtHR, *A. v. United Kingdom* (App. No. 3455/05) (unreported, 19th February 2009), par. 174.

144 See Sageeta Shah, "From Westminster to Strasbourg: *A and others v United Kingdom*" (2009) 9 *Human Rights law Review* 1, p. 487.

145 This reasoning from the case A v. United Kingdom, was repeated in the case *Ciorap v. Moldovia* where the Supreme Court had found a violation of Article 3 ECHR. ECtHR, *Ciorap v. Moldovia* (App. No. 7481/06) (unreported, 20th July 2010), par. 22.

does, however, suggest that the ECtHR is willing to consider the case law of the domestic courts and applies a cooperative approach towards the highest domestic courts which take an active account of the ECHR when scrutinizing domestic legislation.[146] In fact, rather than weakening the Court versus the domestic highest courts, this case law might be a trigger for the highest domestic courts to take greater account of the ECHR and the ECtHR case law as they know that by acting thus the ECtHR will show a wide margin towards their reasoning. In such situation, the ECtHR will actively strengthen the findings of the highest domestic court against the challenges of the domestic authorities.[147]

4. NO PLACE LIKE HOME: PROMISING NEW DIRECTION?

The interaction between the domestic courts and the supranational courts is in general characterized by a remarkable harmony. Conflicts are rare, especially between the ECtHR and the domestic courts. Such harmony might be all the more surprising in the relation between the ECJ and the domestic courts considering that several highest domestic courts have never accepted the supremacy claim of EU law over all constitutional norms. Several have maintained that they might still step in when the core of their constitutional rights and freedoms, by some now labelled as constitutional identity, would be at risk. Even though only some have been specific which constitutional rights could spark resistance, almost any Member State has such sensitive issues related to the protection of constitutional rights and freedoms, e.g. the protection of life concerning abortion in Ireland or the language rights in the Belgian constitution. Yet, the remarks in domestic judgments of limited acceptance have not resulted in contrary judgments with the exception of the European Arrest cases of the Polish, German and Maltese constitutional courts.

This harmony does not mean that there is no need for tools providing for a certain degree of discretion for Member States with regards to the protection of fundamental rights. First, the current harmony of interaction does not mean that it could not change in the future. The ever further expansion of the competences of EU law and expansive jurisprudence of the ECtHR and the ECJ might generate further irritation at the constitutional courts and increase the likeability of

146 In the case *A. v. United Kingdom*, the ECtHR draws heavily on the argumentation of the House of Lords to come to its conclusion. Sageeta Shah, "From Westminster to Strasbourg: *A and others v United Kingdom*" (2009) 9 *Human Rights law Review* 1, p. 487.

147 Such effect of the ECtHR jurisprudence had already earlier been observed. See Wojciech Sadurski, "Partnering with Strasbourg: Constitutionalisation of the European Court of Human Rights, the Accession of Central and East European States to the Council of Europe and the Idea of Pilot judgments" (2009) 9 *Human Rights Law Review* 3, p. 443.

tensions between European law and the core of the constitutional rights and freedoms.[148] Second, there are principled reasons from perspective of fundamental rights protection to allow a certain restraint towards the protection of constitutional rights and freedoms in the domestic legal orders, namely the cultural and social embeddedness of fundamental rights and the supranational position of the European courts. From the perspective of the ECtHR, there is another, more pragmatic reason to provide for a tool allowing for a certain discretionary space for the domestic legal orders with regards to fundamental rights protection, i.e. the enormous caseload and according back logs. Such tool could indicate the responsibilities of the domestic legal orders to protect fundamental rights in the first place resulting in less individual complaints before the Strasbourg court.

A maximisation clause does not offer a viable solution. Crucially, the maximisation concept appears only of limited use because fundamental rights and freedoms cannot be quantified. The balancing of rights and freedoms takes place on principled account and not on a utilitarian basis. The ECtHR elaborated an alternative mechanism to provide manoeuvring space for the Member States, namely the margin of appreciation. However, its application is incoherent, not transparent and based on discussable premises (e.g. the common consensus or practice). The doctrine does not differentiate in principle between the decisions of national authorities and domestic courts. Where the domestic courts do not provide for an additional strict scrutiny of the proportionality of the restrictions, the protection of the ECHR by the Court becomes superfluous. Therefore, the ECtHR should extend the limits of the margin from the prohibition of discriminatory treatment to the requirement of effective domestic procedures to challenge the decision of national authorities restricting fundamental rights.

Promising in that respect is the new direction taken in the case *A v. United Kingdom*. The ECtHR considered that where the domestic highest courts have thoroughly reasoned a case, the Court will need good reasons to overrule such case. In such approach, the ECtHR encourages the domestic courts to provide an effective protection of the conventional rights and freedoms at the domestic level without, however, neglecting its own supervision. Such jurisprudence strengthens the position of those courts which provide for a domestic redress for conventional infringements *vis-à-vis* other domestic authorities. The domestic courts will be inclined to follow the ECtHR from this perspective, but are also enabled to communicate the domestic demands, interests and perspective to the ECtHR. Thereby, the domestic courts could propose an alteration of the current approach of the Court. This approach would enhance active coordination between the

148 See on the ECtHR e.g. Nico Krisch, "The Open architecture of European Human Rights Law" (2008) 71 *Modern Law Review*, p. 184.

ECtHR and the domestic legal orders. In sum, the recent cases of the ECtHR with regards to well-reasoned judgments of the highest courts show great promise, but it is far too early to suggest that such approach will grow into a new approach of the supranational courts.

The accommodation of the constitutional standards of protection and EU law presents a profound challenge. The approach of the ECtHR might not be directly transplanted to the ECJ as the court does not only scrutinize whether domestic law confirms to EU law, including the fundamental rights but is also given the task to ensure the uniform interpretation and application of EU law. Still, with regards to the domestic legal standards of fundamental rights protection the ECtHR approach of restraint in case of profoundly reasoned judgments might give an indication of the way ahead. This approach could ensure a more cooperative relationship with the highest courts. The constitutional courts might in such cases no longer withhold from sending preliminary questions to the ECJ as they know that their reasoning with consideration to EU law in the domestic legal context will be regarded with a certain restraint.[149] This would be in line with the new TEU provision which demands EU law to respect the constitutional and political fundamental structures of the Member States. At first the ECJ appeared to stick to hierarchical approach of the European legal space. In a judgment after the ratification of the Lisbon judgment, the Court reconfirmed that nothing had changed with respect to its primacy case law. In *Winner Wetten*, the ECJ stated that rules of the constitutional order cannot be allowed to undermine the unity and effectiveness of Union law. However, in the recent case *Sayn-Wittgenstein* the ECJ recognised that constitutional identity might be a legitimate reason for a member state to provide an exemption to the freedom of movement. We will have to wait for more jurisprudence on this issue to conclude whether this heralds a new direction, but in any case it signifies that the ECJ as for the ECtHR search for a right balance between effectiveness and diversity.[150]

149 Only a limited number of constitutional courts refer to the ECJ. As a result, the constitutional courts and the ECJ are not directly linked via a formal procedure. It grants these courts a certain flexibility to manoeuvre between EU law as interpreted by the ECJ and their own constitutional jurisprudence.

150 C-208/09 Sayn-Wittgenstein [2010] ECR I-0000, para. 92. It should be noted that the ECJ already accepted Austria's argument on the basis of a legitimate public policy interest.

CHAPTER 4
EUROPEAN HUMAN RIGHTS, SUPRANATIONAL JUDICIAL REVIEW AND DEMOCRACY
Thinking outside the judicial box

Samantha BESSON*

1. INTRODUCTION

Circumstances of legal (or constitutional)[1] pluralism in the European Union (EU) have led to an increased focus on values,[2] on the one hand, and on courts,[3] on the other. Values have been identified as constitutive of the common standards that democratic political and institutional structures and legal rules no longer provide in a context of competing legal orders, regimes and sources[4] – or at least only at the price of very high complexity. Unsurprisingly in those

---

* Professor of Public International Law and European Law at the University of Fribourg, Switzerland. I would like to thank Catherine Van De Heyning, Patricia Popelier, George Pavlakos, Bruno de Witte, Luis Lopez Guerra, Rick Lawson, Leonard Besselink and other members of the audience for their useful feedback at the Seminar *The Protection of Human Rights in the Interaction between the European Courts* held at the University of Antwerp on 27th March, 2009. Many thanks are also due to Catherine Donnelly and Will Phelan and the audience of the *EU Constitution* Seminar at Trinity College, Dublin on 16th April, 2009.

1 Since every legal order can be said to have at least a material constitution, the plurality of overlapping legal orders also implies constitutional pluralism.

2 See A Rosas, 'The European Court of Justice in Context: Forms and Patterns of Judicial Dialogue' (2007) 1:2 *European Journal of Legal Studies*, www.ejls.eu/.

3 See Rosas, *supra* n. 2, M Maduro, 'Interpreting European Law – Judicial Adjudication in a Context of Constitutional Pluralism' (2007) 1:2 *European Journal of Legal Studies*, www.ejls.eu/.

4 It suffices to read the ECJ's recent case-law whenever difficult issues pertaining to the articulation of legal orders or regimes arise to see that human rights are constantly referred to as common standards in the relationship between legal orders, common standards that can provide the equivalence or identity needed to bridge the lack of coincidence between political communities and between legal orders. See e.g. Case C-127/07 *Arcelor Atlantique et Lorraine and Others* [2008] ECR I-9895, Case C-213/07 *Michaniki AE v Ethniko Symvoulio Radiotileorasis and Ypourgos Epikrateias* [2008] ECR I-9999. See also, conversely, BVerfGE v. 30.06.2009 *Lissabonsvertrag*, 2 BvE 5/08, para. 340.

conditions, courts have become the privileged forum of decision-making and have used values as guidance in complex normative conflicts.

This conjunction explains why human rights have become so central to the articulation of European legal orders and regimes in recent years. Human rights are used as common standards of adjudication of normative conflicts. But their multi-level guarantees have also given rise to a legal pluralism of their own. And, in conditions of judicial proliferation in the field, this has triggered further jurisdictional conflicts over their interpretation in Europe. All this in turn explains why supranational adjudication in the field of European human rights is perceived as being so problematic. Discussions of the relationship between the European Court of Justice (ECJ), the European Court of Human Rights (ECtHR) and domestic courts, and generally the revival in discussions of human rights adjudication are a testimony to those concerns.

While it is important to understand the role human rights play in circumstances of legal pluralism and what this implies for judicial interpretation and judicial dialogue between the two European courts, on the one hand, and between each or both of them and domestic courts, on the other, the picture would not be complete without understanding how we got here.[5]

On the one hand, focusing exclusively on the relationship between courts in conditions of legal pluralism provides a skewed image of the challenges lying ahead of us in terms of human rights protection in Europe. Based on their visible effectivity and enhanced role in the European construction, but also on their *prima facie* familiarity to national observers (we all know what a court is and how it works, when we see one), supranational courts are too often understood as singletons vested with quasi-political powers.[6] To broaden our vision and deepen our understanding, we need to place the relationship between courts back into their respective institutional context and especially discuss their relationship to political institutions in their legal order(s).[7] This is even more important as the

5 Discussing the democratic legitimacy of supranational judicial review in the field of human rights in the EU without considering the ECtHR would make no sense given the intricate relationships between the two courts and, as we will see, their complementary nature from a democratic perspective.

6 See e.g. AM Slaughter / A Stone Sweet / JHH Weiler (eds), *The European Court and the National Courts: Legal Change in its Social, Political, and Economic Context* (Hart Publishing, Oxford 1998), A Stone Sweet, 'Why Europe Rejected American Judicial Review, and Why it May not Matter' (2003) 101 *Michigan Law Review* 2744–80, AM Slaughter, 'A Global Community of Courts' (2003) 44 *Harvard International Law Journal* 191, K. Alter, *The European Court's Political Power: Selected Essays* (Oxford University Press, Oxford 2009).

7 This is something Maduro, *supra* n. 3 realizes, but does not do: 'Courts are ultimately bound to the political community to which their legal order is associated and any such debate would lead us into a very difficult inquiry on what exactly would be the new political community or

different courts involved are neither all situated in the same legal order nor at the same level within each legal order. Furthermore, their interactions with democratic institutions in national legal orders are essential to understand how those courts ought to relate not only to domestic courts, but also among themselves. The relationships between the national legal order and other legal orders in Europe and between the national institutional framework and European courts matter especially in this context, as national law remains the primary legal order in which European law and European human rights are received and integrated.

Similarly, on the other hand, (international) human rights are complex moral standards whose relationship to democracy is one of the most difficult issues in contemporary political and legal theory. Clearly, as a result, that relationship needs to be unpacked before a judgement can be made about the interpretation of human rights in a legal pluralist context where human rights are guaranteed by different overlapping legal orders and protected by many overlapping national and supranational courts. In fact, the circumstance that European human rights (at least European Convention on Human Rights (ECHR) rights) were from the beginning intrinsically connected to the strengthening of national democracy, but also to supranational adjudication mechanisms[8] makes the relationship between supranational judicial review and democracy in the context of European human rights a particularly sensitive one.[9]

In short, the key to assessing the role and the legitimacy of European human rights adjudication in circumstances of legal pluralism lies precisely in what has made both human rights and courts the obvious means and place to arbitrate those normative conflicts: the complexity of democratic legitimation in a pluralist European legal order where democratic polities overlap just like the legal norms stemming from them.

True, the relationship between human rights and democracy, on the one hand, and between judicial review and democracy, on the other, are old questions that have kept generations of constitutional theorists and legal philosophers busy. Surprisingly, however, very little has been written theoretically about the legitimacy of *supranational* judicial review of the kind we know in Europe,

---

whether we could abandon such link between courts and the particular legal order whose integrity they are supposed to protect.'

8 See A Moravcsik, 'The Origins of Human Rights Regimes: Democratic Delegation in Postwar Europe' (2000) 54:2 *International Organization* 217–52, 217–8.

9 See G Letsas, *A Theory of Interpretation of the European Convention of Human Rights* (Oxford University Press, Oxford 2008), 18–21.

whether at the ECJ or at the ECtHR.[10] And even less about its democratic legitimacy and about the compared democratic legitimacy of the two courts. Of course, a lot has been written about adjudication, judicial reasoning and judicial discretion/restraint in both courts from a legal or from a political science perspective,[11] but legal and political philosophers have not yet had a chance to address those issues.[12] This is even more important as classical arguments in favour or against judicial review in the domestic context cannot simply be transposed *mutatis mutandis* to the supranational level.[13]

10 This is surprising because supranational judicial review pertaining to human rights is unlike international adjudication between States and over matters that pertain to interstate relations and that cannot be part of domestic law. Supranational human rights review resembles a lot national human rights adjudication in terms of subjects and subject matter.

11 There have actually been more publications about judicial review by the ECJ in this respect than about the ECtHR. See on judicial review by the ECJ: M Volcansek, *Judicial Politics in Europe*, American University Studies –Series X, vol. 7 (Peter Lang, New York 1986), JHH Weiler, 'Journey to an Unknown Destination: A Retrospective and Prospective of the European Court of Justice in the Arena of Political Integration' (1993) 31 *Journal of Common Market Studies* 417, AM Burley / W Mattli, 'Europe before the Court: A Political Theory of Legal Integration' (1993) 47:1 *International Organization* 41–76, JHH Weiler, 'A Quiet Revolution, The European Court and its Interlocutors' (1994) 26 *Comparative Political Studies* 510–34, JHH Weiler, 'Fundamental rights and fundamental boundaries: on the conflict of standards and values in the protection of human rights in the European legal space' in *The Constitution of Europe* (Cambridge University Press, Cambridge 1999), 102–29, Slaughter/Stone Sweet/ Weiler, *supra* n. 6, M Shapiro, 'The European Court of Justice' in P Craig / G de Burca (eds), *The Evolution of EU Law* (Oxford University Press: Oxford 1999), 321–45, G de Burca / JHH Weiler (eds), *The European Court of Justice* (Oxford University Press, Oxford 2001), Rosas, *supra* n. 2 , Maduro, *supra* n. 3, Alter *supra* n. 6, A Stone Sweet, 'The European Court of Justice and the Judicialization of EU Governance', *Living Reviews in EU Governance* (2010), http://europeangovernance.livingreviews.org/Articles/lreg-2010–2/. See on judicial review by the ECtHR, P Mahoney, 'Judicial Activism and Judicial Self-Restraint in the European Court of Human Rights: Two Sides of the Same Coin' (1990) 11 *Human Rights Law Journal* 57–88, R Bernhardt, 'Human Rights and Judicial Review: The European Court of Human Rights' in DM Beatty (ed.), *Human Rights and Judicial Review: A Comparative Perspective* (Martinus Nijhoff, Dordrecht 1994), 297–319, Letsas, *supra* n. 9, A Follesdal, 'The Legitimacy of International Human Rights Review: The Case of the European Court of Human Rights' (2009) 40:4 *Journal of Social Philosophy* 595–607. See on supranational judicial review in general, L Helfer / AM Slaughter, 'Toward a Theory of Effective Supranational Adjudication' (1998) 107 *Yale Law Journal* 273–391, Slaughter, *supra* n. 6, K Anderson, 'Squaring the Circle? Reconciling Sovereignty and Global Governance Through Global Government Networks – Review of Slaughter 2004' (2005) *Harvard Law Review* 1255–312, E Benvenisti, 'Margin of Appreciation, Consensus and Universal Standards' (1998) 31 *NYU Journal of International Law and Politics* 843–54, A Follesdal, 'Why International Human Rights Judicial Review Might Be Democratically Legitimate' (2007) 52 *Scandinavian Studies in Law* 52, 103–122, A Follesdal, 'International Judicial Human Rights Review – Effective, Legitimate or Both?' in J Sihvola / P Korkman / V Mäkinen (eds), *Universalism in International Law and Political Philosophy*, Helsinki: COLLeGIUM, 2008, www.helsinki.fi/collegium/e-series/volumes/volume_4/10_follesdal_2008_4.pdf, L Garlicki, 'Cooperation of Courts: The Role of Supranational Jurisdictions in Europe' (2008) 6:3 *International Journal of Constitutional Law* 509–30.

12 There are exceptions, of course, such as Letsas, *supra* n. 9, Follesdal 2009, 2008 and 2007, *supra* n. 11.

13 Follesdal 2009, *supra* n. 11, 596 seems to think some form of transposition is plausible but does not explain why.

What I would like to do in this chapter, therefore, is assess the types of supranational human rights review exercised by the ECJ and the ECtHR from a democratic point of view,[14] and not only as it is often the case from their respective judicial perspectives or that of domestic courts, or, even more broadly, from that of Member States in general.[15] Normative answers as to what judges ought to do in circumstances of legal and judicial pluralism cannot be found in descriptions of the circumstances of legal pluralism. Nor can they be found within existing sets of judicial duties in monist or dualist and hierarchical legal orders. Thinking outside the judicial box is what is needed, in other words. It will provide us with a clearer view of those supranational courts' respective institutional roles in European democracies, of how to articulate the norms stemming from their respective legal orders and then accordingly of how the respective courts ought to be adjudicating normative conflicts between those orders. Eventually, this will not only help clarify the notion of legal pluralism and ways of addressing a feature of the European legal order that is here to stay, but also the role of human rights in the regional context.[16]

Of course, this approach should not be taken to deny the crucial function of supranational adjudication and the importance of judicial coherence and integrity in circumstances of legal pluralism.[17] The point is merely to place the question in an institutional perspective that goes beyond an interjudicial one and

---

14 Other justifications of the authority of supranational judicial review may be provided than democracy. As a matter of fact, democracy is rarely considered as a major justification of international law and even more rarely of international human rights law (see the discussion in S Besson, 'The Democratic Authority of International Human Rights' in A Follesdal (ed.), *The Legitimacy of Human Rights* (2011) forthcoming). When international law and adjudication become supranational, however, and affect individuals' rights and duties directly, democracy becomes a central concern. This is even more so in circumstances of legal pluralism where international law and especially international human rights can no longer be dissociated from national law and national human rights.

15 Of course, it is easier to focus on courts and judicial relationships: actors are similar across the board and the information readily available. 'Political institutions' or 'actors' are more diverse and numerous, and usually referred to as an indeterminate entity without further efforts: see e.g. Maduro, *supra* n. 3, Weiler, *supra* n. 11. See, however, the more detailed approach to the reception of the ECHR by political actors in Contracting Parties used in the different chapters of H Keller / A Stone Sweet (eds), *A Europe of Rights. The Reception of the European Convention on Human Rights* (Oxford University Press, Oxford 2008).

16 See L Helfer, 'Redesigning the European Court of Human Rights: Embeddedness as a Deep Structural Principle of the European Human Rights Regime' (2008) 19: 1 *European Journal of International Law* 125–159, J Cavallaro / S Brewer, 'Reevaluating Regional Human Rights Litigation in the Twenty-First Century: the Case of the Inter-American Court' (2008) 102 *American Journal of International Law* 768 on the current dangers facing supranational judicial review in regional human rights systems such as the European one.

17 Especially as circumstances of legal pluralism have led to vesting judges with more responsibility in this context. See e.g. Maduro, *supra* n. 3, S Besson, 'From European Integration to European Integrity. Should European law speak with just one voice?' (2004) 10:3 *European Law Journal* 257–281.

hence to understand it better in a multi-level and multi-layered institutional context. True, it would be wrong to oppose supranational courts to domestic political institutions as a whole in an old-fashioned way, thus negating the denationalisation of some of the functions of those institutions (including the judicial function) and hence denying the importance of interjudicial dialogue between national and supranational courts in Europe. However, ignoring the parallel denationalisation of political and especially of legislative institutions, and hence the importance of reconnecting legislative and judicial functions across levels of governance, has become a blind spot in current discussions.[18] In short, we ought and will be looking at the same legal reality, but from a different perspective, thus hoping to shed some light onto other mechanisms and solutions than those usually identified by studies that focus on interjudicial cooperation.

There will be three steps in the argument. First of all, and after a first section in which the terms 'supranational' and 'judicial review' are clarified, I will present the nature and scope of the supranational judicial review exercised by the European Court of Human Rights and by the European Court of Justice, focusing on recent developments and drawing comparisons between the two. In a second step, I will turn to the more philosophical questions raised by the democratic legitimacy of that heightened form of scrutiny exercised by supranational judicial bodies in Europe over the respect of human rights in national legal systems. Not only will the traditional questions have to be reframed to fit the supranational context, but the answers will also be very different from those one usually finds in philosophical discussions of judicial review. A critical assessment of the kinds of judicial review exercised by the two European courts will ensue. Finally, on the basis of the institutional differences between the kinds of supranational judicial review exercised by the two courts identified in the first section, I will draw some implications for the relationship between the two European courts and their national counterparts, but also between them in the context of human rights adjudication in Europe.

2. THE NOTION OF SUPRANATIONAL JUDICIAL REVIEW

Defining supranational judicial review requires a definition of both the terms 'supranational' and 'judicial review'.

---

[18] See AM Slaughter, 'Global Government Networks, Global Information Agencies and Disaggregated Democracy' (2003) 24 *Michigan Journal of International Law* 1041 on this disaggregation. The important thing is to connect those disaggregated functions back again at all levels and across levels.

To start with, the term 'supranational' is used, by contrast to 'international' *stricto sensu*, to identify a type of international organization, institution or law beyond the state that is empowered to exercise directly some of the functions that are in principle reserved to the state, especially in relation to individuals within that state.[19] Supranationality implies, in other words, a greater transfer of or limitation on state sovereignty, either in the establishment of an international organisation, institution or law or in their ability to make decisions which take priority over national law and are directly binding upon states and individuals within those states. Supranationality generally also implies compulsory and binding adjudication within states. This is what one may refer to as 'supranational adjudication'. Supranational adjudication, when it is granted, differs from the non-compulsory kind of adjudication that prevails in international relations and whose decisions are not usually binding within states.

There is no necessary connection, however, between supranational law (e.g. human rights) and supranational adjudication. Human rights law of supranational origin ought to be interpreted, specified and applied by domestic institutions and in particular by domestic courts in priority, without necessarily benefiting from the aid of a supranational court reviewing national law.[20] True, supranational organisations usually have courts such as the ECJ in the EU. However, certain supranational courts exist independently from a supranational organisation and the ECtHR provides a good illustration thereof.

Supranational adjudication may imply the exercise of judicial review –but may not necessarily do so. There is supranational judicial review when supranational courts' decisions that review the compatibility between national law and supranational law are (i) binding within national law and (ii) are directly invocable by individuals (direct effect) (iii) *vis-à-vis* all Contracting States' institutions, whether of a legislative, executive or judicial nature. As in the national context, one ought to distinguish between weak and strong judicial review, depending on whether a judicial decision results in a mere declaration of incompatibility, on the one hand, or in the prohibition of application or even in the striking down of the national act or decision, on the other.[21]

Supranational judicial review may imply some amount of judicial discretion. However, the two questions are distinct. One may regard supranational judicial

19 Helfer/Slaughter, *supra* n. 11, 287.

20 This is a difference Letsas, *supra* n. 9, 39 misses when he argues that the ECtHR's review and judicial reasoning are fully moralized human rights reasoning. While he may be right about ECHR rights being indistinguishable from national human rights, this does not necessarily mean that the ECtHR's reasoning is just the same as that of national courts on ECHR rights.

21 See e.g. W Sinnott-Armstrong, 'Weak and strong judicial review' (2003) 22 *Law and Philosophy* 381.

review as illegitimate independently from the use of discretion by the court. Of course, the use of discretion or even judicial activism in the interpretation of human rights may increase the impact of supranational adjudication on national law. However, judicial review may be exercised without discretion or the activist interpretation of a legal rule. As a result, the debate pertaining to the opposition between judicial activism and judicial self-restraint ought not be conflated with that relative to the legitimacy of supranational judicial review.[22] In what follows, I will try to keep the two issues distinct from each other and will focus exclusively on judicial review.

3. SUPRANATIONAL JUDICIAL REVIEW IN EUROPE

Supranational courts whose jurisdiction is compulsory and whose decisions are binding within states are rare. Recent developments have confirmed that the International Court of Justice's jurisdiction, for instance, is clearly not supranational: it does not have compulsory jurisdiction, its decisions are only binding between states and not within the latter's domestic legal order unless domestic law provides otherwise,[23] and they cannot be enforced judicially whether at the domestic or the international level. The same may be said about international human rights adjudication as there are no international judicial mechanisms of protection *stricto sensu*. Things are different at the regional level, however, where the monitoring of human rights instruments is ensured through regional human rights courts. The two main examples that are usually given of supranational adjudication and judicial review are European: the ECtHR and the ECJ.

Of course, from a European perspective,[24] those two courts have as much in common as they are different. While the ECtHR is the court created by an international human rights convention whose respect of ECHR rights by Contracting Parties is the sole function, the ECJ is the court of a supranational organisation, the EU, and has as its general function to scrutinize the respect of EU law (including EU fundamental rights[25]) by Member States, EU institutions

22 On supranational judicial activism/restraint, see Letsas, *supra* n. 9, Mahoney, *supra* n. 11 for the ECtHR, and Maduro, *supra* n. 3, Weiler, *supra* n. 11 for the ECJ.

23 See e.g. US SCt, *Medellin v. Texas*, 552 U.S. 491 (2008), confirmed (on this point) by the ICJ in *Request for Interpretation of the Judgment of 31 March 2004 in the Case concerning Avena and Other Mexican Nationals* (Mexico v. United States of America), Judgment of 19 January 2009, not published.

24 As opposed to an American perspective: see e.g. Helfer/Slaughter, *supra* n. 11.

25 I am not expanding here on the differences between (EU) fundamental rights and (ECHR) human rights, as this is a complex debate, but it suffices to remember that those European rights themselves are different in their legal nature or at least in their legal function.

and, to a certain extent, individuals. As a result, the two courts have a very different jurisdiction in terms of subjects and subject matters, and they also have a fundamentally different institutional background. Furthermore, both courts have evolved drastically since their creation in the 1950s. While it was clear since the beginning that the ECJ would play a crucial role through supranational judicial review, the ECtHR has only recently started to emancipate from a more subsidiary international-type adjudication. This evolution needs to be borne in mind in what follows, as it is not always easy to compare those two jurisdictions in a chronologically and substantially accurate way.

3.1. SUPRANATIONAL JUDICIAL REVIEW BY THE ECtHR

The ECtHR is an international court based in Strasbourg and an institution created by the ECHR under the aegis of the Council of Europe. It controls the application of the ECHR in the 47 Contracting States that have ratified it to date. It is one of the most accomplished and respected international human rights jurisdictions in the world, thanks in particular to the right of individual application before the European Court of Human Rights.

The ECtHR has recently strengthened its power of judicial review over its Contracting States' laws from what may be referred as a weak review to a stronger review. This has even lead to the constitutional qualification of its review by an increasing number of academics.[26] In order to take the full measure of the kind of judicial review exercised by the ECtHR, it is useful to assess the Convention's status in domestic law before looking more closely into the scope of the jurisdiction of the Court over its Contracting States and the effects of its judgements in domestic law.

3.1.1. *The status of ECHR rights in domestic law*

The ECHR entered into force in its first Contracting States in 1953. Nowadays, the Convention is deeply rooted and well respected in most of its 47 Contracting States. This is due in particular to the specificities of the ECtHR's judicial review and in particular to the right of individual application before the Court. But not only that: the status of the ECHR in the domestic legal order is essential to

[26] See e.g. A Stone Sweet, 'On the Constitutionalisation of the Convention: The European Court of Human Rights as a Constitutional Court' (2009) 80 *Revue trimestrielle des droits de l'homme* 923–44, S Greer, *The European Convention on Human Rights: Achievements, Problems and Prospects* (Cambridge University Press, Cambridge 2006), 173 , L Wildhaber, 'A Constitutional Future for the European Court of Human Rights?' (2002) 23 *Human Rights Law Journal* 161.

understand the scope of the Court's jurisdiction and its judgements' impact on domestic law.

In principle, the status of ECHR rights in a national legal order should vary from one Contracting State to the next depending on the status of international law within each legal order. Although the ECHR is an international treaty, its subject matter and rights-holders have rapidly turned it into supranational law, however. Its status in national law is almost equivalent, as a result, to that of domestic law and to domestic human rights.[27] This is clear from the validity, the effect and the rank of ECHR rights within domestic law.

First of all, the ECHR has immediate validity in most of its 47 Contracting States on the basis of those countries' monism. Even in dualist Contracting States, the Convention has now been incorporated or at least is routinely subsumed under domestic constitutional rights by domestic courts. Secondly, Convention rights are granted direct effect on the basis of Article 1 ECHR and its interpretation by the Court's case-law. Finally, the Convention's rank in most countries is at least that of ordinary legislation and is even sometimes constitutional or quasi-constitutional in the sense that it takes priority over contrary national legislation.

Of course, Convention rights only constitute minimal standards. When national human rights guarantees are more protective, they take priority. This is what the principle of favour contained in Article 53 ECHR foresees. The notion of minimal standards of protection is particularly problematic, however. This becomes clear in case of conflicts of rights where one right is necessarily restricted to protect the other one and where national law may therefore be said to protect the restricted right better. Another difficult case may arise when one right is granted absolute protection under national law and national law therefore precludes balancing in principle.[28] In such instances, the Court is not usually hindered by the principle of favour, provided, of course, it is invoked by a Contracting State to justify a restriction to an ECHR right.

3.1.2. The jurisdiction of the ECtHR

Another reason for the special status given to the ECHR in domestic law by comparison to other international human rights guarantees, and for its

---

27 S Besson, 'The reception of the ECHR in the United Kingdom and Ireland' in H Keller / A Stone Sweet (eds), *A Europe of Rights. The Reception of the European Convention on Human Rights* (Oxford University Press, Oxford 2008), 31–106, S Gardbaum, 'Human Rights as International Constitutional Rights' (2008) 19:4 *European Journal of International Law* 749.

28 *Odièvre v France* (n. 42326/98) EHRR 2003-III.

widespread reception in the domestic case-law in particular, is the supranational control exercised by the ECtHR.

Originally, the type of judicial control exercised by the Court was clearly meant to be and remain international. This becomes clear as the Court's monitoring function is primarily characterized by its subsidiarity. Accordingly, the ECtHR may only be effectively seized once all national remedies have been exhausted. This means that national judges remain the primary judges of the conformity of domestic law to the Convention. This has actually given rise to a rich interjudicial dialogue between national and ECtHR judges in the past.

Recently, however, the Court has started assessing the effectivity of national remedies in a very restrictive way, so as to waive the requirement to exhaust national remedies in an increasing number of cases. This is the case where no clear and rapid remedies are available in domestic law or where future violations are too important for the Court to wait.

In principle, the subsidiarity of the jurisdiction of the Court ought also to be protected with respect to the scope of its jurisdiction. In that context, states are recognized a certain margin of appreciation on issues on which there is no European 'consensus'. It is the case for sensitive moral issues or for intractable political situations.[29]

Regrettably, however, the Court has never been very clear about the notion of 'consensus' and about the exact circumstances in which the margin of appreciation applies. This is an important criterion, as once the Court decides there is a consensus, it can be extremely creative and dynamic in the interpretation of the Convention. In such circumstances, the Court refers to the Convention as a so-called 'living instrument' and makes it fit 'present-day conditions'.[30] As a matter of fact, the Court is increasingly creative even in cases where there is no consensus among Contracting Parties.[31]

At the same time, the Court has repeatedly stated that the margin of appreciation decreases with the importance of the right violated or even with the importance of certain central dimensions of the right being violated.[32] Further, the margin of appreciation does not dispense the Court from assessing the proportionality

29 *Pretty v The United Kingdom* (n. 2346/02) EHRR 2002-III, *Leyla Sahin v Turkey* (n. 44774/98) EHRR 2005-XI, *Pretty v The United Kingdom* (n. 2346/02) EHRR 2002-III.

30 *Fretté v France* (n. 36515/97) EHRR 2002-I, *Christine Goodwin v The United Kingdom* (n. 28957/95) EHRR 2002-VI.

31 *Hirst v The United Kingdom (No 2)* (n. 74025/01) EHRR 2005-IX, *B. and L. v The United Kingdom* (n. 36536/02) Judgment of 13 September 2005, not published.

32 *Jäggi v Switzerland* (n. 58757/00) EHRR 2006-X.

of the measures allegedly violating a Convention right. Again, however, the Court is not very strict in its application of the three classical prongs of the proportionality test (adequateness, necessity and proportionality *stricto sensu*). The test is often interrupted or botched, precisely by reference to the State's margin of appreciation, thus leading to a circular situation where Contracting States cannot invoke the margin of appreciation that is only applied on the basis of the Court's own assessment, but where they cannot rely on the Court's assessment of the proportionality of the measures they have taken either.

3.1.3. The effects of a ECtHR's judgement in domestic law

Besides those increasing inroads into the principle of subsidiarity of its jurisdiction, another element in the Court's practice provides clear signs of reinforcement of the nature and the scope of its judicial review: the impact of its judgements in domestic law.[33] To understand what the effects of a ECtHR's judgement are within domestic law, it is useful to distinguish the consequences of the judgement's binding nature in domestic law, on the one hand, from the mechanisms for the monitoring of the enforcement of the judgement in domestic law, on the other.

It is with respect to the binding nature of the Court's decision, first of all, that its review's supranational nature has gradually become evident.

In principle, and according to Article 46 ECHR, a ECtHR's decision is binding on all national authorities, whether legislative, executive or judicial. It does not have an invalidating effect, however, and is therefore regarded as merely declaratory. Further, it is up to the State's authorities to ensure a *restitutio in integrum*, by guaranteeing that the human rights violation stops, that it does not recur again and that its consequences are remedied. States have a duty of result, therefore, but a free choice of the means to reach that result. It follows that the Court cannot and should not provide directions in its decisions as to how they ought to be implemented. Its decisions are deemed as entirely individualised and hence as pertaining to the violating act or decision only. It is up to a state therefore to decide whether to change its legislation deemed contrary to the Convention, or merely to change its interpretation of that legislation. Nor does the state have to reopen the procedure and revise the judgement deemed in violation of the Convention; revision is recommended by the Committee of Ministers, but does not constitute a duty under the Convention.

---

33 On those issues, see S Besson, 'Les effets et l'exécution des arrêts de la Cour européenne des droits de l'homme – Le cas de la Suisse' in B Ehrenzeller / S Breitenmoser (eds), *Die EMRK und die Schweiz* (Institut für Rechtswissenschaft und Rechtspraxis, St Gallen 2010), 125–199.

In all those respects, and *prima facie* at least, the binding nature of the decisions of the Court stems directly from Contracting States' international obligations and the regime of international state liability, and follows a traditional international approach as a result. The Court's case-law has gradually emancipated, however, leading to a more direct impact of the Court's decisions on domestic law.

To start with, in practice, the difference between the individual violation and the laws that led to that violation is difficult to draw. In most cases, the concerned state has no other choice but to amend or strike down the relevant legal norms. As a result, the Court's decisions are effectively declarations of non-conventionality of national laws, albeit non-invalidating ones. Furthermore, certain countries have recently introduced a revision procedure which enables courts to reopen a procedure and revise a judgement that has been deemed contrary to the Convention by the Court. This may, in certain circumstances, equate to giving an invalidating effect to the ECtHR's decisions. Finally, independently from such revision mechanisms, ECtHR's decisions purport to apply *erga omnes* and hence bind all 47 Contracting States and not only the state against whom the adverse judgement was rendered. As a result, in certain Contracting Parties, ECtHR's judgements have the same effects as Convention rights, whether they pertain to that state or another Contracting State. They are immediately valid, are vested with direct effect, and have a quasi-constitutional rank. They also bind judges prospectively in any future case. Adopted at the 2010 Interlaken Conference on the Reform of the Court, the Action Plan actually entails the objective to generalise the *erga omnes* effect of all judgements of the Court in all Contracting States.[34]

If one refers, secondly, to the mechanisms available for the enforcement of the ECtHR's judgements, the supranational nature of the judicial review exercised by the Court becomes even more evident. It is important to distinguish between the mechanisms used by the Committee of Ministers and those of the Court itself.

The Committee of Ministers, i.e. the executive organ of the Council of Europe, is the institution officially in charge of monitoring the execution of the Court's judgements (Article 46 ECHR). It holds different meetings every year at which it follows up States' implementation (individual and general) measures and can provide help and advice to enhance the effectivity of the Court's judgements. It

34 19 February 2010, available at: www.eda.admin.ch/etc/medialib/downloads/edazen/topics/europa/euroc.Para.0133.File.tmp/final_en.pdf [last accessed 7 July 2010]. See e.g. A Mowbray, 'The Interlaken Declaration – The Beginning of a New Era for the European Court of Human Rights?' (2010) 10:3 *Human Rights Law Review* 519–28, P Wachsmann, 'Entre deux lacs – Quelques réflexions sur la Conférence d'Interlaken sur l'avenir de la Cour européenne des droits de l'homme' (2010) 21:83 *Revue trimestrielle des droits de l'homme* 511–34.

can pressure States through various political means such as interim resolutions. The most powerful means is, of course, suspension from the Council of Europe.

The Committee cannot, however, enforce the ECtHR's judgements on Contracting Parties which are not implementing the judgements. And this has become a sensitive issue in certain countries whose execution backlog is worrying. Given that the effectivity of judgements is part of the credentials of the Court and at the centre of its reforms, recent years have seen the adoption of various reports and measures meant to enhance the enforcement of the Court's judgements. The Protocol 14, that came into force on 1st June, 2010, actually improves the situation to a certain extent. It entails, first of all, the possibility for the Committee to seize the Court of an infringement procedure against a State which does not execute a judgement. Secondly, a follow-up system by the European Commissioner for Human Rights with the help of the European Network of National Human Rights Institutions has been put in place to pressure Contracting States to implement judgements.

In view of the structural difficulties met by some Member States and the repetitive claims made by victims of violations in those States, the Court started a few years ago to deal with the problem itself and to issue directives pertaining to the enforcement of its judgements.

First of all, the Court started, on the recommendation of the Committee of Ministers in 2004, to issue so-called 'pilot judgements' addressing precisely the structural issues to be fixed and indicating how to do so in domestic law. The consequence of pilot judgements is to freeze all similar claims made consecutively until the problems are resolved in the Contracting State concerned.[35] Besides general directives in pilot judgements, secondly, the Court has been issuing implementation directives in ordinary judgements since 2000.[36] It uses individual judgements to recommend general measures to remedy the violation of ECHR rights at hand. Beyond general measures, the Court has also started to recommend individual measures in its judgements, requiring a precise action from the violating state and hence limiting the choice of means available to the state when executing the judgement. The Court has done so, for instance, by requiring the liberation of a detainee in a judgement.[37]

---

35 *Broniowski v Poland* (n. 31443/96) EHRR 2004-V, *Hutten-Czapska v Poland* (n. 35014/97) EHRR 2006-VIII, *Scordino v Italy* (n. 36813/97) EHRR 2006-V, *Sejdovic v Italy* (n. 56581/00) EHRR 2006-II, *Cocchiarella v Italy* (n. 64886/01) EHRR 2006-V.

36 *Scozzari and Giunta v Italy* (n. 39221/98, 41963/98) EHRR 2000-VIII, *Hasan and Eylem Zengin v Turkey* (n. 1448/04) Judgment of 10 October 2007, selected for publication.

37 *Assanidze v Georgia* (n. 71503/01) EHRR 2004-II, *Ilascu and Others v Moldova and Russia* (n. 48787/99) EHRR 2004-VII.

Both types of directives (individual or general measures *per se* or in pilot judgements) have been contested by Member States as reaching beyond the review competences of the Court (and the wording of Article 46 ECHR[38]). It is interesting to see that those States that are most opposed to this assertive development of the judicial review of the Court are Western European States, which base their resistance on democratic grounds. Those cooperating with the Court in pilot judgements, and those at the origins of this new practice, are by contrast Central and Eastern European Countries which see supranational judicial review as an ally to the development of their national democracies. Curiously, in the context of the democratic justification of the 'act of State' doctrine put forward by the Court in its case-law, those very judges from Central and Eastern European Countries that cooperated actively with the Court in pilot cases, have invoked the tyranny of the majority and the risks for national democracies to support the Court.[39] Democracy seems, in other words, to be used both to justify and to object to supranational judicial review and that use of the democratic critique of supranational review seems to vary depending on whether one is an Eastern and Central European State or a Western one.

The Court is showing no sign of weakening, however. It is actually developing means of controlling the implementation of its own cases, besides the possibility to use the new infringement procedure in force since 1st June 2010. There are two developments one may mention in this respect: the decoupling of the judgement on a just satisfaction from the judgement in condemnation, thus granting time for the Contracting State to remedy the situation before discussing the just satisfaction, but also at the same time exercising pressure and directly controlling the implementation of its case-law, and its increasingly intrusive requirements pertaining to the reopening of national procedures on the basis of a violation of Article 46 ECHR.

With respect to the latter, the Court has strengthened its review power lately by developing a new line in its case-law pertaining to the reopening of national procedures in Switzerland.[40] According to the Convention, there is in principle no duty to reopen a national procedure nor to revise a judgement deemed in violation of the Convention. The Committee of Ministers and the Court recommend doing so, but there is no corresponding duty. Of course, in practice, when the *restitutio in integrum* is only possible through a revision, this can create

---

38 In fact the Court never mentions a clear conventional basis and mentions interchangeably Articles 41 and 46 ECHR. See Besson, *supra* n. 33.

39 *Markovic and Others v Italy* (n. 1398/03) Judgment of 14 December 2006, selected for publication.

40 See *VgT Verein gegen Tierfabriken v Switzerland (No 2)* (n. 32772/02) Judgment of 30 June 2009, selected for publication, *VgT Verein gegen Tierfabriken v Switzerland* (n. 24699/94) EHRR 2001-VI.

difficult situations if a Member State's procedure does not allow it. It is the case in criminal proceedings, but most controversially also in private law proceedings. In its *VgT II* judgement, the ECtHR decided that a refusal to revise, as opposed to the absence of a revision process, constituted a new fact that made the claim admissible. It also decided that Switzerland had violated the Convention and that the grounds given by the Swiss Federal Tribunal not to open a revision procedure were 'formalistic'. The implications of this new case-law are extremely important. First of all, States which have a revision procedure almost necessarily have to accept the revision of a judgement deemed contrary to the Court, whereas others do not have the same duties. Secondly, this in turn means that judgements of the Court now *de facto* have an invalidating effect, at least over national judicial decisions.

It is fair to say therefore in light of recent developments that the supranational judicial review exercised by the ECtHR now equates strong constitutional review of the kind we know in certain states in Europe.

3.2. SUPRANATIONAL JUDICIAL REVIEW BY THE ECJ

The ECJ is the second European court whose judicial review may be described as supranational, generally but also in the human rights context. The ECJ was created in 1951 with the first European Economic Community. It is the supranational court of a supranational organisation, the EU. It has since then been regularly reinforced, notably through the creation of a General Court and specialised courts, and through successive revisions of its Statute and procedures. It has jurisdiction over 27 EU Member States – which also happen to be Contracting Parties to the ECHR and are therefore submitted to the review of the ECtHR.

From the beginning, the ECJ's case-law has contributed to changing the nature of EU law. It has a generalist jurisdiction, but one that can issue binding judgements for States, EU institutions and individuals in the EU. As in the previous section on the ECtHR, assessing the supranational features of human rights adjudication by the ECJ requires, first of all, identifying the status of EU fundamental rights in domestic law, before turning to the scope of the ECJ's jurisdiction with respect to those rights and to the effects of its judgements in domestic law.

3.2.1. The status of EU fundamental rights in domestic law

The status of EU fundamental rights within the domestic legal order is the same as that of EU law in general. Their exact status will of course vary depending on their sources within EU law, but they benefit in principle from the immediate validity, the direct effect and the primacy of EU law in domestic law. EU fundamental rights are, in other words, truly supranational law by definition.

The interesting element is that human rights were not part of EU law from the beginning. The founding treaties entailed no fundamental rights provisions. The EU had, and *stricto sensu* still has no competence in the fundamental rights context (see *a contrario* Article 51 EU Fundamental Rights Charter (Charter) or Article 6(1) Treaty on the European Union (TEU)). That competence remains to date an exclusively domestic one.[41] EU fundamental rights were only developed gradually through the ECJ's case-law *qua* general principles of EU law and then codified first by a general clause in the EU Treaty and then later on in the EU Charter of Fundamental Rights. Nowadays, although EU fundamental rights remain general principles of EU law recognised and developed through the ECJ's case-law (Article 6(2) TEU), they are also guaranteed as part of EU primary law (Article 6(1) TEU) and, more specifically, as part of EU constitutional law.[42]

For a long time, in order to compensate for the absence of fundamental rights from EU primary law, the ECJ recognised human rights stemming from national constitutional traditions, the ECHR and other international sources of human rights as general principles of EU law.[43] *Qua* general principles of EU law, their source is formally EU law and they are no longer treated as national law or international law within the EU legal order,[44] but their content remains national and international. As a result, although the ECHR, that is the most important source of EU fundamental rights according to the ECJ (it has 'special significance'[45]), does not directly bind the EU as a Contracting State, but only its

41 See on that issue, O De Schutter, 'L'adhésion de l'Union européenne à la Convention européenne des droits de l'homme: Feuille de route de la négociation' (2010) 21:83 *Revue trimestrielle des droits de l'homme* 535–71, 545–6.

42 Case C-402/05P and C-415/05P *Kadi* [2008] ECR I-6351. This does not affect their binding nature, and that of the ECHR *qua* general principles of EU law, but their rank within the European legal order, vis-à-vis EU fundamental freedoms and vis-à-vis international law norms. See S Besson, 'European Legal Pluralism after *Kadi*' (2009) 5 *European Constitutional Law Review* 237–64. See also B De Witte in this volume, Chapter 1.

43 Case 11–70 *Handelsgesellschaft* [1970] ECR 1125, Case 36–75 *Rutili* [1975] ECR 1219.

44 Their status, rank and effects in the EU legal order are not those of international law norms binding the EU –even by *de facto* succession along the lines of the GATT or through indirect Article 4(3) TEU duties along the lines of UN Security Council Resolutions. Of course, this is clear for the ECHR and the European Social Charter. The status of other international human rights conventions in EU law is a bit more difficult to assess when EU Member States and not the EU itself are parties to those treaties: see T Ahmed / I Butler, 'The European Union and Human Rights: An International Perspective' (2006) 17:4 *European Journal of International Law* 771, Besson, *supra* n. 42, I Butler / O De Schutter, 'Binding the EU to international human rights law' (2008) 27 *Yearbook of European Law* 277.

45 See e.g. Case C-479/04 *Laserdisken ApS v Kulturministeriet* [2006] ECR I-08089. This implies a certain priority when ECHR rights conflict with other international human rights *qua* EU

Member States, it applies *qua* EU fundamental rights within the EU legal order and binds EU institutions and Member States *qua* EU law as result. This has implications for the nature of the duties connected to those rights and their respective content. The latter only reflects that of constitutional guarantees and the ECHR and may differ as a result from those rights' content as it is developed by the ECtHR and domestic jurisdictions.[46] Of course, following the mandate given to the EU by Article 6(2) TEU to accede to the ECHR, and if the negotiations currently held are successful,[47] the EU will one day be a Contracting Party to the ECHR and hence will be bound directly by ECHR rights and their interpretation by the ECtHR.

The ECJ started recognising fundamental rights in reaction to domestic constitutional courts. The latter increasingly faced a dilemma between respecting the primacy of EU law, on the one hand, and respecting their own constitutional rights or the ECHR, on the other. It is essential to emphasize therefore that EU fundamental rights developed negatively to protect Member States and individuals against the EU and its institutions, rather than to protect individuals against Member States themselves. Unlike the ECHR, their original justification was not to strengthen fledgling national democracies, but to reinforce the democratic legitimacy of the EU itself or, more exactly, to protect national democracies from the EU.[48] No wonder therefore that EU fundamental rights bind EU institutions in priority and not Member States. As there is no EU competence to legislate over fundamental rights that apply within Member States, the latter only bind Member States when they apply or derogate to EU law.[49] And this explains, moreover, why EU fundamental rights are more developed in areas in which EU law competences are important and where

fundamental rights. Contra de Witte, in this volume, I do not think that the special significance of the ECHR among sources of EU fundamental rights has any implications in terms of obligations: all EU fundamental rights, whether ECHR-based or not, bind the EU and Member States *qua* EU law (and more precisely both *qua* general principles and primary law).

46 See Case T-99/04 *AC-Treuhand AG v Commission of the European Communities* [2008] ECR II-1501, para. 45. See also for a recent confirmation, Case C-465/07 *Meki Elgafaji and Noor Elgafaji v Staatssecretaris van Justitie* [2009] ECR I-921.

47 Their success requires the unanimous adoption of an international agreement between the EU, the 27 EU Member States, and the other 20 States of the Council of Europe (Art. 218(6) and (8) TFEU).

48 See J Coppel / A O'Neill, 'The European Court of Justice: Taking Rights Seriously?' (1992) 29 *Common Market Law Review* 669, A von Bogdandy, 'The European Union as a Human Rights Organization? Human Rights and the Core of the European Union' (2000) 37 *Common Market Law Review* 1307–1338, S Besson, 'The European Union and Human Rights: Towards a new kind of post-national human rights institution' (2006) 6(2) *Human Rights Law Review* 323–360.

49 See Case C-260/89 *ERT* [1991] ECR I-2925. In spite of efforts to the reverse by the AG Maduro in Case C-380/05 *Centro Europa* 7 [2008] *ECR* I-349, the Court still refuses to regard States as bound by EU fundamental rights in their own sphere of competence.

European integration is most incisive as a result.[50] This difficulty will not be alleviated by the EU's accession to the ECHR as the latter 'shall not affect the Union's competences' (Article 6(2) TEU, Protocol n. 8 to the Lisbon Treaty).[51]

When EU fundamental rights bind States, they do so as EU law and hence benefit from EU law's general status in domestic law. This has actually been particularly useful for the status of ECHR rights within dualist countries such as the United Kingdom or Ireland where EU law has secured the immediate validity of those rights within domestic law *qua* EU law. EU fundamental rights bind states immediately as valid law. They are in principle rights of direct effect that can be invoked directly by individuals against national authorities. And they take priority over any international legal rule *qua* EU constitutional law[52] and over any national legal rule, even a constitutional one.[53]

There are exceptions worth mentioning in that last respect. Horizontal clauses at the end of the Charter clarify the subsidiary role of EU fundamental rights. Those rights are to be considered as minimal guarantees when competing with national and international guarantees binding Member States that are more protective. This also applies to corresponding ECHR rights which would be more protective than EU fundamental rights (Article 53 Charter). Of course, it is difficult to know in practice when an ECHR right is better protected by EU law than by the ECHR. The interpretation of the respective provisions by the two courts' case-law makes the assessment diffuse, but so do conflicts of rights as one of the rights in conflict is necessarily restricted in favour of the other.[54] Another important qualification stems from Article 52(3) Charter which states that when EU fundamental rights 'correspond' to ECHR rights, they should be interpreted as providing at least the same level of protection. Of course, EU fundamental rights may go further. It is difficult, however, to identify when an ECHR right 'corresponds' to an EU fundamental right or vice-versa. This is not only the case *per se* due to different codifications of the same rights, but also due to the two courts' respective interpretations of those rights.

---

50 This convergence between EU fundamental rights practice and the internal market can be noted in the recent case-law pertaining to trade unions in *Viking* (Case C-438/05 *International Transport Workers' Federation and Finnish Seamen's Union v Viking Line ABP and OÜ Viking Line Eesti* [2007] ECR I-10779) and *Laval* (Case C-341/05 *Laval un Partneri Ltd v Svenska Byggnadsarbetareförbundet, Svenska Byggnadsarbetareförbundets avdelning 1, Byggettan and Svenska Elektrikerförbundet* [2007] ECR I-11767).

51 This is a particularly controversial issue as it is difficult to see how the EU may abide by its ECHR duties without competences to adopt positive and negative measures to protect human rights. See e.g. De Schutter, *supra* n. 41, 545–6.

52 Case C-402/05P and C-415/05P *Kadi* [2008] ECR I-6351.

53 Case C-285/98 *Tanja Kreil v Bundesrepublik Deutschland* [2000] ECR I-69.

54 See on conflicts of rights, S Besson, *The Morality of Conflict* (Hart Publishing, Oxford 2005), Ch. 12, E Brems (ed.), *Conflicts between Fundamental Rights* (Intersentia, Antwerp 2008).

3.2.2. *The jurisdiction of the ECJ on fundamental rights*

The ECJ is the institution that first recognized EU fundamental rights *qua* general principles of EU law. EU fundamental rights therefore remain intrinsically jurisprudential in nature even though they have long been guaranteed through primary and secondary law also.

The jurisdiction of the ECJ is not purely fundamental rights-centred, however, and fundamental rights are only a small part of its overall jurisdiction. Even when the ECJ applies EU fundamental rights, the scope and kind of review it applies demonstrate a clear absence of specialisation in the field. Thus, contrary to the ECtHR which specialises in human rights, the ECJ *qua* generalist jurisdiction could go much further than it does with supranational judicial review in the field of human rights. It has the potential but uses it with great restraint.

It is important to start by realising that individuals may only file a human rights complaint to the ECJ against an EU institution and not against Member States, and even then through one single procedure only: the annulment procedure (Article 263 Treaty on the Functioning of the European Union (TFEU)). As a matter of fact, conditions for the individual complaint are very restrictive (Article 263(4) TFEU) thus limiting the number of cases overall.[55] Most human rights decisions taken by the ECJ are decisions against states, however, and decisions that are taken either through the infringement procedure against a state (started by another state or the Commission, maybe on the basis of an individual complaint to the Commission but rarely so, Article 258–9 TFEU) or through the preliminary ruling procedure (started by a national court over the interpretation or validity of EU law, Article 267 TFEU). One should emphasize, however, that it is rare for the ECJ to face a conflict between national law and EU fundamental rights only, most cases will be cases in which EU law (e.g. fundamental freedoms) conflicts with national human rights and hence also with EU fundamental rights, thus giving rise to a balance of interests.[56] This balance of interests is as a matter of fact often in the end even left to the Member States, which have a positive duty to interpret domestic law in conformity with EU fundamental rights.[57]

If the ECJ's jurisdiction in the field of fundamental rights is limited, so is the nature and scope of its review. Its approach to human rights is intentionally

---

55 This is regarded as compatible with Article 13 ECHR and Article 47 Charter given that the duty to ensure effective judicial remedies is a domestic duty in priority (Article 19(2) TEU). See the Explanations relating to the Charter and joined to the Lisbon Treaty.

56 It is important to note that in such cases, it is usually the fundamental right that is restricted in favour of the fundamental freedom (see e.g. Case C-112/00 *Eugen Schmidberger, Internationale Transporte und Planzüge v Republik Österreich* [2003] ECR I-5659, Case C-36/02 *Omega* [2004] ECR I-9609, Case C-438/05 *Viking Line* [2007] ECR I-10779).

57 See e.g. Case C-275/06 *Promusicae* [2008] ECR I-271, para. 65.

eclectic. Thus, the ECJ only addresses human rights issues when the parties to the case raise them and not *motu proprio* as a matter of constitutional order.[58] Contrary to a national constitutional court, the ECJ has no duty to interpret EU law, and even lesser so national law, in conformity with EU constitutional law and hence with EU fundamental rights. Further, even when the parties make a human rights argument, there is no obligation for the Court to settle the case on that basis if there is another ground to solve the issue at stake.[59] Interestingly, Advocate General Maduro has been arguing differently in his opinion in the *Kadi* case where he claims that the ECJ is the constitutional court of an autonomous legal order and therefore ought to review the legality of all acts of the Member States by reference to their compatibility with the EU Treaties *qua* constitutional charter.[60] At least in the *Kadi* case, Maduro was followed by the ECJ on this point.[61]

In all those cases, the ECJ applies the same kind of scrutiny to all violations of fundamental rights without distinction and has no human rights-specific kind of judicial reasoning and balancing. Interestingly, it has not (yet) transposed some of the practices it has developed in the context of the scrutiny of fundamental freedoms' restrictions to the field of fundamental rights.[62] An important question that scope precludes addressing here is whether the ECJ will have to adapt as a consequence of the EU's accession to the ECHR. Based on its new ECHR duties, it may indeed have to examine human rights issues *ex officio* and in a more systematic fashion, and even to specialise its legal reasoning in human rights cases.

Despite those limitations in its scope, the ECJ's jurisdiction on human rights is not strictly speaking subsidiary. It does not require the exhaustion of national remedies. Nor does the Court have more limited discretion and scrutiny on those questions than it would on others. The proportionality test it uses is the same, for instance, and it has no particular duties to respect States' margin of appreciation.

All the same, the lack of EU human rights competence combined with the political nature of human rights, but also the fact that the ECJ *qua* supranational court is ill-equipped to assess facts and balance rights and decides consensually

58 See Case C-301/06 *Ireland v. Parliament and Council* [2009] ECR I-593, para. 57.

59 See Case C-376/98 *Germany v. Parliament and Council* [2000] ECR I-8419. See also Case C-73/07 *Tietosuojavaltuutettu v Satakunnan Markkinapörssi Oy and Satamedia Oy* [2008] ECR I-9831.

60 Case C-402/05P and C-415/05P *Kadi* [2008] ECR I-6351.

61 Contrast the *Kadi* case with Case C-317/04 & 318/04 *Parliament v Council* [2006] ECR I–2457.

62 It suffices here to think of the different kinds of proportionality tests or of the theory of horizontal effect used by the ECJ in the context of fundamental freedoms.

without public majorities and open dissenting opinions of judges, have led to the kind of judicial restraint discussed before. The case-law indicates, for instance, that EU fundamental rights are regarded as minimal guarantees, thus allowing for higher protection by national or international human rights in each Member State (Article 53 Charter). This approach is exemplified by ECJ's decisions such as *Omega* or, most recently, *Arcelor*.[63] Of course, there are also limitations to this minimalist approach as exemplified in the *Michaniki* case: not all human rights arguments can justify a breach of the principle of the primacy of EU law.[64] The difficult question then is how to determine when this is the case.[65]

3.2.3. The effects of an ECJ's judgement in domestic law

To understand what the effects of ECJ judgements pertaining to human rights are within domestic law, it is useful to distinguish the consequences of their binding nature in national law, on the one hand, from the mechanisms available for the enforcement of ECJ judgements, on the other.

With respect to the binding nature of the Court's decision, first of all, its review's supranational nature has always been evident.

The ECJ's judgements are binding and are part of the sources of EU law. Fundamental rights decisions of the ECJ benefit from the same binding nature as other ECJ judgements. Those judgements are immediately valid in domestic law and, most importantly, benefit from the primacy of EU law over national law. This means that ECJ decisions *qua* EU law generate a duty to leave contrary national law unapplied, and even eventually to its amendment. This implies, in other words, an invalidating effect of ECJ judgements on human rights, even if it is only indirectly through the action of domestic authorities themselves.

Of course, the specific effects of ECJ judgements in domestic law will depend on the judicial procedure used to issue that decision. Annulment judgements lead to

---

63 Case C-36/02 *Omega* [2004] ECR I-9609, Case C-127/07 *Arcelor Atlantique et Lorraine and Others* [2008] ECR I-9895.

64 This is exemplified in the discussion by AG Maduro in *Michaniki* (Case C-213/07 *Michaniki AE v Ethniko Symvoulio Radiotileorasis and Ypourgos Epikrateias* [2008] ECR I-9999) and *Arcelor* (Case C-127/07 *Arcelor Atlantique et Lorraine and Others* [2008] ECR I-9895), without there being a clear test or criterion, however.

65 This shows that the minimal v. maximal protection debate is still quite pertinent in the EU albeit in a new context, if the problem originally was the lack of human rights protection in the EU, the problem has now become the breadth of EU human rights protection. See e.g. the exchange between LFM Besselink, 'Entrapped by the maximum standard: on fundamental rights, pluralism and subsidiarity in the European Union' (1998) 35 *Common Market Law Review* 629, and JHH Weiler, 'Fundamental Rights and Fundamental Boundaries: on the Conflict of Standards and Values in the Protection of Human Rights in the European Legal Space' in *The Constitution of Europe* (Cambridge University Press: Cambridge, 1999), 102.

the annulment of EU legal acts deemed contrary to EU law. Decisions pertaining to the validity of national law cannot be taken through the annulment procedure, however, but through the infringement procedure. Infringement decisions are binding, but in a declaratory way, and it is up to national authorities to enforce them. Finally, preliminary rulings bind national courts which have to settle the concrete case, but they bind all national authorities as well and sometimes *ex tunc*. Strictly speaking, therefore, the ECJ's human rights review is weak in that ECJ decisions cannot directly invalidate national law or decisions, or require the re-opening of a national procedure.

This is only a *prima facie* conclusion, however. The preliminary ruling procedure enables the ECJ to play a central role in national adjudication. In the majority of ECJ cases on human rights, i.e. in preliminary rulings, the cooperation between the ECJ and national courts and the fact that the latter retain the competence to decide in the concrete case has helped improve the enforcement rate of ECJ decisions. True, the preliminary ruling procedure has become less and less horizontal and more and more vertical overall and hence supranational in recent times: the national courts have little discretion about the cases they have to submit to the ECJ and about the ways in which they ought to implement them in practice. Furthermore, as indicated before, infringement decisions of the ECJ benefit from the primacy of EU law and this secures sufficient pressure to lead to the indirect annulment of national law or decisions contrary to the judgement.

If one refers, secondly, to the mechanisms available for the enforcement of the ECJ's judgements, the supranational nature of the judicial review exercised by the Court is just as evident. It is important to distinguish, however, between the European Commission and the Court itself.

The Commission reviews the application of infringement judgements and may even launch a further infringement procedure against a State that does not apply such a judgement. Accordingly, a new infringement decision may be released by the ECJ itself (Article 260 TFEU). This could actually apply, in principle, to all ECJ judgements: the non-implementation of any judgement by the Court can give rise to an infringement procedure. Furthermore, there is always the possibility of an action in liability against the State under domestic law but based on EU law principles:[66] a state whose legislative, executive or judicial authorities do not comply with an ECJ decision may be deemed responsible and be condemned to pay damages. As a result, the enforcement of ECJ decisions can

---

66 Joined cases C-6/90 and C-9/90 *Andrea Francovich and Danila Bonifaci and others v Italian Republic* [1991] ECR I-5357, Joined cases C-46/93 and C-48/93 *Brasserie du Pêcheur SA v Bundesrepublik Deutschland and The Queen v Secretary of State for Transport, ex parte: Factortame Ltd and others* [1996] ECR I-1029, Case C-224/01 *Gerhard Köbler v Republik Österreich* [2003] ECR I-10239.

itself be judicial (whether by the ECJ or by national courts) and is not left to interstate cooperation only. This is further evidence, if needed, of the supranational nature of adjudication by the ECJ in the human rights context.

3.3. EUROPEAN SUPRANATIONAL JUDICIAL REVIEW COMPARED

The time has come to contrast and compare the characteristics of supranational judicial review exercised by the two European courts in the human rights context. The result of this comparison will provide the basis for a democratic assessment in the third part of this chapter.

As a preliminary remark, it is important to emphasise that the two courts' jurisdictions have reinforced each other. They have been mutually empowered *vis-à-vis* national institutions through their cooperation and this applies to their respective relations to domestic courts or political authorities.[67] It is because the ECJ has constantly reinforced its jurisdiction that the ECtHR was able to become bolder in the exercise of its own review powers. And in return, it is because EU Member States are so closely scrutinised by the ECtHR in the human rights context that the ECJ has had to strengthen its own control mechanisms in the human rights context. As a result, it is difficult to compare them as completely separate tribunals exercising different and unconnected forms of judicial review.

Clearly, especially when compared with other international human rights courts or bodies, the two European courts qualify as supranational courts, exercising supranational judicial review in the field of human rights. Their jurisdiction is compulsory, their decisions are binding within domestic legal orders *vis-à-vis* all domestic institutions, and they may be invoked directly by individuals.

Of course, when one looks more closely, the ECJ was always a supranational court exercising supranational judicial review in a supranational organisation, whereas the ECtHR started as an international court applying an international Convention in the framework of an international organisation. It is only gradually that the latter has turned into a supranational court both through the supranational status of ECHR rights and the strengthening of its judicial review powers. At the same time, however, individual applications for violations of human rights by states have always been at the core of the ECtHR's jurisdiction,

[67] See Helfer/Slaughter, *supra* n. 11 on this mutual emulation and overall effect. See also L Scheeck., 'The relationship between the European Courts and Integration through Human Rights' (2005) *Max-Planck-Institut für ausländisches öffentliches Recht und Völkerrecht*, available at: www.zaoerv.de, de Witte in this volume.

whereas the ECJ has not always been competent in the human rights field. Even nowadays, it cannot receive individual applications against states and only examines human rights violations by states in the context of preliminary rulings or infringement procedures. Even when it is against EU institutions that individual applications are filed, the conditions for an individual to open an annulment procedure are very strict thus leaving most human rights-based procedures against EU institutions to other applicants than individuals. As a result, there are very few direct human rights cases before the ECJ – although the ECJ is under increasing albeit indirect fundamental rights pressure these days.[68] In fact, it is the place of human rights in the EU legal order that is in question, in contrast to a European Convention entirely dedicated to the protection of human rights: EU fundamental rights developed negatively against the EU to protect national democracies against EU law,[69] whereas the ECHR was adopted to protect national democracies against themselves.

In what follows, I would like to compare the ECJ and the ECtHR with respect to three features of supranational judicial review: the courts' jurisdiction, their scope of review and, finally, the effects of their judgements.

In terms of jurisdiction, first of all, both courts apply the same set of human rights to the same core States, across the board for the ECtHR and in the field of application of or derogation to EU law for the ECJ. The jurisdiction of the ECJ is more limited than that of the ECtHR as a result, but when they overlap, they are largely similar through the evolution of both courts' jurisdiction. First of all, ECHR rights are a sub-group of the rights applicable by the ECJ, albeit the most significant one. Those rights bind states as national human rights would, whereas EU fundamental rights benefit from the status of EU law within domestic legal orders. The supranational status of ECHR rights has been gradually developed through the case-law and state practice. They are minimal guarantees and may be subsided by stronger national rights for ECHR rights, and by stronger national and ECHR rights for EU fundamental rights. Second, not all 47 States submitted to the ECtHR belong to the 27 Member States of the ECJ, but the 27 EU Member States are submitted to both courts' review. Finally, the ECtHR can review the respect of human rights in all areas of national law including those corresponding to EU competences,[70] whereas the ECJ only has jurisdiction in the scope of

---

68 One may mention the development of horizontal effects of fundamental rights, transnational discrepancies in the protection of fundamental rights and the constant restriction of the scope of purely internal situations to which EU fundamental rights do not apply.

69 Even when fundamental rights are said to bind Member States, it is only in the scope of application or derogation to EU law, and primarily to ensure a uniform application of EU law across all Member States and therefore to protect national democracies not so much against themselves, but against others in the EU.

70 See ECtHR, *Bosphorus v Ireland* (n. 45036/98) EHRR 2005-VI.

application of or derogation to EU law. It is important to note that certain political questions are excluded from the scope of jurisdiction of the ECtHR, but (almost) no longer of the ECJ (Articles 275–6 TFEU).

The scope of review, secondly, is similar in both courts. It was not always like that, but with time the ECtHR has gained a scope of review that is less subsidiary, and for instance, its application of the consensus principle and of the margin of appreciation is elastic. By contrast, the ECJ's review was never limited by a consensus or respect for the margin of appreciation of states. True, contrary to the ECtHR's, the ECJ's review is not concrete and individual, as it can only examine human rights violations in preliminary ruling and infringement procedures. However, the ECJ need not wait for the exhaustion of national remedies to be seized of a case, whereas the ECtHR's review remains clearly subsidiary in that respect. Of course, one may argue that since most human rights cases before the ECJ come through the preliminary ruling procedure, the relationship to national courts is as central before the ECJ as before the ECtHR. The recent verticalisation of the preliminary ruling procedure on the part of the ECJ, however, confirms the increasing supranational nature of the review that is exercised in that context as well.

As to the effects of their decisions, finally, both courts exercise weak judicial review in theory: their decisions are binding, but cannot lead to the invalidation of domestic law or decisions. In practice, however, the place of the ECJ in national procedures through preliminary rulings and the individual and general measures ordered by the ECtHR are close to constituting evidence of a strong form of judicial review. The same may be said about the re-opening of national procedures as a result of the primacy of decisions of the ECJ, and of the recent case-law pertaining to the revision of national decisions following the ECtHR's case-law. The monitoring of the enforcement of their decisions differs, however: while it remains very political for the ECtHR – with a few exceptions as confirmed by the increasing role of the ECtHR in the monitoring of its decisions – it is clearly judicial for the ECJ (through an infringement procedure).

In conclusion, one cannot but note the following paradox: the ECJ's supranational strong judicial review is used nowadays in the field of human rights, but only in a belated and bridled fashion and not to its maximal potential, whereas the ECtHR's international judicial review has developed and emancipated in the course of fifty years into strong supranational judicial review, solely focused on human rights and that goes beyond its strictly legal jurisdiction.

This seeming paradox is no longer one when the two courts are placed back into their respective political and institutional context: that of a supranational organisation like the EU for the ECJ (with no human rights competence) and of an international convention like the ECHR and the Council of Europe (solely dedicated to human rights) for the ECtHR. The justification of human rights (notably by reference to democracy), and the democratic legitimacy of judicial review in those two contexts is bound to be entirely different. To understand why, I will, first, discuss the democratic legitimacy of supranational judicial review in general and provide, on that basis, a democratic assessment of the two courts' exercise of judicial review, before coming back to the relationship between them in the final section.

4. THE DEMOCRATIC LEGITIMACY OF SUPRANATIONAL JUDICIAL REVIEW

4.1. THE DEMOCRATIC LEGITIMACY OF JUDICIAL REVIEW *TOUT COURT*

As mentioned before, the question of the democratic legitimacy of (strong) judicial review is a well-known topic in legal and political philosophy. Scope precludes summarising the state of the debate.[71] I will restrict myself to a few reminders as this will shed some light onto my discussion of the legitimacy of *supranational* judicial review.

---

71 See e.g. the arguments presented by e.g.: R Dworkin, *Freedom's Law: The Moral Reading of the American Constitution* (Harvard University Press, Cambridge Mass. 1996), J Elster, *Ulysses and the Sirens, Studies in rationality and irrationality* (Cambridge University Press, Cambridge 1984), J Elster, 'Introduction' in J Elster / R Slagstad (eds), *Constitutionalism and Democracy* (Cambridge University Press, Cambridge 1988), J Elster, 'Limiting majority rule: alternatives to judicial review in the revolutionary epoch' in E Smith (ed), *Constitutional Justice under old Constitutions* (Kluwer, The Hague 1995), J Elster, *Ulysses Unbound* (Cambridge University Press, Cambridge 2000), JH Ely, *Democracy and Distrust* (Harvard University Press, Cambridge Mass. 1980), F Michelman, 'Foreword: traces of self government' (1986) 100 *Harvard Law Review* 4, F Michelman, 'Law's Republic' (1988) 97 *Yale Law Journal* 1493, J Habermas, *Between Facts and Norms* (MIT Press, Boston 1998), S Freeman, 'Constitutional Democracy and the Legitimacy of Judicial Review' (1990) 9 *Law and Philosophy* 327 and the critiques put forward by e.g.: J Waldron, 'Freeman's Defense of Judicial Review' (1994) 13 *Law and Philosophy* 27, J Waldron, *Law and Disagreement* (Oxford University Press, Oxford 1999), Ch. 12 and 13, J Waldron, 'Judicial review and republican government' in C Wolfe (ed.), *That Eminent Tribunal* (Princeton University Press, Princeton 2004), J Waldron, 'The core of the case against judicial review' (2006) *Yale Law Review* 1346, M Tushnet, *Taking the Constitution away from the Courts* (Princeton University Press, Princeton 2000), R Bellamy, 'Constitutive Citizenship versus Constitutional Rights: Republican Reflections on the EU Charter and the Human Rights Act' in T Campbell / KD Ewing / A Tomkins (eds), *Skeptical Essays on Human Rights* (Oxford University Press, Oxford 2001), 15–40, R Bellamy, *Political Constitutionalism: A Republican Defence of the Constitutionality of Democracy* (Cambridge University Press, Cambridge 2007), R Bellamy, 'The Democratic Constitution: Why Europeans should avoid American Style Constitutional Judicial Review' (2008) 7 *European Political Science* 4–8, 9–20.

Arguments for the legitimacy of judicial review abound. For obvious reasons, the most interesting ones, however, are not those based purely on legitimacy, but those based on democratic legitimacy itself.[72] In a nutshell, democracy is the political regime in which all those whose fundamental interests are directly affected by a decision ought to be included among those deciding. Democratic arguments for judicial review often rely on a democratic precommitment argument that justifies the limitations imposed on democracy by reference to some kind of self-commitment, just as one may precommit oneself not to drive when having drunk by handing over one's car keys to a friend, the people in a democracy are claimed to have handed over to judges the right to adjudicate on certain fundamental values on which they disagree and may decide wrongly. On such an approach, judges are part of the democratic process and their function is a contribution to democracy.[73]

More specifically, there are three democracy-based arguments in favour of judicial review, and especially a constitution-based review of democratic legislation in a constitutional democracy.[74]

The first one, widespread in US constitutional theory,[75] pertains to the tyranny of the majority or counter-majoritarian argument and the need to protect the minority against the majority. Judicial review controls the majority's decisions when they threaten the minority. The second argument pertains to the conceptual precedence of human rights and the fact that democracy cannot exist without human rights guarantees and hence without their judicial protection outside of the political process. Judicial review protects the pre-conditions of democracy against democracy itself. The final argument is that of expertise or information. Judges often know better or more at least than parliamentarians, and their

72 See e.g. Harel, A, 'Rights-based Judicial Review: A Democratic Justification', (2003) 22 *Law and Philosophy* 247, Alexander, L, 'Is Judicial Review Democratic? A Comment on Harel', (2003) 22 *Law and Philosophy* 277.

73 See e.g. Habermas, *supra* n. 71, Elster, *supra* n. 71. See for a discussion, Waldron 1999, *supra* n. 71, Besson, *supra* n. 54.

74 Theoretically, the democratic legitimacy of judicial review may be distinguished from that of the constitutional entrenchment of human rights. In practice, however, the more entrenched rights are, the more constrained the legislature is and the more powerful the judiciary becomes when it has judicial review.

75 See the excellent discussion of the American and European models of judicial review by Stone Sweet, *supra* n. 6. Interestingly, judicial review where it exists at the domestic level in Europe came later than supranational judicial review in the 1950s and 1960s and was mostly based on the international example. It is the case, for instance, in Spain or in Germany. It would take to long to discuss the historical connections between the two and how a reconsideration of the democratic legitimacy of supranational judicial review of the kind I am proposing would affect national judicial review where it exists in Europe. It is important to stress, however, that the original connection between supranational judicial review and national democracy may explain why post-1950 national judicial review in Europe may not be considered as as problematic from a democratic point of view as pre-1950 judicial review in Europe and the US.

expertise can enhance or compensate the lack of epistemic qualities of the democratic process. Others stress judges' deliberative quality and hence their contribution to contestation and hence responsiveness that is a central value in a democracy. Both arguments can be used to emphasize the contribution of judicial review to the deliberative quality of judicial debates themselves or, more broadly, of political debates outside the judicial arena.[76]

Objections to those arguments are just as well-known. Generally, the democratic precommitment model is regarded as flawed for different reasons: one may mention the difficulty of the transposition of the model of individual precommitment to a collective subject like a people, the differences between individual incapacity and political akrasia, the epistemic difference between the two situations, the priority of the judgement of a few judges over the deliberation of the many, or disagreements among judges themselves and the use of majority voting between them.[77]

Regarding the three specific arguments mentioned before, various objections may be put forward, albeit in reverse order. First of all, the existence of widespread and persistent reasonable disagreement about issues of justice and morality, even among judges, makes it difficult to assess and compare the epistemic quality of institutions. Further, information may be more diversified among and accessible to parliamentarians than it is to members of the judiciary. Further, the very circumstances of politics also make it important to respect and trust the ability of each of us collectively. In fact, the human rights argument requires giving priority to the judgement of the many over that of the few, since the contrary would imply distrusting the very abilities human rights aim at protecting and furthermore in the very exercise of devising the content of our own mutual rights. Secondly, co-originality may be contested as being never quite granted, in which case one may venture that equality will most probably be the primary or reference value in the mutual relationship between human rights and democracy, thus undermining the legitimacy of judicial review. Finally, political equality justifies majority rule and provided majorities change and people take turn in being in the majority, majority rule protects minority rights in a more egalitarian way.[78]

True, these objections imply guaranteeing (possibly through constitutional entrenchment) a minimal protection of human rights and hence potentially organising a weak judicial review of those rights, without which there could not be a functioning democracy. However, this means in turn that those very rights

---

76 See e.g. Habermas, *supra* n. 71, Michelman, *supra* n. 71, Follesdal 2009, *supra* n. 11, 604–5.

77 See Waldron 1999, *supra* n. 71, Besson, *supra* n. 54.

78 See Waldron 1999, *supra* n. 71, Besson, *supra* n. 54.

are recognised democratically and guaranteed so as to allow (and even trigger) further deliberation in practice. It also implies that judges exercising weak judicial review are democratically elected and accountable. Finally, their exercise of review should not lead to striking down legislation but merely to request new deliberation and decisions on a given question, thus enhancing responsiveness and debate. The point of the present democratic assessment of judicial review is not therefore to reject the latter blankly in a sterile 'either-or' opposition, but to make sure (weak) judicial review is organised so as to be democratically accountable and that the chain of responsiveness between all democratic institutions (including the judiciary) is in place.

4.2. THE DEMOCRATIC LEGITIMACY OF JUDICIAL REVIEW IN THE SUPRANATIONAL CONTEXT

4.2.1. Reassessing the issue

Interestingly, the question of the democratic legitimacy of supranational judicial review has not been addressed extensively yet, at least from a philosophical perspective.[79] This is quite surprising, at least *prima facie*. Questions pertaining to the democratic legitimacy of international institutions and international law have indeed become pervasive. Paradoxically, however, the more intrusive supranational human rights review becomes in the national sphere of sovereignty and hence the more impact it potentially has on domestic democracy, the more effective[80] and hence the more successful it is deemed to be. Its legitimacy is barely ever mentioned or only to stress that it is precisely not in contention.[81]

A first reason for this state of affairs may be that supranational adjudication stems originally from an international agreement and that international law has only recently started to be regarded seriously as law by legal theorists and as an object of moral judgement by political philosophers. Even when international law is regarded as law and its legitimacy is discussed, consent is usually put forward as the major justification for international law's authority. However,

79 See, however, Follesdal 2008 and 2007, *supra* n. 11, Letsas, *supra* n. 9.

80 See the seminal paper by Helfer/Slaughter, *supra* n. 11 referring to the two European courts as paradigms of 'effective supranational adjudication'.

81 See e.g. Gardbaum, *supra* n. 27. This may explain why those who may be cautious about strong judicial review in the national context are ready to endorse it in the supranational context and when asked for justifications, are ready to use a Dworkinian theory of adjudication they would not apply to national circumstances. It is not a surprise, for instance, that the first theory of supranational human rights adjudication at the ECtHR stems from a Dworkinian legal theorist (Letsas, *supra* n. 9).

consent is neither a sufficient nor a necessary condition of legitimacy.[82] Nor is it correct to identify consent with democracy and democratic legitimacy.[83]

Another, more serious reason lies in the largely uncontested legitimacy of international human rights standards. No one would dare contest their justification as readily as one does contest other international law norms' legitimacy. And even if they did, they would not readily submit that justification to the same criteria as other norms of international law – and especially not to consent, but not necessarily to democracy either. This is even more so as international human rights historically found part of their justification in the reinforcement of national democracies. While democracy did not fare that well as a binding international principle, human rights were much more consensual and subsumed other principles such as democracy in particular.[84] Since international human rights and their adjudication mechanisms were regarded as intrinsically connected from the beginning in Europe, it is difficult to contest the legitimacy of supranational human rights adjudication, even on democratic grounds.

As I have argued elsewhere, however, the democratic legitimacy of international human rights is an important albeit complex question that cannot simply be swept away because it cannot be addressed along the same lines as that of other international law norms. True, it calls for a more careful answer given the intricate and mutual relationship between human rights and democracy within any given polity, and the interesting addition of an international dimension in either human rights law or in democratic decision-making.[85] Furthermore, there is no necessary conceptual link between the legitimacy of international human rights and that of supranational human rights judicial review. While it is true that human rights adjudication contributes to the interpretation of human rights and hence, if it is legitimate, to their legitimacy, the reverse is not necessarily the case. International human rights are indeterminate about the best ways of protecting them institutionally. This is the case in domestic law, but even more so in international law given the difference in nature between international and

---

82 See A Buchanan, *Justice, Legitimacy, and Self-Determination: Moral Foundations for International Law* (Oxford University Press, Oxford 2004), S Besson, 'The Authority of International Law – Lifting the State Veil' (2009) 31:3 *Sydney Law Review* 343–80.

83 See Buchanan, *supra* n. 82 , Besson, *supra* n. 82.

84 See Letsas, *supra* n. 9, Moravcsik, *supra* n. 8. Interestingly, the ECHR mentions the notion of 'democratic society' among the conditions set for the restriction to certain rights under the Convention. The Convention thus has its own in-built (human rights-based) definition of what a democratic society is and when that society ought to restrict human rights to protect itself.

85 See Besson, *supra* n. 14, S Besson, 'The Right to Have Rights – From Human Rights to Citizens' Rights and Back' in M Goldoni / C McCorkindale (eds), *Arendt and Legal Theory* (Hart Publishing, Oxford 2011), forthcoming.

domestic human rights and the latter's necessary contextualisation in domestic law and through domestic institutions. Finally, times and circumstances have changed in Europe, national democracies have developed and consolidated, including through national human rights catalogues and judicial institutions of their own and no longer need the kind of supranational law and/or judicial review they put in place in 1945 or at least not necessarily in the same way.[86]

As a result, it is possible, I would like to argue, to isolate the question of the democratic legitimacy of supranational human rights adjudication from that of the legitimacy of international human rights themselves. The difficulty is double, however: does supranational judicial review really raise the same questions as national judicial review in terms of democracy? And how about the answers: are they radically different?

4.2.2. Different questions

Interestingly, the questions raised by supranational judicial review are not entirely the same as the ones discussed before. The concepts of democracy, human rights and judicial review need to be re-qualified in this new context.

First of all, the kind of democracy we are talking about needs to be re-qualified across legal orders in a complex political community such as the European Union. It is unclear indeed which is the polity whose democratic institutions are concerned by the exercise of supranational judicial review and which institutions in that polity are the relevant ones.

On the one hand, democracy needs to be re-qualified *at the European level*. The concern is not only the impact of judicial decisions on national legislative and executive powers, but also on European legislative and executive ones, that is, in other words, on the separation of powers (even of a *sui generis* kind[87]) at the European level. It suffices in this respect to refer to the conflicts between the European Parliament or the European Commission and the ECJ, or between the Council of Europe's Committee of Ministers and the ECtHR, in the context of the execution of the Court's judgements, to understand what is at stake. Furthermore, it is probably impossible and undesirable to separate the different

86 One may even argue that European supranational judicial review was only meant as an example, and as a temporary replacement for what would have to be done eventually at the domestic level. See Stone Sweet, *supra* n. 6 on the relationship between supranational and national judicial review in Europe.

87 The institutional balance principle in the EU may be equated with a *sui generis* form of separation of powers that is both horizontal and vertical. Of course, the specificities of the separation of powers in the EU are a reason for caution in an institution-sensitive discussion of judicial review.

levels of democratic representation given the disaggregation of legislative functions and the re-aggregation of those functions that has occurred at different levels in Europe. Thus, double or even triple forms of democratic representation at the European level (through direct representatives of EU citizens, through representatives of national parliaments, and through governmental representatives of States) make the chain of democratic legitimacy more complex and hence more difficult to unpack in terms of the precise democratic impact of supranational judicial review. A further layer of complexity may be added if non-judicial European institutions side with one of the European courts in its exercise of judicial review of national legislation.

On the other hand, democracy also needs to be re-qualified *at the national level.* National democracy is not only affected in its legislative dimensions, but is impacted as a whole *qua* national sovereignty. This explains the strong national supremacy reactions to supranational human rights adjudication in recent times, both by national executives and even by judicial bodies.[88] Furthermore, supranational judicial review affects the overall institutional balance in a given state. Indeed, not all national institutions are losing equally in democratic power from supranational judicial review. Thus, supranational judicial review affects the national separation of powers. On the one hand, the judiciary in certain European States has been reinforced by the development of the ECtHR's power of review.[89] This is also a well-known reality in the EU where national judges have been empowered by European integration and their cooperation with the ECJ.[90] It is more and more difficult therefore to separate the activity of supranational judges from that of national judges. Of course, the possibility of interjudicial dialogue may actually influence supranational case-law, thus alleviating the impact of supranational judicial review on national democracy. The reverse may also be true: the national legislature may be reinforced by supranational judicial review and the triggering of political remedies at national level. The ECtHR's pilot cases, for instance, and their structural measures have reinforced the position of the Parliament in Poland.[91] In short, therefore, the nature of national democracy itself is evolving as a result not only of post-national law-making processes, but also of supranational judicial review. And sometimes even in opposite directions, which makes the assessment more difficult.

---

88 See e.g. BVerfG, B. v. 14.10.2004 (2 BvR 1481/04 – *Görgülü*), BVerfGE 111, 307 (328).

89 Many European States that had no system of constitutional review of legislation have introduced one after their accession to the EU (e.g. Finland).

90 This has been famously thematized by Weiler, *supra* n. 11.

91 See e.g. the discussion in W Sadurski, 'Partnering with Strasbourg: Constitutionalization of the European Court of Human Rights, the Accession of Central and East European States to the Council of Europe, and the Idea of Pilot Judgments' (2009) 9:3 *Human Rights Law Review* 397–453.

A second qualification is in order: the human rights that constitute the basis of supranational judicial review are a complex set of European human rights applicable across legal orders in the European Union. It is unclear indeed whose human rights are the rights that are applied through judicial review of national laws and what is their relationship to the democratic polity at stake. What remains uncertain, more specifically, is whether these guarantees are entrenched against the democratic will and in what way that entrenchment has been made democratically legitimate.

There is *per se* no entrenchment of European human rights in European law. Of course, some of those rights can be said to have a higher material rank among the norms of European law due to their *jus cogens* nature (e.g. Articles 2, 3, 4 and 7 ECHR based on Article 15 ECHR) or to their nature as general international law norms.[92] However, those categories and the material hierarchies that follow are contested in international law.[93] This triggers difficult questions pertaining to the relation between supranational human rights regimes and other *prima facie* equivalent norms or regimes of international law, such as State or international organisations' immunities, State responsibility, etc.[94] European human rights do not (yet) constitute, in other words, the Constitution of the European legal order.[95] Similar normative conflicts may arise between EU fundamental rights that are deemed constitutional norms of EU law[96] and other norms of EU primary law, as it is often the case between EU fundamental rights and fundamental freedoms.

---

92 See e.g. B Simma / P Alston, 'The Sources of Human Rights Law: Custom, Jus Cogens and General Principles' (1988–1989) 12 *Australian Year Book of International Law* 82 on the sources of international human rights.

93 Of course, this does not apply within the case-law of the ECtHR, as exemplified by the decisions *Waite and Kennedy* (*Waite and Kennedy v Germany* (n. 26083/94) EHRR 1999-I) or *Bosphorus* (ECtHR, *Bosphorus v Ireland* (n. 45036/98) EHRR 2005-VI) and the equivalence test imposed on conflicting international legal regimes such as the law of international organizations. That case-law is not entirely consistent, however, as demonstrated by the *Behrami* case with respect to binding UN law (ECtHR, *Behrami v France* (n. 71412/01, 78166/01) (2007) 45 EHRR SE 10). In this respect, it will be interesting to see what the ECtHR decides in the *Nada v Switzerland* case that is currently pending before it (n. 10593/08). In that case, indeed, the ECtHR is likely to follow its *Bosphorus* presumption and hence abide by the ECJ's *Kadi* decision while at the same time innovating by applying the *Bosphorus* test to UN law and no longer only to EU law. On the potential scenarios, see Besson, *supra* n. 42, A Ciampi, 'The Potentially Competing Jurisdiction of the ECJ and the ECtHR' (2009) 28 *Yearbook of European Law* 601–9.

94 See e.g. *Al-Adsani v The United Kingdom* (n. 35763/97) EHRR 2001-XI, *Markovic and Others v Italy* (n. 1398/03) Judgment of 14 December 2006, selected for publication.

95 Contra: Gardbaum, *supra* n. 27.

96 See Case C-402/05P and C-415/05P *Kadi* [2008] ECR I-6351. The contours of EU constitutional primary law remain to be determined, however. See the discussion in Besson, *supra* n. 42.

Of course, once contextualised or vernacularised at the national level as should be the case,[97] European human rights are usually transformed, or at least identified with constitutional human rights norms – with or without incorporation.[98] This raises the whole democratic question anew from within the national constitutional order. Supranational judicial review is used to enforce the equivalent of a domestic set of human rights on the national political process, albeit from the outside. This contributes to the entrenchment of those rights within the domestic legal order without, however, going through the democratic channels of constitutional entrenchment and thus circumventing the democratic precommitment argument – at least at the domestic level.[99] The same may be said about EU fundamental rights that stem from ECHR rights and national constitutional traditions as those rights benefit from the primacy of EU law over all national legislation, including national constitutional law. They become as a result a source of supraconstitutional rights whose respect can be reviewed from the outside.

This reality also creates a further complexity, however: supranational human rights judicial review sometimes creates hierarchies among supranational and constitutional human rights within national law. In doing so, supranational judicial review interrupts the sensitive balance that has been attained in the domestic legal order between entrenched constitutional human rights and democracy. This has been the case in certain countries, like Switzerland, where constitutional review is weak, but where ECHR rights and supranational review by the ECtHR have introduced unprecedented judicial review at the domestic level as the Swiss Federal Court exercises strong conventional review of domestic legislation. The reverse can also be true, however, as exemplified by Ireland where ECHR rights are not granted the same status as national constitutional rights in constitutional review.[100]

Finally, with respect to the concept of judicial review itself, a few qualifications are needed. There is indeed more than just one supranational court at stake in Europe. It is difficult therefore to single out the institution whose review is under democratic scrutiny.

One may draw at this stage from the flourishing literature that pertains to inter-judicial relations in Europe.[101] On the one hand, supranational courts are not

97 See S Besson, 'Human Rights – Moral, Political, … or Legal? First Steps in a Legal Theory of Human Rights' in T Childress (ed.), *The Role of Ethics in International Law* (Cambridge University Press, Cambridge 2011) forthcoming.

98 See Gardbaum, *supra* n. 27 , Letsas, *supra* n. 9.

99 See my discussion of the democratic qualities of the British and Irish incorporations of the ECHR, especially when compared with Switzerland: Besson, *supra* n. 27.

100 See Besson, *supra* n. 27.

101 See e.g. Maduro, *supra* n. 3, Benvenisti, *supra* n. 11.

one of a kind, thus making the picture more complex. Furthermore, special kinds of strong judicial review exercised by national courts when they apply supranational human rights as opposed to domestic human rights should not be underestimated; supranational judicial review is not only exercised by supranational courts as a result. Of course, national courts are usually the ones in direct contact with supranational courts and the ones distilling their influence in domestic law. It is the case for the ECtHR given the necessary exhaustion of local remedies and for the ECJ in the context of preliminary rulings. This explains the emphasis on judicial dialogue on the part of both the ECJ and the ECtHR. While judicial dialogue with national courts may be seen as a way to alleviate the democratic impact of supranational judicial review, it may also be seen as having a multiplying effect through the convergence of the two European courts on a given issue.

On the other hand, the proliferation of international but also of supranational judicial entities in Europe makes it difficult to isolate one tribunal in particular. When their scopes of jurisdiction overlap, the ECJ and the ECtHR tend in most cases to collaborate and organize their respective jurisdictions along the lines of a complex principle of minimal equivalence (at least from the perspective of the ECtHR).[102] The coordinated exercise of supranational jurisdictions adds a layer of complexity to the appreciation of their democratic impact at the national level. It suffices to think of the cases in which the two Courts' interpretations of the same ECHR rights have diverged and of the quandaries thus created for Contracting States.[103] But the reverse can also be true: a discrepancy between national law and two similar European judicial decisions may reinforce the impact of supranational judicial review on domestic law, triggering the democratic question anew. With the EU's accession to the ECHR, the two courts should coordinate and converge even more on human rights matters, thus reinforcing that difficulty.

102 For a survey of the approaches of each court *vis-à-vis* the other one and their convergence or divergence, especially following the *Bosphorus* case (ECtHR, *Bosphorus v Ireland* (n. 45036/98) EHRR 2005-VI), see de Witte in this volume, and Spielmann in this volume. See also Scheeck, *supra* n. 67, S Douglas-Scott, 'A Tale of Two Courts: Luxembourg, Strasbourg and the Growing European Human Rights Acquis' (2006) 43:3 *Common Market Law Review* 629, Rosas, *supra* n. 2 , G Harpaz, 'The ECJ and its Relations with the ECtHR' (2009) *Common Market Law Review* 105, J Callewaert., 'The European Convention on Human Rights and European Union Law: A Long Way to Harmony' (2009) 6 *European Human Rights Law Review* 768.

103 This has been the case either in terms of diverging interpretations of the same rights in different contexts or in terms of a different balancing of interests or legal qualification of the facts (see e.g. Case C-17/98 *Emesa Sugar* [2000] ECR I-665, or *Koua Poirrez v France* (n. 40892/98) EHRR 2003-X).

4.2.3. *Different answers*

In view of those new qualifications of the questions, the answers are also bound to differ from those put forward at the domestic level. Interestingly, objections to supranational judicial review are even stronger than at the national level, precisely by virtue of some of the inherently democratic qualities of domestic (weak) judicial review, at least in functioning constitutional democracies.

First of all, it is clearly more difficult to put forward a democratic precommitment argument in favour of supranational human rights catalogues and for supranational judicial review on the basis of those catalogues than it is in the domestic context. Domestic human rights, when they are entrenched in a Constitution, do indeed draw part of their legitimation *qua* superior legal norms from the democratic nature of that constitutional entrenchment. One may mention, for instance, an inclusive constituent assembly, high-quality deliberations and the requirement of supra-majorities or unanimity.

ECHR rights instruments take the form of European treaties adopted in an intergovernmental manner.[104] Democratic control mostly occurs at domestic level therefore and usually only in an indirect way (except in countries like Switzerland where a referendum on international treaties may be called for). Even when that democratic control takes place, it is usually through a (parliamentary or even a popular) vote in an all or nothing fashion, rather than through deliberation over the text itself during international negotiations. Moreover, once ECHR rights are granted a constitutional or quasi-constitutional status in domestic law, it is not usually through legislation or constitutional reform, but through judicial practices. As to EU fundamental rights that stem from common constitutional traditions, it is still up to the ECJ to recognise them as general principles and hence to determine whether they are sufficiently widespread to be regarded as common. Once they become part of EU law, those rights benefit from a supraconstitutional status in national law without going through any of the democratic channels for constitutional precommitment of that kind whether at the domestic or at the European level. The democratic credentials of EU fundamental rights that stem from the Charter or other primary or secondary EU law sources are better, of course, at least from an EU perspective but that may also be challenged from a domestic perspective. And this difficulty actually goes to the heart of the matter and explains why there is no EU legislative competence in the human rights context to date.

In any case, it is difficult to see which polity would actually be pre-committing itself: can one speak of a European democratic polity in the Council of Europe? If

[104] See Simma/Alston, *supra* n. 92 on the sources of international human rights law.

there were such a European polity, it would be an imbricated polity made of the 47 European national polities. And if so, along which lines? The Council of Europe's Parliamentary Assembly does not have binding legislative functions and does not actually entail direct representatives of the citizens of the 47 Contracting States but parliamentary delegations. Moreover, it is neither involved in the ECHR drafting and revision processes nor in its interpretation, the former is left to Contracting States and the latter to the ECtHR. The same questions may be replicated with respect to the EU. The EU has gradually developed into a *sui generis demoi*-cracy and a political community of communities that is pluralist, multi-level and multi-layered.[105] It is a democracy of states and individuals and ought not to replace national democracies in Europe. As a matter of fact, one may actually venture that the EU has no human rights competence precisely because of the democratic implications of adopting human rights in any given political community.[106] Instead, it has its own kind of hybrid human rights regime that stems bottom-up from the national traditions and international guarantees of its Member States and corresponds to its special brand of *demoi*-cracy.

All this should make clear how any talk of democratic precommitment, at least in a statist understanding, is clearly precluded with respect to European human rights.

Of course, the difference in European human rights' democratic regime may lie in the difference of nature between international human rights and domestic human rights. One may follow Hannah Arendt and her aporia of international human rights[107] in this respect: given the intricate relationship there is between democracy and human rights, the only international human right there can be is the right to have human rights in a given polity where there can be a democratic justification of human rights *qua* rights of the citizen.[108] If there is one international human right whose legitimacy is to be found outside the democratic polity, it is precisely the right to belong to such a polity and be vested with rights in that polity.[109] Except for that right, however, the primacy of the democratic

---

105 See e.g. K Nicolaïdis, 'We, the Peoples of Europe...' (2004) *Foreign Affairs*, November/December 2004 97–110, S Besson., '*Ubi Ius, Ibi Civitas.* A Republican Account of the International Community' in S Besson / JL Martí (eds), *Legal Republicanism – National and International Perspectives* (Oxford University Press, Oxford 2009), 204–37, S Besson, 'Institutionalizing global demoi-cracy' in L Meyer (ed.), *Justice, Legitimacy and Public International Law* (Cambridge University Press, Cambridge 2009), 59–81.

106 See Besson, *supra* n. 82.

107 See H Arendt, '"The Rights of Man": What Are They?' (1949) 3:1 *Modern Review* 24–36, H Arendt, 'The Decline of the Nation-State and the End of the Rights of Man', in *The Origins of Totalitarianism* (Penguin, London 1951).

108 See Besson, *supra* n. 85.

109 See JL Cohen, 'Rethinking Human Rights, Democracy and Sovereignty in the Age of Globalization' (2008) 36:4 *Political Theory* 578, Besson, *supra* n. 82.

polity is confirmed even more strongly in the case of the protection of other international human rights.

As a matter of fact, the difference in nature and hence in democratic pedigree explains why European human rights are usually drafted as more general norms than national constitutional rights. They are also conceived as minimal requirements rather than as maximal standards. European human rights are, in other words, necessarily incomplete norms that gain their democratic legitimacy from their reception in a national legal order through various reception mechanisms.[110] This difference in nature also reveals how misguided it would be to assimilate too readily European human rights to domestic constitutional rights and to give them the same rank in the domestic legal order or at least to given them the same role in judicial review of democratic legislation.[111] Of course, the buck then passes to those very reception mechanisms which have to be as democratic as possible to account for the rank then granted to those rights in the national legal order. It also implies revisiting the relationship between national and international human rights once they are all 'constitutionalised' at the national level, so to speak. This form of 'constitutional novation', as it were, is analogous to what European and international lawyers see happening to other European and international legal norms in national legal orders, except that it has constitutional rank in the case of human rights and hence generates a constitutional form of pluralism with a complex democratic legitimation.

All this proves, in other words, that European human rights cannot be compared to an entrenched set of constitutional rights protected from the national democratic process albeit on the basis of a democratic decision, and whose protection as a result may be taken away from the hands of national authorities to protect them against their own whim and vested in the hands of the judiciary, be it a supranational judiciary. Except for the right to have rights, they are minimal rights that need to be received and contextualised and hence legitimised democratically before they can be used judicially to review democratic legislation domestically. As to the international democratic legitimation of those minimal rights, it occurs through enhancing the democratic credentials of domestic decision-making processes that contextualise and develop human rights minima,

110 On those reception mechanisms, see Keller/Stone Sweet, 'The Reception of the European Convention on Human Rights in European Legal Orders', *supra* n. 15, 11–36. See also Helfer, *supra* n. 16 on 'embeddedness' of ECHR rights within Contracting Parties' legal order.

111 In this sense, I differ from Letsas, *supra* n. 9 who argues, on the basis of the non-international nature of European human rights, that the concepts of consensus and margin of appreciation have no justification in the ECtHR's reasoning. While I agree with the former prong of his reasoning, I think he too quickly associates European human rights with constitutional rights and hence the Court's reasoning with a national constitutional court's. It is precisely the democratic process of reception of those rights in the domestic order that requires respecting States' margin of appreciation.

on the one hand, and through developing the democratic nature of international decision-making processes, on the other.[112]

Second, if one turns to specific critiques of supranational judicial review itself, the reasonable disagreement objection is even stronger in the context of supranational judicial review than in the domestic context.

To start with the disagreement argument, how could one possibly claim that judges from 47 different countries could disagree less among themselves than judges within each country? Or, to refer to the expertise argument, that they even could know better than those of each respective country or than the legislatures in each respective country? True, judicial politics are often put forward as the way to resolve intractable questions of constitutional pluralism, questions national legislatures have not addressed and left to the judiciary. This argument would seem *prima facie* to be even stronger in the case of an external supranational judge. But why would supranational judges have the legitimacy needed to resolve difficult questions which are, after all, questions left to domestic polities according to the principle of democratic subsidiarity and hence left to national parliaments? How could they do so without reference to the democratic process, however complex, multi-level and multi-layered that process has become? Of course, ECtHR judges are not only selected by Contracting States as ECJ judges are, but also by the CoE Parliamentary Assembly. This does not, however, make them as politically accountable as domestic judges.[113]

These difficulties may actually explain why traditional international judicial review is usually organised so as to remain subsidiary and merely declaratory, but also why it was intended to respect States' margin of appreciation and interpret international human rights in a contextualised and dynamic way that can adapt to the evolution of domestic societies. It also generally aims at enhancing the power of domestic judges by creating interjudicial partnerships and dialogue rather than hierarchies. On that model, domestic judges can remain the ultimate judges to actually exercise weak or strong judicial review of democratic acts or decisions on the basis of supranational human rights law, but according to their domestic democratic arrangements. One may actually venture that the transformation of the ECHR into supranational law and of ECHR rights into quasi-constitutional rights within domestic legal orders, thus associating national institutions to the implementation of those human rights domestically, is a development that may be more legitimate than supranational judicial review. It may somehow even be regarded as antithetic to the latter.

---

112 See Buchanan, *supra* n. 82, A Buchanan, 'Human Rights and the Legitimacy of the International Order' (2008) 14 *Legal Theory* 39–70 , Besson, *supra* n. 82.

113 See also Follesdal 2009, *supra* n. 11, 605.

Hence the reactions of Western democracies, in which ECHR rights are embedded and well received through democratic channels, to the increasingly strong kind of review exercized by the ECtHR. The vernacularisation or reception of European human rights within the political processes in each of the 47 Contracting States, and especially the older ones, constitutes a much more legitimate way of protecting those rights than supranational judicial review. Of course, the situation may well be different in young or disfunctioning democracies. One may draw here on discussions of the justification of constitutional precommitment in post-1989 national democracies in Europe.[114] This is particularly illuminating in the case of the ECtHR since the 47 States are divided on the increase of judicial review powers, which divide actually matches the very border between Western and older democracies, on the one hand, and Central and Eastern and more recent democracies in Europe, on the other.

It is quite paradoxical therefore to observe the Council of Europe recommend a deeper reception of the ECHR within domestic law and hence the reinforcement of the principle of subsidiarity,[115] while at the same time allowing the Court to reinforce its own review powers through its case-law. It is as if, in other words, the ECHR and its Court were facing within its own membership two historical phases at the same moment in time: a new group of States legitimately looking for what the former group got when it first entered the Convention system, but not longer needs and actually legitimately rejects for democratic reasons.

The contrast that lies in this two-speed Europe of rights has become particularly clear within the EU as well. Among EU Member States, the ECtHR's bold supranational velleities are not perceived as well as East of the EU. This is even more the case as supranational judicial review by the ECJ was not meant initially to be used to promote human rights against national legislatures. The ECJ reviews the laws of a complex polity whose laws are integrated in domestic legal orders. The absence of human rights competence of the EU and the way in which European human rights including the ECHR have become sources of EU law and hence benefit from supraconstitutional rank in domestic law sit uneasily with the use of supranational judicial review by the ECtHR in this area, to say the least. And this in turn explains retrospectively the clashes that have occurred between the two courts and culminated in the adoption of the *Bosphorus* test by the ECtHR.[116]

114 See e.g. J Elster, 'Rebuilding the boat in the open sea: Constitution-making in Eastern Europe' (1993) 71 *Public Administration* 169–217, Sadurski, *supra* n. 91.

115 For instance, through an obligation to establish an individual right to constitutional review in domestic law: see the 2010 Interlaken Action Plan (*supra* n. 34).

116 ECtHR, *Bosphorus v Ireland* (n. 45036/98) EHRR 2005-VI.

5. EUROPEAN LEGAL PLURALISM AND THE RELATIONSHIP BETWEEN EUROPEAN COURTS

5.1. THE ROLE OF EUROPEAN HUMAN RIGHTS REVIEW IN CIRCUMSTANCES OF LEGAL PLURALISM

It should be clear by now that the key to the relationship between the two European courts and national courts, but also between themselves, depends on their institutional and political framework, however complex that framework may have become in Europe. When that relationship is assessed from outside the judicial box, the differences between the two institutions become clearer and so should their respective functions in the European legal order *lato sensu*. They are no longer two supranational judicial actors relating to each other and to national judicial actors along mere judicial lines, but they are also institutions relating to other non-judicial institutions at different levels in a complex democratic supranational community. And those relations to non-judicial institutions, once they are unpacked, shed light on the relations European courts ought to have to national courts and to one another.

This conclusion is particularly important in reference to the ways in which supranational human rights review is used to resolve normative conflicts in circumstances of legal pluralism in Europe. The real question behind legal pluralism is one of validity, rank and effect of legal norms stemming from other legal orders within a given legal order. Answers to those questions have to be found in what makes a legal norm legitimate and valid and hence in particular in the democratic community itself.[117] It is only be reverting to democracy that legitimate decisions can be taken in case of normative conflicts and the absence of legal hierarchies. All legal orders cannot be deemed as equivalent and their relationships cannot be organised in a comparable fashion, especially when they have individuals and states or only individuals as subjects.

In the European Union, the very refined *demoi*-cratic regime that was developed within the European legal order during the past fifty years can account for the legitimacy of EU law. It justifies a pluralist relationship between national and EU law within the European legal order. To know which rules should take priority in case of conflict, this implies looking to the processes that are most inclusive of all those potentially affected in their fundamental interests in each case. It is a form of mutual subsidiarity that may go either way: in favour of national or of European law. By contrast, that subsidiarity is only one-way when it applies to

117 See Besson, *supra* n. 42. See also A Buchanan / R Powell, 'Constitutional Democracy and the Rule of International Law: Are They Compatible?' (2008) 16:3 *Journal of Political Philosophy* 326–49.

the relationship between ECHR rights and national law in the absence of a supranational political community and democratic connection between those legal orders.

Of course, judges are among the first institutions to be faced with normative conflicts. However, this does not mean that they are alone with this task. Supranational adjudication ought not be assessed in isolation from other institutions in a democracy. Nor should its judicial review be legitimised without reference to the other national and supranational legislative institutions it relates to.

In the European Union, this implies taking account of the European Parliament, the Council and the Commission, but also of national parliaments. The European political community is indeed a *demoi*-cratic one. Recent efforts in the Lisbon Treaty to connect the Parliament to the election of the ECJ and national parliaments to the ECJ's review mechanisms are to be supported. Clearly, the ECJ should be responsive to both national and European legislative processes. Again, the test of democratic inclusion may work as a legitimate criterion in case of conflicts. By contrast, the ECtHR is not part of a political community, not even a *sui generis* one like the EU and the only political institutions it relates to are national parliaments and executives. Their relation is clearly one that should be more responsive than it is now and should complement the interjudicial relationship between the ECtHR and national courts.

Of course, human rights adjudication is particularly sensitive in the absence of an EU competence in the human rights context. This is particularly obvious given the mutual relationship between human rights and democracy in a political community.[118] The exercize of judicial review in the area was not only belated, as a result, but it is bridled. The fear is indeed that the ECJ may not be able to cope sufficiently well with the need of accountability to national and European democratic institutions in this field. Paradoxically, as we saw before, the ECtHR seems to have had more leeway in the development of a supranational judicial review in the field of human rights, whereas it did not have this kind of review from the beginning. The democratic resistance is only starting to mount now in Western and older democracies in Europe.

The differences between the two courts (belated or original and bridled or unbridled human rights review) do not seem so paradoxical once the connexion

118 See von Bogdandy, *supra* n. 48, Besson, *supra* n. 48. This explains why AG Maduro's proposal in *Centro Europa* (Case C-380/05 *Centro Europa* [2008] ECR I-349) to ensure a mutuality between legal orders in the respect for fundamental rights fails to convince: not only is it contrary to the absence of EU competence in the human rights context, but it is contrary to the kind of *demoi*-cracy in place in the European Union.

between human rights and democracy is revealed. In a complex supranational political community like the EU in which democracy is multi-levelled, human rights protection and human rights review of legislation are more difficult to ensure legitimately. The ECtHR's supranational human rights review, by contrast, is only a concern for national legislatures, as there is no competing political community developing on the basis of those rights at the European level – at least not besides that of the EU.

5.2. THE CONSEQUENCES FOR THE RELATIONSHIPS BETWEEN EUROPEAN COURTS

What is the upshot of all this in terms of judicial relations and interpretation of the same European human rights in different European legal orders? Since those human rights are the human rights of a complex supranational political community, i.e., the EU, democracy ought to constitute the common frame of reference. In those conditions, democratic subsidiarity becomes the guiding principle in supranational judicial review in Europe.[119] This applies between European courts and national courts, as much as between European courts themselves.

In the relationship between either of the two European courts and a national court, on the one hand, it is important to distinguish between what ought to be expected from each of the two European courts.

When the ECJ is competing with national courts and reaches a different interpretation of the same right or a different balancing of the same conflicting rights and interests, democratic subsidiarity requires that the legal norm stemming from the most inclusive institution and decision-making process takes priority. Judicial reasoning based on a common identity and shared values between legal orders cannot resolve difficult normative conflicts.[120] Democratic subsidiarity constitutes the only plausible tie-breaker. This should *a fortiori* also be the case when the ECtHR is in a competition situation with a national court. The fact that the Convention is not part of an autonomous legal order and the Court itself is not part of a supranational or international institutional framework of its own besides that of the Council of Europe explains how democratic

119 On subsidiarity, see Buchanan/Powell, *supra* n. 117.

120 It suffices to see the limitations of that reasoning in *Michaniki* (Case C-213/07 *Michaniki AE v Ethniko Symvoulio Radiotileorasis and Ypourgos Epikrateias* [2008] ECR I-9999) or *Arcelor* (Case C-127/07 *Arcelor Atlantique et Lorraine and Others* [2008] ECR I-9895). This is also confirmed by AG Maduro's reasoning who reverts to the primacy of EU law at the last stage in his argument.

subsidiarity ought to be even stronger between the ECtHR and national courts than between the ECJ and those courts.

With respect to the relationship between the two European courts, on the other, the difference between the two courts and their respective relationships to national courts helps us see more clearly what their mutual duties should be. This argument is the upshot of the *relation à trois* that exists between those courts.[121]

When the ECtHR is competing with the ECJ and reaches a different interpretation of the same right or a different balancing of the same conflicting rights and interests, the former should give way to the latter. It is a form of *subsidiarity within subsidiarity*, if the ECtHR is subsidiary to national courts, it is even more subsidiary to the ECJ which is the supranational court of the European legal order and has closer ties to national and European democracies than the ECtHR.

Interestingly, this approach corresponds to the contextual deference to EU law and the ECJ's case-law recently demonstrated by the ECtHR in areas in which EU law and the ECJ have a more developed and advanced practice but also a practice that corresponds to its own political and social context.[122] This has been the case in the field of anti-discrimination law, for instance.[123] More generally, subsidiarity within subsidiarity seems to have become the rule between the two courts ever since the *Bosphorus* case in 2005.[124] In that case, the ECtHR has established a refragable presumption according to which EU law is presumed to grant equivalent protection to ECHR rights and ought not therefore be reviewed through the control of implementation acts taken by EU Member States, unless that presumption is reversed because the protection ensured is not comparable to that of the ECHR.[125]

The justification of that presumption has been widely disputed by human rights scholars across Europe, and it now has found a clear democratic justification in

121 On this relationship, see Besson, *supra* n. 42.

122 See Spielmann, in this volume, for similar conclusions.

123 See e.g. *Stec and Others v The United Kingdom* (n. 65731/01, 65900/01) EHRR 2006-VI, *D. H. and Others v Czech Republic* (n. 57325/00) Judgment of 13 November 2007, selected for publication.

124 Confirmed in *Kokkelvisserij* (*Cooperatieve producentenorgranisatie van de nederlandse Kokkelvisserij U.A. v The Netherlands* (n. 13645/05), Judgment of 20 January 2009, selected for publication).

125 On the *Bosphorus* case, see B Conforti, 'Le principe d'équivalence et le contrôle sur les actes communautaires dans la jurisprudence de la Cour européenne des droits de l'homme' in Breitenmoser, S, et al. (eds), *Human Rights, Democracy and the Rule of Law. Liber Amicorum Luzius Wildhaber* (Dike, Zürich 2007), 173, C Costello, 'The *Bosphorus* Ruling of the ECHR: Fundamental Rights and Blurry Boundaries in Europe' (2006) 6(1) *Human Rights Law Review* 87–130.

this chapter. It was not a pragmatic decision inspired by the functional division of labour between two courts with similar albeit overlapping jurisdiction, or by mere comity and mutual respect between those courts.[126] As a matter of fact, the democratic argument put forward in this chapter also helps understand that to overrule that presumption, a substantive discussion pertaining to the equivalence of human rights protection will not be enough. The *Solange II* test, on which *Bosphorus* is based,[127] is a much richer test than authors are usually ready to concede. As confirmed by recent revivals of that test in the case-law of the Czech Constitutional Court, democracy is as important a component of the rule of law as human rights. One may even venture that this democratic reservation is what lies behind the ECtHR's position in *Behrami* and further cases in which the Court did not want to mingle with its Contracting Parties' obligations stemming from their membership in other supranational organisations and potentially, one may argue, with the democratic arrangements made in connection to membership in those organisations.[128]

The relationship between the two European courts in the context of human rights protection and review will now go through a process of re-configuration in the context of the EU's accession to the ECHR. While one may be tempted to see the accession as marking the continuation of the *Bosphorus* test, the argument made in this section has hopefully demonstrated that it will toll its knell.[129] As discussed previously, the negotiations aiming at the EU's accession to the ECHR have awakened the sore question of the EU human rights competence precisely because it implies a shift from the current hybrid human rights regime that applies in the EU towards a more municipal model of human rights.[130] And this also means entering into a new stage in the political and democratic development of the EU. In this context, the relationship between the EU legal order and its Member States' legal orders will change, but also that between the ECJ and the ECtHR pertaining to human rights as a result. The ECJ's human rights review of domestic law will have to become bolder and more coherent, while the ECtHR's human rights review of EU law will have to come closer to the subsidiary review it ought to be applying in its relationships to domestic courts[131] and hence less subsidiary than it has been since the *Bosphorus* presumption was put in place.

---

126 And clearly not a *de facto* accession, as some commentators have argued it is: no Contracting Party to the ECHR benefits from a presumption of compatibility with the latter!

127 *Bosphorus v Ireland* (n. 45036/98) EHRR 2005-VI.

128 *Behrami v France* (n. 71412/01, 78166/01) (2007) 45 EHRR SE 10.

129 See also De Schutter, *supra* n. 41, 544, 565.

130 See Besson, *supra* n. 85. See also S Besson, 'International Human Rights and Democracy: Learning from the EU' (2011) 4:1 *Ethics and Global Politics* 19–50.

131 Following De Schutter, *supra* n. 41, 563–6 this does not, however, mean that the exhaustion of local remedies under Article 35 ECHR should necessarily imply the exhaustion of both EU and domestic remedies in cases that pertain to a Member State's decision applying EU law. The respect of the obligation to introduce a preliminary ruling under Article 267 TFEU, when

6. CONCLUSION

This chapter's starting point was that questions pertaining to the articulation between legal orders and courts in Europe would best be answered by thinking from outside the judicial box and by replacing the two European courts in their institutional and political context, both domestic and European. The aim of the chapter was double: it was, first of all, to explore some of the philosophical questions related to the democratic legitimacy of supranational judicial review based on human rights in Europe, and, secondly, to see how that discussion could help clarify practical questions pertaining to recent developments in the human rights review exercised by both courts and difficulties pertaining to their relationship to national courts and among themselves.

My argument was three-pronged. The first step was to define what supranational judicial review means in Europe and to discuss the recent sharpening of the kind of judicial review exercised by both European courts in the human rights context. Important similarities, but also key differences were identified between the two courts in this respect. The ECJ's supranational strong judicial review has been used in the field of human rights, but only in a belated and bridled fashion and not to its maximal potential, whereas the ECtHR's international judicial review has developed in the course of fifty years into strong supranational judicial review that goes beyond its legal jurisdiction. Reasons for those *prima facie* paradoxical differences lie in their respective political and institutional context: that of a supranational organisation for the ECJ (with no human rights competence) and of an international convention (solely dedicated to human rights) for the ECtHR. Supranational judicial review in the EU was only put at the service of human rights late in the history of the EU and not to protect national democracy against itself but against the EU, and hence to consolidate the European political community. As a result, the justification of human rights (notably by reference to democracy), and the democratic legitimacy of judicial review in those two contexts are bound to be entirely different.

In the second part of the chapter, I turned to that very philosophical question and have re-qualified it to fit the European supranational context in terms of democracy, human rights and judicial review. Not only does supranational judicial review raise different questions in terms of its compatibility with democracy, but those questions also call for different answers. I have argued that the democratic objection is stronger at the supranational level than in the domestic context. Paradoxically, however, the more incisive supranational

the conditions of that obligation are fulfilled, is indeed part of Member States' duties under EU law and its violation constitutes not only a violation of EU law and hence of Article 35 ECHR, but also a violation of Article 6(1) ECHR.

human rights review becomes, the more successful it is perceived to be. I ventured that the reason might be that the question cannot be answered satisfactorily before we have a clear idea of the justification of international human rights and of their relationship to democracy. Also, supranational judicial review in the field of human rights was originally intrinsically linked to human rights protection by the ECHR. After untying both questions (European human rights and democracy, on the one hand, and European human rights and judicial review, on the other), I have argued that they have not resisted the passing of time in Western European democracies where democratic legitimacy requires the national reception of human rights and stronger ties between European courts and national ones and between European courts and national parliaments. Differences identified earlier between the two courts (belated or original and bridled or unbridled human rights review) are not so paradoxical when the connexion between human rights and democracy is made. In a complex supranational political community like the EU in which democracy is multi-levelled, human rights protection and human rights review of legislation are more difficult to ensure legitimately. The ECtHR's supranational human rights review, by contrast, is only a concern for national legislatures, as there is no competing political community developing on the basis of those rights at the European level – at least not besides that of the EU.

The third step in my argument was to discuss some implications for the relationship between the two European courts in circumstances of legal pluralism. Since European human rights are the human rights of a complex and *demoi*-cratic supranational political community and European courts ought to relate to many European publics, democracy constitutes the common framework of reference and source of legitimacy of the conflicting sources and norms applicable in each case. In those conditions, democratic subsidiarity becomes the guiding principle in supranational judicial review in Europe. As a result, when the ECtHR and the ECJ are competing with national courts, the most inclusive and democratic legal source should be given priority. It follows from that relationship and from the principle of subsidiarity within subsidiarity, that when the ECtHR is competing with the ECJ on issues of EU law, the former should give way to the latter. This is what the two courts have been doing lately, and the equivalence presumption has now not only found its normative justification, but judicial practice has also gained a richer test of how to go about overturning that presumption when needed.

Three general conclusions may be derived from this study: first of all, the institutional context of European courts explains key features of their own brand of supranational judicial review; second, the institutional framework, and more particularly the democratic context of European judges at the ECJ and at the

ECtHR is very different and arguments for the justification of supranational judicial review by both courts differ accordingly; and, finally, those institutional differences within each legal order affect how both courts ought to relate to national courts, and accordingly to each other in circumstances of legal pluralism within the same European legal order *lato sensu*. Exciting times lie ahead of us with the EU's accession to the ECHR in view and the related re-configuration of the relationship between the two European courts. Let us hope that that new articulation will pay due regard to the inherently democratic nature of human rights and the complex structure of the European democratic polity.

II. THE IMPACT OF THE COEXISTENCE OF THE EUROPEAN COURTS ON THE NATIONAL CONSTITUTIONAL COURTS

CHAPTER 5
BELGIUM
THE SUPREMACY DILEMMA: THE BELGIAN CONSTITUTIONAL COURT CAUGHT BETWEEN THE EUROPEAN COURT OF HUMAN RIGHTS AND THE EUROPEAN COURT OF JUSTICE

Patricia Popelier[*]

1. THE PROTECTION OF FUNDAMENTAL RIGHTS BY THE BELGIAN COURTS

Fundamental rights have taken up a prominent position in the Belgian Constitution since its enactment in 1831. Meanwhile the constitutional list of fundamental rights has extended under the influence of international human rights treaties. Also the protection of human rights has expanded. Originally the Belgian Constitution relied on Parliament to protect individuals against violations of human rights. It displayed however distrust against government, subjecting all regulations and decisions of the Executive to judicial review.[1] The protection of human rights against violation by Statutes enacted by Parliament has developed a twofold track.

1.1. FIRST TRACK: CASE LAW OF THE COURT OF CASSATION (SUPREME COURT)

Although the Belgian Constitution did not explicitly rule out Statutes from constitutional review, the Court of Cassation on several occasions confirmed the

* Professor at the University of Antwerp (Belgium).

1 Originally Article 107, now Article 159 of the Belgian Constitution.

Statute's inviolability.[2] Nevertheless in 1971 in *Franco Suisse Le Ski* the Court of Cassation pronounced the primacy of directly binding international law over national law.[3]

The *Franco Suisse Le Ski* case was a milestone. It introduced a monist view to the relationship between national and international law while the Belgian Constitution remained silent on this issue. The monist approach has on several occasions been confirmed and has been reinforced by recent decisions pronouncing the primacy of international law over the Constitution.[4] The case also illustrates the influence of ECJ case law. In *Costa v. E.N.E.L.* the European Court of Justice (ECJ) clarified the consequences of the accession to a new European legal order, such as the restriction of sovereignty and the primacy of EC law.[5] The Court of Cassation not only accepted this decision but extended it to all self-executing international law, on the ground of the very nature of international law. It thus reversed its attitude towards international law[6] and put an end to the inviolability of Statutes.[7] Although Statutes were still excluded from constitutional review, the *Costa v. E.N.E.L* case made room for the review of Statutes against human rights enacted in human rights treaties.

1.2. SECOND TRACK: THE ESTABLISHMENT OF THE BELGIAN CONSTITUTIONAL COURT

In 1980 the Belgian Constitution allowed for the establishment of a constitutional court with limited competences. The Court, established in 1983, was called 'Court of Arbitration' to emphasize its limitations. The reason for its establishment lay in the emergence of a federal state which implied the co-existence of federal laws and federated laws. Originally the Court of Arbitration's only mandate was the supervision of the division of powers between the federation and the federated entities.

In 1989 however every person with a justifiable interest was given access to the Court and its competence was extended to the review of Statutes against the equality and non-discrimination principle (Articles 10–11 Belgian Constitution)

---

2 Cass. 23 July 1849, *B.J.*VII, 1331, Cass. 16 July 1894 [1894] Pas. I-267, Cass. 10 December 1928 [1929] Pas. I-36, Cass. 21 October 1966 [1967] Pas. 1967, 242.

3 Cass. 27 May 1971 [1971] Pas. I-886.

4 Cass. 9 November 2006, [2005] *C.D.P.K.* 597, Cass. 16 November 2004, [2005] *C.D.P.K.* 610.

5 Case C 6/64 *Costa v. E.N.E.L.* [1964] ECR 1199.

6 M Claes, *The National Courts' Mandate in the European Constitution* (Hart Publishing, Oxford 2006) 199.

7 See however on the problem of the courts' mandate for the review of statutes M Claes, *The National Courts' Mandate in the European Constitution* (Hart Publishing, Oxford 2006) 242–243.

and the rights and freedoms concerning education (Article 24 Belgian Constitution). Since then Government, Parliament as well as every person with a justifiable interest can request the annulment of Statutes originating from federal or federated Parliaments. The petition must be filed within six months after the publication of the law. In addition every court can without time-limit refer a question of unconstitutionality to the Constitutional Court. Where the Constitutional Court finds a violation, the referring court must respect this ruling. Moreover a new six-month term commences in which Government, Parliament or every person with a justifiable interest can bring a direct action for annulment.

As the Court accepts that the Articles 10–11 of the Constitution are combined with other rules and legal principles, it gives protection against Statutes which violate human rights laid down in the constitution or in international treaties. It is not required that the provision in the international treaty is self-executing.[8] According to established case law the comparison test can be omitted when dealing with human rights. Every person is entitled to protection against violations of human rights so that the unjustified infringement of human rights of one person or category implies in itself a discriminatory treatment.[9] Finally in 2003 the Court gained competence to review Statutes directly against all articles in Title II (on fundamental rights) of the Constitution.[10] The Court was also renamed 'Constitutional Court'.

2. THE RELATIONSHIP BETWEEN NATIONAL LAW AND INTERNATIONAL LAW ACCORDING TO BELGIAN LAW

2.1. THE PRIMACY OF INTERNATIONAL LAW: A (MODERATED) MONIST VIEW

Since the *Franco Suisse Le Ski* judgment the primacy of directly binding international law over national law has never been questioned. For the Constitutional Court even the question whether international law is directly binding appears not relevant for assessing whether the law maker has violated international obligations in a discriminatory way.[11]

---

8 Const. Court. No 41/2002, 20 February 2002.

9 See for example Const. Court No 16/91, 13 June 1991, Const. Court No 60/2007, 18 April 2007, Const. Court. No 40/2009, 11 March 2009.

10 The Court is also competent to review to Article 170 and 172 B.C. (rights concerning taxes) and 191 B.C. (which guarantees equal protection against violations of human rights to foreigners on Belgian territory).

11 Const. Court No 106/2003, 22 July 2003.

More controversial is the question whether international law takes precedence over constitutional law. The Court of Cassation has clearly pronounced the primacy of international law over constitutional law.[12] The Council of State seems to side with the Court of Cassation.[13] The Constitutional Court takes up a less outspoken position.

The Constitutional Court reviews parliamentary acts giving assent to international treaties against their compatibility with constitutional clauses including the equality and non discrimination clause.[14] As these acts as such do not contain any substantial clause, this in fact comes down to the constitutional review of the content of the international treaty. This induced Advocate General at the Court of Cassation *Velu* to utter a stern critique,[15] while some constitutionalists appreciated the idea that the Constitution takes precedence over international law.[16] However the Constitutional Court has never openly expressed this view. It merely assesses whether the Constitution allowed Belgium to join the international treaty at the time of access. If this is the case, the international treaty is binding, even if afterwards international or constitutional developments make it contrary to the constitution.[17] Nevertheless the Constitutional Court thus departs from the view taken by the Court of Cassation, according to which international treaties take precedence unless access to the treaty implied a manifest violation of a fundamental rule regarding competence

---

12 Cass. 9 November 2005, [2005] *C.D.P.K.*, 597, Cass. 16 November 2004 [2005] *C.D.P.K.*, 610.

13 Council of State *Orfinger*, No 62.922, 5 November 1996. The case concerned EC law but the wordings of the Council implied also international non EC law. *Contra:* E Ergec, 'La Consécration jurisprudentielle de la primauté du droit supranational sur la Constitution' [1997] *Journal des Tribunaux* 256, P Vandernoot, ' Le concours de questions préjudicielles et l'article 34 de la Constitution: vers un dépassement de la controverse entre les "monistes" et les "dualistes"?' in A Arts, I Verougstraete a.o. (eds.), *Les rapports entre la Cour d'arbitrage, le Pouvoir judiciaire et le Conseil d'Etat* (die Keure, Bruges 2006) 354.

14 The first in line was Const. Court No 26/91, 16 October 1991.

15 J Velu, *Contrôle de constitutionnalité et contrôle de compatibilité avec les traités* (Bruylant, Brussels 1992).

16 T Bombois, 'La restriction des compétences de la Cour d'arbitrage à l'égard des traités internationaux', in *La Cour d'arbitrage vingt ans après* (Bruylant, Brussels 2004) p. 143–150, H Bribosia, 'Applicabilité directe et primauté des traités internationaux et du droit communautaire' [1996] *Revue Belge de Droit International* 76, Ph Brouwers and H Simonart, 'Le conflit entre la constitution et le droit international conventionnel dans la jurisprudence de la Cour d'arbitrage' [1995] *Cahier de Doit Européen* 13–17, C Courtoy, 'Les rélations entre les cours constitutionnelles et les autres juridictions nationales, y compris l'interférence en cette matière de l'action des juridiction européennes' [2002] *Revue Belge de Droit Constitutionnel* 233, F Delpérée, *Le droit Constitutionnel de la Belgique* (Bruylant, Brussels 2000) 686–687, Y Lejeune and Ph Brouwers, 'La Cour d'arbitrage face au contrôle de la constitutionnalité des traités', [1992] *Journal de Tibunaux* 674, F Meersschaut, 'De ondraaglijke lichtheid van de Grondwet' [2005] *Tijdschrift voor.Bestuurswetenschappen en Publiekrecht* 50.

17 See P Popelier, 'De verhouding tussen de Belgische Grondwet en het internationale recht', in *En hommage à Francis Delpérée. Itinéraires d'un constitutionnaliste* (Bruylant, Brussels 2007) 1231–1254.

to conclude the treaty.[18] The law maker has interfered to avoid liability at international level. According to the Special Law on the Constitutional Court the Court has no longer jurisdiction to answer to preliminary references concerning an Act of assent to a EU Treaty or to the European Convention of Human Rights or a Protocol.

In the end the debate on the primacy of international law or Constitution comes down to the concern for the protection of human rights. Irrespective of the question which position each document takes in a hierarchical order, what matters is the maximum protection of human rights. The Constitution does not provide for a maximisation clause or a provision prescribing the interpretation of constitutional clauses in conformity with the ECHR or other human rights treaties. In the following sections it will become clear that the Constitutional Court nevertheless does follow this rule of interpretation.

2.2. EU LAW

The Belgian courts accept the primacy of both primary and secondary EU law. Article 34 of the Belgian Constitution, which allows for the transfer of the exercise of powers to international organisations, provides for a legal basis. It incorporates the entire EU legal system, including ECJ case law and the primacy of EU law over constitutional law.[19]

The question rises whether EU law should still take precedence if this runs counter to fundamental rights. According to the Division Legislation of the Council of State[20] constitutional guarantees can be set aside on the basis of Article 34 Constitution if the implementation of an EU directive would necessitate this.[21] Article 34 Constitution on the other hand does not permit infringement of essential features and basic structures of the constitutional order. If this would be the case the option according to the Council of State would be either to amend the constitution or to withdraw from the EU.[22] The

18 J Velu, *Contrôle de constitutionnalité et contrôle de compatibilité avec les traités* (Bruylant, Brussels 1992) 146. In that case Article 46.1 the Vienna Convention on the Law of Treaties accepts a State to invoke the fact that its consent to be bound by a treaty has been expressed in violation of a provision of its internal law.

19 Council of State *Orfinger* No 62.922, 5 November 1996.

20 The Council of State consists of two divisions. The Division Legislation gives advice to bills and proposals. The Division Administrative Court has power to annul decisions and regulations of the Executive.

21 Council of State, Division Legislation No 39.192/3 of 4 November 2005, *Parl. Doc.* House of Representatives 2005–2006, 51–2189/1, 113–116.

22 Council of State, Division Legislation No 44.028/AV, *Parl.Doc.* Senate 2007–2008, 4–568/1, p. 343.

Constitutional Court seems to agree with this. Some members of the Court have in various doctrinal papers accepted the primacy of primary and secondary EU law over the Constitution.[23] The Court when confronted with the claim that a law implementing an EU directive infringes the Constitution, examines whether the directive gives discretion or not. In the latter case the Court in principle cannot invalidate the law as in doing so it would indirectly invalidate the EU directive. In those cases it must refer a validity question to the Court of Justice.[24] If this does not solve the question and a conflict remains, the law implementing an EU directive can subsist even though it runs counter to the constitution. Article 34 Constitution covers its subsistence.[25] The *Money Laundering* case, however, illustrates that practice is more obscure than the theoretical framework.[26]

3. THE INFLUENCE OF ECHR AND EU LAW ON THE NATIONAL PROTECTION OF HUMAN RIGHTS

3.1. THE INFLUENCE OF THE ECHR ON THE NATIONAL PROTECTION OF HUMAN RIGHTS

The European Convention of Human Rights (ECHR) and the case law of the European Court of Human Rights (ECtHR) have been influential on the case law of the Belgian Constitutional Court.[27]

---

23 A Alen, 'Rechtspraak van het Hof van Cassatie: reden om de bijzondere wet van 6 januari 1989 op het Grondwettelijk Hof te wijzigen?', in A Alen & J Van Nieuwenhove, *Leuvense Staatsrechtelijke Standpunten* (die Keure, Bruges 2008) 4, M Melchior & P Vandernoot, 'Contrôle de constitutionnalité et droit communautaire dérivé' [1998] *R.B.D.C.* 13–14, P Vandernoot, 'Le concours de questions préjudicielles et l'article 34 de la Constitution: vers un dépassement de la controverse entre les "monistes" et les "dualistes"?' in A Arts, I Verougstraete a.o. (eds.), *Les rapports entre la Cour d'arbitrage, le Pouvoir judiciaire et le Conseil d'Etat* (die Keure, Bruges 2006) 353–359.

24 Constitutional Court No 128/2009, 24 July 2009. See also M Melchior & P Vandernoot, 'Contrôle de constitutionnalité et droit communautaire dérivé' [1998] *RBDC* 15–16. In ECJ *Melki & Abdeli* C-188/10 and C-189/10, 22 June 2010, the Court of Justice confirms that the competence of a Constitutional Court to review the constitutionality of a national law, the content of which merely transposes the mandatory provisions of a European Union directive, cannot undermine the jurisdiction of the Court of Justice alone to declare an act of the European Union invalid.

25 M Melchior & P Vandernoot, 'Contrôle de constitutionnalité et droit communautaire dérivé' [1998] *RBDC* 39.

26 See below Section 5.

27 For an overview of cases E De Wet, 'The Reception Process in the Netherlands and Belgium' in H Keller & A Stone Sweet, *A Europe of Rights. The Impact of the ECHR on National Legal Systems* (Oxford University Press, Oxford 2008) 276–282.

This influence manifests itself in two ways.

First the Constitutional Court combines Articles 10 and 11 of the Belgian Constitution with human rights guaranteed in international treaties.[28] It even combines with provisions in international treaties which are not mentioned in the applicant's claim.[29] Although the Court refers to various human rights treaties, the European Convention of Human Rights clearly takes up a dominant position. In its assessment it regularly cites the case law of the European Court of human rights.[30] This may even lead to a reversal of the Constitutional Court's jurisprudence. For example the Constitutional Court originally held the view that the law maker may freely determine the amount of a criminal or administrative fine.[31] Following the ECtHR's *Mamidakas* case[32] the Constitutional Court added a proportionality test.[33]

Secondly the Constitutional Court interprets fundamental rights guaranteed in the Constitution in accordance to analogous human rights guaranteed in human rights treaties. Here as well the ECHR dominates. As soon as the Constitutional Court was given competence to review against the Articles 10 and 11 of the Belgian Constitution, it defined in the *Biorim* case the equality and non-discrimination principle in accordance to the ECtHR case law.[34] The Belgian Court of Cassation and the Council of State follow this reasoning. As soon as the Constitutional Court was given competence to review Statutes directly against fundamental rights in Title II of the Constitution it expressed the 'inextricable' bond between analogous human rights in the constitution and in human rights treaties.[35] For some fundamental rights this is in line with the intention of the Constitution. For example, according to parliamentary documents the introduction of Article 22 of the Constitution holding the right to privacy aimed at being interpreted in conformity with the right to privacy enshrined in Article 10 ECHR.[36] However even constitutional clauses dating from 1831 are interpreted in accordance to the ECHR.

---

28 For the first time in the Pacification Case, Constitutional Court No 18/90, 23 May 1990. A direct link is provided for in Article 24 of the Belgian Constitution: everyone has the right to education, with respect of fundamental rights and freedoms.

29 See J Theunis, 'Grondwettelijk Hof of grondrechtenhof? De evenredigheid van de straf als casus' in A Alen & J Van Nieuwenhove (eds.), *Leuvense Staatsrechtelijke Standpunten* (die Keure, Bruges 2008) 193.

30 See for example Const. Court No 59/2009, 25 March 2009.

31 Const. Court No 60/2002, 28 March 2002, Const. Court No 138/2006, 14 September 2006, Const. Court No 8/2007, 11 January 2007.

32 *Mamidakis v Greece* (App no 35533/04) ECHR 11 January 2007.

33 Const. Court No 81/2007, 7 June 2007. See for this example J Theunis, 'Grondwettelijk Hof of grondrechtenhof? De evenredigheid van de straf als casus' in A Alen & J Van Nieuwenhove (eds.), *Leuvense Staatsrechtelijke Standpunten* (die Keure, Bruges 2008) 173–196.

34 Const. Court. No 23/89, 13 October 1989. Established case law since then.

35 Const. Court No 136/2004, 22 July 2004, Const. Court No 158/2004, 20 October 2004. Established case law since then.

36 *Parl. Doc.* House of Representatives 1993–1994, No 997/5, p. 2. See e.g. Const. Court 162/2004, 20 October 2004.

In most cases the interpretation of fundamental rights in conformity with human rights treaties results in the application of cumulative constitutional guarantees and guarantees included in human rights treaties. For instance the constitutional guarantee that infringement of a human right is based upon a Statute is combined with the conventional guarantee (as interpreted by the ECtHR) that the law is accessible and foreseeable. However, although doctrine states that interpretation in accordance with international treaties cannot result in a weaker protection of the constitutional right,[37] in practice the interpretation exercise may have exactly that result. For example Article 29 of the Belgian Constitution provides for an absolute protection of the confidentiality of letters. According to the Constitutional Court this article must be interpreted in the light of analogous human rights in such a way that it contains a limitation clause.[38] Thus the method of interpretation in conformity with human rights treaties is sometimes used as a means to modernise constitutional clauses, even if this is difficult to explain in the light of the maximisation doctrine.[39]

Two reasons may explain this influence.

The Constitutional Court is a relatively young court. It did not receive an explicit mandate to review Statutes against fundamental rights clauses until 2003. Since 1988 however it made use of the power to review against Articles 10 and 11 Constitution to act as a proper Constitutional Court in the protection of fundamental rights. To this end it could rely on the authoritative and extensive case law of the ECtHR interpreting the well-respected ECHR. Since the ECHR had already played an important role in the case law of the ordinary courts, making use of the ECHR would be rather uncontroversial.

In addition parties are inclined to invoke the ECHR to safeguard a potential appeal at the European Court of Human Rights.

3.2. THE INFLUENCE OF EU LAW ON THE NATIONAL PROTECTION OF HUMAN RIGHTS

Although the Constitutional Court is not competent to review Acts of Parliament directly against EU law, it does take EU law into consideration. The Court states

---

37 J Demeyer, 'L'affirmation des droits fondamentaux dans les constitutions et dans les traités internationaux' in *Le nouveau droit constitutionnel* (Bruylant, Brussels 1987) 254. See similar in Spain E García de Enterría 'Valeur de la jurisprudence de la Cour européenne des droits de l'homme en droit espagnol' in F Matscher and H Petzold (eds.), *Protecting Human Rights: the European Dimenion – Protection des droits de l'homme: la dimension européenne. Mélanges G.J. Wiarda* (Carl Heymanns Verlag, Cologne 1988) 223.

38 Const. Court No 202/2004, 21 December 2004.

39 See for the maximisation doctrine below Section 4.4.

that in linking Articles 10 and 11 of the Belgian Constitution with EU law, it ensures the primacy of EU law.[40]

A requirement is the binding force of the EU law. As long as the EU Charter of Fundamental Rights did not (explicitly) have binding force, the Constitutional Court considered inadmissible the application which links Articles 10 and 11 Constitution with the EU Charter.[41] However, in some judgments it does take the Charter into consideration in so far as it confirms common values of the European Union similar to the values enshrined in constitutional clauses.[42] In these cases the Court does not examine the Statute's conformity with the Charter. The Charter merely strengthens the signification of the constitutional right as a 'common value'.

The Constitutional Court also links the *stand still* clause in environmental law, enshrined in Article 23 Constitution, with EU law, including the ECJ case law.[43] Finally, constitutional clauses may be interpreted similarly to EU law. For example some articles which attribute competences to the federal or federated level are interpreted in conformity to EU law.[44] But also the rule that fundamental rights are interpreted in accordance with conventional human rights is relevant in this respect. Thus the Constitutional Court has pointed out that Article 12 of the EC Treaty (now Article 18 TFEU), in so far as it forbids discriminations based on nationality, is similar to Articles 10, 11 and 191 of the Belgian Constitution concerning the equality and non-discrimination principle of Belgian citizens and foreigners.[45] In the latter case a dispute concerning the interpretation of Article 12 EC Treaty arose, which brought about a preliminary reference to the ECJ. As the Constitutional Court determined the 'inextricable bond' between Article 12 EC Treaty and Articles 10, 11 and 191 of the Belgian Constitution, it indirectly subjects the scope of constitutional clauses to the jurisdiction of the European Court of Justice.

The influence of EU law on the protection of constitutional rights becomes ambiguous when EU directives play a part in the equality and non-discrimination test.

---

40 Const. Court No 151/2003, 26 November 2003.

41 Const. Court No 10/2008, 23 January 2008, Const. Court. No 58/2009, 19 March 2009.

42 Const. Court No 167/2005, 23 November 2005, Const. Court No 101/2008, 10 July 2008. See also Const. Court No 10/2008, 23 January 2008. See also Const. Court No 81/2007, 7 June 2007, where the Court refers to the Charter in order to strengthen the acceptance of the ECtHR ruling that an administrative or criminal fine should be proportional.

43 E.g. Const. Court No 145/2006, 28 September 2006, Const. Court No 135/2006, 14 September 2006, Const. Court No 137/2006, 14 September 2006.

44 E.g. Const. Court No 32/1991, 14 November 1992 and Const. Court No 69/2004, 5 May 2004 (economic and monetary union); Const. Court No 44, 23 December 1987 (waste products).

45 Const. Court No 12/2008, 14 February 2008. Now Article 18 TFEU.

On the one hand, EU law may hinder the justification of a difference in treatment. For example the Social Integration Act in the adjudication of a right to social integration distinguished between two categories of EU-subjects. The Constitutional Court noted that Articles 12 and 17 EC Treaty exclude any justification of such difference in treatment.[46]

On the other hand, EU law may help to justify a difference in treatment. In some cases the Constitutional Court states that when incorporating EU directives the law maker may limit the scope of national laws to categories falling under the EU directive. The law maker does *not* have to justify why other categories, or cases situated within the national legal order, are excluded from protection under this law.[47] In other cases, however, the Court points out that if the EU directive leaves room for a broader scope the law maker *should* justify such a difference in treatment.[48]

4. THE RELATION BETWEEN THE NATIONAL AND THE EUROPEAN PROTECTION OF HUMAN RIGHTS

4.1. THE POSITION OF THE CONSTITUTIONAL COURT IN HUMAN RIGHTS PROCEEDINGS

4.1.1. An exhaustive remedy?

The Constitutional Court links Articles 10 and 11 of the Belgian Constitution (equality- and non-discrimination principle) with human rights enshrined in the ECHR. It also reviews against constitutional clauses containing fundamental rights which are analogous to the human rights implied in the ECHR. Therefore the question arose whether the Constitutional Court fits the ECtHR standing requirement of a domestic remedy to be exhausted, which is a criterion for the admissibility of an application before the European Court of Human Rights (Article 35.1 ECHR).[49] The European Court of Human Rights does not answer

---

46 Const. Court No 5/2004, 14 January 2004.

47 Const. Court No 6/99, 20 January 1999, Const. Court No 28/2001, 24 May 2001, Const. Court No 179/2005, 7 December 2005, Const. Court No 56/2009, 19 March 2009.

48 Const. Court No 110/2001; 20 September 2001, Const. Court No 118/2003, 17 September 2003, Const. Court No 74/2007, 10 May 2007.

49 See A Alen and F Meersschaut, 'Procederen voor het Belgische Grondwettelijk Hof' in M Storme and A Beirlaen (eds.), *Procederen in nieuw België en komend Europa* (Kluwer, Antwerp 1991) 185, P Popelier, *Procederen voor het Grondwettelijk Hof* (Intersentia, Antwerp 2008), 137–138, 141–142, J Velaers, *Van Arbitragehof tot Grondwettelijk Hof* (Maklu, Antwerp 1985), 262–265.

this question by means of a general rule. It assesses in each case the effectiveness of a remedy before the Constitutional Court.[50]

According to Ergec an application before the Constitutional Court is required in case the applicant complains that a Statute violates Article 14 ECHR (equality and non-discrimination principle) combined to other convention rights.[51] The reason is that review of Statutes against the equality and non-discrimination principle constitutes the Constitutional Court's core business. In this case the Court of Cassation and the Council of State both lodge preliminary references before the Constitutional Court.[52] It is not necessary to bring complaints against the violation of Article 10–11 Constitution combined to convention rights before the Constitutional Court if discrimination is not at the heart of the complaint, because in that case ordinary courts can review directly against the European Convention.

Since 2003 however the Constitutional Court can review Statutes against the Constitution's entire Title II on fundamental rights. Many of these rights are analogous to fundamental rights guaranteed by the ECHR. The question whether in that case a reference to the Constitutional Court is necessary in order to lodge an appeal before the ECtHR is dependent upon procedural requirements and the effectiveness of the procedure. Although the will of the law maker was to turn the Constitutional Court into a human rights court it is clear that the Constitutional Court's position does not constitute a monopoly. The judiciary remains competent to review Statutes against Convention rights. Under some circumstances the courts are obliged to refer a case to the Constitutional Court. Surprisingly this is the case particularly when the courts establish a potential violation of a human right. They are not obliged to refer to the Constitutional Court if they uphold a Statute in which case the Constitutional Court could constitute an extra remedy. This will be dealt with in the next paragraph.

4.1.2. Reference to the Constitutional Court in the case of analogous human rights

Until recently the question whether courts in the case of analogous human rights can review Statutes directly against the ECHR or whether they should lodge a preliminary reference before the Constitutional Court, was open to discussion. According to the Special Law on the Constitutional Court whenever a party to

---

50 See *Crnojević v. Croatia* (App no 71614/01) 29 April 2003, *Zovanović v. Croatia* (App no 12877/02) 9 December 2004, *Dragicević v. Croatia* (App no 11814/02) 9 December 2004.

51 R Ergec, 'La Cour d'arbitrage et le juge international et européen' in F Delpérée, A Rasson-Roland and M Verdussen, *Regards croisés sur la Cour d'arbitrage* (Bruylant, Brussels 1995) 211.

52 E.g. Council of State *D'Hondt* No 104.653, 13 March 2002.

the proceedings raises such a preliminary reference these courts were obliged to pose the question to the Constitutional Court. However the Court of Cassation used to reject the preliminary reference on the ground that it is competent to review the Statute directly on the basis of the international treaty.[53] This marked a growing tension between the Court of Cassation and the Constitutional Court.[54]

A recent amendment of the Special Law on the Constitutional Court deals exactly with this point of discussion.[55] It is based upon a compromise elaborated in a seminar which brought together academics, practitioners and judges from the three highest courts.[56] The court is now obliged to first lodge a preliminary reference before the Constitutional Court in case a party claims a violation of a fundamental right which is guaranteed both by the Constitution and international law. This way courts cannot use EU law and preliminary rulings to side-step the Constitutional Court.[57]

There are three exceptions to this obligation. The first exception refers to a general set of circumstances which exempt courts from their obligation to refer preliminary questions in ordinary cases, apart from the analogous human right hypothesis. The second exception expresses the '*acte clair*' theory. No preliminary reference is required when it is obvious that the Statute does not infringe the constitutional clause. Finally an exception applies when a decision of an international court or the Constitutional Court makes clear that either the treaty or the constitutional right is violated.

It is striking that the law maker's main concern relates to the maintenance of Statutes rather than the protection of human rights. The regulation sees to it that constitutional review – directly or indirectly through review against analogous conventional rights – only leads to invalidating a Statute for violation of a human right after having been submitted to the Constitutional Court. If the Court of Cassation decides that a constitutional right obviously has not been violated, the Constitutional Court has no say in the matter. The only exception is the

53 Cass (P040849N) 9 November 2004, Cass (P040644N) 16 November 2004, Cass (P041127N) 16 November 2004.

54 E De Wet, 'The Reception Process in the Netherlands and Belgium' in H Keller & A Stone Sweet, *A Europe of Rights. The Impact of the ECHR on National Legal Systems* (Oxford University Press, Oxford 2008) 251.

55 Special Law of 12 July 2009 amending Article 26 of the Special Law of 6 January 1989 on the Constitutional Court.

56 See Report Velaers, 'Le contrôle des lois, décrets et ordonnances au regard du titre II de la Constitution et des conventions internationales relatives aux droits de l'homme, en cas de concours de droits fondamentaux', in A Arts, I Verougstraete et al. (eds.), *Les rapports entre la Cour d'arbitrage, le Pouvoir Judiciaire et le Conseil d'Etat* (La Charte, Brussels 2006) 144–147.

57 See for this "inter-court competition" notion M Claes, *The National Courts' Mandate in the European Constitution* (Hart Publishing, Oxford 2006) 257–258.

circumstance where an international court has established violation of a conventional human right.

From a human rights point of view, however, the protection of individuals should be the law maker's starting point. The procedure should be organised in such a way that the violation of a human right enshrined in the constitution or in a treaty cannot remain unnoticed by a court specialised in human rights issues. From this point of view another solution seems more logical. If the Court of Cassation establishes violation of a Convention right, it is not necessary for the Constitutional Court to decide whether an analogous constitutional right has been violated as well. If on the other hand the Court of Cassation establishes that a Convention right has not been violated, preliminary reference to the Constitutional Court should remain open. After all, rights enshrined in international treaties such as the ECHR merely offer minimum protection. The Constitutional Court should be able to execute a profound review against constitutional rights after the ordinary courts' initial human rights assessment.

4.2. CONSEQUENCES OF THE *SIMMENTHAL* CASE

In Belgium debate arose concerning the consequences of the *Simmenthal* case.

In this case the ECJ stated: '*[...] any provision of a national legal system and any legislative, administrative or judicial practice which might impair the effectiveness of Community law by withholding from the national court having jurisdiction to apply such law the power to do everything necessary at the moment of its application to set aside national legislative provisions which might prevent community rules from having full force and effect are incompatible with those requirements which are the very essence of community law. This would be the case in the event of a conflict between a provision of Community law and a subsequent national law if the solution of the conflict were to be reserved for an authority with a discretion of its own, other than the court called upon to apply community law, even if such an impediment to the full effectiveness of community law were only temporary. [...] a national court which is called upon, within the limits of its jurisdiction, to apply provisions of Community law is under a duty to give full effect to those provisions, if necessarily refusing of its own motion to apply any conflicting provision of national legislation, even if adopted subsequently, and it is not necessary for the court to request or await the prior setting aside of such provision by legislative or other constitutional means.*'[58]

In the *Mecanarte* case it confirmed: '[...] *the effectiveness of Community law would be in jeopardy if the existence of an obligation to refer a matter to a constitutional court could prevent a national court hearing a case governed by*

[58] Case C-106/77 *Italian Finance Administration v Simmenthal*, [1978] ECR 629.

Community law from exercising the right conferred on it by Article 177 of the EEC Treaty to refer to the Court of Justice questions concerning the interpretation or validity of Community law in order to enable it to decide whether or not a provision of domestic law was compatible with Community law. It must therefore be stated [...] that a national court which in a case concerning Community law declares a provision of national law unconstitutional does not lose the right or escape the obligation under Article 177 of the EEC Treaty to refer questions to the Court of Justice on the interpretation or validity of Community law by reason of the fact that such a declaration is subject to a mandatory reference to the constitutional court'[59]

The question arose whether the obligation to refer a question to the Constitutional Court is in accordance with the case law of the European Court of Justice if the case concerns analogous human rights protected by both the Constitution and EU law. According to some scholars, including the President and the Advocate General of the Court of Cassation, it was doubtful whether the obligation to refer to the Constitutional Court before applying EU human rights law or referring to the ECJ, stood the *Simmenthal* test, which equally applies to temporary impediments to the full effectiveness of EU law.[60][61] This would have undermined a great part of the regulation of preliminary references in the case of analogous protection of fundamental rights, as the human rights enshrined in the ECHR are also part of EU law. However, in the *Melki* case, discussed below, the ECJ had accepted some delay under specific conditions.[62]

The Council of State on the other hand, in its advice to Parliament took another position based on the following arguments.[63] The Simmenthal and Mecanarte judgments concern the situation in which the exclusive competence to review national law against EU law has been reserved to the constitutional court. The Belgian regulation obliges national courts to first refer the constitutional question to the Constitutional Court. It doesn't prevent them from applying EU

59 Case C-348/89 *Mecanarte-Metalúrgica da Lagoa v Alfandega do Porto* [1991] ECR I-3277.

60 Report, *Parl.Doc.* Senate 2007–2008, 4–12/4, 18;.

61 Note in the Parliamentary's Commission report, *Parl. Doc.* Senate 2007–2008, 4–12/4, at p. 18 (see www.senate.be); P Van Nuffel, 'Prejudiciële vragen aan het Hof van Justitie na het Verdrag van Lissabon' [2009–2010] *Rechtskundig Weekblad* 1170–1172.

62 See also W Verrijdt, "Should the EU Effectiveness Principle Be Applied to Judge National Constitutional Review Procedures?", in *Liège, Strasbourg, Bruxelles: parcours des droits de l'homme* (Limal, Anthemis, 2010), 552.

63 Council of State, Division Legislation, Advice No 45.905/AG of 3 March 2009, *Parl. Doc.* House of Representatives 2008–2009, 52–1283/2, p. 8–22 (see www.lachambre.be). The Council adopted the arguments already put forward in J Velaers, 'De samenloop van grondrechten in het Belgisch rechtsbestel' in *Samenloop van grondrechten in verschillende rechtsstelsels, multiculturaliteit in het strafrecht & schuldsanering en collectieve schuldenregeling* (Boom Juridische Uitgevers, The Hague 2008) 123–128.

law afterwards.[64] The ECJ in these cases did not deal with the question whether procedural requirements such as reference to the Constitutional Court may delay direct application of EU law or preliminary reference to the ECJ.[65] Moreover the Council of State drew attention to the ECJ case law concerning the Member States' procedural autonomy.[66] Also in *Mecanarte*, the ECJ confirmed: '*national courts have a discretion as to whether a decision on a point of Community law is necessary to enable them to give judgment*'.[67]

After the coming into force of the Belgian priority rule, the Court of Justice, in the *Melki* case, explained its concerns regarding a national system giving priority to constitutional review by a Constitutional Court: '*To the extent that the priority nature of an interlocutory procedure for the review of constitutionality leads to the repeal of a national law – which merely transposes the mandatory provisions of a European Union directive – on the basis that that law is contrary to the national constitution, the Court could, in practice, be denied the possibility, at the request of the courts ruling on the substance of cases in the Member State concerned, of reviewing the validity of that directive in relation to the same grounds relating to the requirements of primary law, and in particular the rights recognised by the Charter of Fundamental Rights of the European Union, to which Article 6 TEU accords the same legal value as that accorded to the Treaties.*'[68] The Court further clarifies that Article 267 TFEU does not preclude national legislation which establishes an interlocutory procedure for the review of the constitutionality of national law having priority over the review by the other courts and tribunals, on the condition that these courts and tribunals remain free: 1) to refer to the Court of Justice for a preliminary ruling, at whatever stage of the proceedings they consider appropriate, even at the end of the interlocutory procedure for the review of constitutionality, any question which they consider necessary; 2) to adopt any measure necessary to ensure provisional judicial protection of the rights conferred under the European Union legal order, and 3) to disapply, at the end of such an interlocutory procedure, the national legislative provision at issue if they consider it to be contrary to EU law. A fourth condition follows from an *obiter dictum* in which the Court refers to its *Foto-Frost* case law: if the procedure concerns a national law, the content of which merely transposes the mandatory provisions of a European Union directive, the validity of the directive is at stake, which is for the Court of Justice alone to declare.[69]

64 Advice No 45.905/AG, p. 13–14.
65 Advice No 45.905/AG, p. 14.
66 See Cases C-430/93 and C-431/93 *Van Schijndel v Stichting Pensioenfonds voor Fysiotherapeuten* [1995] ECR I-4705, Case C-432/05 *Unibet* [2007] ECR I-2271.
67 Case C-348/89 *Mecanarte-Metalúrgica da Lagoa v Alfandega do Porto* [1991] ECR I-3277.
68 Cases C-188/10 and C-189/10 *Melki and Abdeli* (ECJ 22 June 2010).
69 No. 54. See Case 314/85 *Foto-Frost* [1987] ECR 4199.

It can be argued that the Belgian legislation can be interpreted in conformity with the conditions identified in the *Melki* case.[70] Indeed the obligation to refer a preliminary question to the Constitutional Court does not prevent the court from lodging another preliminary question before the ECJ. Also the law allows the referring court to adopt provisional measures to ensure judicial protection of the rights conferred under the European Union legal order. Lastly the priority given to the Constitutional Court does not prevent the courts and tribunals to review an Act of Parliament against international or EU law of their own accord, even if in doing so they might contradict the Constitutional Court. According to VELAERS the preliminary ruling does not bind the court as far as the review against EU law is concerned, because the Constitutional Court is not able to review directly against EU law but only indirectly, mostly *via* Articles 10 and 11 of the Constitution.[71] In reality however, it is sometimes difficult to separate the Court's constitutional review from the review against EU law. It seems unlikely that the referring court would contradict the Constitutional Court, unless it would base its judgment on a decision of an international court such as the ECJ or the ECtHR. For example, in a case outside the field of human rights, the Brussels Court of Appeal stated as a principle that 'notwithstanding' the decision of the Constitutional Court concerning the implications of EU law in a particular case, the court is still competent to review Acts of Parliament in the light of international treaties.[72] In this case the Court of Appeal did not apply an Act of Parliament. Although the Constitutional Court had judged that the Act was in conformity with the Constitution linked to EU law, the European Court of Justice meanwhile had judged that it did violate EU law.

4.3. PRELIMINARY REFERENCES TO THE EUROPEAN COURT OF JUSTICE

Although a direct test against EU law is excluded, questions concerning the interpretation or validity of EU law do arise before the Constitutional Court. The Court does not question its nature as a court or tribunal in the sense of Article

70 See J Velaers, 'Het arrest Melki-Abdeli van het Hof van Justitie van de Europese Unie: een voorwaardelijk "fiat" voor de voorrang van de toetsing aan de grondwet op de toetsing aan het internationaal en Europees recht", [2010–2011] *Rechtskundig Weekblad* 770–794; W Verrijdt, "Should the EU Effectiveness Principle Be Applied to Judge National Constitutional Review Procedures?", in *Liège, Strasbourg, Bruxelles: parcours des droits de l'homme* (Limal, Anthemis, 2010), 555. A preliminary reference to the ECJ on this matter has been declared inadmissible because there was no link with EU law, C-457/0, *Chartry v Belgian State*, Order of 1 March 2011.

71 See J Velaers, 'Het arrest Melki-Abdeli van het Hof van Justitie van de Europese Unie: een voorwaardelijk "fiat" voor de voorrang van de toetsing aan de grondwet op de toetsing aan het internationaal en Europees recht", [2010–2011] *Rechtskundig Weekblad*, 797–798.

72 Brussels Court of Appeal (AR 1094) 27 April 2009.

267 TFEU.[73] Moreover it does not question its nature as a court falling under the scope of Article 267 par. 3 TFEU:[74] '*Where any such question is raised in a case pending before a court or tribunal of a Member State against whose decisions there is no judicial remedy under national law, that court or tribunal shall bring the matter before the Court of Justice*'. These courts are only exempted from referring a question to the ECJ if they have '*established that the question raised is irrelevant or that the Community provision in question has already been interpreted by the Court or that the correct application of Community law is so obvious as to leave no scope for any reasonable doubt*'.[75] This exemption however only applies to questions concerning the interpretation of EU law.[76]

The Constitutional Court sometimes refuses preliminary reference to the ECJ in cases which do leave 'scope for any reasonable doubt'.[77] Nevertheless compared to other constitutional courts, the Belgian constitutional court demonstrates a remarkable willingness to refer questions to the European Court of Justice. It refers more questions than other constitutional courts[78] and its questions relate to interpretation issues as well as validity issues.[79]

According to Velaers the Constitutional Court's eagerness to avoid contradictory judgments in the case of human rights explains its openness to EU law.[80]

---

73 Ex Article 234 TEU. See also M Claes, *The National Courts' Mandate in the European Constitution* (Hart Publishing, Oxford 2006) 444.

74 Doubtful however in preliminary references cases (opposed to annulation requests) J Velaers, 'De samenloop van grondrechten in het Belgisch rechtsbestel' in *Samenloop van grondrechten in verschillende rechtsstelsels, multiculturaliteit in het strafrecht & schuldsanering en collectieve schuldenregeling* (Boom Juridische Uitgevers, The Hague 2008) 137 at footnote 211.

75 Case C-283/81 *CILFIT v Ministero della Sanità* [1982] ECR 3415.

76 Case C-461/03 *Gaston Schul Douane-expediteur* [2005] ECR I-10513.

77 See P Van Nuffel, 'Het Europees recht in de rechtspraak van het Arbitragehof. Prejudiciële vragen, te veel gevraagd?' in A Alen (ed.), *20 jaar Arbitragehof* (Kluwer, Antwerp 2005) 43–45. Until now the Constitutional Court has referred to the ECJ on fourteen occasions: Const. Court No 6/97, 19 February 1997, Const. Court. No 139/2003, 29 October 2003, Const. Court No 124/2005, 13 July 2005, Const. Court No 126/2005, 13 July 2005, Const. Court. No 51/2006, 19 April 2006, Const. Court No 12/2008, 14 February 2008, Const. Court No 131/2008, 1 September 2008, Const. Court No 103/2009, 18 June 2009, Const. Court No 128/2009, 24 July 2009, Const. Court No 30/3010, 30 March 2010, Const. Court No 133/2010, 25 November 2010, Const. Court No. 149/2010, 22 December 2010, Const. Court No 49/2011, 6 April 2011, Const. Court No 50/2011, 6 April 2011.

78 See for statistics the ECJ's annual reports at http://curia.europa.eu/jcms/jcms/Jo2_11035/rapports-annuels.

79 Preliminary references concerning the validity of EU law were raised in Constitutional Court No 124/2005, 13 July 2005, No 126/2005, 13 July 2005, No 103/2009, 18 June 2009 and No 128/2009, 24 July 2009.

80 J Velaers, 'De samenloop van grondrechten in het Belgisch rechtsbestel', in *Samenloop van grondrechten in verschillende rechtsstelsels, multiculturaliteit in het strafrecht & schuldsanering en collectieve schuldenregeling* (Boom Juridische Uitgevers, The Hague 2008), p. 141.

Vandamme refers to the evolution the Constitutional Court has gone through. Originally established as a court with limited competences, the wide use of Articles 10 and 11 of the Belgian Constitution has allowed it to include international and EU law in its set of norms of control and have helped to obtain its position as a fully-fledged constitutional court.[81] This would explain the Court's openness to enter into dialogue with European courts.

The fact is that the Belgian Constitutional Court was established in the context of a European-minded legal order. The *Franco Suisse Le Ski* rule, giving priority to direct applicable international law, had already become part of the constitutional order. Moreover, contrary to e.g. the German *Bundesverfassungsgericht*, the Belgian Constitutional Court is a relatively young court which is not hindered by a long tradition of constitutional review giving rise to a comprehensive national doctrine of fundamental rights.

4.4. THE MAXIMISATION CLAUSE

In some cases the Belgian Constitution provides for broader protection than analogous conventional human rights. For example Article 25 Constitution in protecting freedom of the 'printing-press'[82] forbids all preventive measures. According to Articles 26 and 27 Constitution also the freedom of association cannot be subjected to preventive measures, except in the case of reunions in the open air. Also the Belgian Constitution often requires that interference must be based upon an Act of Parliament.

Article 53 ECHR contains a maximisation clause which guarantees the highest level of protection. This may come down to a combination of both constitutional and conventional rights. For example according to ECtHR case law interference must be 'foreseen by law'. This does not necessarily imply a Statute but it does refer to quality requirements: the law must provide for a legal basis which is accessible and foreseeable. On the other hand the Constitution may require that interference must be based upon a Statute. In such cases the Constitutional Court combines formal and material legality requirements.[83]

---

81 T Vandamme, 'Prochain Arrêt: La Belgique! Explaining Recent Preliminary References of the Belgian Constitutional Court' [2008] *Eu Const L Rev* 147–148. Compare M Claes, *The National Courts' Mandate in the European Constitution* (Hart Publishing, Oxford 2006): for (other) constitutional courts the ECJ case of law implies a curtailment of their powers.

82 The Court of Cassation interprets this in a strict way. Thus the Article does not apply to other mediums suh as television programs or internet publications. See Cass. 9 December 1981, [1981–1982] *A.C.* 491. Article 19 B.C. protects the freedom of expression in a more general way.

83 Const. Court No 202/2004, 21 December 2004, Const. Court No 131/2005, 19 July 2005, Const. Court No 151/2006, 18 October 2006.

The application of the maximisation clause can however be problematic. It is not always clear which clause provides for the broadest protection. Problems arise especially in the case of conflicts of human rights. Priority for one right may result in a less favourable protection of the other right. For example in Belgian doctrine debate arose concerning the question whether Article 148 Constitution has priority over Article 6 ECHR. The former guarantees publicity of trials in a broader way than the latter, whereas in limiting publicity the latter gives broader protection to the right to privacy.[84]

The ECtHR in these cases does not seem to attach much importance to Article 53 ECHR.[85] Likewise Article 53 ECHR does not take up a prominent role in the case law of the Belgian Constitutional Court. In only a few cases did the Constitutional Court refer to Article 53 ECHR (or the former Article 60 ECHR).[86]

In the first case the Council of State referred a question concerning the validity of the law giving consent to the ECHR in as far as Article 6 ECHR would not apply to disciplinary procedures against clerks of the court. The Constitutional Court upheld the law considering that Article 53 ECHR implies that Article 6 ECHR does not hinder the application of rights granted by national law to clerks of the court.[87] In another case the Constitutional Court reminded that it cannot extend the scope of a conventional right on the basis of Article 53 ECHR.[88] In Case No. 159/2004 the Constitutional Court invoked Article 53 ECHR in order to explain that the law introducing unisex marriages does not violate conventional clauses which protect marriages between men and women. On the contrary the national law maker can extend the right to marry to persons of the same sex.[89] In some other cases the Constitutional Court confirms that on the basis of Article 53 ECHR the material legality principle enshrined in the ECHR must be combined with the formal legality principle in the Constitution.[90]

84 See E Brems, 'Vers des clauses transversales en matière de droits et libertés dans la Constitution belge' [2007] *Rev.Trim.Dr.H.* 374, O De Schutter & S Van Drooghenbroeck, *Droit international des Droits de l'Homme devant le juge national* (Larcier, Brussels 1999) and J Velaers & S Van Drooghenbroeck in Commission Report, 'Les clauses transversales en matière de droits et libertés' *Parl.Doc.* House of Representatives 2004–2005, 51–2304/1, 111–112.

85 *Open Door and Dublin Well Woman v. Ireland* (App no 14234/88; 14235/8819) (1992) Series A no 46–1, *Leempoel & s.a. Ed. Ciné Revue v. Belgium* (App no 64772/01) ECHR 9 November 2006.

86 In four other cases the Article was referred to by the parties but was not considered in the judgment, see Const. Court No 77/94, 18 October 1994, Const. Court 34/96, 15 May 1996, Const. Court No 76/96, 18 December 1996, Const. Court No 49/2001, 18 April 2001.

87 Const. Court No 33/94, 26 April 1994.

88 Const. Court No 81/95, 14 December 1995.

89 Const. Court No 159/2004, 20 October 2004.

90 Const. Court No 202/2004, 21 December 2004, Const. Court No 131/2005, 19 July 2005, Const. Court No 151/2006, 18 October 2006.

The Constitutional Court however has less need to refer to Article 53 ECHR as it already combines constitutional and Convention rights through a process of interpretation. As explained above, this may lead to a restriction of constitutional guarantees in order to balance conflicting fundamental rights.

5. THE PROTECTION OF HUMAN RIGHTS IN CONVERGING LEGAL ORDERS: THE *MONEY LAUNDERING CASE*

A case study illustrates the ambiguous position of the Constitutional Court in relation to both EU law and the ECHR.

In the Money Laundering Case Belgian Bar Associations sought the annulment of certain Articles of the Law relating to the prevention of the use of the financial system for the purpose of money laundering. They argued that certain obligations for lawyers to cooperate with and provide information to the Financial Information Processing Unit, run counter to fundamental principles such as professional secrecy and independence of the lawyer and thus violate the right to a fair trial and the right to defence enshrined in Article 6 ECHR. This law however implements the European Directive 2001/97. As the fundamental rights at stake are also binding to the EU law maker, the Constitutional Court referred a question to the ECJ for a preliminary ruling on the validity of the EU Directive.[91] The legal question finally came down to how far the Directive allows or should allow for derogation to the cooperation and information requirements for lawyers.

The applicants before the Constitutional Court invoked both Article 6 and Article 8 ECHR. In their request for a preliminary reference, however, they focused on Article 6 ECHR. In his Opinion Advocate General Maduro remarked that professional secrecy in the case law of the ECtHR is linked to both Article 6 (fair trial) and Article 8 ECHR (respect for private life).[92] The choice of one of these two bases seemed nonetheless not relevant to him in this case. The ECJ noted that 'the referring court has considered it necessary to ask the Court to review the legality of that directive solely by reference to the right to a fair trial, as guaranteed by Article 6 of the ECHR and Article 6(2) EU.'[93] The Court concluded that the Directive does not infringe the right to a fair trial, account being taken of the fact that the Member States are not obliged to impose the obligations of information and cooperation on lawyers as regards information

91 Const. Court No 126/2005, 13 July 2005.

92 Case C-305/05, Opinion delivered on 14 December 2006.

93 Case C-305/05 *Ordre des barreaux francophones et germanophone and others* [2007] ECR I-5305.

which they have received from a client, or obtained on one of their clients, in the course of ascertaining the client's legal position or in the course of performing their task of defending or representing that client in, or concerning, judicial proceedings, including the giving of advice or instituting or avoiding such proceedings.

The Constitutional Court validated the law on most points, however it annulled a part of one provision.[94]

After having cited the ECJ's ruling it executed its own test against Articles 10–11 of the Belgian Constitution combined to Articles 6 and 8 ECHR. It concluded that the law is in conformity with these Articles, provided that it is interpreted in such a way that it does not apply to lawyers when acting in the course or concerning judicial proceedings, *or* when rendering legal advice. This interpretation is broader than the one provided by the ECJ, but in line with the Advocate General's Opinion.

Finally it annulled the law in so far as it allowed lawyer's employees or representatives to give information concerning a client to the Financial Information Processing Unit whenever the lawyer was unable to do this. According to the Court this was contrary to Articles 10–11 Constitution combined to Article 6 ECHR, although this provision was also a (not literal) transposition of the EU Directive. This part had not been included in the preliminary question submitted to the ECJ and should have been the subject of a new preliminary reference.

According to some authors the Constitutional Court in this case has established the primacy of the Constitution over secondary EU law.[95] The Constitutional Court however does not explicitly confirm this view.[96] In any case it is most regrettable that the Constitutional Court did not extend its prejudicial question to Article 8 ECHR. Likewise it is regrettable that the ECJ did not follow the Advocate General's Opinion where he stated that the ECJ could widen the scope of the preliminary question to that respect.[97]

---

94 Const. Court No 10/2008, 23 January 2008.

95 E Cloots, 'Grondwettelijk Hof plaatst grondrechten boven secundair EU-recht' 165 (12 March 2008) *Juristenkrant* 15, J Stevens & G-A Dal, 'Het arrest van het Grondwettelijk Hof van 23 januari 2008 en de preventie van het witwassen: de Ordes halen hun gelijk' [2008–2009] *R.W.* 104. More hesitant: E Cloots, 'Het Grondwettelijk Hof en de toetsing van secundair Unierecht aan fundamentele rechten', in A Alen & J Van Nieuwenhove (eds.), *Leuvense Staatsrechtelijke Standpunten* (die Keure, Bruges 2008) p. 51–52.

96 See also E Cloots, 'Het Grondwettelijk Hof en de toetsing van secundair Unierecht aan fundamentele rechten', in A Alen & J. Van Nieuwenhove (eds.), *Leuvense Staatsrechtelijke Standpunten* (die Keure, Bruges 2008) 50–52 about the "mysterious" position of the Constitutional Court regarding the relation Constitution and secondary EU law.

97 See also Y Moiny, 'L'arrêt de la Cour Constitutionnelle belge du 23 janvier 2008 et son impact sur le rôle de l'avocat dans le cadre de la lutte contre le blanchement de capitaux ainsi que le financement du terrorisme', [2008] *Cah. Dr. Eu.* 469.

Most important is that the constitutional provisions were merely stepping-stones for a review against the ECHR. The heart of the problem concerns the relation of EU law and ECHR. According to Velaers the Constitutional Court in this case followed the *Bosphorus* case law: there is an assumption that the EU offers equal protection, unless in the specific circumstances of a particular case, it is considered that the protection of Convention rights was manifestly deficient.[98] It is doubtful however whether, as some authors suggest, the ECJ intentionally gave the Constitutional Court liberty to perform a final review to fundamental rights enshrined in the constitution and in the ECHR.[99]

According to Claes the Constitutional Court has found a way out of the supremacy dilemma (supremacy of the Constitution or supremacy of EU law) by declaring that it lacks jurisdiction to pronounce itself on the constitutionality of EU law.[100] The *Money Laundering* case nonetheless makes clear that referral to the ECJ does not solve the dilemma if the ECJ judgment remains unsatisfactory in terms of human rights protection. In this case the Constitutional Court has chosen for the full protection of a fundamental right. Unfortunately it did not explain whether it, in line with the *Bosphorus case law*, deliberately diverted from the ECJ ruling or whether it refrained from new preliminary references to prevent further delays. Its stance therefore remains at this moment quite unclear.

6. CONCLUSION

The Belgian Constitutional Court is said to be 'the least protective and most *communautaire* of all constitutional courts'.[101] It embraces both ECHR and EU law. Constitutional rights are interpreted in conformity with the ECHR and ECtHR case law, even to such an extent that the scope of constitutional rights may be limited. Therefore conflicts between EU law and constitutional law often come down to conflicts between EU law and the ECHR. In an attempt to respect both the primacy of the ECHR and of EU law, the Constitutional Court interprets

---

98 J Velaers, 'De samenloop van grondrechten in het Belgisch rechtsbestel', in *Samenloop van grondrechten in verschillende rechtsstelsels, multiculturaliteit in het strafrecht & schuldsanering en collectieve schuldenregeling* (Boom Juridische Uitgevers, The Hague 2008) 140–141.

99 J Stevens & G-A Dal, 'Het arrest van het Grondwettelijk Hof van 23 januari 2008 en de preventie van het witwassen: de Ordes halen hun gelijk' [2008–2009] *R.W.* 99. They refer to the wordings of the ECJ judgment: "*Member States must not only interpret the national law in a manner consistent with Community law but also make sure they do not rely on an interpretation of wording of secondary legislation which would be in conflict with the fundamental rights protected by the Community legal order or with the other general principles of Community law*".

100 M Claes, *The National Courts' Mandate in the European Constitution* (Hart Publishing, Oxford 2006) 262.

101 M Claes, *The National Courts' Mandate in the European Constitution* (Hart Publishing, Oxford 2006) 641.

constitutional clauses in accordance with human rights enshrined in international law and resorts to the ECJ in case the unconstitutionality of a Statute originates from an EU directive.

The Money Laundering case shows, however, that in the end the Belgian Constitutional Court meets the dilemma as formulated by Monica CLAES: '*In the framework of Community law the constitutional courts thus seem to have an impossible choice to make: either they accept the mandate from the Court of Justice and consequently partly renounce their constitutional mandate to uphold the Constitution; or they continue to protect the fundamental values enshrined in the Constitution and consequently are unable to guarantee, in all cases, the supremacy of Community law.*'[102]

It remains yet uncertain how this dilemma will be solved. It is clear, however, that the Constitutional Court, although rather European minded compared to other constitutional courts, shows more reluctance than the Court of Cassation. It has moderated the traditional monist view in cases where the Parliamentary Act of assent is unconstitutional, whereas the Court of Cassation fully accepts the supremacy of international law over the constitution. Also in practice (though not yet by way of an explicit general ruling) it is reluctant to accept the supremacy of EU law if this would entail manifest infringement of a fundamental right protected both by the constitution and the ECHR.

---

102 M Claes, *The National Courts' Mandate in the European Constitution* (Hart Publishing, Oxford 2006) 388.

CHAPTER 6

EAST EUROPEAN COUNTRIES

ON SECRET LEGISLATION, BLANKET DATA RECORDING, ARREST WARRANTS AND PROPERTY RIGHTS: QUESTIONS ON THE RULE OF LAW AND JUDICIAL REVIEW IN THE EU IN THE LIGHT OF POST-COMMUNIST CONSTITUTIONS

Anneli ALBI*

1. THE CENTRALITY OF THE RULE OF LAW IN THE POST-COMMUNIST CONSTITUTIONAL REFORMS AND THE COMMITMENT TO THE ECHR

In the literature on European constitutionalism, a considerable element of ambivalence and doubt has been expressed with regard to the courts of the new Member States from Central and Eastern Europe (CEE). The ambivalence surrounds four areas in particular. First, there is a general concern about human rights protection in the region, given the background of these countries under the totalitarian regime. Indeed this prompted an unprecedented scrutiny of the countries' record in democracy, rule of law and human rights before their accession to the European Union, under the so-called Copenhagen Criteria.[1] Secondly, there have been concerns as to whether the CEE courts are co-operative

* Senior Lecturer in EU Law, University of Kent (Canterbury, UK). I would like to thank Catherine Van De Heyning and the anonymous referees for their comments. The usual disclaimer applies.

1 For a detailed account of the human rights conditionality, see A. Williams, 'Enlargement and Human Rights Conditionality', (2000) 25 *European Law Review*, 601 and W. Sadurski, 'Accession's Democracy Dividend: The Impact of the EU Enlargement upon Democracy in the New Member States of Central and Eastern Europe', (2004) 10 *European Law Journal*, 371.

with regard to supremacy of EU law, given how recently these countries regained their sovereignty. The received wisdom is that many of them have not been EU-friendly, stubbornly continuing to protect sovereignty. In particular, the Polish Constitutional Court has been described in one leading textbook as representing an approach which 'insists upon the continuing and unconditional sovereignty of the national constitutional order'.[2] According to another leading textbook, these courts have found 'the pull towards rephrasing sovereignty-based objections against the supremacy of EU law ... irresistible'.[3] The Hungarian Constitutional Court has been described as 'slow' to reassess its new role in the aftermath of EU membership, as 'the state organs of new EU members still have to learn the rules of "cooperative constitutionalism".'[4] The third line of criticism is that CEE courts take a formalistic approach to interpretation and are not good at operating with abstract principles and teleological interpretation, which could affect the effectiveness of EU law given the approach used by the European Court of Justice.[5] Fourthly, there is considerable doubt with regard to the independence of CEE judges, and in some countries relevant constitutional amendments have been required by the European Commission.

While questions surrounding the record of CEE countries no doubt continue to be justified in many respects, this paper will argue that the experiences of the post-communist countries make them well placed to make an important contribution to the evolution of the EU constitutional order in at least one important area. It is the German concept of *Rechtsstaat* or the English-language equivalent of the rule of law, which has been central to the post-communist constitutional reforms and has been vigorously defended by the CEE constitutional courts. The heightened commitment to the idea of the rule of law represents a radical departure from the Communist rule. The Communist regime had been marked by the following features: the ruling Communist party's position above the law; teleological use of law to achieve the objectives of a communist society; arbitrary exercise of power by the executive; retroactive imposition of sanctions without a legal base; trampling of human rights; expropriation of private property; absence of a hierarchy of legal acts and of a distinction between legislative and administrative acts; absence of judicial review; adoption of any measures required by expediencies of the 'planned economy'; and overall legal nihilism.

---

2 D Chalmers, C Hadjiemmanuil, G Monti and A Tomkins, *European Union Law* (Cambridge University Press, Cambridge 2006) 198–199 and 201.

3 W Sadurski, "'Solange, Chapter 3': Constitutional Courts in Central Europe", *EUI Law Working Paper* 2006/40, 2–4, as cited in Craig and de Burca, *EU Law. Texts Cases and Materials*, 4th ed. (OUP, 2008), 373–374.

4 A Sajó, 'Learning Co-operative Constitutionalism the Hard Way: The Hungarian Constitutional Court Shying Away from EU Supremacy', (2004) 2 *Zeitschrift für Staats- und Europawissenschaften* 351, 351.

5 See e.g. an influential article by Z Kühn, 'The Application of European Law in the New Member States: Several (Early) Predictions' (2005) 3 *German Law Journal* 565.

In reaction to the Communist regime, strong constitutions were put in place. They accord a prominent position to the principle of the rule of law, which, usually placed at the opening provisions, 'best summarises the idealistic spirit of the post-communist constitutions'.[6] The rule of law implied a hierarchy of norms, at the top of which was the constitution; the principle was intended to ensure limitations to the state power and respect of the individuals' rights.[7] Another element was a strong commitment to the separation of powers, with an elaborate system of checks and balances, including the review of compliance by constitutional courts modelled on the German Constitutional Court. Additionally, the constitutions also accord a central position to fundamental rights, setting out detailed catalogues of rights. The detailed nature of the constitutions and their adjudication by the constitutional courts makes the CEE constitutions more 'legal' in nature, similar to, for example, the German, Italian and Portuguese constitutions which were adopted after the fall of authoritarian regimes. These features distinguish the CEE constitutions from e.g. Nordic and Dutch constitutions and the UK's unwritten constitution, which are more evolutionary in nature.[8]

It is well documented that CEE constitutional courts have enjoyed a prominent and powerful status in adjudicating the constitutionality of parliamentary legislation and government measures, having been widely applauded as vanguards in the protection of fundamental rights.[9] Their case-law is marked by four features in particular, which have been documented in detail elsewhere.[10] By way of a summary, these features include a high ratio of annulment of laws, and frequency of the use of the general principles as grounds for annulment, especially the principle of *Rechtsstaat* or the rule of law, and its sub-principles such as legal certainty, non-retroactivity, proportionality and vested private

---

6 C Dupré, *Importing the Law in Post-Communist Transitions. The Hungarian Constitutional Court and the Right to Human Dignity* (Hart, Oxford 2003), at 20.

7 *Ibid.*, 22.

8 For the two categories of constitutions, see L Besselink, 'The Dutch Constitution, the European Constitution and the Referendum in the Netherlands', in A Albi and J Ziller (Eds.), *The European Constitution and National Constitutions: Ratification and Beyond* (Kluwer, Dordrecht 2006) 113ff. and A Albi, *EU Enlargement and the Constitutions of Central and Eastern Europe* (Cambridge University Press, Cambridge 2005) 22ff.

9 See e.g. W Sadurski (Ed.), *Constitutional Justice, East and West. Democratic Legitimacy and Constitutional Courts in Post-Communist Europe in a Comparative Perspective* (Kluwer, Dordrecht 2002), J Schwartz, *The Struggle for Constitutional Justice in Post-Communist Europe* (University of Chicago Press, Chicago 2000), J Priban, P Roberts and J Young (Eds.), *Systems of Justice in Transition. Central European Experiences since 1989* (Ashgate, Aldershot 2003), W Sadurski, *Rights Before Courts: A Study of Constitutional Courts in Postcommunist States of Central and Eastern Europe* (Springer, 2005) and R Prochazka, *Mission Accomplished: On Founding Constitutional Adjudication in Central Europe* (CEU Press, Budapest, 2002).

10 Including case statistics and references to literature, see A Albi, 'Ironies in human rights protection in the EU: Pre-accession conditionality and post-accession conundrums', (2009) 15 *European Law Journal*, 64ff.

rights. Additionally, while the communist constitutions were designed to foster the development of the planned economy and to shape a socialist society where rights were granted by the party, now precedence is firmly given to individual rights over the interests of the society. Limitations on rights are subject to restrictive conditions, with proportionality scrutiny frequently displacing legislative choices by constitutional courts. As a former Chief Justice of the Hungarian Constitutional Court has put it, constitutional review became 'a kind of symbol of the rule of law'.[11]

To bolster the constitutional reforms, the CEE constitutional courts have granted a notably strong position to the European Convention on Human Rights (ECHR), which has led to a *de facto* 'constitutionalisation' of the Convention in CEE legal orders.[12] CEE constitutional courts very frequently refer to the judgments of the European Court of Human Rights (ECtHR) in their decisions, and the Strasbourg Court ranks highly in the minds of the general public in CEE states.[13] The ECHR has been seen in the region as a key way of making the democratic and human rights reforms more resilient, providing the necessary support for domestic democratic and liberal evolutions and trends.[14]

Against this background, the post-communist judges have faced some interesting conundrums in the context of membership of the European Union and the constraints placed on them by virtue of supremacy of EU law. This paper will consider some recent developments in the EU legislation and court practice that raise a host of questions for the above approach to the rule of law. The paper will start by outlining some of the past criticisms in the literature with regard to the low level of review by the European Court of Justice (ECJ) of the measures of EU institutions in matters of market regulation. The paper will then turn to some recent cases where the low level of review seems to have been extended to certain core areas of the rule of law and constitutional rights: the EU Courts have found that secret legislation is valid; that blanket recording of everyone's electronic communications is acceptable; that criminal sanctions can now systematically

---

11 L Solyom, 'On the Co-operation of Constitutional Courts: Introduction to the 10th Conference of European Constitutional Courts', www.mkab.hu, cited in Prochazka, *supra n.* 9, 25.

12 R Harmsen, 'The Transformation of the ECHR Legal Order and the Post-Enlargement Challenges facing the European Court of Human Rights', in G Martinico and O Pollicino (eds) *The National Judicial Treatment of the ECHR and EU Laws. A Comparative Constitutional Perspective* (Europa Law Publishing, Groningen, 2010), at p. 48.

13 W Sadurski, 'Partnering with Strasbourg: Constitutionalisation of the European Court of Human Rights, the Accession of Central and East European States to the Council of Europe, and the Idea of Pilot Judgments' (2009) 9:3 *Human Rights Law Review*, 436 and 442. For examples of cases e.g. in the Baltic states, see I Jarukaitis, 'Report on Estonia, Latvia and Lithuania', in Martinico and Pollicino, supra n. 12, 177ff.

14 Sadurski, 'Partnering with Strasbourg, *supra n.* 13, 435.

be imposed where an act is not a crime under domestic law and where considerable doubts exist with regard to defence rights; and that large fines can retroactively be imposed without a legal base by using teleological interpretation.

The traditional narrative in the EU law literature, including the main textbooks, has assessed national constitutional and supreme courts from the perspective of how they have gradually come to accept supremacy of EU law or to what extent they remain recalcitrant. This is based on the implicit or sometimes explicit assumption that national constitutions are primarily a manifestation of sovereignty and therefore increasingly represent outmoded, parochial, nationally-oriented values. Therefore, the literature assesses to what extent the national courts remain eurosceptic and reluctant to relinquish sovereignty, or instead act co-operatively and embrace European cooperation that is seen as inherently more progressive and modern.[15]

This paper invites the discourse to consider whether the classic lens of assessing the co-operativeness of national courts remains fit in the light of the cases to be explored, and asks whether co-operation might have perhaps become elevated to an objective in itself, with the actors at times losing sight of the values and rights at stake. In any event, the paper suggests that there seems to be a case for shifting the spotlight from national courts to assessing the Court of Justice in relation to its co-operativeness *vis-à-vis* the national constitutions. The paper will also suggest a reconsideration of the role of national constitutions in the EU law discourse. The post-communist experience reminds us that constitutions are about more than sovereignty: the important values underlying their existence include the protection of constitutional rights and liberties *vis-à-vis* interference by authorities, the rule of law and the separation of powers with due checks and balances, and judicial review to safeguard these values. Upholding these values seems to have a continued relevance in the context of European governance. On a broader level, the paper also explores some trends in the scholarly literature in EU law, and asks how we have come to a situation where critical analysis of problems surrounding the rule of law and protection of rights, which would be normal within states, is in the EU context typically dismissed by a broad-brush approach as euroscepticism.

2. PAST CRITICISMS REGARDING JUDICIAL REVIEW AND RIGHTS PROTECTION BY THE ECJ

The literature in the field of EU law has traditionally focused on and acclaimed the various ways in which the European Court of Justice has developed the EU

15 For some examples, see the European Arrest Warrant section of this paper and the final section.

into an autonomous constitutional order and advanced free movement rights, economic freedoms, the rights of EU citizens and students, immigration rights, and rights relating to gender equality and non-discrimination on other grounds. These are important rights which in very direct ways have enhanced individuals' quality of life and enriched horizons. However, some have noted that these rights tend to fall into areas where EU law has been enforced, and its effectiveness has been expanded, *vis-à-vis* the Member States. The ECJ has typically gone to great lengths by deploying teleological, purpose-oriented interpretation to create and expand the scope of such rights.

Given the special atmosphere that governs the study of EU law, which will be explored in the final section, criticisms of the Court of Justice have been rare. However, a limited number of scholars have nonetheless expressed concern with regard to the EU Courts' low intensity of judicial review of the acts of EU institutions when reviewing compliance with rights.[16] In 1992, Coppel and O'Neill raised the issue of the Court applying a double standards approach. They argued that the Court of Justice's high rhetoric of human rights protection had merely been instrumental in expanding the scope and the impact of EC law with regard to the Member States, with fundamental rights not having been taken seriously by the Court.[17] Such concerns resurfaced in 1990s in the course of the *Banana* saga, where various German courts voiced their open distrust with regard to the protection of fundamental rights by the Court of Justice.[18] A former Court of Justice judge Everling criticized the Court for granting the EU institutions a *carte blanche* and reducing judicial control to a minimum.[19] Others have noted that in matters of economic regulation, the EU Courts take a hands-off approach, and allow the EU institutions considerable discretion, finding an EU measure to be invalid only where the EU institution has made 'a manifest error' or 'clearly exceeded' the bounds of discretion.[20] This approach results in 'the threshold of illegality being placed very high', and in a 'notable' contrast between proceedings before the domestic courts against national authorities, and in proceedings before the European Courts against EU institutions.[21] Some policy fields, such as the Common Agricultural Policy, have been rendered

16 For an overview of the literature, see S Douglas-Scott, *Constitutional Law of the European Union* (Pearson Education, Harlow 2002) 460–461 and 454–458. For an overview of the German literature, see M Herdegen, 'The origins and development of the general principles of Community Law' in U Bernitz, J Nergelius (Eds.), *General Principles of European Community Law* (Kluwer, Dordrecht 2000) 10–12.

17 J Coppel and A O'Neill, 'The European Court of Justice: Taking Rights Seriously?' [1992] CML Rev. 29, 670 et seq. and 692.

18 See e.g. U Everling, 'Will Europe Slip on Bananas? The Bananas Judgment of the Court of Justice and National Courts' [1996] CML Rev. 33, at 401 and Herdegen, *supra n.* 16, 11.

19 Everling, *supra n.* 18, 413, 419.

20 For relevant case law, see Chalmers et al, *supra n.* 2, 436–437.

21 *Ibid.*, 437.

immune from review in the light of certain general principles of law.[22] Additionally, one has to bear in mind that the standing to bring judicial review cases has been extremely limited for private parties, under the notoriously restrictive rules developed by the Court of Justice. Overall, cases where the Court of Justice has found a breach of fundamental rights by the EU institutions have been very rare.[23]

To give some examples, the principle of the rule of law that is central to this paper is not justiciable in EU law. As one recent study shows, the Court of Justice has rarely referred to it and has not directly relied on it to regulate the exercise of EU power.[24] Instead, 'Europeanization' of the rule of law primarily means that references to the rule of law have served as an organisational principle underlining the constitutional character of the Union, and as a value to be exported in the Union's foreign policy and conditionality. The study rejected though the view that the rule of law ought be defined and applied in conformity with national experiences.[25] As regards the principle of proportionality, it is a well-established observation that the Court of Justice is protective of the measures of the EU institutions, hardly ever finding that an EU measure was disproportionate. Meanwhile, many have observed a double standard: the EU Courts readily find breaches of proportionality as well as of other general principles of law in the case of Member States' measures that interfere with the Treaty's economic freedoms; here the EU Courts apply a stricter test and frequently find national measures disproportionately restrictive.[26] As regards the right to property, in no case so far (until *Kadi,* which concerned UN measures) have the EU Courts found a violation.[27] Indeed Judge Ress of the European Court of Human Rights has expressed doubts as to whether the EU Courts' protection granted to property rights under Article 1 of Protocol 1 ECHR corresponds to that granted by the ECtHR.[28] As regards the principle of legitimate expectations, the overwhelming majority of claims have been rejected by the Court of Justice; one can rely on this principle only if specific assurances have been given by the EU institutions.[29] Overall, in the EU the fundamental

---

22 R Barents, 'Recent developments in Community case law in the field of agriculture'[1997] CML Rev. 34, 811, 841, cited in X. Groussot case note in [2007] *Common Market Law review* 44, 772.

23 B De Witte, 'The Past and Future Role of the European Court of Justice in the Protection of Human Rights', in P Alston (ed), *The European Union and Human Rights* (Oxford University Press, Oxford 1999) 869.

24 L Pech, 'The Rule of Law as a Constitutional Principle of the European Union', Jean Monnet Working Paper 04/09, www.jeanmonnetprogram.org, 48, 57–58 and 69–72.

25 *Ibid*, p. 71.

26 Chalmers et al, *supra n.* 2, 450–451. See also Coppel and O'Neill, *supra n.* 17, 670 et seq.

27 T Tridimas, *The General Principles of EU Law* (Oxford University Press, Oxford 2006), 315.

28 Concurring Opinion of Judge Ress, *Bosphorus* v. *Ireland*, 45036/98, [2005] ECHR 440.

29 For a detailed analysis see Tridimas, *supra n.* 27, Ch. 6, and X. Groussot, *General Principles of Community law* (Europa Law Publishing, Groningen 2006), 202–212.

rights involved have not been directly protected as such, but only indirectly as unwritten general principles. Whilst rights can be defined in precise terms and may be restricted only under specified circumstances, principles are relatively vague and uncertain in scope and must inherently suffer exceptions.[30] It remains to be seen whether the Court's approach will change with the recent entry into force of the EU Charter of Fundamental Rights. Although recent literature has suggested that a change may be inferred from cases such as *Omega*[31], *Schmidberger*[32] and *Kadi*,[33] it ought to be borne in mind that none of these cases concerned identification of breaches by EU institutions. The first two cases concerned implementation of EU law by the Member States, and the last one, in essence, concerned implementation of the UN Security Council measures, albeit via an EU regulation.

More recently, concerns regarding the level of review by EU Courts have been reinforced by seven judges from the European Court of Human Rights in their concurring opinions to the *Bosphorus* case. Judge Ress questioned the neutrality of the EU Courts, pointing out that the public interest of the European Union makes it 'rather difficult for the ECJ to find violations' of the general principles of law.[34] Six other judges cautioned against the emergence of 'double standards', where EU Member States 'live under a ... more lenient system' as regards the protection of the ECHR rights in areas where they implement EU law.[35] On the other hand, the other ECtHR judges used in the *Bosphorus* judgment a formula reminiscent of the German Constitutional Court's *Solange II*[36] and *Banana*[37] judgments, finding that the level of protection in the EU is 'equivalent' to that provided by the ECHR. Both the German judgments as well as the ECtHR's *Bopshorus* judgment have been widely acclaimed by the literature as welcome examples of how courts ought to co-operate in the contemporary pluralist setting.

As noted above, the subsequent case studies invite the reader to consider whether the lens of co-operation and 'equivalent protection' remains fit in the light of

30 L Besselink, 'Entrapped by the maximum standard: On fundamental rights, pluralism and subsidiarity in the European Union' [1998] *CML Rev.* 35, 634 et seq., Concurring Opinion of Judge Ress, *supra n.* 28 and De Witte, *supra n.* 23, 879.

31 Case C-36/02, *Omega*, [2004] ECR I-9609.

32 Case C-112/00, *Schmidberger*, [2003] ECR I-5659.

33 Joined Cases C-402/05 P & C-415/05 P, *Kadi and Al Barakaat* v. *Council and Commission*, [2008] ECR I-6351.

34 Concurring Opinion of Judge Ress, *supra n.* 28.

35 Concurring Opinion of Judge Ress, and Joint Concurring Opinion of Judges Rozakis, Tulkens, Traja, Botoucharova, Zagrebelsky and Garlicki, to judgment *Bosphorus* v. *Ireland*, *supra n.* 28.

36 Wünsche Handelsgesellschaft (Solange II), [1987] CMLR 225.

37 Decision of 7 June 2000, 2 BvL 1/97; BVerfGE 102, 147.

recent cases decided by the European Court of Justice. These cases go into the very heart of the fundamental elements of the post-communist rule of law reforms and also show the considerable contrast between the level of judicial review by the EU Courts and that hitherto applied by the CEE constitutional courts. Indeed in a paradoxical way, these cases would seem to have the effect of dismantling some of the core elements of the post-communist reforms, given the constraints placed on the constitutional systems by the supremacy of EU law.

3. RECENT QUESTIONS ON THE REVIEW OF EU MEASURES

3.1. ON SECRET LEGISLATION: *HEINRICH* CASE

One of the most fundamental cornerstones of the post-communist rule of law reforms is the requirement that legislation must be published. This requirement is explicitly stated in most and quite possibly all CEE constitutions. Under the Soviet regime, as well as under the Nazi rule, secret collections of law existed, which were only accessible to officials or members of the ruling party but not to individuals; such laws were tools of *ex post* oppression.[38] Therefore in Eastern Europe and Germany the strictest approach is taken to publication of laws: without publication, an act does not come into existence. In other European countries, the degree of rigidity of the publication requirement varies.[39]

In the context of EU membership, the strict rules regarding publication first had to be revisited in relation to EU measures that had not been translated into the new Member States' languages in time for accession.[40] In *Skoma-Lux* case,[41] a Czech company argued that a sanction cannot be imposed for a breach of an EU customs regulation that had not been published in the Czech language. The printed version of the Special Edition of the Official Journal, the only legally binding and authentic source of EU legislation, did not exist at the time of accession in May 2004; the first volumes were published in summer 2004 and the entire process of publication was not finished until March 2006. The Court of Justice responded that an act not published in the *Official Journal* in the relevant language cannot be imposed on individuals in that State, although the act remains valid and is binding on the Member State concerned. This approach is

38 See M Bobek, 'Case C-345/06, Gottfried *Heinrich*, Judgment of the Court of Justice (Grand Chamber) of 10 March 2009' [2009] CML Rev. 46, 2084 and 2086.

39 For overview, see ibid.

40 For a comprehensive analysis, see M Bobek, 'The Binding Force of Babel: The Enforcement of EC Law Unpublished in the Languages of the New Member States' [2009] *Cambridge Yearbook of European Legal Studies*, 43ff.

41 C-161/06 *Skoma-Lux* [2007] ECR I-10841, para. 37.

more lenient than that normally taken in CEE countries. In Poland, in a case that preceded the *Skoma-Lux* ruling, a regional administrative court had annulled the decision of the customs authority, as it had been adopted on the basis of EU customs legislation that had not been published in Polish and thus breached the requirements of legal certainty and foreseeability of the law.[42] In Estonia, the Tallinn Administrative Court in *Haljas* case[43] noted with regard to the *Skoma-Lux* judgment that EU law is more lenient with regard to publication than the Estonian Constitution and court practice. In Estonia, an act that has a publication defect would have no validity at all, and especially the requirement to publish a norm that imposes obligations on persons is a fundamental and absolute principle of a rule-of-law-based state.

The ECJ's approach could be justified by the exceptional circumstances that surrounded the 2004 accession of a large number of Member States. However, in the *Heinrich* case decided in 2009,[44] the ECJ went further and upheld the practice of deliberate and systematic adoption of secret legislation. In the aftermath of the increased terrorist threat following the September 11 attacks, the EU had adopted unpublished annexes to Regulation 2320/2002 and Regulation 622/2003, concerning civil aviation security. The annexes contained a secret list of measures which were banned from aircraft. On the basis of these measures, Mr Heinrich was not allowed to board an airplane in Austria, because he was carrying in his cabin baggage a tennis racquet, which was among the list of banned items. The requirement of secrecy originated from Article 8(1) of Regulation 2320/2002, which provides a list of measures in the Annex that '*shall be secret and not be published. They shall only be made available to the authorities ..., which shall communicate them only to interested parties on a need-to-know basis, in accordance with applicable national rules for dissemination of sensitive information.*' Further, the requirement that the measures laid down in the Annex to Regulation 622/2003 'should be secret and not be published' in accordance with Regulation 2320/2002 is also stated in the preamble and Article 3 of Regulation 622/2003; Article 3 adds that those measures 'shall be made available only to persons duly authorised by a Member State or the Commission'.

The Austrian court which had referred the case to the Court of Justice noted that keeping secret the rules of conduct with which individuals are required to comply constitutes such a severe impairment of the most elementary principles of the rule of law and the requirements of Article 297 TFEU (then Article 254 EC), as to be legally non-existent and hence cannot be binding. Advocate General

42 For details of the case, see M Bobek, 'The Binding Force of Babel...', *supra n.* 40, 45.

43 Judgment No. 3–07–757 of 13.11.2009, not yet available due to a pending appeal. Extracts on file with the author.

44 Case C-345/06, *Heinrich*, judgment of the Court of Justice (Grand Chamber) of 10 March 2009, nyr.

Eleanor Sharpston in her opinion to the case proposed three possible approaches: (a) Regulation 622/2003 would be valid but not enforceable against individuals; (b) invalidation of the Regulation by the Court; or (c) declaration that the Regulation has been non-existent since the beginning (i.e. as if there had been no legally binding act at all). The Advocate General notably advised *not* to take the first approach, as the Court had never seen the Annex to the 2003 Regulation(!), and would thus not be in the position to assess whether the measure imposed obligations on individuals. Instead the Advocate General advised to take the third approach, and to declare Regulation 622/2003 non-existent. This is because the 'persistent and deliberate disregard of the mandatory publication requirements in Article 254(2) EC in respect of the *whole* substance of the regulation ... is one whose gravity is so obvious that it cannot be tolerated by the Community legal order'.[45] As an alternative option, she advised that the Regulation should at least be invalidated on the grounds of the breach of an essential procedural requirement. The Advocate General went on to warn against the slippery slope that may be involved in public security based exceptions:[46]

> Similar arguments are raised not infrequently in difficult times to justify departure from the ordinary rule of law – whether that be by suspending guarantees of fundamental rights, restricting judicial scrutiny or softening the consequences of such scrutiny. They have no place in a European Union that is governed by the rule of law and whose Court is under the Treaty obligation to ensure that 'the law is observed'.

However, the Grand Chamber of the Court of Justice did not follow the Advocate General's advice. The Court did note that under Article 297 TFEU an EU regulation cannot take effect unless it has been published in the *Official Journal of the European Union*, and that the principle of legal certainly requires that EU rules enable those concerned to know precisely the extent of the obligations which are imposed on them. However, the Court nonetheless decided that secret EU regulation is valid law; it simply cannot impose obligations on individuals. According to the Court, a measure 'which was not published in the *Official Journal of the European Union*, has no binding force in so far as it seeks to impose obligations on individuals'.[47]

In a compelling article, Michal Bobek has noted that while the Court extended the *Skoma-Lux* approach to *Heinrich*, such an approach is misplaced here because the former case concerned accidental temporary non-publication in one official language, which had been caused by the unprecedented scope of the

---

45 Opinion of Advocate General Sharpston to Case C-345/06, *Heinrich*, delivered on 10 April 2008, para. 108.

46 *Ibid*, para. 100.

47 Case C-345/06, *Heinrich*, judgment of the Court of Justice (Grand Chamber) of 10 March 2009, nyr, para. 63.

translation task after the EU's enlargement. *Heinrich*, however, concerned deliberate, systematic, absolute and presumably permanent lack of publication in any of the official languages.[48] Additionally, Bobek notes that while the valid-but-not-enforceable solution is practiced in some countries such as France, where laws can be promulgated by the President instead of publication, the French approach is not suitable in the EU context because the external world can know about the existence EU laws only through the Official Journal. Besides these serious concerns, the *Heinrich* judgment also has potentially alarming consequences for the future of the European constitutional order, especially if one bears in mind the supremacy of EU law:

> In *Heinrich*, the Court basically allowed a grey zone of activities of the Community institutions, where the institutions can adopt secret regulations, withhold information and elaborate legislative schemes the public will never see. This grey zone of institutional activity will only be entered … *de facto* by accident, i.e. when there is someone who knows and objects to such practices and claims that the measure from the grey zone imposed obligations on him. On the whole, however, the measure is allowed to stay – if it is attacked, its enforcement might in certain cases be limited, but the validity of the regulation adopted in violation of all the mandatory procedural requirements, is not questioned.[49]

3.2. ON BLANKET ELECTRONIC SURVEILLANCE: THE EU ELECTRONIC DATA RETENTION DIRECTIVE 2006/24

Another key element of the rule of law for countries which have experienced a totalitarian system is the importance of freedom of expression, freedom of thought and freedom of correspondence. The protection of these classic civil liberties has drawn widespread concerns in the context of the EU Data Retention Directive 2006/24.[50] The Directive, adopted as part of the global 'War on Terror', is widely regarded as one of the most Orwellian measures, requiring the storing of data on everyone's e-mails, text messages, phone calls, website visits etc. Besides mass demonstrations in a large number of Member States against the Directive, in Germany, a historically unique class action was brought to the Constitutional Court by more than 34,000 citizens.[51]

Interestingly, the other constitutional challenges against the national implementing measures were brought in the new Member States in Central and

---

48 M Bobek, 'Case C-345/06, Gottfried *Heinrich*, Judgment of the Court of Justice (Grand Chamber) of 10 March 2009' [2009] *Common Market Law Review* 46, 2090–2091.

49 *Ibid.*, 2093.

50 OJ 2006, L 105/54.

51 For an overview of the legal developments in different countries, see the webpage of Germany's Data Retention Working Group at www.vorratsdatenspeicherung.de/content/view/51/70/lang,en.

Eastern Europe. The Romanian Constitutional Court has been the first to declare in October 2009 the national measure unconstitutional; cases are pending in Hungary and the Czech Republic. In Romania, the Constitutional Court noted the act's 'large applicability – practically to all physical and legal persons'.[52] According to the Romanian Constitutional Court, this is likely to overturn the presumption of innocence, transforming *a priori* all users of electronic communication services into suspects, as well as going against the right to private life, secrecy of correspondence and freedom of expression.

The Romanian Court's concerns were shared by the German Constitutional Court, who found in March 2010 that the national implementing law contravened Germany's Constitution and especially the right to privacy and proportionality.[53] The Court noted that such storage constitutes a particularly serious encroachment with an effect broader than anything in the legal system to date. It allows obtaining detailed information on one's social or political affiliations and on personal preferences, inclinations and weaknesses, making it possible to create personality profiles of virtually all citizens and track their movements. According to the Court, it is part of Germany's constitutional identity that the citizens' enjoyment of freedom may not be totally recorded. The Court found that the law failed to set the barrier high enough for allowing investigators' access to the data and to ensure judicial review, as well as to ensure sufficient data security and encryption should the information be stolen.

On the EU Courts' side, the Court of Justice had earlier rejected Ireland's claim that the Directive was not a single market measure as its aim was to fight terrorism and that it should therefore have been adopted under what was then the third pillar.[54] Human rights arguments presented in the case by Statewatch, a UK-based civil liberties NGO, were not considered due to the restrictive standing rules; on the other hand Statewatch was unable to bring a case itself as direct actions by NGOs and individuals are rarely declared admissible.[55]

3.3. THE EUROPEAN ARREST WARRANT: AN EROSION OF *NULLA POENA SINE LEGE*?

Closely interconnected with the requirement of publication of legislation is the requirement in CEE constitutions that sanctions and especially criminal

52 Decision No. 12581 of Oct. 2009, English translation available at www.legi-internet.ro/fileadmin/editor_folder/pdf/decision-constitutional-court-romania-data-retention.pdf.

53 Judgment of 2 March 2010. For an English summary, see www.bundesverfassungsgericht.de/en/press/bvg10–011en.html.

54 Case C-301/06, *Ireland* v. *Parliament and Council*, [2009] ECR I-0082.

55 See Statewatch Report 'The Shape of Things to Come', 11 September 2008, www.statewatch.org/news/2008/sep/the-shape-of-things-to-come-prel.pdf.

sanctions can only be imposed on the basis of a parliamentary statute. This is a central element of the rule of law in all European countries but particularly so in the countries which have experienced a totalitarian regime, where sanctions had been decided in an arbitrary way by the authorities, often in a retroactive way and without a legal base, using analogy or teleological interpretation.

Questions on the respect for this principle have arisen in the context of the European Arrest Warrant (EAW) Framework Decision.[56] The EAW system renders extradition speedy and automatic: the court that receives an extradition request from another Member State must automatically authorise extradition, with minimum formality and no consideration of evidence. The rule of double criminality is abolished for 32 crimes, and thus a person must be extradited regardless of whether the activity is a crime in domestic law.

While the European Commission officials have described the EAW system as a 'success story',[57] the EAW Framework decision is also a measure that has led the largest number of constitutional courts and supreme courts to express various types of concerns. For example, one dissenting judge at the Czech Constitutional Court painted the following hypothetical scenario:[58] a Czech citizen, who is innocent, is extradited to Greece, where he receives a visit from the 'δικηγορος', presenting lengthy documentation in Greek alphabet. The Czech citizen has to communicate and defend himself via a poorly paid and uninterested interpreter, via English which he does not speak well and with meaning inevitably getting lost in translation. He is unable to find, or in any event to afford, a Czech lawyer who would be familiar with Greek criminal law. Given his absence from work, he loses his job and his marriage breaks apart.

While overall the CEE constitutional courts found a way to interpret the EAW requirements in what was applauded by literature as a 'pro-European' way, some concerns were put to the European Court of Justice by the Belgian *Cour d'Arbitrage*.[59] It requested a preliminary ruling on the legality of the European Arrest Warrant Framework Decision, as a group of defence lawyers asked, *inter alia*, whether the abolition of double criminality is not in breach of the principle of legality in criminal matters (*nulla poena sine lege*). They noted that under national constitutions, criminal legislation must satisfy conditions of precision, clarity and predictability, allowing each person to know whether an act constitutes an offence.

---

56 OJ 2002 L 190/1.

57 I Pérignon, I and C Daucé, 'The European Arrest Warrant: a Growing Success Story', [2007] *ERA Forum* 8, 203–214.

58 Dissenting opinion by Judge Balík to Case No. Pl. ÚS 66/04, available at www.concourt.cz. Some elements of the scenario have been changed or added by the author.

59 Case C-303/05 *Advocaten voor de Wereld* [2007] ECR I-3633.

Despite the fact that the EAW system had prompted an unusually high number of constitutional courts and supreme courts to voice various concerns, the Court of Justice upheld the legality of the measure on the basis of a very laconic reasoning. The judgment has been described as 'disappointing', as the Court 'refused to make any comment on much-contested issues' and made 'little effort to engage with the Court's national counterparts'.[60] The Court's approach seems to represent a practice that has earlier been criticised by eminent authors such as Joseph Weiler, who in an often quoted passage called upon the Court to 'abandon the cryptic, Cartesian style', which is 'not conducive to a good conversation with national courts'.[61] According to Weiler 'it is crucial that the Court display in its judgments that national sensibilities were fully considered and taken into account'.[62] Indeed constitutional court judges at various forums have posed the question whether the Court of Justice actually listens to their concerns, or whether in practice a 'monologue' occurs rather than a 'dialogue'.

At the same time, defence lawyers and NGOs involved in cases on the ground have drawn attention to a host of rather alarming gaps in the protection of rights in the EAW system, which overall appear to have resulted in a degree of erosion of the traditional rule-of-law-based constitutional safeguards for individuals facing criminal proceedings. A number of UK NGOs such as Fair Trials International, Liberty and Justice have called for judicial review before extradition, to ensure that there is a *prima facie* case to answer before a person is extradited. They have used the case of Andrew Symeou as a 'spotlight case':[63] a 19-year old London student, who according to strong evidence appeared to be innocent, was extradited to Greece without any opportunity to defend himself over a period of several months. As it happens, the German Constitutional Court in its European Arrest Warrant judgment[64] had required exactly such a possibility for judicial review before persons are extradited, but was strongly criticised by literature for being eurosceptic and not willing to relinquish sovereignty. Further, while it is inevitably difficult to defend oneself in a foreign language or through translation, the NGOs have highlighted a large number of cases where no translation at all was provided, resulting in miscarriages of justice.[65] For example, a UK national Theresa Daniels, who was sentenced to 10 years in prison in Spain, had assumed

---

60 D Sarmiento, 'European Union: the European arrest warrant and the quest for constitutional coherence', (2008) 6 *International Journal of Constitutional Law* 1, 177–178.

61 J Weiler, 'Epilogue: The Judicial Après Nice', in G de Búrca and JHH Weiler (eds), *The European Court of Justice* (Oxford University Press, Oxford 2001) 225.

62 Ibid, 225.

63 Fair Trials International, www.fairtrials.net/index.php/cases/spotlight/andrew_symeou/; 'Liberty welcomes 'stay of extradition'; 2 June 2009, www.liberty-human-rights.org.uk.

64 Judgment of 18.7.2005, 2 BvR 2236/04, available at: www.bverfg.de/entscheidungen/rs200507182bvr223604.html.

65 Fair Trials International submission to the EU Justice and Home Affairs Council Working Group, 9 July 2009, www.fairtrials.net/campaigns.

until the end of the proceedings (where no translation had been provided) that she had been in the process as a witness. Additionally, the NGOs have expressed concern about cases where the offence had been committed a long time ago or the sentence had been issued *in absentia*,[66] the absence of a network of defence practitioners,[67] and the impossibility for individuals whose names have wrongly been included in the database because of mistaken identity or identity theft to have the arrest warrant removed.[68] Such gaps in defence rights occur against the background where the number of offences caught by the system is considerable: UK officials have noted 'a large volume of trivial extradition requests', with many offences being so minor that they would lead to a caution or no investigation at all in the UK, such as theft of a mobile phone or traffic offences.[69] Indeed while the EAW system was initially aimed at serious crimes such as terrorism, the above NGOs have now called for the introduction of a proportionality test prior to extradition.[70]

Meanwhile, it may also be interesting to note the prevailing approach in the mainstream EU law discourse on the national EAW cases. Few commentators looked at the actual rights involved, especially beyond the abolition of double criminality and the constitutional ban on extradition; those who did were mainly scholars specializing in criminal law and practising defence lawyers. EU law literature predominantly assessed the national constitutional courts' EAW judgments from the point of view of how well the courts performed in the 'contrapunctual' law and cooperation, and in particular to what extent they took account of the Court of Justice's *Pupino* case rather than putting their national constitutions first.[71] Unlike the 'EU-friendly' Czech Court, the Polish and

---

66 'UK grandmother 'wanted' by France', *BBC News*, 26 July 2009, http://news.bbc.co.uk/1/hi/8169357.stm.

67 Justice Report 'The European Arrest Warrant Briefing and Suggested Amendments', September 2009, www.justice.org.uk, paras. 46–47.

68 See e.g. the case of Jan Tabbers, highlighted by Fair Trials International, http://fairtrials.net.

69 See 'Door Thief, Piglet Rustler, Pudding Snatcher: British Courts Despair at Extradition Requests', *The Guardian*, 20 October 2008; 'Extradited for 'stealing' a mobile phone', *Times Online*, 13 August 2009, http://business.timesonline.co.uk/tol/business/law/article6792237.ece.

70 See the articles in the preceding footnote.

71 Including the present writer, see A Albi, 'Supremacy of EC Law in the New Member States: Bringing Parliaments into the Equation of 'Co-operative constitutionalism'' (2007) 3 *European Constitutional Law Review*, 25ff. Among voluminous literature, see e.g. J Komarek, 'European Constitutional Pluralism and the European Arrest Warrant: Contrapunctual Principles in Disharmony', *Jean Monnet Working Paper* No. 10/05, www.jeanmonnetprogram.org, S Siegel, 'Courts and Compliance in the EU: the European Arrest Warrant in National Constitutional Courts', *Jean Monnet Working Paper* No. 5/2008, www.jeanmonnetprogram.org, E Van Sliedregt, 'The European Arrest Warrant: Extradition in Transition', [2007] 3 *EuConst* 2, 244, A Hinajeros Parga, '*Bundesverfassungsgericht* Decision of 18 July 2005 on the German European Arrest Warrant Law' [2006] *CML Rev.* 43, 583–595, O Pollicino, 'European Arrest Warrant and Constitutional Principles of the Member States: A Case Law-Based

especially the German and Cypriot courts were typically described as 'reluctant' to yield sovereignty, not EU-friendly, undermining loyal cooperation, sending 'dark signals', and going against the spirit of *Pupino*. The Italian courts' early cases, where they had put fundamental rights (such as limits to pre-trial detention) first, were regarded as 'formalistic'; subsequent cases where the courts changed their stance were welcomed as more 'Europhile', avoiding national 'particularism' and playing along the contrapunctual principles.[72] We will return this approach that underpins a considerable amount of the literature at the end of the paper.

3.4. ON PROPERTY RIGHTS AND LEGAL CERTAINTY: FROM THE 'BANANA SAGA' TO A 'SUGAR SAGA'

The final central pillar of post-communist constitutional transition to be explored here is the inviolability of property rights. During the communist regime, private property had been expropriated and collective farms created. Under the post-communist constitutions, property rights are declared inviolable; expropriation of property is only allowed in exceptional cases for public purposes, on the basis of a specific parliamentary statute and in return for compensation. The protection of property is accompanied by the requirement that imposition of taxes, fines or pecuniary obligations can only occur under a statute, with any grounds being interpreted narrowly and no retroactivity allowed. This is further protected by the protection of the principles of legal certainty and legitimate expectations.

While these principles are protected in EU law, the standard of protection appears to be different – as seen in the second section of the paper, findings that EU institutions have actually breached property rights or legitimate expectations are extremely rare. As regards the principle of legitimate expectations, the Court of Justice allows one to rely on this principle only if specific assurances have been given by the EU institutions. This interpretation appears to be very narrow compared to that used in the post-communist Member States, where imposition of obligations requires the adoption of a statute with a sufficient lead-in period, and laws that retroactively establish obligations on individuals, let alone pecuniary charges, are simply prohibited and declared unconstitutional.

The difference in the approach to the protection of the above rights created a fault line in a series of cases which, reminiscent of the German '*Banana*-saga',

Outline in an Attempt to Strike the Right Balance Between Legal Systems'[2009] *German Law Journal* 9, 1313 and M Fichera, 'The European Arrest Warrant and the Sovereign State: A Marriage of Convenience?' [2009] *ELJ* 15, 81–82, etc.

72 See e.g. Fichero, *supra n.* 71, 94 and L Marin, 'The European Arrest Warrant in the Italian Republic' [2008] *EuConst* 4, 268–9.

appears to be acquiring the dimensions of 'a sugar saga'. It involves the General Court (formerly the Court of First Instance) judgments on the direct actions brought by the Polish, Cypriot and Estonian governments against various EU sugar regulations, and domestic cases in Hungary, Estonia and Cyprus regarding the protection of constitutional rights when implementing EU regulations, as well as WTO rules. The EU and domestic cases have been explored in detail in earlier articles. Here a brief summary will be provided first of the main issues regarding the property rights and legitimate expectations of undertakings, followed in the second sub-section by a recent EU General Court judgment regarding the property rights of individuals.

3.4.1. Retroactive fines on undertakings: Overview of direct actions and domestic cases

By way of a background to the 'sugar saga' cases, in order to prepare for the EU's 2004 enlargement, the Act of Accession authorized the European Commission to adopt transitional measures to prevent the purchase of certain foodstuffs for speculative purposes, which could distort prices on the common market. The European Commission adopted two regulations to this end: Regulation 1972/2003 on the transitional measures regarding trade in agricultural products[73] and Regulation 60/2004 on the sugar sector.[74] The latter, which is central to this section, required undertakings to eliminate surplus sugar stocks (by export, use in the combustibles sector, or by denaturation for animal feed) in view of transition to the Common Agricultural Policy (CAP). The regulations obliged the new Member States to ensure that, upon their entry into the EU, the stocks of sugar would not exceed the average of the preceding years. Under the regulations, excess stocks had to be eliminated or were to be penalized by fines. For any surplus stocks not removed, the governments had to impose a fine on the undertakings, and the governments themselves had to pay a hefty fine to the European Commission.

The Polish[75] and Cypriot[76] governments lodged direct actions to the General Court of the EU against Regulation 60/2004 on the sugar market. They argued, in essence, that a system which obliges the new Member States to compel their companies to eliminate the sugar bought before accession, or to pay a corresponding fine, was *impossible to implement in practice* without interfering with rights such as non-retroactivity and the right to property. The Polish Government's action was declared inadmissible on procedural grounds, but an

73 OJ 2003, L 293/3.

74 OJ 2004, L 9/8.

75 Case T-258/04, *Poland* v. *Commission*, Order of 10 June 2009, nyr. Under appeal as Case C-336/09, *Poland* v. *Council*, pending.

76 Joined Cases T-300/05 & T-316/05, *Cyprus* v. *Commission*, judgment of 2 Oct. 2009, nyr.

appeal is pending. Cyprus' claims, all of which were rejected by the General Court by reference to the Commission's wide margin of discretion in CAP, centred around the following issues. Firstly, Cyprus pointed out that the undertakings had imported sugar before accession, and government interference with the right to property is not allowed unless required by general interest and the interference is proportionate. Furthermore, the obligation on undertakings to pay the fine for non-elimination would constitute a retroactive sanction. The General Court rejected the claim, as in EU law the principle of legitimate expectations can only be invoked if the EU itself has previously provided specific assurances that would have given rise to such legitimate expectations. Normal diligent operators are assumed to know, as of the publication of the Act of Accession, that the new Member States were obliged to eliminate excess stocks. Secondly, Cyprus argued (to no avail) that by not having shown that less restrictive measures were unavailable, the Commission had breached the principle of proportionality. Given that Cyprus had imported sugar solely from the EU, the Commission could have simply prevented the accumulation of stocks by not subsidising exports to Cyprus, and Cyprus had in fact been unable to legally limit its imports without breaching WTO agreements. Thirdly, Cyprus claimed that the Commission had exceeded its powers because the imposition of pecuniary sanctions on the new Member States had gone beyond Article 41 of the Act of Accession, which only allows measures that are 'strictly necessary' for the transition to CAP. The Court rejected the claim by recalling Annex IV point 4 of the Act of Accession, according to which the surplus quantities have to be eliminated at the expense of the new Member States.

Meanwhile, the issue of property rights of undertakings in having to eliminate their surplus sugar, along with the principles of legitimate expectations and non-retroactivity, had become a heated constitutional issue in the domestic courts of Estonia, Hungary and Cyprus. The legislatures had struggled to find a way to require undertakings to eliminate surplus sugar or to pay a corresponding fine under EU Regulation 60/2004 in a way that would respect constitutional rights. While prior to EU membership such undertakings would have been certain to win, the national courts readjusted the protection standards to avoid undermining the supremacy of EU law, although some cases are still pending. The details of these cases have been provided elsewhere.[77]

3.4.2. Impossibility of removing stocks held by private individuals and households

The amount of surplus sugar stocks with regard to individual new Member States was subsequently determined by the European Commission Regulation 832/2005

77 See A Albi, 'Ironies in human rights protection...', *supra n.* 10, 46–69.

of 31 May 2005.[78] This led to the imposition of fines by Commission Decision 2006/776[79] on five new Member States: Estonia, Latvia, Slovakia, Cyprus and Malta. Regulation 832/2005 was challenged by Cyprus and Estonia. Cyprus argued that it breached the principles of proportionality and non-retroactivity, as well as being insufficiently reasoned given the serious financial consequences. In particular, Cyprus pointed out that according to Regulation 60/2004, the only possible ground for determining stocks as surplus would have been speculation, while in Cyprus the surpluses had been caused by increased annual consumption and establishment of new large undertakings. Furthermore, whilst the Preamble of the contested Regulation refers to surpluses resulting from an increased production, Cyprus does not in fact produce sugar. The General Court rejected all claims, recalling the Commission's wide margin of discretionary power.[80]

In the Estonian case, the European Commission had gone a notable step further. Whilst the wording of the underlying Regulation 60/2004, along with the past accession practice, appeared to indicate that only *undertakings* were required to remove surplus sugar, in Regulation 832/2005 the Commission imposed a hefty fine of 45 million EUR for sugar held not only by undertakings but also by *private households* (i.e. individuals and families). The Estonian Government's direct action focused on this element in the Regulation and did not raise the point regarding undertakings, despite the very real and on-going difficulties in implementation as demonstrated by domestic court challenges. By way of background, of the total surplus stocks of 91,500 tons held in Estonia, approximately half, 42,700 tons, had been held by private households. Consequently, half of the dramatically large fine of 45 million EUR corresponds to sugar held by households. With threefold price rises expected after accession, people had stored large quantities of sugar to continue making delightful, organic home-made jams in the forthcoming years. Traditionally 96 per cent of jams, 92 per cent of compotes and 54 per cent of fruit juices are prepared by the families themselves in summer and autumn months, doing so with great enthusiasm and passing recipes on from generation to generation. It comes as no surprise that such a baffling fine fuelled considerable perplexity and disenchantment with the EU, especially as it came at a time when social benefits, public services and public sector salaries have seen drastic cuts due to the financial crisis.

The EU General Court's judgment in case *Estonia* v. *Commission*[81] is fascinating. The General Court upheld the validity of the Regulation, despite its agreement

[78] O.J. 2005, C 271/24.

[79] O.J. 2006, L 314/35–36.

[80] Joined Cases T-300/05 & T-316/05, *Cyprus* v. *Commission*, judgment of 2 Oct. 2009, nyr., paras. 166–201.

[81] Case T-324/05, *Estonia* v. *Commission*, judgment of 2 Oct. 2009, nyr. Appeal (Case C-535/09) pending.

with the Estonian Government that there had been no textual basis for the requirement to eliminate private household sugar, and furthermore, despite its agreement that, in practice, it had been impossible to require households to eliminate sugar. Furthermore, the Court did not find it problematic that the Commission had not provided any warnings about, or reasons for, its change of policy; in fact the first instrument that had included the private household stocks was the contested Regulation of May 2005, adopted one year after accession. The Court simply based its judgment on three general considerations of teleological or consequential nature: (a) *the need to avoid distortions on the common market*; (b) *macroeconomic indicators*; and (c) the capacious principle of effectiveness of EU law. The case leaves one even more baffled after learning that 80 per cent of the sugar had been exported to Estonia from the EU, with the support of EU subsidies, and that the European Commission had in fact discouraged the Estonian Government from adopting trade barriers. The reasoning of the General Court has been explored in detail in another article;[82] here a short summary will be provided as the case raises important questions given the central theme of the article regarding the level of judicial review over EU institutions by EU courts.

The Estonian Government's central claim concerned the fact that no treaty, regulation or other EU instrument or any previous practice or case-law had contained a reference to the need to eliminate private household sugar. Furthermore, domestic households cannot abuse the market by selling sugar on for a higher price or by exporting it with the support of EU subsidies. Exploring the relevant documents, the General Court indeed confirmed that there had been no textual basis for the inclusion of household stocks.[83] However, whilst in the post-communist constitutional systems the grounds for interfering with private property have to be express and interpreted narrowly, the EU General Court strikingly considered the Commission's wide interpretation of the term 'stocks' more plausible.[84] The Court invoked the much cherished EU law doctrine of *effet utile* or effectiveness of EU law, finding that in case of ambiguity, an interpretation should be chosen that ensures the effectiveness of obligations arising from EU provisions.[85] If small quantities of sugar were excluded, the relevant provisions would lose their effectiveness because many small quantities in total could undermine market stability.

The second key claim of the Estonian Government was that in practice it was, in fact, impossible to require elimination of surplus stocks held by private

---

82 A Albi, 'From the *Banana* saga to a Sugar Saga and Beyond: Could the Post-communist Constitutional Courts Teach the EU a Lesson in the Rule of Law?'[2010] *CMLRev.*, 791–829.

83 Case T-324/05, *Estonia* v. *Commission*, judgment of 2 Oct. 2009, nyr., para 108.

84 Ibid., para 115 et seq., especially para 136.

85 Ibid., paras. 108, 210–211.

households (i.e. individuals and families). The modes of elimination provided in Article 6(2) of Regulation 60/2004 are: (a) by export without refund from the EU; (b) by the use in the combustibles sector; (c) by denaturation without aid for animal feed. None of these, however, can be used with regard to stocks acquired by domestic households. Furthermore, household stocks had in fact already been removed from the market, by having been purchased by the self-same private households. The Court indeed reluctantly acknowledged that it may not be possible to eliminate households' sugar by using the modes provided in Article 6(2).[86] However, the Court then got round the impossibility argument by mounting a *suggestion* that the *Estonian Government could have fulfilled the obligation to eliminate sugar, by purchasing a quantity of sugar corresponding to that owned by households.*[87] The lengthy and technical reasoning by which the Court reached this *suggestion* was explored in detail elsewhere.[88] It was suggested that the reasoning appeared to have been based on several leaps of faith, a considerable element of teleological reasoning, and an interpretation of the key provisions which at times seemed to go against the spirit and the wording of the provisions. For example, Article 6(3) of Regulation 60/2004 had required the relevant authorities of the new Member States to put in place a system to determine the quantities of sugar held by 'main operators concerned'. The Court noted that although this provision leaves out surplus stocks held by less important undertakings, it does not mean that sugar held by less important undertakings or even private households can nonetheless not be included.[89]

Overall, a draconian and retroactive pecuniary obligation on a government was upheld by the General Court of the EU on the basis of vague, teleological, poorly linked leaps of faith. The Court *suggested* that the Estonian Government should have spent a lot of taxpayers' money to buy sugar, without there having been any legal basis or even any indications to that end from the past accessions. In essence, the first the Estonian Government heard of such a suggestion was this very judgment of the General Court in 2009. The first legal act informing the Government of the inclusion of household stocks was the contested 2005 Regulation, adopted one year after accession. Thus, the Court's *suggestion* would not only seem simply absurd, but also a judicial approval of an arbitrary exercise of power and of a retroactive imposition of a pecuniary obligation. The case seems to squarely corroborate the concerns expressed by the former Court of Justice judge Everling at the time of the *Banana* judgment, where despite 'the extremely unjust effects of the Bananas Regulation', the EU Courts had granted the EU institutions a *carte blanche* and reduced judicial control to a minimum.[90]

---

86 Ibid., see paras. 173 and 178.

87 Ibid., para 178.

88 Albi, 'From the *Banana* saga to a Sugar Saga…', *supra n.* 82, 803ff.

89 Case T-324/05, *Estonia* v. *Commission*, judgment of 2 Oct. 2009, nyr., para 174.

90 Everling, *supra n.* 18, 413, 419, 433.

The Estonian Government's third main claim concerned property rights: forcing the Estonian people to eliminate sugar bought for consumption would have constituted a disproportionate and intolerable interference with property rights and a forced expropriation. The Court rejected this with a very laconic statement that Regulation 60/2004 did not oblige the Estonian households to eliminate sugar; only the Estonian Republic was obliged to remove surplus stocks or to pay a relevant fine. The credibility of this finding depends on the reader's assessment of the Court's above reasoning regarding the *suggestion* that the Estonian Government should have purchased sugar, without any textual basis for doing so.

The Estonian Government additionally raised the following points. First, the European Commission had not provided any reasons for the inclusion of household stocks, which goes against good administration and represents an abuse of power. Secondly, the Estonian Government argued that Regulation 832/2005 breached the principle of proportionality: the inclusion of private household stocks led to the doubling of the fine, while such stocks were a negligible 0.32 per cent of the EU sugar market and did not cause speculation, as they could not be sold on. Thirdly, the Commission had breached legitimate expectations which it had created by virtue of its 2002 and 2003 letters to Estonian institutions, where it had made references to the previous accessions and indicated that only undertakings had to be prevented from accumulating stocks. Fourthly, Estonia invoked the principle of good faith, echoing a point raised in Cyprus' direct action: 87 per cent of Estonia's sugar had in fact originated from the EU and had been supported by EU export subsidies; the Commission had even obstructed Estonia from taking protective measures against EU imports. Finally, Estonia also claimed that the Regulation breached the principle of collegiality, as it had been adopted by one Commissioner. None of the arguments found favour, with the General Court referring to the wide margin of discretion of EU institutions. The Court also found that the contested Regulation 832/2005 is merely an administrative measure regarding calculation, and not a decision of principle, even though the obligation of elimination was extended to private household stocks unlike ever before.

4. SUPREMACY OF EU LAW: A CASE FOR RIGOROUS RATHER THAN MINIMAL JUDICIAL REVIEW?

While the introduction noted various criticisms with regard to CEE courts, their past rule-of-law case-law allows one to confidently assume that none of the main measures explored in this article would have withstood scrutiny in a typical Central and Eastern European constitutional court. Yet such measures comfortably passed the threshold of legality in the assessment of the EU Courts. The cases considered seem to corroborate the concerns noted in the second section of this paper. Indeed as regards the *Heinrich* case on secret legislation, Bobek expressed concern that the Court of Justice showed 'apparently unshakeable trust' in the European Commission, having decided on the legality of the secret measure without ever having seen it. He found this 'disquieting' given that institutionally only the EU Courts can oversee the legality of the European Commission's activities.[91] Overall the low intensity of review, combined with the very limited admissibility for actions brought by private parties, appear to effectively place EU measures beyond judicial review.

An important issue that has received little attention so far is that the level of judicial review has very direct consequences for the legal orders of all twenty-seven Member States, as they are bound by the supremacy of EU law. As Weatherill's well-known quote puts it, 'even the most minor piece of technical Community legislation ranks above the most cherished constitutional norm'.[92] Furthermore, one has to bear in mind that according to different estimates, more than half of national legislation today represents implementation of EU law, and is thus virtually beyond the control of national constitutional courts. Indeed national courts that have raised the prospect of reviewing measures that implement EU law have been fiercely criticized by commentators as 'eurosceptic' or as not understanding their new role as European judges.

Furthermore, when adjudicating in the extensive areas of law where the Member States' authorities implement EU law, the European Courts' judgments become *de facto* precedents for national courts. Thus the latter effectively have had to import the lower level of judicial review and of the protection of rights and of the general principles of law. Indeed the national courts have in various ways adjusted their standards. The Czech Constitutional Court recently declared its previous fundamental rights standards '*excessive*' and decided to apply the principle of '*constitutional self-restraint*'.[93] It did so after having carried out an extensive examination of the EU Courts' case law as regards the protection of the principles of legitimate expectations, legal certainty, non-retroactivity and non-discrimination, the right to undisturbed engagement in economic activity, and property rights. The Czech Court noted the high margin of discretion left by the Court of Justice with regard to implementing EU law; indeed as regards the principle of proportionality it noted the '*highly deferential standard*' and that

91 M Bobek, 'Case C-345/06, Gottfried Heinrich, Judgment of the Court of Justice (Grand Chamber) of 10 March 2009, Nyr. (Case Note)' [2009] *Common Market Law Review* 46, 2092 and 2094.

92 S Weatherill, *Law and Integration in the European Union* (Oxford University Press, Oxford 1995), 106.

93 Pl. ÚS 50/04, 8 March 2006; English translation available at <www.concourt.cz/view/726>.

fundamental rights 'may be subject *even to significant limitation*'. With regard to the Hungarian Constitutional Court's sugar stocks case, Andras Sajó has noted that cooperation at the EU level involves trade-offs: the concerns of uniform application and effectiveness of EU law 'seem to have forced certain countries to give up elements of their rule of law, e.g. legal certainty in administrative procedure, and even national versions of fundamental rights'.[94] According to him, '[i]t is ironic that in the Hungarian case[,] the learning [of cooperative constitutionalism in the EU] is made difficult by a historically determined serious commitment to ... fundamental rights'.[95] But such concerns have also surfaced in some older Member States, most notably in Germany during the above-discussed *Banana* saga where various German courts voiced their open distrust with regard to the protection of fundamental rights by the Court of Justice. By way of other examples, in the Netherlands the *Affish* case[96] has been characterized as one where the national administration was put in 'a nasty position', due to the obligation of loyal implementation which applies even if the governments are in doubt about the validity of an EU decision concerned and even where it would go against the principles of proper administration or procedural rules.[97] In Finland, the Constitutional Law Committee of Parliament has deemed it important to stress that the domestic implementation of EU law may not weaken the level of national protection of constitutional rights.[98] In Belgium, in the above-mentioned EAW preliminary ruling request, a group of defence lawyers raised a question about the protection of the right to equality of individuals, given that certain defence rights are no longer available to those individuals who are extradited under EU rules. Additionally, widespread concerns about prioritising market rights over social rights has been prompted in a large number of Member States by the ECJ judgments in cases such as *Laval* and *Viking*[99] regarding the right to strike, minimum pay and the social protection of workers.

In the EU law literature, it has become a well-established view that when applying the general principles of law in the EU context, the Court of Justice has 'Europeanized' the principles, by defining the content of these principles primarily in the light of the distinct features and the needs of the Union legal order.[100] The case studies in this paper would appear to suggest that in a paradoxical way, in some areas 'Europeanization' may have led to a reduction

94 Sajo, *supra n.* 4, at 367–8.
95 *Ibid*, at 371.
96 Case C-183/95, *Affish*, [1997] ECR I-4315.
97 E Steyger, *National Traditions and European Community Law: Margarine and Marriage* (Ashgate, Aldershot 1997) 190ff.
98 T Ojanen, 'The Impact of EU Membership on Finnish Constitutional Law', (2004) 10 *European Public Law*, at 542 and 545.
99 Case C-341/05 *Laval* [2007] ECR I-11767; Case C-438/05 *Viking Line* [2007] ECR I-10779.
100 As summarized by Pech, *supra n.* 24, at 6.

rather than an enhancement of standards. Indeed it was seen earlier that seven judges of the European Court of Human Rights have asked similar questions about application of a more lenient standard when EU Member States act within the field of EU law. This issue warrants further scrutiny but remains beyond the scope of this paper. It would also be interesting to explore whether the Member States' courts will in the future preserve a differential treatment of EU cases and cases falling outside the scope of EU law, or whether a downwards unification across the board may gradually occur in practice.

In any event, such far-reaching consequences of the EU Courts' judgments to national constitutional orders seem to warrant an open discussion about the role of judicial review over EU institutions and the objectives being sought with the current practice. Would supremacy of EU law not mandate a stricter rather than minimal judicial review? Otherwise, hard-won liberties and rights seem to be in the process of being eroded with no public discussion or wider awareness. As regards the Data Retention Directive, four years after the adoption of the measure, calls are emerging at political level to abolish the directive or leave it to national parliaments and constitutional courts to decide whether they wish to implement this policy or not.[101] With regard to the European Arrest Warrant, the Fair Trials International has noted 'the lack of public engagement in the area of defence rights and the almost total absence of political debate on the subject'.[102] It has taken several years of lobbying for the NGOs to put legislation on defence rights on the EU agenda. Although the Lisbon Treaty and the Stockholm Programme envisage improvements in the area of defence rights, this work starts more than eight years after the adoption of the EAW Framework Decision. Additionally, serious questions have been raised with regard to the suitability of introducing the principle of mutual recognition from trade and internal market regulation into the field of criminal law, as the logic of these two fields of regulation is entirely different.[103] Fletcher and Lööf have developed a detailed analysis showing that the classic spillover argument, which the EU has traditionally used to justify expansion of its competence, has tenuous empirical justification in the context of criminal law and that its use in this field is theoretically flawed.[104]

---

101 'German Minister wants to end EU-wide communications data retention', Press release of 14 November 2010 by the Working Group on Data Retention, <www.vorratsdatenspeicherung.de/content/view/305/79/lang,en/>.

102 Fair Trials International submission to the EU Justice and Home Affairs Council Working Group, 9 July 2009, www.fairtrials.net/campaigns, p. 4. On the need for democratic debate, see also V Mitsilegas, 'The Constitutional Implications of Mutual Recognition in Criminal Matters in the EU' [2006] *CMLRev* 43, 1309.

103 For a summary of the criticisms, see Mitsilegas, *supra n.* 102, 1280.

104 M Fletcher and R Lööf with B Gilmore, *EU Criminal Law and Justice* (Edward Elgar, Cheltenham Gloss 2008) 22–31.

But the principle of mutual recognition has also caused questions about the rule of law and rights in the context of civil matters. In Estonia, considerable media attention has been given to a case of a truck driver, who in 2009 discovered all of a sudden that his bank account was 6.7 million Estonian *kroons* (430,000 EUR) in debit, as Estonian customs authorities had automatically executed a customs tax request issued by German authorities.[105] Earning only 11,000 Estonian *kroons* (700 EUR) a month, the driver had little choice but to declare bankruptcy. He had been acquitted nine years earlier in Germany from cigarette smuggling charges, but Germany nonetheless requested a customs tax with interest that had accrued. This case led lawyers to raise the question of whether it is compatible with the Estonian Constitution to enforce foreign administrative acts without judicial review by a local court, as required by the relevant EU directives.

It may also be interesting to note that public concerns with regard to the above measures have predominantly emerged in the process of, or after, the national implementation of the measures rather than in the course of the EU legislative process. Furthermore, the public protests have been directed to national governments, with little understanding that these measures were required by the EU. This may well vindicate some of the German Constitutional Court's concerns expressed in the *Maastricht* decision with regard to the level of development of European public space and democratic deliberation; the literature at the time was very critical of what was regarded as the German Court's old-fashioned, ethno-cultural view to democracy.

5. TELEOLOGICAL INTERPRETATION AND EFFECTIVENESS OF EU LAW: QUESTIONS REGARDING BALANCING, LIMITS, FINES AND DOUBLE STANDARDS

The Estonian sugar case considered above also raises important questions with regard to the use of teleological interpretation and the all-important principle of effectiveness of EU law by the European Court of Justice. While their use has led to great benefits in rights concerning economic freedoms and free movement, one has to ask whether the same approach can be used when imposing large fines on Member States. As Bobek has observed with regard to the use of the doctrine of *effet utile* in EU law, it entitles the EU judges 'to do pretty much anything'; 'purposive reasoning is often reduced to one and only one purpose: the full effectiveness of Community law, which is turned into the crucial principle not

105 'Saksamaa nõuab eestlaselt miljoneid kroone' (Germany requires millions of kroons from an Estonian), *Postimees* 04.11.2009, www.postimees.ee.

allowing for any balancing or opposition'.[106] He notes with regard to the extensive use of teleological interpretation and *effet utile* in the EU Courts' case law that '[h]eretical though it may sound, there are some striking similarities between the communist/Marxist and Community approaches to legal reasoning …'[107] The early Stalinist phase of Marxist law required that judges disregard the remnants of the old bourgeois legal system. They had to apply the law in an anti-formalistic, teleological way, directing their aim towards the victory of the working class and the communist revolution. In EU law, the purpose also comes first, leading to reasoning that consequentially follows from the purpose, using open-ended clauses such as *effet utile*. These take precedence over a textual interpretation of the written law.[108] As Bobek notes, '[t]he only visible difference is that the universal "all-purpose" argument has changed – from the victory of the working class to the full effectiveness of EC law'.[109]

This historical background also helps to explain the reservations that CEE judges have with regard to teleological reasoning, and for which they have received considerable criticism as noted in the introductory section. However, the above cases show that such reservations may well be justified in some respects. In particular, it has been an essential tenet of the constitutional systems based on the rule of law that imposition of obligations and sanctions is only permissible on the basis of a statute; sanctions cannot be applied in a retroactive way and they have to be construed narrowly. Sanctions cannot be inferred by virtue of teleological reasoning out of objectives and aims, with no textual basis, or by virtue of analogy.[110] Let us recall that this is exactly what occurred during the communist regime, where administrative and criminal sanctions were arbitrarily imposed, using purposive reasoning and analogy, often in a retroactive manner. One cannot help being perplexed that elements of such a practice have to be restored because of EU membership, and not only in market matters but also with regard to criminal sanctions imposed on individuals.

Furthermore, the use of teleological interpretation to impose fines to the tune of 45 million EUR[111] also raises important questions about a potential conflict of interests, given that the EU's own budget is formed in part by such fines and, as seen above, the European Commission can expect virtual immunity from

106 M Bobek, 'On the Application of European Law in (Not Only) the Courts of the New Member States: 'Don't Do as I Say'?' [2007] *Cambridge Yearbook of European Legal Studies*, 10 and 21, citing Procházka, 'Prekážka rozhodnutej veci – judikatúra Súdneho dvora ES a jej dopad *na konanie vnútroštátnych súdov*' (*Res iudicata* – the Case law of the Court of Justice and its Impact on the Procedure before National Courts) 10 *Justičná revue* (2007), 1240, 1248.

107 Bobek, 'On the Application of European Law…', *supra n.* 106, 23.

108 *Ibid.*, 23–24.

109 *Ibid.*, 24.

110 I am grateful to Michal Bobek for highlighting this point.

111 Half of this fine corresponded to sugar held by individuals.

judicial review of its measures. This point was in fact indirectly raised by Latvia, which had supported the Estonian Government in the above sugar stocks case. Latvia pointed out that the objective of Regulation 60/2004, rather than burdening the state budgets of the new Member States, was to burden the budgets of undertakings that had bought sugar for speculative purposes. When looking at how the Commission had calculated the fine set out in Regulation 832/2005, Latvia suggested that it was impossible to achieve the objectives of Regulation 60/2004. In any event, the Estonian sugar case seems to reinforce questions regarding transparency that have earlier been raised in the context of infringement proceedings, in relation to how the European Court of Justice reaches its judgments on calculation of fines. Ian Kilbey's detailed case studies show that the Court has approved the Commission's 'all-embracing approach', typically dismissing Member States' arguments, e.g. as regards proportionality or where compliance has meanwhile been achieved.[112] Kilbey's study ends by noting that given the perilous financial position of a number of Member States in the context of the on-going financial crisis, and the on-going protests by citizens against the austerity measures, there are question marks as to how citizens would react if they realised how many millions of Euros are paid to the EU in penalties.[113]

While the Court has used teleological interpretation to minimise the review of EU institutions, it is increasingly drawing attention for the continued relentless use of teleological interpretation to find Member States' measures in breach of EU law and to expand the scope of EU competences *vis-à-vis* the Member States. In a recent article entitled 'Stop the European Court of Justice',[114] Roman Herzog, the former President of Germany and the former President of the German Constitutional Court as well as the President of the Convention that drafted the EU Charter of Fundamental Rights, explored the Member States' concerns regarding the expansion of EU competences in recent cases such as *Mangold*. Herzog notes that the ECJ has 'squandered a great deal of the trust it used to enjoy', as its justifications for 'interfering heavily in their legal systems are becoming increasingly astonishing'. According to Herzog,

> The cases described show that the ECJ deliberately and systematically ignores fundamental principles of the Western interpretation of law, that its decisions are based on sloppy argumentation, that it ignores the will of the legislator, or even turns it into its opposite, and invents legal principles serving as grounds for later judgements.

---

112 I Kilbey, 'The Interpretation of Article 260 TFEU (ex 228 EC)', [2010] *European Law Review* 3, 373–377.

113 *Ibid.*, 385.

114 R Herzog and L Gerken, 'Stop the European Court of Justice', www.euobserver.com, 10.09.2008.

A similarly strongly worded title, 'The only solution is to refuse to comply with ECJ rulings', has recently been used by Fritz Scharpf, Director emeritus of the Max Planck institute for Social Research in Cologne,[115] summarising the widespread concern with regard to the ECJ's judgments such as *Laval, Viking, Rueffert and Commission v Luxembourg.*[116] He draws attention to the ECJ's 'radical approach to the integration of the single market' whereby 'the most minor difficulty of exercising a basic freedom' has become 'a pretext to scrap an important element of national law', including fundamental social matters such as minimum pay, the right to strike and collective agreements.[117]

The requirement to make ample use of teleological interpretation and the principle of effectiveness has also led to considerable problems and diminished legal certainty in the Member States' constitutional orders more generally. Among more recent cases, considerable criticism has been expressed with regard to the far-reaching implications of the ECJ's *Köbler* judgment[118] for the principle of *res judicata*, which has been at the core of every European legal system based on the rule of law.[119] For example, Peter Wattel, Advocate General in the Supreme Court of the Netherlands, in an article entitled 'We can't go on meeting like this', asks what is so special about EU law that cases should be procedurally forced even beyond *res judicata*.[120] He suggests that *Köbler* is a major source of legal uncertainty, not least because of a large number of incoherent, contradictory or 'enigmatic' ECJ cases, as well as 'illegible' EU rules.[121] He also suggests that the EU itself should be held liable for damages caused not only to individuals but also to taxpayers by manifest errors on the part of the ECJ and for overstepping competence.[122] Wattel and others have questioned how *Köbler* complies with national judicial hierarchies (as lower courts will rule on the degree of wrongfulness of higher judicial decisions), and with the principle of separation of powers (as the executive becomes liable to pay damages for the actions of a body independent of them – the judiciary).[123]

---

115 F Scharpf, 'The Only Solution Is to Refuse to Comply with ECJ rulings', Interview with C. Girndt, *Social Europe Journal*, 2008, at 16-21, www.social-europe.eu.

116 Case C-341/05 *Laval* [2007] ECR I-11767; Case C-438/05 *Viking Line* [2007] ECR I-10779; C-346/06 *Rüffert* [2008] ECR I-1989; Case C-319/06 *Commission v Luxembourg* [2008] ECR I-4323.

117 Scharpf, *supra* n. 115, at 17.

118 Case C-224/01 *Köbler* [2003] ECR I-10239.

119 L Heuschling, *État de droit, Rechtsstaat, Rule of Law* (2002), cited in M Ruffert, 'case note on Case C-173/03, *Traghetti del Mediterraneo*' [2007] *CMLRev.* 44, 479.

120 PJ Wattel, '*Köbler, CILFIT* and *Welthgrove*: We Can't Go on Meeting Like This' [2004] *CML Rev* 41, 190.

121 *Ibid.*, 181–182.

122 *Ibid.*, 183–186.

123 *Ibid.* See also G Davies, 'The humiliation of the state as a constitutional tactic', in F Amtenbrink and P Van Den Berg (eds), *The Constitutional Integrity of the European Union* (Asser Press, The Hague 2010), 164.

As it happens, questions on the limits of teleological reasoning were recently raised by the High Court in the UK, in an unprecedented decision to send a preliminary ruling judgment for a reconsideration to the ECJ, given that the original EU regulations had spoken about compensation for air passengers in case of cancellation, but the ECJ had extended the compensation to cases of delay.[124] There may be merit in carrying out a systematic study of Member States judges' views in relation to the challenges encountered in their constitutional systems when applying EU law. In an on-going empirical research project, Urszula Jaremba has shown that Polish judges have been very keen to implement EU law and go to great lengths to do so correctly; however, the judges' anonymous answers to her questionnaires nonetheless reveal considerable challenges in practice.[125] For example, the judges' comments include the following remarks:

> 'ECJ goes too far in its judgments. Even though it is not (in) the written law, the Court still decides otherwise.'
> 'The Court itself adjudicates *contra legem*.'
> 'The quality of Community legislation is very low.'
> 'The ECJ decides something far-reaching and we must find the way out of this hell of national procedure, Community law and national rules.'
> 'ECJ decides something and does not care that we often have enormous problems with its judgment.'

Gareth Davies has gone further and looked at the landmark ECJ cases regarding preliminary rulings and free movement rights from the point of view of what he regards as very disorientating, destabilising and contemptuous effects on the national constitutional structures, structures which have evolved over time and have strong reasons for their existence.[126] He describes the ECJ's approach as one of 'the humiliation of the state as a constitutional tactic', where the ECJ 'repeatedly and consistently … diminishes the power, status, and capacity of the states in the eyes of its citizens'. He notes that ECJ's motto is one of 'divide and conquer' in action, where the cases attempt

> … to turn national courts upon each other; to reverse the hierarchy; to instruct lower judges to judge higher ones; to punish the state for things it cannot help; and to encourage citizens to ignore the administration. It is all perfectly sensible from an EU law policy perspective, but it is a world turned upside down for the traditional constitutionalist, as well as for the constitutionally aware citizen. The inability of the

124 'Air delay compensation claims suspended by High Court', *BBC News*, 17 August 2010, www.bbc.co.uk/news/business-10991631.

125 Slides accompanying U Jaremba's presentation on her on-going empirical PhD research project conducted among Polish civil judges, presented at the workshop 'Central and Eastern Europe and the European Union Court System', Loughborough University, 14 November 2009, on file with the author and cited with U Jaremba's permission.

126 Davies, *supra n.* 123, pp. 159–165.

> state to defend itself – and there have been no serious attempts to challenge these doctrines of the Court – is then the final disillusionment. The state has been made small.[127]

Overall the justification for applying double standards in the Court of Justice's approach to the EU institutions and to the Member States needs to be addressed and discussed, along with the rationale, added value and the *telos* that such an approach might seek, especially given the high level of integration that has already been achieved to date. While teleological interpretation was essential in the earlier phases of development of the EU legal order, the time seems ripe for a discussion whether such an approach still remains appropriate given the sheer extent of powers that the EU has acquired, especially after the Lisbon Treaty.

6. REVISITING THE ROLE OF CONSTITUTIONS AND CONSTITUTIONAL COURTS IN EU SCHOLARLY DISCOURSE: BEYOND THE LENS OF SOVEREIGNTY AND EURO-FRIENDLINESS

As noted in the introduction, in the EU law discourse national constitutions have come to be viewed primarily as a manifestation of sovereignty, and hence any arguments based on them have increasingly been dismissed offhand as passé and nationalistic. The literature has focused on the need for constitutions to open up to European level in the new context of multilevel constitutionalism and constitutional pluralism. Constitutional courts are judged on the basis of whether they take an 'EU-friendly' approach, embracing the more progressive and modern European cooperation, or whether they remain reluctant to relinquish authority and sovereignty. To bring just one example from the voluminous literature, one leading EU law textbook assesses the constitutional courts' judgments from the perspective of whether their approach represents 'European constitutional sovereignty', 'unconditional national constitutional Sovereignty' or 'constitutional tolerance'.[128] Some other examples were brought in the context of the EAW decisions. This literature captures important transformative trends that have occurred in recent decades. However, the analysis of the recent developments in EU law in the light of the post-communist constitutional reforms leads to four suggestions for a reconsideration of some of the main received wisdoms in the literature.

The first concerns rethinking the role of national constitutions. Rather than consigning them to history as a relict of sovereignty, the post-communist experience reminds us that there are other important values that underlie the

127 Davies, *supra n.* 123, p. 165.
128 Chalmers et al, *supra n.* 2, 198ff.

existence of national constitutions, such as the protection of constitutional rights and liberties *vis-à-vis* interference by authorities, the rule of law and the separation of powers with due checks and balances. It would appear that these important values may have increasingly been overlooked in the literature's focus on *sovereignty, authority* and pragmatic, EU-friendly cooperation by courts. It ought to be recalled that by invoking these values, historically constitutional courts have served as catalysts for improvements in the EU's constitutional order, in particular the German Constitutional Court by virtue of its *Solange I* decision,[129] which prompted the Court of Justice to introduce fundamental rights protection. It is hoped that the case studies showed that safeguarding these values remains of considerable importance in the European context. Indeed while the concern about constitutional rights has hitherto primarily been seen as a peculiar German and Italian preoccupation, the CEE accession shows that the concerns of countries that have strong constitutions merit a greater weight in the EU's constitutional balance. Having spent years at the receiving end of the EU's and the Council of Europe's human rights conditionality, the recent constitutional and fundamental rights reforms of CEE countries make them well placed to offer valuable contributions to the EU's evolving fundamental rights agenda. Indeed it is submitted here that the constitutional courts of the post-communist Member States would have a strong mandate to put some awkward questions about constitutional rights and the rule of law in the EU. As Radoslav Prohazka succinctly describes the post-communist ethos, the post-communist citizenries have become 'accustomed to the availability of mechanisms designed to protect their autonomy and rights from excessive interference by government. The notion that a citizen is both worth, and entitled to, institutional protection against government abuse has become *a constitutive element* of the *consciousness of the former Homo sovieticus* (emphasis added).'[130] It would appear paradoxical to expect that after 'return to Europe', the former *Homo sovieticus* can no longer count on such protection as a result of the constraints placed on national authorities by virtue of supremacy of EU law. It is indeed somewhat striking that the post-communist states, with their very recent experience of pervasive state control of personal freedoms, have not been considerably more vocal with regard to the Data Retention Directive as well as the other developments highlighted in this paper.

Secondly, it may also be necessary to explore how the rights of the states could be better entrenched *vis-à-vis* the EU institutions, especially in cases where they may be required to implement rules that would manifestly go against national constitutions. This also concerns matters which have sparked strong public opposition, for example in the case of the demonstrations against the blanket

---

129 *Internationale Handelsgesellschaft (Solange I)*, [1974] 2 CMLR 540, 549.

130 Prochazka, *Mission Accomplished…, supra n.* 9, 266.

electronic surveillance or the strong public opposition to the approval of genetically modified foods by the European Commission. At present, non-implementation on any ground simply leads to infringement proceedings by the European Commission and the possibility of imposing sizeable fines on the Member States.

Thirdly, while the literature mainly appears to expect cooperation and self-restraint on the part of national courts in deference to the EU Courts, it seems time to shift the spotlight on assessing the co-operativeness of the European Court of Justice with regard to national constitutional concerns. In the wake of the *Banana* decision in the 1990s, Everling called for a reconsideration of the attitude by the Court of Justice, as it is no longer imperative for it to primarily act as an 'integration motor', but, as 'a real Constitutional Court, it has to ensure a balanced equilibrium between the competences, rights and functions of the institutions, Member States and citizens'.[131] The recent developments seem to give little indication that the Court of Justice has taken any notice of such calls. Therefore, some commentators, including Roman Herzog in the above-noted article, have called for reviving the debate on the creation of an independent European Constitutional Tribunal.[132] While in terms of human rights protection, the ECJ will become subject to the oversight of the ECtHR after the Union's expected accession to the ECHR, such a system may well render the system of protection of rights even more byzantine than at present and, in any event, concerns remain with regard to a fair and neutral policing of competences between the EU and the Member States. Given that the creation of a new tribunal would appear an unlikely development, it is suggested here that the only way to balance the ECJ would be if the constitutional courts beyond Germany were to voice their concerns in a firmer and more co-ordinated way. It is hoped that the detailed case studies in this article show that instead of parochially protecting their turf, constitutional courts have a legitimate role to fulfil in the European constitutional system. The debate ought be reframed and moved to a new level: instead of assessing whether courts are EU-friendly, the arguments based on national constitutions ought to be re-legitimized, discussing in a meaningful way how constitutional values can be preserved in a pluralist legal environment. Otherwise, perhaps there is a danger of forging ahead towards the elusive *telos* of an ever closer union, while inadvertently dismantling the hard-won constitutional rights and guarantees which have strong historical reasons and clearly remain of continued importance in the contemporary pluralist setting.

---

131 Everling, *supra n.* 18, 435–436.

132 See Herzog and Gerken, *supra n.* 114. For earlier calls, see J Weiler, *The Constitution of Europe. 'Do the new clothes have an emperor?' and other essays on the European Integration* (Cambridge University Press, Cambridge 1999) 350ff.

The final question that needs addressing is how we have come to a situation where critical analysis of the European Court of Justice has typically been dismissed as euroscepticism. In a paradoxical way, to a post-communist writer this evokes uncanny memories from the Communist regime, where one was either for or against the system, with no substantive deliberation on the rules. In the national legal orders of EU Member States, the focus of legal analysis has shifted from the content and shaping of law to whether EU law is implemented correctly by the authorities and applied in an EU-friendly manner by judges. In the political discourse, the debate is typically about Member States' national interests versus European interest, rather than on substantive policy choices. For example, in Germany, it has been noted that the 'right-left' political dichotomy, which is often found in public law works at national level, is largely absent from European legal study. Instead the division is between 'integration friendly' and 'integration sceptical' camps.[133] In France, the divide appears to be between 'integrationists' and 'souverainists'. To bring the example of the on-going financial crisis, there has been virtually no discussion of whether the EU technocrats might have made policy errors; the solution to the crisis is seen in 'more Europe', transferring further economic competences to the Union and creating new EU financial institutions.[134] When the EU recently sought to increase its budget by 6% at a time when national governments have had to impose severe cuts to public services, the Member States opposing the increase were described by high-ranking EU officials as 'anti-Europe'.[135]

In the emergence of such a mind-set, a central role appears to have been played by lawyers. It is well established that European integration has been a legal project developed largely through the interpretation of the Court of Justice, rather than by political process. Scholars studying the sociology of law have additionally noted the role of EU legal scholars in creating and sustaining the notion of the Community/Union as a juristic idea with its technical, autonomous and specific nature, given that scientific authority has been an essential device for political legitimacy.[136] In a recent study, Antoine Vauchez has documented the historical evolution of the main EU law doctrines through self-referential

---

133 A Von Bogdandy, 'A birds-eye view on the science of European Law: Structures, debates and development prospects of basic research on the law of the European Union in a German Perspective', [2000] *European Law Journal* 6, 210.

134 H-J Schlamp, 'More Power to Brussels: Crisis Forces Europe to Unite on Financial Reform', 13.09.2010. www.spiegel.de and A Rettman, 'EU economic governance inevitable, Belgian PM says', www.euobserver.com, 16.03.2010.

135 V Pop, 'Buzek clashes with EU leaders over 'un-European' budget, www.euobserver.com, 28.10.2010.

136 See e.g. H Schepel, R Wesseling, 'The Legal Community: Judges, Lawyers, Officials and Clerks in the Writing of Europe' [1997] *European Law Journal* 3, 165–188, J Shaw, 'European Union Legal Studies in Crisis? Towards a New Dynamic' [1996] *Oxford Journal of Legal Studies* 16, 231–253, 240, A Vauchez, 'The transnational politics of judicialization. *Van Gend en Loos* and the making of the EU polity' [2009] *European Law Journal* 16, 1.

writings of EU lawyers in their often simultaneous roles as EU officials, judges, law professors and members of editorial boards of key journals.[137] Indeed he argues that Europe's powerful meta-narrative of 'Europeanisation through case-law' owes its success to the requirement that anyone wishing to authoritatively take part in the EU debates and to access positions within the EU polity should possess legal credentials and know-how.[138] Another study, analysing the articles published in the main EU law journals that have traditionally set the research agenda, notes a 'process of reciprocal legitimisation' by contributors who move in their career paths between the EU institutions, the Court of Justice and academia.[139] This community of lawyers advances a shared mind-set that seeks to depoliticise European integration 'by creating an opposition between a realm of European "law" as a rational force towards the inevitable and a realm of *national "politics" as the articulation of the illogical, irrational and ideological*' (emphasis added).[140] The articles in such journals are typically reactive to recent developments in EU law, representing a learned treatise on how Community law has made 'yet another step forward' in the 'forward march of European integration', or a scholarly follow-up of Commission White Papers and discussion documents.[141]

A central effect of the above developments is that EU law has been developed into a specific area of study, disconnected from other disciplines, especially comparative law. Indeed historical accounts have documented the considerable investment by the European Commission in founding specialised EU law journals and university centres, with the aim to shift EU studies away from a comparative analysis of national laws (which would aim to identify common principles) to the study of the own 'specificity' of EU law, focusing on the relationships between EU law (and ECJ) and national law (and courts).[142] EU law has become the province of the specialist EU lawyer, 'untouchable by outsiders not initiated into its special techniques';[143] it is studied and taught as 'a highly technical set of rules, a dense doctrinal thicket'.[144] Overall, EC/EU legal studies have been 'to a large extent insulated from the theoretical, methodological and contextual influences which have been felt in most other fields of legal study', and EU lawyers broadly have a reputation as a doctrinal, uncritical, unreflective, atheoretical and unidisciplinary group.[145] The limited critical work that exists

[137] Vauchez, *supra n.* 136.
[138] Ibid, 4.
[139] Schepel and Wesseling, *supra n.* 136, 174, 183–184.
[140] Ibid, 186.
[141] Ibid, 175–176, 180.
[142] Vauchez, *supra n.* 136, 20–21.
[143] Shaw, *supra n.* 136, 235–236.
[144] F Snyder, 'New Directions in European Community Law' [1987] *Journal of Law and Society* 14, 167, cited in Shaw, *supra n.* 136, 234.
[145] Shaw, *supra n.* 136, 236–237, and Schepel and Wesseling, *supra n.* 136, 165–188.

with regard to the Court of Justice has typically not been well received or has even been vehemently criticised.[146] Indeed ECJ judges, who have traditionally played a particularly prominent position in EU legal commentary, have even discouraged comparative, politico-sociological and contextual method, especially if 'contextual' strays into 'critical'.[147] Despite various calls for a change, a cursory look at recent law journals and conference papers typically reveals a continued focus on exposition of the very complex and fast-changing treaties, legislation and case-law, and assessing national implementation from the point of view of uniformity and coherence of EU law, with minimal critical discussion.

Such an approach to the study of EU law in its own specificity, disconnected from comparative constitutional context, might go some way towards explaining why the literature in EU law typically celebrates the very fact that EU law proclaims the protection of the rule of law and fundamental rights and the Europeanization of the general principles, and that the considerable fall in the standard of protection of some of the classic constitutional rights has by and large escaped the literature's notice. Instead of comparative studies on how the protection in practice compares with that provided by constitutional courts, the latter are presumed to be parochial. Instead the focus of study is on the nature of the ECJ as a constitutional, federal court. Indeed in leading books and articles in the field, the expression 'European constitutional law' has come to signify EU constitutional law largely developed by the ECJ rather than comparative European constitutional law.

As an aside, it might also be interesting to consider the role that the English language has played in shaping the scholarly discourse: research agendas and trends in the mainstream discourse on EU constitutionalism often appear to have been set by scholars and law journals based in the UK and the Benelux countries. Some of the Benelux countries have evolutionary, flexible constitutions;[148] the UK is the only country in the EU which does not have a written constitution and where human rights have been systematically listed only since 2000, following the adoption of the Human Rights Act 1998. In fact, it has been noted that the principles of legitimate expectations and proportionality were mainly introduced in the UK via EC and ECHR law.[149] The absence of explicit constitutional provisions and adjudication by a constitutional court in the UK may well have channelled the scholarly discourse in terms of regarding

146 E.g. Hjalte Rasmussen's work questioning the extension of competences by the ECJ, and the above-discussed article by Coppel and O'Neill on fundamental rights protection; for an overview of the literature see Schepel and Wesseling, *supra n.* 136, 184.

147 For references to literature, see Schepel and Wesseling, *supra n.* 136, 186.

148 See Besselink, 'The Dutch Constitution …', *supra n.* 8 and the accompanying text.

149 J Usher, 'General Principles and National Law – a Continuing Two-Way Process', in U Bernitz, J Nergelius and C Cardner, C. (eds) *General Principles of EC Law in a Process of Development* (Kluwer, Dordrecht 2008) 402–410, 415.

the more flexible approach towards the general principles as a standard, and the stricter approach taken by the German and Italian constitutional courts as a deviation.

It is hoped that the cases explored in this article demonstrate the need for a critical comparative analysis to identify areas where EU law has posed genuine constitutional problems for the Member States. As Follesdal and Hix[150] have pointed out in the context of research on the European Commission, the Commission's activities 'should be open to rigorous contestation and criticism. Such criticism should not be interpreted as euroscepticism or anti-federalism, but rather as an essential element of democratic politics at the European level…' In the context of the debate on the ECJ's prioritisation of market freedoms over 'social Europe', Scharpf has noted that

> pro-European legal discourses and political rhetoric are still shaped by the idealistic commitment to promoting European integration against what they consider protectionist impediments and nationalistic opposition. As a consequence, there are no meaningful public exchanges between pro-European elites and national non-elites about the impact of integration …[151]

According to him, '… good Europeans need to draw a distinction between their continuing support for political and social integration in Europe on the one hand, and their unquestioning acceptance of policy choices dictated by a nonaccountable judicial authority on the other hand'.[152] In a similar vein, the problems faced by national courts when applying EU law legitimately merit scrutiny, without being dismissed as eurosceptic. There is no question that European integration has brought about long-standing peace, prosperity, freedom of movement and a wealth of other benefits, especially so to the new Member States. However, this does not mean that asking questions about the rule of law and the quality of constitutionalism would in any way undermine the underlying European idea. It is submitted here that given the present stage of the EU's development and the extensive powers that the EU has post-Lisbon virtually in all areas of regulation, it would no longer seem acceptable to reduce far-reaching policy issues to technical matters of legal doctrine, on which only handful of lawyers mastering the highly specialised vernacular of EU law can authoritatively speak on, dismissing any critical analysis as euroscepticism.

---

150 A Follesdal and S Hix, 'Why there is a Democratic Deficit in the EU: A Response to Majone and Moravcsik' [2006] *Journal of Common Market Studies* 44, 554.

151 F Scharpf, 'The Double Asymmetry of European Integration Or: Why the EU Cannot Be a Social Market Economy', MPIfG Working Paper 09/12, www.mpifg.de/pu/workpap/wp09-12.pdf, at 21; reprinted in *Socio-Economic Review* (Oxford U. Press) 2010, Volume 8, No 2, at 211-250.

152 Ibid, at 34.

CHAPTER 7

FRANCE

THE IMPACT OF EUROPEAN FUNDAMENTAL RIGHTS ON THE FRENCH CONSTITUTIONAL COURT

Laurence BURGORGUE-LARSEN*

1. INTRODUCTION. THE 'EUROPEANIZATION' OF THE FRENCH CONSTITUTION

It took quite some time for the European Union to make its entrance into the French Constitution of 4th October 1958. Indeed, the altogether rather limited space allotted to international law in the Constitution clearly demonstrates the fate the constituent powers of the time intended to reserve for the 'exterior' sphere. While on the one hand the existence of international engagements and a certain peace ideal were to be recognized (paragraph 14, Preamble 1946)[1], on the other hand the country was wary of pledging allegiance, no matter the cost, to any supranational structure (paragraph 15, Preamble 1946).[2] Besides the dated phrases in the Preamble, the Constitution contained a very classic[3] Title VI 'International Treaties and Agreements', composed originally of only four

* Professor at the Ecole de droit de la Sorbonne (Université Paris I), Vice-Director of the Institut de Recherche et d'Etude en Droit international et européen (IREDIES).

1 Paragraph 14 of the Preamble is written as follows: "*The French Republic, true to its traditions, conforms to the rules of international public law. It will not undertake any war with a view to conquest and will never use its force against the liberty of any one people*".

2 The reference of paragraph 15 of the Preamble to the requirement of reciprocity reveals this established fact: "*Subject to reciprocity, France consents to the sovereignty limitations necessary for the organization and the defence of peace*".

3 In accordance with a tradition stemming from the 19th century, the constituent powers of the Fifth Republic perceived the theme of international relations above all in terms of procedures. They endeavoured to designate the authorities empowered to represent the State *ad extra* in the Constitutional Charter, to attribute the *treaty making power* and to determine the rank of international treaties in the internal organization.

clauses.[4] Not only did this title betray a certain reserve towards international law, but it also left a major institutional innovation of the time undocumented: the creation of sectoral Communities in 1951 (the ECSC) and in 1957 (Euratom and the EEC). This silence in itself was an extraordinary paradox. The founding speech of 9th May 1950 was delivered by a Frenchman (Robert Schuman, Minister of Foreign Affairs), in France (in the illustrious drawing room *Salon de l'Horloge* of the *Quai d'Orsay*). Its promoters were Frenchmen (Jean Monnet in particular) and its intention was nothing less than Franco-German reconciliation and peace on the European continent. Nevertheless, the constituent power of 1958 did not breathe one word of this new political order that would transfigure post-war international relations. This was in part due to the dispute over the ratification of the ECSC treaty and the stillborn EDC treaty (1954). It has to be said that the three institutional treaties – all ratified on the basis of pertinent clauses in the Constitution of the Fourth Republic – already implicated France as of 1st January 1958. This was already more than enough for the constituent power of 1958, taking care not to go any further and mention the European 'fact', so as not to give rise to any federal thoughts, so fiercely fought by Gaullists.

However, France was not able to stay on the side-lines of the process of integrating the Community structures into the constitutional domain. It would take until 1992 before the country resigned to integrating Europe in its Constitution, thanks to the workings of the procedure of Article 54 in the Constitution, as it instituted the facultative and *a priori* control of international treaties. In case of a discrepancy, detected by the Constitutional Council, between an international treaty and the French Constitution, the latter must be revised so as to enable the process of ratification or approval of the international engagement.[5] In this respect, the Treaty on European Union (TEU), adopted in Maastricht, was the trigger. It was decried and criticized, in France as well as in other countries. It must be said that it required a 'leap' towards a Community structure that was not merely a symbolic one. The Maastricht Treaty demanded, among other things, for countries to transfer to the European Community a competence so archetypical of sovereign states: minting coins. And so the French Constitution was Europeanised. Following the decision of *9th April 1992, Maastricht 1*[6], which led to constitutional law nr. 92–554 of 25th June 1992, a new

4 These four original clauses of Title VI are related to the powers of the President of the Republic as regards international relations (Article 52), to the classification of treaties from a ratification or approbation viewpoint (Article 53), to the preventive mechanism of control by the Constitutional Council and its consequences (Article 54), and finally to the place of the treaties in the legal organization (Article 55).

5 It reads as follows: "*If the Constitutional Council, called upon by the President of the Republic, by the Prime Minister, by the President of either assembly or by sixty deputies or sixty senators, has declared that an international engagement contains a clause contrary to the Constitution, the authorization of ratifying or approving said international engagement cannot intervene until the Constitution has been revised.*"

6 Cons. const., 9 April 1992, *Treaty on the European Union* (*Maastricht I*), No. 92–308 DC.

Title XV was added at the end of the constitutional text[7], entitled 'Of the European Communities and the European Union', amendable in the event of further elaboration of the European structure, if the Council decides that this needs to be accommodated by a revision of the Constitution. It is therefore that after the decision of *31st December 1997, Treaty of Amsterdam*[8], which led to constitutional law nr. 99–49 of 25th January 1999, Title XV was at once removed, developed and added back in. It was through the decision of *13th December 2007, Lisbon Treaty*[9] – the basis for the constitutional law of 4th February 2008[10] – that Title VX was renamed *'Of the European Union'* and was extended with several clauses taking into account the role of the French Parliament in controlling subsidiarity (Article 88§6) and in implementing simplified revision procedures (88§7). Europe is thereby 'constitutionalized', which is the progressive nature of European integration. Both the Treaty on European Union of 7th February 1992 (Article 88–3) and the Lisbon Treaty, as signed on 13th December 2007 (Article 88§1 and 88§7), made a remarkable entrance in the 'European' part of the French Constitution, seeing that they are cited *expressis verbis*. When an 'international constitutional law'[11] started to emerge, a 'constitutional law of the European Union' took shape in the Constitutional Charter, and it is seen by many as largely sufficient and satisfactory.

This 'Europeanization' of the French Constitution is also the work of the constituent power spurred on by the decisions made by the Constitutional Council, which has participated, thanks to the power of the *a priori* verification of international treaties, in shaping the contours of references to the European Union in the French Constitution.[12] We shall see that these elements have had a significant influence on the French Constitutional Council's attitude *vis-à-vis* the legal principles of the European Union (Part I). As to the connections between the Constitutional Council and the European Convention on Human Rights, that is a completely different issue. We shall see that, while the European Court's control over constitutional decisions and procedures is quite real and visible, there is still no trace of any reference to said court's jurisdiction in the

7 This is a consequence of the technique of "additional revision".

8 Cons. const., 31 December 1997, *Amsterdam Treaty*, No. 97–234 DC.

9 Cons. const., 20 December 2007, *Lisbon Treaty*, No. 2007–560 DC.

10 Constitutional Law No. 2008–103 of 4 February 2008, *Traité de Lisbonne modifiant le traité sur l'Union européenne et le traité instituant la Communauté européenne, JORF*, 5 February 2008.

11 This expression traditionally refers to the clauses dedicated to international relations and to international law in the Constitutions. Its inventor is B Mirkine-Guetzevitch, *Droit constitutionnel international* (Paris, 1933) 300 p. This now-classic term has been taken up and somewhat popularized or at least given a French flavour by J Rideau "Constitution et droit international dans les Etats membres de l'Union européenne", [1990] 2 *RFDC* 259–296 and L Favoreu, "Le contrôle de constitutionnalité du Traité de Maastricht et le développement du 'droit constitutionnel international'" [1993] *RGDIP*, 39–65.

12 It is actually interesting to note that the *a priori* control of Article 54 has been performed on international engagements several times.

Constitutional Council's decisions. In reality, Strasbourg's case law does have an impact on the members of Palais Montpensier, but for the time being this influence remains 'invisible' (Part II).

2. THE CONSTITUTIONAL COUNCIL AND EUROPEAN UNION LAW

Two points require a closer look when discussing the confrontation of the Constitutional Council with the existential principles inherent to the law of integration. First the question about respecting absolute primacy, asked by the Court of Justice[13], and then the question about the necessity of the 'reference for a preliminary ruling' (*renvoi préjudiciel*), asked by Article 267 TFEU, actually one of the consequences of the first question. These two themes have given rise to very extensive case law in recent years.

2.1. THE CONSTITUTIONAL COUNCIL AND PRIMACY

Generally speaking, and depending on each 'constitutional context', one can distinguish two kinds of attitudes of the Constitutional Courts regarding the place of European Union law in the internal legal orders. The first attitude consists of staying in the background, not partaking in the debate and holding on to one's constitutional positions without engaging in 'dialogue' with the Luxemburg Court, leaving the latter in the hands of ordinary jurisdictions in charge of conventionality control. The second attitude is for the constitutional judge to take sides, partaking in the debate and possibly risking a head-on collision with the Court of Justice. The French Constitutional Council has successively had both kinds of attitudes. It has moved from indifference to being "involved". This evolution stems from the transformation of the French Constitution, which from 1992 onwards has constitutionalised the phenomenon of European integration.

However, in his decision of 15th January 1975 about 'Voluntary Pregnancy Termination' (i.e. abortion)[14], the constitutional judge clearly distanced himself from conventionality control. He considered that assessing the compatibility of international (and Community) law with French law was not a matter of constitutionality control. Consequently he referred this control to the ordinary courts. In this context, the supreme judges of the legal and administrative order

---

13 Case C 6/64 *Costa v. E.N.E.L.* [1964] ECR 1199; Case 106/77 *Italian Finance Administration v Simmenthal*, [1978] ECR 629.

14 Cons. Const., 15 January 1975, *IVG*, No. 1975-54 DC.

were the ones who ended up accepting the primacy of Community law, but only over laws (including subsequent laws)[15] and under no circumstances over the French Constitution.[16] All this would change with the 'Europeanization' of the French Constitution. Since the introduction of Title XV, certain authors deemed early on that they were witnessing a kind of constitutionalisation of the European standards mentioned in this title.[17] As a result, it seems that the position of the Council in its decision on abortion is logically becoming harder and harder to uphold, with the European standards mentioned in Title XV being 'constitutionalised' – i.e. transformed into constitutional standards – yet all the while keeping their initial quality. Consequently, constitutionality control and conventionality control tend to get mixed up and the division of roles with ordinary judges, too, tends to become blurred. The Council's case law as from 2004 provides striking proof of this. It reveals both the involvement of the Council in the *disputatio* relating to primacy and the difficulties in trying to draw a simple line between constitutionality control and conventionality control. This raises the question of how long this precarious balancing act will manage to last.

As from the decision of *19th November 2007*, which examined the constitutionality of the *Treaty Establishing a Constitution for Europe*[18], the Council was induced to take a position in the primacy debate. It did not go about this blindly. While moderating the authority of the system of the Union, the judge ultimately preserved the French Constitution.[19] Although absolute primacy is *in fine* impugned by the constitutional judge, this is done in such a way that the denial is not all too blunt. By not detecting any discrepancy between Article I-6 of the Treaty Establishing a Constitution for Europe[20] and the pertinent clauses of the French Constitution, the Palais Montpensier judge finds the legal motivations for a *conciliation* of systems thanks to a new interpretation of Article 88 §1 of the Constitution[21] to which a 'normative

15 Cass. (mixed chamber) 24 May 1975, *Société des Cafés J. Vabre*; CE, ass., 20 October 1989, *Nicolo*.

16 Cass., (plenary assembly) 2 June 2000, *Fraisse*; CE, ass. 30 October 1998, *Sarran et Levacher*.

17 E Picard, "Vers l'extension du bloc de constitutionnalité au droit européen?" [1993] *RFD adm.* 47.

18 Cons. const., 19 November 2004, *Treaty establishing a Constitution for Europe*, No. 2004–505 DC. The doctrinal analyses were countless, so we will refer to the Constitutional Council's website for further reading (www.conseilconstitutionnel.fr).

19 Here, France joins the majority of Constitutional Courts that did not fail to issue "constitutional reservations" (*réserves de constitutionnalité*), both to enforce the principle of competence attribution and to preserve a high level of protection of fundamental rights.

20 We know that this article had codified the primacy principle: "*The Constitution and the law adopted by the institutions of the European Union, in exercising the competences attributed to them, take precedence over Member State laws*", see §§ 9 through 13 of the decision of 19th November 2004.

21 It read as follows in 2004: "*The Republic participates in the European Communities and in the European Union, composed of States that have freely chosen, by virtue of treaties establishing*

value'[22] is attributed.; and also to consider that the primacy of European Union law results quite simply from the constitutional clauses and from Article 88§1 in particular. Even if the conciliation was acquired at the cost of issuing a 'constitutional reservation' (*réserve de constitutionnalité*)[23], this did not make the conciliation of opposites (primacy of the Constitution vs. primacy of EU law) any less real. The normative content attributed to Article 88§1 had made its appearance a few months earlier in the decision regarding *The Digital Economy* of *10th June 2004*[24], within the scope of controlling the constitutionality of laws (Article 61 of the Constitution). In this decision, the Council had considered that the translation of the Directives into internal law resulted from a constitutional requirement. Therefore, the judge showed that the Constitution consented to its own subordination, which *in fine* amounted to demonstrating, at the same time, its authority and, by doing so, its superiority. The constitutional judge did, however, issue a 'constitutional reservation' (*réserve de constitutionnalité*) to this primacy accepted by the constitution. Indeed, the constitutional immunity imparted to the Directives caused discrepancies with the '*express clauses of the Constitution*'[25], which '*do not have an equivalent in the Community's legal order*'.[26] Certainly sensitive to numerous doctrinal criticisms[27], the Council reformulated its reservation in 2006 in the decision about *Copyright*. It continued to limit the primacy of Directives (and more generally of European Union law) by considering that '*the transposition of a Directive cannot run counter to a rule or a principle inherent to France's constitutional identity, except for instances to which the Constituent power has consented*'.[28] The constitutional reservation relating to the 'constitutional identity' made its appearance in French constitutional case law; we know that it was emulated in Germany.[29] The wording of former Article I-5 of the Treaty Establishing a Constitution for Europe must not have been incompatible with it,

---

them, to exercise jointly a number of their competences." Since the commencement of the Lisbon Treaty, this clause reads as follows: "*The Republic participates in the European Union, composed of States that have freely chosen to exercise jointly a number of their competences by virtue of the Treaty on European Union and the Treaty on the Functioning of the European Union, as they result from the treaty signed in Lisbon on 13th December 2007.*"

22 For a presentation of the history of the integration of this clause into the Constitution and its current interpretation by the Constitutional Council, see J Rideau & F Picod, "Article 88§ 1" in, F Luchaire, G Conac & X Prétot (ed) *La Constitution de la République française* (Paris, Economica, 2009, 3th ed.), 1864–1916.

23 It had been worded a few months earlier in the *Digital economy* decision (see note 24).

24 Cons. const., 10 June 2004, *Economie numérique*, No. 2004–496 DC.

25 Cons. const., 10 June 2004, *Economie numérique*, No. 2004–496 DC, § 6.

26 This was stated explicitly in this decision: Cons. const., 29 July 2004, *Bioéthique*, No. 2004–498 DC.

27 Such is the analysis of J Roux, *Droit général de l'Union européenne* (Litec, Paris 2010, 3th éd) 268.

28 Cons. const., 27 July 2006, *Droit d'auteur*, No. 2006–540 DC, § 19.

29 German Constitutional Court, 30 June 2009, *Lisbon judgment*.

as it valued 'the national identity' of States[30], which is still the case, for that matter, in the Treaty on European Union, as revised in Lisbon by adding a reference to 'local and regional autonomy'.[31]

Such a jurisprudential policy had an impact on the outline of constitutionality control, and consequently also on the outline of conventionality control. Indeed, today the office of the Constitutional Council breaks down in both a negative and a positive obligation. The former is the *incompetence* to control the *constitutionality* of transposed laws (except for the constitutional reservation); the latter is the *competence* to verify the *compatibility* of laws with the Directives they are meant to transpose. It is clear that this second element is an exception to the case law regarding abortion and implicates the Council in the universe of controlling conventionality. This implication may be indirect and filtered, but this does not make it any less effective[32], which results in a considerably complex jurisdictional landscape in France. Add to this the introduction in France – based on the new Article 61§1 of the Constitution[33] – of *a posteriori* control of laws through the technique of the *'question prioritaire de constitutionnalité'* (commonly abbreviated as QPC), and the resulting extreme complexity becomes a distinct characteristic of the French system.[34] Above all, there is a point there which, in concrete terms, collides with one of the requirements that follow from the primacy of EU law, namely the integral acceptance of the logic of the reference for a preliminary ruling in Article 267 of the Treaty on the Functioning of the European Union (TFEU). Therefore, although the reservation relating to the 'constitutional identity' remains very theoretical and is unlikely to be

30 M Blanquet, "Article I-5", in L Burgorgue-Larsen, A Levade & F Picod (ed), *Traité établissant une Constitution pour l'Europe,* Parts I and IV *"Architecture constitutionnelle"* (Bruylant, Brussels, 2007).

31 Article 4§ 2 of the Treaty on European Union: "The Union respects the equality of Member States before the treaties as well as their *national identity, inherent to their fundamental political and constitutional structures, including with regard to local and regional autonomy.* It respects the essential functions of States, in particular those meant to ensure their territorial integrity, to maintain public order and to safeguard national security. National security in particular remains the sole responsibility of each Member State." (underlined by us).

32 Cons. const., 30 November 2006, *Secteur de l'énergie,* No. 2006–543 DC. The control *in casu* has been limited, but effective. The Council penalizes *"only glaring errors in transposition"*, because of the brief period granted to deliver a verdict (one month). In this case, the Council censured Article 17 of the law submitted for review, as it maintained regulated rates, while the objective of the Directive was to open the energy market to competition.

33 It was introduced after the constitutional reform of 23rd July 2008 (constitutional act n°2008–724). It read as follows: *"When, during the proceedings before a jurisdiction, it is upheld that a legislative clause undermines the rights and liberties guaranteed by the Constitution, this question may be submitted to the Constitutional Council upon referral by the Council of State or the* Cour de Cassation, *which will give a verdict within a set timeframe. An organic law determines the conditions of application of the present article."*, we refer to V Bernaud, "Article 61–1", F Luchaire, G Conac & X Prétot (ed) *La Constitution de la République française,* (Economica, Paris, 2009, 3th ed), 1438–1467.

34 G Alberton, "Peut-on encore dissocier l'exception d'inconstitutionnalité et exception d'inconventionnalité?", [2008] *AJDA*, 967 a.f.

activated one day, the creation of the QPC does elicit a very real confrontation between two kinds of prejudicial procedures: the constitutional procedure (QPC) and the European procedure (267 TFEU).

2.2. THE CONSTITUTIONAL COUNCIL AND THE REFERENCE FOR A PRELIMINARY RULING (ARTICLE 267 TFEU)

The introduction in France of the QPC closed an old debate which had taken shape in the early 1990s, about a procedure which was then called the 'unconstitutionality exception'.[35] Early on, many enlightened jurists[36] had considered that an *a posteriori* control mechanism[37] was needed to strengthen the protection of rights in France. This mechanism ultimately came into being after two failed attempts in 1990 and 1993. This was a genuine 'jurisdictional big bang'[38] for France. The preparations demonstrate perfectly that it was a matter of reinstating the Constitution at the heart of the French judicial architecture.[39]

35 Regarding terminology issues – which are not to be ignored as they have obvious and substantial implications – we refer to the special issue of the *Revue française de droit constitutionnel* published in 1990 entitled "L'exception d'inconstitutionnalité. Le projet de réforme de la saisine du Conseil constitutionnel" and particularly the analysis of T S Renoux, "L'exception, telle est la question", [1990] 4 *RFD Const.*, 651–658.

36 Among them, special mention is appropriate for Bruno Genevois who, as Secretary-General of the Constitutional Council, played a major role in the entourage of Robert Badinter to give an impetus to the constitutional reform project of 1990. To take stock of this influence, one need only refer to the tribute of Robert Badinter *in* "L'exception d'inconstitutionnalité" in *Le dialogue des juges. Mélanges en l'honneur du Président Genevois (*Paris, Dalloz, 2009) 39–49.

37 We refer to the snappy wordings of Robert Badinter in the *Mélanges Ryssdal*, stating that the persons subject to a trial in France were quite paradoxically treated as constitutional "minors", whereas conventionally they were considered "of age", see R Badinter, "La Convention européenne des droits de l'homme et le Conseil constitutionnel", in P Mahoney (ed), *Protection des droits de l'homme: la perspective européenne / Protecting human rights: the european perspective, Mélanges à la mémoire de Rolv Ryssdal* (Carl Heymanns Verlag KG, 2000) 79–85, spec. p. 84.

38 D Rousseau, "La question préjudicielle de constitutionnalité: un big bang juridictionnel?" [2009] 3 *RDPub.*, 631–644.

39 Councillor Olivier Dutheillet de Lamothe was very clear when, during a visit of the Constitutional Council to Madrid in early April 2009, he affirmed without beating about the bush: "it follows from the preparatory work for the 2008 constitutional revision that by adopting the prejudicial question of constitutionality, the constituent power intended to re-establish a certain priority of constitutionality control over conventionality control." Indeed, he considered that it was not sound for conventionality control, and consequently the treaties, to take up more room in the internal order than constitutionality control. O. Dutheillet de Lamothe, visit to the Spanish Constitutional Tribunal (2–4 April 2009), text available on the Council's website (www.conseil-constitutionnel.fr). The Keeper of the Seal also mentioned this when she presented the organic bill to the Assembly: XIII legislature, Questions to the Government, 8 April 2009. Answer by Rachida Dati to a question posed by Ms Anne Grommerch. When asked to present the general philosophy behind the organic bill, the Keeper of the Seal replied as follows: "*This text represents a major leap forward in the*

Although the organic bill presented by the Minister for Justice in April of 2009[40] had taken into account the requirements ensuing from EU law[41], the National Assembly and the Senate removed the specificity of EU law in their examination, casting serious doubts on conformity to certain requirements, such as those in the *Simmenthal* judgment. Flouting criticism that had been issued in the legal doctrine, the constituent power adopted the '*organic law of 10th December 2009*' giving constitutional priority to the conventional obligation, including when EU law is involved.[42] Therefore, when an ordinary jurisdiction is presented with matters contesting both the constitutionality of the law and the conformity of this law to the '*international engagements of France*', the jurisdiction first and foremost has to decide on the referral of the question of constitutionality to the Constitutional Council. Only in effect since 1st March 2010, the QPC has given rise to quite an action-packed judicial saga, centred around the problem of the articulation of referrals and so also of 'priorities'. Although the wording of the organic law did not allow any doubt to remain by imposing the 'constitutional priority', the *Cour de Cassation* (France's highest judicial court) did not hesitate to express its scepticism *vis-à-vis* the conformity of such a procedure to EU law.

---

respect of liberties, since it awards French citizens, especially those to be tried, a new fundamental right; as a matter of fact, it is not about a simple procedure, but about real, drastic changes. Henceforth, any person to be tried will be able to invoke before all jurisdictions a possible violation of the Constitution to better defend their rights. Until today, this was not possible, even though the person to be tried could invoke the European Convention on Human Rights before the courts. It was our wish that the Constitution, containing all the fundamental rights and principles, could be invoked before our jurisdictions." National Assembly, *JO*, p. 3495.

40 Bill of "*loi organique relatif à l'application de l'article 61§ 1 de la Constitution*", 8 Avril 2009.

41 In accordance with the wording of paragraph 4 of Article 23-2 of the organic bill. It reads as follows: "In any case, when the jurisdiction is presented with means contesting, in a similar way, the conformity of the clause to the Constitution and to France's international engagements, it must first give a verdict about the constitutionality question, *subject to the requirements resulting from article 88§ 1 of the Constitution, if need be.*" (Underlined by us). This mention of Article 88§ 1 was a way of bringing up the requirements of European integration and consequently also those induced by the reference for a preliminary ruling as interpreted in the *Simmenthal* judgment, see L Burgorgue-Larsen, "Question préjudicielle de constitutionnalité et contrôle de conventionnalité. Etat des lieux de leurs liaisons (éventuellement dangereuses) sur la base du projet de loi organique appliquant l'article 61§ 1 de la Constitution", [2009] 4 *RFD adm.*,787–799. For an *a posteriori* and recapitulative analysis, particularly taking into account the organic law of 10th December 2009, see M Gautier, "La question prioritaire peut-elle rester prioritaire?", [2010] *RFD adm.* 449–466.

42 Organic Law No. 2009–1523 of 10 December 2009. The Constitutional Council, inevitably called upon by virtue of Article 61 of the Constitution for the assessment of the organic bill, validated the law's constitutionality in its decision of *3rd December 2009.* Could it really have gone differently? Could anyone have believed that the Council would have cut off the very branch that was going to propel it into the heart of a completely overhauled jurisdictional system? Be that as it may, the Council perfectly values the procedural aspect of the priority so as not to (overly) harm the primacy requirement, A Levade, "Priorité n'est pas primauté ou comment articuler contrôle de constitutionnalité et contrôle de conventionnalité", [2010] 2 *Constitutions. Revue de droit constitutionnel appliqué*, 229–233.

Indeed, on *16th April 2010*[43], the *Cour de Cassation* referred two prejudicial questions to the Court of Justice of the EU, one of which distinctly questioned the conformity of the QPC to European Union law. Obviously, this question boldly challenged the mechanism provided by the constituent power and fine-tuned by the organic legislator. This was the trigger for a dialogue among judges characterised not only by discord, but also by concord – basically all the elements inherent to the judicial exchange of standpoints.[44]

In one respect the Constitutional Council, faced with the European loyalty of the *Cour de Cassation* – awkward, but quite real[45] – promptly agreed to subject the QPC procedure as such to the rules of the game of European Union law, so as to defuse the politically contentious situation embodied by the decision of 16th April 2010. Indeed, it opted in its decision of *12th May 2010*, regarding *Online games*[46], to deliver a 'Europe-compatible' interpretation of the QPC in order to preserve the essence of the mechanism, thereby indirectly saving its own function. This was in a way a pre-emptive offensive[47], which was joined – obviously with a view to systemic coherence – by the Council of State in a decision of *14th May 2010, Rujovik.*[48] One need only read the 12th preamble of the *Online games* decision to realise to what extent the interpretation of the QPC delivered by the Council entails the eradication of what until now had seemed imperative: the priority of the constitution.[49] Its supremacy, so fiercely stressed only a few months earlier by the Constitutional Council in its decision of *3rd December 2009*[50], disappeared in favour of a consensual formula introducing

---

43 Cass., 16 April 2010, No.10–40–001, *Aziz Melki* and No. 10–42.002, *Selim Abdeli.*

44 For an attempt at conceptualizing the dialogue of the judges and how it manifests itself on the international level, see L Burgorgue-Larsen, "De l'internationalisation du dialogue des juges. Missive doctrinale à l'attention de Bruno Genevois", in *Le dialogue des juges. Mélanges en l'honneur de Bruno Genevois* (Paris, Dalloz, 2009) 95–130.

45 Awkward, because in these cases, the *Cour de Cassation* merged and fully assimilated constitutionality control and conventionality control, the result of which was that any and every violation of EU law was considered to be a violation of the French Constitution. Eventually, of course, such an interpretation destroyed the constitutional priority.

46 Cons. const., 12 May 2010, *Loi relative à l'ouverture à la concurrence et à la régulation du secteur des jeux d'argent et de hasard en ligne,* No. 2010–605 DC.

47 Labayle spoke of "preventive counter-fire", H Labayle, "Priority question of constitutionality and prejudicial question: bringing order to the judges' dialogue", [2010] *RFD adm*, 659 a.f.

48 Council of State, 14 May 2010, *Rujovik c. OFPRA*, No. 312305.

49 It reads as follows: "Neither article 61§ 1 of the Constitution, nor articles 23§ 1 and following of the aforementioned order will obstruct the judge entrusted with a lawsuit in which the incompatibility of a law with European Union Law has been invoked, to do, *at every moment*, what is necessary to prevent any of the legislative clauses obstructing the full efficiency of EU standards to be applied in this lawsuit." (Underlined by us).

50 Cons. const., 3 Decembre 2009, *Loi organique relative à l'application de l'article 61§ 1 de la Constitution,* No. 2009–595 DC, cons. 14: "The organic legislator has intended to ensure the respect of the Constitution and to stress its place at the top of the internal legal order; that this priority has the sole effect to impose, in any case, the order of examination of means brought up before the called-upon jurisdiction." The commentary in the Council's notebooks (*les Cahiers*) was eloquent: "*The jurisdiction must examine the means based on conformity with*

some flexibility (towards ordinary judges, increasing their freedom of choice) and clearly conveying a diplomatic message to the Court of Justice. This message reached its goal as the Court of Justice, in a particularly constructive spirit of concord, decided in its important judgment of *22nd June 2009, Melki*, not to collide head-on with the French QPC system, by recognising its conformity to European Union law and simultaneously conditioning the conformity of this declaration.[51] In other words, the QPC 'does have priority as long as it is not impeded by the obligation to ensure the full effect of European Union law'.[52] The Constitutional Council's honour was intact. Going further still, following the example of Advocate General Mazak, in the single interpretation of the 'framework of the lawsuit' as presented by the *Cour de Cassation*, the Grand Chamber of the Court of Luxemburg decided to take into account the context in its entirety and to incorporate in it the 'interpretations' by the Montpensier and Palais Royal judges[53] (items 48, 50, 51). It saved the QPC[54], at the cost of taking into account the 'Europe-compatible' interpretations of both constitutional and administrative judges.

The *Melki* judgment is a manifestation of the Court of Justice's wish to arrive at an interpretation of French law in accordance with European Union law. This judgment was such a concession to the classics of EU case law, however, that it was quite necessary for the Court of Justice to simultaneously introduce '*the use of coercive measures*'[55] towards the national jurisdiction. Indeed, declaring a mechanism such as the QPC to be in accordance with EU law is, in and of itself, likely to generate a shockwave throughout Europe – first and foremost in Belgium, a country that has opted for an equally far-reaching mechanism and the jurisdictions of which have also called upon the Court of Justice in order to

---

the Constitution before the means based on conformity of a law with France's international engagements." To avoid any ambiguity, this clause confirms the priority character of the QPC.

51 Case C-188/18 *Melki*, 22 June 2010, § 57.

52 Hearing of J-M Sauvé (Vice-President of the Council of State), 1st September 2010, 9 h session, *compte rendu* No. 81 *Commission des lois constitutionnelles et de la législation et de l'administration générale de la République*, p. 21.

53 Case C-188/18 *Melki*, 22 June 2010, §§ 48, 50, 51.

54 Item 57 of the judgment clearly shows there has been a "rescue operation" because the Court begins: "In consequence, there is cause to respond to the first question asked that Article 267 TFEU opposes a legislation of a Member State implementing an incidental procedure for constitutionality control of national laws, insofar as the result of this priority character is, either before the transmission of a constitutionality question to the national jurisdiction entrusted with constitutionality control of laws or, if need be, after the decision of this jurisdiction about said question, to prevent that any other national jurisdictions exercise their faculty or satisfy their obligation to submit prejudicial questions to the Court". The Court goes on to indicate very clearly that *"On the other hand, article 267 TFEU does not oppose such a national legislation, insofar as the other national jurisdictions remain free to..."* followed by a reiteration of the three conditions stemming from constitutional and administrative case law.

55 D Sarmiento, "L'arrêt Melki: esquisse d'un dialogue des juges constitutionnels et européens sur toile de fond française", [2010] 3 *RTD eur.* The author wants to thank D Sarmiento for having been so kind as to send over his text before publication.

assess the Belgian law that will introduce a similar priority mechanism.[56] Therefore the Court demands that the Constitutional Council submit, under certain circumstances, to the working of Article 267 TFEU. This was the big surprise of the decision of 22nd June 2010, a procedural surprise that the Constitutional Council[57] will have to get used to, and (let's hope) also abide by.

We are aware of the objections made in the legal doctrine in order to recognise the technical impossibility for the Constitutional Council to activate the prejudicial mechanism within the scope of *a priori* abstract control of laws. The prejudicial mechanism does not apply insofar as the submission of a case does not belong to those submitting it, no 'party' presents itself before it, there is no 'request', there is not necessarily a motivation, there is no interest in taking action and no conclusions exist either.[58] How does one then postpone giving a verdict in order to ask a prejudicial question about the interpretation or the validity of Community law? The Council reinforced these doctrinal analyses with its decision of *27th July 2006, Copyright*, by advancing another argument: the time period. It affirmed clearly in preamble 20 that – faced with giving a verdict before the promulgation of the law within the foreseen timeframe by Article 61 of the Constitution – it was unable to call upon the EU Court of Justice. Logically, it threw the issue right back at the ordinary jurisdictions.[59] It confirmed this approach in its now-famous decision of *12th May 2010, Online games,* in preamble 18.[60] The current contentious configuration allows the

---

56 In other words still, the fact that the Court of Justice takes a constitutional specificity into account should not contribute to the disintegration, in the medium to long term, of its jurisdiction on the outlines of referral obligations in the hypothesis of coinciding procedures, nor should it be a pretext for all kinds of rebellions in other Member States.

57 This position was supported in doctrine by D Sarmiento (note 55) and H Labayle (note 47). We join this position.

58 J-P Camby [1997] 1 *RDP* 6–12.

59 It reads as follows: "20. Considering, secondly, that, *faced with reaching a verdict prior to the promulgation of the law within the time allotted by article 61of the Constitution, the Constitutional Council may not submit the prejudicial question, provided for in article 234 of the Treaty establishing the European Community, to the Court of Justice of the European Communities*". (Underlined by us).

60 It reads as follows: "18. Considering that when a law aiming to transpose a community Directive into internal law is submitted to the Constitutional Council under the conditions provided for in Article 61 of the Constitution, it is up to said council to ensure that this requirement is met. However, its control in this matter is doubly limited: firstly, the transposition of a Directive cannot run counter to a rule or a principle inherent to France's constitutional identity, except for instances to which the Constituent power has consented; *secondly, faced with reaching a verdict prior to the promulgation of the law within the time allotted by article 61of the Constitution, the Constitutional Council may not call upon the Court of Justice of the European Union based on article 267 of the Treaty on the Functioning of the European Union.* As a consequence, only a legislative clause blatantly incompatible with the Directive it is meant to transpose can be declared as not in accordance with Article 88-1 of the Constitution. *In any case, it is up to the legal and administrative jurisdictions to control the compatibility of the law with regard to France's European engagements and, if need be, to call upon the Court of Justice of the European Union on a prejudicial basis.*" (Underlined by us).

problem to be revisited to remove these different kinds of objections. The QPC is part of a mechanism of concrete *a posteriori* control of the law, which has entailed a 'jurisdictionalisation' of the Council before which the parties plead their case, publicly and duly heard.[61] And even if it is often repeated that the Council is judge of the law and not of the substance with this new mechanism, all the same the very nature of the control is radically different. The citizens are the main actors in the new procedure, presenting themselves as the exclusive promoters of activating it, while the judges are not authorised to take up an obvious constitutionality issue of their own accord. Then, and above all, the *obiter dictum* of the Court of Justice in the *Melki* judgment in item 54 and the effects of this *obiter dictum* in item 56 of the judgment could not be clearer. We know that the Luxemburg Court has indeed expressly broached the particular hypothesis of a grievance regarding unconstitutionality being directed at a law '*which is limited to transposing the imperative clauses of an EU Directive*'. The Court of Justice here strongly repeats its exclusive competence in '*determining the invalidity of an act of the European Union*' (item 54). As a result, the priority attributed to the QPC is erased in favour of the 'preliminary character' of the question of the Directive's validity (item 56), because if not, that would mean that the Constitutional Council indirectly controls the validity of an act of the European Union. Also, the following mention is addressed not only to the Supreme Courts, but also to the Constitutional Council: 'Before the incidental constitutionality control of a law, the content of which is limited to transposing the imperative clauses of a Directive […], the national jurisdictions – the decisions of which are not susceptible to a jurisdictional appeal of internal law – are in principle obliged, under Article 267 §3 TFEU, to interrogate the Court of Justice about the validity of this Directive'. Item 56 *in fine* of the judgment confirms this by hinting at the timeframe – '*capturing the duration of investigations by national jurisdictions in a strict timeframe cannot foil the reference for a preliminary ruling relating to the validity of the Directive in question*'. This is quite certainly a response to the technical temporal argument, stating that the very short deadlines for the Council to give a verdict make it impossible to activate the reference for a preliminary ruling (*renvoi préjudiciel*). The QPC's timeframe of three months is not an obstacle, especially when taking into consideration the accelerated procedure, which enables the Court of Justice to respond urgently to a reference for a preliminary ruling.

Looking through the lens of French constitutional case law, such a submission of the Council to the reference mechanism is at risk of significantly disturbing the case law according to which the Council does not carry out conventionality control. The case law inaugurated in 2004 and refined in 2006 – no matter what the Constitutional Council says about it in its various decisions and no matter

61 This element will be discussed in the second part of this study.

what the majority of the doctrine may think[62] – very seriously erodes the foundations of the 'Voluntary Pregnancy Termination' case law. It is becoming ever more complex and delicate to establish a completely watertight barrier between constitutionality control and conventionality control. This barrier is most certainly still 'blurred' by the submission of the Constitutional Council to the reference for a preliminary ruling as imposed, it would seem, by the Court of Justice. This is such a sensitive issue in France that the National Assembly's Commission of constitutional laws decided to carry out a first evaluation of the QPC barely six months after it came into force, whereas the organic law mentioned a period of three years[63] When looking at the points of view expressed on 1st September 2010 during the hearing of certain representatives of academic and legal circles – who had been asked to give their views on the *Melki* judgment of *22nd June 2010* – it is significant to note the striking absence of any mention of the idea of a possible reference for a preliminary ruling being activated by the Constitutional Council itself.[64] The issue must therefore be monitored to see if one day the Palais Montpensier judge himself will venture to activate Article 267 TFEU at the risk of disrupting the fragile balance with the supreme judges even more, by permanently burying the 'Voluntary Pregnancy Termination' case law.

Should the decision of 17 December 2010 17 December 2010 decision be regarded as a further encouragement in that direction? The Constitutional Council confirmed in the first place that it was not competent "in the absence of

62 For an exception, see J Rideau, "Contrôle de constitutionnalité et contrôle de conventionnalité: les orphelins de la pyramide", [2009] 3*RDpub*., 601–630.

63 National Assembly, XIII legislature, *Commission des lois constitutionnelles, de la législation et de l'administration générale de la République*, Wednesday 1st Septembre 2010, 9 h session, *Compte rendu* No. 81. Presided by M. J-L Warsmann, Chairman. Accessible for free on the National Assembly's website.

64 The university professors heard either do not evoke this aspect of the matter at all (Denys Simon), or evoke it, but only use it for an analysis which never broaches the hypothesis of direct submission by the Constitutional Council of the ECJ (B Mathieu and G Carcassonne for the "constitutionalist" doctrine and J-M Sauvé on behalf of the Council of State as its Vice-President). Roughly speaking, they are of the opinion that the obligation of reference for a preliminary ruling *on account of the preliminary character of the validity question* is exclusively directed at the Supreme Courts (Council of State and *Cour de Cassation*) and considers the question solely in terms of the existence of a double reference: QPC on the one hand, prejudicial question on the other. As a result, they reckon that the "preliminary character" of the validity question would impose the necessity for the CC to postpone giving a verdict (within the scope of the examination of a QPC) so as to await the ECJ's response regarding the question of the Directive's validity, asked either by one of the two Supreme Courts (given their obligation set out in Article 267 TFEU, par. 3), or by the Ordinary Court (given the faculty set out in Article 267 TFEU, par. 2). Bertrand Mathieu considers that this would require a modification of the organic law so as to enable the Constitutional Council to postpone giving a verdict and to dismiss the period of 3 months. Conversely, Guy Carcassonne considers that a modification would not be necessary and that the constitutional judge, thanks to the workings of interpretation and by combining Articles 61§ 1 and 88§ 1, could sidestep the deadlines constraining the constitutional judge's office.

the entrenchment of a rule or principle inherent to the constitutional identity of France...to control the conformity of legislative provisions which are the necessary consequences of unconditional and precise provisions of a directive of the European Union with the rights and liberties which the Constitution guarantees". The Court could have limited itself to that statement, but it further indicated that it appears to fall to the judge of the European Union exclusively to control the conformity of the directive with the fundamental guarantees of Article 6 TFEU by means of a preliminary reference procedure (para. 3). Does this mean that the Constitutional Court accepts to put the preliminary procedure in motion?

3. THE CONSTITUTIONAL COUNCIL AND THE POWER OF THE EUROPEAN CONVENTION ON HUMAN RIGHTS

We know that in the eyes of the European Court *'the State as a whole is responsible in the international order. As a consequence, this concerns all the authorities of the State, including constitutional authorities'*.[65] This broad meaning of European control – which touches upon the national constitutional bases – is important. It implies that *no constituted power is free from the Court's control.* The representatives of the executive[66], legislative[67] and judicial[68] powers have therefore not escaped European control. In this context, it would seem unavoidable for the constitutional jurisdictions – although they are strictly speaking not a part of the judicial organization – to fall into the conventional grip of Europe as well. The Constitutional Council has therefore not escaped the European Court's control (A). Furthermore, it is noteworthy that it has not been able to escape the European Court's jurisprudential influence either. Even though the decisions of the Council must be scrutinized carefully to detect the effects of European case law, this does not make those effects any less real (B).

---

65 G Cohen-Jonathan, "La France et la CEDH – Synthèses et perspectives" [1999] *Europe*, October, p. 32.

66 *Wille v. Liechtenstein* (App no 28396/95) 28 October 1999. With 16 votes to one, the Court decided that the highest authority of the Principality of Liechtenstein, that is to say the "Prince", who together with the people holds the "State power" by virtue of Article 2 of the Constitution of 24th October 1921, violated Article 10 of the Convention.

67 *Marckx v. Belgium*, 13 June 1979, Series A-222.

68 *Djaid v France* (App no 38687/97) 29 September 2009; *Brumarescu c. Roumanie* (App no 28342/95) 28 October 1999.

3.1. THE CONSTITUTIONAL COUNCIL IS CONTROLLED BY THE EUROPEAN COURT OF HUMAN RIGHTS

Taking stock of the jurisprudential side of the matter, we see that the European Court has chronologically judged the *decisions* of the Constitutional Council (1). The introduction of the QPC now places the matter of the *procedure's* submission to European requirements before the Constitutional Council (2).

3.1.1. Decision control by the Constitutional Council

The grip of European control on constitutional decisions no longer needs to be proved, as it is all too clear. On the one hand, the Court has penalised a number of the Constitutional Council's decisions for being 'unconventional' (negative control), but on the other it has also awarded some proverbial 'gold stars' for other decisions (positive control). In both cases, the European judge obviously always has the last word on the way the Constitutional Council assesses conventional requirements.

It was the case of 28th October 1999, *Zielinski and Pradal and Gonzalez and others vs. France*, that directly rejected the Constitutional Council's jurisdiction in the field of legislative validations. In its decision nr. 93–332 DC of 13th January 1994 regarding the *Law on public health and social protection*, the Council had declared this endorsing act to be in accordance with the Constitution, so it was promulgated on 18th January 1994. Upon reading the decision, one cannot find room for any diverging interpretations of the 'corrective action' imposed on the French High Constitutional Jurisdiction, which had regularly accepted without discussion the government's purely financial arguments to foil the normal *res judicata*. Paragraph 59 is especially significant in this matter: '*The Court considers that the financial risk indicated by the government (§53) and expressly brought up by the Constitutional Council to motivate its decision (§26), in itself, shall not allow the legislator to substitute himself either for the parties to the collective convention or for the judges to settle the lawsuit*'. And it continues: '*Along with the Commission, the Court considers that the decision of the Constitutional Council does not suffice to establish conformity of article 85 of the law of 18th January 1994 to the clauses of the Convention*'. The European Court *actually* reminds the Council that a law it has declared in accordance with the Constitution may still be incompatible with a treaty, in this case the European Convention, and that this discrepancy is penalised, as the Council cannot escape European control. This *Zielinski* decision was quite a turning point. At first they saw eye to eye, but now the Strasbourg Court and the Constitutional Council were diametrically opposed. Since this decision, the Constitutional Council has considerably tightened its control so as to be more in line with European requirements. Based on Article 16 of the Declaration of the Rights of Man, interpreted as imparting the right to an effective jurisprudential appeal, it has established the notion of '*sufficient general interest*' as a parameter of real proportionality control[69], drawing closer to the European Court, which as we know ardently upholds the notion of an '*overriding general interest*'. Despite this coming together, certain decisions of the Council continue to be penalised by the Court, as is demonstrated by the *Cabourdin*[70] case.

The European Court's control over the Council's decisions is not systematically negative. It also takes on a positive form by valuing either the constitutional text itself *through* the interpretation of a legislative norm implementing it, or more generally the interpretation the constitutional judge himself has derived from it. The decision of irreversibility of 24th October 2000 made in the case *Thivet vs. France* is proof of this second hypothesis. The Court aligned itself *expressis verbis* with the Constitutional Council's case law, more precisely with decision nr. 99–425 DC of 29th December 1999 made in light of the tumultuous and ardent dispute regarding the indemnification of Russian loans.[71] The express alignment of the Court with the motives put forward in good time by the Council to declare the text in accordance with the Constitution is so rare it deserves a mention here. By evoking that Article 1 of Protocol nr. 1 does not guarantee the right to full compensation in all cases – insofar as legitimate objectives 'of public use' can campaign for a reimbursement lower than the full market value[72] – the judge in Strasbourg agreed with the reasoning of the guardian of the Constitution, who had focused on the solidarity objective pursued by the legislator and had therefore deemed it necessary to reconcile the different interests of both categories of shareholders: modest and other.[73] The

69 In the judgment of 29th December 1999 (99–425 DC, *loi de finance rectificative pour 1999*) the Council decided that: "*the general interest attached to such a validation is more important than questioning the taxpayer's rights, which would result from the token irregularity that the validation is actually meant to eliminate*". *See* decision of 21 December 1999 (99–422 DC, *loi de financement de la sécurité sociale pour 2000*) which annuls, see B Mathieu, [2000] 4 *D.* p.VII.

70 *Cabourdin v. France* (App no 60796/00) 11 April 2006. And yet, despite the fact that in the *Cabourdin* judgment the European Court demonstrates to the Palais Montpensier judges that it has taken note of evolutions in their case law, more in line with the conventional parameters – "*the Constitutional Council, inspired by the Court's case law, henceforth demands a 'sufficient general interest'*" (§ 36) – it still unanimously condemns France and clearly penalizes the Constitutional Council once more by stressing that its decision "*would not manage to establish conformity of article 87 of the law of 12th April 1996 to the clauses of the Convention.*" (§ 36).

71 Although Article 48 of the rectified 1999 finance law defined the conditions for implementing the indemnification of claims by determining that each bearer was to receive a fixed amount, increased with an amount proportional to the total value of the portfolio up to a certain maximum, the applicant upheld that because of this capped compensation, the amount she was to receive did not in the least correspond to the value of the bonds in her possession and she argued that her property rights were violated, as well as the equality principle.

72 *The Holy Monasteries v Greece* (App No 13092/87; 13984/88) 9 December 1994.

73 He had been able to consider that the discrepancy between the sum of the indemnity and the amount of the despoilments suffered does not allow for a strictly proportional indemnification without reducing to nothing the possibilities for compensation of holders of modest portfolios.

case *Stella vs. France* of 18th June 2002[74] did not cause a great deal of controversy, as decisions of irreversibility delivering certificates of conventionality go mostly unnoticed, contrary to the sensational decisions of violation. And yet, this case should be remembered as a sort of positive counterpart to the *Zielinski, Pradal, Gonzalez and others* judgment. When the Constitutional Council declares an endorsing act to be in accordance with the Constitution (decision of 18th December 1997) in consideration of motives of general interest (i.e. the social security deficit) and this does not incur any conventional 'penalty', then at least it should be made known, especially when the decision brings up important points, also evoked by the government in its defence. Therefore, '*the case law of organs of the Convention has never allowed for an imbalance in the equality of arms to result in measures "anticipating" in some way an as yet nonexistent lawsuit, and it would be going too far to elaborate this theory with a sort of analogy.* (*National organization of liberal nurses vs. France*, 29th August 2000, App 39971/98)". In reality any imprecise, not to say erroneous, interpretation of the Council of State's judgment of 28th March 1997 by the applicants is brought up in great detail by the Court. While the legislative validation enabled the State to avoid putting excessive strain on the social security budget deficit for 1996 and the following years, in reality it did not block the impact of the Council of State's judgment, which was fully implemented by internal authorities. And it was affirmed (as a disguised warning for the future?) '*that, although the applicants deny it, the Court considers that their interpretation as to the scope of the judgment of 28th March 1997 carries risks of legal insecurity, since it would be inadmissible for any jurisdictional decision about a calendar year to have de facto* res judicata *with regard to subsequent years, thus jeopardizing the legislative and regulatory power's margin of appreciation and this, by the way, over an undetermined period of time. Such a situation would be even less acceptable since the right to allocation, if not contested in principle by the government, still does not entail an intangible right to a fixed amount of this allocation.*' The aside is far from trivial, especially for States and how they conduct their social policies. Do we owe it to the sagacity of French *ad hoc* judge Bruno Genevois? All conjectures are permitted. We still need to underline that if the attitude of the Constitutional Council in reality was not the Gordian knot in the overall issue, this is because there was no retroactive law designed to thwart the execution of a judicial decision.[75] The Court has gone about demonstrating it item by item, thereby nonsuiting the applicants.

---

74 *Stella and the National Federation of Families in France v France* (App. No 45574/99) 18 June 2002.

75 In this matter, the Council decided to align itself with the criteria derived by the European Court, as can be seen in decision 2002–458 DC 7 February 2002, *loi organique portant validation de l'impôt foncier sur les prévôtés bâties en Polynésie française* (*JO*, 12 February 2002, p. 2783), *see D.*, Chr., 2002, n°18, note B Mathieu, p. 1439–1441.

3.1.2. Procedure control before the Constitutional Council

The jurisprudential saga of establishing the European Court step by step as the judge of constitutional procedures is well-known. It is generally characterized by the submission of the 'constitutional process' to the rules of the equitable process.[76] In France, the first procedure likely to come under the control of the European Court was the procedure taking place before the judge of *the application of the law*, before the constitutional reform in 2008 questioned the control of the procedure used by the judge of constitutionality of the law.[77]

As long as the exception of unconstitutionality was not a part of the French constitutional landscape, the abstract constitutionality control of laws in France could not fall into the grip of Article 6§1 ECHR. Before the judge of constitutionality of the law, the constitutional procedure benefited from a conventional immunity. Then again, notwithstanding the absence of a concrete form of constitutionality control, the Constitutional Council, as *electoral judge, judge of the application of the law*, was put under 'heavy surveillance' by the European Court through the judgment in the case *Pierre-Bloch vs. France* of 21st October 1997.[78] Indeed, even if in the case in point a Chamber of the Court had agreed, with seven votes to two, that Article 6§1 could not be applied to the electoral dispute – which found itself suddenly out of reach of the right to an equitable trial – it followed from the analysis of the judgment that a deputy deprived of his mandate, who would find himself facing one of the sentences mentioned in Article L.113§1 of the Electoral Code (a fine of 25,000 francs and/or a sentence of one year in prison), could choose to invoke, most likely with success, Article 6§1 of the Convention, these sentences coming under the penal domain. The European Court decided to establish as a general rule the *dictum* of the *Pierre-Bloch* judgment, since it declared two requests inadmissible on the grounds that they were *ratione materiae* incompatible with the clauses of the Convention. The first, the *Masson* case[79], tied into the *Pierre-Bloch* case since it

---

76 L Burgorgue-Larsen, "L'influence de la Convention européenne sur le fonctionnement des Cours constitutionnelles", [2008] *Revue internationale de droit comparé*, 2, p. 265–282.

77 F Sudre, "Question préjudicielle de constitutionnalité et Convention européenne des droits de l'homme", [2009] *RD pub.* 3, p. 671–684.

78 L Burgorgue-Larsen, "Le face à face entre le juge constitutionnel et la Cour européenne", note *sub* ECHR, 21 October 1997, *Pierre-Bloch c. France,* [1998] *AJDA*, 20 January 1998, 65–71.

79 *Masson v France* [App No 41944/98] ECHR 14 September 1999. The applicant was faced with sanctions that did not come under Article L113§ 1 of the Electoral Code. If they had been pronounced, they would undoubtedly have fallen into the "penal sphere" and have carried along the applicability of Article 6 § 1 to the trial of the electoral dispute. It was in any case the only foreseeable "breach" insofar as the Court confirmed its argumentation in terms of the "civil domain" by affirming that "*the dispute in question concerned the regularity of electoral operations; notwithstanding its possible implications on the personal assets of the applicant, it did not have to do with a contestation of rights and obligations of a civil nature [...]. As a consequence, article 6§ 1 cannot come into play from a civil angle.*" (§ 3).

involved a member of Parliament whose election was invalidated by the Constitutional Council, while the second, the *Cheminade* case, concerned an unsuccessful candidate for the presidential election of 1995.[80]

After the constitutional reform of 23rd July 2008 and the introduction of the QPC on the grounds of famous Article 61§1 of the Constitution, the issue took a new turn.[81] In what became known as a 'little revolution', the French jurisdictional landscape underwent a metamorphosis through radical changes in the country's legal customs. Lawyers both discovered and tamed the Constitution, since neither the European Convention nor EU legislation held any more secrets for them. Furthermore, all the 'quirks' in the workings of the Council (namely working behind closed doors and not hearing the parties)[82] had to be done away with: indeed, they could no longer subsist, now with the existence of a concrete form of constitutionality control of the laws. Consequently, by adopting a decision on *4th February 2010* regarding an *interior regulation of the procedure followed before the Constitutional Council for the QPC*[83], the Council – brilliantly and logically – submitted to a series of requirements stemming from the conventional European domain.[84] It quite simply took the standards set by the Strasbourg Court seriously. In spite of the particularly successful adaptation with regard to the submission of the constitutional process to the equity requirement, though, we will see that the situation is undoubtedly less praiseworthy when it comes to the submission of the constitutional jurisdiction as such to the impartiality requirements. In this matter, the adaptation leaves much to be desired.

Equity consists of two parts: the hearing, and 'equality of arms' (*l'égalité des armes*). For the European Court, the hearing (*le contradictoire*) is '*the faculty of a party to be informed about observations or pieces of evidence presented by the other*

---

80 *Cheminade v France* [App No 31599/96] ECHR 26 January 1999: "*The Court reiterates that in principle, the procedures concerning the electoral dispute do not come under article 6, insofar as they concern the exercise of rights of a political nature and therefore are not about rights and obligations of a civil nature.*"

81 It is interesting to point out that the "legal diplomacy" has manifested itself between the French constitutional judges and the Strasbourg judges, which confirms that the dialogue *of* judges also entails a dialogue *between* judges. We refer to the Constitutional Council's website, which has published judge F Tulkens' intervention following a visit by a delegation of several members of the European Court to the Constitutional Council, see F Tulkens, "Convention européenne des droits de l'homme et Cours suprêmes" at www.conseil-constitutionnel.fr/conseil-constitutionnel/root/bank_mm/cedh_13fev2009/cedh_ftulkens_130209.pdf.

82 D Schnapper, *Une sociologue au Conseil constitutionnel* (Paris, Gallimard, 2010) 141.

83 M Guillaume, "Le règlement intérieur sur la procédure suivie devant le Conseil constitutionnel pour les questions prioritaires de constitutionnalité", *Les petites affiches,* No. 38 and *Gazette du Palais* No. 54 of 23 February 2010.

84 It needs to be said that this adaptation was announced in organic Law nr. 2009–1523 of 10th December 2009 pertaining to the application of Article 61§ 1: it referenced the "future" regulations of the Constitutional Council adopted on the basis of Article 56 of the organic Law nr. 58–1067 about the Constitutional Council of 1958.

party, and its right to discuss them'.[85] The lessons learned from the *Ruiz Mateos* judgment – which aided in the complete renewal of the Spanish procedure of the constitutionality question[86] – forced the French Constitutional Council to take action and stay up to date in this matter. Article 1 of the internal regulations links the *a quo* trial's parties to all the steps in the procedure and elevates them up to the level of real parties to the constitutional trial.[87] As to equality of arms, we know that it '*requires a fair balance between the parties: each party must be offered a reasonable possibility to present its cause in conditions that do not place it in a position of net disadvantage compared to its adversary or adversaries*'.[88] Reading the internal regulations reveals that these requirements have been taken into account, particularly by valuing the role of the parties' lawyers[89] and by putting a stop to the secret of the Council's workings, i.e. the way the hearings are conducted, to be exact. Article 8 organizes the public nature of the hearing, conducted under the direction of the president of the Constitutional Council, responsible for 'keeping order in the hearing' (Art. 8 of the regulations). This hearing will be open to the public, in the sense that it is transmitted via an audio-visual broadcast to a dedicated room within the Council's building complex (Article 8, par. 2). Moreover, the hearing may, upon agreement of the parties, be broadcast on the website of the Constitutional Council (Article 9, par. 2). Only under a limited set of circumstances, stipulated in the regulations, will a hearing be conducted behind closed doors (Article 8, par. 3). There is no manifest incompatibility here with the case law of the European Court of Human Rights. Indeed, the public nature is the sole guarantee for a fair trial, limited by the very text of Article 6§1 of the Convention: it stipulates a series of hypotheses where public access to the courtroom may be restricted. A number of these hypotheses are included in the procedural regulations of the Council, which is rather orthodox in this respect by making provision for '*the President to restrict the public nature of the hearing upon request of a party or as a matter of course, in the interest of minors or to protect the privacy of persons who so require. He may only order the debates to be conducted behind closed doors in exceptional cases and on those grounds alone*'.

This mechanism in its entirety is innovative; it testifies of a modernisation in the means used to satisfy the equity requirements for the constitutional procedure.

---

85 *Ruiz-Mateos v Spain* [App No 12952/87] 23 June 1993, § 63.

86 F Rubio Llorente, "La relation entre les juridictions espagnoles et les juridictions européennes", *Renouveau du droit constitutionnel. Mélanges en l'honneur de Louis Favoreu* (Paris, Dalloz, 2007) 1401; P Bon, "Tribunal constitutionnel espagnol. Importantes modifications de sa loi organique en 2007", *Le dialogue des juges. Mélanges en l'honneur du Président Genevois* (Paris, Dalloz, 2009), 72–73.

87 F Jacquelot, "La procédure de la question prioritaire de constitutionnalité devant le Conseil constitutionnel", [2010] *AJDA* 951.

88 *Kress c. France* [App No 39594/98] 7 June 2001, § 72.

89 They are heard (art. 10 of the regulations) while the Constitutional Council may notify them of the proceedings.

In contrast, the Council's impartiality requirement is more problematic. The adaptation to the European requirements undertaken by Article 4 of the internal regulations is evident, but seems insufficient. This clause makes provision for both an *abstention duty,* prohibiting that any member sit on the Council if his impartiality can be questioned, and for the *right* of any party to ask for such a member's *removal* if his impartiality is questionable.[90]

It is paragraph 1 of Article 4 of the internal regulations that makes provision for the possibility to abstain.[91] This clause does institutionalise, however, a practice that had eventually become established in the Constitutional Council as a part of the *a priori* constitutionality control of laws and within the scope of the Council's competences in electoral matters (legislative and referendum elections). Nevertheless, this simple possibility does not suffice and the doctrine has already revealed loopholes in the text. First of all, nothing is said about the reasons for abstention, since there is 'not any obligation for justification'.[92] What if the disastrous potential of such an absence of justification manifests itself in the concrete organization, putting the smooth workings of the Council at risk? Indeed, there are 9 members[93] and we know that the necessary *quorum* for deliberation is still 7 sitting members. Article 14 of the order of 7th November 1958 pertaining to this matter has not been amended.[94] As abstentions are not limited, falling under the discretion of the judge, several judges may decide, for various reasons, to remove themselves from the same case, which would pose a significant threat to the proper functioning of the procedure. Also, there is no form of control by the Constitutional Council itself on this possibility of abstention. Lastly, these abstentions are only known *ex post*, that is to say only after the decision has been made and its text has been published online, becoming accessible to the public, followed by publication in due form.

Paragraphs 4 and 5 of the article of the internal regulations are the ones making provision for *challenging* a member of the Constitutional Council.[95] In

---

90 P Bon, "Récuser un membre du Conseil constitutionnel", [2010] *Dalloz* 2009.

91 It reads as follows: "Any member of the Constitutional Council who *deems* it necessary to abstain from sitting informs the president." (Underlined by us).

92 M Verpeaux, "Question prioritaire de constitutionnalité et libre administration des collectivités territoriales", [2010] *AJDA* 1594.

93 These are, as of 12th October 2010: M. Jean-Louis Debré, President, M. Jacques Barrot, Ms Claire Bazy Malaurie, M. Guy Canivet, Michel Charasse, Renaud Denoix de Saint Marc, Ms Jacqueline de Guillenchmidt, M. Hubert Haenel and Pierre Steinmetz.

94 M Verpeaux, "Question prioritaire de constitutionnalité et libre administration des collectivités territoriales", [2010] *AJDA* 1594.

95 They read as follows: "A party or its representative, equipped to this end with a special proxy, may ask for a member of the Constitutional Council to be challenged via a specially motivated letter accompanied by documents suited for justification. The request is only admissible if registered with the general secretariat of the Constitutional Council before the date set for receipt of the first observations.
The request is communicated to the Constitutional Council member concerned. The latter announces whether (s)he acquiesces to the challenge. If not, the request is examined without participation of the members whose challenging is requested.

the vast majority of other European countries, the judges come from two worlds: academia, in particular Faculties of Law; and the legal world, especially that of ordinary justice. For both, the risk of being challenged is low in France.[96] In reality, the problem in France is that most of the members of the Constitutional Council come from the political world and that this general profile may favour the development of multiple challenges. As Dominique Schnapper revealed in his indispensable book, 'of the 66 councillors appointed until 2007, more than half (thirty-five) originate directly from the domain of active politics, and this is without taking into account *ex officio* members, former Presidents of the Republic, who by definition come from the political world. Among those are twenty-two former ministers or junior ministers, as well as six deputies and seven senators.[97]' To cut a long story short, 'many constitutional judges used to be members of Parliament, ministers, prime ministers, party leaders or Presidents of the Republic, which might legitimately undermine their neutrality and their impartiality if they were to judge the constitutionality of a law they themselves had drafted a few years before. If taken to the extreme, these reasons for challenging might lead to a situation where a Council meeting becomes impossible[98]!' Yet an alternative has been imagined in the procedural regulations of the Council, inspired by the Belgian[99] and German systems. It is mentioned in paragraph 4 of Article 4: '*The sole fact that a member of the Constitutional Council has participated in the elaboration of the legislative clause whose constitutionality is in question, does not in itself constitute grounds for a challenge*'. However, as made clear by the Secretary-General of the Constitutional Council, challenging will be possible 'if the accomplished actions entail that their author has made an assessment of the constitutionality of this norm'. Will this be sufficient? The specificity of the composition of the Constitutional Council is such that we will have to be on the lookout, for it just might be called into question before the European Court of Human Rights...

The sole fact that a member of the Constitutional Council has participated in the elaboration of the legislative clause whose constitutionality is in question, does not in itself constitute grounds for a challenge".

96 Since the beginning, professors of Law have always been a minority; especially since the renewal of 1997 – now there are none.

97 D Schnapper, *Une sociologue au Conseil constitutionnel* (Paris, Gallimard, 2010) 146. The renewal of February 2010 hardly contradicts this fact: no need to remind ourselves of the political careers at the local, national and European levels of Messrs Barrot, Charasse and Haenel. While this finding may be qualified in light of the latest appointment when we go over Mrs Bazy-Malaurie's career (who was appointed by the president of the National Assembly in August 2010, after the death of Mr Pezant), it still remains unchallenged.

98 D Rousseau, *Droit du contentieux constitutionnel* (Paris, Montchrestien, 2010) 264.

99 Article 101 of the special law of 6th January 1989, modified on the Belgian Court of Arbitration.

3.2. THE CONSTITUTIONAL COUNCIL UNDER THE INFLUENCE OF THE EUROPEAN COURT OF HUMAN RIGHTS' CASE LAW

Does the Constitutional Council apply the European Court of Human Rights' case law? From a strictly technical point of view, the answer to this question is negative. The reference to the European norm as interpreted by the European Court is non-existent and does not appear in the *ratio decidendi* of French constitutional judges. Everything is arranged as if the Convention did not exist or rather, everything is arranged to be in line with the text of the Declaration of 1789 and not with the text of 1950, since the latter is not integrated in the set of standards referred to as the *bloc de constitutionnalité* (Constitutional Block). However, this deliberate absence of referral to European case law and the exclusive reference to the sole constitutional referent does not prevent the judge from being inspired by either the European Convention or Strasbourg case law.[100] He is all the more inclined to do so as there is a certain similarity between the fundamental rights protected on the constitutional and conventional level.[101] Without going so far as to consider the two catalogues to be materially *identical* – so much so that certain authors have proposed to merge them[102] – it is still known at the same time[103] not only that both types of control are fundamentally of the same nature[104], but also that they have the same scope, particularly seeing as the reference standards for conventionality control and constitutionality control of laws are the same. Although the Constitutional Council and the European Court of Human Rights have long ignored one another, it is well-

100 L Burgorgue-Larsen, "L'autonomie constitutionnelle aux prises avec la Convention européenne des droits de l'homme", [2001] *Revue Belge de Droit constitutionnel*,1, p. 31–64; G Carcassonne, "Le Conseil constitutionnel et la CEDH", *Cinquantième anniversaire de la Convention européenne des droits de l'homme,* Droit et justice (Brussels, Bruylant, 2002) 231–239; O Dord, "Systèmes juridiques nationaux et Cours européennes – De l'affrontement à la complémentarité", [2001] *Pouvoirs*, No 96, p.5–18; P Gaia, "Les interactions entre le Conseil constitutionnel et la Cour européenne des droits de l'homme", [1996] *RFDconst.*, No 28, p. 725 a.f.; P Tavernier, "Le Conseil constitutionnel français peut-il échapper au contrôle de la Cour européenne des droits de l'homme?", *Mélanges en l'honneur de Gérard Conac* (Paris, Economica, 2001) p.255–273.

101 As of the 1990s, legal doctrine already focused on the proximity of the constitutional and conventional catalogues. See D Rousseau, F Sudre (eds.), *Le Conseil constitutionnel et la Convention européenne des droits de l'homme* (Paris, STH, 1990); during the 9th Constitutional Courts Conference, the Constitutional Council itself was not secretive about its conventional inspiration, see [1993] *RFD adm.* 864.

102 G Alberton, "De l'indispensable intégration du bloc de conventionnalité au bloc de constitutionnalité?", [2005] *RFD adm.* 249–268; G Alberton, "Peut-on encore dissocier exception d'inconstitutionnalité et exception d'inconventionnalité?" [2008] *AJDA*, 2008, 967.

103 O Dutheillet de Lamothe, "Contrôle de constitutionnalité et contrôle de conventionnalité", *Mélanges en l'honneur du Président Labetoulle* (Paris, Dalloz, 2007) 315–327.

104 Both very often use the same governing principles to orchestrate control and to succeed in reconciling conflicting rights. Nevertheless, this does not imply *ne varietur* an equivalent level of protection, as the specificities of each system, like the specificities pertaining to each.

known that this era of indifference has come to an end and has been replaced by a 'dialogue without words', as it was so aptly expressed by former constitutional judge O. Dutheillet de Lamothe in his tribute article to Bruno Genevois.[105] Interpretative reconciliations, symptomatic of a strong legal syncretism, have irrigated the fields of freedom of expression[106], guarantees provided as far as repression is concerned[107], and even the rights of defence.[108] In the decision concerning the *Rome Statute of the International Criminal Court*[109], the Palais Montpensier judge came even closer to European case law by elevating the principle of the public nature of judicial debates[110] to the constitutional level. Such dialectics have also penetrated the domains of the protection of privacy, of family life[111], of contractual liberty and also of legal security. Even the principle of human dignity was at the heart of this 'dialogue without words'.[112] The question causing debate for many years now is how long this case law policy will remain tenable and desirable. Since the Constitutional Council has shown no intention of referencing the Strasbourg Court's case law in the *ratio decidendi* of

105 O Dutheillet de Lamothe, "Conseil constitutionnel et Cour européenne des droits de l'homme", *Le dialogue des juges. Mélanges en hommage au Président Genevois* (Paris, Dalloz, 2009) 403–417.

106 Compare *Handyside v United Kingdom* [App No 5493/72] 7 December 1976, A24 with Cons. const., *Entreprises de presse* 10–11 October 1984; compare *Informationsverein lentia v Austria* [App No 13914/88; 15041/89; 15717/89; 15779/89; 17207/90] 23 November 1993, A276 with Cons.const., 29 July 1986.

107 Compare *Engel a.o. v the Netherlands* [App No 5100/71; 5101/71; 5102/71; 5354/72; 5370/72] 8 June 1976, A22; *Luedicke, Belkacem et Koc* [App No 6210/73; 6877/75; 7132/75] 23 November 1978, A29; *Oztürk v Germany* [App No 8544/79] 21 February 1984, A73 with Cons.const., 17 January 1989, *CSA*.

108 Compare *Delcourt v Belgium* [App No 2689/65] 17 January 1970, A11; *Golder v United Kingdom* [App No 4451/70] 21 February 1975, A18 with Cons.const., 19–20 January 1981, *Sécurité et liberté*.

109 Cons.const., 22 January 1999, *Traité portant statut de la Cour pénale internationale*.

110 Compare with *Axen v Germany*, 8 December 1983, A72.

111 In the decision of 28 January 2011, Corinne C. et al. (prohibition of same sex marriage) n°2010–92 QPC, the Constitutional Council considered that the notion of family in the meaning of the Preamble of 1946 included same sex couples. The Council appeared to be inspired by the jurisprudence of the ECtHR on this matter (ECtHR, Schalk and Kopf v. Austria, 24 June 2010, para. 94–95). In the same judgment the Council held that the justification of the difference in treatment established by the legislator between heterosexual and homosexual couples which prohibited the latter to marry was conform to the Article 6 of the Declaration of the rights of men which upholds the principle of equality. The Council held that: "in maintaining the principle that marriage is a union between a man and a women, the legislator has, in the exercise of its competences attributed by Article 34 Constitution, considered that the difference in the situation between a couple of the same sex and a couple composed of a man and a woman can justify the difference in treatment with regards to the rules of family law; that it does not fall upon the Constitutional Council to substitute its appreciation for that of the legislator with regards to the consideration, in this field, of this difference in situation; that, in consequence, the complaint based on a violation of Article 6 of the Declaration of 1789 needs to be dismissed" (para. 9).

112 The Constitutional Council infers this from the Preamble of the 1946 Constitution, Cons. const., 27 July 1994, No 94–343/344 DC.

its decisions, we must also note here that said Council is therefore not the judge of conventionality. The introduction of the QPC in constitutional litigation law most certainly reopens the debate.[113]

* *
*

The Constitutional Council has most certainly arrived at a turning point in its history. Its office has undergone a metamorphosis, which completely changes its relations with the Supreme Courts on the one hand (the *Cour de Cassation* and the Council of State) and with the European Courts on the other (ECJ and EHCR). The future will need to be examined carefully to see if this metamorphosis ruptures the lines dividing the different offices of the French judges.

113 J Roux, "L'abandon de la jurisprudence IVG: une question d'opportunité ou de logique?" [2009] *RDPub.* 3, p. 645–670.

CHAPTER 8
GERMANY
THE FEDERAL CONSTITUTIONAL COURT OF GERMANY IN THE CONTEXT OF THE EUROPEAN INTEGRATION

Rainer ARNOLD*

1. THE DUAL FUNCTION OF THE CONSTITUTIONAL COURT

1.1. CONSTITUTIONAL COURT AND THE EU: SOME BASIC OBSERVATIONS

The Constitutional Court is the guardian of the national constitution. In the internal hierarchy, constitutional law is the supreme law of the land. But states are also bound to international law and, as in Europe, the Member States of the European Union (EU) are integrated into a supranational legal order. National constitutions give the authorisation for a State to join such a supranational organisation. Thus, on the basis of an international treaty, Member States of the EU, such as Germany, have transferred internal competences, referred to by the Basic Law (BL) in its Articles 23 and 24 as 'sovereign powers' (Hoheitsrechte), to the multi-national body and in doing so have created a new autonomous legal order, whose nature is, due to its particular characteristics, *supranational*.[1]

The link between the national and the supranational order is the international treaty by which such a transfer has been effectuated and, on the national side, an Act of Parliament approving this treaty (Zustimmungsgesetz).[2]

---

* Professor at the Universität Regensburg.

1 The German Constitutional Court uses this term for the first time largely in the *Lisbon* decision of 2009, vol.123, p. 267.

2 Federal Constitutional Court (FCC), Rep. Vol. 73, p. 339, 375.

The national constitution therefore has a national as well as an inter/supranational dimension: the integration norms of the constitution, namely the above mentioned articles, permit in general the creation and the membership of such a multi-national organisation. For the realisation of this in concrete cases, the Act of approval, based on the integration norm, is the essential instrument which links the international treaty and therefore the supranational with the internal order. This Act is and remains, in the eyes of the Constitutional Court, the legal basis for the transfer of national competences and thus for the integration process. It describes the 'integration programme' and with that, the limits of the supranational power, as stated by the Court in the Maastricht decision.[3]

The Constitutional Court therefore has a dual function: it assures the conformity of internal actions with the Constitution and controls the external, inter/supranational dimension of state activity.

The German Constitutional Court legitimises its control of the limits to which the supranational legislation is submitted, by referring to the internal Act of approval, a German Act, as the link to the external order. This Act is the basis for judicial control of the limits for supranational activity resulting from the national Constitution, not only with respect to an excess of competences by the supranational institutions, for *ultra vires* acts in a *formal* sense[4], but also for *ultra vires* actions in a *substantive* sense. This is the case if supranational institutions act formally within the competences attributed to them by the Member States but in violation of substantive law. There are two possibilities: contradiction with supranational primary law or with national (constitutional) law. The first mentioned case falls within the jurisdiction of the ECJ and is outside the competence of the national Constitutional Court. The conflict which arises in the second case is normally resolved according to the principle of the primacy of supranational over national law. In so far as a Member State considers its Constitution or a part of it, a nucleus of constitutional law identifying the State order – its constitutional identity[5], as sacrosanct, intangible by supranational law, the national Constitutional Court feels competent to make a decision in this conflict. From the national perspective the legitimisation for such a 'substantive *ultra vires* control' is again the aforementioned Act of approval.

1.2. THE CONSTITUTIONAL COURT AND TRADITIONAL INTERNATIONAL LAW

Here the role of the Constitutional Court is less dramatic. Due to the dualistic approach, deep-rooted in Germany, international treaties are transformed into

3 Vol. 89, p. 155.

4 See vol. 89, p. 155, 187–188 (Maastricht decision); vol. 123, p. 353–355 (*Lisbon* decision).

5 See FCC vol. 123, p. 267, 353–355 (also with respect to the identity control).

internal law by the Act of approval. While EU law which is directly valid in the Member States is introduced, also by the Act of approval, under the specific rules of Art. 24 and 23 BL, rules which take into account the particularities of supranationalism, Art. 59 §2 BL is applied to treaties of a traditional type. They are regarded as equivalent to ordinary Federal law and underlie therefore the '*lex posterior*' principle. The dualism concept hinders primacy in a hierarchical sense and even in the sense of 'application primacy' (*Anwendungsvorrang*)[6], typical for supranational law, though the international treaty obligation remains. This separatist view is anachronistic and not adequate for the impact of national law even on international Human Rights treaties such as the ECHR. As a certain response to this dualistic separatism, the Constitutional Court, in seeking to moderate its unfortunate consequences, has developed some concepts reflecting a sort of *intermediate monism*. These will be examined later.

General international law is conceived as a type of norm which has immediate normative validity in the state order, ranking superior to ordinary laws but inferior to the Constitution (Art. 25 BL). Art. 100 §2 BL prescribes that in the case of dispute, within judicial proceedings, on the existence or the content of such a general rule, the Court of *Karlsruhe* has to be addressed for a final decision on these questions.

1.3. THE JURISDICTIONAL MEANS OF CONTROL

As is well known, the Federal Constitutional Court in Germany disposes of a wide range of competences. The Act of approval of an international treaty and even of the EC/EU reform treaties (Maastricht Treaty, Lisbon Treaty!) underlies the judicial control of the Constitutional Court: frequently individual plaintiffs impugn, by *Verfassungsbeschwerde* (individual constitutional complaint), these Acts of approval and thereby invoke the violation of fundamental rights. Also possible is the *Normenkontrolle,* in its abstract and concrete form, the review of this Act by the initiative of a state institution under Art. 93 §1 n. 2 or of a tribunal under Art. 100 §1 BL. For State institution even a review *a priori* (that is before the treaty enters into force) is admitted to avoid the dilemma of the incompatibility of an internationally binding treaty with the national constitution.

Constitutional review of an international treaty is not limited by a political question doctrine, as is the case in some other States, because the advanced Rule of Law concept does not tolerate issues exempt of judicial control.

6 See vol. 73, p. 339, 375.

A certain change has taken place in regard to the EU: the judicial review system, as created by the *Grundgesetz,* was appointed for internal conflicts. Therefore an individual constitutional complaint could only be directed against an action of German public power and the judicial legislation review was limited to German laws. Secondary EC law as regulations were considered as autonomous legal acts stemming from a legal order distinct from German law. There was no procedural possibility to review such acts under national law. The Constitutional Court refused to admit an individual complaint directed against an EEC regulation due to its non-German origin.[7] A certain exception was made by the Constitutional Court in 1974[8] when it was addressed by the Frankfort Administrative Court under Art. 100 §1 BL for the examination of whether an EC regulation applied by a German authority was compatible with German constitutional law. The Court, by making recourse to an analogy, broadened the admissibility requirements for reasons of an effective protection against the impact of supranational law. This was a heavily criticised early predecessor of the general procedural extension of German Constitutional Court control power to supranational acts if they are deemed (formally) *ultra vires.*[9] This extension, pronounced by the Court in its Maastricht decision, is kept alive by subsequent jurisprudence and seems to be extended to cases of intrusion into the State's constitutional identity, as seen in the Lisbon decision.[10] The only limitation is established by the *Solange II* concept which excludes individual complaints (or other judicial actions) aimed at a control of incompatibility of a supranational legal act with German BL fundamental rights. Such complaints are rejected by the Constitutional Court as inadmissible[11] because the Court no longer applies German fundamental rights when examining EU legal acts (a task which is left to the ECJ applying EU Charter rights), not for the reason that a regulation is not German law which had initially been the argument.

What has aggravated the situation was the Constitutional Court's (implicitly expressed) denial to involve the ECJ/ECJ in the decision process by a preliminary question procedure. The national Court claimed for itself the exclusive competence to decide on *ultra vires* and constitutional identity. The *Mangold* decision[12] seems to have expressly re-confirmed the national Constitutional Court's obligation to involve the supranational Court according to EU law.

7 FCC vol. 22, p. 2.
8 Vol. 37, p. 271.
9 Vol. 89, p. 155, 188.
10 Vol. 123, p. 267, 353.
11 See for example the *Banana market* decision FCC vol 102, p. 147.
12 Of July 6, 2010 – 2BvR 2661/06.

1.4. APPROXIMATION OF THE NATIONAL AND INTER/ SUPRANATIONAL ORDERS BY INTERPRETATION

The German Constitution is 'open' in a twofold sense: for a long time the Constitutional Court has classified Germany as an 'open State' (*offene Staatlichkeit*)[13] which reflects the basic attitude of the State towards the international community and international law. 'Friendliness', in this sense, means 'acting in favour of international law' (*Völkerrechtsfreundlichkeit*) and also *interpreting* internal law, even constitutional law favourably inclined towards international law (*völkerrechtsfreundliche Interpretation*).[14] Such a mechanism helps to overcome the harsh consequences of dualism between national and international law and to adapt *a priori* national law to the requirements of binding international law. The limit of this conflict reducing and even method of avoidance is the clear, unequivocal will of the legislator which cannot be overridden by interpretation without prejudice towards the separation of power.

The recent jurisprudence of the Constitutional Court, namely in its Lisbon decision, has used the instrument of the 'interpretation in favour of EU law' (*europarechtsfreundliche Auslegung*), applicable also to the interpretation of the national Constitution.[15] The Polish[16] and the Czech[17] Constitutional Court had already applied this interpretation maxim before the German Lisbon decision. This maxim helps to reduce, even to minimize, normative conflicts between the two orders but reaches its limit in the same way as has been pointed out above for the field of international law.

2. THE BASIC ORDER OF THE EUROPEAN COMMUNITIES AND ITS ACCEPTANCE BY THE FEDERAL CONSTITUTIONAL COURT

2.1. THE THREE ELEMENTS OF THE SUPRANATIONAL ORDER

The Constitutional Court accepted from very early on what the European Court of Justice (ECJ) had described as the structural features of the new supranational

13 See K Vogel, *Die Verfassungsentscheidung des Grundgesetzes für die internationale Zusammenarbeit* (Mohr, Tübingen 1964) 42.
14 See for example the *Görgülü* decision of the FCC vol. 111, p. 307, 317–319.
15 Vol. 123, p. 267.
16 K 18/04.
17 Pl.ÚS 19/08 (*Lisbon* I) and Pl. ÚS 29/ 09 (*Lisbon* II).

order: its autonomy constituted by the transfer of sovereign powers, ie internal competences of the Member States; the direct effect of the norms of this legal order ie their immediate normative validity in the national legal orders, and, as a third element, its primacy over national law.

This 'constitutional structure' of the European Communities, as pointed out by the ECJ in the well known decisions *van Gend & Loos*[18] as well as *Costa/ ENEL*[19], are, even today, essential for qualifying the legal nature of the EU. The supranational character of the European Communities and of the EU of today has been recognised by the German constitutional jurisprudence at an early period. The term *supranationality* was not used at that time by the Constitutional Court and was only introduced into the constitutional jurisdiction by the Lisbon Decision of 2009.

However, it was quite clear, not only to the German Constitutional Court, but also to the ECJ, that Community Law is quite different from traditional international law. The Karlsruhe Court also made clear that Community Law is not State law[20] which corresponds to the later statement of the Court in the Maastricht decision (confirmed by the Lisbon judgement) that the EU is not a State.[21]

2.2. THE EU NOT A STATE BUT A 'STAATENVERBUND' – THE VAGUENESS OF THIS TERM

It should be mentioned that later decisions, particularly the Maastricht Decision of 1993, brought about the term '*Staatenverbund*'[22], a term which indicates the uniqueness, the *sui generis* character of the supranational organisation. This new term is nothing other than what has already been stated by the Constitutional Court in its early jurisprudence that European Community law is neither traditional international nor internal State law. In addition to distinguishing this, the word *Staatenverbund* should also express that the EU is neither a federation nor a confederation but rather something in between.

When using this – rather vague, until then not used in jurisprudence – term in both the Maastricht decision and the Lisbon decision, the Constitutional Court aimed to make clear the limits of supranational power by stressing that *Staatenverbund* is to be understood as an intergovernmental body where the Member States are 'the masters of the Treaty'.[23] This is important for the question of whether a new transfer of competences to the supranational order

18 Case 26/62 *Van Gend & Loos v Administratie der belastingen* [1963] ECR 1.
19 Case 6/ 64 *Costa v E.N.E.L.* [1964] ECR 585.
20 Vol. 22, p. 293.
21 Vol. 89, p. 155, 186; vol. 123, p. 267, 348.
22 See note 21.
23 Vol. 89, p. 155, 190; vol. 123, p. 267, 348.

would lead to the creation of a European State which would not be possible under the existing Constitution. By introducing the term *Staatenverbund* the Court denies the State character of the EU and thus avoids declaring the Maastricht Treaty, as well as later the Lisbon Treaty, to be unconstitutional.

The main argument of the Maastricht decision against qualifying the EU (which was created by the Maastricht Treaty) a State was that the EU had no so-called 'competence of competence' (*Kompetenz-Kompetenz*)[24], ie the legal power to create any competence whatever by its own will; if the EU (what was of course true also for the then existing EC) shall have additional competences, an unanimous consent of the Member States as the 'masters of the Treaty' to a further competence transfer is indispensable (apart from very particular exceptions of a simplified Treaty reform laid down in the new Article 48 (7) EU Treaty).

The discussion on the legal nature of the EC/EU was and is typically connected with the problem whether the creation of the supranational organisations with their particular state-like features endanger the sovereignty and statehood of the EU members. German statehood (*Staatlichkeit*) was an important issue in the Maastricht decision and, under the perspective of the future integration development, also in the Lisbon judgment. Will German statehood be suppressed if the EU is or becomes a Federal State? Or, besides that, is the power transfer to the EU effectuated by the Maastricht Treaty undetermined, so unlimited that would as such destroy statehood and be contrary to the existing national Constitution? These questions denied by the Court in the Maastricht case came up again in the Lisbon case but with a different accentuation[25]:

How far must democracy (in particular electoral equality as understood in German constitutional law) correspond to State criteria (i.e. German criteria) in an intergovernmental 'Staatenverbund' as the EU is in the eyes of the Constitutional Court? The Court accepts the specific equality deficiencies in the EU Parliament electoral system as tolerable in an intergovernmental organisation, but not in a – possible – future European State. In such a case democracy and with it the electoral systems must completely satisfy the 'ideal' as it seems to be realized in German constitutional law (to which the Court refers as its guardian). This argumentation is rooted in Art. 23 §1 BL which prescribes a (functional) parallelism between German and EU basic constitutional structures.

Sovereignty is a new judicial argument[26] and largely used by the Constitutional Court for the first time in the Lisbon decision. By the way, the term 'supranational' formerly avoided by the Court is now a common expression in this judgement.

24 FCC vol. 89, p. 155, 181, 192.

25 Vol. 123, p. 267, 340–344, 370.

26 The FFC referred marginally to sovereignty also in its Maastricht decision, see vol. 89, p. 155, 189.

Sovereignty and statehood are now reflected under the aspect of a 'competence reserve' indispensable for a State: the Court enumerates a series of fields where competences of 'substantive weight' must remain for national legislation[27], ie a substantive competence core which is deemed to be the fundament of statehood. This rigid and inflexible view has understandably aroused a lot of critics.

As a summary: the Court stated that the EU is no State but an intergovernmental '*Staatenverbund*' (Maastricht, Lisbon) with a supranational legal order (Lisbon). Sovereignty is preserved in this organisation though in a limited form (Lisbon). German statehood can be endangered by further transfers of competences; a remaining competence substance is therefore indispensable (Lisbon). A European State cannot be created under the existing German Constitution.

3. CONSTITUTIONAL LIMITS OF THE EUROPEAN INTEGRATION

3.1. FORMAL AND SUBSTANTIVE LIMITS – ARTICLE 23 §1 BL

The Constitutional Court, though having accepted, as has been pointed out above, the basic features of supranationalism, has been anxious to define the limits of the integration power.

There are formal and substantive limits of the integration process as laid down by the constitution. Both types of limits are connected with Article 23 §1 BL, the integration norm for the EU which came into force in 1993. The preceding integration norm was Article 24 §1 BL which was the basis for the creation of European Economic Communities in the fifties. The nucleus of both articles is the 'transfer of sovereign powers' (*Hoheitsrechten*) which has the same functional content in both provisions.

What is new in Article 23 §l is the procedure which requires since 1993 (1) a two-thirds majority of parliamentary consent (in the Federal Parliament as well as in the Federal Council) and (2) the explicit consent of the Federal Council to such a point. The two-thirds majority reflects the fact that the transfer of internal competences to the supranational order is a substantive constitutional reform; as it is necessary for a formal constitutional reform to have a two-thirds majority in the legislative organs, this requirement is extended, as expressed in Art. 23 §1 BL, to the creation of the EU as well as to reforms of their foundation treaty or similar reforms which would modify or complement the German BL in its contents or authorise such reforms or complements. The Constitutional Court did not make

27 Vol. 123, p. 267, 358–363.

a decision on these formal requirements because they were fulfilled in all cases with the Maastricht Treaty as well as with the Nice and the Lisbon Treaty.

The substantive limits laid down by Article 23 §1 BL are the constitutional requirement that the EU adheres to democratic, rule of law, social and federal principles and to the principle of subsidiarity as well as that they guarantee a fundamental rights protection which is, in its essential contents, comparable to that of the German BL.

The Constitutional Court's jurisprudence has examined, especially in its Lisbon Treaty decision of 2009, the compatibility of the Lisbon Treaty with the democratic principle as referred to in Article 23 (1) BL.[28]

3.2. THREE SUBSTANTIVE INTEGRATION LIMITS DEVELOPED BY THE JURISPRUDENCE

Independent of the constitutional provision of Article 23, the Constitutional Court has, since the entry into force of the Maastricht Treaty in 1993, developed in its jurisprudence *three essential substantive limits* for the European integration process: the requirement of constitutional parallelism, the *ultra vires* concept and the demand that constitutional identity should not be overruled by EU law.

3.2.1. *Constitutional parallelism*

The first aspect, *constitutional parallelism*, was already an important criterion before Article 23 BL was created in its EU-oriented form. The two *Solange* decisions, *Solange I* (1974) and *Solange II* (1986), were concerned with the question of sufficient fundamental rights protection in the supranational order which is similar to that of the German BL. It seems that these decisions were the incentive for introducing such limiting requirements for a transfer of sovereign powers and the intensification of the integration process into the German Basic Law itself. Furthermore, the Lisbon Treaty decision largely examined, as previously mentioned, the compatibility of the existing democratic system at the supranational level with that required by the German BL.

3.2.2. *The ultra vires concept*

The second limit formulated by the Constitutional Court is of great importance: the *ultra vires concept* which has been elaborated by the Maastricht decision[29]

28 Vol. 123, p. 267, 340–344.

29 Vol. 89, p. 155, 188; vol. 123, p. 267, 353–355; decision (*Mangold*) of July 6, 2010, 2 BvR 2661/06.

and reaffirmed by the Lisbon Treaty decision but relative to the Mangold decision of July 2010. In short, the supranational institutions are not allowed, under German constitutional law, to act outside the competences attributed to them by the Member States. It would be a violation of national sovereignty if the multinational organisation acted without being given authorisation by the integration treaties.

3.2.3. Constitutional identity

A third limit is that which was developed by the Lisbon Treaty decision of 2009 which declares *constitutional identity*[30] protected against intrusions from supranational law.

3.3. VALUES AND SUBSTITUTIVE PARALLELISM: A FUNCTIONAL INTEGRATION APPROACH

3.3.1. The dignity of man as a basis of fundamental rights

European integration must be based on the respect of fundamental rights. The German Constitution as well as the Constitutions of the other Member States, guarantee an effective protection of fundamental rights for the individual. The idea of the dignity of man is inherent in the orders of these states. A supranational body which replaces most of the national competences would not be thinkable without such an ideological basis. Therefore EC/EU institutions must respect fundamental rights.

3.3.2. Supranational fundamental rights for the supranational order

As these institutions create and apply legal norms deriving from their own legal order, the fundamental rights they have to observe must be of the same origin. Supranational institutions are not bound by national fundamental rights because these rights are part of a different legal order. Their own supranational order must contain superior norms that protect the individual to which the supranational institutions have to refer. This means that the supranational order itself needs to contain a set of fundamental rights.

3.3.3. From unwritten to written fundamental rights in the EU

As is well known, the judges of the ECJ have developed unwritten fundamental principles that have the effect of fundamental rights. In doing so they have

[30] Vol. 123, p. 267, 347/ 350.

discovered existing, yet unwritten values which they shaped on the example of the fundamental rights traditions of Member States as well as on the international covenants guaranteeing such rights, particularly noticeable in the example of the European Convention of Human Rights. These principles of European Community law have been regarded as superior to the secondary legislation of the EC/EU so that these national fundamental rights could bring about full normative effect.

On 1st December 2009 the European Union Charter of Fundamental Rights came into force, having been first drafted ten years ago. Nowadays, fundamental rights protection within the EU is effectuated on the basis of this Charter. Complementing this are unwritten rights that judges have determined which fill in the gaps in the written system.

3.3.4. *Joining the ECHR*

It is well known that the European Convention of Human rights (ECHR) has not yet fully joined the EC/EU because only a unilateral normative attachment to this Convention by supranational law existed as such (see Article 6 §3 of the Union Treaty of 1993 as well as Article 6 §3 of the new EU Treaty). But a reform of the Convention as well as the entry into force of Article 6 §2 of the new EU Treaty will enable the EU to join the ECHR in the near future. This will lead to a double protection of fundamental rights, by the EU Charter in the internal supranational order as well as, as a second guarantee, by the Strasbourg Convention.

3.4. NATIONAL OR SUPRANATIONAL FUNDAMENTAL RIGHTS? – THE *SOLANGE I* AND *II* DECISIONS

Supranational legal acts executed by national authorities have to respect fundamental rights. But the question arises: which fundamental rights, the national (because national authorities are acting) or the supranational (because these national authorities are executing a supranational legal act) are applicable?

The EU Fundamental Rights Charter of today answers this question very clearly: supranational fundamental rights apply in such a case. But this was not so clear in former times. Here the famous *Solange* jurisprudence of the German Constitutional Court has to be taken into consideration.

In 1974, the Karlsruhe Court rendered a first *Solange* decision[31]: the individual has to be protected against public power, both national and supranational power, which intervenes within this sphere of liberty of the individual. Fundamental

31 Vol. 37, p. 271.

rights are values and indispensable for a public power based order. If public authorities (national or supranational) have the competence to restrict the freedom or property of a person, they must respect the basic values expressed by their legal order.

In 1974 neither a written catalogue of fundamental rights nor a sufficiently developed fundamental rights charter created by judges had existed. For that the German constitutional judges applied the German fundamental rights. But they declared that at the moment when the supranational order itself creates a fundamental rights catalogue, the Constitutional Court of Germany will refrain from applying their own national rights. By this judges recognised that the supranational order should have its own rights to which the legal acts of the supranational order would have to conform. Until this moment, the national order offers the necessary protection of the individual, in a subsidiary way.

In 1986, 12 years later, the second decision, *Solange II*[32], was adopted by the Federal Constitutional Court. Here the Karlsruhe judges acknowledged the existence of fundamental rights in the supranational order, not in the written catalogue but developed by the judges as a coherent system of unwritten general principles protecting the individual. The German Court enumerated in its decision all the ECJ jurisprudence guaranteeing rights and found that this was equivalent to the German protection as foreseen by the BL. This was the reason that the German court refrained from applying German fundamental rights and attributed to the ECJ the power to examine supranational acts under EC fundamental rights.

But the Constitutional Court had a stipulation: only if the existing standards of protection of fundamental rights at the supranational level were maintained, would the German Constitutional Court refrain from applying German rights. If the level of protection in the EC/EU would essentially be reduced, the German Court would re-establish its jurisdiction in this field and again reapply the German fundamental rights. As long as the standards of protection as they existed in 1986 were valid, then the Constitutional Court would not intervene.[33] For this reason this decision is called the *Solange II* decision. This is the legal situation of today, confirmed in the banana market decision of the Constitutional Court in 2000.[34]

With the entry into force of the EU Fundamental Rights Charter on 1st December, 2009, there is no longer any doubt about the stability of the existing fundamental rights standards in the EU. Therefore it seems impossible that the case of essential reduction of these rights would occur and the Court of Karlsruhe would re-establish its jurisdiction.

---

32 Vol. 73, p. 339.

33 Vol. 73, p. 339, 387.

34 Vol. 102, p. 147.

The Constitutional Court declared itself exclusively competent to decide on whether the fundamental rights protection standards in the EU have essentially decreased or not. This role cannot be carried out by other courts, it has been monopolised by the Constitutional Court.[35]

3.5. THE FUNCTIONAL-SUBSTITUTIVE APPROACH OF THE CONSTITUTIONAL COURT

The jurisdiction of the Constitutional Court which has been examined above can be qualified as a functional approach: what is crucial is the efficient protection of the individual realised either by the supranational order itself or, in a subsidiary way, by the national order as it was pointed out in the *Solange I* position of 1974. This means that the protective function of legal order is what is important, not which legal order it is.

The national protection of fundamental rights must have its parallel in the supranational order. This does not mean that there must be a congruence in instruments or modalities. It is sufficient that the same function is fulfilled in an effective way. If there is a parallel which functionally meets the requirements of an efficient protection of fundamental rights, this parallel protection system on the supranational level substitutes for the national protection system. It can therefore be said that the German constitutional jurisprudence maintains the idea that the *function* of fundamental rights must be fulfilled on one of the two levels, the national *or* the supranational level. If the supranational level fulfils it sufficiently, the national guarantees do not apply. The supranational system substitutes for the national one.

3.6. RULE OF LAW

What has been said regarding the protection of fundamental rights is also valid for the rule of law aspects. The ECJ has developed, in close similarity to the German constitutional jurisprudence, a set of elements which are essential for rule of law: the principle of legality, the protection of legal confidence including the prohibition of retroactivity, the principle of proportionality, the prohibition to act arbitrarily etc.[36]

From a German constitutional law standpoint the EC/EU must also meet the rule of law requirements in a certain parallel to the state system. But also here it

---

35 See FCC [1987] *EuR (Europarecht)*, p. 269.

36 See for example ECJ Case 11/70 *Internationale Handelsgesellschaft mbh* [1970] ECR 1125, 1137; Case 261/81 *Rau v De Smedt* [1982] ECR 3961, 3972; Case 265/87, *Schräder v Hauptzollambt Gronau* [1989] 2237, 2269.

can be said that the supranational order has to develop its own rule of law concept. At a supranational level rule of law is developed in a parallel manner as it is in Member States such as Germany. Therefore these elements, for example the principle of proportionality, are applicable in the supranational form when the supranational legal acts are to be executed by German authorities. Thus, in this field also, a *substitutive parallelism* between national and supranational order is possible.

3.7. LIMITS OF INTEGRATION: *ULTRA VIRES* AND CONSTITUTIONAL REVIEW

3.7.1. The principle of compétences d'attribution and ultra vires actions

A basic principle of EC/EU law is the principle of *compétences d'attribution*, meaning that the supranational institutions can only act if this is permitted by a competence attributed to them by the Member States.

If supranational institutions act outside of their competence, they are acting in an *ultra vires* way. Such an act would violate the sovereignty of the Member States. As the competences attributed to the supranational institutions are laid down in the primary law of the EU, this act would also be a violation of primary EU law. The consequence would be that this *ultra vires* legal act is illegal and can be annulled by the ECJ.

The *ultra vires* action also has a *national* dimension: as already pointed out, a transfer of national competences to the supranational organisations took place on the basis of the constitutional consent of the Member States. This requirement, resulting from the integration norm, has in Germany always been effectuated by the Act of approval of the founding or reform treaties of the EC/EU. Therefore the primary law shows whether or not a competence existed for a supranational action.

So the national dimension of the *ultra vires* problem is therefore the fact that the supranational institutions have passed the limits drawn by the Act of approval and have therefore also violated the national constitution. This is the basis for the intervention of the national Constitutional Court.

3.7.2. The obligation to address the ECJ

It must be stressed in this context that the interpretation of the primary law of the EC/EU containing the competences, has been made by the ECJ/ECJ as a last resort. In the case of the annulment of an *ultra vires* action by the ECJ/ECJ, it is this court which interprets the competence norms in question and states whether this law has been trespassed or not. If the national Constitutional Court (or other national courts) are involved in the charging for an *ultra vires* action of the EC/

EU, they have no exclusive interpretation competence in regard to the primary law. The national Constitutional Court as well as the last instance ordinary or administrative court of a Member State concerned with the interpretation of primary law, ie of the competence norm, have to make a preliminary request to the ECJ in order to get its final decision on the interpretation of the competence norm. This obligation arising from Article 267 of the Treaty on the functioning of the EU (former Article 234 of the EC Treaty) had for a long time not been recognised by the German Constitutional Court. This has changed with the *Mangold* decision of 2010.[37]

3.7.3. *The Maastricht decision and the ultra vires concept*

The decisive question is: which institution can ultimately decide whether or not a legal act of the supranational power is outside the attributed competence? The German Constitutional Court attributes this competence exclusively to itself without referring to the obligation of last instance tribunals to address the ECJ for interpretation. Only in the new *Mangold* decision[38] does the court take this mechanism prescribed by EU law into consideration.

In fact, the tribunals of the Member States are obliged to make a preliminary ruling under Article 267 of the new Treaty on the functioning of the EU (the former Article 234 of the EC Treaty) which has the consequence that the ECJ has itself the exclusive power to decide whether or not supranational legal acts are *ultra vires*.

The German Constitutional Court pointed out that in the event of an *ultra vires* act (*ausbrechender Rechtsakt*[39]) it will declare this act to be not applicable in Germany. But such position is contrary to EU law which reserves such a non-applicability statement to the ECJ.

3.7.4. *The journey back to EU law conformity: The Mangold case*

The Mangold decision of 2010 concerning the existence of an unwritten principle of EU law embodying the prohibition of age discrimination, has had two major points:

In the Mangold case the Constitutional Court expressly states that it is obliged to address the ECJ but it does not give up the ultimate decision on *ultra vires*. It has recognised that it is the task of the supranational Court to interpret the primary law competences of the EU.

Apart from this aspect it is highly important what the court says on the *ultra vires* concept; only in cases where the lacking compliance with the competence

37 Decision of 6 July 2010, 2 BvR 2661/06.

38 See note 37.

39 Vol. 89, p. 155, 188.

attribution is manifest and is so serious that the competence distribution system existing between the EU and the Member States would be shifted in a seriously detrimental way for the Member States. This means that an act can only be regarded as *ultra vires* if it has such serious consequence and is not only a simple excess of competence. It must be a *qualified* trespassing of the competence with the above mentioned serious consequences.

Thus, the strict *ultra vires* concept originally maintained by the Constitutional Court has been relativised to the aforementioned extent.

3.8. LIMITS OF INTEGRATION: CONSTITUTIONAL IDENTITY

3.8.1. Constitutional identity through Article 79 §3 BL?

In the Lisbon decision, the Federal Constitutional Court has referred to the 'constitutional identity' of the German legal order. This nucleus of the constitutional law should not be submitted to the primacy of EU law. The Court has defined identity in this sense by referring to Article 79 (3) of the BL. This article applies to a formal constitutional reform and saves some most important principles from being modified. For this reason this clause is also called the '*Ewigkeitsgarantie*', the Eternity Clause. As is well known, Article 1, the dignity of man, as well as the principles of Article 20, ie. democracy, rule of law, social state principle as well as federalism (which is mentioned elsewhere in this article) are sacrosanct and cannot be overruled by any constitutional reform, not even by a two-thirds majority.

This article, dedicated to a formal reform, is also implicitly applicable for a 'substantive reform' (*materielle Verfassungsänderung*). The transfer of sovereign power to the supranational institutions is such a substantive reform and, as is pointed out by Article 23 (1) BL, falls also under the regime of this eternity clause.

In its decision on the Lisbon treaty, the Federal Constitutional Court has used this clause for defining constitutional identity.[40]

3.8.2. National identity in the sense of Article 4 §2 of the new EU Treaty

In this context it should be noted that that primary law of the EU, Article 4 §2 of the new EU Treaty, also speaks of 'national identity' and includes, by defining this notion, the fundamental principles of the constitutional law of a Member State. It seems that national identity (a vague notion already laid down in Article 6(3) of the EU Treaty of 1993) is now enlarged by the inclusion of the nucleus of the constitutional law in the Member States.

---

40 Vol. 123, p. 267, 347/350.

But it is obvious that the interpretation of national as well as constitutional identity in the sense of Article 4 of the new EU Treaty has to be based on a *supranational* perspective while the *national* constitutional identity clauses can only be interpreted in light of the national law. Nevertheless a harmonisation between the two notions must be found, a problem which has not been dealt with by the Constitutional Court.

3.8.3. The term of constitutional identity going back to the Solange jurisprudence

The term constitutional identity is not absolutely new in the jurisprudence of the German Constitutional Court. In 1974, when the Court rendered the *Solange I* decision, it already qualified fundamental rights as one of the identifying elements of our constitutional order.[41] But this did not launch a debate over the concept of constitutional identity; only 35 years later, in the Lisbon Treaty decision, did the argumentation surrounding constitutional identity expand considerably and acted as the starting point for a vehement discussion on what identity is in this sense. It can be said that this has expanded into a Europe-wide debate.

The Constitutional Court reserves for itself the exclusive competence to decide on whether a supranational legal act is contrary to constitutional identity and, in the eyes of the Constitutional Court, therefore not applicable in Germany.

3.8.4. A functional approach to identity?

An important question has been left open by the Court: we must look back at the *Solange II* decision where the Court accepted that the protection of fundamental rights directed against supranational acts could be executed by means and in forms of the supranational legal order. The Court has preferred a functional approach in that it was considered a requirement of the German Constitution that the *function* of adequate protection of fundamental rights of the individual needs to be fulfilled, by whichever means, national or supranational. As explained above, the Court did not state in the *Solange* I decision that Community acts should always be submitted to German fundamental rights which would have been a serious limitation of the principle of primacy of Community law over national law. Such a perspective would have been a *substantive* approach referring exclusively to the institutional existence of national fundamental rights. The *functional* approach goes beyond and is more flexible and more adapted to the dynamic integration process.

Is a functional approach possible without endangering constitutional identity? The Constitutional Court has not yet reached a decision on this question. In my view, a functional approach is possible and compatible with a guarantee of the constitutional identity.

---

41 Vol. 37, p. 271, 279.

3.8.5. *The involvement of the ECJ*

The more crucial question arises in the fact that the Constitutional Court claims exclusive power to decide whether the German constitutional identity is affected resulting in the non-applicability of the supranational act in question on German territory. This is contrary to the legal thinking of the ECJ which denies the possibility for national courts to stop the application of supranational legal acts.[42] In a similar way, as in the field of *ultra vires* acts, the Constitutional Court has the obligation to address the ECJ, putting forward the preliminary questions as to the contents of the supranational legal acts. The Luxemburg Court has to interpret the legal act which is important for the question of whether it intrudes on national constitutional identity. So the previously mentioned *Mangold* decision of 2010 is also important in this context: we can deduce from this position a general rule that the Constitutional Court has to involve the ECJ to discover the exact substantive range of the supranational act in question.

3.8.6. *Harmonising the national and supranational perspectives on constitutional identity*

There is a further problem: on the one hand it is obvious that national constitutional identity can only be examined by the national Constitutional Court as far as the national dimension is concerned. On the other hand there must be a harmonisation with the EU perspective of national identity including constitutional identity. Article 4 §2 of the new EU treaty has to be interpreted by the Luxembourg Court. Both, this supranational interpretation as well as the national interpretation of what, in the concrete case, constitutional identity is, have to be adequately harmonised. Here a cooperation of both courts is inevitable. Such a harmonisation can only be effectuated if the ECJ makes a decision about what comprises national and constitutional identity in the sense of Article 4 §2 of the EU Treaty. This should be made in an abstract way. The national Constitutional Court has to point out which supranational act is affecting which constitutional identity element *in concreto*. If this element is comprised by the supranational notion of constitutional identity (which is combined here with the supranational notion of national identity), the national Constitutional Court has to, by means of the preliminary question mechanism, address the ECJ, indicating the possible violations of national constitutional identity and asking the Luxembourg Court to examine whether the points in question are covered by EU primary law, ie by Article 4 §2 of the EU Treaty. If the supranational act affects national constitutional identity, the Luxembourg court could annul or declare the EU act inapplicable. A clear solution has not yet been developed by either the ECJ or by the doctrine.

---

42 Case 314/85 *Foto-Frost v Hauptzollamt Lübeck-Ost* [1987] 4199.

4. THE CONSTITUTIONAL COURT AS A PROTECTOR OF SUPRANATIONAL LAW

4.1. THE CONSTITUTIONAL COURT AS A GUARDIAN OF THE ECJ

While the role of the Constitutional Court is mainly the protection of the national Constitution, it has also assumed the task of protecting the EU legal order, specifically the cooperation between German tribunals and the ECJ according to Article 267 Treaty on the Functioning of the EU.

The supranational Court is functionally connected with the German judicial system, on the basis of the constitutional integration norms. The guarantee of the 'lawful judge' (*gesetzlicher Richter*) foreseen by Art. 101 §1 BL is the instrument used by the Constitutional Court to safeguard this 'dialogue of judiciaries' between Member State and EU.

The traditional guarantee of Article 101 BL has been extended, from an earlier understanding involving only national courts, to a more supranational perspective, a consequence of the European integration.

4.2. WHAT IS A VIOLATION OF THIS GUARANTEE?

However, the main problem in this context is knowing under which circumstances this guarantee is violated, ie someone is removed from the jurisdiction of her/his 'lawful' judge which has been determined by Article 267 of the Treaty on the Functioning of the EU linked to the national legal order by the German Act of approval.

A mere error in procedure (*error in procedendo*) is not sufficient, as the Constitutional Court says. It must be a 'qualified' (particularly serious) violation of this guarantee[43]: if the national court does not consider at all the possibility of referring a preliminary question, then Article 101 BL has been violated. Besides that, if a national court does not make preliminary rulings according to the aforementioned Article 267 of the Functioning Treaty because it has interpreted the procedural rules of EU law in an unacceptable way (*unvertretbare Auslegung*[44]), then a violation has also occurred.

This can also be true in other cases: for example if a court of last instance does not make a preliminary ruling whereas the court of first instance, in the same case, had made such a reference to the Luxembourg Court and had arrived at a particular interpretation of supranational law which was not accepted by the national court of last instance. This was the case when the Federal Finance Court

43 Recently FCC decision of August 30, 2010, 1 BvR 1631/ 080.

44 FCC vol. 88, p. 159, 195–196.

denied that EC directives could not be directly applicable. The first instance finance tribunal had made a reference to the Luxembourg Court and received the answer that the direct applicability of directives has been developed by the jurisprudence of the ECJ and is valid in interpretation. This was denied by the last instance *Bundesfinanzhof* which did not launch a preliminary question procedure and refused to follow the interpretation decision of the Luxembourg Court initiated by the first instance. The Constitutional Court considered this case a violation of the lawful judge guarantee and annulled the Federal Finance Court decision.[45]

A recent decision of the Federal Constitutional Court was rendered in August 2010 confirming the former jurisprudence. The decision rendered by the Federal Court of Justice (*Bundesgerichtshof*) was annulled because this Court did not address the Luxembourg Court and did not take EU law into consideration which would have been, alongside German law, applicable in this case.

4.3. THE 'COOPERATION' BETWEEN THE CONSTITUTIONAL COURT AND THE ECJ

Thus the German Constitutional Court protects the ECJ by national constitutional means. In the Maastricht decision the Federal Constitutional Court described the role of both courts as a 'cooperation relationship' (*Kooperationsverhältnis*[46]), referring to the fundamental rights. Indeed, a cooperation can be seen in the fact that the German Constitutional Court, based on the *Solange II* concept, no longer examines a legal act of the EU under German fundamental rights. It recognises that the Luxembourg Court has to take over this task of applying supranational fundamental rights. What remains for the Constitutional Court, in the field of fundamental rights, is to observe whether the general standards of the fundamental rights protection at the EU level are being maintained sufficiently or whether they have essentially decreased. In such a case, as was pointed out above, the Karlsruhe Court would reopen its doors and resume its jurisdiction, applying national fundamental rights for supranational acts executed by national authorities.

This cooperation system has even been enlarged in the perspective of Article 101 BL because in doing so the *Bundesverfassungsgericht* goes beyond cooperation and assumes a protective role for the Luxembourg Court and therefore, for the uniform and adequate interpretation of supranational law.

45 Vol. 75, p. 223, 235.
46 Vol. 89, p. 155, 178.

5. THE CONSTITUTIONAL COURT AND THE EUROPEAN CONVENTION OF HUMAN RIGHTS (ECHR)

5.1. THE ECHR AS AN INTERNATIONAL TREATY TRANSFORMED INTO GERMAN LAW

Formally the ECHR is an international treaty transformed under Article 59 §2 BL by the Act of approval with the consequence that it is equivalent to federal ordinary law. As already pointed out, federal law adopted later than this Act of approval would be able to repeal it. Such a repeal would be valid at the internal level though it would violate international law. Politically, it is very improbable that this would occur intentionally. Nevertheless it can happen without being recognized as such.

5.2. CONSTITUTIONALISING THE ECHR

The German Constitutional Court refers to the ECHR very seldom. It seems that the fundamental rights of the Basic Law have reached such a high standard through the 60 years of constitutional jurisprudence that the Court normally refers to these national rights which have the rank of constitutional law. In preparation of its decisions the Court takes into account the Strasbourg jurisprudence in order to harmonise, to a certain extent, the contents of both types of rights and to avoid a censure by the Human Rights Court.

Despite the ordinary law rank of the ECHR, the Constitutional Court used the Convention as an instrument of interpretation. The presumption of innocence was declared an element of the German Rule of Law concept as laid down in a very general term in Article 20 BL.[47]

5.3. THE MONISTIC EFFECT OF RULE OF LAW

Obedience to international law is a demand of Rule of Law, independent of the dualism in the traditional German perspective of the relationship between international and national law. In the famous *Görgülü* decision[48] the Constitutional Court confirmed its competence to examine whether national courts have duly applied the ECHR and the jurisprudence of the European Court of Human Rights. It would be a violation of Rule of Law and the fundamental rights relevant in the particular case if a national institution, in particular a

47 FCC vol. 35, p. 311, 329; vol. 74, p. 358, 370; vol. 82, p. 106, 114/115.

48 Vol. 111, p. 307, 317, 329–330.

court, would not try to interpret the national fundamental right in the light of the Strasbourg decision. This is a consequence of the obligation of the courts (and of other State institutions) to interpret internal norms in favour of the international law. This principle, resulting from the basic rule of '*Völkerrechtsfreundlichkeit*'[49], characteristic of the 'open State' (*offene Staatlichkeit*[50]) as well as the Rule of Law principle, helps to overcome, in part, the normative deficiencies of the dualism.

5.4. THE *GÖRGÜLÜ* DECISION AND ITS DEFICIENCIES

The *Görgülü* decision of the Federal Constitutional Court clearly shows the dilemma between Germany's orientation as an 'open State', that is a State which fully accepts international law and is in favour of the international community, on the one hand, and the dualist tradition on which the Constitution is based, on the other hand. Human rights are recognised as the very essence of a legal er their origin being in human dignity, the highest value in German constitutional law, but if they are embodied in an international treaty such as the ECHR they do not have the rank in internal law which would be merited in accordance to their importance: being equivalent in their normative force to ordinary federal laws they have no controlling power on national legislation. The attempt of the Court to attenuate this effect by interpreting national laws in the light of the international treaties is a step in the right direction but does not compensate for the deficits which result from the dualist approach. It seems anachronistic to uphold a concept which has been developed in the nineteenth and early twentieth century in the closely interconnected globalised world of today. A State which assumes an international obligation cannot keep its internal legislation separated from it and only require conformity with the Constitution.

The *Görgülü* case demonstrates that a Constitution-oriented legislative solution in a dualist system can lead to a conflict with the different approach of the international treaty. Thus, in this case, German family law was regarded as a coherent and equilibrated system which has been shaped in conformity to Article 6 BL and which should be accepted, as to the Constitutional Court, also under the perspective of the ECHR. The conformity to the German Basic Law seemed sufficient to the Court; in the Court's view the ECHR should leave this system intact because it could not be regarded as being as differentiated as the national system. Thus it can easily be seen that dualism makes it possible to have separated perspectives at the internal and external level. A monist system, however, would harmonize these perspectives.

---

49 Vol. 111, p. 397, 317–319.

50 See note 13.

It corresponds to this view that priority is given to the legislative solution based on constitutional conformity and it is only allowed (and required) to interpret the legislative approach in the light of the ECHR if it allows for such an interpretation. The 'open State' concept is therefore limited by dualism.

In summary it can be said that the dualistic view, as seen in the *Görgülü* decision, is to a certain extent a barrier to a full internal acceptance of the ECHR but also shows the tendency of the Constitutional Court to attenuate the consequences of dualism in order to avoid a violation of the international law obligation.

CHAPTER 9

ITALY

THE IMPACT OF THE EUROPEAN COURTS ON THE ITALIAN CONSTITUTIONAL COURT*

Giuseppe MARTINICO and Oreste POLLICINO

1. THE PROTECTION OF FUNDAMENTAL RIGHTS BY THE ITALIAN COURTS

In order to describe the content of many European constitutions and their attention to the fundamental rights dimension, a famous Italian constitutionalist, Costantino Mortati, devised the formula 'Constitution born from the Resistance'[1], conceiving the constitutional principles included in this document as the ultimate axiological wall against the ghosts of Nazi fascism. This also explains why the principles recalling these values usually represent the untouchable core of new constitutions. Thus fundamental rights clauses and democratic principles typically are core to the Italian constitutional experience.

Despite that, the Constitutional Court can hardly be described as a 'judge of rights' *stricto sensu* conceived, since no direct action before it is provided for individual citizens. Obviously this does not exclude the importance of the Constitutional Court's case law in matters of protection of fundamental rights, on the contrary, one '*fil conducteur*' in the tale of these two courts (the European Court of Justice (ECJ)[2] and the Italian Constitutional Court) can be seen in the constant disagreement about the level of protection offered by the supranational

---

* Sections I and II were written by Giuseppe Martinico, while Section III was written by Oreste Pollicino. Section IV is jointly written. Giuseppe Martinico is García Pelayo Fellow at the Centro de Estudios Politicos y Constitucionales, Madrid, Max Weber Fellow at the European University Institute, Florence, Researcher at the Centre for Studies on Federalism, Turin; Oreste Pollicino is Associate Professor in Comparative Public Law at the Bocconi University, Milan.

1 C Mortati, *Lezioni sulle forme di governo*, Cedam, Padua, 1973.

2 The official name is Court of Justice of the European Union.

level. Traditionally, thus, the 'counter-limits' doctrine is described as an attempt by the Italian Constitutional Court at constitutionalizing the EC/EU legal order (something similar might be said with regard to the *Solange* doctrine of the German Constitutional Court).

If the literature on this bottom-up phenomenon (i.e., the contribution of the national courts to the improvement of the ECJ case law on issues of fundamental rights) is massive, few readings exist on the contribution of the ECJ to the development of the national courts' jurisprudence in this field. Obviously there is a totally different discourse for the European Court of Human Rights which has had, as we will see, a very important impact on the activity of Italian courts.

A potential turning point in the relationship between the EU and national levels might be represented by the EU Charter of Fundamental Rights, although the ECJ has only recently paid attention to this document and although this Charter has only recently been attributed with binding effects thanks to the coming into force of the Lisbon Treaty.

2. THE RELATION OF NATIONAL LAW AND INTERNATIONAL LAW ACCORDING TO ITALIAN LAW

2.1. ITALIAN DUALISM AS A STARTING POINT OF THE NATIONAL CONSTITUTIONAL COURT

Italy is usually seen as a country characterized by a strong dualist tradition, according to which the international and national legal systems are conceived of as autonomous.

There are two fundamental provisions in the Italian Constitution regarding the relationship between international and domestic law; Articles 10[3] and 11.[4] These two articles provide the first important distinction existing in this field in Italy; the distinction between the general rules of international law and international treaties. As for the former, Article 10 provides an automatic

3 "*The Italian legal system conforms to the generally recognised principles of international law. The legal status of foreigners is regulated by law in conformity with international provisions and treaties.*
A foreigner who, in his home country, is denied the actual exercise of the democratic freedoms guaranteed by the Italian constitution shall be entitled to the right of asylum under the conditions established by law.
A foreigner may not be extradited for a political offence".

4 "*Italy rejects war as an instrument of aggression against the freedom of other peoples and as a means for the settlement of international disputes. Italy agrees, on conditions of equality with other States, to the limitations of sovereignty that may be necessary to a world order ensuring peace and justice among the Nations. Italy promotes and encourages international organisations furthering such ends*".

procedure of adoption, in the sense that such norms are directly incorporated into the Italian system.

According to Italian scholars, the general rules of international law (which would correspond to the customary international law) belong to the constitutional level.[5] According to some scholars, the international customary law existing before the entry into force of the Italian Constitution could prevail over the constitutional provisions (because of the application of the chronological criterion) but this does not apply with regard to the principles belonging to the untouchable core recalled by Article 139 of the Constitution[6] (this untouchable core, according to the judgment 1146/1988, also includes the supreme principles included in the first part of the Italian Constitution).[7]

As for international treaties, it is necessary for there to be a national act transforming the international act into national law. The intervention of the national legislature is not required for all treaties, since Article 80 provides the necessity of legislation enabling the ratification only with reference to some particular treaties.[8] The procedure of ratification is also governed by Article 87, which empowers the President of the Republic to ratify international treaties.[9] When the intervention of parliament is required, it intervenes with a normal

---

5 G de Vergottini, *Diritto costituzionale*, Cedam, Padua, 2004, 32.

6 "*The form of Republic shall not be a matter for constitutional amendment*".

7 For an overview of the debate see: "Commento art.10 della Costituzione", in G Branca (ed.), *Commentario della Costituzione*, vol. *Principi fondamentali.* Artt. 1–12, Zanichelli, Bologna, 1975, 485 ff., 502. According to R Quadri, the automatic procedure shall be applied to the international treaties but this remains a minority view. This theory was based on the fact that one of the general rules of international law is given by the principle *pacta sunt servanda.* R Quadri, *Diritto internazionale pubblico*, Naples, 1989, 64.

8 "*Parliament shall authorise by law the ratification of such international treaties as have a political nature, require arbitration or a legal settlement, entail change of borders, spending or new legislation*".

9 "*The President of the Republic is the Head of the State and represents national unity.*
The President may send messages to Parliament.
The President shall:
- authorise the introduction to Parliament of bills initiated by the Government;
- promulgate laws and issue decrees having the force of law, and regulations;
- call a general referendum in the cases provided for by the Constitution;
- appoint State officials in the cases provided for by the law;
- accredit and receive diplomatic representatives, and ratify international treaties which have, where required, been authorised by Parliament.
The President is the commander-in-chief of the armed forces, shall preside over the Supreme Council of Defence established by law, and shall make declarations of war as have been agreed by Parliament.
The President shall preside over the High Council of the Judiciary.
The President may grant pardons and commute punishments.
The President shall confer the honorary distinctions of the Republic".
In this regard, one should note that the final paragraph of Article 72, provides that: "*The ordinary procedure for consideration and direct approval by the House is always followed in the case of bills on constitutional and electoral matters, delegating legislation, ratification of international treaties and the approval of budgets and accounts*".

legislative statute. According to the majority of scholars, this confers a primary force in the national hierarchy of law to norms derived from international treaties.

Despite that, the Italian Constitution recognizes a particular force to the laws related to international obligations. Article 75, paragraph 2 (devoted to the referendum) provides: '*No referendum may be held on a law regulating taxes, the budget, amnesty or pardon, or a law ratifying an international treaty*'.

Apart from Articles 10 and 11, another fundamental provision is entrenched in Article 117[10] which will be discussed in the next sections of this contribution. What we would like to specify here is that, because of the dualist tradition, international treaties acquire the strength of the domestic statute adopted for their incorporation. This explains why, at the beginning, both the European Convention on Human Rights (ECHR) and EC law were considered as primary sources in the Italian legal system.

Another important feature of the Italian legal order is the fact that, unlike in other countries like Portugal and Spain, no specific status is accorded to treaties devoted to human rights. This is another important point to be kept in mind when analysing the Italian Constitutional Court's judicial developments in this field.

2.2. EU LAW

The Constitutional Court originally established the basis for accepting EC law as a supranational law with primacy and direct effect on the Article 11 of the Italian Constitution. This acceptance, however, did not come about immediately. On the contrary, it was the result of a long series of judgments. One of the reasons for this can be attributed to the absence of an explicit European clause in the Italian Constitution. As a matter of fact, Article 11 was originally conceived to deal with the Italian membership of organizations like the United Nations rather than to justify the consequence of supranationalism (a phenomenon that was unknown when the Italian Constitution came into force). This changed in 2001 with the constitutional reform of Title V of the second part of the Italian fundamental charter.

The Italian Constitution's new Article 117, paragraph 1, expressly codifies the limit that supra-national obligations represent for domestic law by providing that: '*Legislative power belongs to the State and the regions in accordance with the constitution and within the limits set by European Union law and international obligations*'. Looking at the judicial parameter, we will see that this provision

10 Other relevant provisions in this field are given by Article 26: "*Extradition of a citizen may be granted only if it is expressly envisaged by international conventions*". In any case, extradition may not be permitted for political offences.

provoked interesting innovations in the Italian Constitutional Court's case law. Soon after the reform, the interpretation of this provision created a division among scholars.[11] According to some, Article 117, paragraph 1, would simply codify the pre-existing situation: it would grant a sort of *a posteriori* assent to the European primacy[12] as it was developed by the ECJ and accepted across the European Community. Other scholars, on the other hand, emphasized the importance of the constitutional *status* given to the European primacy, and asserted that Article 117 paved the way for the acceptance of the Italian monist thesis.[13]

2.2.1. *The Italian Constitutional Court before EU law: The counter-limits doctrine*

Another feature of the approach of the Italian Constitutional Court to the EU law is given by the counter-limits doctrine, devised by the *Consulta* in 1973 soon after the well known judgment of the ECJ in *Internationale Handelsgesellschaft*.[14] In this judgment, the European Court of Justice pointed out the primacy of the EC law over the national law including the national constitutional principles.[15]

In this respect the Italian position – along with the German one – is relevant for a complete understanding of the reasons of the 'resistance'. The Constitutional Courts have claimed to maintain their own role (the role of the guardians of the national constitutional identity) without exceptions. They have denied the acceptance of dangerous monist visions in order to preserve the constitutional identity of their legal orders. On the contrary they have raised some ultimate barriers against the penetration of the EU law in order to define the fundamental principles of the legal orders for which they are the guardians. Hypothetically, if an EU provision conflicted with the fundamental principles of the national legal order, the Constitutional Court could strike down the national statute executing the EC Treaty/TFEU, thus causing a 'rupture' between national and supranational legal orders. The Constitutional Courts in fact normally have jurisdiction over

---

11 For an overview, see R Chieppa, "Nuove prospettive per il controllo di compatibilità comunitaria da parte della Corte costituzionale", in *Il Diritto dell'Unione Europea*, 3/2007, 493–511, 499 ff; A Ruggeri, "Riforma del titolo V e giudizi di "comunitarietà" delle leggi", 2007, www.associazionedeicostituzionalisti.it/dottrina/ordinamentieuropei/ruggeri.html.

12 C Pinelli, "I limiti generali alla potestà legislativa statale e regionale e i rapporti con l'ordinamento comunitario", in *Foro italiano*, V, 2001, 194 ff.

13 F Paterniti, "La riforma dell'art. 117, 1° co. della Costituzione e le nuove prospettive dei rapporti tra ordinamento giuridico nazionale e Unione Europea", in *Giur. Cost.*, n. 2/2004, 2101 ff; A Pajno, "Il rispetto dei vincoli derivanti dall'ordinamento comunitario come limite alla potestà legislativa nel nuovo Titolo V della Costituzione", in *Le Istituzioni del federalismo*, 2003, 814–842.

14 ECJ Case 11/70 *Internationale Handelsgesellschaft* [1970] ECR 1125.

15 "*Therefore the validity of a Community measure or its effect within a member State cannot be affected by allegations that it runs counter to either fundamental rights as formulated by the constitution of that State or the principles of its constitutional structure*".

national legislation (including the legal source of execution of treaties) but not over the EU provisions: the latter are beyond their jurisdiction because, in their argumentation, they belong to another legal order.

Starting from this approach, one can understand why the Constitutional Courts have refused the possibility of striking down the EU law provisions, since the acceptance of this option would have implied the adhesion to the monist theory of the ECJ. It is by a legal fiction that it is possible to defend the hard core of constitutional legal orders by preserving the formal autonomy of the national and supranational orders and the jurisdiction of the ECJ. The identification of these barriers to European integration represents the essence of the counter-limits doctrine (*dottrina dei controlimiti*), devised in case 183/73, the so called *Frontini* judgment[16] (but see also case 170/84, the so called *Granital* judgment[17]) by the Italian Constitutional Court. The consequence of a possible declaration of invalidity could spell Italy's withdrawal from the EU: according to Cartabia[18] in these two cases, in fact, the counter-limits test was conceived as a way to carry out an exceptional control on the respect of the conditions of constitutionality of the Italian adhesion to the ECs.

Following this reconstruction, the counter-limits worked as conditions for evaluating the legitimacy of the limitations of sovereignty accepted by the Italian adhesion to the European venture.

Later on (with the decision no. 232/1989, the so called *Fragd* judgement[19]), the nature of the counter-limits doctrine changed, transforming itself from an exceptional control into a 'simple' control of compatibility of the EU law with the Constitution that cannot put in discussion the Italian membership to the EU.

Because of the 'transformation' of this doctrine, the counter-limits have worked as a limitation to the European primacy: that is why, according to the same scholarship, from the *Fragd* judgement, the Italian Constitutional Court has implicitly admitted that the possible conflict with the Constitution would not cause invalidity of the statute of execution of the EC Treaty/TFEU, but just the non-applicability of the EU rule.[20]

2.2.2. Preliminary references to the European Court of Justice

The preliminary ruling mechanism illustrates the imperfect coincidence between the position of the Italian Constitutional Court and the ECJ. Well-known is the

16 Corte Costituzionale, sentenza 183/73, Frontini: [1974] 2 CMLRev 372.

17 Corte Costituzionale, sentenza n. 180/1974. Granital: [1984] CMLRev 756: "*nella sent. n. 183 del 27 dicembre 1973, già avvertito come la legge di esecuzione del Trattato possa andar soggetta al suo sindacato, in riferimento ai principi fondamentali del nostro ordinamento costituzionale e ai diritti inalienabili della persona umana*". About this see: M Cartabia, *Principi inviolabili e integrazione europea,* Giuffrè, Milan 1995.

18 M Cartabia, *Principi inviolabili cit,*.110.

19 *Corte Costituzionale*, sentenza n. 232/1989, in www.cortecostituzionale.it. In English: Fragd: [1990] 27 CMLRev 93.

20 See M Cartabia and JHH Weiler, *L'Italia in Europa*, Bologna, 2000, 171–172.

constitutional courts' refusal to conceive of themselves as judges under Article 234 of the EC Treaty (now Art. 267 TFUE) and the Italian *Consulta* was one of the pioneers in this respect. On 15 April 2008, for the first time in its history, the Italian Court agreed to refer a preliminary question to the ECJ.[21]

The Italian Constitutional Court limited its referral decision to direct proceedings, stressing the different structure characterizing the indirect form of constitutional review of legislation. The distinction made by the Court in this case seems to be in accordance with its previous case law. One should not overestimate the value of this *revirement*: the Court was careful to prevent the revolutionary component of the decision from spreading and causing unexpected consequences. This distinction also seems to be very coherent with the previous case law of the Constitutional Court. We would argue against an extension to indirect proceedings of the conclusions reached by the Italian Court with regard to direct proceedings: in the logic of interpretive competition, such an extension could lead to the loss of control over the national common judges who are fundamental to the activity of the Italian Constitutional Court.

Another factor that should be taken into account is the self-exclusion of the Italian *Consulta* from the preliminary mechanism, which did not produce the automatic denial of any form of dialogue with the ECJ. On the contrary, over the years, the Italian Court has devised some alternative modes of dialogue with the Luxembourg Court in order to combine respect for EU obligations with the preservation of the constitutional core.[22] Our impression is that in the near

---

21 ICC, *ordinanza* No. 103/2008, available at www.cortecostituzionale.it.

22 See G Martinico and F Fontanelli, "The Hidden Dialogue: When Judicial Competitors Collaborate", *Global Jurist 8.3*, available at www.bepress.com/gj/vol8/iss3/art7, 2008. By the formula "hidden dialogue" we mean that unexplored side of the relationship between Constitutional Courts and the ECJ which feeds itself with the somehow non-orthodox ways of judicial communication (that is, ways of judicial communication that are different from the preliminary ruling and are not formalized according to the letter of the Treaties, i.e., Art. 234 ECT). From the domestic courts' perspective there are two ways of cooperating with the ECJ: the former represents the "official" route provided by Art. 234 ECT (although entirely "governed" by the interpretative competitor: the ECJ), the latter is the parallel and informal route whose dynamics are mostly discretionary (so that both the procedures and the outcome of such a cooperation can be bargained). The second way is the one historically preferred by the Constitutional Courts, which have traditionally opted for levelling the playing field, thus avoiding the preliminary ruling (as the ECJ's domain), which would have implied the loss of interpretative sovereignty, given the fact that the game within the preliminary ruling's field is governed by the Treaties, the competitor's (i.e. the ECJ's) fundamental charters. As we know both the Constitutional Courts and the ECJ conceive of their own documents (respectively the national Constitutions and the Treaties) as the highest law and claim the ultimate authority in the interpretation of the legal materials in the multilevel legal system. This context was described as interpretative competition (K Alter, "Explaining National Court Acceptance of European Court Jurisprudence: A Critical Evaluation of Theories of Legal Integration", in A Slaughter, A Stone Sweet and JHH Weiler (eds), *The European Court and National Courts – Doctrine and Jurisprudence. Legal Change in its Social Context*, Hart, Oxford 1997) and it represents the judicial and dynamic side of the struggle for sovereignty. Schematically, we have identified the following techniques of hidden dialogue:

future the Italian Constitutional Court will rely on this kind of alternative mode of dialogue in the field of indirect proceeding, especially in the dual preliminarity mechanism.[23]

According to the technique of dual preliminarity (*doppia pregiudizialità*), the Constitutional Court could be asked to solve a question of constitutionality regarding an Italian norm in cases where such a question is strongly related to another preliminary ruling question contemporarily raised before the ECJ (either by the same or by another ordinary judge) on the meaning/validity of an EU act.

Should these two questions be strongly related, the Italian Constitutional Court can decide either to return the question (declaring it 'inadmissible') to the ordinary judge (decision no. 536/1995) or to 'wait for' the ECJ to pronounce itself before judging (decision no. 165/2004).

This way the Constitutional Court acknowledged an interpretive priority to the questions pending before the ECJ and *de facto* suspends its own trial by reaching an effect that is equivalent to that requested by Article 267 TFUE (i.e. the stay of the trial) without using the preliminary ruling mechanism.

As we can see, the dual preliminarity is a technique by which the Italian Constitutional Court acknowledges 'priority' to the ECJ and to Article 234 ECT (now 267 TFEU) questions; at the same time, it can work as a 'safety valve', since it avoids a conflict with the ECJ with regard to the possible violation of counter-limits. In the *Berlusconi* case, for example, the Italian Constitutional Court (165/2004) waited for the ECJ's answer, preparing itself for a decision that could possibly be incompatible with its fundamental principles. Thanks to dual preliminarity, the Italian Court allows the ECJ to decide whether to challenge the risk of a jurisdictional 'clash' or not. On the other hand, perhaps one can read the *Berlusconi* case as an attempt to avoid such a danger and as a chance to show the maturity of the EU system about fundamental rights. This technique is based upon a judicial triangle and obviously this can only happen in the framework of *incidenter* proceedings. Thanks to dual preliminarity, the Italian Constitutional Court can maintain control over the national ordinary judges and, at the same time, a symmetrical dialogue with the ECJ.

(a) introduction of a new step in the hierarchy of legal sources;
(b) distinction between "primacy" and "supremacy";
(c) admissibility of *recurso de amparo* against the domestic judges' refusal to raise the preliminary ruling;
(d) acknowledgment of *erga omnes* effects for ECJ's interpretive rulings;
(e) dual preliminarity (*doppia pregiudizialità*);
(f) distinction between disapplication and non-application.

23 On dual preliminarity see: M Cartabia, "Il processo costituzionale: l'iniziativa. Considerazioni sulla posizione del giudice comune di fronte a casi di 'doppia pregiudizialità', comunitaria e costituzionale", 1997 5 *Il Foro italiano*, 1997, 222–225. For a very similar point of view about the dual preliminarity, see M Cartabia, "'Taking dialogue seriously'. The renewed need for a judicial dialogue at the time of constitutional activism in the European Union", *Jean Monnet Working paper*, 12/07, 2007, www.jeanmonnetprogram.org/papers/07/071201.html.

2.2.3. *The impact of the EU Charter of Fundamental Rights on Italian case law*

Although originally the EU Charter of Fundamental Rights was not binding from a *stricto sensu* legal point of view, its proclamation favoured the emergence of a huge debate among scholars, especially among constitutional lawyers in continental Europe. Even before the coming into force of the Reform Treaty, the ECJ had already begun to quote the Charter and refer to it[24], in spite of the failure of the Constitutional Treaty to come into force and of the delay of the Lisbon Treaty, which made it legally binding (although the position of some Member States, such as the UK and Poland, is not clear because of the so-called opt-out signed by these countries[25]).

More generally, the proclamation of the Charter of Fundamental Rights of the EU brought new life into the debate about the drafting of a European Constitution and the possibility of a Bill of Rights at EU level, since it testified to the possibility of providing rights through a written instrument at supranational level, overcoming the ECJ's logic of *ius praetorium* in this field.[26] This explains why some Italian judges used the Charter in a very different way for supporting their decisions.[27]

---

24 Among the other cases, see: Case C-438/05, *The International Transport Workers' Federation and The Finnish Seamen's Union*, [2007] ECR I-10779 and Case C-341/05, C-341/05 *Laval un Partneri Ltd /Svenska Byggnadsarbetareförbundet* [2007] ECR I-11767.

25 Scholars (J Ziller, *Il nuovo Trattato europeo*, Il Mulino, Bologna, 2008) have stressed the absurdity of the so-called opting out by Poland and the UK with regard to the EU Charter of fundamental rights and the exclusion of the Charter itself from the text of the Reform Treaty. Article 6 EUT states that:
"*The Union recognises the rights, freedoms and principles set out in the Charter of Fundamental Rights of the European Union of 7 December 2000, as adapted at Strasbourg, on 12 December 2007, which shall have the same legal value as the Treaties*".
This article makes the Charter of fundamental rights part and parcel of EU primary law. In order to escape the risk of being subject to this document's provisions, the UK and Poland insisted on signing a specific protocol (no. 30), to the effect that:
"Art. 1:
1. The charter does not extend the ability of the Court of Justice of the European Union, or any court or tribunal of Poland or of the United Kingdom, to find that the laws, regulations or administrative provisions, practices or action of Poland or of the United Kingdom are inconsistent with the fundamental rights, freedoms and principles that it reaffirms.
2. "*In particular, and for the avoidance of doubt, nothing in Title IV of the charter creates justiciable rights applicable to Poland or the United Kingdom except in so far as Poland or the United Kingdom has provided for such rights in its national law.*"
"Art. 2
To the extent that a provision of the charter refers to national laws and practices, it shall only apply to Poland or the United Kingdom to the extent that the rights or principles that it contains are recognised in the law or practices of Poland or of the United Kingdom".

26 ECJ Case C-540/03, *Parliament v. Council* [2006] ECR I-5769.

27 For an overview of the Italian case law using or just mentioning the Charter, see: A Celotto and G Pistorio, "L'efficacia giuridica della Carta dei diritti fondamentali dell'Unione europea (rassegna giurisprudenziale 2001–2004)"; www.associazionedeicostituzionalisti.it/materiali/anticipazioni/carta_diritti_ue/index.html; B Caruso and M Militello, "La Carta di Nizza nel diritto vivente giurisprudenziale: una ricerca sulle motivazioni dei giudici (2000–2008)", in

Italian scholarship[28] has identified two groups of decisions in which the Charter has been applied by domestic judges; the first group of judgments refers to the indirect application of the document while the second refers to cases of direct application of the Charter. For instance, in a decision of 16 October 2007, the Italian *Corte di Cassazione*[29] mentioned the Charter as authority for the principle of free and informed consent as inferable from the right of physical integrity. In another judgment, the Italian Constitutional Court ruled on 24 April 2002[30] on measures limitative of personal domicile, quoting the EU Charter in support of its conclusion.

A similar use can be found in another judgment of the Italian *Corte di Cassazione*, of 9 July 2008[31], where the Court recalled the Charter as a fundamental part of the common principles and the European constitutional traditions. The same idea is present in a judgment of the Italian Constitutional Court of 23 December 2008[32], regarding the right to informed medical treatment, mentioning the Charter among the European and domestic relevant legal sources in this field.[33]

The general idea behind these decisions is that the Charter has interpretative value, although lacking in binding force (before the coming into force of the Lisbon Treaty) as the Constitutional Court acknowledged in two judgments.[34]

The Charter has been also referred to by some common judges (*giudici comuni*, i.e., ordinary and administrative courts[35]), for example, in a judgment of the *Tribunale* of Salerno on 21 April 2008.[36] Actually these judges were the main actors of the second group of judgments where the Charter has been applied directly, and in a hard rather than in a soft or persuasive way. The first

---

Rivista Italiana di Diritto del Lavoro, 2009, III, 147–189, 182 ff.; F Amici, V Papa and E Sacca, "L'uso giurisprudenziale della Carta di Nizza", www.lex.unict.it; V Sciarabba, *Tra fonti e corti: diritti e principi fondamentali in Europa*, Giuffrè, Milano, 2008, 144–145; M Cartabia and A Celotto, "La giustizia costituzionale in Italia dopo la Carta di Nizza", in *Giur. cost.*, 2002, 4477 ff.

28 Caruso and Militello, 2009, 182 ff. Almost all the judgments quoted here are reviewed in that article.

29 Corte di Cassazione, Sez. I, 16 October 2007, n. 21748.

30 Corte Costituzionale, sentenza n. 135/2002, available at www.cortecostituzionale.it.

31 Corte di Cassazione, Sez. III, 9 July 2008, n. 18849.

32 Corte Costituzionale, sentenza n. 438/2008, available at www.cortecostituzionale.it.

33 Corte di Cassazione, Sez. III, 3 July 2008, n. 18203 where the Corte di Cassazione used the new condition of the Charter under the Reform Treaty for considering decisions nos 348 and 349/2007 of the Constitutional Court.

34 Corte Costituzionale, n. 251/2008 and 349/2007, both available at www.cortecostituzinale.it. The Italian Constitutional Court has used the Charter in other decisions: sent. n. 135/2002, sent. n. 445 del 2002; sent. n. 49, 148 and 307/2003; sent. n. 382 2004; sent. n. 45 and 345, ord. n. 154 and n. 464/ 2005; sent. n. 190, 393 and 394/2006; sent. n. 349/2007 and ord. n. 93 and 266/ 2007. See Sciarabba, 2008, 144.

35 Among others: *Tribunale* of Avellino of 2 March 2001; T.A.R. Emilia Romagna, 20 June 2002 n. 959; T.A.R. Sicilia, 10 December 2003 n. 79. See Sciarabba, 2008, 144; T.A.R. Marche, 23 February 2004, n. 67.

36 Quoted by Caruso and Militello, 2009, 185.

case to be cited concerns the decision of the *Corte di Appello* of Roma[37], which decided to apply Article 47 of the Charter of Nice directly although this document lacked binding legal force. This episode has been strongly criticized by scholars since it was based on an evident misunderstanding of the Charter. A decision of the *Corte d'Appello* of Florence applied Article 34.2 (social security and social assistance) of the Charter in order to argue the necessary non-application of a domestic norm in a case concerning discrimination between regular and non-regular foreigners.[38] Another relevant case is that of a decision of the *Tribunale* of Ravenna, which decided to disapply the domestic law conflicting with the Charter of Fundamental Rights for the same reason.[39] There are other cases in which Italian judges have quoted the Charter, looking at it as a possible ground for arguing the fundamental nature of the protection in the event of unjustified dismissal (Article 30 of the Charter), despite the fact that many national constitutions do not include such a right in their letter.[40]

Furthermore, the Charter is seen as a fundamental element to be taken into account when reconstructing the general legal frame applicable for solving a concrete case because of its nature as a compendium of the common constitutional traditions. This is the idea behind two interesting cases of the *Corte d'Appello* of Roma regarding Article 31 of the Charter.[41] After the coming into force of the Lisbon Treaty, the Charter was referred to in two judgments of the *Corte di Cassazione*, regarding, respectively, professional deskilling[42] (where the Charter was recalled *ad adiuvandum*), and the relationship between parents (irregular extra-EU foreigners) and their children.[43]

In conclusion, although the Italian judges have referred to the Charter often, in the majority of cases they rely on it just to enrich their motivations while just in few cases the judges have acknowledged a direct effect and applicability to its provisions, by not applying conflicting domestic norms.

There have also been cases where the Charter of Fundamental Rights was confused with other EU legal materials. The most famous case is the *Federfarma* judgment of the State Council (*Consiglio di Stato*).[44] In this decision, the State Council identified another exception to the *Cilfit* doctrine[45], following a very

37 Corte d'Appello di Roma, Sez. lavoro – ordinanza 11 April 2002.

38 Corte d'Appello di Firenze, 9 June 2007.

39 Tribunale di Ravenna, 16 January 2008.

40 Corte di Cassazione, 11 November 2002, n. 15822.

41 Corte d'Appello di Roma, 4 October 2007 and 6 June 2008.

42 Corte di Cassazione, 2 February 2010, n. 2352.

43 Corte di Cassazione, Sex. I, 19 January 2010, n. 823.

44 Cons. St., sez. V, sent. n. 4207/ 2005.

45 In the well known *Cilfit* case, where it excluded the duty of the national judge of last instance to raise the question, also when: "*previous decisions to the Court have already dealt with the point of law in question, irrespective of the nature of the proceedings which led to those decisions, even though the questions at issue are not strictly identical.*" (emphasis added). This is further confirmed by Art. 104, para. 3, of the ECJ Rules of procedure, where no distinction can be traced (under this perspective) between the preliminary ruling and other proceedings.

eccentric reasoning: since a contested discipline had been interpreted by the Constitutional Court in a certain way, it had to be conceived as constitutional in nature since the interpretative judgment of the Italian Constitutional Court '*had been issued by the Constitutional Court to safeguard the right to health, which amounts to a "counter-limit" to European law insofar as it is situated in an area, that of fundamental rights*'.[46] As a result of this characterization, '*it, therefore, made no sense to refer to the ECJ for a preliminary ruling which cannot be taken into account*'[47], i.e., which was immaterial to the case[48]: '*If we cannot use the ECJ's decision, why refer to the ECJ?*'. This rhetoric seems to be the essence of the State Council's decision. The *Federfarma* case, however, is just one of many judgments based on an evident misunderstanding of the basic elements of EC/EU law by the Italian national judges: in *Federfarma*, the State Council confused the Charter of Fundamental Rights of the EU with the Nice Treaty.[49]

It is interesting to have a look at the academic debate. On the one hand, it has been said that such a utilization of the Charter by the national judges can be explained by the closeness of many provisions of the document with the national constitutional provisions devoted to fundamental rights: in this sense, the Charter would be an opportunity to overcome the rigid opposition to the rigid vision of the counter-limits doctrine.[50] On the other hand, as was pointed out by Cartabia and Celotto[51], this document was not perceived as something revolutionary, since it codifies years of ECJ case law and reflects years of dialectic interaction between the ECJ and the Constitutional Courts. That is why – so far at least – it cannot be argued that the Charter had a great impact on the Italian Constitutional Court's case law.

Some authors[52] have also stressed – but this goes beyond the issue of the Charter of Fundamental Rights – the risk of a new climate of activism (writing

---

The State Council interpreted this case as a test of utility/necessity of the decision of the Court. ECJ, Case C-283/81, *SRL Cilfit e Lanificio di Gavardo SPA v. Ministero della Sanità*, 1982. ECR 3415.

46 G Itzcovich, "Fundamental Rights, Legal Disorder and Legitimacy: The Federfarma Case", Jean Monnet Working Paper, 12/08, http://centers.law.nyu.edu/jeanmonnet/papers/08/081201.html, 2008, 17.

47 Cons. St., sez. V, sent. n. 4207/ 2005.

48 Itzcovich, 2008, 17.

49 See O Pollicino, "Il difficile riconoscimento delle implicazioni della supremazia del diritto europeo: una discutibile pronuncia del Consiglio di Stato (A margine di Cons. St., sez. V, sent. n. 4207/ 2005)", available at www.forumcostituzionale.it, 2006.

50 On the evolution of the relationship between the Italian Constitutional Court and the ECJ, see: A Tizzano, "Die Italienische Corte Costituzionale und der Gerichtshof der Europäischen Union", *Europäische Grundrechte Zeitung*, 2010, 1 ff; A Tizzano, "La Corte di giustizia delle Comunità europee e i diritti nazionali", *Il Diritto dell'Unione Europea*, 2005, 839–852; A Tizzano, "Ancora sui rapporti tra Corti europee: principi comunitari e c.d. controlimiti costituzionali", *Il Diritto dell'Unione Europea*, 2007, 734–744.

51 Cartabia and Celotto, 2002, 4480.

52 See M Cartabia, "L'ora dei diritti fondamentali nell'Unione europea", in M Cartabia (ed.), *I diritti in azione*, il Mulino, Bologna, 2007, 13–66, 58; M Cartabia, "'Taking dialogue seriously'.

about a '*judicial colonialism*') in the rights field by the ECJ, underlining the danger connected to some judgments in the field of family and marriage law but, here again, there is no evidence of such a thesis, at least from examining the Italian scenario.

3. THE EUROPEAN CONVENTION ON HUMAN RIGHTS

If the EC/EU law is perceived as a very peculiar extra-national law, something similar may be said with regard to the European Convention on Human Rights (ECHR), as the Italian Constitutional Court has acknowledged over the years. However if the Italian Constitutional Court has, after a period of strong resistance, admitted the particular status of EU law under Article 11 of the Constitution, the same could not be said with regard to the status of the ECHR in the Italian legal system. In this regard we should differentiate the position taken by constitutional scholarship from the position of the Constitutional Court.

In relation to the former, long before the adoption of Article 117, paragraph 1, legal scholars had tried to find a constitutional basis for the ECHR in order to justify a higher position for the Convention in the hierarchy of law. That basis has been identified by a first group of authors in Article 10 of the Italian Constitution, by a second group in Article 11, and by third group in Article 2.[53] According to the first thesis, the ECHR includes general rules which are part of the generally recognised tenets of international law, to which Article 10 attributes a special status. This would imply that the ECHR rules, independently of any formal ratification, could find direct access, at a constitutional level, to the Italian legal system through its duty, provided by Article 10, to conform to the tenets of international law. According to the second group of authors, the ECHR's constitutional foundation could be found in Article 11 of the Italian Constitution, which admits '*the limitations of sovereignty necessary for an order that ensures peace and justice among nations*'. With regard to the third view, the reference to the inviolable rights recognized and guaranteed by Article 2 of the Constitution is taken into consideration. This clause would allow constitutional protection for 'new fundamental rights' arising after the adoption of the Constitution of 1948.

The renewed need for a judicial dialogue at the time of constitutional activism in the European Union", *Jean Monnet Working paper*, 12/07, 2007, www.jeanmonnetprogram.org/papers/07/071201.html. Cartabia's conclusion stems from the analysis of cases like *K.B.*, *Richards* and *Kreil*.

53 Art. 2 of the Italian Constitution provides that: "*The Republic recognises and guarantees the inviolable rights of the person, as an individual and in the social groups where human personality is expressed. The Republic expects that the fundamental duties of political, economic and social solidarity be fulfilled*".

Among these rights, those provided by the ECHR would find a (constitutional) place.

In its case law, the Constitutional Court has not shown any great enthusiasm towards these attempts to give special constitutional protection to the ECHR. In relation to Article 10 of the Constitution, the Constitutional Court has specified that the privileged constitutional status enjoyed by the tenets of international law as generally recognized rules cannot extend to international obligations – as is the case of the ECHR – undertaken by the state under an international treaty.[54]

Regarding Article 11, the Constitutional Court, treating the issue as if it were beyond dispute[55] affirmed that no international treaty – irrespective of its subject area – can entail any limitation on sovereignty under the terms provided by Article 11 of the Constitution. In relation to interpreting Article 2 of the Constitution as an open clause suitable to give constitutional protection to new fundamental rights, the Constitutional Court did not assess the issue with specific reference to the ECHR. In more general terms, it clarified that the guarantee provided by Article 2 is intended to refer only to the rights expressly enunciated in the Constitution and to those directly connected to them.[56]

By rejecting any attempt (before judgments nos. 348 and 349 of 2007[57], which we will discuss in depth below) to find a constitutional basis for the ECHR applied to the latter, the Constitutional Court has substantially confirmed the dualistic matrix of the Italian legal system. In particular, it has argued that the ECHR, as well as all ratified international treaties, have the same position in the hierarchy of Italian sources of law as mandated by the national statute through which they have been assigned in the internal legal order.[58]

Given the fact that the ECHR, like other international treaties, has been implemented via an ordinary statute[59], the Constitutional Court, apart from an isolated decision[60], has attributed to the ECHR the legal value proper to an ordinary statutory law prior to delivering the judgments analysed here. To put it simply, according to this jurisprudential orientation, the ECHR could be abrogated by any successive statutory law that conflicts with it. The abrogative effect, in the absence of any constitutional protection for the ECHR, would result in the rule of *lex posterior derogat legi priori* being applied in order to solve the

54 Constitutional Court, judgments No. 48/79, No. 32/60, No. 104/69, No. 14/64, No. 323/1989.

55 Constitutional Court, judgment No. 188/1980.

56 Constitutional Court, judgment No. 98/1979.

57 Corte Costituzionale, sentenze n. 348 and 349/2007, both available at www.cortecostituzionale.it.

58 Corte Costituzionale, sentenze n. 188/1980, n. 153/1987, n. 323/1989 and n. 315/1990, available at www.cortecostituzionale.it.

59 Law 4-8-1955 n. 848.

60 Decision no. 10/1993, in which, in relation to the ECHR and its ratification by ordinary law, the Constitutional Court speaks in terms of an "atypical source of law". This special status enjoyed by ECHR, according to this judgment, would place it in a higher position in the hierarchy of sources of law with respect to the ordinary legal order.

conflict between two statutes placed in the same position on the scale of sources of law.

At the end of the 1990s, the Constitutional Court, without changing its opinion about the place occupied by the ECHR in the hierarchy of Italian sources of law, began looking at the relationship between the Italian constitutional legal system and the ECHR in a different and complementary way. In particular, in decision no. 388/1999 the Court seems to have drawn a distinction, in relation to the sources of international law, between the content, the material area on which the international treaty is concluded, and its container, the ordinary statute which transforms the international source into a national law. In this regard, it is argued by the Constitutional Court that in cases where the content is characterized by the aim to protect human rights, those rights should enjoy a constitutional guarantee independent of the position of the bearer of these rights. In other words, starting with this decision, the Constitutional Court began to appear more interested in looking not only, from a formal(istic) point of view, at the static position of the ECHR in the hierarchy of the sources of law, but, from a substantial and axiological point of view, and due to its fundamental rights-based content, at its suitability to complement the recognition of inviolable fundamental rights protected by Article 2 of the Constitution.[61]

The constitutional scenario described above has been integrated by the adoption of the new Article 117, paragraph 1, in 2001, as mentioned at the beginning of the chapter.

3.1. THE SIMMENTHAL DOCTRINE FOR THE ECHR? THE VIEWPOINT OF THE NATIONAL NON-CONSTITUTIONAL JUDGES

In the meanwhile, at the beginning of the new millennium, some ordinary judges started looking at the relationship between the ECHR and the national legal order in a surprising, if not revolutionary, way, making almost no reference to 'new' Article 117, paragraph 1. The *Tribunale* of Genoa[62], in order to solve a conflict between ordinary national laws and ECHR principles, started to apply the same solution according to which, since the historic decision of the Constitutional Court in *Granital* in 1984[63], ordinary judges have applied the priority of EC law in cases of conflict between national law and EC law. It has been followed in this position by other courts of first and second instance. This

61 D Tega, "La Cedu e l'ordinamento italiano", in M. Cartabia (ed.), *I diritti in azione*, Il Mulino, Bologna, 2007, 67 ff.

62 *Tribunale* of Genoa, 23-11-2000; Corte d'Appello di Roma, 11-4-2002; Corte d'Appello di Firenze, 20-1-2005.

63 Constitutional Court, judgment, 6 June 1984, No. 180.

approach, supported by the highest ordinary and administrative courts[64], has mainly been founded on the consideration that due to the incorporation of the ECHR in the European dimension, by the bridge provided by the general principles of EU law mentioned in Article 6 of the Treaty of the European Union, it seems logical to provide the same constitutional protection to EU and ECHR law. In other words, this brave new judicial approach interpreted the well known paragraph 16 of the landmark decision of the ECJ in *Simmenthal*[65] as applying to ECHR law as well.

Based on how the Constitutional Court reacted when it first had the opportunity to take the floor in this debate, the Court's disdain towards the period of its forced silence on the interpretation of the new Article 117, paragraph 1, of the Italian Constitution with regard to the relationship between national law and the ECHR becomes apparent.

3.2. THE LANDMARK DECISIONS OF 2007

Two decisions handed down by the Italian Constitutional Court at the end of October 2007 now seem finally to be having an impact on one of the Italian Constitution's fundamental principles: the notion of openness to international law, embodied in Articles 10 and 11 of the Constitution and above all Article 117, paragraph 1, – the provision chosen by the Constitutional Court in the judgments being examined – which was added by the constitutional revision of 2001. In particular, the two decisions focus on the relationship between the Italian constitutional legal order and the ECHR.

The final outcome of the decisions being considered may be summarized as follows:

(a) Article 117, paragraph 1, of the Constitution is identified by the constitutional judges as the correct parameter to give the ECHR a higher status than domestic ordinary laws. This means that in case of conflict between the ECHR and a national statute subsequent to the statute (no. 848/1955) that gave the ECHR effect in the domestic legal system, the judge hearing the case must suspend it and request the intervention of the Constitutional Court.
(b) The Constitutional Court clearly specifies that the exact meaning of the ECHR can be ascertained only as it is interpreted by the European Court of

64 Corte di Cassazione section I, 19–07–02, No. 10542; Corte di Cassazione, section I, 11–06–2004, No. 11096; Corte di Cassazione, United Sections, 23–12–2005, No. 28507; Consiglio di Stato, section I, 9–4–2003, No. 1926.

65 ECJ Case C-106/77 *Simmenthal* [1977] ECR I-62, para. 21, according to which: "*Every national Court must in a case within its jurisdiction, apply Community law in its entirety and protect rights which the latter confers on individuals and must accordingly set aside any provision of national law which may conflict with Community law, whether prior or subsequent to the Community rule*".

Human Rights. In the cases under discussion, it is the right to property, provided by Protocol 1 and the right to a fair process, contemplated in Article 6, as 'living in the case law of the European Court of Human Rights' that are taken as parameters to value the constitutionality of the domestic law under judicial scrutiny. The first point identified under (a) deserves a separate analysis at this stage.

3.2.1. *The new parameter of Article 117, paragraph 1, of the Constitution*

It is evident that, by identifying Article 117, paragraph 1, as the constitutional parameter that enables the Constitutional Court to ascertain a possible violation of the ECHR by a successive domestic statute, the Court has managed to halt the activist approach adopted in recent years by the ordinary courts. This approach involved putting aside the statutory law conflicting with the ECHR by applying the analogy that the Constitutional Court has finally authorized ordinary judges to deal with statutes in violation of Community law after 20 years of 'bloody war' with the European Court of Justice.[66] In other words, with regard to the interpretation of the ECHR, the Constitutional Court is not willing to be bypassed by the ordinary courts. The primary role of the constitutional judges, according to the relevant decisions of the *Corte di Cassazione*[67], is to correct their (ordinary) colleagues, by stating how the difficulty of identifying the ECHR role wrongly gave rise to the judicial attitude of directly setting aside any statute in conflict with the ECHR on the main basis of the asserted 'communitarization' of the ECHR through the reference in Article 6 of the TEU.

All the remaining arguments of the Constitutional Court focus on trying to explain why this approach is not constitutionally correct. The constitutional judges recognized that the consolidated case law of the European Court of Justice has affirmed that the fundamental rights protected by the ECHR are part of the general principles of European law, and that this orientation has been codified in Article 6 of the Treaty of the European Union and extensively in the provisions of the European Charter of Fundamental Rights. Directly challenging the main grounds of reasoning used by the ordinary judges, the constitutional judges argued, however, that it is nonetheless not possible to apply, by analogy to ECHR law, the same treatment reserved to EU law. This is because, according to the constitutional judges, the ECHR legal system has distinct structural and functional legal features in comparison with the European Union legal order. This difference is confirmed, according to the constitutional judges, by the language of Article 117, paragraph 1, which distinguishes between the constraints

66 See *Granital*, *supra* n. 60. See above in this chapter.

67 As was specified above (*see* para. 4), the *Corte di Cassazione* supported the test of non-application to the case of the statutory law in conflict with the ECHR in decision No. 672/1998 and especially No. 28507/2005.

deriving 'from EU law and those deriving only from international obligations'. On this point, the Constitutional Court draws an unconvincing distinction, to which we will return later, between 'the EC provisions, which have direct effect, and the ECHR provisions, which are international law sources binding only States, without providing any direct effect in the internal legal order such as to make the national judges competent to put aside the national provisions in conflict with them'.

The peculiarities of the ECHR legal system, starting with the very intrusive powers granted to the ECtHR and the possibility of a direct access to individual justice, are not 'peculiar' enough, according to the Italian constitutional judges, to perceive any transfer of sovereignty in the terms provided by Article 11 of the Italian Constitution. Furthermore, the Constitutional Court adds, quoting the relevant case law of the ECJ[68], that the fundamental rights of the ECHR enjoy the status of general principles of EU law only in relation to national rules that are within the scope of EU law. In other words, according to the Constitutional Court, in the situation under discussion, characterized by an exclusively domestic relevance, the ECJ would have denied its jurisdiction to ascertain the eventual violation by national law of ECHR fundamental rights in their role of general principles of EU law.[69]

The Constitutional Court is well aware of the 'schizophrenic' nature of the ECHR in domestic law, considered to be an ordinary law from a formal point of view and constitutional law in its substance.[70] However, the Court still denies that the Convention deserves privileged constitutional protection with respect to 'ordinary international law'.

We have seen that the doctrine has proposed three possible interpretations in this regard: Article 10, Article 11 and Article 2 of the Constitution. In relation to the first interpretation, the Constitutional Court confirms its previous case law by arguing that the privileged constitutional status enjoyed by the tenets of international law, as generally recognized, does not extend to international obligations based on an international treaty such as the ECHR. According to the constitutional judges, however, a different conclusion is possible, where there is a small opening for a pluralistic and values-based vision in a reasoning dominated by a formal hierarchical approach, only if the international treaty in question '*reproduces general consuetudinary principles of international law*'.[71]

With regard to the second interpretive option, the Constitutional Court states that the European legal system alone has the character of an autonomous legal order, which implies the transfer of a portion of sovereignty from the national to the supranational dimension under Article 11 of the Constitution. In order to

---

68 ECJ Case C-159/90, *Society for the protection of unborn children* [1991] ECR I-4685; Case C-299/95 *Kremzow* [1998] ECR I-2629.

69 Corte Costituzionale, sentenza No. 349/2007, para. 6.1.

70 Corte Costituzionale, sentenza No. 348/2007, para. 4.3.

71 Corte Costituzionale, sentenza No. 349/2007, para. 6.1.

support this statement, the constitutional judges emphasized the constitutional parameter (Article 11) used by the ordinary judges that give constitutional protection to EU law and noted that it is not apt to obtain the same effect for the ECHR making references to the established precedent mentioned above.[72] Moreover, considering that the ECHR like other international treaties (irrespective of subject matter), cannot entail a limitation on sovereignty under Article 11, the constitutional judges have rightly held that '*the ECHR is "only" a multilateral international public law Treaty which does not entail and cannot entail any limitation on sovereignty in the terms provided by Article 11 of the Constitution*'.[73]

In relation to the possible identification of a constitutional basis for the ECHR in Article 2 of the Constitution, and with reference to inviolable, constitutionally protected rights, the hope had been expressed that after a long silence on this subject, the Constitutional Court would finally follow the thesis of the speciality *ratione materiae* of the Treaties in the human rights area in relation to all other international treaties.[74] The truth is that, by basing the priority of the ECHR over conflicting national law on Article 2, the Constitutional Court would have shifted from a formal hierarchy to a substantial one. Consequently, this shift would have legitimated the judicial trend, inaugurated by the ordinary judges, of setting aside domestic national legislation that conflicts with the ECHR. This is exactly what the Constitutional Court wanted to avoid. The silence of the Court in relation to Article 2 of the Constitution is, then, not surprising.[75]

3.2.2. A possible alternative judicial path for the Constitutional Court?

The Constitutional Court, following the line emerging from its latest precedent (case 388/1999, *supra*) could have taken a different, values-based approach, and by recognizing the substantial constitutional character of the ECHR, it also could have differentiated its status from that of 'ordinary' international treaties. Instead, the Constitutional Court decided to follow an interpretation-based approach, relying on formal logic within the perspective of a hierarchy of sources of law according to which all international treaties, the ECHR included, are a step higher in that hierarchy. They no longer have the same status as ordinary

---

72 Corte Costituzionale, sentenza n. 188/1980, quoted in judgment no. 349/2007.

73 Corte Costituzionale, sentenza n. 348/2007, para. 6.1.

74 C Pinelli, "Sul trattamento giurisdizionale della CEDU e delle leggi con essa configgenti", in *Giurisprudenza costituzionale* [2008].

75 See, for a deeper analysis of the above mentioned decisions, and for a general framework of the impact of the EU and ECHR laws on the domestic jurisdictions of EU Member States G Martinico and O Pollicino (eds), *The National Judicial Treatment of the ECHR and EU Laws. A Comparative Constitutional Perspective* Europa Law Publishing, Groningen, 2010 and O Pollicino, *Allargamento dell'Europa ad est e rapporti tra Corti costituzionali e Corti europee. Verso una teoria generale dell'impatto interordinamentale del diritto sovranazionale?*, Giuffrè, Milan, 2010.

laws, but, as the Constitutional Court explained: '*they are to a degree subordinated to the Constitution, but are intermediate between the Constitution and ordinary status*'.[76] This upgrade applies to *all* international treaties ratified by Italy. Subject to the condition that they are not in conflict with the Constitution, they can then lead to the annulment by the Constitutional Court of *all* subsequent ordinary statutes in conflict with them.

Unfortunately, the clarity of this formal hierarchically-based approach has a number of drawbacks. The first drawback is the one we have already witnessed: the exclusion of any power for common judges to set aside national legislation in conflict with ECHR and the consequent risk of losing the effectiveness of ECHR law. It would be naïve to think that the *effet utile* is an exclusive prerogative of EU law. If it were possible to agree that the protection of fundamental rights must be assured in the domestic legal order in the most timely and direct way, then the same logic seems, *a fortiori*, applicable to domestic legislation conflicting with ECHR law. The second drawback is the unavoidable generalization that every judicial approach based on a certain degree of simplification implies. Is it not confusing to put the ECHR and the Treaty on Principles Governing the Activities of States in the Exploration and Use of Outer Space, Including the Moon and Other Celestial Bodies, on the same level only because they are formally both international treaties ratified by Italy?

More problematically, the choice of putting all international agreements on the same level has serious repercussions. For example, a hypothetical international treaty ratified by Italy which is in conflict with the ECHR's lesser guarantee of the freedom of expression will have to be considered, by the mere application of chronological criteria, as prevailing over the protection accorded by Article 10 of the ECHR.

Even more problematic is that equating all treaties elevates international treaties concluded by the government in the so-called simplified form to the level of ordinary treaties. According to authoritative doctrine, these treaties in simplified form are binding on the State when they are concluded on the international level, notwithstanding the absence of parliamentary approval and ratification by the president.

Following the interpretation of the Constitutional Court, these treaties will be on the same level as ordinary treaties and will equally limit the normative powers of the legislature, with the minor detail that, unlike the former, the latter have never received parliamentary approval.

In reality, behind the form, there is the substance, and in the case of the EHCR, the latter has a constitutional character, as the Constitutional Court itself has substantially admitted. This admission came about when the Constitutional

[76] Corte Costituzionale, sentenza n. 348/2007, para. 4.5.

Court noticed the 'substantial coincidence' between the principles contained in the EHCR and those included in the Constitution.[77]

The fact that the ECHR is accorded a higher value in the hierarchy of law sources than ordinary statutes does not mean that it occupies a level equal to that of the Constitution. On the contrary, the Constitutional Court clearly specifies that the status of the ECHR is intermediate, between the ordinary law and the Constitution. It is for this reason that, in the judgments being discussed, the Constitutional Court, having established that ordinary law was in conflict with Article 6 and Protocol 1 of the ECHR, examined the question whether these provisions and the relevant case law conformed to the Constitution with a positive result.

The final step of the Constitutional Court's reasoning, as we have argued above, was to declare the law unconstitutional. Then again, there is a difference of treatment with European law, which is considered to have particular status (a quasi-constitutional status, with the *caveat* pointed out in the first part of the chapter) and is consequently subordinated, not to the entire Constitution, but only to its fundamental principles. The emphasis on the aforementioned differentiation between the obligations stemming from the EU legal order and those deriving from the ECHR is perhaps the weakest point of the decisions. Instead of equating ECHR law to every other source of international law (under Article 117, paragraph 1), the Constitutional Court could have looked, not to the end, but to the beginning of the Constitution in order to identify in Article 11 the adequate constitutional parameter for the ECHR, as it has done in the past with regard to European law. The benefit of this method is that it would adopt a substantial approach aimed at underlining the constitutional nature of the ECHR provisions. The reasons adduced by the Court to justify the exclusion from Article 11 are not completely convincing. The formalistic approach to the ECHR, 'as every international Treaty cannot entail any limitation on sovereignty in the terms provided by Article 11 of the Constitution', seems to forget several key 'small details'. When the Constitution was drafted, the Founding Fathers who wrote about limitations of sovereignty in Article 11 had Italy's entrance into the United Nations in mind. In this respect, it is possible to argue that, especially in light of the latest reforms in judicial procedures under the ECHR, the latter has a greater impact on the limitation of national sovereignty than the United Nations. Moreover, the Constitutional Court's qualification of the ECHR as a 'multilateral international public law Treaty' could be put in doubt, since the European Court of Human Rights has underlined the peculiar nature of the ECHR in relation to other treaties,[78] defining it as 'a constitutional instrument of European public

---

[77] Constitutional Court, judgments no. 388/1999, no. 129/1967, no. 7/1967.

[78] In the decision *Ireland* v. *United Kingdom*, 18-1-1979 (para. 239), the ECtHR has clarified that "Unlike international Treaties of the classic kind, the Convention comprises more than mere reciprocal engagements between contracting States. It creates, over and above a network

order (*ordre public*)'.[79] Apart from this 'self-qualification argument', it should be objectively noted that it does not seem enough to cite, as the constitutional judges did, a 27-year-old precedent,[80] pursuant to which the ECHR may not entail any limitations on sovereignty in the terms provided by Article 11 of the Constitution to justify the exclusion of the constitutional protection provided by the said constitutional provision.

In 27 years, many things have changed, mainly due to Protocol XI. These changes, which in 1998 gave the ECJ compulsory jurisdiction over individual complaints, had a far reaching impact; from eliminating the jurisdiction of the Council of Ministers to decide complaints on their merits to suppressing the role of the Commission to filter claims. It also made the hearing procedure entirely public (previously, 95% of complaints were decided in a confidential way).

In this sense, the Constitutional Court seems to forget that ECHR law, more than a legal act that could be statically 'photographed', is a dynamic process or a constitutional work in progress that is constantly emerging, thanks mainly to the growing constitutional character of Strasbourg case law. Moreover, ECHR law is slowly revealing more of its constitutional nature.[81]

Another 'historical' component undervalued by the Constitutional Court is that the Italian participation in the system of protection of fundamental rights provided by the ECHR may be considered more functional to the achievement of constitutional goals, as embodied in Article 11, to guarantee of peace and justice among nations, than was the European Economic Community originally, as it was oriented, at least directly, to economic-based goals.

3.2.3. A look at the follow up to such decisions

During the two years following the decisions commented on above, the Italian Constitutional Court had the opportunity to develop and, in a way, go beyond the position taken in the judgments of 2007. In highlighting the main features of the new developments, two paths are underlined:

(1) First, a judicial trend which, without putting in discussion the conclusion related to the rank of the ECHR in the light of the application of a formal

---

of mutual, bilateral undertakings, objective obligations which, in the words of the Preamble, benefit from a 'collective enforcement'."

79 European Court of Human Rights, 23-3-1995. *Loizidou* v. *Turkey*, para. 75.

80 Decision no. 188/1980, quoted in decision no. 349/2007.

81 In relation to the emerging constitutional character in Strasbourg case law, it is enough to recall the recent attitude of the ECtHR of identifying in its judgments, where there was a finding of a violation of the ECHR, what it considers to be an underlying systemic problem and the source of that problem. In these cases, the Court, in order to assist the condemned State in finding the appropriate solution, *suggests* the appropriate general measures to adopt in order to solve the systemic problem. *See* European Court of Human Rights, 22-6-2004, *Broniowsky,* ric, 31443/96. This new proactive approach was oriented towards Italy, for the first time, some months later, with the judgment of 10-11-2004, *Sejdovic*, ric. 56581/00.

sources of law-based approach, is directed to favour to the latter the application of a substantive value-based approach.

(2) Second, a partial *revirement* with regard to the position taken in the decision of 2007, commented on above, in relation to the identified parameter able to give a constitutional basis to the ECHR provisions.

With regard to the first novelty, in decisions nos. 348 and 349 of 2007 the Constitutional Court, as has been stated above, did not pay much attention to emphasizing the added value of the ECHR in interpretative terms, because it was preoccupied with differentiating the judicial treatment of EU law and ECHR law. In the subsequent judgments, however, the constitutional judges attributed much higher value to the obligation of the political and judicial actors to respect the case law of the European Court of Human Rights. In particular, the Constitutional Court's decision no. 38 of 2008 held that the peculiarity of the ECHR provisions, within the context of the scope of application of the relevant parameter of Article 117 of Constitution, is that 'the contracting states are bound, except in the case of the ascertainment of the constitutional conformity of the ECHR provisions, to follow the interpretation that on those provisions is given by the European Court of Human Rights'.

With regard to the issue of reopening the national *res iudicata* and giving full effectiveness to the judgments of the Strasbourg judges, the Constitutional Court in 2008 expressly affirmed that '*this Court wants to address the legislator with the aim to make the urgent invitation to adopt the reforms needed in order to give the possibility to the nation legal order need to conform itself to the decisions of the European Court of Human Rights which have ascertained a violation, in the criminal proceeding, of Article 6 of the ECHR*'.[82]

The most evident amplification, in relation to the Constitutional Court's previous decisions and their binding effect, of the case law of the European Court of Human Rights, however, is evidenced by the obligation imposed on the common national judges and on the Constitutional Court itself to give to the ECHR the meaning which emerges in the case law of the European Court of Human Rights. After having underlined that the common judge is obliged to do everything possible to interpret the national legislation in conformity to the ECHR as interpreted by the European Court of Human Rights, in a more recent decision rendered at the end of 2009, the constitutional judges added that: '*the Constitutional Court itself is prevented from putting in discussion the interpretation that the European Court of Strasbourg, in its case law, has given to the ECHR*'.[83]

This is not the only passage from which it is possible to infer that the new strategy of the Constitutional Court seems to favour the application of a

82 Corte Costituzionale, sentenza 39/2008.

83 Corte Costituzionale, sentenza 311/2009.

substantive and values-based logic founded on a pluralistic vision of the relationship between legal orders, rather than a logic based on the formal hierarchy among the sources of law. Needless to say, the former is the opposite of what emerged in the reasoning of decisions nos. 348 and 349 of 2007, commented on above. In particular, the decisions of 2007 argued that '*it must be emphasised that the judgments of the Strasbourg Court are not unconditionally binding for the purposes of the verification of the constitutionality of national laws. Such controls must always aim to establish a reasonable balance between the duties flowing from international law obligations, as imposed by Article 117(1) of the Constitution and the safeguarding of the constitutionally protected interests contained in other articles of the Constitution.*'.

More recently, in decision no. 311 of 2009, the constitutional judges not only amplified the binding value of the Strasbourg case law, but they also developed the idea of a bidirectional balancing between conflicting norms which until that point was only unidirectionally expressed in the abovementioned judgments of 2007.

By applying a value-based theory and not a source of law-based theory, the unidirectional sense of the statement in the decisions of 2007 recognizes that a provision of the ECHR, despite its conformity with the Constitution, could be set aside by the Constitutional Court itself. This is due to the fact that the ordinary statute, in contrast to the ECHR, is found to safeguard the relevant constitutional principles better. The Constitutional Court, in the above mentioned decision no. 317 of 2009, instead integrated the described value-based reasoning, admitting that the ECHR, as interpreted by the European Court of Human Rights, could prevail over the Constitution itself, if the protection of the relevant fundamental rights is higher at the ECHR level than at the constitutional level.

In relation to the second element that has been identified, it is worthwhile to recall a passage of decisions nos. 348 and 349 of 2007 relating to the opening of the Constitutional Court to identify an alternative constitutional parameter for the ECHR in place of Article 117, paragraph 1. In those decisions, the Court found that ECHR provisions are excluded from the reach of Article 10(1) of the Constitution, which provides for the automatic adaptation of Italian law with the generally recognized rules of international law on the ground that the said constitutional provision '*applies exclusively to general principles and the rules of customary international, whilst it does not apply to rules contained in international treaties which do not reproduce principles or rules of customary international law*'. In contrast, in decision no. 311 of 2009, the Constitutional Court admitted for the first time, *apertis verbis*, the possibility that Article 10 of the Constitution could constitute the relevant parameter of the ECHR in cases where the relevant provisions of the ECHR are found to be the expression of a rule of customary international law that is generally recognized.

Independently of how many times in the future the Constitutional Court will accord such a status to the ECHR provisions, the statement noted above of the Constitutional Court is of utmost importance because it confirms that the constitutional judges could imagine, at least for some provisions of the ECHR, a formal constitutional status that gives some provisions the strength to prevail over the Constitution itself.

4. THE KEY ROLE OF THE ORDINARY JUDGES: FROM THE RISK OF A 'DOUBLE STANDARD' TO THE REACTION OF THE ORDINARY JUDGES

Most of all, the refusal of the Constitutional Court to assimilate the status of EU law and ECHR law under the 'common constitutional roof' of Article 11 creates a double standard with the protection of fundamental rights embodied in the ECHR. This double standard is rendered by the fact that depending on whether the Constitutional Court applies only to domestic situations (in which case they have an intermediate level between ordinary statutes and constitutional law) or to situations of EU law relevance. It is evident that, by creating a situation of reverse discrimination, it may lead to a violation of the constitutional principle of equality embodied in Article 3 of the Italian Constitution.

In the end, despite these criticisms, it would not be fair to underline only the negative aspects of the path taken by the Constitutional Court with these decisions. The main positive effect is that the qualification of the Constitutional Court as the only tribunal in Italy competent to solve conflicts between ordinary laws and the ECHR, is forced to take up the challenge to become the arbiter of the protection of fundamental rights in that critical area in which the constitutional dimension encounters the supranational and the international ones. This could, perhaps, lead to an attenuation of the judicial hesitation the Court has shown up to now. Moreover, this could also lead to the Court taking an active role in the new season of European co-operative constitutionalism. It is not a coincidence that, four months later, after 50 years, in the middle of February 2008[84], the Constitutional Court requested a preliminary ruling under Article 267 TFEU from the ECJ.

After the Constitutional Court's *dicta* banning common judges from putting aside the national law that was in conflict with the ECHR was published in 2007, many speculated on how the said judges would react to this ban. Apart from some early exceptions[85], the majority of the common judges have shown

84 See above in this chapter.

85 See, for example, *Tribunale* of Ravenna, decision 501/2007, in which the judges expressly refused to raise the constitutionality issue, in the light of Article 117, par. 1, before the Constitutional Court and preferred instead to put aside the national law in contrast with the

obedience to the rule handed down by the Constitutional Court. This does not imply, however, a definitive loss for the common judge of any interpretative freedom. On the contrary, as the Constitutional Court previously underlined[86], the common judge has to challenge his or her interpretative tools by attempting to interpret the national law in conformity with the ECHR. Only after that will he be allowed to raise the question of constitutionality before the Constitutional Court, assuming that the contrast still persists.

When looking at the development of the relationship between the ECHR and national law, one can find further evidence of the key role played by the common judges in the multilevel system: since they are involved in the application of all the legal materials present in such a context, the analysis of their case law is essential for understating the real impact of the extra-national laws on the domestic systems.

Another feature of the Italian case is the fact that the treatment of the external legal materials (i.e. ECHR and EU) is a motive of conflict between common and constitutional judges. Finally, when looking at the case law of the common judges – and despite what the Constitutional Court has argued over the years – one can appreciate a sort of convergence in the judicial treatment, favoured by the extension of the *Simmenthal* doctrine to the ECHR.

ECHR. See I Carlotto, "I giudici comuni e gli obblighi internazionali dopo le sentenze n. 348 e n. 349 del 2007 della Corte costituzionale: un'analisi sul seguito giurisprudenziale", in www.associazionedeicostituzionalisti.it [2008]; and E Lamarque, "Vincolo alle leggi statali e regionali derivante dagli obblighi internazionali nella giurisprudenza comune", in www.associazionedeicostituzionalisti.it [2009].

86 Italian Constitutional Court, decision n. 239/2009, in which the constitutional judges specified that, in the absence of an attempt by the common judge to interpret the national law in conformity with the ECHR, the issue of constitutionality raised by the *a quo* judge will be rejected as inadmissible.

CHAPTER 10

THE NETHERLANDS

A CASE OF CONSTITUTIONAL LEAPFROG

Fundamental rights protection under the Constitution, the ECHR and the EU Charter in the Netherlands

Monica Claes* and Gert Jan Leenknegt**

1. INTRODUCTION

In comparative treatises on judicial constitutional review or on the relationship between international and national law, or even on the domestic effect of European law, the Netherlands usually features as an outlier, an exception which provides the interesting contrast with most of the other systems.[1] The Netherlands legal system does not provide for *judicial review of the constitutionality* of Acts of Parliament. Article 120 of the Constitution even explicitly precludes the courts to review the constitutionality of statutes and of treaties. The roots of this stance on judicial constitutional review go deep, and go back to a time when the principle of parliamentary sovereignty reigned everywhere in Europe. In most other countries, constitutional review has since those days been introduced, most often at the occasion of a regime change after times of war or dictatorship (such as in Germany, Spain or Hungary), a change

* Monica Claes is professor of European and Comparative Constitutional Law at Maastricht University. This paper has been drafted in the framework of the EuNaCon project, financed by the European Research Council.

** Gert Jan Leenknegt is associate professor of Constitutional Law at Tilburg University.

1 Examples can be found in A-M Slaughter, A Stone Sweet and JHH Weiler, The European Courts and National Courts: Doctrine And Jurisprudence (Oxford: Hart Publishing, 1997); H Keller and A Stone Sweet, The Reception of the ECHR in National Legal Orders (Oxford: Oxford University Press, 2008); V Ferreres Comella, Constitutional Courts and Democratic Values. A European Perspective (Yale University Press, 2009).

in the system of government (France) or the federalisation of a previously unitary state (Belgium). None of these events – *constitutional moments* – have taken place in the Netherlands. Neither have the Netherlands joined the smaller group of European States which have more recently embraced a form of decentralised review (Sweden, Finland, Norway, Denmark).[2]

The Netherlands assumes a similarly exceptional position when it comes to the *domestic effect of treaties and of European law*. In the spectrum between the extremes of monism and dualism, the Netherlands approach comes closer to the monist extreme than any other Member State of the European Union. No other national system in the EU is so unconditionally open and receptive to international treaties as the Netherlands, where directly effective treaties and decisions of international organisations are given a rank even over and above the Constitution. They are considered to form part of the broader constitution[3] of the Netherlands.[4] In fact, in the absence of constitutional review of primary legislation, they operate as a default constitution for the review of such legislation. This is true even during the legislative process, when legislation is drafted by government and debated by parliament, and when its legality is reviewed by the Council of State.[5] In all of these instances, international and European law can be said to have more authority and be more efficient in guiding and limiting the government and the legislature, than the Constitution.[6] The ECHR has in practice become the chief document for human rights protection in the Netherlands. In the near future, it may have to compete for that position with the EU Charter. The Constitution, in many countries the focal point for fundamental rights protection, seems to have become much less relevant in this respect in the Dutch discourse.

This chapter aims to explain this *exception hollandaise*, and to analyse how in a monist legal system with no constitutional court, the courts relate to the

2 These systems differ from the American system in that the constitution was amended in those countries in order to explicitly provide for the power of every court to review the constitutionality of acts. In addition, review is restricted to cases in which the unconstitutionality is obvious or blatant.

3 In the Dutch language, a distinction can be made between the document containing the formal constitution (*'grondwet'*) and the category of fundamental rules and principles governing the relationship between the State organs, between the domestic and the international legal order and between the State and the individuals (*'constitutie'*).

4 This is interesting in itself, since it would be more correct to say that these treaties are supra-constitutional. This is further developed below.

5 So W Konijnenbelt, 'Grondwetsinterpretatie door de Raad van State: wetgevingsadvisering en grondrechtenbepalingen in de Grondwet', in R de Lange, *Wetgever en grondrechten*, (Nijmegen: WLP, 2009, p.61, at p.74–75.

6 See e.g. JA Peters, 'Geen groen maar rijp voorstel. De angst voor constitutionele toetsing (Het wetsontwerp-Halsema)', in PPT Bovend'Eert and others (eds), *De staat van wetgeving. Opstellen aangeboden aan prof. mr. C.A.J.M. Kortmann*, Deventer: Kluwer (2009), 99–127; LFM Verhey, 'Wetgever en constitutie: enkele beschouwingen over de mug en de olifant', in HR Schouten (ed), *Wetgever en constitutie*, Vereniging voor wetgeving en wetgevingsbeleid (Nijmegen: Wolf Legal Publishers 2009), 1.

European Court of Justice (ECJ) and the European Court of Human Rights (ECtHR). We will also look into the on-going debate on whether or not the Dutch position should on both points be changed and brought in line with the structures that exist in most EU Member States. A proposal is currently pending to amend the Constitution and provide for some form of judicial constitutional review.[7] With respect to the prevailing supra-constitutionality of treaties and EU law, the debate turns on whether the absolute primacy of international law should become conditional upon compliance with the fundamental core of the Dutch Constitution. The contribution concludes with some observations on the place of Dutch courts in the European judicial dialogue.

2. INTRODUCING THE ACTORS: A BRIEF OVERVIEW OF THE DUTCH COURT SYSTEM

Judicial constitutional review is explicitly ruled out in the Constitution, and no Constitutional Court exists. Moreover, there is not one single court that is the sole highest court for the country. Instead, several courts and tribunals serve as the highest courts in their respective fields of jurisdiction. The Supreme Court of the Netherlands (*Hoge Raad der Nederlanden*, HR) is the highest court in civil law, criminal law, and fiscal law, while the Administrative Jurisdiction Division of the Council of State (*Afdeling bestuursrechtspraak van de Raad van State*, AbRvS) is the highest court in general administrative law.[8] In addition, there are two specialized highest administrative courts.[9] The Central Appeals Court (*Centrale Raad van Beroep*, CRvB) decides on conflicts in the field of social security, and on cases regarding the legal position of civil servants;[10] the competence of the Trade and Industry Appeals Tribunal (*College van Beroep voor het Bedrijfsleven*, CBb) concentrates on the field of social and economic administrative law.[11]

All of these courts are highest courts in their respective sectors. They decide on the application and interpretation of the law within their fields of jurisdiction, including international and European law. These highest courts may disagree about the interpretation of the Constitution or on the direct effect, the

---

7 The proposal, known as the 'Halsema proposal' to amend the Constitution has been adopted in the first reading in both houses of Parliament: Act of 25 February 2009, *Stb.* 120; for the second reading, see: *Kamerstukken II* 2009/2010, no. 32 334. See para. 3 on the substance of the proposal.

8 Article 26 ff., 37 of the Wet op de Raad van State.

9 Until 2000, the Tariff Commission was the single highest court with regard to customs issues; it is now part of the Amsterdam Court of Appeal.

10 Www.rechtspraak.nl/Gerechten/CRvB/Over+de+Raad/English+summary.htm; see also the Beroepswet.

11 Www.rechtspraak.nl/Gerechten/CBb/; see also the Wet bestuursrechtspraak bedrijfsorganisatie (Wbbo).

interpretation and application of the relevant provision of international law, and none of them is bound by the decision of the other on these matters. None of them holds 'ultimate' authority to decide such a conflict.[12] As a result, the case law of these courts sometimes differs with respect to the application of international law, even on the same international or European legal provision.[13]

3. CONSTITUTIONAL REVIEW: NOT A JUDICIAL MATTER

Article 120 of the Dutch Constitution prohibits constitutional review of Acts of Parliament by the courts. The provision has been interpreted as precluding review both of the substance and the procedural aspects of those Acts.[14] In addition, the *Hoge Raad* has understood article 120 as also prohibiting review in the light of the Statute of the Kingdom of the Netherlands,[15] and of unwritten principles of Dutch constitutional law.[16]

Article 120 of the Constitution is the successor to article 131, which used to provide even more radically that 'Acts of Parliament are inviolable'.[17] But from the very inception of that provision in 1814, the issue of judicial constitutional review has occupied pride of place in the debate. One of the fathers of the Dutch Constitution, Thorbecke, was a fierce defender of judicial constitutional review, but he had to give way to the legislature who wanted to protect its position in the Constitution. The chief argument against judicial review is traditionally couched in terms of democracy and the anti-majoritarian difficulty. The debate is on-going to this day. Many scholars now hold the view that the courts should be awarded the power of constitutional review in some form, in order to strengthen

---

12 The presidents of the various courts have regular meetings and consultations, but these mainly regard the uniform interpretation and application of the General Administrative Law Act (algemene wet bestuursrecht); see MC Burkens e.a., *Beginselen van de democratische rechtsstaat*, 6th ed., Kluwer 2006, p. 163, footnote. Furthermore, there is a Council for the Judiciary (*Raad voor de Rechtspraak*), which performs mainly budgetary and supportive functions within the judiciary, but no coordinating tasks in a substantive sense.

13 A recent example is the case on the SGP, a political party which in its statutes excludes women as candidates. Women cannot feature on the list of the SGP for the elections. The Administrative Jurisdiction Division of the Council of State did not find a breach of article 7 of the CEDAW in a case brought before it concerning the financing of the SGP (AbRvS, 5 december 2007, LJN BB9493), the Hoge Raad did (Hoge Raad, 9 April 2010 (LJN BK4549 and BK4547). See e.g. on article 7 ICESCR, HRBM Kummeling, 'Internationaal recht in de Nederlandse rechtsorde. Over een onduidelijke grondwet(gever) en verwarrende jurisprudentie', in: *De Grondwet als voorwerp van aanhoudende zorg* (Burkens-bundel), Zwolle 1995, p. 369–386 (377 ff.).

14 Hoge Raad 27 January 1961, *NJ* 1963, 248 (Van den Bergh/Staat der Nederlanden).

15 The Statute of the Kingdom of the Netherlands (Statuut voor het Koninkrijk der Nederlanden) is the legal basis for the relations between the countries that make up the Kingdom of the Netherlands: the Netherlands and the islands of Aruba, Curaçao and St. Maarten.

16 Hoge Raad 14 April 1989, *NJ* 1989, 469 (Harmonisatiewet).

17 In the 1983 revision of the Constitution, the provision was amended to its current wordings.

the authority of the Constitution in general, or of the fundamental rights catalogue in its first chapter in particular.[18]

In 2002, the debate was given a new impulse when a private members bill was tabled in the Lower House (the Halsema proposal). The proposal is to add a second paragraph to article 120, giving the courts the power to review Acts of Parliament in the light of listed so-called classical fundamental rights in the Constitution.[19] The original proposal was to introduce a decentralized or diffuse system of review; the setting up of a Constitutional Court was not envisaged.[20] The bill was adopted in the first reading,[21] albeit that the majority in the Upper House was extremely slim: the bill was carried by a majority of one single vote. The second reading is currently taking place. During this second stage, the Constitution requires approval by a two-thirds majority in both houses. This may well prove difficult given the legislative history of the proposal so far, and the extremely critical treatment the proposal met, especially in the Upper House.

In contrast to Acts of Parliament, all secondary legislative acts (such as Royal decrees, and ministerial, provincial and municipal by-laws) as well as administrative decisions, may be reviewed by any court in the light of the Constitution. But in those cases too, the ECHR and EU law often steal the light.

Review of the constitutionality of bills is first and foremost the responsibility of the legislature.[22] The Government must consider the constitutionality of the bills it tables.[23] The Lower House of the States General (*Tweede Kamer der Staten-Generaal*) must consider the constitutionality of the bills it debates. However, the focus of its attention will mainly be on the political and socio-economical aspects of those bills.[24] Limited staff and means make it rather utopian that the Lower House would indeed carry out a careful and thorough analysis of the legal constitutional implications of the legislative proposals before them, irrespective of the political issues involved. The Upper House (*Eerste Kamer*) acts more as a

---

18 For an overview see G Van der Schijff, Rethinking the justification for constitutional review of legislation in the Netherlands, p. 129, footnote 1, in: RAJ van Gestel en J van Schooten (red.), *Europa & de toekomst van de nationale wetgever* (Eijlanderbundel), Nijmegen.

19 *Kamerstukken II*, 2001/2002, 28 331, nrs. 1–3.

20 Since the proposal was tabled, the creation of a constitutional court has been suggested and proposed several times, see further below.

21 Constitutional amendments under article 137 of the constitution require two readings in consecutive legislatures, whereby they must be adopted with simple majority in both Houses in the first reading and a two thirds majority in the second reading.

22 'The legislature' is here used to refer to the primary legislature, i.e. the Government, and the States-General (Lower House and Upper House) acting together (article 81 of the Constitution).

23 See Aanwijzingen voor de regelgeving.

24 See e.g. LFM Verhey, Wetgever en constitutie: enkele beschouwingen over de mug en de olifant, in: *Wetgever en constitutie, Verslag van het symposium, gehouden op 23 april 2009 ter gelegenheid van de algemene ledenvergadering van de vereniging voor wetgeving en wetgevingsbeleid*, (Nijmegen: WLP, 2009); and L De Lange (ed), *Wetgever en grondrechten* (Nijmegen: WLP, 2008).

chambre de réflexion, and is less political in character than the Lower House.[25] The Upper House traditionally pays special attention to constitutionality issues and to questions regarding compliance with international and European law. Yet, it lacks both the power to initiate bills, and to amend them; it can either accept or reject bills that have already been passed by the Lower House.[26]

During the legislative procedure, the Advisory Division of the *Council of State* advises Government and Parliament on all bills and proposals for Royal decrees.[27] In its advice, the Council traditionally focuses on three elements in its analysis of proposed legislation: policy considerations, legality issues and technical questions. The review of the constitutionality of a proposal forms part of the second element of the analysis. Nevertheless, the Council seems to give more weight, in its advice, to compatibility with treaties and European law (both ECHR and EU law), than to the constitutionality of the proposal.[28] Since especially the ECHR often substantially overlaps with what the Constitution prescribes, it will not matter a great deal for the result of the analysis whether the advice is based on the Constitution or on treaties or European law. It is, however, telling for the authority of the Constitution that an alleged incompatibility with treaties or European law seems to carry more weight in the legislative procedure, than an alleged unconstitutionality. One explanation could be that there is no deterrent in the form of judicial review when it comes to the constitutionality of legislation. As for to the compatibility with treaties and European law, there is a double deterrent, in the form of judicial review by the Dutch courts and the threat of an infringement of Treaty law or European law and the State liability which may ensue from it, declared by a European Court.

---

25 CAJM Kortmann, *Constitutioneel recht*, 5th ed. (Deventer: Kluwer, 2005), p 238–239; PPT Bovend'eert and HRBM Kummeling, *Het Nederlandse parlement*, 10th ed. (Deventer: Kluwer, 2004), p. 34 ff.

26 Articles 82–87 of the Constitution. When the Eerste Kamer does encounter a problem with a certain part or provision of a bill, and persists that the bill cannot be accepted because of that, it can suspend the reading of that bill to allow for the government and the Tweede Kamer to make the necessary amendments to that bill, and then reassume the second reading of the amended bill. Thus, it avoids having to reject the bill completely and definitively. This so-called 'novelle-procedure' has no explicit constitutional basis, but is an accepted constitutional practice. Bovend'Eert and Kummeling, *supra*, p. 34–35, 43, 188.

27 Article 73, para. 1, of the Constitution.

28 See e.g. LFM Verhey, Wetgever en constitutie: enkele beschouwingen over de mug en de olifant, in: *Wetgever en constitutie, Verslag van het symposium, gehouden op 23 april 2009 ter gelegenheid van de algemene ledenvergadering van de vereniging voor wetgeving en wetgevingsbeleid*, (Nijmegen: WLP, 2009). In its 2009 Annual Report, the Council of State pledged that it would step up its efforts with respect to the constitutional review of legislative proposals. The Council admitted that in the past, it had often been rather short and vague in its analysis of the compatibility of legislative proposals on their compatibility with the Dutch Constitution, see Annual Report (2009), p. 54. To that end, a constitutional council was set up inside the Council of State, in order to pull together the existing constitutional knowledge and know how in the Council, so as to be able to work more efficiently and more effectively.

As this is only an *advice*, neither government nor parliament are legally bound by it. However, if the Council declares that in its view a bill or proposed decree is unconstitutional, government and parliament will not dismiss it lightly. Such criticism will usually lead to the amendment or withdrawal of the bill or proposed decree. Nevertheless, the Council of State is often not very outspoken in its advice, and usually restricts itself to saying that 'there may be some tension between the proposal and the Constitution' or to asking the government to amplify its analysis of the legality of the proposed piece of legislation.[29]

4. DUTCH LAW AND INTERNATIONAL LAW

With regard to the effect of international law in the national legal system, the Netherlands again stands out and is situated at the extreme end towards monism on the monism-dualism spectrum. Dutch monism – the notion that international law is effective in the domestic legal order in and of itself – is not codified and was accepted by the Supreme Court in 1919.[30] Article 93 of the Constitution, originally introduced in 1953, restricts the direct effect (having direct effect on citizens' rights and freedoms) to those provisions in international treaties that have been published. Article 94 of the Constitution awards priority to directly effective provisions of treaties and decisions of international organisations over conflicting provisions of national law, including the Constitution itself. This priority of directly effective international law over the Constitution is exceptional when compared to other States in Europe. It implies that in Dutch legal thinking, international treaties are generally given a higher rank than the Constitution. They are, so to say, supra-constitutional.

As with the constitutionality of legislation, the conformity of national norms with international law is assessed in various instances: it is, of course, not just the business of the courts. The Government and both Houses of Parliament must make sure during the legislative process that they do not adopt legislation which infringes treaties which the Netherlands have ratified, or EU law. As already explained, the Council of State conducts a review of the compatibility with international treaties in general and ECHR and EU law in particular, when it looks into the legality of proposed legislation it is asked to advise on. Article 94 makes all Dutch courts review courts, and this is true also when the provision under review is contained in an Act of Parliament. If national law conflicts with directly applicable international law, the courts must apply international law,

---

29 For a critique, see GJ Schutte, 'Op weg naar volwaardige constitutionele toetsing', in *Verslag van het symposium van de Raad van State op 25 mei 2010. Rol en betekenis van de Grondwet*, 2010, pp. 25–30.

30 Hoge Raad 3 March 1919, *NJ* 1919, 371 (Grenstractaat Aken).

setting aside the national norm.[31] The provision that is thus set aside is kept intact and remains valid, but it is not applied to the case in hand.

For a couple of years, there has been some debate as to whether a limit should be placed on the now unconditional openness towards international law. Should a provision of international law, which infringes the core values of the Dutch Constitution, really be given effect in the Dutch legal order and bind citizens? Or should the effect of international law be limited to the extent that it passes muster in the light of the core principles of the Dutch Constitution?[32] The debate is complicated by the fact that the Constitution does not identify its core principles, and that several of the principles that are generally considered to be fundamental – such as the principle of legality and the rule of law – are not mentioned in the text of the Constitution. The question is debated at a time when critics, both in academia and in the public debate, have challenged the authority of the 'activist' European Court of Human Rights for curbing the sovereignty of the Netherlands.[33] Support for EU integration has dropped. In addition, there is an undeniable trend towards nationalism in the Netherlands, demonstrated also by the rise of populist parties (mainly Geert Wilders' PVV) and anti-Islam movements. The Dutch, like other peoples and states, are in search of their national identity.[34] In a sense, one could say, the call for a reconsideration of the absolute priority of international law reflects these nationalistic tendencies in the country. For others, however, it is a legitimate rethinking of a legal constitutional question, in the light of the present day circumstances of globalization, in which international law has developed in a way the drafters of the 1953 Constitution could not have imagined.

---

31 Article 94 of the Constitution contains no addressee, and it would seem therefore, that the duty to set aside conflicting provisions of national law applies equally to other state bodies, including administrative authorities, so CAJM Kortmann, *Constitutioneel Recht*, 6th ed., (Deventer: Kluwer, 2008), p. 189.

32 So e.g. Raad van State, Annual Report 2009; M van Emmerik, 'De Nederlandse Grondwet in een veellagige rechtsorde', *Rechtsgeleerd Magazijn Themis* (2008), p. 145–161; LFM Besselink and RA Wessel, *De invloed van ontwikkelingen in de internationale rechtsorde op de doorwerking naar Nederlands constitutioneel recht. Een 'neo-monistische' benadering* (Kluwer 2009).

33 See for instance T Baudet, 'Het Europees Hof voor de Rechten van de Mens vormt een ernstige inbreuk op de democratie', NRC 13 November 2010; T Zwart, 'Bied dat mensenrechtenhof weerwerk', NRC 17 January 2011.

34 Consider, for instance, the mandate of the Staatscommissie, which was asked to draft a preamble, which according to some could be the expression of the national identity in the Constitution. The comment of Princess Màxima, the Argentinian wife of the successor to the throne, at the occasion of the presentation of a report 'Identification with the Netherlands', that after seven years of residence in the country she had not yet discovered '*the* Dutch identity', caused an enormous public upheaval and critical comments in the Lower House, not only from Wilders' party, but also of the Christian democrats (CDA) and the liberals (VVD). Immigrants are required to integrate and follow citizenship courses, which focus on Dutch traditions and Dutch culture. On a more prosaic note, consider the TV game show 'I love Holland' – which focuses entirely on Dutch culture and traditions, Dutch music, and the Dutch language – or the rise of traditional Delft blue and traditional colours and patterns in pottery, interior decorating and gadgets.

In 2008, the Government passed the question concerning these core principles of the Dutch Constitution and whether they should be protected against international law to the *Staatscommissie Grondwet*, an advisory body set up to advise the Government on constitutional amendment in a number of areas. The *Staatscommissie* suggested that a general provision *(algemene bepaling)* be inserted in the Constitution, making explicit some of its core values, such as respect for fundamental rights and constitutional principles, the rule of law and the principle of legality. In line with the traditional openness to the international legal order, the commission emphasised that the 'fundamental rights' referred to in the provision included those derived from international treaties. In the view of the commission, therefore, international fundamental rights, including the ECHR and the EU Charter, are among the core principles of the Dutch Constitution.

Treaties impinging on these principles should not be entered into: the Government should not conclude them and Parliament should not give its approval to such treaties. The commission was split, however, on the question as to what the courts should do if after entry into force, a treaty would prove to conflict with these core values, or if a decision of an international organisation would breach them. Half of the members defended the view that article 94 of the Constitution should be amended so as to mandate the courts to enforce the core principles in those cases, and to let them prevail over those treaty provisions and conflicting decisions of international organisations. The remaining half advised that article 94 should remain unaltered.

5. THE DUTCH CONSTITUTION AND THE EUROPEAN UNION: DON'T ASK, DON'T TELL

The Dutch Constitution does not mention the EU or EU membership. Where relevant,[35] the effect of European law in the Dutch legal order is considered to be governed by the provisions of the Constitution that apply to international law in general.[36] Thus, no special majority is required in Parliament to approve treaties attributing competences to the EU, and there are no legal limits to such attribution. The government is under a constitutional obligation to contribute to the development of the European legal order, which would seem to come under the wider obligation to contribute to the development of the international legal order laid down in article 90 of the Constitution. The Constitution continues to apply when the government or other state organs act in the context of the European Union. These bodies cannot, for instance, infringe on their

35 As explained above, the tendency in Dutch legal thinking still is that European law takes effect with precedence over national law in the Dutch legal order, on the basis of the very nature of European law, because the ECJ has so stated it in *Van Gend en Loos* and *Costa v ENEL*.

36 Articles 90 to 94 of the Constitution.

constitutional obligations when participating in the Council of Ministers or other organs in which they represent the state. The relationship between the Dutch government and parliament is governed by the usual rules, and the ordinary principles of ministerial responsibility and the duty to inform the Parliament and so forth continue to apply. EU law is effective and takes precedence, even over the Constitution, on the basis of Article 93 and 94 of the Constitution, or of its own motion.

There is some discussion on the question whether a Europe provision should be inserted into the Dutch Constitution.[37] In its advice on the approval bill for the Treaty Establishing a Constitution for Europe, the Council of State mentioned the issue as well, but it did not draw conclusions. A private member's bill is currently pending, proposing to amend the Constitution so as to require a two-thirds majority in both Houses of Parliament for Acts approving Treaties amending the Treaty on the European Union.[38] Some other suggestions have been made as well. One of those is to introduce a simplified legislative procedure with respect to the implementation of EU law.

On the whole, there is a growing awareness of the fact that the EU is missing in the Constitution is an anomaly. Yet, none of the proposed concrete amendments have gained enough support to see the light of day. The Constitution is difficult to amend, and moreover, there is no legal urgency to introduce the EU into the Constitution. The Constitution as it stands does not hinder Dutch membership and does not prevent European law from having its full force and effect in the Dutch legal order. In addition, while the view that Europe at times harms Dutch interests is currently widespread, it is not considered to threaten the principles and values of the Constitution. Accordingly, while the absence of the EU may be an anomaly, it does not complicate membership and the added value of one or more provisions concerning the EU and EU membership is not obvious.

The *Staatscommissie* advised the Government to consider introducing the words *'and European'* in the text of Article 90 of the Constitution which would accordingly read: 'The [government][39] contributes to the development of the international *and European* legal order'. The addition seems rather meagre at first

---

37 See e.g. the motion by senator Jurgens, *Parliamentary proceedings (Senate)* 2000/01, 26 200 VI, nr. 65, nr. 37b; LFM Besselink et al., *De Nederlandse Grondwet en de Europese Unie*, Groningen, 2002; ML van Emmerik, De Nederlandse Grondwet in een veellagige rechtsorde, in: *RMThemis* 2008, nr. 4, pp 145–161 (155 ff.). See more recently the advice of the Scientific Council for Government Policy (*Wetenschappelijke Raad voor het regeringsbeleid – WRR*) has proposed two additions to the Constitution: a provision that explicitly states the value and objectives of the Dutch EU-membership, and a provision that aims to ensure the autonomy of the Netherlands within the framework of the EU. The Government rejected the proposals as vague.

38 The so-called Van der Staaij-proposal, 30.874 (R1818).

39 A majority also advised that the obligation should be addressed to all public bodies, rather than to the government alone, in order to reflect that international relations and international law are no longer the responsibility of the government alone.

sight, but the commission preferred this to a mere statement that 'The Netherlands is a member of the European Union'. Indeed, its inclusion in Article 90 imposes a constitutional obligation to participate in the EU and to do so with a view to the development of the European legal order. The provision has to be read in the context of the entire constitution, which binds the government and other public officials who act in the context of European integration: the Constitution continues to apply to their participation in the European context. The EU would not be mentioned in so many words, but feature under the broader concept 'European', which also covers the ECHR.

The Constitution also does not contain provisions on the domestic effect and application of EU law specifically, and the general provisions therefore would seem to apply. The case law of the ECJ on direct effect and primacy of EU law fell on constitutionally fertile ground in the Netherlands and never posed a serious problem.[40] Yet, while the constitutional provisions seem highly apt to allow for the direct effect and primacy of EU law, the prevailing view is that they have no bearing on the effect of EU law. There is still some discussion on the question whether the basis for the primacy of European law over Dutch law is to be found in Articles 93 and 94 of the Constitution, or rather in the case law of the ECJ or EU law itself.[41] Many argue that the effect of EU law in the national legal order is based on the case law of the ECJ, rather than on the Constitution.[42] The courts have never dwelled much on the issue, but in a very brief and thinly motivated judgment in 2004, the *Hoge Raad* merely stated that Articles 93 and 94 of the Constitution do not apply to EU law.[43] It should be remembered, however, that these provisions were inserted in the Constitution in 1953 precisely with a view to facilitate the Dutch participation in the rapidly developing process of European integration. Moreover, in the course of the 1983 revision of the Constitution the Government confirmed that European law takes effect with primacy through these provisions of the Constitution.[44] On this view, then, the Constitution is still very open towards EU law, but the direct effect and primacy of EU law are based on the acceptance of these principles in the Constitution, not on case law of the ECJ or the nature of EU law itself. In any case, the issue remains rather theoretical

40 See M Claes and B De Witte, 'Report on The Netherlands', in *The European Courts and National Courts – Doctrine and Jurisprudence. Legal Change in its Social Context*, A-M Slaughter, A Stone Sweet en JHH Weiler (eds) (Oxford, Hart Publishing, 1998), 171–195; B De Witte, 'Do Not Mention the Word: Sovereignty in Two Europhile Countries, Belgium and the Netherlands', in N Walker (ed), *Sovereignty in Transition*, (Oxford: Hart Publishing, 2003), 351-366.

41 For the discussion on this issue, see: E.A. Alkema, noot onder HR 2 November 2004, *NJ* 2005, 80; LFM Besselink e.a., *De Nederlandse Grondwet en de Europese Unie*, Groningen 2002, pp. 28–39; ML van Emmerik, De Nederlandse Grondwet in een veellagige rechtsorde, in: *RMThemis* 2008, nr. 4, pp 145–161 (149–150); LFM Besselink, noot onder HR 1 October 2003, LJN: AO8913 en HR 2 November 2004, LJN: AR1797, in: *SEW* 2005, nr. 7/8, pp 336–339.

42 More specifically the *Van Gend en Loos* and *Costa/Enel* cases.

43 Supreme Court 2 November 2004, *LJN* AR1797 (www.rechtspraak.nl).

44 Van Emmerik, *supra*, p. 149; Besselink, *supra* 2005.

and the courts adopt a highly pragmatic approach. Nor is this the subject of much academic debate when compared to countries like Germany or Italy. One way or the other, Dutch courts are held to give directly applicable EU law effect in the Netherlands, setting aside Dutch law if necessary, and they do.

6. EU LAW IN DUTCH COURTS: ROUTINE, OR IS IT?

The national judges embraced their European mandate as developed in the case law of the ECJ easily, and much more smoothly than in any of the other founding Member States.[45] Much of the explanation for this can be found precisely in the absence of a constitutional court, in the Dutch version of monism and a pragmatic approach to such grand concepts as sovereignty, transfer of powers and integration.

Dutch courts seem to be keen to make references to the ECJ, and they have been since the very beginning. Ten of the first thirteen questions referred to the ECJ came from Dutch courts. Between 1952 and 2008, Dutch courts referred a total of 719 references.[46] This is roughly in the same range as the number of references made by French (755) courts during the same period.[47] Among the Dutch courts, the high number of references by the Trade and Industry Appeals Tribunal can be explained by the fact that it is the competent specialized court in matters in the field of socio-economic administrative law. Dutch references enjoy a very good reputation in Luxembourg: they are usually well drafted, contain the necessary information, and suggest directions for answers.[48] In fact, the high number of questions referred may well be caused by the high level of expertise on EU law in these highest courts.[49]

When compared to other Member States, the lower courts strikingly refer less often than highest courts, while in most Member States, it is the lower courts which make more references than highest courts. Evidence is scarce on this issue, but there may be several explanations for this. Firstly, suspending the procedure and making a reference delays the decision of the court by a considerable period of time. Lower courts often prefer to decide a case quickly in order to satisfy the

---

45 For a comparative analysis, see M Claes, *The National Courts' Mandate in the European Constitution* (Oxford: Hart Publishing, 2006).

46 Between 1952 and 2008, the Administrative Jurisdiction Division of the Council of State made 59 references, the Supreme Court 177, and the Administrative High Court referred 46 times, the Trade and Industry Appeals Tribunal 137 times. The Tariff Commission, which no longer exists as a separate tribunal since 2000, asked for a preliminary ruling 34 times. Other courts or tribunals made266 references.

47 Annual report of the ECJ and the Court of First Instance, http://curia.europa.eu/jcms/jcms/Jo2_7000/ annual-report, Statistics, table 20: General trend in the work of the Court (1952–2008) – New references for a preliminary ruling (by Member State and by court or tribunal).

48 Information received from a source in the ECJ.

49 See www.europa-nu.nl/id/vi32he7z6bzj/nieuws/nederlandse_en_belgische_rechters_vaak?ctx=vg9obtulslrn, citing a spokesperson for the ECJ.

parties involved, and therefore refrain from asking for a preliminary ruling unless they really have to.[50] Secondly, decisions of the highest courts have strong authority in the lower courts. Complex issues of European law are passed on to the highest courts more often than in other countries. In any case, lower courts can be confident that the highest courts will in principle be willing to apply EU law and to make a reference if they should consider it necessary. The Dutch highest courts have never been among those which were reluctant to make references. Lower courts most likely have not felt the need to 'revolt' against the highest courts and team up with the ECJ, as may have been the case in other countries.[51]Also, European law has not had a central position in law programmes at Dutch universities until relatively recently. Therefore, many of the current judges are not very familiar with substantive European law, especially with regard to the protection of human rights. Perhaps these judges tend to avoid judging cases on the basis of European law, and rather decide cases on arguments derived from national law or the ECHR when possible. Of course, many of these circumstances may be relevant in other European countries, too, but we suspect that they play a stronger role in the Dutch legal system when compared to other countries.

EU law is part of daily legal practice and EU law permeates all areas of national law. Nevertheless, the perception still is that EU law can be highly complex and technical, and not all judges are familiar with details of substantive EU law or feel confident to apply it. Contrary to the smooth acceptance in principle of EU law in the domestic legal order, the practice appears less comforting. EU law is still very much seen as 'foreign law'.[52] Transforming national courts in veritable *juges communs de droit européen* requires a lot more than acceptance in principle of that role. To some extent, this is probably a matter of time, and for the younger generation of judges, this task may well be less daunting than it is for older judges. In the meantime, efforts are made to assist the courts.

Justices and legal staff take part in seminars on European Union Law as a form of the *education permanente* which is provided for by the *Raad voor de Rechtspraak*.[53] A complicating factor is, however, that the frequency of cases with a European law aspect is still low for many judges who are not specialised in EU law, so that in practice it remains difficult for them to build up a solid experience.

---

50 S Prechal, RH van Ooik, JH Jans & KJM Mortelmans, *'Europeanisation' of the Law: Consequences for the Dutch Judiciary*, Research Memoranda nr. 2.vol.1, 2005, p. 13 (the text is available on www.rechtspraak.nl/gerechten/rvdr).

51 For an explanation of the national courts acceptance of the European mandate along these lines, see K Alter, Establishing the Supremacy of European Law: The Making of an International Rule of Law in Europe (Oxford University Press, 2001).

52 Prechal, Van Ooik, Jans and Mortelmans, *supra*, p. 4–6.

53 The Council for the Judiciary is part of the judiciary system, but does not administer justice itself. The Council supports the courts with respect to allocation of budgets, supervision of financial management, personnel policy, ICT, housing. It promotes quality within the judiciary system and advises on new legislation, which has implications for how justice is administered.

In 2000, the Dutch Minister of Justice presented a Project Plan concerning the reinforcement of the European law knowledge infrastructure for the judiciary, known as 'the Eurinfra project'.[54] This project was set up to cope with the problem of the identification of EU law cases, the accessibility of sources of EU law, and the insufficient knowledge of EU law among judges. As a result of this project, judges and staff lawyers have access via web technology by entering *Porta Europea*, as a subpart of the overall web system, *Porta Iuris*, to sources of European law in a user-friendly and rapid manner from their desks.[55]

One of the most important results of the Eurinfra project is the creation of a Network of court coordinators for EU law (*Netwerk gerechtscoördinatoren Europees recht*). At this moment the nineteen district-courts, the five courts of appeal and the two specialised administrative courts, the Council of State and the Supreme Court have designated in their court so-called 'court coordinators on European Law' (CCE's).

These coordinators form a network to facilitate the sharing of information on EU law. Within their own court they collect questions from judges and staff members in the field of EU law, give advice or refer these questions to experts. This network of coordinators on EU law, chaired by the President of the Trade and Industry Appeals Tribunal, is supported by a justice and a senior law clerk. These latter from time to time act as experts on questions coming from the CCE network.

None of the highest courts in the Netherlands has a research unit dedicated specifically to EU law or ECHR law. The library of the Supreme Court produces summaries of all ECHR and ECJ case law, which can be accessed by the judges. It is for the individual judges to keep their expertise with respect to ECHR and ECJ case law up to date. If a judge feels that a specific case requires more information on a subject of European law or ECHR law, further research is conducted by the Research Bureau of the Supreme Court. The Bureau is not dedicated to issues of European or ECHR law, but supports the work of the Supreme Court on any area within its competence.

Roughly the same applies to the Administrative Jurisdiction Division. The judges are supposed to have adequate knowledge of European law and ECHR

54 Www.rechtspraak.nl/NR/rdonlyres/5C1D99EC-AB32-4BD9-A65E-744A34539097/0/Eurinfra2007NL.pdf; most of the information in this paragraph was provided by RR Winter, president of the Trade and Industry Appeals Tribunal.

55 The following sources are available: Dutch legislation and regulations (in force and consolidated); European conventions and treaties; European legislation; Netherlands implementation regulations; Dutch case law; decisions of the ECJ, the GC and of the ECtHR; cases pending before the ECJ (including references as for preliminary rulings); texts and commentaries from inter alia the leading Dutch legal journals; decisions of Netherlands Courts and Tribunals in cases in which European law has been applied or explained; a toolkit with checklists (such as checklist concerning the reference for preliminary rulings), manuals and tutorials on the basis of handbooks and training materials; a 'source of information', including inter alia information by and about the network of courts coordinators European Law (CCE); a 'news column' (Commission, Council, ICER, etc.).

law. The supporting staff provides the necessary information with respect to all relevant legal topics, including international and European law.

Within the Trade and Industry Appeals Tribunal, the expertise of individual judges supposedly suffices in most cases where EU law or ECHR law is involved. When this is not the case, the Network of court coordinators for EU law can be of assistance. Although the Tribunal is a rather small court – 18 justices, legal staff, law clerks and administration staff, altogether approximately 60 people – the Court employs a researcher who concentrates specifically on EU law.

At the Central Appeals Court too, the assumption is that the expertise of individual judges should suffice. Basic issues, such as the application of article 6 of the ECHR, are dealt with properly by all judges. When a case involves a more complex issue of international law (including EU and ECHR law), the case is referred to the International Chamber of the Court, which consists of judges with specific expertise on the relevant matters.[56]

7. THE ECtHR: A SUBSTITUTE CONSTITUTIONAL COURT?

The influence of the ECtHR case law, and of the Convention itself, on Dutch legal practice can hardly be overestimated. With respect to the protection of fundamental rights, the Convention has become a 'substitute constitution', so much even that the *Staatscommissie Grondwet* did not feel it necessary to insert fundamental rights into the Constitution, if they were already included in the ECHR.[57] As the Dutch Constitution prohibits judicial constitutional review of Acts of Parliament, review in the light of international treaties is the only alternative in the hands of the courts. The Netherlands are a party to many human rights treaties, both in the context of the UN and the Council of Europe, but for Dutch legal practice the ECHR is without a doubt the single most important treaty among those. Even when alleged fundamental rights violations concern subordinate legislation or administrative acts, which the courts may review against the fundamental rights provisions in the Constitution, the ECHR is often used alongside or instead of the Constitution. The ECHR may also offer additional protection, as many of its provisions have a wider scope than the corresponding articles of the Dutch Constitution. An example is article 8 of the ECHR, which the ECtHR has interpreted broadly as covering the protection of the environment,[58] while article 10 of the Constitution does not. Furthermore, the ECtHR case law has developed a vast body of case law on the notion of

56 Information provided by the 'Afdeling voorlichting en communicatie' (information and communications department) of the Central Appeals Court.

57 Rapport van de Staatscommissie Grondwet, 2010.

58 *Lopez Ostra v. Spain*, 16798/90 [1994] ECHR 46 (9 December 1994).

proportionality, which has become increasingly important for the fundamental rights protection by Dutch courts.

The ECHR has become the baseline for the domestic system of fundamental rights protection, so much so that the ECHR – clearly intended to offer minimum protection and to introduce a subsidiary protection mechanism – has come to be seen as *the* standard. Dutch courts tend to feel bound by the interpretation given by the ECtHR, and often seem to feel that they are not in a position to offer a higher level of protection at the national level.[59] Paradoxically, the ECtHR's case law may thus have a chilling effect on fundamental rights protection in the Netherlands.

8. COMPETITION FROM THE OTHER EUROPE? THE ECJ AND FUNDAMENTAL RIGHTS

The ECJ has so far been much less influential for the protection of fundamental rights,[60] though there have been cases in which EU law was of more assistance than the ECHR. A striking case, is that of *Eman and Sevinger* concerning voting rights for Dutch nationals living in Aruba, where the ECJ did find a breach of the equality principle, while the ECtHR in a very similar case did not.[61]

Whether the impact of EU law and the ECJ will increase with the entry into force of the EU Charter is difficult to predict. Politically, there has been much resistance against the inclusion of the EU Charter in the Constitutional Treaty. In part, this reluctance had to do with the constitutional aura of the Charter, but others opposed the idea of an EU Charter because it would jeopardize the ECRH. In the process of de-constitutionalisation and the negotiations of the Lisbon Treaty, the Dutch government strongly insisted on the removal of the Charter from the Treaty.

Over the past decade or so, Dutch case law shows different modes of appreciation of the EU Charter by various courts and tribunals.[62] So far, there have been no cases in which a court has explicitly applied provisions of the Charter to decide a case. Cases in which the Charter could apply are decided on other grounds and when the Charter is mentioned, it is, in most cases, only in passing. Below, we will give an summary of all cases in which the Charter is mentioned in any way.

---

59 See critically on this Dutch version of the mirror principle JH Gerards, 'Samenloop van nationale en Europese grondrechtenbepalingen – hoe moet de rechter daarmee omgaan?', 1 *Tijdschrift voor Constitutioneel Recht* (2010), p. 224–255.

60 The market freedoms are not here considered as fundamental rights.

61 Case C-300/04 *Eman and Sevinger* ECR [2006] ECR 1–8055.

62 We must limit our overview to the case law that has been published through www.rechtspraak.nl. This database contains all the case law of the Administrative Jurisdiction Division of the Council of State, and a broad selection of case law from other courts (selected by those courts themselves).

Initially, courts seemed to *avoid giving an opinion concerning the character or substance* of the Charter. In six cases decided by lower courts between 2001 and 2003, when the Charter was merely a document solemnly proclaimed by the European institutions, plaintiffs invoked the Charter in their arguments, but the courts did not dwell on the character or content of the Charter, or even mention it, and concentrated on other elements to decide the case.[63]

After 2003, when the Charter was made an integral part of the Draft Treaty Establishing a European Constitution, it *featured in the arguments* supporting the decisions of Dutch courts in various ways. In the period between 2003 and 2008, the Supreme Court, several lower courts, and the Administrative Jurisdiction Division of the Council of State simply mentioned the Charter in nine cases but they did not specify its character or substance.[64] In three cases (2007–2008), district courts referred to the preambles of directives and framework decisions, which in turn refer to the Charter, but then decided the case without using the Charter in their reasoning.[65]In three cases, the Charter was mentioned briefly along with the corresponding provisions of the ECHR, but without any statement on the character or substance of the Charter.[66]

In some cases, a court simply stated that a *contested decision did not conflict* with the rights and freedoms laid down in the Charter. In three cases (2002, 2009), plaintiffs invoked rights in the Charter, and the courts took into consideration the substance of the arguments of the plaintiffs, but without making an explicit reference to the Charter. The courts rejected the arguments of the plaintiffs on substantive grounds, and did not touch upon the character of

63 Gerechtshof 's-Hertogenbosch 17 December 2001, 95/03084, www.rechtspraak.nl, LJN: AE5186; Rechtbank 's-Gravenhage 14 November 2002, KG 02/1190, www.rechtspraak.nl, LJN: AF0505; Rechtbank Rotterdam 11 March 2003, 02/00092 meded, www.rechtspraak.nl, LJN: AF5745; Rechtbank Rotterdam 11 March 2003, 02/00091meded, www.rechtspraak.nl, LJN: AF5735; Rechtbank Zutphen 8 October 2009, 102240, www.rechtspraak.nl, LJN: BK4206; Raad van State 25 November 2009, 200905898/1/V3, www.rechtspraak.nl, LJN: BK4678.

64 Rechtbank 's-Gravenhage, zittingsplaats Zwolle 3 July 2008, Awb 07/35971, www.rechtspraak.nl, LJN: BD6344; Raad van State 19 December 2007, 200604981/1, www.rechtspraak.nl, LJN: BC0537; Rechtbank 's-Gravenhage, zittingsplaats Haarlem 21 December 2005, AWB 05/299, www.rechtspraak.nl, LJN: AU8416; Rechtbank 's-Gravenhage 21 December 2005, 207614, www.rechtspraak.nl, LJN: AU8410; Hoge Raad 16 January 2009, 43143, www.rechtspraak.nl, LJN: AZ6922; Gerechtshof 's-Gravenhage 5 June 2003, 02/1609, www.rechtspraak.nl, LJN: AF9613; Hoge Raad 19 May 2006, C05/157HR, www.rechtspraak.nl, LJN: AV1110; Hoge Raad 16 December 2005, C04/020/HR, www.rechtspraak.nl, LJN: AT2056.

65 Rechtbank 's-Gravenhage, zittingsplaats 's-Hertogenbosch 5 October 2007, AWB 07/10115, www.rechtspraak.nl, LJN: BB6223; Rechtbank Amsterdam 28 December 2007, 13.497.431–2006, www.rechtspraak.nl, LJN: BC9789; Rechtbank 's-Gravenhage, zittingsplaats Middelburg 3 July 2008, AWB 08/4469, www.rechtspraak.nl, LJN: BD9291.

66 Rechtbank Amsterdam, 3 July 2009, 13.497.470–2008, www.rechtspraak.nl, LJN: BJ1772; Rechtbank Amsterdam 3 July 2009, 13.497.522–2008, www.rechtspraak.nl, LJN: BJ1773; Rechtbank Amsterdam 18 September 2009, 13.497.394–2009, www.rechtspraak.nl, LJN: BK2118.

the Charter.[67] In one case (2007), the Central Appeals Court held that the contested decision did not conflict with the rights and freedoms protected by the Charter, and therefore it found no need to elaborate on the direct effect of the Charter.[68] In 2008, the Administrative Jurisdiction Division of the Council of State without discussing the character of Charter, decided that a case fell outside the scope of the Charter.[69]

An interesting line of reasoning in the Dutch case law further stresses the *intricate relation between the ECHR and the Charter.* In two cases the Administrative Jurisdiction Division of the Council of State held that the contested decision did not conflict with the rights and freedoms laid down in the ECHR, and *therefore* did not conflict with the Charter.[70] In November 2009, the Administrative Jurisdiction Division, held that since the Charter had not yet entered into force,[71] the complaint was to be understood *as if it were* a complaint based on article 1 of the First Protocol, and on article 8 of the ECHR, but it found no violation.[72] In October 2010, the Administrative Jurisdiction Division held, on grounds of a similar wording of article 47 of the Charter and article 6 ECHR, that these provisions must therefore be interpreted and applied identically.[73]

The November 2009 case is one of only five in which the *binding character of the Charter was addressed* in a more explicit manner. In 2005, the Trade and Industry Appeals Tribunal held that the Charter was not binding, as it was not a treaty in the sense of articles 93 and 94 of the Dutch Constitution. It could accordingly not prevail over Dutch law.[74] In 2007, the district court of Almelo stated that the Charter was but a 'declaration of intent', and that national legislation may regulate and limit the exercise of the fundamental rights laid down in the Charter.[75] In 2008, the Supreme Court noted that the Charter was not binding, but then stressed its importance, as well as the fact that it would acquire a binding character in the near future. In the text of the judgment, however, it is not clear whether the Charter played a role in deciding the case.[76]

---

67 Rechtbank 's-Gravenhage 14 August 2002, KG 02/953, www.rechtspraak.nl, LJN: AE6513; Rechtbank Haarlem 19 May 2009, AWB 08/3086, www.rechtspraak.nl, LJN: BI4860; Rechtbank Haarlem 19 May 2009, AWB 08/3084, www.rechtspraak.nl, LJN: BI4862.

68 Centrale Raad van Beroep 2 August 2007, 06/3938 MAW, www.rechtspraak.nl, LJN: BB1528.

69 Raad van State 20 August 2008, 200708387/1, www.rechtspraak.nl, LJN: BE8853.

70 Raad van State 22 November 2006, 200600657/1, www.rechtspraak.nl, LJN: AZ2769; Raad van State 22 November 2006, 200600612/1, www.rechtspraak.nl, LJN: AZ2766.

71 We may assume that the Court actually meant to refer to the non-binding character of the Charter until the coming into force of the Lisbon Treaty.

72 Raad van State 25 November 2009, 200807964/1/M1, www.rechtspraak.nl, LJN: BK4313.

73 Centrale Raad van Beroep 3 October 2010, 10/2968 WW, www.rechtspraak.nl, LJN: BO1242.

74 College van Beroep voor het bedrijfsleven 28 September 2005, AWB 04/474, www.rechtspraak.nl, LJN: AU3987.

75 Rechtbank Almelo 26 October 2007, 06/789 GEMWT AQ1 A, www.rechtspraak.nl, LJN: BB6684.

76 Hoge Raad 12 December 2008, 44102, www.rechtspraak.nl, LJN: BD5493.

And finally, in March 2010 the Amsterdam Court of Appeal stated that the Charter had entered into force.[77] It declared that the Charter applied together with the corresponding provisions of the ECHR, but it did not explicitly debate the substance of the Charter or the ECHR respectively.[78]

The case law shows that Dutch courts and tribunals have been reluctant to rely on the Charter to decide cases *before* the entry into force of the Lisbon Treaty. In the cases mentioned, the Charter is referred to only in passing. In three cases, all decided after the Dutch referendum on the Treaty Establishing a Constitution (1 June 2005), the courts explicitly pointed out that the Charter had no binding character. In 2008, the Supreme Court did emphasise the importance and future binding character of the Charter, perhaps in the light of the ratification by the Netherlands of the Lisbon Treaty (10 July 2008).[79] In the first case that was decided after 1 December 2009, the court acknowledged the binding character of the Charter, but it did not rule on its substance in an explicit way.

The overview further shows that Dutch courts seem to regard the ECHR and Charter as equivalent expressions of the same fundamental rights and principles. In their arguments and motivations, they tend to lump the applicable articles of the ECHR and the Convention together, and then decide the case in a general statement on their combined meaning for the case. Furthermore, they tend to rely on the ECHR rather than the Charter, perhaps not just because of its non-binding character until 1 December 2009, but also because the Convention is simply much more familiar to them. It has acquired a central place in Dutch legal practice over the last decades and therefore courts may feel more comfortable to apply it in concrete cases.

9. CAUGHT IN THE MIDDLE? DUTCH COURTS AND CONFLICTS BETWEEN ECtHR AND ECJ CASE LAW

During the debate on the Constitutional Treaty before the negative referendum, both academics and the Council of State warned that the coexistence of the ECHR and the EU Charter could create conflicts between the ECtHR and the ECJ.[80] The Council of State emphasised the importance of regular informal

77 Again, we must assume that the Court actually means that the Charter 'has become binding'.

78 Gerechtshof Amsterdam 4 March 2010, 08/00703 en 08/00704, www.rechtspraak.nl, LJN: BL6952.

79 Act of 10 July 2008, *Stb.* 301; entry into force 11 July 2008.

80 See e.g. G Overkleeft-Verburg, Het Handvest van de Grondrechten, in: *Getuigend Staatsrecht. Liber Amicorum A.K. Koekkoek*, Nijmegen, 2005, p. 176; SC van Bijsterveld, EMH Hirsch Ballin, *De integratie van het Handvest van de Grondrechten van de Europese Unie in de Constitutie van de Europese Unie* (WRR-paper), Den Haag, May 2003, p. 18–19.

consultations between both, and suggested that a coordinating mechanism should be designed to prevent clashes.

In the same period, the Dutch government saw two main problems with respect to the Charter. Firstly, it argued, EU accession to the ECHR would make the Charter superfluous. There was accordingly no need for yet another bill of rights that would make the system of protection unduly complicated. Secondly, the Charter would become substantive EU law that could result in direct claims by individual citizens against their government, leading to a competence creep on the part of the EU.[81]

Consider then the conflict of allegiance a Dutch court could be confronted with if ECJ and ECtHR should diverge on the scope and level of protection. In such a case, there is no rule awarding precedence to one over the other as a matter of principle.

The recent case law on the Charter demonstrates that Dutch courts regard the ECHR and Charter as equivalent expressions of the same fundamental rights and principles. They tend to lump together the applicable provisions of the ECHR and the Convention. Some courts have expressed the view that the Charter *must* be interpreted in conformity with the ECHR.[82] There is however no reason in EU law or in ECHR law, why the Charter could not be interpreted as offering better protection than the ECHR. Accordingly, there is some room for divergence between the two legal codes.

10. TALKING TO THE NEIGHBOURS: ON JUDICIAL DIALOGUES

Dutch courts have traditionally been active participants in European judicial dialogues. In the context of EU law, Dutch courts, including the highest courts, are keen users of the preliminary reference procedure. The type of questions varies. Some are rather technical, and seem to have a rather limited impact on other national systems but are crucial in the Dutch legal system. Other references have laid the foundations of the European legal order, such as *Van Gend en Loos*. Yet, none of the landmark cases in which the ECJ built its fundamental rights case law came from the Netherlands.[83] This may well be a consequence of the poor tradition of judicial fundamental rights protection at the time, when

81 Discussed in Van Bijsterveld and Hirsch Ballin, WRR paper 2003, p. 4–6.

82 See Gerards, *supra*, p. 242–243 and the relevant case law mentioned there.

83 Reference to the landmark cases in the field can be found in the Digest of the case law on the ECJ website. None of the cases during the formative stages were referred by a Dutch court. The only two Dutch cases on the list were direct actions, one brought by a company Emesa Sugar, C-17/98 [2000] ECR I-665, where the applicant held that the procedure before the ECJ infringed article 6 ECHR; and one by the state of the Netherlands, Case C-377/98 The Netherlands v Parliament and Council [2001] I-7079.

compared to, say, German or Italian courts. The primacy of European law was not challenged in the Netherlands – there is no Dutch version of *Solange* – and the Dutch courts accordingly did not challenge the ECJ on the issue of fundamental rights protection.

Dutch courts apply the case law of the ECJ and of the ECtHR in their daily practice and refer to it in their decisions.[84] In the field of fundamental rights protection, the ECHR has developed into the main point of reference, both for the legislature and for the courts. The courts are well aware that in multilevel systems such as the EU and the ECHR, the actual implementation and application of European law ultimately depends on the national authorities including the courts.[85]

Dutch courts also play a leading role in European judicial networks, such as the ACA-Europe, the Association the Councils of State and the Supreme Administrative Jurisdictions of the European Union.[86] Still, the Dutch courts do not seem to be convinced that there may also be a value in *exporting* their case law. While courts in other European countries make available their landmark cases, which they believe can have an impact on legal development elsewhere, in other languages, predominantly English, Dutch courts have not yet turned to translation.[87] In this respect, they do not seem convinced that they are part of a 'market of law' in which law has become a commodity, competing with other systems on the market.[88]

---

84 E de Wet, 'The Reception Process in the Netherlands and Belgium', in: H Keller & A Stone Sweet (eds.), *A Europe of Rights: The Impact of the ECHR on National Legal Systems* (Oxford University Press, 2008), p. 229–309; E Mak, 'Report on the Netherlands and Luxembourg', in: G Martinico & O Pollicino (eds.), *The National Judicial Treatment of the ECHR and EU laws: a constitutional comparative perspective* (Groningen: Europa Law Publishing, 2010), p. 303–325.

85 This is nicely illustrated by the speech of the president of the Supreme Court at the Dialogue between Judges seminar 'The Convention is yours', held at the occasion of the opening of the judicial year in Strasbourg, 2010, available at www.echr.coe.int/NR/rdonlyres/3F410EB0-4980-4562-98F1-B30641C337A5/0/DIALOGUE_2010_EN.pdf.

86 Www.aca-europe.eu/en/home_en.html. On judicial networks, see M Claes and M de Visser, 'Courts United? On European Judicial Networks', in B De Witte and A Vauchez, *The European Legal Field*, (Oxford: Hart Publishing, 2011), forthcoming; M Claes and M De Visser, 'Are You Networked Yet? On European Judicial Networks', forthcoming in *Utrecht Law Review* (2011). The same is true in other fields as well: the membership of FIDE is high in the Netherlands, the Dutch contingent often being one of the largest to attend the conferences. Several European journals published in English are based in the Netherlands, such as the Common Market Law Review and the European Constitutional Law Review. Dutch academics often publish their work in English, and Dutch universities are open and attract scholars from abroad. Dutch academia thus seems to participate much in the European academic debate.

87 On this trend, see M-C Ponthoreau, *Droit(s) constitutionnel(s) compare(s)* (Paris: Economica, 2010), at p. 140–141.

88 See for instance the work of Jan M Smits, for instance his *Legal Tourism: on Civil Codes and Constitutions beyond the State*, Tilburg, 2010.

CHAPTER 11

SPAIN

THE IMPACT OF THE EUROPEAN CONVENTION OF HUMAN RIGHTS AND THE CHARTER OF FUNDAMENTAL RIGHTS OF THE EUROPEAN UNION ON SPANISH CONSTITUTIONAL LAW: MAKE A VIRTUE OF NECESSITY

Enrique GUILLÉN LÓPEZ[*]

1. PRELIMINARY OBSERVATIONS. LAW AND RIGHTS IN THE FORMATION OF A NEW EUROPE

The European legal system is continuously evolving.[1] This new legal system recognizes that the concept of constitutionalism has provided the basis of power and guaranteed fundamental rights since the 'Declaration of the Rights of Man and of the Citizen', and fundamental rights continue to play a key role in the construction of this legal system.[2] It is worth noting, however, that the definition and mechanisms for recognizing and guaranteeing these rights have undergone

* Lecturer in Constitutional Law, Universidad de Granada, enriqueg@ugr.es. This work has been made within the framework of research project SEJ 2007-66427: "Constitutional interaction between the EU and Member States as a factor in the development of European constitutional law". I wish to thank Gregorio Cámara, Francisco Balaguer, Javier Roldán, Miguel Azpitarte, Tomás Requena, Juan Barrilao, Angelo Schillaci and Simon Campa for extremely valuable comments and discussion.

1 N Colneric, D Edward, JP Puissochet and D Ruiz Jarabo Colomer (eds.) *Une communauté de droit. Festschrift für Gil Carlos Rodríguez Iglesias* (Berliner Wissenschafts-Verlag, Berlín 2003). On ambiguity see A Rodriguez, *Unión Europea y Derechos Fundamentales* (Cívitas, Madrid 2001).

2 To the point where Europe can be described as: "The land of rights" in the sense used by MA Glendon, *Rights talk. The Impoverishment of Political Discourse* (The Free Press, New York 1991).

a major transformation with respect to their historically parallel discovery and affirmation. Specifically, during the emergence of nation-states, the concepts of 'Demos' and 'We' initiated claims for freedoms and were subsequently translated into rights. However, within the framework of European construction, rights are initially recognized and the definition of the right holder, conceived in the widest possible sense, is practically irrelevant. Several reasons can be argued to justify this strategy. The first reason is practical: bonds of solidarity between people are strengthened by their adherence to the same legal community. In other words, first the right is established and then a common political consciousness develops. The historical subject then emerges along this tentative route.

Another reason is the changing perception of entitlement to rights. It is now widely held that basic rights are the simple reflection of human dignity.[3] As a result, fundamental rights are now undisputed and as universal as their own metaphysical justification (leaving aside the profound debate about the weaknesses of the concept of human dignity as the foundation of rights). It is clear that these rights are undisputed. States sign legal instruments with other states recognizing the international nature of their citizens' rights (rights that citizens do not have to fight for). In this way, Court's confirmation of a right is constituent to the guarantee of a specific right – and the judges and courts must enforce these rights during a specific process that weighs the positions of the parties and whose effects are usually limited to those parties.

As mentioned above, the process of rights being granted without the citizen having previously fought for those rights is a very substantive change when seen from a historical perspective. During the English Revolution (the Glorious Revolution), as well as the American and French revolutions, or the years following the Second World War (with huge differences in the constituent processes), the sequence began with the identification of historical subjects (citizens, the people, slaves, workers) who form a shared consciousness. These subjects fought for liberties which were translated into legal rights and freedoms such as the freedom of belief, right to participation, right to strike, etc. These claims were then added to the social contract (sic) of what later was formalised in a constitutional document. These claims would further be developed by parliamentary debate and legislation, as well as media discussion. In the case of the French Revolution, these activities were led by political bodies because judicial independence was yet to be fully established, and this was the obvious political nature of the early concept of fundamental rights – a political nature that meant that the recognition of these rights was celebrated as a collective victory. However,

---

3 Article 10.1 of the Spanish constitution – taken from text on the concept of human dignity in Bonn's basic law (Grundgesetz). The pronounced German impact on the constitution on the subject of rights and the design of mechanisms for guaranteeing rights shows that constitutionalism is increasingly a process of evolution from earlier texts (Häberle).

much of this process has since been inverted – as we have already mentioned. The rights recognised by our states through international treaties have not been requested by popular demand. Instead, these rights have been assumed by those who did not contribute to winning them. In addition, the essentially judicial mechanisms for their guarantee lack the capacity for major social change.

'My rights are alien to me' – *I did not fight for them. I do not guarantee them. I will not use them to change the world.* Thus, fundamental rights became a part of an exclusively legal environment. The inclusive capability of these rights is limited because they are recognized through legal instruments and guaranteed judicially.[4] It is not my intention to undervalue the judicial contribution to the extension of rights, nor do I deny that certain rights have been very widely developed as a result of court decisions. However, the judicial contribution has not resulted in the creation of a new awareness of what these rights signify in the development of a new political community.[5] Both the European Convention on Human Rights and the Charter of Fundamental Rights of the European Union confer rights. However, awareness among citizens is limited to that tiny percentage of the population able to reach the European Court of Human Rights or the European Court of Justice because, for instance, they are suffering unbearable noise and smells (*López Ostra v Spain*[6]). The primary right is the right to a fair trial – rather than participation. The 'prime mover' is law such as it is established and the corresponding judicial decisions.[7] The 'prime movers' are not events arising from the all-encompassing parliamentary actions of our elected representatives – who determine the general interest using public and contradictory procedures.[8]

In short, fundamental rights have always been the indisputable assets of constitutionalism and must recover their traditionally conflictive meaning if Europe intends to overcome its appraisal as an 'emerging' legal system and instead develop into a real political community. This approach proposes a reinterpretation of the concept of constitutionalism that does not avoid the

---

4 On the limitations of partial judicial activities see F Balaguer Callejon, 'Derecho y Derechos en la Unión Europea', in J Corcuera Atienza (ed.), *La protección de los derechos fundamentales en la Unión europea* (Dyckinson, Madrid 2002).

5 "It must not be forgotten that rights only exist as an expression of power in relationships". See A Lopez Pina and I Guttierez, 'Sobre los Derechos fundamentales en Europa', in F Balaguer Callejon (ed.), *Derecho constitucional y cultura. Estudios en homenaje a Peter Häberle* (Tecnos, Madrid 2004) 495.

6 European Court of Human Rights, Case López Ostra v. Spain, 9 December 1994.

7 On the characteristics of producing regulations using case law and a comparison with legislative procedures see F Balaguer Callejon, 'Niveaux et techniques internes et internationaux de réalisation des droits en Europe' [1995] *Revue française de Droit constitutionnel.*

8 Here there is some convergence with the argument offered by F Rubio Llorente, 'Derechos fundamentales, derechos humanos y Estado de Derecho'[2006] *Fundamentos, Cuadernos monográficos de Teoría del Estado, Derecho Público e Historia constitucional* 4, 209.

consensual element and does not completely neglect the role that conflict is bound to play as a mechanism of integration.[9] It is sometimes more difficult to swim in calm and oily seas than in stormy seas. In the process of building a new political structure, we need a European political space[10] for the definition and defence of rights – so that the delicate balances achieved between the judicial and political elements in the national constitutions can be re-established. Europe could develop from a stage for raising national interests[11] into the new 'political arena'. Of course, this requires the presence of a European public opinion that has only very occasionally been glimpsed. The guiding principle in the following conceptual analysis is that it is necessary to change from territorial to ideological pluralism.

The main purpose of this paper is twofold; it will initially analyse the constitutional framework that enables the integration of supranational texts on fundamental rights; and the contribution then separately analyses the difficulties of incorporating rights from the two organizations concerned: the Council of Europe and the European Union. It should be immediately noted that there are inherent – and widely known – differences between the two structures. This difference can be expressed by noting that the Council of Europe, historically the first milestone towards a new Europe, is constituted as an instrument of legal cooperation with rights primarily based on a judicial mechanism of protection – the European Court of Human Rights. It is not the intention of this court to define a new space between individuals and society. However, this has been the aim of the EU since Maastricht when a qualitative leap was made towards political integration and constitutionalisation – a work that is still in progress. During this process, fundamental rights have occupied a predominant role in discussions about the EU and it has been necessary to specify these rights in the Charter of Fundamental Rights of the EU. These two realities have not yet converged[12] and this requires a differential treatment. However, the most

9 K Hesse, *Escritos de derecho constitucional* (Centro de Estudios Constitucionales, Madrid 1983).

10 P Häberle, '¿Existe un espacio público europeo?' [1998] *Revista de Derecho Comunitario Europeo* 3. Also see my observations E Guillen Lopez, 'El Parlamento Europeo' [2005] *Revista de derecho constitucional europe* 3. Copy available at: www.ugr.es/~redce/ReDCE3/04enriqueguillen.htm.

11 It can be seen that this approach is incorrect by observing the manner in which the states behaved before the European parliamentary elections in June 2009; and the support given for the candidacy of Durão Barroso.

12 Although the aim is contained in article 6 of the Treaty of the European Union where it says: "The Union shall accede to the European Convention for the Protection of Human Rights and Fundamental Freedom". In the judgment of some authors (Alvarez Ossorio Micheo and A Saiz Arnaiz), when this adhesion was specified, the convention became the cornerstone for the European model of fundamental rights. See A Saiz Arnaiz, 'El Tribunal de Justicia, los Tribunales Constitucionales y la tutela de los derechos fundamentales en la Unión Europea: entre el (potencial) conflicto y la (deseable) armonización. De los principios no escritos al

attractive hypothesis for the protection of fundamental rights in Europe remains the definition of community policy by a single mechanism.[13]

Furthermore, consideration of the impact will be based on the doctrine of the Spanish constitutional court – because the Spanish constitutional system has adopted the concentrated-control model established according to Kelsenian principles.[14] It is the constitutional court that leads the way and chooses the path for implementing decisions made by other legislative and judicial (such as the Supreme Court) bodies.

2. THE THEORETICAL FRAMEWORK OF THE IMPACT OF THE DOCTRINE OF THE EUROPEAN COURT OF HUMAN RIGHTS AND THE EUROPEAN COURT OF JUSTICE ON THE FUNDAMENTAL RIGHTS EXPRESSED IN THE SPANISH CONSTITUTIONAL SYSTEM. THE LEGAL INSTRUMENTS FOR INTEGRATION

The Spanish constitution of 1978 was an extremely ambitious endeavour: aiming to serve as a legal and political vehicle for a new European democracy. This objective is reflected in each chapter. However, the ambition of the Spanish constitution does not stop here – as it expresses the certainty that the intended constitutionalism is closely linked with the reality beyond our borders. Therefore, articles from other constitutions considered workable in our own society have been openly imported into the text.[15] This is not the only way in which our constitution recognizes the outside world. The international context is also

catálogo constitucional, de la autoridad judicial a la normativa' in M Cartabia, B De Witte and P Perez Tremps, *Constitución Europea y Constituciones Nacionales* (Tirant Lo Blanch, Valencia 2005), F Alvarez Ossorio Micheo, 'Los derechos fundamentales' in P Cruz Villalon (ed.) *Hacia la europeización de la Constitución Española. La adaptación de la Constitución española al marco constitucional de la Unión Europea* (Fundación BBVA, Madrid 2006).

13 See the report of the state council (Consejo de Estado) on the integration of European law in the Spanish legal code – published 14 February 2008, 268. Available at: www.consejo-estado.es/pdf/Europa.pdf.

14 See E Guillen Lopez, 'Judicial Review in Spain: The Constitutional Court' (2008) *Loyola of Los Angeles Law Review* 41.

15 This incorporation is not only about the acceptance of rules or foreign constitutional institutions (especially the German and Italian). It also touches on the principles behind the doctrines and the resolution of conflicts. See M Azpitarte Sanchez and F Balaguer Callejon, 'Das Grundgesetz als ein modell und sein einfluss auf die Spanische Verfassung von 1978' [2010] *JöR*, forthcoming and M Presno Linera, 'Impresiones de un constitucionalista español sobre la Constitución italiana en su 60° aniversario' [2008] *Giornale di Storia costituzionale* 16.

reflected in its provisions.[16] It is within a geographical, economic, and cultural context that the constitution clearly seeks to establish a variable association.

This openness is reflected in a variety of legal instruments.[17] First, among these instruments are international treaties. International agreements with other states, or other subjects of international law, are covered in Articles 93–96 of the constitution. The keynotes determining the legal position are:

1) Treaties are considered sources of law and form part of the internal legal order once officially published in Spain.[18]
2) Article 96 states that 'their provisions may only be repealed, amended, or suspended in the manner provided in the treaties themselves, or in accordance with the general rules of international law'.
3) A cohesive manner to prevent conflict between a treaty and the constitution is set out in Article 95 – which creates a preventive control mechanism under the constitutional court.[19]
4) However, the constitutional court may declare the unconstitutionality of a treaty in accordance with Article 27 of its own organic law. This has been recently verified by the constitutional court itself (judgment 38/2007[20]).[21]
5) The constitution does not clarify the exact position of treaties in the system of legal sources, and especially their relationship with the legal ordinary laws.[22] However, a council of state report on the introduction of European law in the Spanish legal system (published 14 February 2008)[23] stated that such laws had a supralegislative value when referring to the interpretation of fundamental rights and public freedoms (as a result of Article 10.2 of the Spanish constitution).
6) International treaties form a homogenous legal category,[24] yet follow varying procedures in obtaining consent from the state. The principle is the following:

---

16 A Schillaci, *Obblighi internazionali e parametro di costituzionalità*. Doctoral thesis forthcoming.

17 See "Constitutional law and integration". A Rodgriguez, *Unión Europea y Derechos Fundamentales, supra.*

18 Article 96 of the Spanish constitution.

19 See P Cruz Villalon, 'Europeización de la Constitución española: una introducción al problema', in P Cruz Villalon (ed.), *Hacia la europeización de la Constitución española, supra* In this sense, declaration 1/2004 of the constitutional court emphasises that this article is not only functional for assuring the constitutional supremacy, but also guarantees the international order established in the treaties. See legal basis (FJ) 1.

20 Constitutional Court. Decision 38/2007, 15 February 2007.

21 The consequences of unconstitutionality are discussed in detail. See legal basis (FJ) 3 of the cited decision.

22 In relation with constitution, the system offers enough certainties to establish the constitutional court as a cornerstone.

23 P. 290.

24 F Balaguer Callejon, *Fuentes del Derecho II, Ordenamiento general del Estado y Ordenamientos Autonómicos* (Tecnos, Madrid 1992).

> the more substantial the content entrenched by the treaty, the greater the requirement becomes for parliamentary participation. In that respect the article 93 of the constitution is of specific relevance as it requires that an organic law[25] is passed to accommodate a treaty if 'powers derived from the Constitution are to be vested in an international organisation or institution'. Article 94.1 specifies the types of treaties that require a prior authorization by the Cortes Generales (the Spanish parliament). While Article 94.2 states that both houses of the Cortes Generales (Congress and the Senate) need only be immediately informed of the signing of other types of treaties.

This briefly summarises the constitutional position of international treaties in the Spanish constitution. We can see immediately some elements in these regulations that will have enormous significance in the following pages. This clearly underlines the fact that although joining the EU was not expressly stated,[26] membership appeared as a hypothesis for the near future. As a result, a formal and abstract reference is made to what could occur to our legal system if 'powers derived from the Constitution are vested in an international organisation or institution.' Here we find the assumption of a technique for transferring powers (the difference between the right to exercise a power and its actual exercise is referred to in Article 150.2 of the constitution when detailing the process of conferring powers to Spain's autonomous regional communities).[27] This represents a radical innovation: ensuring, for example, the effective regulation of delegated powers; or determining the execution of judgments given by non-state judicial bodies. As the state holds the right to exercise these powers, it formally remains 'Master of the Treaties'.[28]

Article 93 of the constitution remains an essential key[29] to the understanding of the integration of European law in Spain and, especially, the relationship between the constitution and European law. It should be emphasized that the constitutional court has followed an interpretative path that is consistent with the gradual process of constitutionalisation of the European Union.[30]

---

25 A law requiring an absolute majority in Congress in a final vote on the whole of the project (article 81).

26 As occurs with other constitutions. See J De Miguel, 'España' in J Tajadura and J De Miguel (eds), *Justicia Constitucional y Unión Europea. Un estudio comparado de las experiencias de Alemania, Austria, España, Francia, Italia y Portugal* (Centro de Estudios Políticos y Constitucionales, Madrid 2008). Also see P Cruz Villalon, 'Europeización de la Constitución española. Una introducción al problema', *supra*.

27 Article 150.2.

28 The same is true of the organic law of transfer and delegation. See JA Montilla Martos, *Las leyes orgánicas de transferencia y delegación. Configuración constitucional y práctica política* (Tecnos, Madrid 1998).

29 Declaration 1/2004, 13 December 1004, FJ 2.

30 Noted in this sense by A Lopez Castillo, *Constitución e integración* (CEC, Madrid 1996).

Therefore, the Declaration 1/1992 of the constitutional court[31] concerning the possible contradiction between the Maastricht Treaty and the constitution, clearly stressed the formal nature of article 93 (and therefore the fact that it is the regulatory procedure for transferring 'the exercise of powers derived from the Constitution', but it cannot dispense with the Constitution itself, contravening or allowing a contravention of its provisions"[32]). Article 93 became more 'material' in Declaration 1/2004[33] which analysed the compatibility of the treaty establishing a constitution for Europe. In a correction to its earlier ruling, the court demonstrated its receptiveness to the true nature of European integration by the manner in which it inferred that a state instrument may have powers that go beyond the formal and procedural. This decision was justified not by the progressive 'constitutional advances' of the EU (which would perhaps be more exact, but more committed for other motives[34]); but was justified for the more prosaic reason that the earlier declaration was limited to an analysis of a specific case (an examination as to whether an exception could be made to Article 13.2 so that foreigners could vote in local elections).[35] Without denying this aspect, Article 93 is also a substantive material expression[36] of the primacy of community law as expressed in the constitutional treaty – once the counter-limits doctrine[37, 38] has been taken into account.

In comparison with the problems presented by the treaties referred to in Article 93, the approach applied to the remaining treaties that are dealt with under Article 94 is completely different in as much as the article postulates a criterion of interpretation that is related to the material content of the obligations contained in the text. This aspect is relevant to the two defining moments in the treaties: the provision of consent and the determination of the effect on the internal legal order. It was, for example, discussed whether the decision by Spain to join NATO should have been agreed using Articles 93 or 94.1 (the instrument actually relied upon in this case).[39] In addition, as Article 94 does not permit the granting of powers derived from the constitution itself, there is an excellent legal argument for denying the direct enforceability of the

31 Available at www.tribunalconstitucional.es/es/jurisprudencia/restrad/Paginas/DCC11991en.aspx.

32 Legal basis (FJ) 4.

33 Available at www.tribunalconstitucional.es.

34 More committed because it was intended from the start to open a debate about the benefits – and whether they were sufficient.

35 See legal basis (FJ) 2.

36 Both points of view can be clearly seen in legal basis (FJ) 2 of the declaration.

37 Legal basis (FJ) 2.

38 Analysis of the indicated evolution and reveals its contradictions. J De Miguel, 'Capítulo III: España' in J Tajadura and J De Miguel (eds), *Justicia constitucional y Unión Europea., supra.*

39 Instrument announced on 29 May 1982. See A Remiro Brotons, *La acción exterior del Estado* (Tecnos, Madrid 1984).

judgments of the European Court of Human Rights in the Spanish legal system.

Article 93 was used for Spain's joining the EU; while 94.1 was used as a base for ratifying the North Atlantic Treaty for NATO membership and, more relevant for this work, the European Convention on Human Rights.[40]

A second major element in the Spanish constitution that provides an opening to the outside world is the second section of Article 10. This contains an interpretive rule that operates over a specific regulatory body. Specifically, it establishes that: 'The principles relating to the fundamental rights and liberties recognized by the constitution shall be interpreted in conformity with the Universal Declaration of Human Rights and the international treaties and agreements ratified by Spain'. In its literal interpretation, Article 10.2 is not a mechanism for creating fundamental rights but instead determines a new criterion for the interpretation of such norms. The norms defining fundamental rights are restricted to those recognized by the constitution. This is the starting point for constitutional court rulings. For example, see below court judgment 236/2007 (November 7):

> 'Our case law has frequently emphasised the usefulness of international treaties ratified by Spain in order to configure the meaning and scope of fundamental rights pursuant to the terms of Article 10.2 of the Spanish constitution (constitutional court judgment 38/1981 (23 November) LC 4; 84/1989 (10 May) LC 5). In particular, we have explained the significance of "interpretation" as referred to in Article 10.2 indicating that "such international treaties and agreements do not become an autonomous canon validating the rules and acts of public authorities from the perspective of fundamental rights. If this were the case, the constitutional declaration of such rights would be superfluous, with it being sufficient for the constitutional assembly to have referred to the International Declarations of Human Rights, or in general, to the treaties to which Spain is a party on fundamental rights and public freedoms. In contrast, having made the aforementioned statement there can be no doubt that the validity of the provisions and acts appealed should be measured solely through reference to the constitutional precepts which acknowledge the rights and freedoms likely to be protected in this type of dispute, with the international texts and agreements of Article 10.2 being the interpretive source contributing to the best identification of the content of the rights whose protection is requested for this constitutional court" [constitutional court judgment 64/1991 (22 March) LC 4 (a)]'.

In short, the constitutional court considers that Article 10.2 cannot be used in an unintended manner; and that its interpretation should match the scope of the international obligations assumed by Spain. Therefore, it is these obligations that

40 Instrument of ratification 26 September 1979. In the same way as all the main Spanish reference texts on human rights, ratification occurred at the same time democracy was founded.

enable us to establish who is responsible for determining rights. Accordingly, this is not an independent channel for inferring rights that are not directly recognised in Spain (because they are not in the constitution); or indirectly (because the transfer of the exercise of regulatory powers has not been authorised). This is the key reference – and not the current of thought expressed in various international texts and court interpretations on the effects of judgments. In the same way that treaties cannot be unilaterally modified by a state, nor can the terms on which an international organization is founded be altered by that organization.

However, the situation is quite different when the ruling on rights is made by a supranational court (the European Court of Justice, for example) because in this case the framework of the law is not defined by the Spanish constitutional system while the norms defining the exercise of the right have been transferred to a supranational organization. In this case, Article 10.2 is not a factor. Put simply, we are looking at the execution of a judgment that determines which law is applicable once its exercise has been transferred by the state.

The presence of the two elements mentioned earlier as a part of the constitutional law of integration creates doctrinal difficulties. From the moment that article 10.2 was introduced in the constitution there were serious reservations by leftist political groups, fearing that rights not recognized in chapter 2 of the constitution could be introduced by this route. In particular, it was feared that this would serve as an indirect route to secure the right to private education – something not contemplated in Article 27.[41] This argument is interesting, because it nevertheless shows the fallacy of supposing that the widening of rights generates only positive impacts on the democratic nature of a legal-political structure. There are rights (such as the right to private education) that may challenge the collective definition of a society. The right to education becomes a major issue for an individual committed to a secular state. This example goes to show that the reassurance of the public via the principle that treaties provide a minimum level of protection which can only be supplemented by the national protection of rights (the maximisation principle)[42] does not preclude controversies in concrete cases on the balancing of rights.[43]

---

41 See A Rodriguez, *Unión europea y derechos fundamentales, supra.*

42 This principle is also recognised in the Charter of Fundamental Rights of the European Union (article 53). See G Camara Villar, 'Los derechos fundamentales en el proceso histórico de construcción de la Unión Europea y su valor en el Tratado Constitucional' [2005] *Revista de Derecho constitucional europeo*.4 (Available at www.ugr.es/~redce/REDCE4/articulos/01camara.htm).

43 This is also very clear in those cases where the rights are related to each other in such a way that increasing one right (for example, the freedom to information) means reconsidering another right (for example, the right to privacy). Another example is the right to abortion and the right to life.

In short, once the various concurrent elements are highlighted, it must be concluded that the Spanish constitutional framework requires reform. Such a reform is urgent and must include the essence of the European Convention on Human Rights[44] and the EU[45] in the constitution. Almost all the Spanish legal experts have emphasized that without this inclusion we will eventually undermine the legal effectiveness of the Constitution as the source of supreme law – something that has been achieved after great effort. Other problems include the fact that the constitution continues containing only generic clauses that do not account for the profound change they represent in the legal framework for citizens and public authorities. The constitution moreover lacks specific elements for rationalization of the conflicts that arise in an increasingly fragmented context.

However, there are more implications. The internal process of territorial distribution of power between the central state and the regional autonomous communities also faces a similar dilemma: an absence of a consensus about reforming the constitution means that constitutional changes are made outside the constitution and through the statutes regulating regional government. This means that the constitutional court becomes the cornerstone of the whole process, with the resulting judicial pressures. As a result of the above, a great challenge lies ahead for Spanish constitutional law.

3. THE EUROPEAN CONVENTION ON HUMAN RIGHTS AND THE CASE LAW OF THE EUROPEAN COURT OF HUMAN RIGHTS, CONFLICT AND DIALOGUE

The Spanish constitutional court uses a dual approach for the integration of decisions and judgments from the European Convention on Human Rights and the European Court of Human Rights. The first concerns the possible inclusion of these texts as parameters of constitutionality; and the second (derived logically from above) is a consequence of the role of the constitutional court in the legal system.

---

44 Including all the protocols – in the opinion of F Alvarez-Ossorio Micheo, 'Los derechos fundamentales', *supra*.

45 In this sense, see the report of the state council of 14 February 2008. For a criticism of the approach to law in the EU, M Azpitarte Sanchez, 'El Estado autonómico unitario y el Informe del Consejo de Estado sobre la inserción del Derecho europeo en el Ordenamiento Español' [2009] *Revista d'Estudis autonòmics y federals* 9. Among the doctrinal contributions see, for example, the proposals of P Cruz Villalon, F Alvarez-Ossorio Micheo, A Carmona Contreras, M Medina Guerrero and A Ruiz Robledo, *Hacia la europeización de la Constitución española, supra*.

The first question concerns the list of Spanish fundamental rights and freedoms as defined in the Constitution (Chapter 2 of part 1) in contrast to other constitutional texts. The writers of the constitution chose to recognize a specific list of rights and only allow some flexibility in the 'interpretation of those rights' (retaining the traditional distinction between creation and interpretation). In my view it was correct to conceive these rights as elements that define the scope open to citizens from a certain conception of society and state. This ought to be considered an act of foundation and was therefore made in the full awareness that new rights alter the foundations which define the society politically.[46] I do not wish to subscribe to any form of strict originalism[47] that might prevent a broader understanding of the opening clauses. However, I intend to show that the constitution is rightfully open to interpretation in terms of rights. Does the constitution prevent the creation of new rights through case law? Not if the creation is the result of action by the constitutional court. Such interpretation is justified for two reasons. Firstly, the formal argument that the constitutional court is the supreme interpreter of the constitution (Article 1 of the organic law regulating the court) and its judgments inevitably negate its characterization by Kelsen as a negative legislator. Second, the constitutional court is an adequate place within a state for discussion and debate although preferably not in majoritarian terms. The creation of new rights by international courts does not occur in such a communicative environment (unless we reduce public communication to a dialogue between courts). Therefore, the role of the international courts should be limited to simply interpreting those rights that the Spanish people believe to have arisen from human dignity.

3.1. THE THEORETICAL FRAMEWORK BEHIND THE CONSTITUTIONAL COURT. ARTICLE 10.2 AS AN INTERPRETATIVE MANDATE AND NOT AS A MECHANISM FOR CREATING NEW RIGHTS (CONSTITUTIONAL COURT JUDGMENT 236/2007)

As noted earlier, the Spanish constitutional court views Article 10.2 as suitable for handling the provisions and judgments of the European Convention on Human Rights and the European Court of Human Rights. Its efficacy is

46 We currently have a derivation of this argument in Spain with respect to the inclusion of rights in the statutes of autonomous communities. The arguments are given in LM Diez-Picazo, '¿Pueden los Estatutos de Autonomía declarar derechos, deberes y principios?' [2006] *Revista española de derecho constitucional* 78 and the answering response in F Caamano Dominguez, 'Sí, pueden: (Declaraciones de derechos y Estatutos de Autonomía)' [2007] 27 *Revista española de derecho constitucional* 79.

47 I refer to the debate regarding originalism in the American context. See a critical explanation in LG Sager, *Justice in Plainclothes. A Theory of American Constitutional Practice* (Yale University Press, New Haven 2004).

interpretative. However, this does not alter the fact that in some cases[48], the dialogue with the doctrine of the European Court of Human Rights is so fluid that there is no doctrinal distinction between the doctrine of the European court and the doctrine of the constitutional court (another factor is that once the constitutional court accepts the doctrine of the European Court of Human Rights the constitutional court makes that doctrine its own[49]). For example, in a case where the constitutional court ratified the constitutionality of an article in the criminal code penalizing genocide justification (235/2007)[50], its references to European case law were constant and formed an inherent part of each of the court's concluding arguments. In this case, it is not strictly possible to discuss the interpretative efficacy of European case law – but rather its integrative efficacy. A look at this judgment reveals that the European Convention on Human Rights and the Spanish constitution (through its supreme interpreters) are integrated within a single legal definition of rights. This reality remains implicit.

This does not, however, alter the general rule that is perfectly exemplified by the previously discussed constitutional court judgment 236/2007; the role of the European case law is effectively interpretative but interpretation cannot ignore what is already written in the constitution.

3.2. THE CONSTITUTIONAL COURT IS AS AN INSTRUMENT FOR THE PROTECTION OF FUNDAMENTAL RIGHTS ENSHRINED IN THE SPANISH CONSTITUTION – AND NOT OTHER RIGHTS

In accordance with the above, the Spanish constitutional court has maintained that its role is limited to being the ultimate guarantor[51] of fundamental rights recognized by the constitution. Among other judgments 99/2004 stipulates that: 'it is not for this court, when hearing an application for judicial review, to monitor compliance or failure of international instruments to which Spain subscribes. However, it is for this court to verify compliance or violation of

48 A systematization of the various uses of the doctrine of the European Court of Human Rights can be seen in: A Queralt Jiménez, *La interpretación de los derechos: del Tribunal de Estrasburgo al Tribunal Constitucional* (Centro de Estudios Políticos y Constitucionales, Madrid 2008).

49 See A Queralt, *supra*.

50 Constitutional Court. Decision 235/2007, 7 November 2007.

51 This characteristic of the court as an organ of protection of fundamental rights and which acts only when the ordinary guarantee of rights offered by the lower-level courts fails – was heightened by the reform of the organic law regulating the constitutional court: LO 6/2007 (24 May).

constitutional principles that recognize fundamental rights and civil liberties under review' (legal basis 3).[52]

This interpretation is contested by those observers who base their arguments on the integration of EU law with the European Convention for Human Rights.[53] For these observers, when treaties assume rights derived from European case law, these rights become rights to be observed by the state when applying EU law (and so form parameters by which the constitutional court should judge any infringement of a given right). In this way, the European Convention on Human Rights acts at the margins of Article 10.2 on cases regarding the application of EU law to state law, and Article 10.2 is used interpretively in those cases where the courts are resolving purely internal conflicts. It seems difficult with this new dynamic to insist that the Spanish constitutional court can limit its role to exclusively protecting rights enshrined in the constitution given the limited opening for interpretation offered by article 10.2. A new and more fragmented framework will open in the next two scenarios: the entry into force of the Charter of Fundamental Rights of the European Union and adhesion to the European Convention on Human Rights by the European Union (Article 6 of the Treaty of the European Union). In addition to this new and uncertain framework, we should respond by anticipating the formation of formalized structures of communication and dialogue between the European Court of Justice and the constitutional courts.[54]

3.3. ANALYSIS OF THE INTERNAL CONSTITUTIONAL CASE LAW CITED FOR VARIOUS RIGHTS UNDER THE EUROPEAN CONVENTION ON HUMAN RIGHTS. ANALYSIS OF THE RIGHTS THAT MAY CREATE A NEW FRAMEWORK[55]

We have already seen how the Spanish constitutional court makes considerable – although ambivalent – use of the doctrine of the European Court on Human

52 Constitutional Court. Decision 99/2004, 27 May 2004.

53 See for example, JA Montilla Martos, 'El derecho a la reagrupación familiar' in E Aja Fernandez (ed.), *Los derechos de los inmigrantes en España* (Tirant Lo Blanch, Valencia 2009).

54 F Balaguer Callejon, 'Los Tribunales Constitucionales en el proceso de construcción europea' (2007) *Revista de Derecho constitucional europeo* 7. Available at: www.ugr.es/~redce/REDCE7/articulos/12franciscobalaguercallejon.htm.

55 An exhaustive analysis of the question can be found in two fundamental works: A Saiz Arnaiz, *La apertura constitucional al derecho internacional y europeo de los derechos humanos: el artículo 10.2 de la Constitución española*, Consejo General del Poder Judicial, Madrid, 1999; and in the previously mentioned book by A Queralt Jiménez, *La interpretación de los derechos, supra*.

Rights.[56] In addition, since judgment 5/1981[57] the court has been unchallenged in its practice of referring to the European convention and case law of the European Court on Human Rights as if the two were indivisible. It is interesting to regard those areas where such practices have been particularly significant and the specific reasons for the ambivalence with which this doctrine is accepted. We will also see how these cases largely represent new challenges regarding fundamental rights – although some cases are only indicative of a breakdown in those mechanisms protecting rights.[58] Finally, we will discuss the possibility of amending the consequences of the doctrine of the European Court of Human Rights and differently designating some rights, even though a specific occurrence of the argument referred to in the case law of the constitutional court has not occurred.[59]

3.3.1. Sexual equality (Article 14 of the European Convention on Human Rights)

The Spanish constitution has been involved in controversy several times with regard to real and effective sexual equality. This interest has been triggered by affirmative action in various spheres and, recently, under the right to political participation.[60] The 12/2008[61] judgment of the constitutional court has shown the court's continuing doctrine. Court judgment 236/2007[62] was the starting point. Despite the 'relevance' of the arguments of international law and comparative law, the debate should focus on the Spanish constitutional order.[63] However, with this exception the constitutional court uses international instruments to deduce objectives that are in line with those proposed in the legislative bill under discussion. In this way, the argument emerges that: 'every

56 Many treaties in addition to the European Court of Human Right remain unratified by Spain (especially the protocol no. 7). In my opinion, it is legally unsound to include unratified treaties in the legal bases for judgments. It appears that treaties ratified or not, are used as part of a set of arguments to discretionally fall back on. This habit creates further doubts about their effectiveness in the Spanish legal system. Other well known texts such as the European Social Charter are constantly invoked to indicate the position of the unions.

57 Constitutional Court. Decision 5/1981, 13 February 1981.

58 A systematic and comprehensive analysis that distinguishes between those cases in which the European canon is used as mere support of constitutional doctrine, and other cases in which there is an integration of the European canon in the constitutional system can be seen in: A Queralt Jiménez, *La interpretación de los derechos: del Tribunal de Estrasburgo al Tribunal Constitucional, supra.*

59 The aim here is not to fully review the case law of the constitutional court which reflects the doctrine of the European Court of Human Rights, but to only review those cases where the doctrine of the European court is integrated – and perhaps creating new developments in internal law.

60 See organic law 3/2007 (22 March) regarding effective sexual equality.

61 Constitutional Court. Decision 12/2008, 29 January 2008.

62 Constitutional Court. Decision 236/2007, 7 November 2007.

63 Ibid., legal basis (FJ) 2.

text emphasizes that the search for formal and material equality between the sexes is a cornerstone of international human rights' (legal basis 2).

Faced with claims from one of the parties that positions in Italy or France may support arguments against the establishment of the proposed measures, the court closed its arguments at the very place it had begun: 'The Spanish Constitution is obviously our only canon of constitutionality' (legal basis 2). This statement shows how European standards are met by the constitutional court with reservations and qualifications when they lead to conclusions that differ to those the court intends introducing into the constitutional doctrine. The example given shows this unfounded fear. Such fear is unfounded in this case because it would have been sufficient to clearly differentiate the differing legal effects of the arguments put forward by the parties, i.e. between a highly effective argument regarding treaties and agreements ratified by Spain and a purely interpretive argument regarding comparative law and contexts from other states with differing constitutional parameters. By not accepting this solution, references to the situation in Europe are reduced to a quotation of texts that authorize measures encouraging real and effective equality for women. No importance is given to Article 14 of the European Convention on Human Rights, or Article 1 of the additional protocol 12.[64]

In short, neither the rules nor the doctrine of equality under the European Convention on Human Rights play defining roles in the Spanish constitutional framework. Considered as a truly minimal standard, the constitutional court has not considered sufficient rulings to enable the extraction of the parameters necessary to precisely judge when affirmative action is admissible – and this is the main challenge posed by the principle of equality.

3.3.2. *Right to a fair trial (Article 6 of the European Convention on Human Rights)*

The acceptance by the constitutional court of the doctrine contained in Article 6 of the European Convention on Human Rights is crucial.[65] The reason is obvious given that the vast majority of judgments from the constitutional court relate to the entitlement to an effective remedy under Article 24 of the constitution.[66] The

---

64 As cited in other decisions of the constitutional court such as 41/2006 (02/13/2006) determining if homosexuality can be considered a circumstance relevant to the banning of discrimination. Legal basis (FJ) 3.

65 P Perez Tremps, 'Las <<Cartas>> y los Tribunales' in X (ed.) *Estudios sobre la Constitución Española. Homenaje al Profesor Jordi Solé Tura* (CEPC, Madrid 2008).

66 It is important to note that Spain belongs to the states that have established a specifical mechanism in order to protect fundamental rights. This remedy, very similar to the German "Verfassungsbeschwerde, is called "Recurso de Amparo". According the article 53. 2 of the Constitution: "Any citizen may make a claim to the liberties and rights recognized in

general trend is the integration of the legal outlines of the doctrine of the European Court of Human Rights. It is clear that the doctrine of 'European rights' is increasingly becoming the 'European right to a fair trial'. Proof of this is the acceptance of the doctrine of undue delay ('everyone is entitled to a fair and public hearing within a reasonable time');[67] judicial impartiality ('everyone is entitled to a fair and public hearing (...) by an independent and impartial court established by law');[68] the presumption of innocence ('everyone charged with a criminal offence shall be presumed innocent until proven guilty according to law');[69] or the right to counsel ('everyone charged with a criminal offence has the following minimum rights (...) to defend himself in person or through legal assistance of his own choosing or, if he has not sufficient means to pay for legal assistance, to be given it free when the interests of justice so require.').[70]

---

article 14 and the First Section of the Second Chapter before the regular courts through a process based on the principles of preference and speed and through the recourse before the Constitutional Court. This last recourse shall be applicable to the objections of conscience recognized in article 30". From the beginning, many appeals for protection arrived at the Constitutional Court (almost 90 per cent of the registered cases), most of them claiming Article 24 violations of the Spanish Constitution: effective protection from the judges. See, e.g. VC Jackson and M Tushnet, *Comparative Constitutional Law* (Foundation Press, New York 1999).

67 See, for example, Constitutional Court Decision 124/1999, 28 June 1999, Legal basis (FJ) 2.

68 Queralt emphasised this point as "the formula used by the constitutional court is the presentation of article 24.1 of the Spanish constitution and article 6 of the European Convention of Human Rights." *La interpretación de los derechos, supra*, 294. This parallel use can be seen in the crucial Constitutional Court Decision 5/2004, 16 January 2004 in which the court rejected the appeal for a judicial review made by Batasuna of the judgment of the special court constituted under article 61 of the organic law of judicial power that decreed the illegalisation of Batasuna. See legal basis (FJ) 2.

69 Decision of the Constitutional Court 25/2003, 10 February 2003, legal basis (FJ) 3. Regarding the presumption of innocence there are aspects that are not shared between the Spanish legal code and the doctrine of the Strasbourg court. In this respect, see the judgment of the European Court of Human Rights *Puig Panella v Spain* (25 April 2006) which condemned Spain on the basis on which a violation of article 6 of the European convention when the state refused an indemnification to somebody who had spent several months in prison before being released because of an absence of proof. In the judgment of the European Court of Human Rights, the refusal of indemnification supposes the suspicion of guilt for someone who had been formally declared innocent. See L Martin Rebollo, 'Presunción de inocencia y responsabilidad del Estado: una relación ambigua (a propósito de la sentencia TEDH de 25 de abril de 2006)' in X. (ed.) *Derechos fundamentales y otros estudios en homenaje al Prof. Dr. Lorenzo Martín Retortillo,* Vol. I (Universidad de Zaragoza, Zaragoza 2008). The report of the council of state of the 14 February indicated that Spain was condemned not because it refused indemnification, but because the motive for refusing such indemnification undermined the presumption of innocence, 318.

70 Decision of the Constitutional Court 13/2000, 10 January 2000 legal basis (FJ) 2.

It has been rightly pointed out[71] that this material convergence[72] regarding the meaning of legal protection in the European constitutional model has been one that presents itself as an opportunity to witness the dialogue among the courts. A demonstration, among others, of this dialogue can be found in the European Court of Human Rights judgment *Cañete de Goñi v. Spain.*[73] In this ruling the European Court of Human Rights did not consider that Article 6 of the convention had been breached after observing how the constitutional court had scrupulously respected the doctrine of the Strasbourg court.

We cannot end this section without noting that Spanish doctrine has correctly resolved the question[74] created by parliamentarians claiming the right to an appeal in line with constitutional interpretation of Article 2 of the 7th protocol of the European Convention of Human Rights. It is noteworthy that the text which should serve as an interpretive model is not the aforementioned protocol, not yet ratified by Spain, but Article 15 of the UN International Covenant on Civil and Political Rights. This option is not, however, the product of an error or an attempt to extend the convergence of rights beyond the purely formal ratification, but the consequence of the fact that the 7th protocol supports the interpretation of Article 71.3 already made by the constitutional court.

3.3.3. Right to respect for private and family life (Article 8.1 European Convention on European Rights)

The legal problems arising from noise pollution are of great importance in Spain – one of the world's noisiest nations. The fundamental reference in the constitutional system is Article 43 of the Spanish Constitution which recognizes the right to an adequate environment. However, in reality this is not a right but rather a constitutional principle. The application of Article 53.3 of the constitution means that it only becomes a right if legislation subsequently develops this principle. Moreover, an application for judicial review by the

---

71 JM Bandres Sanchez-Cluzat, 'El derecho a un proceso equitativo en la reciente jurisprudencia del Tribunal Europeo de Derechos Humanos' in AAVV (ed.) *Derechos humanos y otros estudios en homenaje al prof. Dr. Lorenzo Martín Retortillo,* Vol. I (University of Zaragoza, Zaragoza 2008), 1345.

72 It must be remembered that the European Court of Human Rights has condemned Spain on various occasions for violating the right to a trial in a reasonable period of time. See A Rodriguez, 'Hable con él. Las resoluciones del Tribunal constitucional español previas a las sentencias condenatorias del Tribunal Europeo de Derechos Humanos (Primeras reflexiones sobre las dificultades de un diálogo)' in F Balaguer Callejon (ed.) *Derecho constitucional y cultura. Estudios homenaje a Peter Häberle* (Tecnos, Madrid 2004). The most recent guilty judgment against Spain for this reason was handed down on the 9 June 2009 in *Bendayan Azcantot and Benalal Bendayan v Spain.*

73 European Court of Human Rights, *Cañete de Goñi v. Spain* (App no 37703/97), 15 October 2002.

74 See again A Queralt Jiminez, *La interpretación de los derechos, supra,* 375–392.

constitutional court cannot be used to claim the violation of an environmental 'right'. Given this lack of protection and the seriousness of the noise problem in various areas, another interpretation has been tested. This new argument attempted to present the rights to privacy and inviolability of the home from a functional standpoint. In this way, it could be understood that the right to privacy in the home is an instrument for protecting the establishment and free development of the personality. A home that suffers permanent interference from outside is in distress, and denied the freedom to enjoy the rights that enable the free development of the individual. This doctrine was upheld by the European Court of Human Rights in *Lopez Ostra Case v Spain.*[75] The Spanish constitutional court endorsed this doctrine in judgment 119/2001[76], and this supposedly extended rights to new boundaries.[77] However, this acceptance did not lead to the granting of judicial relief since it was not considered to be sufficiently proven that there was a link between the damages claimed and the level of noise pollution in the area affected.

It is precisely this fact which comes into play in the European Court of Human Rights judgment *Moreno Gómez v. Spain*[78] This ruling followed an appeal lodged by the appellant after the rejection by the constitutional court of a request for judicial review in the case quoted above. This judgment did not achieve a greater precision in the conceptual scope of the right to privacy or privacy of the home. The judgment reconsidered the conditions under which alleged damages are to be recognized. In this case, the European Court of Human Rights noted that the protection that must be offered to the appellant cannot be undermined by demanding from the appellant exhaustive tests of sustained noise when noise levels in the area are already clearly established. This closes the circle of integration in this area of the criteria of the European Court of Human Rights. The constitutional court extended the concept of damages to privacy of the home in cases where the interference is due to noise – or other elements capable of inhibiting the free development of the personality. In addition, it was found that the appellant cannot be obliged to prove in excessive detail the existence of damages when there is already objective proof to evidence these damages. This is a case in which the constitutional framework was convinced by the case law produced by the European Court of Human Rights. However, as already emphasized, it was not considered similarly appropriate to reassess the right to

75 European Court of Human Rights, *López Ostra v. Spain* (App no 16798/90) 9 December 1994.

76 Constitutional Court. Decision 119/2001, 24 May 2001.

77 To the point of assuming new concepts such as the right to privacy in the home – a hybrid between the right to privacy and the inviolability of the home. A criticism of this approach can be found in R Martin Morales, T Requena Lopez and E Guillen Lopez, *El régimen constitucional de "la movida"* (Grupo Editorial Universitario. Granada 2001).

78 European Court of Human Rights, *Moreno Gómez v. Spain* (App no 4143/02), 16 November 2004.

family reunification as an extension of the right to privacy as stated in Article 18 of the constitution. Judgment 236/2007indicated that there is no place for this new right.[79]

3.3.4. *Confidential correspondence (Article 8 of the European Convention on European Rights)*

The arguments of the European Court of Human Rights on the right to privacy and confidentiality of communications have been especially relevant in the doctrine of the constitutional court. The reason has already been cited earlier: namely, the need to resort to the European Court of Human Rights in cases revealing gross inadequacy in the Spanish mechanism for the protection of rights. Indeed, our legal system did not offer the guarantees required by the European Court of Human Rights and this led to a series of judgments against Spain.[80] In these judgments damages were assessed for breaches of confidentiality in communications in the absence of foreseeable and comprehensible legislation establishing the circumstances under which confidentiality might be breached. In this way, European case law was making apparent the omissions in Spanish national mechanisms for protecting rights and which could only be fully corrected by legislation. This is one of those cases in which legislative inaction cannot be remedied by the protective interpretations of the constitutional court. Such doctrine cannot take the place of the necessary 'comprehensible and accessible legal empowerment'.[81] The same occurs in European Court of Human Rights judgment *Burgallo Prado v Spain*[82] which condemned Spain for the same reason for offenses committed before the amendment of the Criminal Procedures Act of 25 May 1988.[83]

This modification and new corresponding case law[84] have resulted in the convergence of Spanish law with Europe on the protection of confidentiality of correspondence.[85] In short, the regime of confidentiality of correspondence is a clear case of intervention by the European Court of Human Rights in defining

79 Constitutional Court. Decision 236/2007, 7 November 2007.

80 Judgment of the European Court of Human Rights, *Valenzuela Contreras v Spain* (App no 58/1997/842/1048) 30 July 1998.

81 Constitutional court Decision 49/1999, 5 April 1999 has been rightly criticised because after establishing that the legislation was insufficient, the decision did not consider it necessary to automatically determine the damages arising from the breach of the right to confidential correspondence. See Queralt, *La interpretación de los derechos*, *supra*, 324–330.

82 European Court of Human Rights, *Prado Bugallo v. Spain* (App no. 58496/00) 18 May 2003.

83 Organic law 4/1988.

84 Especially in the proceedings of the Naseiro case in the second court of the supreme court (18 June 1992).

85 As can be deduced from the decision of inadmissibility given on 25 September 2006 in *Abdulkadir Coban v Spain*. See A Queralt, *ibid*.

the national framework of rights protection. European case law was not called upon to support rights that were well defined constitutionally or to discover new profiles. The European Court of Human Rights discovered that the national protection mechanisms were insufficient and the Spanish legal system responded by filling the legislative gap.[86]

3.3.5. Freedom of expression (Article 10 European Convention on Human Rights)

The legal regimes for the freedom of expression have become similar in European nations. This approach has been due to reasons more closely related to the very essence of democracy than specific regulatory requirements. Indeed, as the freedom of expression appears as an essential element in a democracy (associated with a free public opinion, or from a procedural standpoint, the creation of a free communications structure[87]) so every nation seems to understand the concept in similar terms. This explains, for example, why Spanish constitutional case law has begun accepting the American doctrine of 'preferred position'.[88] The model for freedom of expression and its possible limitations is almost universal. However, this does not prevent serious problems arising over rules such as 'maximum scope for the expression of dissent' (especially when the information affects politicians) and 'extreme care when interpreting its restrictions'.[89] We have already shown above how the references of the European Court of Human Rights in this area of constitutional case law have been constant and have become a bastion of argument for responding to conflicts such as the constitutional admissibility of genocide denial crime (235/2007).[90] A recent case reveals new perspectives on the problem. This case caused controversy following the publication by a Spanish newspaper '*El Pais*' of photographs taken inside the summer house of the Italian Prime Minister Silvio Berlusconi. This case is extraordinarily important because from the beginning it emerged as a transnational dispute against the backdrop of European parliamentary elections on the 7 June 2009. Discussion centred on reconciling the right to privacy with the freedom of information regarding public figures. The European case law rather than the national framework served as a reference for each of the opposing views.[91]

---

86 The jurisprudence of the European Court of Human Rights has been conclusive in determining that when the violation of rights is directly attributable to legislation then the corresponding law should be repealed. European Court of Human Rights, *Vermeire v Belgium* (App no 12849/87) 19 November 1991.

87 See Decision of the constitutional court 237/2007, 8 November 2007, legal basis (FJ) 4.

88 See FJ Bastido Freijedo, *El régimen jurídico de la comunicación social* (Instituto de Estudios Económicos 1994).

89 See European Court of Human Rights, *De Haes and Gijsels v Belgium* (App no 7/1996/626/809) 24 February 1997, para. 49.

90 Constitutional Court. Decision 235/2007, 7 November 2007.

91 See the article by M Carrillo, 'La intimidad y el primer ministro', *El País* wednesday, 10 June 2009.

3.3.6. Right to free elections (Article 3 of the Additional Protocol)

As has become evident in the previous case, one of the more relevant aspects of the doctrine of the European Court of Human Rights has been the determination of elements fundamental for democracy and the state guarantees for its protection. On numerous occasions references to the European Court of Human Rights have been made with respect to these principles (from the right to participate, the most obvious, to the freedom of religious choice,[92] etc.) resulting in a coherent body of doctrine. This doctrine has been constructed within the framework of the judicial and extra-judicial situation that resulted from the approval of organic law 6/2002 and the subsequent orders issued by the special chamber of the supreme court. Indeed, constitutional court judgment 48/2003 determined the constitutionality of the Political Parties Act and its controversial Article 9 which provided for the outlawing of ideologies offering direct or indirect support for terrorism. This judgment carefully follows the doctrine established by the European Court of Human Rights, and especially those concerning the banning of the Refah Partisi party.[93] This European court doctrine was also closely followed by the constitutional court in judgments on the legal appeals brought by the outlawed parties. Such compliance was appreciated by the European court and action brought by Batasuna, the outlawed party, was decided in a judgment of 30 June 2009[94] which declared that Spain had not committed any violation of the convention.

This sentence is a key factor in dealing with the problem of ETA terrorism because it closes the door to the political process for groups that support violence. Any recent history of Spain will include the moment that the European court provided the '*compte tenu de la situation existant en Espagne depuis de nombreuses années concernant les attentats terroristes, plus spécialement dans la « région politiquement sensible » qu'est le pays basque (voir, mutatis mutandis, Leroy c. France, no 36109/03, §45, 2 octobre 2008), ces liens peuvent être considérés objectivement comme une menace pour la démocratie*'. (p.89).

3.3.7. Protection of property (Article 1 of the Additional Protocol)

A final example considers the influence of the European Court of Human Rights on the legal definition of property rights and liability when legislation causes

---

92 See E Guillen Lopez, 'La inescrutabilidad de los caminos del señor: comentario de la Sentencia del Tribunal Europeo de Derechos Humanos "Leyla Sahin c. Turquía' (num. 44774/98) de 29/06/2004" (2004) *Revista de Derecho constitucional europeo* 2. Available at: www.ugr.es/~redce/ReDCE2pdf/enriqueguillen.pdf.

93 European Court of Human Rights, *Refah Partisi (The Welfare Party) and others v. Turkey* (App. No. 41340/98, 41342/98, 41343/98, 41344/98) 13 February 2003.

94 European Court of Human Rights, Herri Batasuna and Batasuna v. Spain (App no 25803/04 et 25817/04) 20 June 2009.

damage to property. The constitutional court had not yet considered the issue itself, but certain doctrinal scholars supported the following reading.[95] The right to property as defined by the European Court on Human Rights case law requires compensation for any damage to property, whatever the body responsible for the damage. The Constitution contains the principle of liability where the administration causes damages (Article 106)[96] but it is argued that this model excludes important cases that require repair, and specifically excludes injuries caused by the failure to transpose EU directives (*Francovich and Bonifaci and others v Italian Republic*). These insufficiencies enabled the principle of financial liability to reach previously unscaled heights. This principle of financial liability now extends to the legislature and judiciary (Köbler[97]) under community law and does not stop there. This is because, as we have noted, the effect is to create a new right to indemnation for the damage to property caused by legislation (or, at least, legislation subsequently declared to be unconstitutional)[98] and this right is based on the doctrine of the European Court of Human Rights on ownership rights. This case law may become a topic of debate regarding European confirmation[99] of a doctrine of widening liability for the protection of property, both objectively and subjectively. But acceptance or rejection of the doctrine must be preceded by a complex examination of what it means to assume new rights and in particular, the impact of confirming case law principles that affect the scope for new legislation. Therefore, it implies a continuous national tension between democracy and rule of law. Again, welcoming new rights without deliberation is not a solution unless the aim is to avoid an ideological debate.[100]

In short, the brief summary of reviewed case law clearly shows the variability of situations and relationships impacting on the European convention and Spanish constitutional law. The convention sometimes provides a real minimum standard (gender equality), while in other cases it serves to confirm national standards

---

95 See JI Moreno Fernandez, 'La responsabilidad patrimonial del Estado-legislador frente a disposiciones legales declaradas contrarias a la Constitución o al derecho comunitario' (2008) *Revista General de Derecho Constitucional* 5.

96 Developed in an unsatisfactory manner in article 139 of the act regulating public administrations and procedures (known in Spanish as LRJAPPAC).

97 C-224/01 Gerhard Köbler v Republik Österreich [2003] ECR I-10239.

98 See M Ahumada Ruiz, "Responsabilidad patrimonial del Estado por las leyes inconstitucionales (o el derecho a no ser perjudicado por una ley inconstitucional)", *REDC*, num. 62, 2001.

99 See the revealing opinion of Miguel Poiares Maduro, Advocate General at the European Court, in judgment C-120/06. He indicated that a principle only recognised in a few states of the EU could become a general principle if it was applicable to the construction of the European community (p. 55).

100 Weiler reminds us that this has characterised the regulatory production of the court from its earliest days. See JHH Weiler, 'Viaje a lo desconocido: Pasado y futuro del Tribunal de Justicia en el campo de la integración política', in X (ed.) *Europa, fin de siglo* (CEC, Madrid 1995).

(right to a fair trial, freedom of expression, right to free elections). There are cases in which the convention helps reveal the lack of internal mechanisms for the protection of rights and this causes condemnatory judgments followed by legislative change (confidentiality of correspondence). The European convention and constitutional court case law have enabled new profiles to be found in constitutionally recognized rights – so creating new rights in an indirect way (right to privacy).

3.4. CONDEMNATORY JUDGMENTS MADE AGAINST SPAIN BY THE EUROPEAN COURT OF HUMAN RIGHTS

Below we will look at a particular type of impact on the Spanish constitutional law code resulting from the European Convention on Human Rights: the impact derived from judgments of the European Court of Human Rights that condemn Spain for violations of the convention.

The elements we have to consider are the terms expressed in Article 46 of the convention and how these terms are made effective. With respect to the first point, it must be remembered that Article 46 requires that states 'undertake to abide by the final judgment of the Court in any case to which they are parties'. In the case of Spain, it must be mentioned that the European Convention on Human Rights was adhered to through Article 94 of the constitution – and not Article 93. This means that 'powers derived from the constitution' were not transferred and that the judgments of the international tribunal are not immediately executable.

This was clearly highlighted in a report of the state council (Consejo de Estado) on the integration of European law into Spanish law (14 February 2008). The report also revealed how only one of the claims for judicial review brought before the constitutional court and citing a declaratory judgment of the European Court of Human Rights was, in fact, evaluated.[101] Neither have the lower courts accepted the condemnatory sentences of the European Court of Human Rights as sufficient reason to grant annulment proceedings (article 240 of the organic law regulating the judiciary); nor have European judgments been accepted as a justification for judicial review claims. The solution to this problem is the establishment of suitable legal mechanisms. Following the second recommendation (19 January 2000) of the Committee of Ministers of the Council of Europe, the Spanish council of state proposed that Spain would follow the model of France and Belgium by giving the supreme court 'jurisdiction over appeals and, if necessary, the power to revise sentences or, if this is not possible

[101] Constitutional Court Decision 245/1991, 16 December 1991 regarding the *Bultó* case.

in view of the nature of the violation, to order nullity proceedings and refer the matter to the court in which the violation occurred'.[102]

4. FUNDAMENTAL RIGHTS WITHIN THE EUROPEAN UNION AND THE SPANISH CONSTITUTIONAL SYSTEM

The history of the Charter of Fundamental Rights of the European Union is well known.[103] Clearly, it is not a Bill of Rights of Man and Citizen nor the European Convention on Human Rights. Let's say that it is an exact example of the thesis proposed in this paper. Indeed, the charter was not written to enshrine rights for which historical subjects have fought. The charter was created to 'make rights visible', that is, to protect rather than enable rights. The charter explains the application of community law and does not confer any new powers for European legislation. It was not created to transform, but to prevent any damaging transformations occurring to the minimum framework agreement. In fact, as a charter, it virtually surrenders its conceptual autonomy. The specific starting point is the convention and the case law of the European Court of Human Rights (see the accompanying explanations) and its end-point is the same convention to which the EU adheres. The charter is not all-encompassing, as those rights are inspired by the concept of human dignity as enshrined in the Spanish, German, or Italian constitutions. The Charter of Fundamental Rights of the European Union is, in other words, a necessity for the construction of Europe as a legal entity. In this European context, the expression 'fundamental rights' has both symbolic and ancestral resonance.

The charter is the result of the widespread assumption (arising initially from national constitutional courts,[104] the *Solange* and *Frontini* cases, and then from within the bodies of the EU) that constitutionalism is the future of the union. Furthermore, if the aim is to go beyond mere economic integration, then a constitution and bill of rights are inseparable realities. To understand what the charter means, we must understand what led the European Union on 7 December 2000 to continue along the path taken with Article 6 of the Treaty of the European

---

102 Report of the state council (Consejo de Estado) (p.317).

103 See, e.g. J Roldan Barbero, 'La Carta de Derechos Fundamentales de la UE: su estatuto constitucional' (2003) *Revista de Derecho comunitario europeo* 6 and FJ Matia Portilla (ed.), *La protección de los Derechos Fundamentales en la Unión Europea* (Cívitas, Madrid 2002).

104 For information on how the material was handled in Germany, Spain, and Italy see C Vidal Prado, *El impacto del nuevo derecho europeo en los Tribunales Constitucionales* (Colex, Madrid 2004).

Union[105] and which announced the creation of the Charter of Fundamental Rights of the European Union.[106] In this context, we must understand that the charter is not currently part of the treaties although it is recognized as having the same legal force (Article 6 – Treaty of the European Union).

The mechanism for incorporating the charter into the Spanish code was Article 93 of the constitution. Therefore, with the authorisation for the ratification of the Lisbon Treaty, organic law 1/2008[107] states in Article 2 that: 'Under the provisions of paragraph 2 of Article 10 of the Spanish constitution and paragraph 8 of Article 1 of the Treaty of Lisbon, the rules relating to fundamental rights and freedoms recognized by the constitution shall be interpreted in accordance with the provisions of the Charter of Fundamental Rights, as published in the Official Journal of the European Union on 14 December 2007 (…)'. The organic law later reproduced the content of the charter and so the legal basis for its application is twofold: the legal value provided by the Lisbon Treaty (once in force)[108] and that derived from the organic law which reproduces the content. It should be understood that the only objectives of the reproduction were those given in the statement of purpose namely, to demonstrate transparency and provide a source text that is more easily understood by the public. As is the case with regulations[109] it is the charter itself[110] that contains the formal legal text which can displace existing and contradictory instruments (in line with the principle of primacy). This is not the only noteworthy feature of the above act. The express mention of Article 10 of the constitution is also interesting because the wording and probable consequences (which we have already had occasion to examine) could lead to an interpretation in which the European convention is reduced to the level of interpretative effectiveness expressly referred to in the provision. It may therefore be argued that the act intends to make clear that the charter is not a treaty[111] and is accepted in the legal system with the specific

---

105 M Azpitarte Sanchez, 'La cultura constitucional de la Unión Europea. Análisis del artículo 6 TUE', in F Balaguer Callejon (ed.) *Derecho constitucional y cultura. Estudios en homenaje a Peter Häberle*, (Tecnos, Madrid 2004).

106 See G Camara Villar, 'Los derechos fundamentales en el proceso histórico de construcción de la Unión Europea y su valor en el Tratado Constitucional', *supra*.

107 Organic law 1/2008 of the 30 July authorised the Spanish ratification of the Lisbon Treaty, which modified the European Union Treaty and the Constitutive Treaty of the European Economic Community. It was signed in Lisbon on 13 December 2007.

108 It could be understood that this instrument may enable the charter to be authorised before the Lisbon treaty enters into force.

109 Especially the arguments referring to the confusion about where to position the regulation in the system of legal sources and the position of the controlling body (C-39/72, *Commission v. Italy* [1973] ECR I-101.

110 Azpitarte Sanchez discusses this question in his chronicle. M Azpitarte Sanchez, "Crónica política y legislativa del año 2007" [2008] *Revista Española de Derecho Constitucional* 82.

111 This argument is additionally supported by the literal interpretation of article 53 of the charter which says: "Nothing in this *Charter* shall be interpreted as restricting or adversely

reservation that it does not create any new rights which cannot be drawn from the constitution itself.

This interpretation could be supported by the fact that the charter is not, as noted above, formally a treaty and that the organic law facilitates the signing of specific treaties (as in the case of Organic Law 1/2008, which authorizes signing the Treaty of Lisbon). As a result, the inclusion of the charter (included in the organic law only to ease the task of relating the legal texts) does not permit the inclusion of the powers that derive from it (particularly actions by the Court of Justice of the European Union in compliance with its rulings). Ultimately, if the charter occupied a place in the Spanish legal code on the basis of Article 10.2 instead of on Article 93, then the legal consequences would be quite different. Certainly, these arguments can only be encouraged from the literal reading of an unfortunate, in my view, organic law in combination with the problematic fact that the charter has not been formally integrated into the treaties.[112] But from the moment a treaty recognizes a text as being of equal legal value, it also recognizes an identical position in the legal code.[113] This interpretation changes the terms by which the charter is used so that the rights recognized in the charter become the only standard reference when the state implements community law[114] (unless, as we shall see, the protection provided by the constitutional procedure is greater). This only constitutes a mechanism for the interpretation of internal constitutional rights in cases outside EU law. In the latter case, the charter would operate in a similar way to the European Convention on Human Rights. However, if the first case transpired it would inaugurate a dynamic process very different to that which has been hitherto examined. This is because it would represent a new text on rights that would operate in a supranational, rather than international dimension. As a result: (1) new rights may be created (which implies extending the constitutional catalogue); (2) internal rules on

---

affecting human rights and fundamental freedoms as recognised, in their respective fields of application, by *Union law...*".

112 See J Baquero Cruz, 'What's left of the Charter? Reflections on Law and political mythology' [2008] *Maastricht Journal of European and Comparative Law* 15.

113 It is worth mentioning at this point the theory of Prof. BALAGUER regarding the concept of 'value' in the analysis of the system of legal sources. See F Balaguer Callejon, *Fuentes del Derecho II, supra.*

114 Or more precisely, when there is a sufficient connection with EU law. See JI Ugartemendia Eceizabarrena, 'La incorporación (nacional) de los Derechos Fundamentales de la Unión Europea como límites a la actuación del poder público estatal' in AAVV (ed.) *Estudios sobre la Constitución Española, Homenaje al Profesor Jordi Solé Tura* (CEPC, Madrid 2008). The communitisation of the third pillar should be considered from the Maria Puppino judgment. See D Sarmiento, 'Un paso más en la constitucionalización del Tercer Pilar de la Unión Europea: la sentencia Maria Pupino y el efecto directo de las Decisiones marco' [2005] *Revista electrónica de Estudios Internacionales.*

rights that contradict the new text would be displaced;[115] (3) the Court of Justice of the European Union would be positioned at the top of the legal pyramid in the system for protecting and recognizing rights;[116] (4) judgments on rights would acquire an immediate executive character.

With this new outlook the Spanish constitutional court[117] would be able to abandon the myth that it has used for years to avoid conflict. This myth has been based on the view that constitutional law and EU law are two parallel lines that only cross when it is necessary to avoid chaos.[118] The charter itself leaves theoretical room for this argument when it states in Article 51:[119] 'The provisions of this Charter are addressed to the institutions and bodies of the Union with due regard for the principle of subsidiarity and to the Member States only when they are implementing Union law. They shall therefore respect the rights, observe the principles and promote the application thereof in accordance with their respective powers'. But it has been observed[120] that there are some aspects that may lead to rights contained in the charter being extended beyond their original mission.[121] These aspects include: an extension of the powers of the EU,[122] the crosscutting nature of community freedoms together with the doctrine of implied powers and the expansion involved in determining the remit of the community,[123] the decision by a state to exclude the application of EU law as an

---

115 "Artículo 53". Comments by J Martin and Perez De Nanclares in A Mangas Martin (ed.), *Carta de los Derechos Fundamentales de la Unión Europea. Comentario artículo por artículo* (Fundación BBVA, Madrid 2008).

116 Advantage could be taken of the situation to convert the court in an authentic constitutional court. That is, a court that decides on questions with authentic constitutional content; in contrast to its current situation where the court handles both constitutional and ordinary legal matters. See R Alonso Carcia, *Justicia constitucional y Unión Europea* (Civitas, Madrid 2005). It is worth emphasising that a transformation in this sense would create a new deliberative structure at the centre of the EU. Such a move would increase public space at a European level.

117 See F Balaguer Callejon (ed.) *Manual de Derecho Constitucional* (Tecnos, Madrid 2008).

118 This is more or less the hypothesis put forward in declaration 1/2004 – which refers to the constitutional court as the final guarantor in the event of a conflict.

119 Also see the explanation regarding article 51.

120 See A Saiz Arnaiz, 'El Tribunal de Justicia, los Tribunales Constitucionales y la tutela de los derechos fundamentales en la Unión Europea: entre el (potencial) conflicto y la (deseable) armonización. De los principios no escritos al catálogo constitucional, de la autoridad judicial a la normativa', *supra*.

121 It should also be noted that the displacement that may follow favouring the charter over the internal code for rights does not operate the same way in all other respects. Because this shift only occurs as stated in article 53, the protection afforded by the Charter is greater than that received from the national law. This will not remove the primacy of community law, insofar as it is the Charter itself that determines the possible preferential application of national law. However, this point adds a new twist. Clearly against this point is J Martin Perez De Nanclares in A Mangas Martin (ed.) *supra*, 858.

122 See A Mangas Martin, 'Comentario al artículo 51', in A Mangas Martin (ed.) *supra*,. 820.

123 This element has to be seen together with the improved accuracy of the EU remit detailed in the Lisbon Treaty.

aspect of EU law[124] and the expansive force of the principle of non-discrimination.[125] This probably represents another step further along the path of 'multilevel constitutionalism' (Ingolf Pernice)[126] and inaugurates a new dynamic in which the Court of Justice of the European Union and the constitutional court participate in an extremely fluid dialogue[127] on deference.[128] That is, the deference of the Court of Justice of the European Union towards the constitutional courts and deference of the constitutional courts towards the Court of Justice of the European Union.[129] Evidence relevant to the doctrine of the judgment of the *Köbler* case in the *Court of Justice*[130] can be found, namely precautions are being taken to ensure that the conduct of the judiciary can be considered a 'sufficiently serious violation' of EU law.

We must distinguish between various situations when considering the impact of the fundamental rights of the EU itself on the Spanish constitutional system. Firstly, the situation occurred after the acceptance of the rights recognized in the original law and prior to the charter. Secondly, the situation of those rights is specifically recognized in the charter. Both situations vary to the extent that, in the first case, the rights involve regulatory authorization in favour of the EU for their development while in the second case, the rights are situated on the margins of the competences as specifically recognized in Article 51.2. It therefore emerges that the primary role is to provide limits on the performance of public authorities when implementing EU law.

---

124 See A Mangas Martin, 817 (citing C-285/98 Tania Kreil [2000] ECR I-69).

125 JI Ugartemendia Eceizbarrena, 'La incorporación (nacional) de los Derechos Fundamentales de la Unión Europea como límites a la actuación del poder público estatal', *op.cit.*

126 I Pernice, 'Multilevel Constitutionalism and the Treaty of Ámsterdam: European Constitution-Making Revisited?' [1999] *CMLRev.* 36.

127 See M Azpitarte Sanchez, *El Tribunal Constitucional ante el control del Derecho comunitario derivado* (Civitas, Madrid 2002). See as well Carrillo Lopez, 'El diálogo entre Tribunales como condición necesaria para la tutela de los derechos fundamentales', in H Lopez Bofill (ed.), *La Constitución europea* (Tirant Lo Blanch, Valencia 2006).

128 I believe this principle of deference is consistent with the position of the constitutional courts that Cruz Villalon maintains with respect to the national constitutions. See P Cruz Villalon, 'El papel de los tribunales constitucionales nacionales en el futuro constitucional de la Unión' in N Colneric *et al.* (ed.) *Une communauté de droit. Festschrift für Gil Carlos Rodríguez Iglesias, supra* understandably, in the public imagination the constitution and the constitutional court have one and the same. Also see G Cruz Villalon, 'La Constitución inédita. La dificultad del debate constitucional europeo' in X (ed.), *La Constitución inédita. Estudios ante la constitucionalización de Europa* (Trotta, Madrid 2004).

129 Referred to by Saiz Arnaiz the formula: "separated Courts, sharing doctrines". See Saiz Arnaiz, 'El Convenio de Roma, el Tribunal Europeo de Derechos Humanos y la cultura común de los Derechos fundamentales en Europa' in X. (ed.) *Estudios sobre la Constitución Española. Homenaje al Profesor Jordi Solé Tura, supra.*

130 C-224/01 Kobler v Austria [2003] ECR I-10239.

I pointed out earlier that some rights were recognized before the Charter's recognition. For example,[131] since the Treaty of Amsterdam the ban on sex discrimination has occupied a key position in the treaties. In this sense, the Court of Justice of the European Union has been developing case law that focuses on identifying what is meant by discrimination, and on the permissibility of affirmative action. But, as witnessed when we analysed the relationship between internal constitutional debate on the subject and Article 14 of the European Convention on Human Rights, the protection afforded by the Spanish legal system is better than that offered by the judgments *Kalanke* and *Marschall*. These cases are ambiguous and the arguments presented by the parties have not been assumed by the constitutional court.[132] The same applies to the regulatory references (directives) because the protection that is offered is sometimes overtaken by the transposed national measures.[133]

The other situation refers specifically to the acceptance of the charter by the constitutional court. It should initially be pointed out that this has not been as extensive as the integration of the texts from the European Convention on Human Rights and the European Court of Human Rights. However, the text appears in a set of judgments that will be discussed below and placed in context. The first are contemporary, or even older than the charter itself.[134] This can be seen in Constitutional Court Decision 292/2000[135] declaring the unconstitutionality of certain parts of the Organic Law on Data Protection and based on the charter with respect to the delimitation of law.[136]

An even earlier judgment by the constitutional court on computing freedom, 290/2000[137], included a reference to the charter in a dissenting opinion by Judge Manuel Jiménez de Parga which intended to demonstrate that the paradigm of rights should not remain anchored within the constitutional formula. By reading between the lines, it is possible to deduce a position that differs from the dominant position and the judge finds in the new texts on rights a method for adapting the Spanish constitution to reality (including his interpretation of case law[138]). However, his proposal for reform remains within a context in which the reform of the constitution is a pipe dream. Indeed, an important aspect in the Spanish debate on formal reform of the constitution (according to Part 10) is that

131 Among others, for example, the rights involved in policies on visas, asylum, and immigration have been largely *communitarised by the Amsterdam treaty.*
132 See Constitutional Court Decision 12/2008, 29 January 2008.
133 Assumed in Constitutional Court Decision 92/2008, 21 July 2008.
134 See, among others, P Ridola, *supra*, 464 (fn 4).
135 Constitutional Court. Decision 292/2000, 30 November 2000.
136 See legal basis (FJ) 8.
137 Constitutional Court. Decision 290/2000, 30 November 2000.
138 Also effected in Constitutional Decision 119/1991, 3 June 19991.

reform has proved politically impossible.[139] The impossibility of reform has led part of the doctrine and case law to accentuate other mechanisms for modifying the basic rules. In particular, this accentuation has been applied to the case law of the constitutional court and the references to international instruments that enable further modelling of constitutional rights. The example given is a good demonstration.

The Charter has been cited in other statements. Yet, specific references are made without attaching binding legal effect to this document.[140] In these cases the Charter is included as an argument to support the decision reached, but not as the decisive factor. The aim has been to show the level of agreement between international texts[141] and especially the European Convention on Human Rights.[142]

In some cases, however, the charter has been playing a more important role than merely supporting the established case law of the constitutional court. In this regard, we must look again at some of the criticisms directed at Constitutional Court Decision 236/2007.[143, 144] These objections rest on the idea that the absorption of immigration policy by the EU rests entirely on the doctrine of the European Court of Human Rights with regard to related rights (the right to family reunion, in this case). The judgments of the European Court of Human Rights form a reference parameter beyond the Charter of Fundamental Rights of the European Union (thanks to the explanation that when the Charter and the European Court of Human Rights include the same rights, then they should be interpreted in the same way, i.e. according to the doctrine of the European Court of Human Rights). However, the constitutional court has not made such a leap and uses Article 10.2 as an interpretative perspective from which to analyse the Spanish model.

Therefore, we must again conclude that it is essential to reform our constitutional framework in order to clarify the relationships between existing constitutional levels. Reform is urgent. At this point in the discussion about rights we should refer to the content of the charter and the value added to the horizontal clauses by the process of progressively extending rights from extra-state organizations.

---

139 The only reform until now has been made to article 13.2 of the constitution. Constitutional court declaration 1/2004 wanted to make clear the lines of separation between the transfer of competences of Article 93 and the wider issues of constitutional reform.

140 See for example Constitutional Court Decisions 17/2006, 30 January 2006,;273/2005, 27 October 2005 and 138/2005, 26 June 2005.

141 As indicated by A Queralt, *supra*, 220.

142 An example of this use can be seen in Constitutional Court Decision 138/2005, 26 May 2005, legal basis (FJ) 4.

143 Constitutional Court. Decision 236/2007, 7 November 2007.

144 See Montialla Martos, 'El derecho de reagrupación familiar', *supra*.

This process must be seen alongside the relevance that rights have in the definition of a political society. New political dynamics create new rights but not necessarily new political societies.[145]

5. CONCLUSIONS

This chapter examines a very complex question. The question is built on some of the key Western legal concepts. The nature and scope of sovereignty, the tension between democracy and rule of law, the very notion of rights, the description of various levels of competence and jurisdiction in the protection of rights.

The recognition of rights within a supranational framework has been primarily the work of the judiciary, especially the action of the European Court of Human Rights. This court has provided a framework for asserting rights within Europe with the Charter of Fundamental Rights of the EU.

The integration of the various texts on rights in the Spanish constitutional system has been possible because of the articles of the constitution that enable the state to sign international treaties (Articles 93 and subsequent) and the rule contained in Article 10.2 that obliges us to interpret 'our' rights in agreement with international agreements signed by Spain. Articles 93 and 10.2 have become crucial in understanding the possibilities and limits of the expansion of European rights in the Spanish constitutional code.

These constitutional articles do not specifically mention the EU or the European Convention on Human Rights. The Spanish constitutional framework requires an urgent reform that must include in the constitution the essence of the European Convention on Human Rights and the EU.

The Spanish constitutional system has become a large and variable echo of the doctrine of the European Court of Human Rights. This can be clearly seen in the doctrine of our constitutional court as set by two basic references: (1) Article 10.2 as an interpretative mandate and not as a mechanism for creating new rights and (2) the constitutional court as an instrument for the protection of fundamental rights enshrined in the EU and not other rights.

As regards the fundamental rights of the EU, the debate focuses mainly on the Charter of Fundamental Rights of the European Union. This charter will generate a new dynamic in comparison with the previous approach despite the fact that the charter has been integrated into the Spanish system in a confused and incoherent manner. The Charter of Fundamental Rights of the European Union has already created a new reality because: (1) it may clearly lead to new rights (which implies extending the constitutional catalogue); (2) internal rules

---

[145] For example, the concept of freedom of information as an obstacle for a monopoly on television (on the basis of the free provision of services) shows the consequences of widening the profiles of those covered by fundamental rights.

on rights that contradict the new text will be displaced; (3) the Court of Justice of the European Union will be placed at the top of the legal pyramid in the system for protecting and recognizing rights; (4) judgments on rights would acquire an executive character. Multilevel constitutionalism has inexorably reached the level of fundamental rights and this requires a multilevel protection in which internal constitutional courts and the Court of Justice of the European Union reach an understanding based on the principle of deference.

CHAPTER 12

THE UNITED KINGDOM

THE INFLUENCE OF EUROPEAN LAW ON THE PROTECTION OF FUNDAMENTAL HUMAN RIGHTS IN UNITED KINGDOM LAW

Brice DICKSON*

1. INTRODUCTION

The stance of the United Kingdom (UK) in relation to sources of law in Europe has for long been bi-polar. On the one hand the UK has professed a desire to be 'at the heart of Europe', supporting extension to membership of the European Union (EU) and driving forward initiatives aimed at spreading democracy and the free market. On the other hand the UK has resisted developments which it interprets as a sacrifice of sovereignty or as a step towards the creation of a federal Europe.

In the field of human rights this bi-polarity has manifested itself in an enthusiasm for the system that protects fundamental rights through the European Convention on Human Rights (ECHR) but in a parallel suspiciousness of the system that allows for Directives and other EU initiatives to be developed through the European Commission and Council of Ministers. The former is evidenced by the facts that officials from the UK played a central role in drafting the ECHR in 1949,[1] that the UK was the first country to ratify the Convention in 1951, and that several judges from the UK have contributed long and

* Professor of International and Comparative Law and Director of the Human Rights Centre, Queen's University Belfast.

1 G Marston, 'The United Kingdom's part in the preparation of the European Convention on Human Rights' (1993) 42 *ICLQ* 796.

distinguished service to the European Court of Human Rights.[2] It is true that the UK did not accept the right of individual petition to Strasbourg until 1966,[3] that the Convention was not treated as part of domestic UK law until 2000,[4] and that on occasions the UK government has been quick to derogate from the Convention and slow to implement the judgments issued against it,[5] but on the whole the UK's interaction with the Strasbourg organs has been a positive one.[6] The relationship between the UK and the EU, however, has been and remains quite strained. When Mrs Thatcher was Prime Minister (1979–90) she insisted on reclaiming large annual rebates from the European Community because the UK was not benefiting as much as other countries from the Common Agricultural Policy, her government fought several key battles in the European Court of Justice (ECJ) over defective implementation of Directives, and she negotiated an opt-out for the UK from the Social Chapter of the Maastricht Treaty.[7] Subsequent Labour Prime Ministers[8] gave up that opt-out but then refused to support the idea of an enforceable Charter of Fundamental Rights.

It has to be admitted that common to both of these contrasting attitudes to the European way of protecting rights is what many see as a certain British arrogance, which doubtless stems from the longevity of its democracy, from its colonial history and from its crucial role in the defeat of fascism in World War II. Central to this mind-set is the phenomenon of the common law, the system whereby judges in the UK can create law on the basis of precedents constructed around principles that are considered to best serve society. Ever since the 17th century the common law has been a hugely important factor in the UK constitution. Today its role is as great as ever, the more so given that previous faith in the omniscience and incorruptibility of Parliament is not as strong as it used to be.[9] In the UK it is judges who are increasingly viewed as the prime protectors of human rights.

---

2 Two of the 10 Presidents of the Court have been British: Lord McNair (1959 to 1965) and Sir Humphrey Waldock (1971 to 1974). Waldock was also a member of the European Commission of Human Rights from 1954–62. The current UK judge at Strasbourg, Sir Nicolas Bratza, has been working there since 1993.

3 Anthony Lester, 'UK acceptance of the Strasbourg jurisdiction: what really went on in Whitehall in 1965' [1998] *Public Law* 237.

4 The Human Rights Act 1998 came fully into effect on 2 October 2000.

5 For recent accounts of the UK's record on implementation see the reports of the Parliamentary Joint Committee on Human Rights (JCHR): 15th Report of 2009–10 (HL 85 / HC 455); 31st Report of 2007–08 (HL 173/ HC 1078); 16th Report of 2006–07 (HL 128 / HC 728).

6 The JCHR has concluded that '[t]he UK can generally be proud of its record on national implementation of the Convention' and that '[t]he UK's record on implementing judgments of the European Court of Human Rights is also generally a good one': 15th Report of 2009–10 (n. 5 above) at paras. 18 and 19 respectively.

7 On the last two points see the text at no. 38–42 below.

8 Tony Blair (1997–2007) and Gordon Brown (2007–10).

9 For a good recent summary of the impact of the common law see Justin Leslie, 'Vindicating common law constitutionalism' (2010) 30 *Legal Studies* 301.

In this chapter I will first explore the influence of what is now called the EU on the protection of human rights in the UK, drawing particular attention to the contribution it has made to the human rights of employees. I will then sketch the pre-2000 position of the UK *vis-à-vis* the ECHR before looking in more detail at the impact of the Human Rights Act 1998 (HRA) on UK law since 2000. Due to shortage of space the coverage throughout will be rather general and will focus on just three aspects of the HRA's impact – its influence on legislators within Parliament, its effect on how judges interact with legislation, and its role in the development of the common law *per se*. This is a good time to be considering such matters because we may be on the cusp of a change in the nature of the relationships between judges and Parliament in the UK, and also, perhaps, between judges in the UK and the European Court in Strasbourg.

2. FUNDAMENTAL HUMAN RIGHTS PROTECTION AT THE EU LEVEL

It is safe to assume that when the UK joined the European Economic Community (EEC) in 1973[10] no-one thought that a prime reason for doing so was to enhance the protection of human rights. This was partly because at that time the very concept of human rights, in the West at least, was largely confined to civil and political rights. There was confidence within the UK government that UK standards in those fields were already as high as those in Continental Europe and, even if they were not, there was a strong feeling that it should be left to the UK Parliament to decide whether to improve them, not some institution in Brussels or Luxembourg. Yet the fact that the Treaty of Rome expressly protected four fundamental freedoms within the EEC – the free movement of goods,[11] and of persons, services and capital[12] – suggested that the protection of economic and social rights in the UK *would* soon be affected by membership of the EEC. The context in which this first occurred was that of social policy,[13] in particular the policy that men and women should receive equal pay for equal work.[14]

In 1970 the UK Parliament had passed the Equal Pay Act in an attempt to ensure that women received the same remuneration as men for the work they did. The Act was not actually brought into force until 1975, by which time it had already

10 Membership took effect in the UK because Parliament passed the European Communities Act 1972.

11 Arts. 9–37.

12 Arts. 48–73.

13 Arts. 117–128 of the Treaty of Rome.

14 Art. 119. This began by saying: 'Each Member State shall...ensure and subsequently maintain the application of the principle that men and women should receive equal pay for equal work'.

been amended by the Sex Discrimination Act 1975[15] to make it clear (amongst other things) that the implied equality clause in employment contracts 'shall not operate in relation to a variation between the woman's contract and the man's contract if the employer proves that the variation is genuinely due to a material difference (other then the difference of sex) between her case and his'.[16] In *Macarthy's v Smith* the question arose whether the amended Act could benefit a woman who had been employed to do a job which had been vacated several months earlier by a man who had been paid more money. The Court of Appeal of England and Wales was inclined to hold that it could not, but it referred the issue to the ECJ and that court ruled that Article 119 of the Treaty of Rome did extend to protecting a woman in this situation. The Court of Appeal then applied that ruling and held for Mrs Smith. The head of the Court of Appeal at the time, Lord Denning MR, said:

> *It is important now to declare – and it must be made plain – that the provisions of Article 119 of the EEC Treaty take priority over anything in our English statute on equal pay which is inconsistent with Article 119. That priority is given by our own law. It is given by the European Communities Act 1972 itself. Community law is now part of our law: and, whenever there is any inconsistency, Community law has priority. It is not supplanting English law. It is part of our law which overrides any other part which is inconsistent with it.*[17]

Not long after this decision the significance of the priority of EEC law in the UK was even more starkly revealed in another sex discrimination case, *Johnston v Chief Constable of the RUC*.[18] Here the ECJ ruled, on a reference for a preliminary ruling in a case from Northern Ireland, that Article 6 of the Council Directive on Equal Treatment[19] took priority over a provision in a UK statute which precluded a claimant from challenging a certificate issued by a government Minister asserting that if any sex discrimination had occurred it was because of the need to safeguard national security and protect public safety and order.[20] In the course of its judgment the ECJ said:

> *The requirement of judicial control stipulated by [Article 6] reflects a general principle of law which underlies the constitutional traditions common to the member states.*

15 In order to comply with Council Directive 75/117/EEC on equal pay.

16 Equal Pay Act 1970, s. 1(3), as substituted by Sex Discrimination Act 1975, s. 8(1).

17 [1981] QB 180, at 200E.

18 Case 222/84, [1987] QB 129. At this time the President of the ECJ was from the UK, Lord Mackenzie Stuart.

19 "Member States shall introduce into their national legal systems such measures as are necessary to enable all persons who consider themselves wronged by failure to apply to them the principle of equal treatment within the meaning of Articles 3, 4 and 5 to pursue their claims by judicial process after possible recourse to other component authorities." (Council Directive 76/207/EEC).

20 Sex Discrimination (NI) Order 1976, art. 53(2).

> *That principle is also laid down in Articles 6 and 13 of the [ECHR]. As the European Parliament, Council and Commission recognised in their joint declaration of 5 April 1977*[21] *and as the court has recognised in its decisions, the principles on which that Convention is based must be taken into consideration in Community law.*[22]

The ECJ had already decided in previous infringement proceedings that the UK had not properly implemented the Equal Pay Directive of 1975[23] because it had made it a requirement that a right to equal pay for work of equal value should be available only if a job evaluation study had been carried out with the employer's consent.[24] The ECJ had also condemned the UK for totally excluding persons employed in private households from the protection of the Equal Treatment Directive of 1976 and for not legislating to allow provisions in collective agreements or in rules governing independent professions to be declared void if they breached the principle of equal treatment of men and women.[25]

The superiority of EC law struck home even more forcibly in the UK when a challenge was mounted to provisions in the Merchant Shipping Act 1988 on the ground that they discriminated against foreign nationals when stipulating what vessels could be registered as British. After an eight-day hearing in the UK's top court, the House of Lords, it was held that a court had no power under UK law to suspend the operation of an Act of Parliament for being in breach of EC law, but the House did refer to the ECJ the question whether it had such a power under EC law.[26] The ECJ ruled that if a rule of national law precluded a national court from granting interim relief in a case concerning EC law then the rule of national law had to be set aside.[27] When the case was sent back to the House of Lords for this ruling to be applied the House decided to exercise its discretionary power to grant the interim relief sought because the applicant's challenge to the Act's requirements concerning residence and domicile was, on its face, a strong one and there was no countervailing public interest that outweighed the damage being caused to the applicants while the matter remained unresolved.[28]

This *Factortame* case was a key turning-point in the relationship between UK law and EC law and deserves to be highlighted here even though the rights at stake were hardly human rights (unless one argues that the applicants' pre-existing property rights had been improperly interfered with as a result of the

21 OJ 1977 No. C 103 p. 1.
22 N. 18 above, at 147G (para. 18).
23 75/117/EEC.
24 *Commission of the EC v UK* Case 61/81, [1982] ICR 578.
25 *Commission of the EC v UK* Case 165/82, [1984] 1 All ER 353.
26 *R v Secretary of State for Transport, ex p Factortame Ltd* [1990] 2 AC 85.
27 *R v Secretary of State for Transport, ex p Factortame Ltd (No. 2)* [1991] 1 AC 603.
28 *Ibid.*

changes made to the rules on registration of vessels by the 1988 Act). Whether the result is attributable to common law *per se* (because the judges decided to defer to the ECJ's ruling) or to Parliament (because the European Communities Act 1972 required the judges to seek and apply such a ruling) is not as important as the fact that EC law was, unequivocally, given priority. That this was then accepted as a constitutional fact is clear from the case of *R v Secretary of State for Employment, ex parte Equal Opportunities Commission*,[29] for there the House of Lords disapplied a provision in another Act of Parliament without even bothering to seek a preliminary ruling from the ECJ. The case concerned statutory provisions which limited the right not to be unfairly dismissed, and to receive compensation if made redundant, to those employees who had worked continuously for specified periods.[30] The House held that these provisions were indirectly discriminatory against women because the UK government had not objectively justified the difference in treatment by showing that it would result in greater availability of part-time work than would otherwise have been the case.

Decisions by the ECJ in two other cases concerning discrimination in the employment context also brought about changes in UK law. *P v S*[31] led to the making of the Sex Discrimination (Gender Reassignment) Regulations 1999, which extended the protection of the Sex Discrimination Act 1975 to persons who intend to have, are having, or have had, gender reassignment surgery. And in *Coleman v Attridge Law*[32] the ECJ ruled that the prohibition of discrimination on the basis of disability in a Council Directive of 2000[33] protected not just employees who were themselves disabled but also employees who were treated less favourably because of their association with a person who was disabled. This decision meant that people who were the primary carers of people with disabilities gained protection against discrimination and the change has now been embedded in the law of England, Scotland and Wales (though not very obviously, and not in Northern Ireland) by the Equality Act 2010, which defines direct discrimination as A treating B less favourably than others 'because of' a protected characteristic such as disability.[34] This definition applies not just in the employment context but also in the context of access to goods and services.

---

29 [1995] 1 AC 1.

30 Employment Protection (Consolidation) Act 1978, ss. 54, 64, 68, 71, 81, 151, and Sch. 13.

31 Case No. C-13/94, [1996] ICR 795. The ECJ held that Council Directive 76/207/EEC, on equal treatment between men and women, did extend to discrimination arising from gender reassignment.

32 Case C-303/06, [2008] ICR 1128.

33 2000/78/EC.

34 S. 13(1).

EC or EU law has also influenced the development of human rights in the UK by requiring protection to be granted to workers against dangers in the workplace,[35] although the government of the day did try (unsuccessfully) to challenge the legitimacy of the Working Time Directive.[36] Brussels has also greatly influenced the way in which personal data is kept confidential in the UK, with the Data Protection Act 1998 implementing a Council Directive of 1995.[37] Otherwise, because EU competence in areas such as housing, education and health care is not yet very extensive, the protection of human rights in those fields has not been greatly impacted by European developments. As is well known, when a 'Social Chapter' was included in the Treaty of Maastricht in 1992[38] (the Treaty of European Union), the UK negotiated an opt-out. But when a Labour government came to power in the UK in 1997 it immediately announced that it was abandoning the opt-out and supporting the revisions to the Social Chapter proposed for the Treaty of Amsterdam later that year. Those revisions still do not include collective rights, such as the right of association, the right to strike or the right to impose lock-outs.[39] However, shortly afterwards, in 2000, the EU's Charter of Fundamental Rights was approved by the European Council and European Parliament and the UK government again proved recalcitrant. When the Council agreed, in 2007, that a 'reform treaty' would replace the draft constitutional treaty that had been rejected by referenda in France and the Netherlands in 2005, the UK government secured another 'opt-out'. This came in the form of Protocol 30 to the Treaty of Lisbon,[40] which has the effect of ensuring that the Charter is not justiciable in UK courts.[41] In other words, the Charter cannot be used to challenge UK laws, regulations or administrative provisions, practices or action, or to create new rights in UK law, and the jurisdiction of the ECJ in such matters is also excluded.[42] To the extent that the ECJ gradually applies the Charter's standards in its own case-law, and equates them to general principles of law, this could eventually impact on the

---

35 See generally Phil Hughes and Ed Ferrett, *Introduction to Health and Safety at Work* (4th edn, 2009).

36 93/104/EEC. This was in *UK v Council of the EU* [1997] ICR 443.

37 95/46/EEC. This built upon the Data Protection Act 1984, which implemented a Council of Europe Convention of 1981. The main change brought about by the 1998 Act was that protection was extended to non-computerised records.

38 It took the form of Protocol 14 to the EC Treaty on Social Policy and the Agreement on Social Policy. The Social Protocol was itself based on the Community Charter of the Fundamental Social Rights of Workers, agreed by all Member States except the UK in 1989. The very first article of the Treaty of Amsterdam of 1997 confirms the attachment of all Member States to fundamental social rights as defined in the European Social Charter of 1961 and the Community Charter of the Fundamental Social Rights of Workers of 1989.

39 Catherine Barnard, 'The United Kingdom, the "Social Chapter" and the Treaty of Amsterdam' (1997) 26 *Industrial Law Journal* 275, 276.

40 Protocol on the Application of the Charter of Fundamental Rights of the EU to Poland and the UK.

41 Nor in the courts of Poland.

42 Protocol 30, Art. 1(1).

UK's human rights law *indirectly*, but this is not likely to occur in the near future. At present there is greater potential for an impact on social and economic rights in the UK to be derived from ECHR law, an area to which we now turn.[43]

3. PRE- AND POST-2000 APPROACHES TO THE ECHR

Until the coming into force of the Human Rights Act 1998, on 2 October 2000, the status of the ECHR in UK law was not high, but nor was the document completely ignored. Parliament was under no national legal obligation to pay attention to it when enacting legislation and the furthest the courts would go in applying the ECHR was to use it as a tie-breaker in situations where ambiguous legislation could be interpreted in a way which either did or did not comply with the Convention or where the exercise of a public authority's discretion was being considered in an application for judicial review.[44] The courts would sometimes refer to the Convention when developing the common law, but they were not obliged to do so, let alone to treat the pronouncements of the European Court of Human rights as binding precedents. It was not until the 1990s that opinion amongst senior judges in the UK began to swing in favour of incorporating the Convention into national law.[45] Towards the end of its long period in opposition the Labour Party published a consultation document on 'bringing home' the Convention[46] and in its manifesto for the 1997 general election it promised to make Convention rights part of national law. After it won that election the Labour government issued a White Paper proposing, in effect, formal incorporation of the Convention. This was because existing law was defective:

> *In this country it was long believed that the rights and freedoms guaranteed by the Convention could be delivered under our common law. In the last two decades,*

---

43 UK readers who are interested in the interaction between EU law and the principles of ECHR law should consult J Wadham et al, *Blackstone's Guide to the Human Rights Act 1998* (4th edn, 2008), ch. 7.

44 See Piers Gardner and Chanaka Wickremasinghe, 'England and Wales and the European Convention' in Brice Dickson (ed.), *Human Rights and the European Convention* (1997), 95–112; Conor Gearty, 'The United Kingdom' in Conor Gearty (ed.), *European Civil Liberties and the European Convention on Human Rights* (1997), 65–83; R Gordon and R Wilmot-Smith (eds.), *Human Rights in the United Kingdom* (1996).

45 In a debate in the House of Lords in 1995 two serving Law Lords, Lord Browne-Wilkinson and Lord Lloyd, spoke in favour of incorporation: HL Debs., Vol. 560, cols. 1148–50 and 1152–1154 (25 January). See too Lord Bingham (Lord Chief Justice of England and Wales at the time), 'The European Convention on Human Rights: Time to Incorporate' in Gordon and Wilmot-Smith, n. 44 above, ch. 1.

46 *Bringing Rights Home* (1996).

> *however, there has been a growing awareness that it is not sufficient to rely on the common law and that incorporation is necessary.*[47]

One of the great debating points at this time was whether domestication of the ECHR should be accompanied by giving UK courts the power to 'disapply' legislation if they found it to be in breach of the Convention. In the end a compromise approach was adopted, partly modelled on New Zealand's Bill of Rights Act 1990: the courts would not be allowed to disapply legislation but they would be allowed to declare it to be incompatible with the ECHR and the government would be given a fast-track mechanism for remedying any such incompatibility (if it so wished) through the making of secondary legislation.[48] Courts would themselves be placed under a duty, as public authorities, to act in a way which is compatible with Convention rights,[49] and would also be required, 'so far as it is possible to do so', to read and give effect to primary and secondary legislation in a way which is compatible with Convention rights.[50] When determining a question arising in connection with a Convention right the courts would have to 'take into account' (i.e. consider but not necessarily follow) existing case law from Strasbourg.[51]

The HRA was revolutionary in that it required a whole new mind-set to be adopted by UK judges. Appropriately, an extensive judicial training programme was put in place, one reason why the commencement of the Act was delayed for almost two years. Looking back now over the first decade of judicial responses to the Act, one can safely say that it has had a hugely significant impact on how judges go about their business. The number of reported cases in which judges have made reference to Strasbourg jurisprudence is legion and between one-third and one-half of all appeals decided by the UK's highest court – which was the Appellate Committee of the House of Lords until October 2009 and is now the Supreme Court[52] (with the same judges sitting in a different building) – involve the interpretation of Convention rights.

---

47 *Rights Brought Home: The Human Rights Bill*, Cm 3782 (1997), para. 1.4. Cf. para. 1.15: '[I]n the Government's view the approach which the United Kingdom has so far adopted towards the Convention does not sufficiently reflect its importance and has not stood the test of time.'

48 HRA 1998, ss. 4 and 10 respectively. The lawyer-politician who claimed most credit for the Act was Lord Irvine of Lairg, the Lord Chancellor at the time. See 'The Impact of the Human Rights Act: Parliament, the Courts and the Executive' in Lord Irvine, *Human Rights, Constitutional Law and the Development of the English Legal System* (2003), ch. 8.

49 *Ibid.*, ss. 6(1) and 6(3)(a).

50 *Ibid.*, s. 3(1).

51 *Ibid.*, s. 2(1).

52 Provided for by the Constitutional Reform Act 2005, ss. 23–60. Moving the top court out of the precincts of Parliament (for the House of Lords is the upper chamber of the UK's bicameral Parliament) was itself partly inspired by the need to avoid a violation of Art. 6 of the ECHR, which requires courts to be impartial and independent.

However, alongside this judicial enthusiasm for the ECHR there has been a strong current of dissatisfaction in the popular press and amongst more right-wing elements of society. This opposition so concerned Tony Blair's government that in 2006 it published a report which attempted to explode some of the myths and misperceptions that had grown up around the HRA.[53] This did not prevent the same government from bitterly complaining when judges took decisions on human rights grounds which appeared to undermine anti-terrorism measures it had pushed through Parliament.[54] The remainder of this chapter will focus on what changes have occurred in UK law during the last decade that are directly attributable to the incorporation of the ECHR through the HRA. It looks first at the influence on Parliament, then at the impact on how judges interact with Parliament, and finally at how judges have developed the common law *per se* by relying on the ECHR.

4. INFLUENCES ON THE UK PARLIAMENT

The Human Rights Act expressly requires the Minister who is in charge of a Bill in either House of Parliament to make a statement indicating whether, in his or her view, the provisions of the Bill are compatible with Convention rights.[55] Not surprisingly, nearly all such statements have so far indicated complete compatibility. Only in three instances has the government indicated incompatibility.[56] Of course the statements are not binding on the courts, being intended mainly as reassurance to MPs and peers that the government has given serious thought to the human rights dimension of the Bill in question.

In addition, examples abound of Acts of Parliament since 2000 which expressly refer to the need to adhere to Convention rights. The Extradition Act 2003 states that any judge who is considering whether a person can be extradited from the UK to a non-EU state must first decide if the extradition would be compatible with Convention rights.[57] The Crime (International Co-operation) Act 2003 allows UK courts not to give effect to overseas freezing orders only if giving effect to them would be incompatible with a Convention right.[58] The Civil

53 Department for Constitutional Affairs, *Review of the Implementation of the Human Rights Act.*

54 See, e.g., the interview on Sky News with former Home Secretary David Blunkett on 2 July 2006: www.skynewstranscripts.co.uk/transcript.asp?id=228 (last accessed 16 May 2011).

55 S. 19. This section was brought into force on 24 November 1998, nearly a year ahead of the rest of the HRA: HRA 1998 (Commencement) Order 1998 (SI 2882).

56 Local Government Bill 1999, Civil Partnership Bill 2002, and Communications Bill 2003. For details see David Feldman, 'The impact of human rights on the UK legislative process' (2005) 25 *Statute Law Review* 91.

57 S. 87(1). The Convention rights in question do not necessarily have to be those of the extraditee (they could be those of his or her family members).

58 S. 90 and Sch. 4, para. 3, inserting para. 11E(4) into Pt. I of Sch. 4 to the Terrorism Act 2000.

Contingencies Act 2004 requires emergency regulations issued by senior government ministers to be compatible with Convention rights.[59] The Legislative and Regulatory Reform Act 2006 prohibits a government minister from ordering the removal of a legislative burden from any person if this involves amending or repealing any provision of the HRA.[60] The Justice and Security (NI) Act 2007 provides that the limitations it imposes on challenges to a decision of the Director of Public Prosecutions in relation to juryless trials in Northern Ireland are subject to claims that a public authority has infringed a Convention right. The Banking Act 2009 requires the government, the Bank of England and the Financial Services Authority, when adopting a special resolution regime for banks that are encountering financial difficulties, to have regard to the objective of avoiding interference with property rights in contravention of the ECHR.[61] All of these Acts show that Parliament takes the ECHR very seriously. In 2002 the government promised to provide specific information on human rights aspects of government Bills when publishing Explanatory Notes to those Bills. The current advice to departments says '[t]his assessment of the impact of the Bill's provisions on the Convention rights should be as detailed as possible setting out any relevant case law and presenting the Government's reasons for concluding that the provisions in the Bill are Convention compatible'.[62]

5. INFLUENCES ON THE RELATIONSHIP BETWEEN UK JUDGES AND THE UK PARLIAMENT

As already noted, the HRA requires judges to read and give effect to legislation in a way which is compatible with Convention rights 'so far as it is possible to do so'.[63] To date judges have exercised this power quite readily.[64] Indeed on one or two occasions they have been accused, with some justification, of overstepping the boundaries of what is 'possible'.[65] In *R v A*[66] the House of Lords applied section 3 of the HRA when ruling that a defendant who was charged with rape could be allowed to cross-examine the complainant about a prior consensual sexual relationship she had had with him, despite this being apparently

59 S. 20(5)(b)(iv).

60 S. 8(b).

61 S. 4(8).

62 UK Cabinet Office, *Guide to Making Legislation* (2010), para. 11.63.

63 S. 3(1).

64 For a fuller exposition of the case law see Alec Samuels, 'Human Rights Act 1998 Section 3: A New Dimension to Statutory Interpretation?' (2008) 29 *Statute Law Review* 130.

65 Lord Bingham described such overstepping of the mark as 'judicial vandalism': *R (Anderson) v Secretary of State for the Home Dept* [2002] UKHL 46, [2003] 1 AC 837, [30].

66 [2001] UKHL 25, [2002] 1 AC 45.

prohibited by a legislative provision.[67] In *Ghaidan v Godin-Mendoza*,[68] where the question was whether a surviving same-sex partner was entitled to succeed to his deceased partner's statutory tenancy as his 'spouse',[69] the House of Lords held that he was, even though the legislation in question dated from 1977 when very few people would have referred to a gay partner as a spouse. In *Secretary of State for the Home Dept v MB*[70] the House of Lords sent two cases back to the High Court with an instruction that the judge there should deal with the challenges to a control order imposed on a suspected terrorist by reading and giving effect to the relevant statutory provisions in a way which was compatible with Article 6 of the ECHR; when one of the controlees returned to the Lords nearly two years later the Lords held that, on the facts, Article 6 had not been complied with.[71]

At times the interpretative approach of section 3 is not adequate to meet the defect in the legislation at issue. In *R (Wright) v Secretary of State for Health*,[72] for example, the question was whether the Care Standards Act 2000,[73] which authorised the keeping of a list of people who were considered unsuitable to work with vulnerable adults, was compatible with Convention rights because it did not provide for according such people a hearing before their names were placed on that list. The Court of Appeal held that, although the statutory provision looked as if it precluded such a hearing, in fact it could be interpreted under section 3 of the 1998 Act as permitting such a hearing.[74] The House of Lords, on the other hand, preferred to issue a declaration of incompatibility under section 4 of the HRA. It felt that the defects in the Care Standards Act could not be wholly cured by reading in the words 'after giving the worker an opportunity to make representations' because there would still be no swift method of hearing both sides of the story before irreparable damage was done to the reputation of the person accused.[75]

Nevertheless, while the interpretative power in section 3 may, on the face of it, look less significant than the power conferred by section 4, the opposite is often the case because a ruling by the highest court based on section 3 can be reversed only if full standard Parliamentary procedures are used, whereas government

---

67 Youth Justice and Criminal Evidence Act 1999, s. 41(3)(c).
68 [2004] UKHL 30, [2004] 2 AC 557. Lord Millett dissented.
69 Under the Rent Act 1977, Sch. 1, paras. 2 and 3(1).
70 [2007] UKHL 46, [2008] AC 440.
71 *Secretary of State for the Home Department v AF (No 3)* [2009] UKHL 28, [2010] 2 AC 269.
72 [2009] UKHL 3, [2009] AC 739.
73 S. 82(4)(b).
74 [2007] EWCA Civ 999, [2008] QB 422.
75 [2009] UKHL 3, [2009] AC 739, [29] (per Lady Hale). The other four Law Lords agreed with Lady Hale.

can react to a declaration under section 4 simply by issuing a remedial order under the procedures allowed for elsewhere in the HRA.[76]

By 1 August 2006 courts in the UK had issued 14 declarations of incompatibility, as well as at least six others which were later overturned on appeal.[77] There have been at least three further declarations since then.[78] In every case the government has taken heed of the declaration by issuing a remedial order[79] or otherwise ensuring a change in the law.[80] In this way the statute book is being made fully ECHR-compliant. In Scotland a full-scale review of the compatibility of existing laws with the ECHR was carried out at the time the HRA was due to come into force. This resulted in the Scottish Parliament enacting the Convention Rights (Compliance) (Scotland) Act 2001 in order to correct some of the alleged incompatibilities. When the House of Lords later held that the HRA's one-year limitation period[81] did not apply to legal proceedings which challenged actions taken by the Scottish Executive,[82] the Scottish Parliament stepped in to amend the Scotland Act 1998 so as to reassert a one-year limitation period.[83]

6. INFLUENCES ON THE UK'S COMMON LAW PER SE[84]

The ECHR has also been influential on the development of 'pure' common law, quite apart from cases where the interpretation and/or compatibility of legislation has been under consideration. In general, though, one might have expected a much greater influence than has in fact occurred, because the HRA expressly

76 S. 10 and Sch. 2. There is a standard procedure for making remedial orders (Sch. 2, para. 2(a)) and also an emergency procedure (Sch 2, para. 2(b)).

77 Details are given in the report issued by the Department for Constitutional Affairs referred to at n. 53 above. The Table is available online at www.dca.gov.uk/peoples-rights/human-rights/pdf/decl-incompat-tabl.pdf.

78 *R (Clift) v Secretary of State for the Home Department* [2006] UKHL 54, [2007] 1 AC 484; the *Wright* case, n. 72 above; and *R (F) v Secretary of State for the Home Department* [2010] 1 UKSC 17, [2010] 2 AC 992. In *Doherty v Birmingham City Council* [2008] UKHL 57, [2009] 1 AC 367 the House of Lords held a legislative provision to be incompatible with the ECHR but did not issue a declaration because Parliament had already amended the provision in question.

79 E.g. Mental Health Act 1983 (Remedial) Order 2001.

80 E.g. by enacting the Gender Recognition Act 2004.

81 S. 7(5).

82 *Somerville v Scottish Ministers* [2007] UKHL 44, [2007] 1 WLR 2734.

83 Convention Rights Proceedings (Amendment) (Scotland) Act 2009. Likewise, after the UK Supreme Court held that Scottish law's denial of access to a solicitor for persons arrested was a violation of Art. 6 of the ECHR (*Cadder v HM Advocate* [2010] UKSC 43, [2010] 1 WLR 2601), the Scottish Parliament rectified matters by enacting the Criminal Procedure (Legal Assistance, Detention and Appeals) (Scotland) Act 2010.

84 For a summary of the views on the extent to which common law can protect human rights see R Clayton and H Tomlinson, *The Law of Human Rights* (2nd edn, 2009), paras. 1.36 –1.46.

requires courts to act in ways that are compatible with Convention rights,[85] so if counsel do not raise Convention points when arguing their cases the judges themselves should do so. Moreover, in cases where the common law *has* been developed the judges often suggest that they would have come to the same conclusion even if the HRA had not compelled them to consider the ECHR and in a recent interview the Deputy President of the UK Supreme Court implied that if the HRA were to be repealed it might not make much difference because the common law could still protect Convention rights.[86] The approach generally adopted by UK judges to arguments that they should go beyond the ECHR is that which was clearly set out by the Senior Law Lord, Lord Bingham, in *R (Ullah) v Special Adjudicator*:

> *It is of course open to member states to provide for rights more generous than those guaranteed by the Convention, but such provision should not be the product of interpretation of the Convention by national courts, since the meaning of the Convention should be uniform throughout the states party to it. The duty of national courts is to keep pace with the Strasbourg jurisprudence as it evolves over time: no more, but certainly no less.*[87]

6.1. THE RIGHT TO PRIVACY AND REFUSAL TO DEVELOP THE COMMON LAW

Perhaps the area of common law in which UK judges have most obviously failed to live up to expectations as regards Convention rights is that of privacy law. Despite the requirements of Article 8 of the ECHR, and decisions by the European Court such as that in *Von Hannover v Germany*,[88] UK judges still refuse to confirm that there is a full-blown right to privacy in English law and they deny that Article 8 requires such a right. In one case, where a woman and her disabled son were strip-searched when visiting a relative in prison (at a time before the HRA came into force), the House of Lords held there was no breach of the common law and it intimated that even if the HRA had been in force at the time there would still have been no violation of a Convention right.[89] But when the case was taken to Strasbourg the European Court ruled that Article 8 had indeed been violated.[90] Similarly, in the disturbing case of Diane Pretty, who suffered from motor neurone disease and wanted her right to an assisted suicide to be recognised under the Convention, the House of Lords held that Article 8

85 S. 6(1) and 6(3)(a).

86 See http: //ukhumanrightsblog.com/2010/08/05/repeal-of-human-rights-act-would-make-no-difference (last accessed 16 May 2011).

87 [2004] UKHL 26, [2004]2 AC 323, [20].

88 (2005) 40 EHRR 1.

89 [2003] UKHL 53, [2004] 2 AC 406. See in particular [32] – [35] (per Lord Hoffmann).

90 *Wainwright v UK* (2007) 44 EHRR 40.

was not even engaged.[91] The European Court again had to correct this[92] and when a later case on assisted suicide reached the Lords they accepted that Article 8 was engaged and ordered the Director of Public Prosecutions to issue new guidelines on the factors that would be taken into account when deciding whether to prosecute someone for assisting a suicide.[93]

A further context in which UK courts have failed to apply Article 8 in the manner preferred by Strasbourg is that of police powers. In *R (S) v Chief Constable of South Yorkshire Police*[94] the House of Lords held by 5 v 0 that the police's power to retain fingerprints and DNA samples of persons not convicted of criminal offences did not constitute an unjustifiable interference with Article 8.[95] This too did not survive scrutiny in Strasbourg, where all 17 judges in the Grand Chamber found a breach of Article 8.[96] This is as marked a difference of opinion between top UK judges and the European Court as there has ever been and is all the more remarkable given that the UK's top court is now staffed by some of the most liberal judges yet to have served in that capacity. Yet the House also failed to meet the European Court's standards when it was asked to adjudicate on whether a power conferred on the police to stop people at random and search them for articles that could be used in connection with terrorism was compatible with the ECHR. The Law Lords again held unanimously that it was,[97] but the European Court unanimously begged to differ, finding that there was a violation of Article 8 on the basis that the powers to authorise and confirm the use of such stops, as well as the stops and searches themselves, were neither sufficiently circumscribed nor subject to adequate legal safeguards against abuse and so were not 'in accordance with the law' as required by the ECHR.[98] The current UK government, a coalition elected in May 2010, has suspended the use of this stop and search power and has issued a remedial order temporarily replacing it until it is permanently replaced with provisions in the Protection of Freedoms Bill currently before Parliament.[99]

On other occasions UK courts have said that they might have decided cases differently if the facts had arisen after the HRA had come into force, but they have still not plugged the gap in the law by developing the common law. A

91 *R (Pretty) v DPP* [2001] UKHL 61, [2002] 1 AC 800.
92 *Pretty v UK* (2002) 35 EHRR 1.
93 *R (Purdy) v DPP* [2009] UKHL 45, [2010] 1 AC 345. This was the last set of judgments issued by the House of Lords before that court was replaced by the UK's Supreme Court in 2009.
94 [2004] UKHL 39, [2004] 1 WLR 2196.
95 All of the judges except Lady Hale went so far as to say that the retention of the data did not even engage Art. 8!
96 *S and Marper v UK* (2009) 48 EHRR 50.
97 *R (Gillan) v Commissioner of Police for the Metropolis* [2006] UKHL 12, [2006] 2 AC 307.
98 *Gillan and Quinton v UK* (2010) 50 EHRR 45, para. 87.
99 Terrorism Act 2000 (Remedial) Order 2011 (SI 631).

notable instance of this is *In re McKerr*,[100] where the House of Lords had to decide whether the UK government was obliged to conduct an Article 2-compliant investigation into a death occurring before the HRA came into force and whether, if not, there was a common law right to arrange for a comparably effective investigation. The House held against the applicant on both points,[101] with Lord Nicholls observing as follows:

> *I have grave reservations about the appropriateness of the common law now fashioning a free-standing positive obligation of this far-reaching character. Such a development would be far removed from the normal way the common law proceeds. But I need not pursue this wider question. The submission fails for more straightforward, orthodox reasons. The effect of counsel's submission, if accepted, would be that the court would create an overriding obligation on the state, corresponding to Article 2 of the Convention, in an area of the law for which Parliament has long legislated. The courts have always been slow to develop the common law by entering, or re-entering, a field regulated by legislation. Rightly so, because otherwise there would inevitably be the prospect of the common law shaping powers and duties and provisions inconsistent with those prescribed by Parliament.*[102]

A comparable reluctance to develop the common law was apparent in *Jain v Trent Strategic Health Authority*.[103] There the House of Lords criticised Parliament for the 'lamentable lack… of reasonable safeguards' in the provisions of the Registered Homes Act 1984 relating to cancellation of the registration of a nursing home,[104] but it refused to move away from the precedent it had itself set in *X (Minors) v Bedfordshire County Council*,[105] which limits the beneficiaries of the duty of care owed by state authorities acting under legislative powers to those whom the legislation in question was designed to protect, thereby excluding others whose interests might be adversely affected by the exercise of the powers. Although the House said that, had the HRA been in force at the time of the application by the local authority to cancel the registration of the claimants' nursing home, the claimants might have argued successfully that their Convention rights to a fair trial and to protection of their property had been breached, the court was unable to conjure up a remedy for the claimants under

100 [2004] UKHL 12, [2004] 1 WLR 807.

101 Even though, remarkably, in two other appeals heard by five different Law Lords but decided on the same day as *In re McKerr*, the House ruled that the regime for holding inquests in England and Wales did not provide an Art. 2-complaint investigation of a death in custody even though the deaths had occurred before the HRA came into force: *R (Middleton) v West Somerset Coroner* and *R (Sacker) v West Yorkshire Coroner* [2004] UKSC 10 and 11, [2004] 2 AC 182.

102 N. 100 above, [30]. See too [51] (per Lord Steyn), [70]-[71] (per Lord Hoffmann), [91] (per Lord Brown).

103 [2009] UKHL 4, [2009] AC 853.

104 *Ibid.*, [36] (per Lord Scott).

105 [1995] 2 AC 633.

the common law. However, in other sensitive cases where the need to balance Article 8 considerations against Article 10 considerations have arisen, the House of Lords appears to have got the balance right because no disappointed litigant has since gone on to win on the point in Strasbourg.[106]

6.2. DEVELOPING THE COMMON LAW BEYOND THE ECHR

On at least three occasions UK judges *have* been able to develop the common law in order to protect fundamental rights in ways which the ECHR did not do. The first case relates to the admissibility of unfairly obtained evidence, the second to prison law, and the third to adoption law. In *A v Secretary of State for the Home Department (No. 2)*,[107] a follow-up case to the landmark ruling by the House of Lords that the indefinite detention without trial of non-British citizens reasonably suspected of involvement in terrorism was contrary to Article 5 of the ECHR (despite a derogation notice being in place under Article 15),[108] the issue was whether a UK court could admit evidence which had been, or may have been, procured by torture inflicted by officials of a foreign state, with or without the complicity of British authorities. In their search for guidance on this basic point, judges in the House of Lords surveyed the jurisprudence emanating from Strasbourg but could not find a definitive ruling. In the end the court relied first and foremost on principles of the common law to justify the conclusion that such evidence could not be admitted:

> *I accept the broad thrust of the appellants' argument on the common law. The principles of the common law, standing alone, in my opinion compel the exclusion of third party torture evidence as unreliable, unfair, offensive to ordinary standards of humanity and decency and incompatible with the principles which should animate a tribunal seeking to administer justice.*[109]

Unfortunately the majority of their Lordships immediately undermined this conclusion by ruling that the burden of proving that the evidence in question has been wrongfully procured rests on the defendant, an almost impossible burden

---

106 The two principal cases here are *In re S (A Child) (Identification: Restriction on Publication)* [2004] UKHL 47, [2005] 1 AC 593 and *In re British Broadcasting Corporation* [2009] UKHL 34, [2010] 1 AC 145. For a House of Lords' decision in an Art. 10 case involving a broadcaster's right to refuse to broadcast offensive material see *R (ProLife Alliance) v British Broadcasting Corporation* [2003] UKHL 23, [2004] 1 AC 185; the losing applicant appears not to have later lodged an application in Strasbourg.

107 [2005] UKHL 71, [2006] 2 AC 221.

108 *A v Secretary of State for the Home Dept* [2004] UKHL 56, [2005] 2 AC 68.

109 N. 107 above, [52] (per Lord Bingham). Cf. Lord Carswell, at [151]: 'I am satisfied that the common law can accommodate the principles involved'. See too [64] (per Lord Nicholls), [97] (per Lord Hoffmann], [113] (per Lord Hope), and [137] (per Lord Hope).

to discharge, even if the standard of proof required is merely the balance of probabilities.[110] In a wholly separate case, moreover, UK judges refused to go beyond the European Court's established position regarding civil remedies for torture: they refused to allow victims of torture committed abroad to sue the authorities of that country in the courts of the UK.[111] Sadly, both of these decisions would probably have been no different had the issues been considered in Strasbourg.[112]

The prison case is *R (Smith) v Parole Board*,[113] where two prisoners had been recalled to prison for breaching the conditions of their release on licence but were denied an oral hearing by the Parole Board when it was considering whether to revoke their licences. The House of Lords held that there was no breach of Articles 5(1) or 6(1) of the ECHR, but that there was a breach of the common law duty of procedural fairness. This, in turn, meant that there was also a breach of Article 5(4) because it is a feature of Article 5 that it requires detention to be lawful in accordance not just with the minimum requirements laid down by Article 5 itself but also with whatever additional requirements are laid down by the national legal system in question. Hence, in Lord Hope's words:

> *Procedural fairness is a requirement of the common law. It is not in itself a Convention requirement. But it is built into the Convention requirement because Article 5 (4) requires that the continuing detention must be judicially supervised and because our own domestic law requires that bodies acting judicially, as a court would act, must conduct their proceedings in a way that is procedurally fair.*[114]

The adoption case is *In re G (Adoption: Unmarried Couple)*,[115] an appeal from Northern Ireland to the House of Lords. Under the Adoption (NI) Order 1987[116] only couples who were married could jointly adopt a child. In this case an unmarried heterosexual couple complained that this was a violation of their rights under Article 8 of the ECHR. In the courts of Northern Ireland they lost,[117] because the judges saw the legislation as representing a deliberate choice on the part of Parliament which reflected the comparatively conservative nature of Northern Ireland society (elsewhere in the UK the right to jointly

---

110 Only Lords Bingham, Nicholls and Hoffmann thought that the burden of proving that the evidence was not so obtained lay on the party seeking to adduce it.

111 *Jones v Ministry of Interior of Saudi Arabia* [2006] UKHL 26, [2007] 1 AC 270.

112 This is certainly so as far as civil liability for torture is concerned: *Al-Adsani v UK* (2002) 34 EHRR 11.

113 [2005] UKHL 1, [2005] 1 WLR 350.

114 *Ibid.*, [75].

115 [2008] UKHL 38, [2009] AC 173.

116 Art. 14.

117 [2007] NICA 20, [2007] NI 251.

adopt had already been extended to unmarried couples, whether heterosexual or homosexual). But in the House of Lords four of the five Law Lords were prepared to treat the legislative provision as invalid because of its undue interference with Article 8. This was so even though the right to adopt is not one which the European Court of Human Rights has unequivocally recognized, although it has held that if the right to adopt does exist in a national legal system it should not operate in a way which discriminates against adopters depending on their sexuality.[118] Lord Hoffmann approached the issue head on:

> *I...do not think that your Lordships should be inhibited from declaring that article 14 of the 1987 Order is unlawful discrimination, contrary to Articles 8 and 14 of the Convention, by the thought that you might be going further than the Strasbourg court. But what if you were?...[This is] a case in which Strasbourg has deliberately declined to lay down an interpretation for all member states, as it does when it says that the question is within the margin of appreciation. In such a case, it is for the court in the United Kingdom to interpret Articles 8 and 14 and to apply the division between the decision-making powers of courts and Parliament in the way which appears appropriate for the United Kingdom.*[119]

6.3. HESITATION AND DOUBTS

There are other cases, however, where the UK's highest court has found the domestic law to be compatible with the ECHR, where it has nevertheless identified other anomalies in the law that it felt should be rectified, but where it has left the rectification to be conducted by Parliament rather than make the change itself. One such case is *R (Black) v Secretary of State for Justice*,[120] where the House of Lords found that the Home Secretary's statutory power[121] to reject the Parole Board's recommendation that a prisoner serving a determinate sentence of more than 15 years should be released was compatible with Article 5(4) of the ECHR.[122] The domestic court went on to add that the Home Secretary's power was indefensibly anomalous, given that it did not apply in cases where the prisoner was serving either an indeterminate sentence or a determinate sentence of less than 15 years. The power, said their Lordships, should be removed, but this should be done by Parliament not by the courts. The Court of Appeal below had been bolder, declaring that the domestic legislation in question

118 *EB v France* (2008) 47 EHRR 21.

119 [2008] UKHL 38, [2009] AC 173, [29], [36] and [37]. Lord Walker dissented. For him the decision to change the law in Northern Ireland 'is one that ought to be made by a democratically-elected legislature' (ibid., [82]).

120 [2009] UKHL 1, [2009] AC 949.

121 Criminal Justice Act 1991, s. 35(1).

122 Lord Phillips, the President of the Court, dissented.

was incompatible with Article 5(4).[123] The problem facing the House of Lords was that, having found that Article 5(4) was not even engaged on these facts, it could not then fall back on any common law power to override the express words of an Act of Parliament or to develop the content of Article 5(4) through expanding the common law as it had done in *R (Smith) v Parole Board*.[124]

While the UK courts have displayed considerable respect for the jurisprudence of the European Court of Human Rights in the past decade, there have recently been tell-tale signs that the relationship is not as harmonious as it used to be. A lecture delivered by Lord Hoffmann to the Judicial Studies Board of England and Wales a few months before he retired as a senior judge in 2009 left his audience in no doubt that in his view the European Court had begun to go too far in 'correcting' UK judges on whether aspects of UK law were fully compatible with the ECHR.[125] He was particularly critical of the European Court's judgments in *Saunders v UK*[126] on the right to silence, in *Al-Khawaja and Tahery v UK*[127] on the hearsay rule, and in *Hatton v UK*[128] on night flights at Heathrow airport. He felt that the Strasbourg court should not have interfered with conclusions reached by the top UK court on matters which were essentially within the margin of appreciation of the Member State. He did not think the Strasbourg court was like the ECJ in Luxembourg:

> *The Strasbourg court, on the other hand, has no mandate to unify the laws of Europe on the many subjects which may arguably touch upon human rights. Because, for example, there is a human right to a fair trial, it does not follow that all the countries of the Council of Europe must have the same trial procedure. Criminal procedures in different countries may differ widely without any of them being unfair. Likewise, the application of many human rights in a concrete case, the trade-offs which must be made between individual rights and effective government, or between the rights of one individual and another, will frequently vary from country to country, depending upon the local circumstances and legal tradition.*[129]

There have been similar, though not such strongly worded, sentiments expressed by at least two other senior UK judges, Dame Mary Arden[130] and Lord Judge

123 Also reported at [2009] AC 949.

124 N. 113 above.

125 'The Universality of Human Rights' (19 March 2009), available at www.justice-for-families.org.uk/reports/JStudiesBoardLecture0309.htm (last accessed 16 May 2011).

126 (1996) 23 EHRR 313. Lord Hoffmann also poured scorn on the two dissenting Strasbourg judges in *O'Halloran and Francis v UK* (2008) 46 EHRR 21.

127 (2009) 49 EHRR 1.

128 (2003) 37 EHRR 28 (GC).

129 N. 125 above, para. 24.

130 Speech at a seminar to mark the opening of the judicial year at the European Court of Human Rights, 29 January 2010: www.globalgovernancewatch.org/docLib/20100310_LJA_Speech_at_2010_Opening.pdf (last accessed 16 May 2011).

(the current Lord Chief Justice).[131] And in one case, again on the hearsay rule, the UK's Supreme Court Justices have gone to extraordinary lengths to make it clear why they think the European Court of Human Rights should come to the same conclusion as that favoured domestically.[132] Given that other highly sensitive cases are currently pending before the European Court – on issues such as deportation to countries where torture (or the death penalty) is routinely practised[133] and the extra-territorial operation of the ECHR[134] – it is possible that significant clashes will soon occur. If this were to happen most commentators are likely to see it as a set-back for the influence of European law on UK human rights law. A minority will suggest that it is time the European Court pulled in its horns and began to pay more attention to the particularities of national legal cultures.

7. CONCLUSION

It can be seen from the foregoing pages that UK human rights law has indeed been deeply impacted by both EU law and ECHR law, despite the fact that the UK has opted out of the Charter of Fundamental Rights and took so long to make the ECHR part of its domestic law. That influence will undoubtedly continue, but at the same time the law-making organs of the UK will strive to preserve their own role in protecting human rights in ways which accord with the legal traditions of the common law. There is no reason for unseemly clashes to occur between national positions on human rights issues and the positions adopted in Brussels, Luxembourg and Strasbourg. Complementarity should be the name of the game.

---

131 Annual lecture of the Judicial Studies Board, 17 March 2010: www.judiciary.gov.uk/NR/rdonlyres/F019E590–827B-463F-8069-A40376DC3C4B/0/lcjjsblecture2010.pdf (last accessed 16 May 2011).

132 *R v Horncastle* [2009] UKSC 14, [2010] 2 AC 373.

133 *RB (Algeria) v Secretary of State for the Home Department* [2009] UKHL 10, [2009] 2 AC 110; *Al-Saadoon v UK* (2010) 51 EHRR 9.

134 *R (Al-Jedda) v Secretary of State for Defence* [2007] UKHL 58, [2008] 1 AC 332.

CHAPTER 13

PROTECTION OF EUROPEAN HUMAN RIGHTS BY HIGHEST COURTS IN EUROPE

The art of triangulation

Wim VOERMANS*

'(...) As if it harm'd me, giving others the same chances and rights as myself – As if it were not indispensable to my own rights that others possess the same.'

Walt Whitman, Leaves of Grass (1867)

1. AT THE HEART OF THE MATTER: OBSERVING EUROPEAN HUMAN RIGHTS REQUIRES CONSTITUTIONAL BALANCING

In his contribution '*The Jurisprudence of Constitutional Conflict: Constitutional Supremacy in Europe before and after the Constitutional Treaty*,' Mattias Kumm in 2005 observed that:

> "The question how to deal with constitutional conflicts is perhaps the most enduring controversial issue in contemporary European constitutional theory and practice. Forty years after the Court of Justice declared the law of the European Communities to be the supreme law of the land in Europe, controversy over the relationship between EU Law and national law remains very much alive."[1]

* Wim Voermans is professor of Constitutional Law at Leiden University, Dean of the European Academy of Law and Legislation and vice-president of the International Association of Legislation.

1 M Kumm, 'The Jurisprudence of Constitutional Conflict: Constitutional Supremacy in Europe before and after the Constitutional Treaty,' *European Law Journal*, Vol. 11, No. 3, May 2005, pp. 262–307.

Six years later we can only say that his observation still holds true and – especially after the enlargement of the EU with Eastern European States – the debate is still on-going, notwithstanding or even due to the constitutional settlements in the Lisbon Treaty. Constitutional conflicts in the EU arise for many reasons. First of all the constitutional order of the EU is still relatively young – 50 years of age more or less, depending on one's perception of the starting moment[2] – and developing. Secondly there is (increasing) political controversy over the content of EU Constitutional law related to questions as regards the direction the EU should take and the speed and depth of political and economic integration. Third: the EU's constitutional order is not an isolated system but a part of a complex "compound constitutional system"[3] consisting of the Treaties, enacted EU law, case law, conventions,[4] soft law,[5] international law and the constitutional law of the Member States. Interpreting and applying European constitutional law, as the EU courts (including both the domestic courts and the Court of Justice of the European Union)[6] are required to do, is a perpetual balancing act with rules on conflict resolution and coordination that are themselves constantly evolving or – worse – not even there at all.

Different jurisdictions grapple with the many conundrums the EU's compound constitutional system presents, especially the courts who have to reconcile the demands of constitutional law welling from different sources. This is why the study of the interaction between the European Court of Justice, the European Court of Human Rights and the national constitutional courts, in case of the protection of human rights is interesting and topical both from an academic point of view as well from a practical perspective. The 2009 seminar on the protection of human rights in the Interaction between the European Courts[7] – inviting judges and referees of the Luxembourg and Strasbourg courts and academics alike – and the indeed rich contributions to this study prove that beyond any doubt.

---

2 One might argue that the constitutional order of the European Community started with the EEC treaty (entering into force in 1958) or, on the other hand, that the order came about by the ruling of the Court of Justice in the cases of Van Gend en Loos (Case 26/62, [1963] ECR 1) and Costa Enel (Case 6/64, [1964] ECR 585). So, emerging from 1963 or 1964 onward depending on one's view.

3 A Peters, 'The Globalization of State Constitutions' in J Nijman and A Nollkaemper (eds), *New Perspectives on the Divide between National and International Law* (OUP, Oxford 200), p. 251–308.

4 See for a very interesting study on conventions as a source of EU constitutional law T Beukers, *Law, Practice and Convention in the Constitution of the European Union*, PhD thesis University of Amsterdam, Amsterdam 2011.

5 L Senden, *Soft Law in European Community Law*, PhD thesis Tilburg University. OUP Oxford 2004.

6 Which after the Lisbon treaty in turn consists of three courts: the Court of Justice, the General Court (created in 1988) and the Civil Service Tribunal (created in 2004).

7 Held on 27 March 2009, University of Antwerp.

In this contribution I will try to distil some common threads from the discussions (which involved very open – Chatham house rule – debates between justices, referees and academics) and from the contributions to this study. The account in this chapter will neither be comprehensive (the material is too rich for that) nor will it be comparative in the true sense of the word. The constitutional systems, the way domestic highest constitutional courts – to which the domestic element of this study is restricted – are set up, the way the courts review and apply and interpret human rights differ to an extent that does not easily allow for comparison.

2. THE EUROPEAN COMPOUND HUMAN RIGHTS SYSTEM: SHARING RIGHTS AND COURTS

The system of human rights protection in Europe is hard to explain when travelling abroad and meeting colleagues from other parts of the world. Indeed, most of continental Europe shares a common pool of human rights, the bulk of it expressed in the European Convention on Human Rights (ECHR). This Convention, signed in Rome in November 1950, is binding on the 47 Member States of the Council of Europe. The 1950[8] Convention establishes a European Court of Human Rights (ECtHR) which enforces the ECHR rights by way of providing legal recourse of last resort for individuals and other contracting parties who feel that their human rights have been violated by a contracting party to the Convention. The human rights catalogue of the ECHR has developed substantially by way of elaboration in case law and by way of 14 ratified Protocols[9] to date.[10] The common core of the European rights, the rights expressed in the ECHR proper, can in nearly all signatory states be invoked directly in proceedings before domestic courts[11]and – if all domestic remedies have been exhausted – in proceedings before the ECtHR. Contracting parties to the ECHR can address the

---

8 Entering into force in 1953.

9 Actually less, because some of the protocols (e.g. 11 and 14) merely amend the European Convention.

10 March 2011.

11 Depending on the constitutional system of reception and implementation of international law of a jurisdiction. If a constitution gives direct effect to international law (monistic system) violations of ECHR-rights may be appealed right away. Constitutional systems that are dualistic in nature – meaning that international law needs to be transposed and incorporated into domestic law before it can have direct legal effect – resist direct invokability and direct application of international law before or by national courts. Some states that are formally dualist (Belgium) or that have traditionally denied the direct applicability of treaty law in the domestic legal system (like Austria) have nonetheless conferred on the Convention rights constitutional or quasi-constitutional status, with truly transformative effects. In the United Kingdom, for instance, a special Act (the Humans Rights Act 1998) was enacted to give 'further effect' (meaning more or less the same as a sort of mitigated direct effect) to the ECHR. See Alec Stone Sweet and Helen Keller, 'The Reception of the ECHR in National Legal

Strasbourg Court right away in case of alleged violations by another contracting party.

A second source of supranational fundamental rights emerged in the European legal order, namely EU fundamental rights. Originally, the Treaties did not have a 'traditional' list of human rights, such as civil rights and political freedoms. However, since the human rights of the ECHR were common to all of the European Communities Member States the Court of Justice as far back as 1970 ruled that the ECHR rights are an 'integral part of the general principles of [European Community] law', with the effect that they also impose restrictions on community institutions.[12] In later cases the ECJ emphasized that these fundamental rights also bind Member States when executing EU norms (agency-type actions as mentioned in the case Wachau – case 5/88, 1989, ECR 2609) or when legitimately derogating from EU law (ERT-type actions). In short, when domestic measures fall within the scope of EU law they are required to respect fundamental rights.

The EU reinforced its fundamental rights credentials through four crucial steps. First, fundamental rights were enshrined in the TEU as general principles of Union law and thus binding all EU institutions as Member States with regard to all measures falling within the scope of EU law. Article 6 ECHR holds that these fundamental rights follow from the ECHR and rights common to the constitutional traditions. Secondly, a Charter on EU fundamental rights was solemnly proclaimed by the EU institutions in the year 2000.[13] Since December 2009 the EU Charter – consisting of 54 articles – under Article 6 of the Treaty on the European Union (EU Treaty) has the same legal value as the European Union treaties themselves, although it still remains a separate act. Third, Article 6(2) of the EU Treaty stipulates that the EU shall accede to the European Convention for the Protection of Human Rights and Fundamental Freedoms. The EU has already sprung into action. On 17 March 2010 the EU Commission proposed negotiation directives for the EU's accession to the ECHR. Finally, the EU improved its fundamental rights credentials through elaborating several norms

---

Orders', *Faculty Scholarship Series*, Paper 89, 2008, 28–29. http://digitalcommons.law.yale.edu/fss_papers/89.

12 Case 228/69, Internationale Handelsgesellschaft mbH v. Einfuhr und Vorratsstelle für Getreide und Futtermittel [1970] ECR 1125. The community institutions endorsed this 'Handelsgesellschaft'-ruling in 1977. Joint Declaration by the European Parliament, Council and the Commission concerning the protection of fundamental rights and the ECHR (*OJ* C 103, 1977, p. 1–2) A statement to this effect was added to the Maastricht Treaty of 1992. Article F of the Maastricht Treaty, *OJ* 2002, C 191.

13 On the benefits of such Charter in addition to the ECHR see e.g. T Barkhuysen and AW Bos, 'De betekenis van het Handvest van de Grondrechten van de Europese Unie voor het bestuursrecht (The meaning of the Charter of Fundamental Rights of the European Union in Dutch administrative law)', *JB plus* (*Journal for Administrative Law*), 3 [2011], p. 3–34.

on specific fundamental rights issues (e.g. gender discrimination). In addition, several fundamental rights with human right character are to be found in the EU Treaty (e.g. the principle of equal treatment, the rights to vote and to be eligible, etc.) and the Treaty on the functioning of the EU (TFEU) (e.g. privacy rights such as the right to protection of personal data, respect for religion, the principle of non-discrimination, etc.).

The fact that all 27 members of the European Union are contracting party to the ECHR makes Europe's fundamental rights protection complex. The EU accession to the ECHR further intertwines the two supranational systems of fundamental rights protection. Thus, the protection of fundamental rights of the ECtHR and the ECJ interact as well as affect fundamental rights protection at the domestic plane. Besson argues convincingly that while many similarities between both supranational systems exist, there also remain key differences which render the interaction even more complex as with regards to the protection of fundamental rights and democratic credentials (see Chapter 4).

This complexity is even more increased due to the existence of several procedures which allow applicants to challenge norms which violate their fundamental rights. E.g., applicants can demand the protection of the ECHR before national courts. If all domestic procedures have been exhausted, the applicants can lodge a complaint before the ECtHR. The same ECHR rights can – as principles – be invoked in proceedings before the ECJ as well: after the Treaty of Lisbon citizens with an interest can, under the new Article 263 TFEU, directly challenge EU action if it violates ECHR rights, but they can also take the indirect route of the request for a preliminary reference procedure. Under this injunction-like procedure (Article 267 TFEU) national courts may, and sometimes must, turn to the Court of Justice and ask that it clarify a point concerning the interpretation or application of EU law, in order, for example, to make sure their national legislation complies with that law. Correct application of ECHR rights – in the guise of EU principles – is an issue that may require this kind of clarification and – on a request of one of the applicants – may prompt a national court to refer the issue to the Luxembourg Court during national proceedings. Four forms of legal recourse for the observance of ECHR rights. Mind boggling. If courts do not take due account of the position of other courts this might result in incoherencies and open conflicts.

In a similar fashion the supranational procedures might undermine the domestic fundamental rights protection. The UK has limited the competence of judges to set aside legislation on the grounds of incompatibilities with the ECHR by a procedure called the Declaration of Incompatibility entrenched in the Human Rights Act 1998. Judges cannot set aside legislation, but only signal the incompatibility of an act of parliament with the Human Rights Act (see Chapter

12). In order to decrease the potential of judges setting aside domestic legislation with regards to supranational fundamental rights law, the UK has opted out of the EU Charter. However, one may for instance wonder what will happen to the system if British litigants find the short-cut of using the rights in the EU Charter and the preliminary reference procedure to get a quick answer to a European right complaint. Will British courts, when confronted with a preliminary ruling on a human rights complaint, saying that a British Act does not comply, still refer the matter to Parliament? Difficult questions all in all.

The complexities of the triangular human rights review (domestic, Luxembourg and Strasbourg) in Europe affects national courts, especially the highest courts, as well. Domestic 'last resort courts', i.e. a court against whose decisions there is no judicial remedy under national law (like a Supreme Court, High Court or a Constitutional Court) shoulder important responsibilities. First of all they are – when it comes down to ECHR rights protection – the gateposts and switch points to the European Courts. Only when all domestic remedies have been exhausted the ECtHR can deal with complaints (Article 35(1) ECHR) and last resort courts are obliged to refer cases involving the validity or interpretation of EU law to the ECJ under Article 267 TFEU. Secondly they are the joints between the domestic constitutional/legal system and the EU legal orders. The crossroads here are governed by the complex constitutional relations of compound – or if you prefer 'pluralistic' – legal orders. Although one would expect otherwise, there are only few rules that govern these constitutional relations between the European legal orders and the domestic ones. This implies that these last resort courts have to establish their own position in this legal network of fundamental rights jurisprudence. When scrutinizing the interactions between these different actors we can observe two common threads: first, the search for coherence and secondly, the dilemma of autonomy.

3. CONSTITUTIONAL CALIBRATION OF EUROPEAN HUMAN RIGHTS REVIEW

3.1. THE SEARCH FOR COHERENCE

Open conflicts with regards to fundamental rights protection are rare. There is a simple reason for that: courts have sensibly developed flexible mechanisms to avoid open conflicts. It is clear from the Member State contributions that the ECJ and the ECtHR jurisprudence play a defining role in the domestic protection of fundamental rights. While the legal rank of EU law or ECHR law in the domestic legal order might diverge (legislative, sub-constitutional or constitutional), the constitutional courts take due regard of the ECJ and the ECtHR case law when interpreting constitutional rights. Arnold explains how the German

Constitutional Court holds that ordinary judges must take due account of the ECtHR case law when interpreting constitutional rights even though the ECHR is in principle only of legislative rank (Chapter 8). The constitutional systems of the EU Member States give – in one way or other – direct effect to the ECHR rights, more or less regardless of their constitutional system of reception of international law. This produces the net effect that ECHR rights override domestic law albeit that the consequences thereof may be mitigated by national law (e.g. the UK Human Rights Act 1998 or the judicial ban on constitutional review of parliamentary acts in the Netherlands, as the contributions of Dickson and Claes & Leenknegt show, see Chapter 10).

Most constitutional courts refer explicitly to the ECtHR case law when reviewing. Constitutional courts might even function as the main protector of the ECtHR. E.g. the German Constitutional Court has argued that it will scrutinize whether the neglect of ECtHR case law by ordinary courts amounts to a violation of constitutional rights (see Chapter 8). The Italian Constitutional Court qualified itself as the only tribunal in Italy competent to solve conflicts between ordinary laws and the ECHR and therefore forced to take up the challenge to become the arbiter of the protection of fundamental rights in that critical area in which the constitutional dimension encounters the supranational and the international ones (see Chapter 9). The French Constitutional Council appears exceptional in the fact that it does not rely explicitly to the ECtHR jurisprudence. The contribution of Burgorgue-Larsen argues that such lack of explicit references does not mean that the Constitutional Council's jurisprudence remains free from Strasbourg influence. On several occasions a shift in the case law was influenced directly by new ECtHR jurisprudence. She speaks of an "Europeanization" of the French Constitution (see Chapter 7).

Similarly, fundamental rights developed at the EU level have played a considerable role in the domestic protection of fundamental rights. Guerra Lopez indicates in a detailed manner how EU fundamental rights law has had an impact on the Spanish constitutional protection of fundamental rights. This influence has been enabled by the constitutional provision which requires that constitutional rights are interpreted in the light of all equivalent international norms. Guerra Lopez argues that the influence of ECJ case law on fundamental rights protection will only increase with the introduction of the Charter as this Charter will generate a more visible role for the ECJ as protector of fundamental rights (Chapter 11).

There appears to be a general tendency among constitutional courts in Europe to read constitutional rights in the light of the ECtHR or ECJ case law in order to avoid conflicts and guarantee respect for the supranational obligations of the Member State. We observe similar efforts on behalf of the ECJ and the ECtHR to ensure coherent fundamental rights adjudication in the European legal order.

The EU accession to the ECHR is an attempt to improve the coherence. Still, this sort of compilation of European human rights – in our experience – puzzles outside observers, because how does one accede to a Convention that has already been incorporated into a separate EU Charter? And which Court will ultimately decide on the observance of what fundamental rights? The Babushka-like nature of human rights protection undoubtedly will continue to raise questions, conflicts and coordination problems in the near future. In order to avoid such problems both courts – ECJ and ECtHR – try to avoid such conflicts. De Witte highlights the manner in which the ECJ applied the ECtHR case law when interpreting and applying EU fundamental rights (Chapter 1). The EU Charter links the interpretation of this document firmly to the ECHR and the ECtHR case law.

Lawson and Van de Heyning observe that the ECtHR tries to avoid frictions by providing for considerable restraint when scrutinizing indirect EU action, namely applications directed against Member State actions which execute their obligations under EU law (Chapter 2). E.g. in *Kokkelvisserij v The Netherlands*[14] applicants complained – in brief – that the EU system of multi stage judicial review (beginning with legal recourse before a domestic court) held less rights to present and argue a case than is required under Article 6 ECHR. The ECtHR observed that:

> "State action taken in compliance with such legal obligations [Article 1 ECHR WV] is justified as long as the relevant organisation is considered to protect fundamental rights, as regards both the substantive guarantees offered and the mechanisms controlling their observance, in a manner which can be considered at least equivalent to that for which the Convention provides (...) By 'equivalent' the Court means 'comparable'; any requirement that the organisation's protection be 'identical' could run counter to the interest of international cooperation pursued (...). If such equivalent protection is considered to be provided by the organisation, the presumption will be that a State has not departed from the requirements of the Convention when it does no more than implement legal obligations flowing from its membership of the organisation. However, any such presumption can be rebutted if, in the circumstances of a particular case, it is considered that the protection of Convention rights was manifestly deficient".

With this ruling the Court assessed that the guarantees offered in the Article 267 TFEU preliminary reference procedure are comparable to the ones required under Article 6 ECHR and that there is no strong evidence to the contrary either.[15] In relation to the EU jurisdiction the ECtHR is – in sum – in certain

---

14 ECtHR Kokkelvisserij v The Netherlands 2009-I 48 *EHRR* SE18.

15 See Tobias Lock, 'Beyond Bosphorus: The European Court of Human Rights' Case Law on the Responsibility of Member States of International Organisations under the European Convention on Human Rights', *Human Rights Law Review* (2010) 10 (3), p. 529–545.

respects prepared to recognize and presume an equal level of protection unless the presumption can be rebutted by evidence that the protection of ECHR rights is manifestly deficient (raising the bar quite high).

For domestic last resort courts the *Kokkelvissers* case means that they can work under the presumption that when an applicant invokes an ECHR right in a case involving EU law the protection the EU legal recourse offers is sufficiently comparable to the level of protection by the ECHR. The *Bosphorus* doctrine as applied in the *Kokkelvissers* case indicates that the European courts recognize the importance of a peaceful interaction between the ECtHR and the ECJ. When the ECJ or the ECtHR alters its attitude towards the other court, this might generate a considerable impact on the relationship between either courts with the domestic courts, in particular the constitutional courts. Therefore, it must not surprise that the question how the ECtHR should scrutinize indirect actions, namely actions against domestic measures implementing EU law, is given due consideration in the negotiations between the COE and EU with regards to the EU accession to the ECHR.

3.2. THE DILEMMA OF AUTONOMY

While the impact of the ECtHR and ECJ case law on constitutional adjudication is considerable, several constitutional courts struggle with the dilemma between the respect for their international obligations, on the one hand, and their mandate to protect constitutional rights, on the other. In her contribution Popelier shows how the Belgian Constitutional Court is sometimes faced with an impossible choice: either accept the mandate of the Strasbourg Court and consequently partly to renounce their constitutional mandate to uphold the constitution or – on the other hand – uphold the national constitutional values and default on EU or ECHR obligations (Chapter 5). It appears that this dilemma is a common thread to most domestic contributions.

Arnold discusses how the German Constitutional Court has tried to combine Germany's orientation as a State which fully accepts international law, on the one hand, with the dualist tradition on which the Constitution is based, on the other hand (Chapter 8). E.g. in the *Gorgülü* case the Constitutional Court confirmed its competence to scrutinise whether ordinary courts had given due regard to the ECHR and the ECtHR, thereby strengthening the importance of the Strasbourg case law in the domestic jurisprudence.[16] At the same time, the Constitutional Court argued in the same case that the constitutional identity does place certain limits to the penetration of ECtHR case law of the German constitutional order.

16 Vol. 111, p. 307, 317, 329–330.

In addition, the German Constitutional Court refers to the ECHR very seldom, but rather refers to constitutional rights. Moreover, the ECHR is only of legislative rank in the German system. Arnold argues that currently a state cannot keep internal legislation separated from its international obligations and only require conformity with the Constitution. Similarly, Dickson indicates that, while UK courts until now have displayed considerable respect for the jurisprudence of the Strasbourg Court, in the last decade there are tell-tale signs that the relationship is not as harmonious as it used to be. E.g. the UK government authorized a study on the possibility to leave the ECHR (Chapter 12).

These examples illustrate that present European human rights adjudication is not merely about procedure and rights but on constitutional supremacy and sovereignty as well. In more dualistic states the idea of transnational European human rights, enjoying supremacy over national (constitutional) law, handed down by a supreme European Court challenges the idea of constitutional sovereignty at the core. While such dilemmas on the balance between constitutional protection and respect for international obligations might be inherent to most constitutional orders, it generally takes a specific, political and societal gripping case to spark unrest. The present UK controversy over the case of voting rights for prisoners – in which the Cameron administration is not inclined to give effect to the ECtHR judgment *Greens and M.T. v. UK* of 2010[17] – provides evidence for this. Similarly, Italian voices to leave the ECHR followed the ECtHR's Chamber judgment in Lautsi, which concerned the highly sensitive issue of crosses in class rooms.

A similar dilemma can be observed with regards to EU law. Constitutional courts in general take the ECJ case law in regards when interpreting constitutional rights and freedoms. They accept the effectiveness of EU law as an important interest. Still, most constitutional courts do not refer preliminary references to the ECJ. The willingness of the Belgian Constitutional Court to refer both interpretation and validity issues to the ECJ, is a remarkable exception in this respect (Chapter 5). In addition, the protection of constitutional rights has been relied on by constitutional courts to delineate the limits of the ECJ's potential in the constitutional legal order. Most famous are the German Constitutional Court's feuds with the ECJ (the *Solange* cases and the recent *Lisbon* judgment). The Court held that it would only accept the primacy of EU law if it would offer a level of fundamental rights protection equivalent to German constitutional rights and freedoms. This resistance has evolved to a

[17] Judgment of 23 November 2010 (Applications nos. 60041/08 and 60054/08), to be retrieved at http://cmiskp.echr.coe.int/tkp197/view.asp?action=html&documentId=877343&portal=hbkm&source=externalbydocnumber&table=F69A27FD8FB86142BF01C1166DEA398649.

more cooperative stance whereby most constitutional courts accept the primacy of EU law but still set the essence of constitutional values, including constitutional rights, as ultimate barriers. E.g. the Italian constitutional court early on red-lined the limits of EU law with regards to the domestic legal order, but has recently referred its first preliminary reference to the ECJ and referred to the EU Charter even before it became legally binding (see Chapter 9). Yet, the Italian Constitutional Court has not explicitly dismissed its former declaration that it maintains the ultimate say in conflicts between constitutional rights and EU law. Similarly, Dickson argues that EU law has significantly influence on the UK protection of fundamental rights (Chapter 12). However, at the same time the UK legislature and courts will continue to safeguard their own role in protecting fundamental rights in accordance with the common law traditions.

Albi argues that rather than dismissing such constitutional rights defence by constitutional courts as "historic relicts" or old-fashioned sentiments for national sovereignty, we should explore how such rights could be better entrenched *vis-à-vis* the EU institutions. She demands for the debate to be moved from assessing whether courts are EU-friendly to discussing in a meaningful way how constitutional values can be preserved in a pluralist legal environment (Chapter 6).

The dilemma of autonomy presents itself in the supranational legal systems as well. While the ECJ regularly relies on the ECtHR case law to interpret fundamental rights, it is also weary for the loss of autonomy. With regards to the EU accession to the ECHR, the ECJ itself argued that such accession cannot undermine its autonomy. The negotiators of the EU accession dedicate special attention to the effects on the position of the ECJ as supreme court of the EU legal order.

4. COORDINATION AND CONFLICT RESOLUTION STRATEGIES

As we have seen from the former sections, courts, domestic and European alike, grapple with the challenges of human rights protection in the compound legal systems in Europe. Human rights are expressed in different catalogues and applied and interpreted by different courts which risks collisions and divergent interpretation and possible compromise of constitutional integrity and thereby loss of legitimacy (of systems, courts and catalogues alike). Highest national courts are at the centre of gravity of these different relations: their job is to balance, or better, to triangulate the protection of human rights in Europe.

At the 2009 workshop in Antwerp the discussants observed a proliferation of source documents of human rights in Europe after World War II and the establishment of institutions (courts) for the observance of the rights. This affects domestic legal and political systems in different ways. First of all EU legal systems have under the human rights genesis grown more interdependent. Secondly, national constitutional systems (most of them essentially based in the Westphalian concept of a sovereign state) are confronted with these new volumes of European human rights law with, de facto, direct effect. Third: the traditional set up of the separation of powers is affected by it; under the influence of an increased set of European human rights, domestic courts and judges have – in their relation to the legislature and administration – become a more corrective power, even in parliamentary systems based on the concept of parliamentary sovereignty.[18] There are no easy answers here. The dynamics of compound legal orders are new and there are no definite contours as of yet. Most of the discussants agreed that a coherent theory or a theoretical framework is still missing in the debate on European human rights and their observance in the increasingly pluralist legal systems of European states. In order to come up with solutions we need to be prepared to look beyond the lens of sovereignty and euro-friendliness as Albi in her contribution puts it (Chapter 6).

To avoid collisions, divergent interpretation and constitutional debates there is little black letter law to fall back on, but some strategies can be discerned. The first strategy is that of *pluralism* itself. Worldwide case law of courts is available on the internet, even in translation. Judges and courts draw inspiration from that,[19] they are even prone to cite from foreign jurisprudence in their judgments as a means of rationalizing their own argumentation. This already results in what Burgorgue-Larsen in her contribution calls 'interpretative reconciliations' (Chapter 7). The second strategy consists of *coordination*. This may be brought about by law or by other means, it may be explicit or implicit. Different methods were discussed during the workshop. Let us address the legal ones first. Within the common European legal framework of the EU and ECHR legal orders, written legal rules on coordination exist – albeit it few. Some of them express principles of *priority*. For instance we have the substantive norms on the priority of the right rendering the highest level of protection (Article 53 ECHR and Article 53 EU Charter – see Chapter 3). There are procedural rights to this effect as well, e.g. in the form of the obligation to exhaust all domestic remedies before one can lodge a complaint before the ECtHR or the competence (or as the case may be obligation) of domestic courts in the EU to ask for a preliminary ruling in case there are questions on the validity or interpretation of EU law. Some of

---

18 K Malleson, *The New Judiciary; the effects of expansionism and activism*. Ashgate 1999.

19 Eyal Benvenisti, 'Reclaiming Democracy: The Strategic Uses of Foreign and International Law by National Courts', *American Journal of International Law* 2008, Vol. 102.

the coordination rules expressing priority even express supremacy. The *Hannover* case provides an illustration of this. In mirror image there are constitutional coordination rules in some jurisdictions trying to uphold the domestic integrity of the constitutional legal order as well. Mechanism like dualistic or (mitigated) monistic approaches to international law provide examples hereof. It may even go further down the road. The German *Görgülü* case and the British Human Rights Act 1998 provide examples of constitutional red lines.

There are unwritten sets of priority rules as well. They are the classic legal rules on priority expressed by legal maxims like '*lex posterior derogat legi priori*' and '*lex specialis derogat legi generali*'. These unwritten rules are ingrained in the European legal framework and applied by the courts. They might prove even more important than now, once the EU accesses to the ECHR.

A second set rules on coordination concerns *rules of recognition*. On the basis of these rules a court may decide that the way a human right is protected in another jurisdiction is of equal value. This technique of deference we saw for instance used in de the cases of *Kokkelvissers* and *Bosphorus*. Some of the 2009 discussants raised some flags here. Does Strasbourg deference not give too much leeway to the EU and ultimately lead to substandard protection of ECHR rights in the EU? Will it trigger EU strategies to fence of Strasbourg review by simple EU statements that EU law 'is in full conformity with ECHR provisions'?

An informal way of coordination, that is becoming more important, is *dialogue*. This may be brought about by informal contacts between judges of different courts and from different institutions (contacts between the Strasbourg and Luxembourg courts are frequent) but also by learning and citing from each other's case law.

A last strategy the discussants observed is that of *integration*. In *Costa/Enel* the ECJ found that with the EEC Treaty a new legal order had been established. This in effect integrated the Member State legal orders in that of the European Community (now EU) and gave precedence to the community's legal order over the domestic ones. None of the discussants believed this to be a likely panacea for human rights protection in Europe. The ECHR legal order and that of the EU are more or less parallel legal orders but with different rationales and different settings. Integration would dilute this and bring about complex constitutional issues and legitimacy problems in its wake.

5. IN CONCLUSION: ADDING TO EUROPE'S COMMON HUMAN RIGHTS GENE POOL

Where does this leave us in Europe anno 2011? The EU, transformed as it is after the Lisbon Treaty, is on the brink of accessing to the ECHR. Although all of the EU Member States are signatories to the ECHR proper,[20] they did not all sign up for all of its protocols and some of them have better records when it comes down to the observance of ECHR rights than others. Also, let us not forget the issues of constitutional integrity some jurisdictions face as regards the ECHR jurisdiction. One might wonder whether the EU is up to collective membership, especially when not all problems of coordination and collision between domestic, Luxembourg and Strasbourg courts seem to be thought through.

On the basis of the evidence produced in the different contributions to this project, we feel that there is no need to fear. First of all the internationalization and increase of human rights in domestic legal orders in Europe is not as much the effect of a single political act of accession, it is a fact of life, a result of a process of more than five decades. Under the influence of internationalization, globalization and advances in information technology, domestic jurisdictions have opened up more than ever before, especially so in Europe, and in particular as it regards human rights. After the fall of the Berlin wall in 1989 European states seem – instinctively – to have understood that they have in common what Cheryl Saunders[21] has called a common constitutional gene pool of shared human rights values and rights. Developments in the EU since 1989 went at breakneck speed and now – maybe not surprisingly – sometimes backlash effects occur. European human rights will be controversial in future as well, since with present volumes and character, it touches upon key political and constitutional questions. Effective human right protection in the EU therefore at this juncture requires that they are consolidated in the parallel legal orders of Europe. Accession of the EU to the ECHR seems a sensible step – especially with an eye to the needs of coordination. And as for the unanswered questions remaining? Every effective solution, we believe, begins with a sound analysis. We hope this project contributes to just that.

---

20 The UK has opted out for the EU Charter however.

21 Cheryl Saunders, 'Toward a global constitutional gene pool', (2009) 4 *National Taiwan University Law Review* 3, p. 1–38.

ABOUT THE AUTHORS AND EDITORS

THE EDITORS

Patricia Popelier is professor in constitutional law at the University of Antwerp, where she is the co-director of the research group on Government and Law. She is also a member of the board of the Centre for Law and Cosmopolitan Values, and vice-president of the International Association of Legislation. Her Ph.D. on legal certainty as a principle for proper law making won the Fernand Collin Price in 1998. Since then, she has published various books and articles in the field of constitutional law and legislative studies.

Catherine Van de Heyning is a researcher at the research group Government and Law of the University of Antwerp and a member of the Centre of Law and Cosmopolitan Values. She obtained a Ph.D. from the University of Antwerp and an LL.M of University College of London. She has published various articles in the field of European human rights law and constitutional rights protection.

Piet Van Nuffel is professor in European law at Leuven University and visiting professor at the College of Europe (Natolin). He is a member of the Legal Service of the European Commission. Previously, he has been administrator at the European Commission (DG Competition) and legal secretary (référendaire) at the General Court and the Court of Justice of the European Union. He has published extensively on various fields of EU law, including *Constitutional Law of the European Union* and *European Union Law* (with Koen Lenaerts).

THE AUTHORS

Anneli Albi is a Senior Lecturer in European Law at the University of Kent (Canterbury, UK). She obtained her doctorate in 2003 from the European University Institute in Florence. Her doctoral thesis was published by Cambridge University Press as a book entitled *EU Enlargement and the Constitutions of Central and Eastern Europe* (2005). More recently, she completed the British Academy and European Commission funded project *The European Constitution and National Constitutions: Ratification and Beyond*, which led to a book published by Kluwer (2006, co-edited with Prof. Jacques Ziller). Amongst a variety of consultancy work, she serves as an expert to the European Commission's Gender Equality Network.

Rainer Arnold holds a Chair of Public Law and the Jean Monnet Chair ad personam "Legal relations of the EU with Central, Eastern and South Eastern Europe" at the University of Regensburg. He held the Jean Monnet Chair of EU Law. He is a visiting Professor of Charles University Prague and is the Director of German Law Studies Programme at the Law Faculty of Lomonosov State University Moscow.

Samantha Besson is Professor of Public International Law and European Union Law at the University of Fribourg in Switzerland and Co-director of the European Law Institute of the Universities of Fribourg, Bern and Neuchâtel. Her current research focuses on European and international human rights theory, and on the philosophy of European and international law more generally. Some of her recent publications include *The Philosophy of International Law*, Oxford: Oxford University Press 2010 (edited with John Tasioulas) and *Legal Republicanism: National and International Perspectives*, Oxford: Oxford University Press 2009 (edited with José Luis Martí).

Laurence Burgorgue-Larsen is Professor in Law at the Sorbonne Law School at the University Paris I, professor in Madrid (Institute Ortega y Gasset, Master in Law and International Relations; University Autonoma, Master in European Law) and co-Director of the "Institut de Recherche en droit international et européen de la Sorbonne" (IREDIES). She researches in the areas of Human Rights Law, Comparative Law and European and International Law. She has published several French, Spanish and English articles on fundamental rights and human rights protection.

Monica Claes is professor of European and Comparative Constitutional Law at the Maastricht University where she is a researcher at the Maastricht Centre of European Law (M-Cel) and a member of the Ius Commune Research School. She obtained a Ph.D. from Maastricht University. She is a member of De Jonge Akademie and the Royal Commission on the Review of the Constitution. She previously was a professor at Tilburg University. Monica is the director of the European and National Constitutional Law Project EuNaCon, funded by the European Research Council. She is a member of the editorial board of the European Constitutional Law Review and the Tijdschrift voor Constitutioneel Recht.

Bruno de Witte is professor of European Union law at Maastricht University (the Netherlands), and part-time professor at the Robert Schuman Centre of the European University Institute (EUI) in Florence. Previously, from 2000 to February 2010, he was professor of EU law at the EUI, and co-director of the Academy of European Law there. He is the author of many publications on European constitutional law and on the law of cultural diversity. He is editor of the volume *Ten Reflections on the Constitutional Treaty for Europe* (2003) and co-editor of the volumes *Genesis and Destiny of the European Constitution* (2007), *Social Rights in Europe* (2005) and *EU Foreign Relations Law – Constitutional Fundamentals* (2008).

Brice Dickson is Director of the Human Rights Centre and Professor of International and Comparative Law at the School of Law, Queen's University Belfast, Northern Ireland. From 1999 to 2005 he served as the first Chief Commissioner of the Northern Ireland Human Rights Commission, a statutory body established in the wake of the Belfast (Good Friday) Agreement. His most recent book is *The European Convention on Human Rights and the Conflict in Northern Ireland* (Oxford University Press, 2010) and he is currently writing a book for the same publisher on the protection of human rights by the UK Supreme Court.

Enrique Guillén López is full time Professor in Constitutional Law (*Profesor Titular de Universidad*) at the University of Granada (Spain) where he is editor of the "European Constitutional Law Review" and member of the Research Project "Constitutional rights in the context of the internal market". Previously, he has been Secretary of the Master and Ph.D "European Constitutional Law" (Jean Monnet Chair, University of Granada). He has published various books and articles in the field of Spanish constitutional law and European constitutional law.

Rick Lawson is a professor of European Law at the University of Leiden where he currently functions as the Dean of the Law faculty. He holds the Kircheiner chair. He obtained his Ph.D. at Leiden University on the topic of the interaction between the ECHR and the European Communities. Rick published various articles on the theme and holds several scientific positions including the presidency of the Commission Scientific Expenses of the Leiden University Fund.

Gert-Jan Leenknegt is a professor in Public law at Tilburg University where he is a member of the Department for Public Law, Jurisprudence and Legal History. He published various articles on constitutionalism in the Netherlands, Parliamentary History and Educational Law.

Giuseppe Martinico is currently García Pelayo Fellow at the Centro de Estudios Politicos y Constitucionales (CEPC), Madrid. Before joining the CEPC he was Max Weber Fellow at the European University Institute, Florence. Giuseppe got a PhD in Law from the Scuola Superiore Sant'Anna (Sant'Anna School of Advanced Studies) Pisa, Italy, where he also conducted two years of post-doctoral research. In Pisa he also serves as STALS Editor (www.stals.sssup.it). He has held the position of visiting researcher at the University of Barcelona, Université de Montréal, University of Geneva, King's College, London, and the Tilburg Institute of Comparative and Transnational Law (TICOM). He is also Researcher at the Centre for Studies on Federalism, Turin.

Oreste Pollicino is Associate Professor in Comparative Public Law at the Bocconi University. After taking a Master in European Law at the University of Bologna and a LLM in European Law at the College of Europe in Bruges, he obtained a PhD in Constitutional Law at the State University of Milan.

He published books and articles in the field of European Constitutional Law and European Media Law.

Law and Cosmopolitan Values

In this series, the editors envisage monographs and collections of essays that address fundamental topics in law and globalisation, which range over doctrinal as well as normative questions of International and European law, human rights, justice and democracy. A main purpose of the series is to encourage scholarship that explores and transcends the categories and assumptions on which contemporary debates on globalization are conducted, and to stimulate reflection upon questions concerning the interplay between law, policy and principle. Recognizing that there is no occasion sharply to distinguish theoretical and systematic work in the field from an analysis of law in context, the editors welcome studies from a wide variety of methodological traditions. Contributions to the series, inevitably crossing disciplinary lines, will be of interest to students, researchers and professionals in public law, international law, human rights law, political science, legal, and political philosophy. Although the series aims in the first place to reflect the diverse scholarly activity within the Centre for Law and Cosmopolitan Values, University of Antwerp, submissions of manuscripts by anyone who is working in the same field are strongly encouraged.

Submissions of Manuscripts

Manuscripts can be forwarded to any of the editors at any time.
If the entire manuscript or a minimum of 2 chapters are available then the author is required to submit a detailed table of contents and brief proposal (up to 3 pages) outlining methodology, likely public, and the contribution the book is – or is likely to make. If no manuscript is available then the proposal should, in addition to the above, contain summaries of all chapters (no longer than 10 pages).

Every contribution should be accompanied by a statement that it is the author's own original work, that it is not being considered for publication elsewhere, and that it does not constitute a substantial repetition of work published or to be published elsewhere.

Selection Process

Manuscripts that are deemed worth of further consideration will be forwarded by the editors to a member of the advisory board or an external expert for a second review. Peer review reports are signed and should be detailed, describing and commenting on content, methodology, likely public, and the contribution the book makes – or is likely to make. In case of disagreement between first and second reviews, the editorial board will ask a third reviewer for a further opinion.

It is expected that the reviewing process will not exceed 2 months in each case.

www.lcv.ua.ac.be